THE MINOAN DISTANCE

THE MINOAN

The Symbolism of Travel

Photographs by LaVerne Harrell Clark

Away from the encircling hills . . . ,
away from the outreaching land to the north,
and over the edge of the open sea.
                    — D. H. LAWRENCE
                    Sea and Sardinia

DISTANCE

in D. H. LAWRENCE

L. D. CLARK

THE UNIVERSITY OF ARIZONA PRESS
Tucson

About the Author . . . .

L. D. CLARK has concentrated his study on the travels of
D. H. Lawrence since graduate school days. In more recent
years he has been involved in the editing of *The Plumed
Serpent* for the Cambridge Edition of Lawrence. *Dark
Night of the Body* (1964), Clark's first critical study of
The Plumed Serpent, was the result of research done by
Clark and his wife, LaVerne Harrell Clark, in Mexico and
the Southwest.

Clark is also author of two novels, *The Dove Tree* (1961)
and *The Fifth Wind,* as well as a collection of short stories
entitled *Is This Naomi? and Other Stories* (1980). He has
taught in the English Department of the University of
Arizona since 1955.

THE UNIVERSITY OF ARIZONA PRESS

Copyright © 1980
The Arizona Board of Regents
All Rights Reserved
Manufactured in the U.S.A.

Library of Congress Cataloging in Publication Data
Clark, L D
  The Minoan Distance.
    Includes index.
    1. Lawrence, David Herbert, 1885–1930 — Criticism and
interpretation. 2. Lawrence, David Herbert, 1885–1930 —
Journeys. 3. Travel in literature. 4. Authors,
English — 20th century — Biography. I. Title.
PR6023.A93Z62137   823'.912   80-18844

ISBN 0-8165-0707-4
ISBN 0-8165-0712-0 (pbk.)

Contents

Illustrations

Acknowledgments

On a subject as massively investigated as D. H. Lawrence, any critic who has read published research while slowly building his own commentary is bound to owe his colleagues much that he would be hard put to identify. To know the full extent of his debts would call for a record kept over the years of each time a fellow critic presented ideas that he accepted and in part adopted, or confirmed ideas he already held, or stirred him to further exertions by expounding ideas with which he disagreed. But this is not the sort of knowledge amenable to record-keeping, at least not with the procedure for learning about Lawrence which comes naturally to me and which I have always followed.

From undergraduate days on, I have read Lawrence, and along the way many works of criticism. Each time I went back to a Lawrence book perspectives changed and opened the way to new evaluations. At times these changes owed something to critics whose views I had come across between readings, and at times they were due simply to maturing opinions of my own. Most often, new assessments arose from both sources at once: in effect from multiple sources, for the views of other critics had become echoes going back a long way and difficult to distinguish. It would have been useless to attempt singling out any individual as the guide or the opponent of the moment. Today, when the shifting perspectives of the years have united to culminate in the present book, it is often next to impossible to know which fellow-workers to thank and how much to thank them.

All the same, I am conscious of having derived great benefits from certain works of scholarship and criticism. Those looming largest are the several primary sources, without which any study of Lawrence could hardly begin. I am indebted to the following people in various degrees from a few facts to constant dependence:

(Publication data is given only for those works not found in the "Works Cited" section.) Harry T. Moore, *Collected Letters of D. H. Lawrence;* Warren Roberts, *A Bibliography of D. H. Lawrence* (London: Rupert Hart-Davis, 1963); Gerald M. Lacy, *An Analytical Calendar of the Letters of D. H. Lawrence;* Aldous Huxley, *The Letters of D. H. Lawrence;* Edward Nehls, *D. H. Lawrence: A Composite Biography;* George Zytaruk, *The Quest for Rananim;* Harry T. Moore, *The Intelligent Heart* and *The Priest of Love;* E. W. Tedlock Jr., *The Frieda Lawrence Collection of D. H. Lawrence Manuscripts;* Keith Sagar, *The Art of D. H. Lawrence* (Cambridge University Press, 1966) and *D. H. Lawrence: A Calendar of His Works;* James T. Boulton, *Lawrence in Love;* Armin Arnold, *The Symbolic Meaning;* Frieda Lawrence, *Not I, But the Wind . . .* and *Memoirs and Correspondence;* Helen Corke, *D. H. Lawrence: The Croydon Years;* Lawrence Clark Powell, *The Manuscripts of D. H. Lawrence* (Los Angeles: The Public Library, 1937); Witter Bynner, *Journey with Genius* (New York: The John Day Co., 1951); Dorothy Brett, *Lawrence and Brett;* D. H. Lawrence, *Letters to Martin Secker;* Mabel Dodge Luhan, *Lorenzo in Taos;* D. H. Lawrence, *The Centaur Letters;* Earl and Achsah Brewster, *D. H. Lawrence: Reminiscences and Correspondence;* Jessie Chambers, *A Personal Record;* Ada Lawrence, *Young Lorenzo;* Compton Mackenzie, *My Life and Times;* Knud Merrild, *A Poet and Two Painters* (London: George Rutledge and Sons, 1938); David Garnett, *The Golden Echo.*

And in spite of the impossibility of keeping a true record during the research, I am aware of debts to a number of critical works in one of the senses mentioned earlier: for ideas accepted and in part adopted; for ideas confirming those I already held; for ideas with which I could not agree but which stirred me to further exertions in solidifying my own: Armin Arnold, *D. H. Lawrence and America* (New York: Philosophical Library, 1958); David Cavitch, *D. H. Lawrence and the New World* (New York: Oxford University Press, 1969); Colin Clarke, *River of Dissolution: D. H. Lawrence and English Romanticism* (New York: Barnes and Noble, 1969); James C. Cowan, *D. H. Lawrence's American Journey* (Cleveland: The Press of Case Western Reserve University, 1970); H. M. Daleski, *The Forked Flame* (Evanston: Northwestern University Press, 1965); Émile Delavenay, *D. H. Lawrence: L'Homme et la genèse de son oeuvre: les années de formation (1885-1919)* (Paris: Klincksieck, 1969), and also *D. H. Lawrence and Edward Carpenter* (London: William Heinemann Ltd., 1971);

William Arthur Fahey, *The Travel Books of D. H. Lawrence: Records of a Spiritual Pilgrimage* (Unpublished Ph.D. Dissertation, New York University, 1964); George Ford, *Double Measure: The Novels and Stories of D. H. Lawrence* (New York: Holt, Rinehart and Winston, 1965); Sandra M. Gilbert, *Acts of Attention: The Poems of D. H. Lawrence* (Ithaca: Cornell University Press, 1972); Christopher Hassall, "D. H. Lawrence and the Etruscans," *Essays by Divers Hands,* new series, vol. XXXI (London: Oxford University Press, 1962); Graham Hough, *The Dark Sun* (London: Duckworth and Co., 1956); Frank Kermode, *D. H. Lawrence* (New York: The Viking Press, 1973); F. R. Leavis, *D. H. Lawrence: Novelist* (London: Chatto and Windus, 1955); Tom Marshall, *The Psychic Mariner* (New York: The Viking Press, 1970); Julian Moynahan, *The Deed of Life* (Princeton: Princeton University Press, 1963); Edward Nehls, *The Spirit of Place in D. H. Lawrence* (Unpublished Ph.D. Dissertation, University of Wisconsin, 1953); Sylvia Sklar, *The Plays of D. H. Lawrence* (New York: Barnes and Noble, 1975); Mark Spilka, *The Love Ethic of D. H. Lawrence* (Bloomington: University of Indiana Press, 1955); Richard Swigg, *Lawrence, Hardy and American Literature* (New York: Oxford University Press, 1972); William York Tindall, *D. H. Lawrence and Susan His Cow* (New York: Columbia University Press, 1939); Eliseo Vivas, *D. H. Lawrence: The Failure and the Triumph of Art* (Evanston: Northwestern University Press, 1960).

I am also indebted to many people for direct encouragement and assistance, and I wish them to know my gratitude. The following have contributed to this book in outstanding fashion:

William York Tindall introduced me to the work of Lawrence at Columbia University a good many years ago, a beginning which is still producing gratifying consequences today.

Warren Roberts kindly opened to me the enormous resources of the Humanities Research Center, University of Texas at Austin, and gave me great assistance toward my first publications in Lawrence studies.

James Cowan has been an unfailing support in the exchange of knowledge, in publishing work of mine in the *D. H. Lawrence Review,* and in his excellent management generally of that periodical essential to Lawrence studies.

Frank Wardlaw did a remarkable job of publishing and marketing my first book on Lawrence, *Dark Night of the Body,* when he was Director of the University of Texas Press.

John Unterecker gave me a good opportunity for expanding my work on Lawrence by inviting me to contribute to *Approaches to the*

Twentieth-Century Novel (New York: Thomas Y. Crowell, 1965), a volume of which he was general editor.

Émile Delavenay, with his wife Katherine in full participation, has given added incentive to my work by the exchange of knowledge, and by his part in my invitation to the University of Nice as a *professeur associé* in 1973-74, a location from which I was able to complete some Lawrence work in France and Italy.

Lawrence Clark Powell has often shared with me the valuable discussion of a knowledgeable colleague.

Harry T. Moore, aside from his monumental labors in scholarship, of great value to every Lawrence scholar, has given me his personal encouragement and support on numerous occasions.

I wish also to express my appreciation to the following people: To David Farmer for aid in securing Lawrence materials; to Gerald Lacy for information on Lawrence correspondence; to George Zytaruk for being always ready to exchange knowledge on Lawrence; to Keith Sagar for enlightenment in discussion; to Edward Tripp for editing done on past Lawrence work of mine; to Marshall Townsend and others of the staff of the University of Arizona Press, in particular Patricia Shelton for editing the manuscript; to Donald Powell, Gladys Bean, Lois Olsrud and John McKay for library assistance; to Patricia Brandt for assistance in research and proofing; to Jane Ninde, Boleyn Baylor, Phyllis Gibbs, Patricia White and Patricia Hepworth for typing the manuscript.

The following institutions and agencies have given me support for which I am grateful: The Humanities Research Center of the University of Texas at Austin, the Morgan Library of New York, the Dartmouth College Library, the Library of the University of California at Berkeley and the Library of the University of New Mexico gave me access to necessary Lawrence materials; the Fulbright Commission awarded travel funds that put me within reach of essential research; the University of Arizona provided me with sabbatical leaves and faculty research grants.

Grateful acknowledgment for quotation of Lawrence material is made to the following: Laurence Pollinger Ltd., the Estate of Frieda Lawrence Ravagli, Alfred A. Knopf Inc., Cambridge University Press, Viking Penguin Inc., William Heinemann Ltd., the Houghton Library of Harvard University, the Humanities Research Center of the University of Texas at Austin.

To conclude these acknowledgments, I wish to express my gratitude to the many who were kind and hospitable to my wife, LaVerne Harrell Clark, and me, as we traveled in foreign lands, especially to the Albertoni family of Mandas, Sardinia, and to Eliseo and Adriana

Quadrini of Villa Latina, near Picinisco, Italy. This gratitude extends to the passing acquaintances whose names I never knew or no longer recall: like the peasant in the market at Cagliari, Sardinia, who gave us such a cheery welcome in a dialect beyond our comprehension, or like the news vendor in Rome who saved for me a precious notebook I had left lying on his counter. These are but two of the many who gave us aid, directions and information, or the simple pleasure of communicating with citizens of fascinating countries in languages half-understood, as we went about with notebook and camera from Mexico to Italy.

L. D. CLARK

Key to Works Cited

Works cited are identified by the following symbols placed in the margin of the text, with appropriate page numbers, next to the line on which a reference begins (except for a few additional citations to be found in the footnotes). All quotations are printed in italics.

AC   Gerald M. Lacy. *An Analytical Calendar of the Letters of D. H. Lawrence* (Unpublished Ph.D. Dissertation, University of Texas at Austin, 1971).

AL   S. Foster Damon. *Amy Lowell: A Chronicle.* Boston: Houghton Mifflin Co., 1935.

AN   E. M. Forster. *Aspects of the Novel.* New York: Harcourt Brace, 1927.

AP   D. H. Lawrence. *Apocalypse.* New York: Penguin Books, 1976.

AR   ———. *Aaron's Rod.* New York: Penguin Books, 1976.

BB   ——— and M. L. Skinner. *The Boy in the Bush.* New York: Thomas Seltzer, 1924.

CB   Edward Nehls. *D. H. Lawrence: A Composite Biography.* Madison: The University of Wisconsin Press: vol. 1, 1957; vol. 2, 1958; vol. 3, 1959.

CE   D. H. Lawrence. *The Centaur Letters,* with an introduction by Edward D. McDonald. Austin: University of Texas Humanities Research Center, 1970.

CG   George Santayana. *The Idea of Christ in the Gospels or God in Man.* New York: Charles Scribner's Sons, 1946.

CL   *The Letters of D. H. Lawrence,* vol. 1, edited by James T. Boulton. Cambridge: Cambridge University Press, 1979.

CM   Compton Mackenzie. *My Life and Times: Octave Five, 1915–1923.* London: Chatto and Windus, 1966.

CO   D. H. Lawrence. *The Complete Plays*. New York: The Viking Press, 1965.

CP   _____. *The Complete Poems,* edited by Vivian de Solo Pinto and Warren Roberts. New York: The Viking Press, 1964.

CS   Mrs. Henry Jenner. *Christian Symbolism*. London: Methuen and Co., Ltd., 1910.

CY   Helen Corke. *D. H. Lawrence: The Croydon Years*. Austin: The University of Texas Press, 1965.

DN   Paul Delany. *D. H. Lawrence's Nightmare: The Writer and His Circle in the Years of the Great War*. New York: Basic Books, 1978.

DR   *The D. H. Lawrence Review*. Published at the University of Arkansas, Fayetteville: James C. Cowan, editor.

EC   D. H. Lawrence. *The Escaped Cock,* edited with a commentary by Gerald M. Lacy. Los Angeles: Black Sparrow Press, 1973.

EG   John Burnet. *Early Greek Philosophy*. London: Adam and Charles Black, 1948 (reprint of the 3rd edition, 1920).

EP   D. H. Lawrence. *Etruscan Places,* in the double volume *Mornings in Mexico and Etruscan Places*. London: William Heinemann Ltd., 1956.

ER   *The English Review*. London, September 1913.

FL   D. H. Lawrence. *The First Lady Chatterley*. London: William Heinemann Ltd., 1972.

FR   *Fortnightly Review*. London, July 1, 1913.

FU   D. H. Lawrence. *Fantasia of the Unconscious,* in the double volume *Fantasia of the Unconscious and Psychoanalysis and the Unconscious*. London: William Heinemann Ltd., 1961.

GA   John Bunyan. *Grace Abounding to the Chief of Sinners,* edited with an introduction by Roger Sharrock. London: Oxford University Press, 1966.

GE   David Garnett. *The Golden Echo*. New York: Harcourt, Brace and Co., 1954.

HL   *The Letters of D. H. Lawrence,* edited with an introduction by Aldous Huxley. London: William Heinemann Ltd., 1932.

HT   The Harvard University typescript of *Quetzalcoatl,* first and unpublished version of D. H. Lawrence's *The Plumed Serpent*.

IH   Harry T. Moore. *The Intelligent Heart*. New York: Farrar, Straus and Young, 1954.

IP   *The Imagist Poem,* edited with an introduction by William Pratt. New York: E. P. Dutton, 1963.

JC   Jessie Chambers. *D. H. Lawrence: A Personal Record*. London:

Frank Cass and Co., Ltd., 1965.

JL   D. H. Lawrence. *John Thomas and Lady Jane.* New York: The Viking Press, 1974.

KA   _____. *Kangaroo.* New York: Thomas Seltzer, 1923.

KL   *The Quest for Rananim: D. H. Lawrence's Letters to S. S. Koteliansky,* edited with an introduction by George I. Zytaruk. Montreal: McGill-Queen's University Press, 1970.

LA   Dorothy Brett. *Lawrence and Brett, A Friendship,* with introduction, prologue and epilogue by John Manchester. Santa Fe, New Mexico: The Sunstone Press, 1974.

LB   D. H. Lawrence. *The Ladybird,* in *Short Novels,* vol. 1. London: William Heinemann Ltd., 1956.

LC   _____. *Lady Chatterley's Lover.* New York: New American Library, 1959.

LG   _____. *The Lost Girl.* New York: Penguin Books, 1976.

LL   *Lawrence in Love: Letters to Louie Burrows,* edited with an introduction by James T. Boulton. Nottingham: University of Nottingham Press, 1968.

LS   D. H. Lawrence. *Letters to Martin Secker.* Privately published: MS, 1970.

LT   Mabel Dodge Luhan. *Lorenzo in Taos.* New York: Alfred A. Knopf, 1935.

MC   Frieda Lawrence. *Memoirs and Correspondence,* edited by E. W. Tedlock Jr. New York: Alfred A. Knopf, 1964.

MH   D. H. Lawrence. *Movements in European History,* with an introduction by James T. Boulton. London: Oxford University Press, 1971.

ML   *Collected Letters of D. H. Lawrence,* edited with an introduction by Harry T. Moore. New York: The Viking Press, 1962.

MM   D. H. Lawrence. *Mornings in Mexico,* in the double volume *Mornings in Mexico and Etruscan Places.* London: William Heinemann Ltd., 1956.

NW   Frieda Lawrence. *Not I, But the Wind...* New York: The Viking Press, 1934.

PA   James Fenimore Cooper. *The Pathfinder.* New York: G. P. Putnam's Sons, 1896.

PH   *Phoenix: The Posthumous Papers of D. H. Lawrence,* edited with an introduction by Edward D. McDonald. London: William Heinemann Ltd., 1936.

PL   Harry T. Moore. *The Priest of Love: A Life of D. H. Lawrence.* Carbondale: Southern Illinois University Press, 1977.

PS   D. H. Lawrence. *The Plumed Serpent.* London: William Heinemann Ltd., 1955.

PU   _____. *Psychoanalysis and the Unconscious,* in the double volume *Fantasia of the Unconscious and Psychoanalysis and the Unconscious.* London: William Heinemann Ltd., 1961.

PX   *Phoenix II: Uncollected, Unpublished and Other Prose Works of D. H. Lawrence,* edited with an introduction and notes by Warren Roberts and Harry T. Moore. London: William Heinemann Ltd., 1968.

RA   D. H. Lawrence. *The Rainbow.* New York: Penguin Books, 1976.

RC   Earl and Achsah Brewster. *D. H. Lawrence: Reminiscences and Correspondence.* London: Martin Secker, 1934.

RE   Keith Sagar, "Three Separate Ways" (Unpublished D. H. Lawrence Letters to Francis Brett Young), *Review of English Literature,* vol. 6, no. 3, July 1965, pp. 93–105.

RL   Unpublished letters of D. H. Lawrence to Ida Rauh, Humanities Research Center, University of Texas at Austin.

RS   Martin Green. *The von Richthofen Sisters.* New York: Basic Books Inc., 1974.

SA   D. H. Lawrence. *St. Mawr,* in *Short Novels,* vol. 2, London: William Heinemann Ltd., 1956.

SC   _____. *Studies in Classic American Literature.* New York: Penguin Books, 1976.

SD   G. G. Coulton. *From St. Francis to Dante.* London: David Nutt, 1906.

SH   D. H. Lawrence. *Complete Short Stories,* in three volumes. New York: Penguin Books, 1976.

SL   _____. *Sons and Lovers.* New York: Penguin Books, 1976.

SM   _____. *The Symbolic Meaning: Uncollected Versions of Studies in Classic American Literature,* edited by Armin Arnold. Fontwell Arundel: Centaur Press Ltd., 1962.

SR   Keith Sagar. *D. H. Lawrence: A Calendar of His Works.* Manchester: Manchester University Press, 1979.

SS   D. H. Lawrence. *Sea and Sardinia.* London: William Heinemann Ltd., 1956.

TB   E. W. Tedlock Jr. *The Frieda Lawrence Collection of D. H. Lawrence Manuscripts.* Albuquerque: University of New Mexico Press, 1948.

TE   Raymond Bloch. *The Etruscans,* translated by Stuart Hood. London: William Heinemann Ltd., 1956.

TF   D. H. Lawrence. *The Fox,* in *Short Novels,* vol. 1, London: William Heinemann Ltd., 1956.

TI   _____. *Twilight in Italy.* London: William Heinemann Ltd., 1956.

TR   _____.*The Trespasser.* London: Duckworth and Co., 1912.

TS   _____. *Letters to Thomas and Adele Seltzer,* edited by Gerald M. Lacy. Santa Barbara, California: Black Sparrow Press, 1976.

VG   _____. *The Virgin and the Gipsy,* in *Short Novels,* vol. 2, London: William Heinemann Ltd., 1956.

WL   _____. *Women in Love.* New York: Penguin Books, 1976.

WP   _____. *The White Peacock.* London: William Heinemann, 1911.

YL   Ada Lawrence and G. Stuart Gelder. *Young Lorenzo.* New York: Russell and Russell, 1966.

Prologue

Over a decade ago, enticed by Lawrence's vision of place and dissatisfied with knowing it from his writing alone, I set out to retrace his paths in Europe and America. I began with the half-formed thought that observation on the scene might assist me in writing a critical analysis of those Lawrence texts classified as travel works, apart from any relation they might have to other writings of his. But the more I learned of Lawrence's commitment to travel, the better I understood that to consider the travel works alone would be to force limitations on the transitory vision of place which they share with everything else that came from his pen, not only fiction and poetry and essays but even the letters he wrote from day to day. And I came to think that his vision of place, as it takes shape in page after page, presented maybe the clearest outlines obtainable of the meaning of Lawrence's life and art, reaching down into the psychological sub-structure of the man, touching the complex web of sexual and religious conflicts which compelled Lawrence to be what he was, and which as he confronted his condition led him on to be a great man and a great artist.

As I visited the site of a Lawrence sojourn, or followed the route of some Lawrence journey, I began to see that Lawrence's vision of place — and, by extension, of space — was equally a vision of time, and that the vision could never have come to exist and exercise its overwhelming influence on him without that spirit of travel, of transience, which kept him so much on the move and convinced him that his geographical movements constituted a spiritual quest, a pilgrimage. His imagination eventually came to be controlled by the concepts of voyage, of pilgrimage, of abandoning the known and outworn world for the new world, as if by death and rebirth.

This demand from within to seek out existence between geographical opposites seen as opposite poles of being was the grounding of the many oppositions in Lawrence whose interplay was the source of all his growth and change. In terms of time, his imagination moved always in awareness of the opposition between past and present, present and future, between the temporal and the eternal, between all that stood for actual time and time imagined. As for place, that too revolved perpetually in his mind as the present against the absent, the near against the remote, the ideal against the actual. Within all this lay Lawrence's vision of human nature, fed by the stresses of his intricate and sensitive character. A whole range of opposites revolved there in unending interaction with his place-time mystique: the interaction between an interior and an exterior landscape, and all the features of each one ultimately the landscape of Lawrence's soul, in which he carried out an exploration of strange lands synonymous with the exploration of self. It was a search for identity, an all-absorbing endeavor to reconcile the conflicts of religion and sex and disease within, and the identity he sought was the fullness of a strong and vital manhood, the struggle for physical and psychological health all but identical with a search for artistic expression.

So the following of Lawrence's trail came to be engrossing to a degree unsuspected at the start in that it grew to be the exploration of a man's soul. And the pleasures of carrying out the task increased with time, to be enjoyed at several levels.

For one thing, the exercise of simple curiosity in trying to recapture a shadow of Lawrence's original impressions of a scene. To visit any place embraced and re-created by an author is always something of a re-visit. Having envisaged the place in his books, you experience on actual arrival the pleasure of comparing what you see around you with what you conjured up as you read. This is never a disappointing moment, though you recognize at every turn a great difference between the real and the described place. The experience is similar to what happens when you return to places from your own past. These are never the same as you remember them, but you don't feel called upon to give up either the memory or the new vision. You only feel delight in the potentialities of vision inherent in place, in the very contradiction between the recollected and the present vision. In reading, a faculty of your own was at work in cooperation with the author's faculties to create a scene in his book, and now you treasure that as a memory, projecting your nostalgia upon the literal scene in front of you.

Still, through such rewarding distortions you try to keep in mind that you most desire a shadow of the author's impressions, that in some sense you wish to verify his faithfulness to his scene. With Lawrence this is an exhilarating activity. He had an uncanny way of singling out the qualities of a place and putting them into words with the most concise and vivid directness. He saw deeply beneath the surface, which may change from year to year, into that which does not change, what he called "spirit of place." And he identified this spirit in such a way that a later visitor can still touch the direct bond between Lawrence's words and what the place itself communicates. In Italy the hills above the little bay of Fiascherino may now surround a crowded beach resort, but many more olive trees will have to be cut down to take away the ancient atmosphere which Lawrence perceived and which still reigns inside the groves a few yards from the vacation cottages. This, by the way, was one of the several places I visited where the present dwellers have learned of Lawrence's stay there and added something about it to their other tourist attractions. On a mural in the Hotel Shelley-Delle Palme in nearby Lerici, Lawrence stands with other famous visitors to the area: Dante, Goethe and Shelley. Beside Lawrence is a short quotation from a letter of his describing the region. Unfortunately, the thought of the passage has been mutilated by translation from the racy prose of a Lawrence letter to "literary" Italian.

A brilliant surface and a deeper rhythm of place translated into language at one and the same time — this was the vision that Lawrence cultivated out of an inexhaustible talent for seeing. And he understood very well how the frantic rush to know and experience in modern times has stunted the travel instinct in man. Here are two significant comments he made on the deterioration of man's relation to place, one on home as a strange place, the other on the wide world. Both comments date from the last years of Lawrence's life, when thoughts of travel underlay nearly all his contemplation. The comment on world travel came to mind when he was writing in retrospect of New Mexico, which in memory urged itself as *the greatest experience* PH, 142 *from the outside world* that he had ever known. He says, *Superficially,* PH, 141 *the world has become small and known. Poor little globe of earth, the tourists trot round you as easily as they trot round the Bois or round Central Park. There is no mystery left, we've been there, we've seen it, we know all about it. We've done the globe, and the globe is done.* But, as he goes on to say, *The more we know, superficially, the less we penetrate, vertically. It's all very well skimming across the surface of the ocean, and saying you know all about the sea. There still remain the terrifying under-deeps, of which we have utterly no experience.*

By a similar operation of spirit Lawrence confronted his home region late in life in much the same way: *Now I am turned forty, and* PX, 257 *have been more or less a wanderer for nearly twenty years, I feel more alien, perhaps, in my home place than anywhere else in the world.* The once-familiar has become strange through absence, and has to be discovered anew like one strange place after another during those twenty years. Lawrence remembers that when he was young, *the whole population lived very much more **with** the country. Now, they rush and tear along the roads, and have joy-rides and outings, but they never seem to touch the reality of the country-side.* But to him there is still that *certain glamour about the country-side. Curiously enough, the more motor-cars and tram-cars and omnibuses there are rampaging down the roads, the more the country retreats into its own isolation, and becomes more mysteriously inaccessible.* This trait Lawrence observed on one of his last visits to England, and that still-visible *glamour* out of which England could be regenerated is the spirit of place that informs *Lady Chatterley's Lover.*

Since Lawrence identified quickly and for a time completely with a place, when you arrive there yourself, you are eager to recapture what he left almost in the atmosphere. After a while you become accustomed to feeling the nearness of his spirit. You need only say to yourself "Lawrence was here" to sense that Lawrence is still here, and constantly the thought recurs of what Lawrence had to say about immortality, how the dead never really die but enter into the spirits of the living, how their haunting is not envious and inimical but nourishing: *The living soul partakes of the dead souls, as the living breast partakes of the outer air, and the blood partakes of the sun.* You might almost breathe the drifting spirit of Lawrence as you stand in New Mexico, or in Oaxaca, or near the Lago di Garda, and breathe the air he breathed. . . .

In Italy you walk up from Gargnano one fall day to San Gaudenzio, with a thunderstorm threatening and Lake Garda sinking below as you climb. You come to where the road is sloughing down the cliff. This might be the same *landslip* that Lawrence mentions. Then you arrive at the wall and the narrow gateway of the little farm, San Gaudenzio, with nothing changed much in fifty years.

But while you were prepared for all this, you are not for what occurs next. As you walk through the gateway and come to a high terraced bank level with the roof of a cowshed, you are stopped cold by a man raising his head above the bank and saying, merely, "Lorenzo?" It takes a couple of seconds to realize that he is not addressing you by that famous name, but that he knows on whom these syllables will have a magical effect. No foreigner would be struggling up here on a stormy day who was not in search of the shade of Lorenzo.

Another time you follow Lawrence's way from Oaxaca to Huayapam, the village described in *Mornings in Mexico,* slipping into the depths of the Mexican countryside just as he did. You are not accompanied by a Rosalino, an Indian boy who sweeps the patio of your house and whose ambition, half-wild as he is from the hills, is to

PX,
257–258

PX, 257

FU, 149

TI, 83

learn Spanish. No, but you left just such a boy, of almost identical character and ambition, in the courtyard of the hotel this morning. Nowhere on your way to the village do you meet a woman with a basket of fruit who gives you *chirimoyas* and won't take money for them because they are not as ripe as they ought to be. No, but you meet the *pastora* Pacheca — so she introduces herself, though for the moment she is without her sheep — who carries coffee branches and tells you volubly how that rare freeze which descended on the valley last night may have been the ruin of those trees on which so many people in the valley depend. With a worried but friendly and curious look, she makes you a present of the coffee branch, and you carry it along to study. You think how Lawrence would have loved her.

So many things the same, though not quite the same. You too see people bathing in the streams. This time it is not the boys of *Mornings in Mexico* but two girls, a sudden apparition of lovely brown flesh against the dry rocks and cactus, who bolt for cover when they see you like Ixtaccihuatl vanishing before the eyes of Popocatepetl. And when you arrive in Huayapam, a fiesta is even going on, as woebegone a celebration as the one Lawrence stumbled upon fifty years before.

But most surprising of all, in the utter disregard that truth has for coincidence, is what happens when you return to Oaxaca that day, in the still clear noon all the more wonderful after a morning of frost. You walk across a piece of barren ground toward a little yellow stucco restaurant with your eye on the doorway of swinging bead-strands and the menu hanging on the wall outside. On a tree next to the building hangs a cage with a huge parrot whose many-colored feathers gleam in the sun. You stop to exchange looks with him. You remember Lawrence's word sketch of the little white dog Corasmín and the parrot that jeers at him by calling out *perro, perro* all day long. You look and chuckle, and when both the parrot and you are satisfied that nothing further is to be gained from mutual observation, you turn away. You expect Corasmín to appear at any instant. He doesn't. Still, just as you turn your back on the parrot he begins calling out *perro, perro*.

You could hardly have been more surprised if the red-bearded hero of your researches had pushed aside the swinging bead-strands of the restaurant doorway.

But the one place in which Lawrence seems closer than elsewhere is Kiowa Ranch, above Taos, New Mexico. You and your wife have arrived there to stay for two weeks in the cabin where Lawrence and Frieda lived. It is your first visit to this ranch that became the realization of the wild spirit of the American wilderness in *St. Mawr*. In this cabin where he lived in the early 1920s, you can still make use of the things that Lawrence used, like the chairs and the bedstead. You can look out at the giant pine keeping guard, as Lawrence put it, a little way from the front door, the host and spirit of the ranch. You can chop wood in the backyard as he did, and comfort yourself with a fire in the fireplace he used. And at night, of course, you will be visited by the descendants of the packrats that kept him awake, whose feet whisper on every timber above your head, as they did above his. . . .

It is now night, your first hours of darkness here. You and your wife go to bed. You lie back with your head toward the window and watch over the footboard of the bed the few tracings of ember left in the heavy ash of the nearly dead fire. You hear the first scuttling of the packrats over the roof and in the rafters. You hear the pine breathe low. You think that Lawrence and Frieda could not be far away, closer maybe than their graves fifty yards up the mountainside.

Then you notice a new thing, a strange thing. The wall above the fireplace is whitewashed and bare. It would gleam a little on a dark night, and this is the darkest of nights. But this is not simply a gleam you see. The wall glimmers, glimmers. A faint play of light shimmers over the whole expanse of whitewash, from the dark line of the mantelpiece upward to the dark line of a rafter.

You take a deep breath. You force your muscles to go limp. Yet you think, there's no light you could dream of within miles of here. Unless maybe, my God! Unless maybe somebody is standing out by the pine with a dim flashlight trained on the window above your head, somebody with a trembly hand.

A few seconds pass before the fright and stiffening of this thought will let you muster courage enough to look. When you do rise to your knees and swing around to peer out over the headboard, you see the pine, the dark sky, the piercing stars. You settle your chin on top of the headboard, you scan and scan. You think, now where is the axe? In the chopping block behind the house, no doubt. Where is the hunting knife? Maybe in the car, maybe who knows where?

But what could be out there that any weapon, if you had a weapon, could protect you against?

No one is out there, and no light either, to break the still and silent surface of what is supposed to be there. Now the light on the wall glimmers and now it doesn't, but nothing in the dark outside changes, whether the wall glimmers or not.

After dividing your attention between the dark of the yard and the light on the wall for a couple of minutes, you think of a remotely possible explanation, and you wonder how to phrase it in answer to your wife's anxiously repeated question, "What do you think it is? What do you think it is?"

Well, it could be a reflection on the blank surface from the coals of the fire beneath. But how? How could such tiny streaks of glow from far below the mantelpiece, even if bright enough to reflect, cast their light on the window to be cast back to the wall?

It sounds more far-fetched as you say it.

Or — explanations having started to come out — you offer another: It's the starlight shattered and filtered by the barely moving branches of the pine.

The first jangle of fear has settled to a steady thumping of the heart. You and your wife lie back close together and watch the coming and going of the glimmer. You have a little control over your fear now. And being a divided man of the modern world, you are prepared both to accept the light as a sign and to reject it. Your reason tells you this couldn't be the ghost of Lawrence, and you wouldn't think of denying the clamors of reason, right to the point of scoffing at the thought that this *could* be the ghost of Lawrence. At the same time, your instincts tell you it *is* the ghost of Lawrence, and you accept that too. You catch yourself halfway opening your mind to receive what he has to tell you.

Now you dare to half rise up and lean on an elbow to watch, with your head turned so that you have the wall in full view and in a corner of your eye the dim outline of the window over the headboard.

You catch a tiny distant flicker from the window. Your fear rushes back. The flashlight again!

You pitch over and get to your knees. You press your face to the window.

What you think you see, an instant later, is a far-off bump of cloud flickered over by a moment of lightning.

So! Now you begin to see, to laugh, to tell your wife: "Of course, of course, that's what it is!" You climb out of bed and head for the door with her calling for you to come back.

"It's all right, it's all right," you answer. You walk out to the porch facing Lawrence's guardian pine. Now you can see across Taos valley far below to another uplift of the Sangre de Cristo range. On those remote peaks thirty or more miles away, a thunderstorm is in progress, invisible except for those instants of fire, pulse after pulse of glow through the long rough body of clouds humped up in a clash of elements. And in utter darkness a tiny gleam can reach over the great distance and come back to life on a white wall. . . .

Which is all the explanation that reason needs. It wasn't Lawrence's spirit, of course. Reason knew that all along, and reason is comforted to have its conclusions verified by causes discovered in natural phenomena.

As for the instincts, which is where Lawrence's spirit would still be glimmering with life, if anywhere . . . well, the instincts are better off if left to travel a road of their own.

THE MINOAN DISTANCE

1

Perhaps It Is My Destiny
To Know the World

I

Near the end of 1911, in his twenty-sixth year, Lawrence reached a climax of troubles which had been building for a long while. The slow death of his mother from cancer the previous December had driven him to the verge of despair and subjected him to lingering grief. Having already broken with Jessie Chambers, in large part because his mother disliked her, he abruptly turned to Louie Burrows, who agreed a week before his mother's death to marry him. But his heart was never in the engagement. It only became one element in the growing crisis. He was also involved — but not as much as he often wished — with Helen Corke. This interest dated from before his mother's illness, when he set out to base a novel on his friend's recent and disastrous love affair: a literary undertaking in some ways an elaborate and unsuccessful attempt at seduction. Other women briefly attracted him too. Lawrence was all but frantic for a sexual union and without the means to achieve it except by a marriage he could not afford nor believe in. An equally tormenting state of affairs had developed out of the several false starts at making a novel out of his mother's unhappy life and his hypersensitive attachment to her. Conflicting demands between the teaching position to which he had never been devoted and his increasing literary commitments added overwork to the other strains. All these great professional, sexual and filial problems — the last two difficult to distinguish — came to a head in a nearly fatal bout with pneumonia.

During his lengthy convalescence Lawrence made drastic changes. He resigned from teaching. He ended his engagement to Louie Burrows. Plans for the future which began half by chance and half by resolution grew to momentous decisions that determined the whole course of his life. He hoped to live by his pen, but when German relatives by marriage invited him to visit, he decided that an extended stay on the Continent would for one thing give him sufficient command of German and French to qualify if need be for a higher teaching post. The Continent would likewise provide scope for the great restlessness which had seized him after weeks of being bedfast. A complete break from the past and the narrow confines of England was now a necessity.

Then came a coincidence that had profound effects. As he was preparing for departure Lawrence met Frieda von Richthofen Weekley, whose aristocratic freedom was a new and captivating influence. The attraction between them materialized quickly into a love affair. In a matter of weeks Frieda had consented to leave her husband and three children and accompany Lawrence to Germany. The two interconnected choices, of the woman and a new way of life abroad, transformed Lawrence as man and artist.

The elopement was the beginning of a chiefly itinerant life together. From this time until Lawrence's death in 1930, they never remained long in one spot. In later years Frieda came to complain regularly of never settling down, but Lawrence seldom expressed any such desire. As time went on he only became more confirmed as a traveler, pursuing over the world an endless journey that he once described as a ML, 736 *savage enough pilgrimage.* He led Frieda, who eventually became his wife, through many brief sojourns in various foreign lands: Germany, Italy, Ceylon, Australia, New Mexico, Mexico, France and Spain; and from place to place in England when he was forced by circumstances to be in his native country. And all the while their marriage resembled their wanderings: the course of it was as full of abruptness and reversal as the course of their travels.

This wayfaring became to Lawrence a quest for self-realization that he felt he could not achieve by any other means, and not by this means either unless Frieda shared the journeys, even though hate and fear came to control his dependence on her as much as love. It was this process that created the Lawrence we know. Its essence is con- CP, 688 tained in the phrase *the Minoan distance* from a late poem. But the roots of this complex vision of time and place go far back, not just to the association with Frieda, for that matter, but deep into Lawrence's origins.

Lawrence was a traveler born. In his native valley, friends saw him as a natural explorer, in whose company a walk through the country was like landing on a new continent. Years later, after Lawrence had added much of the earth to his sphere, what he told Richard CB, Aldington of his *wandering adventurous life sounded wholly fascinat-* vol. 3, *ing and rewarding. . . . Lawrence had the remarkable gift — in his* 86 *writing and especially in his talk — of evoking his experiences so vividly and accurately that his listeners felt as if they had been present them-selves, with the supreme advantage of being gifted with Lawrence's unique perceptions.*

This talent for communicating the unusual could sometimes lead to exaggerated impressions on a listener. Frederick Carter, for instance, made a supposed voyage of Lawrence's sound like something out of a popular thriller: *He was full of tales of his travel and the vastness of* CB, *forgotten cities, lost in wild places, overgrown and tumbledown and* vol. 2, *hard to reach even now, though once more found again. Up immense* 316 *rivers they had journeyed to them, carrying their meat alive in the boat. A goat to be killed on the way. And when it was slaughtered the genitals were offered to the white woman as the chiefest delicacy. They were declined by his wife — by him also, no doubt, for he was by habit extremely sensitive in most things.* This incident is reported to have taken place in Mexico. But nothing of the sort ever happened to the Lawrences anywhere, and since there is no other record of his having gone in for such yarns, it seems likely that Carter either confused something Lawrence mentioned having read with something he had done — for Lawrence was himself a great reader of travel and adven-ture books — or else Carter was half-consciously impelled to render in concrete terms the air of exotic adventure that Lawrence lent all his travel accounts, oral or written.

Some of Lawrence's contemporaries recognized in his devotion to travel more than an uncommon knack for absorbing and recounting curiosities. To Aldous Huxley, Lawrence's fundamental nature was engaged in his wayfaring: *His travels were at once a flight and a* HL, *search: a search for some society with which he could establish con-* xxvi– *tact. . . . and at the same time a flight from the miseries and evils of* xxvii *the society into which he had been born. . . .*

His search was as fruitless as his flight was ineffective. . . . and he never found a society to which he could belong. In a kind of despair, he plunged yet deeper into the surrounding mystery, into the dark night of that otherness whose essence and symbol is the sexual experience. In Lady Chatterley's Lover *Lawrence wrote the epilogue to his travels.*

This early estimate of Lawrence's wanderings, made about two years after his death, contains much that is still of value, but it stands in need of radical qualification. The chief error is that it imposes an external pattern, a search for a literal place, on what was principally an internal condition of the traveler himself, a search for a state of being at best symbolized by literal places. In a nearby passage to the one just quoted, Huxley does indicate an awareness of the psycho-logical ends of Lawrence's restlessness, but he does little to follow up

HL,
xxviii–
xxix

the insight: *I remember very clearly my first meeting with him. The place was London, the time 1915. But Lawrence's passionate talk was of the geographically remote and of the personally very near. Of the horrors in the middle distance — war, winter, the town — he would not speak. For he was on the point, so he imagined, of setting off to Florida — to Florida, where he was going to plant that colony of escape, of which up to the last he never ceased to dream. Sometimes the name and site of this seed of a happier and different world were purely fanciful. It was called Rananim, for example, and was an island like Prospero's. Sometimes it had its place on the map and its name was Florida, Cornwall, Sicily, Mexico and again, for a time, the English countryside. That wintry afternoon in 1915 it was Florida. Before tea was over he asked me if I would join the colony, and though I was an intellectually cautious young man, not at all inclined to enthusiasms, though Lawrence had startled and embarrassed me with sincerities of a kind to which my upbringing had not accustomed me, I answered yes.*

Fortunately, no doubt, the Florida scheme fell through. Cities of God have always crumbled; and Lawrence's city — his village, rather, for he hated cities — his Village of the Dark God would doubtless have disintegrated like all the rest. It was better that it should have remained, as it was always to remain, a project and a hope.

We are closer, now, to the metaphysical plane on which Lawrence's travels evolved. The dream of Rananim was ultimately its own reason for being. That it never came to realization in a utopian colony was due not so much to practical difficulties as to what Huxley suggests: a City of God best exists in the heart of the believer and not in the material world. The same interpretation can be applied to all of Lawrence's constant changes of place: they were nothing so much as a symbolic transference onto the outer world of the flight and search always in progress in Lawrence's soul and having its goal there as well as its beginning.

Another statement by a contemporary touches also on the sources of Lawrence's migrancy. When Rebecca West first met him in Florence in 1921 and listened to his account of the journey he was then on, she

CB,
vol. 2,
63

sensed an underlying purpose: *Lawrence traveled, it seemed, to get a certain Apocalyptic vision of mankind that he registered again and again and again, always rising to a pitch of ecstatic agony.* That he was already committing his vision of Florence to paper, though just arrived, made her at first suspicious of his insight. But on recalling the

CB,
vol. 2,
66

incident nine years later she could say this: *I know now that he was writing about the state of his own soul at that moment, which, since our self-consciousness is incomplete, and since in consequence our*

*vocabulary also is incomplete, he could only render in symbolic terms;
and the city of Florence was as good a symbol as any other.*

Rebecca West was remarkably perceptive to glimpse this quality
in Lawrence at so early a date. Even so, she reports, she could not
have explained it from the writing alone, without her knowledge of
him as a friend. We know so much more about Lawrence today than
she could have known that the pattern in question emerges clearly
enough from the work on close study.

The symbolism of place in apocalypse is as old as the form itself:
Babylon, Jerusalem and the like. With Lawrence the places were
multiple and shifting to a far greater degree than with the apocalyptists
of ancient tradition. And while he did travel, as Rebecca West suggests, for an apocalyptic vision of humanity, he was engaged first and
foremost in a search for a whole vision of the self, a search to unify
those states of soul symbolized by places. The further vision came by
extension from the primary quest, and in its widest reach it embraced
not only the condition of mankind but also a cosmology defining new
dimensions of time and space. The quest unfolded through a long succession of strange places and familiar places made strange by absence:
across the face of the earth and at the same time across the inner landscape of Lawrence's spirit.

What Lawrence sought was a primeval male identity. His experience and his own nature drove him to embody that identity through
a symbolism both topological and sexual. To begin with the sexual,
he was prevented from reaching a normal male independence after
puberty by the possessiveness of his mother. And the rejection of her
domination, which did not come about till after her death, was incomplete and subject to a lingering guilt. But against this guilt stood
another, no less potent for being late realized. His mother had taught
him to despise his father. When Lawrence finally came to see the
injustice of his attitude, his father grew in his esteem until he became
something of a model to emulate in seeking the completeness of manhood. This mother-father conflict underlies all the others entangled
in Lawrence's character. It contributed in large part to making him a
soul divided against itself — in an apt phrase of his own, *a multitude*   SC,15
of conflicting men. These contraries emerged in a typical response to
an oedipal background: an assertive maleness to overcome fears of
incest-tainted mother domination, a male-female ambivalence, and
an inclination to homosexuality.

But if we arrive easily at a clinical statement of Lawrence's sexual
complications, this is plainly only the beginning of the matter. One of
the best ways to proceed toward a fuller understanding of the man and

his accomplishments is to consider his uncompromising genius for self-analysis — not forgetting, of course, that even such honesty as Lawrence's is sometimes self-deluding.

Lawrence had great faith in the potential of the unconscious. In his view emotional stresses and psychological maladjustments, while they might be hurtful now and again in the foreground of the battle for unity of self, were at an underlying level a beneficial influence. He held that the unconscious in its depths is pure and wholly creative: WL, VIII *Nothing that comes from the deep, passional soul is bad, or can be bad.* He disagreed, then, with the psychoanalytic theory that the way to a greater equilibrium of self is through exposing and eradicating harmful subliminal impulses. The harm lies not in the original nature of our impulses but in the distorting and stigmatizing accretions they have suffered from civilization. For instance, the incestuous urges of infancy. From his never-conceded premise that all human attachment is physical, Lawrence was bound to support an intimate physical bond PU, 203 between mother and son. But he denied that the bond, if traced to *the pristine unconscious in man,* is sexual. The contention that the incest craving is inborn, Lawrence argues, stems from a mental concept that the rational mind, in its arrogant exclusiveness and tyranny over the pre-mental soul, merely attributes to the unconscious: *The incest-craving is propagated in the pristine unconscious by the mind itself, even though unconsciously. The mind acts as incubus and procreator of its own horrors,* **deliberately unconsciously.** *And the incest motive is in its origin not a pristine impulse, but a logical extension of the existent idea of sex and love.*

Lawrence attempted the same stance on common views of homosexuality as he took on those of mother-son incest. He wanted to see a physical but nonsexual closeness between men as a natural thing, and to blame the sinful mind for the perversion of all blood warmth into sexual attraction. Deep in the unconscious such warmth between men was not homoerotic. However, as might be expected, Lawrence had more difficulty here with distinguishing between a *pristine impulse* and a mental distortion than he did with incest. He could not fail to recognize on occasion a strong set of truly homoerotic urges in himself, as recorded, for instance, in the long-unpublished "Prologue" to *Women in Love.* Birkin, Lawrence's surrogate here, has a full knowledge of his passion for other men. He has refused homosexual practice, but still he does not believe in the advisability, the impossibility PX, 106 aside, of denying these urges toward a physical sympathy: *A man can no more slay a living desire in him, than he can prevent his body from feeling heat and cold.* The language of this rejected "Prologue" is in fact so sexually charged that it fails altogether to reach any psychic source that is not erotic. In *Women in Love* as published, Lawrence does with some success touch upon such a source, as we will see in discussion of that novel. The attempt agrees with Lawrence's consistent recommendation for psychic growth: like any other, the homoerotic impulse is not to be erased through suppression. If pursued far enough it can be rediscovered as a nonsexual male intimacy which can in fact contribute to a greater sort of manhood, even to the extent of forming a new basis for civilization. This is what the novel tries to tell us. The eliminated "Prologue" conveys another and contradictory meaning: that the homoerotic impulse is primary after all and guilt-ridden from its origin, that only by admission and transformation, and not by seeking a purity in the source, can it be turned into creative channels.

Lawrence's male-female ambivalence, either caused or exacerbated by the overshadowing of the mother, comes out in his work in a variety of ways, not always in agreement with one another. He could take a Platonic approach: that male and female may be one in eternity but are doomed to be separate and distinct in time, with a sexual difference in individuals absolute from birth. But again he spoke of proportions of male and female in one person.[1] In any case, a deep sympathy with a feminine point of view came naturally to him, putting his women among the most credible produced by any male author. And while these heroines may be half-admitted versions of himself, he was motivated in their creation by a desire to do justice to women that has another cause than a fictional transference of identity. Lawrence's mother had instilled in him the belief that he must in some fashion compensate for what she had lost through her unhappy marriage to his father. Consequently his women are in part attempts to incorporate into his growing horizon of male existence that substance of his mother's life from which she was cut off by an unfulfilled marriage and a sorrowful death.[2]

One force outweighs all the others, though, in Lawrence's treatment of women, and this stems from a deep mistrust of the feminine. He did not so much fear becoming a woman as he dreaded domination by a woman. A woman may stand in the way of a man becoming a man, by a sort of perverse confusion of her functions as mate and mother. Resistance to this power led Lawrence ultimately to subordinate the feminine in his work, to create a world where woman finds her greatest fulfillment in conjunction with a supreme maleness and subject to a male's authority. The perils along this path were many. As a man is once born of his mother, so must he be reborn of the woman he loves on the way to his highest achievement — which of course puts the mate dangerously close to the overpowering mother. Woman is often pictured too as the intermediary between man and the divine vision he must seek in order to be a man, or even as the very substance of the deity to be discovered.[3] Yet for all her universal significance, woman is never more than half aware of her roles. The male must make her aware. And not only this. He must, paradoxically, shape her to these roles before submitting temporarily to her, as he moves on into new realms, guiding all mankind to a new flowering of the godhead. Man is never finally responsible to woman or to the race, but only to the deity. And to achieve this divine accountability a man must learn to be perfectly alone, even though, again, such isolate integrity cannot be reached without alternating moments of intense harmony with the woman.

Paradoxes of this sort required of Lawrence unremitting efforts at solution. His questioning of the whole intricate structure brought him often to formulations of what really constitutes the integrated self. Sometimes he emphasized multiplicity: *I am many men. . . .* SC, 15 SC, 22 *This is what I believe:*

> '*That I am I.*'
> '*That my soul is a dark forest.*'
> '*That my known self will never be more than a little clearing in the forest.*'
> '*That gods, strange gods, come forth from the forest into the clearing of my known self, and then go back.*'
> '*That I must have the courage to let them come and go.*'

But if Lawrence could hold the self to be a succession of unforeseeable phantoms from the great unknowns of space and time, we should not overlook the antithesis contained in the very creed just quoted: *I am I,* which is close to Yahweh's identification of himself to Moses and a claim to the utmost singleness. Here is an equally representative passage, which finds the traveler or pilgrim bearing his holy singularity along among complementary individualities of the universe: PH, 403 *The fluttering, singing nucleus which is a bird in spring, the magical spurt of being which is a hare all explosive with fulness of self, in the moonlight; the real passage of a man down the road, no sham, no shadow, no counterfeit, whose eyes shine blue with his own reality, as he moves amongst things free as they are.* On the one hand, a man is an unbreachable unity. On the other, he is a living vessel of selves flowing in and out without his knowledge. Lawrence found no inconsistency in these two views—though we may—simply because he equated the courage to let "the gods" come and go with the sole integrity of the free man whose male strength and authority are bestowed directly by some dark deity of power and glory, the source of all these passing avatars in the soul.

The vision of unity and the vision of multiplicity have this prominently in common: both demand a fluid relation with the strangeness of the road or the forest. The necessity for a symbolism of place and movement in order to face conflicts arising out of a cleavage of loyalties in childhood did not take firm precedence in Lawrence's life until that crucial spring of 1912, when the search for equilibrium with the oppressive spirit of the dead mother fell into conjunction with a search for equilibrium with the new-found mate. In this first loosing of the bonds of England originated the opposing motives of all the later flights. England became the land of death, the death of the mother, and not long after, death by war and industrial blight. England became the land of the crushed hope for gaining manhood. The Continent, specifically the alpine region from southern Germany across Austria and into Italy, became the first visionary as well as the first actual place where the son and lover might expect to win newness of life through the woman who had so miraculously appeared to free him, in an act of love synonymous with their fleeing together from England to the Alps. It became Lawrence's way, no matter if achievement never did live up to expectation, to see his life with Frieda, unfolding in journeys from lands condemned toward lands redeemed, as a bursting of the bonds of death and a hope of entrance into a resurrected life. She became both the presiding genius and eventually, altogether too much on the order of the mother, the nemesis of the salvation Lawrence sought: that recapture of a semi-divine maleness which largely out of his own condition he came to believe the world had lost, but which he could glimpse over and over and which he never despaired of recovering. The unity he pursued in multiplicity was *a strange and*   SC, 15 *fugitive self shut out,* a self beckoning far off in the compelling distance, countries and continents away and yet as near as the core of the seeker's own soul. Such a self lured Lawrence the traveler also into the far reaches of time, assuming a splendid male integrity in the misty ages of the Egyptians and the Minoans and promising an imminent return.

Place became an entity momentarily arrested in the streaming past of the world. Out of this preoccupation Lawrence arrived at his belief in space and time, as purely psychological: *Time,* he said, is *only the*   VG, 66 *current of the soul in its flow*—and for him it was a soul always in movement through space. The soul could flow backward also, and in so doing surround the ancients, dividing the history of man into two conditions: the fallen and the unfallen. To the unfallen belonged the Egyptians, the Minoans, and others of the golden ages in which man lived out his fortunate life poised between the mind and the instincts. Then came the fall and the beginning of the present iron age of life by the mind alone. But the decisiveness of this fall did not signify that the golden age was irrevocably past. It was Lawrence's belief that such a time could and would eventually be recaptured, and for that matter, time being only the flow of the soul, that golden age could be re-entered at any moment and in any place, if one had the gift.

In the days when man lived by his whole psyche, Lawrence believed, space was concomitant with time and would never have been thought of apart from it. Man then always lived at the quick of time, in the present instant, the true realm of immortality.[4] The gods came and went, or more properly, the divine light played upon all and in all, man included. Man knew, in that he felt it at the root of his being, the whole cosmic system, from his own heartbeat to the furthest stars. The individual was the source and the sole vessel of life, but so concentrated was his awareness that he could easily project the flow of soul, what we call time, through all space and make it live, from whence it came back to him magnified many times and in different forms.[5] Lawrence read a simplification of Einstein's theories when he was at work on *Fantasia of the Unconscious,* in 1921, and was thankful to

KL, 224   him for having taken *out the pin which fixed down our fluttering little physical universe.* Not that he agreed, to be sure, with Einstein's hypothesis that time is only a dimension of the spatial universe, but he felt that the upsetting of old mechanistic theories left the way open for his own psychological theories of a time and space originating in the dynamic continuity of the individual being.

So Lawrence needed a sense of unconfined time and space to

SC, 69   carry out his *onward adventure of the integral soul:* integral principally in the hope of putting a host of inner identities under the control of a metaphysically conceived male self. Actual geographical space was of the greatest importance to this quest, the constant removal of limits imposed by horizons. Lawrence absorbed the places to which he traveled and drew them out of himself as landscape to respond to his ideal of time and space. His sense of history matched his sense of place, the two conjoined as the basic fabric of much of his work. The poem alluded to at the start of this section states the aim of Lawrence's imaginative endeavors: the discovery of a sphere of being where the distant in space and the far-off in time unite with the immediate present, the eternal passing moment, to make incarnate the deepest impulses of the human soul:

Middle of the World **CP, 688**

This sea will never die, neither will it ever grow old
nor cease to be blue, nor in the dawn
cease to lift up its hills
and let the slim black ship of Dionysos come sailing in
with grape-vines up the mast, and dolphins leaping.

What do I care if the smoking ships
of the P. & O. and the Orient Line and all the other stinkers
cross like clock-work the Minoan distance!
They only cross, the distance never changes.

And now that the moon who gives men glistening bodies
is in her exaltation, and can look down on the sun
I see descending from the ships at dawn
slim naked men from Cnossos, smiling the archaic smile
of those that will without fail come back again,
and kindling little fires upon the shores
and crouching, and speaking the music of lost languages.

And the Minoan Gods, and the Gods of Tiryns
are heard softly laughing and chatting, as ever;
and Dionysos, young, and a stranger
leans listening on the gate, in all respect.

As Lawrence looks out upon the Mediterranean, the middle-of-the-world sea, and watches the progress of modern journeys, he sees a second world-center and another journey told in the symbols of eternity. But the symbols are not of eternity only. For Lawrence these entities once existed as entities in history, in the golden age, and they would come to exist again in the perfected future. Thus the vision yields to the imaginary traveler a double satisfaction. An accomplished fact of the past will revive in the future. At the same time the vision offers to the actual man contemplating a literal journey the symbols that can bring him the transubstantial world here and now.

One of the most important conclusions to be drawn from the implications of this poem is that the psychological quest counts for more than the physical quest. Lawrence was never truly as Huxley saw him, an expatriate seeking an unspoiled country with a population whose outlook might be in accord with his own. Nor, as we will see, was he ever in the final analysis dedicated to communes like the proposed Rananim. His forever deteriorating and forever renewed quest for a golden time in a golden space was carried on more in the imagination than in actuality, and the constant travel was essential to keeping the imaginative quest alive.

II

If Lawrence's manner of transforming experience into language had to be summed up in a single word, it might well be the one that E.M. Forster chose in 1927: *prophetic*. While Forster confessed that he had no clear idea of what Lawrence was prophesying — it was nothing so simple as his pronouncements of doom against technological civilization, prophetic as these may turn out to be — we note that his response was similar to that of Rebecca West, who found Lawrence "apocalyptic," and this cannot be far from what Forster meant. Assessments of Lawrence in this prophetic vein have continued, with gratifying results, into current times.[6] Lawrence belongs to apocalypse by virtue of a certain puritan tradition which descends strongly into his life and work. His well-known assertion that *one has to be so terribly religious, to be an artist,* makes it plain that he drew no distinction between the sphere of imaginative literature and that of religious experience. And religion became for him a religious pilgrimage, a puritan pilgrimage. He was a man on a journey with disaster all around him and his face set toward a new creation. His apocalyptic imagination, like that of Bunyan or Blake, was wrapped up in visions of destruction and renewal of the world with himself at the center of the great mystical drama of catastrophe and regeneration.

The puritan imagination functions through a curious duality. One stereotype of the puritan has always been that of a practical, sober and industrious member of society. But we do not forget that while he thrives in this world and acts on strict principles of community responsibility, he is also a lawless visionary who holds in his heart a vivid tableau of flashing doom and shining salvation: as he walks through a town he walks as well in a myth from the City of Destruction to the Celestial City. This radical duality of outlook leads the puritan naturally to allegory and symbolism. The common things of earth become cosmic symbols, and each small turning of the puritan's inner experience takes on eternal significance. Lawrence's view of the metamorphosis of everyday life, as well as the place that his own immediate experience assumes in his work, aligns him with this puritan tradition: the *beauty* of the greatest literature, he declared in one of his most apocalyptic works, lies in *the identity of daily experience with profound mystic experience.*

We might think of symbolic transformations such as Bunyan's, where the lanes and country fairs of England are concrete features of Christian's mysterious journey. And there is also fantasy-making like Blake's: he had words with a soldier, was accused of treason though acquitted, and then incorporated the episode in a drama of

AN, 143

ML, 189

SM, 239

cosmic proportions, his allegorical poem *Jerusalem*. The puritan independence of mind, often extreme to the point of arrogance, may
remove all limits to the exercise of fantasy. This is what sometimes
happens in Lawrence. In the hoped-for resolution of his sexual stresses
he saw not just emotional well-being but religious salvation. And he
saw his own salvation as the type for that of all mankind. The sexual
mystery, he became convinced, was the only one left through which a
restitution of divine communication was possible for modern man.
His uncompromising puritan honesty and his conviction of the significance of the individual led him to as frank a treatment of sex as he
could imagine, relying always on his own sexual impulses for material
and projecting these into fantasy and allegory. A Lawrence story
will sometimes read, on the face of it, like the most private of sexual
fantasies — *The Ladybird* or *The Escaped Cock,* for instance — sexual
fantasies held improbably but convincingly into the light of religious
vision.

The appeal — or the equally strong aversion — awakened by these
writings in the reader points to an essential trait of puritan self-
dramatization: a powerful prophet's alluring mystery of message is
at bottom a mystery of character. He compels belief by magnetism,
not by reason. If the puritan who attributes eternal meaning to each
impulse and action happens also to possess a bewitching personality
which overflows even into his writing, then the conviction he transmits
of the universal importance of his every experience and utterance
is all but inescapable to anyone of a nature sympathetic to his. This
may appear to come down to a claim that the prophetic in literature
has its value not in what is said, but in who says it. What I mean is
that the two streams are inseparable, but that the prophet himself
provides the primary force. A parallel from ancient times — concerning
one of the Hebrew prophets who were the first puritans — may serve
to strengthen the point. The prophet Hosea, when his will-to-act
and his will-to-be issued in choice, selected a prostitute from a pagan
temple for his wife — because he couldn't help doing so, perhaps. But
his prophetic ambitions were as strong as his sexual urges, and his
talent for fantasy directed him to unite these in allegory: as his faithless
wife was to him, so was Israel to Yahweh. This was what he preached
to Israel: that Yahweh had commanded him to marry a whore in order
to set a living example of infidelity before the eyes of God's unfaithful people. Which makes of Hosea a natural for psychoanalysis, by
whose tenets his sexual distortions are almost ludicrously clear. But I
see a Hosea more difficult to comprehend and far more fascinating
than any that psychoanalysis might describe. Our involvement with
life is substantive and purposive, not analytical and theoretical: and

our involvement with prophecy and poetry is the same. The substance out of which purpose grows is not ultimately of prime importance, so long as that purpose is beneficial to the heightening of life, toward the TI, 45 *living, growing truth,* as Lawrence put it. If Hosea built out of his odd sexuality a vision of such quality that it led him and the Israelites, and leads his readers in later ages, toward a greater realization of life, then that is where the value of his vision lies, and that is the plane on which it is to be studied, not in quibbling about detachment and subjectivity, or in supposition that the vision is any the less of value because it can be traced to sexual maladjustments in the author's personality.

The difference in eras considered, Lawrence's translation of sexual problems into religious vision is analogous to Hosea's, and the appeal is of the same order, in the very intensity with which common standards are flouted and in the clarity of the vision. Lawrence too looks steadily into the darkness of sexual problems where Adam and Eve crouch in guilty knowledge — not to mention Onan and the Sodomites — and seeks to gaze unflinching at what Adam and Eve could not face: an accusing God walking in the garden in the cool of day. He put it so in a poem:

CP, 231   *I'm not afraid of God.*
Let him come forth.
If he is hiding in the cover
let him come forth.

Now in the cool of the day
it is we who walk in the trees
and call to God "Where art thou?"
And it is he who hides.

As Lawrence expected to arrive at a prophetic truth through a transvaluation of sexual cravings, he expected to do the same through a metamorphosis of place and an extension of the two sorts of experience combined into concepts of space and time. As a prophetic ideal, this mystique conforms to a definition offered by George Santayana CG, 252   in *The Idea of Christ in the Gospels:* Prophecy *sees in a vision as an accomplished fact, though hidden from vulgar apprehension, a secret ideal of the heart, and helps to render that ideal clearer and more communicable.*

The *secret ideal,* for Lawrence as for the Biblical prophets, was a new moral world: a revived human selfhood and a reawakened spirit of place: a new concept of a "holy land" and a "chosen people." Lawrence's prophetic sense emerges here through the special gift he had for seeing into the soul of place as he traveled and looked into his own soul. The spirit of place and the spirit of travel, to Lawrence, were much more than the cultivation of a sustaining feeling of kinship with nature and with mankind. He reached out for the divine spirit residing in any spot on earth, and one of his chief reasons for traveling was that continual change of scene kept him alert to the forever shifting manifestations of the universal spirit of place with which man must re-establish contact if he is to be redeemed. So the *"questing*   HL, 551 *beast"* in Lawrence was drawn to distance, or to the turning of the distant into the near-at-hand, in order to penetrate the secret of being.[7]

NOTES

[1] *See* PH, 443, 459–460; FU, Chapters 8 and 9; RA, Chapter 5. *Compare* Plato's *Symposium.*

[2] *See* "Everlasting Flowers: For a Dead Mother," CP, 226–227, and "Spirits Summoned West," CP, 410–412.

[3] *See* what Lawrence called a "Foreword to *Sons and Lovers*," written in a letter to Edward Garnett, HL, 95–102.

[4] *See* "Poetry of the Present," CP, 181–186.

[5] *See* especially FU, Chapter 13.

[6] For example, Frank Kermode, *Lawrence* (London, 1973); Horace Gregory, *D. H. Lawrence: Pilgrim of the Apocalypse* (New York, 1933); L. D. Clark, "The Apocalypse of Lorenzo," *D. H. Lawrence Review,* vol. 3, no. 2, Summer 1970, pp. 141–160.

[7] *The Questing Beast* (1914), a novel by Ivy Low, who became an admirer and friend of Lawrence's after reading *Sons and Lovers.*

2

The Bright Doorway

While Lawrence's search for emotional wholeness through a symbolism of time and place did not become a commitment to geographical change in company with the beloved until after his elopement with Frieda, his life before 1912 holds much vital background to this decisive step. The attraction of distance may first have come to him in his native Eastwood, a town winding shabby along the top of a ridge that commands a sweep of country. At least the view from a home doorstep remained firm in memory years afterwards: *Go to Walker St — and stand in front of the third house — and look across at Crich on the left, Underwood in front — High Park woods and Annesley on the right: I lived in that house from the age of 6 to 18, and I know that view better than any in the world.* It was a vista of nearness and distance combined. Across from the houses packed high and narrow on the uphill side of Walker Street, the lower side in Lawrence's boyhood lay open toward the valley and the rises beyond: the well-tended hills with their checkering of hedges, all intimate and familiar and yet stretching to horizons far off. It was a landscape across which the clash between nature and technology, eventually to govern so much of Lawrence's writing, was evident at every hand. The coal mines ate away at the smoked-over green of the earth, leaving mounds of coal rubbish scattered as abominations among the natural hills. The worsening of these ravages over Lawrence's stretch of Nottingham and Derby during his lifetime contributed to shaping his final vision of the necessity for destruction and re-creation of the world.

ML, 952

If Lawrence's mother had lived to see him into maturity, he might never have become a traveler at all. At any rate, when he left home in 1908 to teach in Croydon, just south of London, he felt at first like an exile and returned to Eastwood as often as he could. He took no trips abroad, and only a few in England, practically always accompanied by his mother. One of these, a holiday to the Isle of Wight in the summer of 1909, wakened in Lawrence that dazzling curiosity for strange places that became so evident in his later travels, so that the crossing by ferry to the Isle of Wight might almost be described as Lawrence's first trip overseas. This was the best excursion he ever took with his mother: his first discovery of a "foreign" place with a beloved woman. So the island assumed a great importance after his mother's death sixteen months later, in the struggle to rid himself of the domination of her memory.

The Isle of Wight vacation occurred just when Lawrence was going through several torments at once: of breaking with Jessie Chambers, of powerful and frustrated sexual desires, of incipient realization that closeness to his mother was twisting his life. Yet he was happy during the days spent on the island, and so was his mother: for one reason, Jessie was not one of the group, as she had often been at other holiday places in previous years. Lawrence was enthralled with the island, calling it *the most charming place imaginable.* On a boat trip ML, 55 around the coast, which together with the ferry ride from the mainland was Lawrence's first exposure to the sea, he was captivated by the *shimmering iridescent running water* of the Solent and Spithead. ML, 56

But the significance of the Isle of Wight to this early phase of Lawrence's life arose only in part from its beauty and its lingering association with his mother. It happened that Helen Corke, whom he scarcely knew then but was later to court, was also on the island at the time and experienced there the greatest emotional crisis of her life. She was with her lover, a married man, who committed suicide shortly after their return to the London area. Soon after the opening of the fall term — they did not teach at the same school but in the same town — Lawrence and Helen Corke became friends, and his sympathy was of great aid to her in her battle with shock and grief. He drew her out of absorption with her dead lover by his ever-ready understanding, reading Greek tragedy to her and helping her to a greater knowledge of German poetry. By February he was calling on her to assist in the final revision of his first novel, subsequently entitled *The White Peacock.* Soon he learned that since her lover's death, as a kind of therapy, she had written an account in the form of a diary about her stay on the Isle of Wight. Lawrence insisted on reading it, and having done so declared that she ought to do something with these heart-searchings. She declined, of the opinion that the writing had served its purpose in providing emotional relief. Lawrence would not hear of this. Writing must be read. In a remark typical of this man who pursued without mercy the revelation of himself and his friends in fiction, he declared

CY, 7   *that human experience is the common property of humanity.* He was eager to take the account out of Helen Corke's hands and transform it into a novel, with her active participation. She agreed to allow him use of the material if she could act as a guide only, and not a collaborator. The outcome, after complications unforeseeable at the time, was Lawrence's second novel, *The Trespasser,* published in 1912.

ML, 61   Lawrence told Helen Corke at one point that he was writing the novel from *a second consciousness,* and she too understood that he was putting himself in the place of her dead lover: but as an artist and not as a man, though Lawrence recognized no such division of intent. His excitement over the story was due to several impulses. He had finished his first novel, in which he appears largely as an impersonal observer, and he now felt ready to tackle more directly the problem of understanding himself. Still, he was proceeding by a curious indirection, telling Helen Corke's story as hers and seeking to make it his own as well. Whatever his conscious purpose at the start, the re-creation in prose of the brief and tragic love affair was all the while bringing Lawrence nearer to claiming a role as Helen Corke's lover in life as well as in art.[1] But more was involved than simply ingratiating himself with a woman by an elaborate act of sympathy. Always at work in Lawrence was the deep-felt need to reconcile male and female being, often expressed by taking experience from a woman with whom he felt a kinship and trying to shape and interpret this experience as his own. Such collaboration was tantamount to spiritual parenthood, yet on a further level Lawrence himself played a dual sex role: he could achieve an identification with the heroine but also play the more gratifying part of the male reborn of her, who controls and yet relies on her. In his first creative gropings Lawrence had looked upon his mother in this fashion, with himself as the gifted, dependent yet masterful son. The next woman who filled the place was Jessie Chambers. Drawing away from Jessie now, he meant for Helen Corke to be next. Looking ahead after the stage of *The Trespasser,* we see Lawrence turning to Frieda to such a degree that he could declare his artistic creed in terms like this: the only way for the world to reach a new vision in his day

ML, 291   was for the artist to submit his soul to being *fertilised by the **female***
ML, 280   and to consider art *the joint work of man and woman.* This cannot be taken as Lawrence's final conviction, but he held it from 1912 to 1916, his most concentrated period of great work.

In setting a pair of lovers in *The Trespasser* within a strange and fascinating landscape beyond their everyday world, Lawrence's purpose was to free himself from the infantile attachment to his mother as beloved that he had suffered — and enjoyed — on the same landscape.

How strong this transference of disturbing passion was, at first, is hard to say, but in the two years between the first and last writing of the novel, Lawrence's mother died, he despaired almost to suicide, and he suffered a critical illness, from which he was convalescing when he last worked on the book. By then, the need to exorcise the mother image and replace her with a mate had become imperative, necessitating the sort of therapy undertaken in *Sons and Lovers* — indeed Lawrence interrupted work on an early version of this novel to revise *The Trespasser*. The intensification of his problems had carried him, however, beyond the fictional potentialities of the original involvement with Helen Corke, toward whom he was increasingly indifferent by early 1912. She was not the woman to release him from the oppressive shade of the mother, even if he had been able to project himself fully into the original for Siegmund, hero of the novel, whose dilemma all the while grew less and less like his own. The result of all this in the novel is confusion.

Yet this quest on a dream island for psychic balance in love and for accord with the great realities of sea and land contains much of value toward assessment of the mature Lawrence.

Siegmund leaves the city to join Helena on the Isle of Wight as *elated as a young man setting forth to travel* — Lawrence was pondering, TR, 22 as he completed the book, his first trip to the Continent. Siegmund nears the island with the feelings of a hero: thinking how *like the* TR, 23 *beautiful women in the myths, his love hid in its blue haze,* thinking in the Wagnerian terms that so pervade the book. The island has at once begun to exercise its influence over the course of the love affair. The cliffs offer the danger and mystery of death, and other allurements of the great beyond. The sea offers the ceaseless rolling splendor of life, and with its margin of clean beach, a purification that Siegmund achieves embracing the waves and the sand as he swims or lies on the beach. The island can be a vessel bearing the couple like *two grains* TR, 56 *of life in the vast* whirling of the spheres, *travelling a moment side by side.* Now and again Siegmund is overtaken by a desire to exist in time and timelessness at once, but for the most part this vision cannot reach beyond literary allusion: *He could not yet fully realize that he was* TR, 99 *walking along a lane in the Isle of Wight. His surroundings seemed to belong to some state beyond ordinary experience — some place in romance, perhaps, or among the hills where Brünhild lay sleeping in her large bright halo of fire.* On occasion Lawrence does maneuver his hero into an expression of harmony with the natural world foreshadowing the great symbolic union of the later novels, sometimes to the point of undermining the credibility of Siegmund's suicide later on. Glimmerings also occur of fictional rhythms where gratuitous behavior springs from unconscious potencies, rhythms drawn so regularly in the mature Lawrence from relationship to landscape. But here they carry little conviction, as much because of the style as anything ML, 93   else. Lawrence recognized in this a *fluid, luscious quality* that he was ready to renounce even before he completed the book.

As Lawrence could not bring this landscape to interweave with the deeper promptings of his characters, neither could he bring any unity to Siegmund's ambivalence toward Helena. The mother and the beloved are embodied in the same woman. Often Siegmund is tempted to slip back into the fear and clinging of childhood, with Helena looming over him like the demon Lawrence sought to cast out even as he clutched it to his bosom. For example, Siegmund lies half-conscious TR,   at Helena's feet, and *as he lay helplessly looking up at her some other* 93–94   *consciousness inside him murmured: "Hawwa — Eve — Mother!" She stood compassionate over him. Without touching him she seemed to be yearning over him like a mother. Her compassion, her benignity, seemed so different from his little Helena.* In later years Lawrence came to detest these *pietà* postures with the great mother sorrowing over the limp son. Even in other parts of the present novel, he goes so far as to condemn mother and son alike in oedipal situations. Toward the end of his rapid deterioration, Siegmund appeals even to his nine-year-old daughter for the mothering he craves, with the author's scorn manifest. Another pattern is set up in Siegmund's repudiation by his own household, with all the children pitted against him, which is reminiscent of what happened to Lawrence's father. This rejection hastens Siegmund's destruction. Then his wife triumphs in vicarious motherhood by setting up a boarding house and ruling over young men in gentle, solicitous tyranny.

Siegmund is aware that a weakness of his own contributes to his downfall, but he lays the chief blame on women, who are implied to be insidiously destructive. Lawrence has a double appear to warn Siegmund against the female peril. The principal means in the woman's denial of life becomes, for Siegmund, not the assumption of magna materhood but the negation of physical passion. He is capable of masculine boldness and wisdom in the amorous mystery, of initiating his beloved. But Helena resists. She is too much the Victorian spiritual TR, 35   woman. She lacks *brightness and vividness of blood.* With her, *passion* TR, 68   *exhausts itself at the mouth,* and she would like to reject *the "animal" in humanity.* She feels *blasted* when the man has taken her completely. She will sooner offer herself as a sacrifice than as a partner in sensual adventure: the same complaint that Paul has against Miriam in *Sons and Lovers.*

In all the entanglements of the Siegmund-Helena affair, then, Lawrence was reaching out blindly for a fictional form of the turmoil within, but for all his description of Seigmund's suffering, he never makes convincing the supposed sense of excruciating failure that hurries Siegmund to his self-inflicted end. Lawrence could only in an obscure way attribute his difficulties to Siegmund. He could not put himself in Siegmund's skin.

When the lovers must leave the Isle of Wight, they stand gazing out into the beyond for a moment, where they know life cannot lead them: *They looked down the cliffs at the beach and over the sea. The* TR, 166 *strand was wide, forsaken by the sea, forlorn with rocks bleaching in the sun, and sand and sea-weed breathing off their painful scent upon the heat. The sea crept smaller, further away; the sky stood still. Siegmund and Helena looked hopelessly out on their beautiful, incandescent world. They looked hopelessly at each other.* All they can do is retreat from the outer Eden to the city, he to meet death and she disillusion.

Helen Corke was disappointed with Lawrence's final rewriting of *The Trespasser.* One of the greatest losses, to her, was a number of *grandly symbolic passages* that he had written under the inspiration CB, of the landscape, sea and sky of the Isle of Wight. This objection only vol. I, shows how far the two had by now diverged in emotional requirements. 97 As seen from the author's standpoint, the landscape of the published work could hardly have been made more symbolic than it is, however much it refuses to cohere with the human elements of the story.

The symbolism of islands underwent a long cycle of change in Lawrence's career, now objectifying a new world of manageable limits, now a prison of the soul. But at the last he was uneasy with islands, and it may well be that the unsuccessful metamorphosis of the Isle of Wight — that first breaking of geographical horizons which failed to break emotional horizons — contributed as initial defeat may to final dislike.[2] In any event, no liberation could be gained within the boundaries of the British Isles, and *The Trespasser,* so full of that disappointment just under the narrative surface, served only as a prelude to escape.

During those months in 1910 while his mother wasted away with cancer, Lawrence came to feel a pressing need, as if by psychological compensation, for a woman who could devote her life to him and still meet with maternal approval. He may even have felt that he could never marry if death cut off forever his mother's consent. Certainly he wished to cling still to what had been his undoing: a soul-union with his mother. This hope, as revealed in letters of the time, indicates the extent of his emotional disruption. Inevitably, he confided in an older woman, in Rachel Annand Taylor, a poet of recent acquaintance:

ML, 70   *Muriel [Jessie Chambers] is the girl I have broken with. She loves me to madness, and demands the soul of me. I have been cruel to her, and wronged her, but I did not know.*

Nobody can have the soul of me. My mother has had it, and nobody can have it again. Nobody can come into my very self again, and breathe me like an atmosphere. Don't say I am hasty this time — I know. Louie — whom I wish I could marry the day after the funeral — she would never demand to drink me up and have me. She loves me — but it is a fine, warm, healthy, natural love.

That very day Lawrence had on impulse proposed to Louie Burrows, a friend of several years, and she had accepted him. The rationalization of his actions shows how much, and yet how little, he saw into his own plight. He could not yet condemn his mother for having taken his soul: he was still in love with his servitude. He saw plainly, however, that a union with Jessie Chambers might mean a shifting of ownership from mother to wife, and this recognition had played its part, along with his mother's disapproval, in the rupture with Jessie. But he seriously miscalculated in his belief that he could have a *warm* and *natural* marriage with Louie Burrows on a purely physical level, that she would live with him in simple wifely obedience and sacrifice, without demands on his deeper self. He did not even seem to understand that demands could be made on the deeper self in any *natural* way, and indeed in his experience this was true. He was some time in realizing his errors, and much longer in making any headway against them. Meanwhile, at least, he had the solace of knowing that he had stilled one of his torments: he had wrung from his mother her grudging death-bed consent to his marriage with Louie. Clearly he had counted on this, and it figured large, no doubt, in his even asking Louie to marry him.

For the moment, this young woman seemed to Lawrence the promised land of uncomplicated bliss. He wrote her so three days after his proposal, and just three days also before the death of the mother:

LL, 57   *You will be the first woman to make the earth glad for me: mother, J [Jessie] — all the rest, have been gates to a very sad world. But you are strong & rosy as the gates of Eden. We do not all of us, not many, perhaps, set out from a sunny paradise of childhood. We are born with our parents in the desert, and yearn for a Canaan. You are like Canaan — you are rich & fruitful & glad, and I love you.*

Sensuality cast in Biblical language was to be increasingly natural to Lawrence as time went on, a characteristic way of lending his emotional processes universality. Identifying his love with a mythical place to be attained by pilgrimage may here suggest exaggeration to overcome doubts, but we see forming nonetheless a habit of thought which was to become an indispensable part of his imaginative make-up.

Lawrence had indeed been wandering in the wilderness of his parents' unhappy marriage for years, and the only visible way out at the time was to enter a settled maturity as quickly as possible. Not long before, he had said to Helen Corke: *"When I'm middle-aged, I shall probably be married and settled, and take my family to church every Sunday .... Best so ...."* Still, early in his engagement to Louie Burrows he admitted he might not have the instinct necessary to such staidness: *I cannot accumulate things. Possessions all go under the heading 'Impedimenta' — for me.* He hastened to add that he must mend his ways, but he never could have done so. CB, vol. I, 96   LL, 58

As he watched his mother fade into death, Lawrence saw his native landscape alter with her. From her bedside he would *turn to look out of the window at the bright wet cabbages in the garden, and the horses in the field beyond, and the church-tower small as a black dice on the hill at the back a long way off, and I find myself apostrophising the landscape 'So that's what you mean, is it?' — and under the mobile shadowy change of expression, like smiles, on the countryside, there seems to be the cast of eternal suffering.* He could not yet know, but the realization of sorrow under joy in landscape was but the first step toward another revelation it contained: eternal renewal to offset suffering. He soon took the first step, too, in loosing the bonds of his mother's domination. In October 1910, two months before her end, he began a novel purportedly to be her story but transmuted into his own before its completion as *Sons and Lovers.* PL, 122–123

But Lawrence could not tell this story till he found the woman who could bring him relief from excessive mother-love. The engagement with Louie lasted for about a year, and given Lawrence's half-hearted commitment, it is no wonder he could not discover freedom in that direction. Some fifteen months after his mother died and shortly after he broke the engagement with Louie, he met Frieda. He could never have gone to her, he confessed, if his mother had lived, for certainly she would never have approved of Frieda. The power of mutual attraction was such, however, that even this weighty objection fell away, bringing Lawrence his first real victory over the past.

Frieda von Richthofen Weekley was not literary and soulful and possessive through humility like Jessie Chambers. She did not have the claim to intellectual equality plus the fidelity to a lover's memory which had stood in Lawrence's way with Helen Corke. Frieda had all the physical desirability of Louie Burrows, but she was not, like her, ruled by convention in most things. She had a strong belief in the potency of physical love, acquired in the Bohemian circles of Munich, where eroticism amounted to a religion and where such theories as Freud's were a constant topic. She overflowed with warmth and vitality and was a few years older than Lawrence: perfect as lover and mother MC, 388 & 460 in one to his frustrated spirit. If a readiness to abandon her family did not in itself prove a willingness to devote her life to his welfare, she also harbored an ambition to be the feminine power behind a genius. RS, 59–62 She had been picked as perfect for that role and offered the opportunity of filling it, by Otto Gross, who during their love affair a few years earlier had written begging her to be his nurture and inspiration. She had declined, but only, it seems, because Gross did not have his feet planted on the earth. But with her ambition intact, Lawrence's appearance on the horizon of her dull existence as a professor's wife in Nottingham must have seemed as providential to her as her appearance did to him.

Lawrence did not attempt to put their flight from England into imaginative prose until a couple of years had elapsed. When he did describe their crossing of the Channel, he did so with the intensity of recording a voyage into outer space or a journey through death to life. The narration occurs in *Women in Love,* and Lawrence divides his feeling between the hero and the heroine. The lovers go forward WL, 378–379 to *near the very point of the ship, near the black, unpierced space ahead. Here they sat down, folded together, folded round with the same rug, creeping in nearer and ever nearer to one another, till it seemed they had crept right into each other, and become one substance. . . .*

In Ursula, the sense of the unrealised world ahead triumphed over everything. In the midst of this profound darkness, there seemed to glow on her heart the effulgence of a paradise unknown and unrealised. . . .

But he [Birkin] *did not know the ecstasy of bliss in fore-knowledge that she knew. To him, the wonder of the transit was overwhelming. He was falling through a gulf of infinite darkness, like a meteorite plunging across the chasm between the worlds. The world was torn in two, and he was plunging like an unlit star through the ineffable rift. What was beyond was not yet for him. He was overcome by the trajectory.*

No experience went deeper with Lawrence than the forging on into unknown places. In the re-creation of his travel adventures, this two-fold response of the male and the female is common also, elaborated often with the overtones of religious pilgrimage. We note above that Ursula has her heart set on the goal, the *paradise,* while to Birkin the journey itself is all in all. In Lawrence the woman perennially seeks a point, a fixed center, while the man seeks an outflinging of movement for its own sake. These are the complementary halves of any venture.

One of the first new imaginative roles that the resolution to travel and the coincidental discovery of the right companion brought to

Lawrence was that of the dark wanderer, who pursues a solitary integrity outside the ordinary confines of life, a figure who after many appearances culminates in the figure of Jesus in *The Escaped Cock*. In conjunction with the dark wanderer is the wayfaring woman, now discovered in Frieda but also in one aspect of himself. The whole of their migrant life together is epitomized in one of the first poems about their love: the "Ballad of a Wilful Woman" that Lawrence wrote during the first week of their elopement.

The woman in the poem is Mary, who on the plodding donkey makes for Egypt with Joseph and the child. As they pause on a hilltop above the sea, *a dark-faced stranger* beckons to her, and handing the CP, 200 child to Joseph, she drifts away with the stranger. Obviously, this is Frieda as young wife leaving her older husband in charge of the children, renouncing a life of duty for one of exploring the unknown with a fascinating lover. Under his first incarnation in the poem, the dark man leads Mary to Cythera, to know the ways of Aphrodite. At length she returns to Joseph, willing to take up the journey again, but far wiser than when she was only a *mother mild*. Over and over, in several CP, 201 forms, the dusky wanderer appears. Once he rows Mary away to live *in a huge, hoarse sea-cave,* where she submits to his instruction in how to see spirits from the world beyond *crowding the bright doorway,* which is visible far off through the dark of the cave. This doorway is the egress from his dark troubles that Lawrence's first excursion with Frieda promised.

Later, Mary and the stranger sojourn in Patmos, to taste visions like those of St. John the Divine. Time after time she comes back to Joseph, only to follow again the irresistible alien. In the last of the six sections of the poem he becomes a beggar, and lures Mary away for good. Here Lawrence was surely thinking of Frieda's straying from her husband in earlier love affairs, and of himself as the final and impecunious lover. The beggar is demanding. He leads the woman through harsh places where strange winds blow. At night she makes love with him, and dreams too of her deserted family. He gathers wild berries for her to distill. The *flame-wild drops* of her brewing he sells CP, 203 in the town — words, of course, or the poems engendered by the great adventure:

> So she follows the cruel journey
> That ends not anywhere,
> And dreams, as she stirs the mixing-pot,
> She is brewing hope from despair.

While Lawrence was soon to arrive at more effective expression than this "ballad," nowhere is his appraisal of his own experience plainer. The woman is led into mysterious realms by the man, the revealer of life. But she is the support of his quest: he cannot wander without her. She thus fulfills the perfect function of woman as Lawrence at this time understood it. The woman in the poem is also CP, 201   the creative imagination of Lawrence pursuing two ways at once, *the slow, mean journey* of mundane life and the pilgrimage through bitterness and beauty to religious vision. The poet identifies at will with either the masculine or the feminine figure of the wanderer, but here too the woman serves first to glorify the quest for greatness of the bold and adventurous male. This dark man, usually bearded, we will encounter again and again on the way to his final incarnation in the Christ of *The Escaped Cock:* in *The Plumed Serpent* and *The Virgin and the Gypsy,* for instance. The woman will be recognizable in such figures of quest as the heroines of *St. Mawr, The Plumed Serpent* and *Lady Chatterley's Lover.*

The "Ballad of a Wilful Woman" is also one of Lawrence's earliest poems to employ a thoroughgoing Biblical parallel as a framework for experience. The young man who thought of his fiancée as Canaan and himself as Israel had reached his first real elaboration of such a theme.

To note the variety that Lawrence the traveler experienced, we might turn from the epic wanderer or the religious pilgrim to the amused and genial observer who could catch in a few words the brilliance of life's surface, who could display a ready sympathy with foreigners and draw them out, with a capability to see and describe what seem whole lives from the briefest of contacts. We detect this mood in Lawrence's first "travel sketches": "German Impressions," hastily written for the *Westminster Gazette* soon after his arrival in Germany.

Having spent the first few days in Metz, Frieda's native town, Lawrence went on alone to Trier, forced to leave Metz sooner than intended when mistaken for a British officer too curious about fortifications. He stayed in Trier only three days, on the second of which he wrote an "impression" of Metz called "French Sons of Germany." PH, 72   Beyond the many soldiers and the *imitation-medieval church* uneasy on a peninsula in the river, he had found little that was German about the town. Enough to repel him, however. He had to admit, after thinking it over, *a temperamental aversion* to the national character of the PH, 71   German, in whom he found a *tiresome split between his animal nature and his spiritual.* Lawrence first detects here the cleavage that he later saw in all modern men and not just certain nationalities. Insights in this direction always continued to come to him through powers of observation sharpened by travel in foreign countries.

The hostility to Germans in this sketch, which became so pronounced in others that the *Westminster Gazette* refused to print them, must have been due partly to Lawrence's brush with the military in Metz. He responded quite differently in other instances, as in his admiration of how deeply the folk spirit was rooted in German soil. But in Metz it was the French he liked. For one reason he could speak their language better at that time. With them he was genial and communicative, drawing glowing and memorable little portraits of the tradespeople and the school children, all based on his view that the French did not suffer from a split between the physical and the spiritual as the Germans did.

Lawrence's few days in Trier, where Frieda came to join him briefly, were extraordinarily active. Besides one or more sketches, he composed the more than eighty lines of "Ballad of a Wilful Woman," wrote at least four letters, and as if this was not enough to keep him busy, thought over a new novel. For at the moment he believed that the Paul Morel novel, as he now neared the end of the third draft, would not detain him long.

Frieda returned to Metz after her visit and Lawrence went on to Waldbröl, a little town in the hills east of Bonn, to pay a visit to the Krenkows, relatives by marriage on his mother's side — this connection had been one of his original reasons for contemplating a trip to Germany. It was a roundabout train ride from Trier up to Waldbröl, through the valleys of the Moselle and the Rhine. The last of four changes came at Hennef, on the River Sieg, where Lawrence had an hour's layover just at twilight. Here he quickly set down a poem different in form and tone from the "ballad" of a day or two before. And although the "ballad" was the first poem on his affair with Frieda, it was the second poem, in free verse and titled "Bei Hennef" from the scene of its composition, that Lawrence later on recognized as opening a new phase of his career, a whole cycle inspired by his stay on the Continent with Frieda.

A new facet of Lawrence's enchantment with place is the key to this poem. A little village the poet is passing through, an instant of time at dusk, a small river whose flowing is an image of the constantly changing yet never changing present: all these combine to bring an unforgettable moment of truth, the knowledge that

> *And at last I know my love for you is here;*   CP, 203
> *I can see it all, it is whole like the twilight.*

Here does not really designate a geographical location but a sudden presence. The love for the woman does not reside in the village, nor in

Germany either. The locale has become a metaphor. From the hugeness and wholeness of twilight and the sound and motion of the stream, the poet derives vision to see the inner landscape of his love, which the anxieties of escape from the homeland have concealed up to now. The landscape is symbolic as an immediate embodiment of pain and joy in love, yet the place never ceases to be itself while it serves this purpose: a procedure Lawrence was to utilize often in his poetry from now on.

If we compare this poem with the "ballad," two significant new directions of Lawrence's talent emerge. The "ballad" also takes a passage through strange places as symbolic, but in it the method is that of myth-making, not the suggestive realism of "Bei Hennef." This sort of narrative myth-making Lawrence was more often to exploit in prose than in poetry.

To grasp the poetic insight Lawrence had gained by entry into an unfixed life, we have only to contrast another poem of this later vein with one on a former affair where the circumstances were similar.

CP, 61   The early poem, entitled "Lightning," concerns Lawrence and Jessie Chambers. The two lovers stand in close embrace in darkness. After a description in two five-line stanzas of the delight in clinging together, in the heartbeat and breathing of the woman, the man leans to kiss her and at that instant a flash of lightning illuminates her face. In this glimpse he sees her fear of physical love and a grieving determination to sacrifice herself for his sake. His desire dies. His arms fall limp. He comes near to hating her and himself, the place where they are, and the cold rain that seems to speak, telling him to go home, for the lightning has made their predicament all too clear.

The poem has a rhyme scheme of no apparent relation to the theme — in rhyming, the early Lawrence often mistook facility for spontaneity. The realization of the lover, the justification for the poem, is drawn out for thirty lines, in contradiction to the suddenness of the discovery. The use of natural events is clumsy. The key moment, the lightning, is conveyed in words effective enough, but not so the look on the woman's face. The metaphor comparing her to snow slipping from a roof and weeping at its own death is strained. And the rain speaking, putting into words what the lightning has communicated, is even less effective. Such looseness and inexactness is typical of a great many of the early poems in which Lawrence attempts to bring human feeling and natural surroundings together. Even one of the

CP, 35   better ones, "Dog-Tired," consists really of disjointed halves: a vivid description of a hay-field at dusk beside an evocation of the man's desire to rest his head on the woman's lap, with no sealing of the two themes into one substance.

A poem from the sequence that "Bei Hennef" introduces, working with elements similar to those of the "Lightning" poem, does all that the early poems do not do, in only fourteen lines of verse free in rhythm but echoing the sonnet form:

On the Balcony

CP,
208–209

In front of the sombre mountains, a faint, lost
        ribbon of rainbow;
And between us and it, the thunder;
And down below in the green wheat, the labourers
Stand like dark stumps, still in the green wheat.

You are near to me, and your naked feet in their sandals,
And through the scent of the balcony's naked timber
I distinguish the scent of your hair: so now the limber
Lightning falls from heaven.

Adown the pale-green glacier river floats
A dark boat through the gloom — and whither?
The thunder roars. But still we have each other!
The naked lightnings in the heavens dither
And disappear — what have we but each other?
The boat has gone.

The earlier poem could only be over-explicit to exhaustion. Here the surroundings carry the message by suggestion, not by awkward metaphor. The universe in the midst of which the lovers stand is made up of ephemeral things, whose truth is *naked* as they pass, none giving comfort to the pain and wonder of the flesh yet all serving to unite the lovers by pitting human love against immensity. By simple analogy a real landscape, while remaining itself, is transformed into symbol.

In such poems Lawrence made far-reaching strides during his first months in new lands with his new love, toward a mature theory and practice of poetic utterance incorporating his beliefs on the nature of self, place, and time. When these poems had accumulated and ripened into a recognizable sequence, some five years later, he published them in an independent volume, *Look! We Have Come Through!, as an essential story, or history, or confession, unfolding* CP, 191 *one from the other in organic development.* The "Argument" introducing the volume presents the *confession* in a quasi-religious light, where pilgrimage to distant places and the attainment of felicity in marriage are inseparable halves of the same quest:

After much struggling and loss in love and in the world of men,
the protagonist throws in his lot with a woman who is already
married. Together they go into another country, she perforce
leaving her children behind. The conflict of love and hate goes on

between the man and the woman, and between these two and the
world around them, till it reaches some sort of conclusion, they
transcend into some condition of blessedness.

But even at that time, early 1917, Lawrence had not come to a
finished hypothesis of what he was about, and did not reach one till
over two years later, in a piece written to introduce the American
edition of *New Poems* (1920). This statement he belatedly recognized
as rightly a foreword to *Look! We Have Come Through!* The vision
of time, place and self incipient in the poetry of 1912 arrives at a summation here, at the end of one cycle whose doctrine was nevertheless to carry over into the next, was indeed to evolve as the core of
Lawrence's poetic beliefs for the rest of his life. Chiefly this hypothesis
concerns a relationship between theme and form which Lawrence
conceived under the term "free verse," and which he held in almost
mystical reverence.

If we survey both the poems and the poet's comments about them
from *Look! We Have Come Through!* to the culminating work of
the next cycle, *Birds, Beasts and Flowers* — probably Lawrence's greatest poetic achievement — we find that without half realizing it he meant
much more by "free verse" than merely the line structure of a poem.
Actually he includes under verse called "free" some poems with
definite rhyme scheme. And his division of the later *Collected Poems*
— under "Rhyming Poems" mainly early work, under "Unrhyming
Poems" mainly what begins with *Look! We Have Come Through!* —
makes little sense if taken literally. Poems nominally in free verse occur
in the "Rhyming Poems" section, and though he trumpeted his breaking into new territory with the "free verse" of *Look! We Have Come
Through!,* more than half the poems in this volume cling to a rhyme
pattern, frequently one quite traditional. The real cleavage between
rhyme and free verse, by line structure, does not come until *Birds,
Beasts and Flowers.*

What Lawrence really meant in heralding "Bei Hennef" as the
dawn of a new era in his poetry was that he was suddenly capable of a
more flexible composite of language and emotion than ever before.
He could express the instantaneous and soul-dazzling revelations that
unforeseen moments in love can bring, and could do this without undue
attention to scansion: he could write "On the Balcony," no longer
constrained to the limitations of "Lightning." The discussion of "free
verse" in the "Introduction" to the American *New Poems* means more
if accepted in this sense.

Free verse is the only one, Lawrence here claims, that can lay hold
of the pulsing present, as opposed to forms best suited to the past or the
CP, 185   future. Free verse alone can be *instantaneous like plasm,* can contain
CP, 183   *the seething poetry of the incarnate Now.* In other words, Lawrence

speaks of a practice opposite to making poetry out of emotion recollected in tranquility. The aim instead is to seize the essence of the
experience close to the moment of its occurrence and shape it in words
at once, the form compelled by the strength and immediacy of the
emotion rather than a traditional technique.

These ideas of poetry presuppose a certain view of the nature of
time. The present, the ever-fleeting moment of consciousness, is the
only form under which time can be truly experienced. Lawrence
could first have met with this thought in Schopenhauer, whose work
had struck him as brilliantly true in college days, or he could have
learned it through his passion for experience, his avidity for cultivating
the whole presence of life in every feeling and act.[3] He wished to perceive time as he perceived place, each minute and each feature of his
surroundings a mysterious terrain for exploration. But far from being a
renunciation, as such, of past and future, or of distance, this perception
was an all-inclusive concentration of time and place like that exemplified in the *Minoan distance* phrase, a simultaneous awareness of all
time and place, unified in one burning substance of feeling and language. The terminology of the "Introduction" can easily apply to either
time or place: *One realm we have never conquered: the pure present.*   CP, 185
One great mystery of time is terra incognita to us: the instant.

In 1928, about ten years after the above reckoning with poetic
theory, Lawrence restated what were basically the same convictions
from another slant: his preoccupation with the self rather than time
and place. He had by now decided that from the start of his poetic
vocation two voices had habitually made themselves heard in his verse.
Only one of these spoke in real poetry, though, and Lawrence's description of how this voice operated explains why he would prefer "free"
verse over any other. One voice was that of the versifier, a clever
literary man who self-consciously "composed" poems in a pleasant
vein. Lawrence calls him *the commonplace me.* The other self, the   CP, 852
author of his real poetry, he calls his *demon,* and gives an extended
account of how he first made the acquaintance of that mysterious spirit:
I used to feel myself at times haunted by something, and a little guilty   CP, 849
about it, as if it were an abnormality. Then the haunting would get
the better of me, and the ghost would suddenly appear, in the shape of
a usually rather incoherent poem. Nearly always I shunned the appa-
rition once it had appeared. From the first, I was a little afraid of my
real poems — not my "compositions," but the poems that had the ghost
in them. They seemed to me to come from somewhere, I didn't quite
know where, out of a me whom I didn't know and didn't want to know,
and to say things I would much rather not have said.

Lawrence never states, here, that the demon inclined to one certain variety of verse. A great many of the poems he classified as

demon-inspired are in rhyme. But he does insist on the spontaneity
CP, 851   of form: *The demon, when he's really there, makes his own form
willy-nilly, and is unchangeable.* And clearly the demon came to prefer
free verse, for as the years advanced and with them the force of
Lawrence's expression, he grew to write in almost nothing else.

If the demon was ubiquitous, he was also elusive. When Lawrence
was going over his poems for collected volumes, he often revised,
especially the earlier poems, to allow the veritable voice of the demon
to come through. This practice seems to contradict the view of the true
poetic self: if the demon had spoken, in his inevitable form, selection
should have been no more than weeding out the failures attributable
to the clever literary self and harvesting the true grain of the demon.
Lawrence's justification — and the distinction is none too clear — is that
CP, 850   the *commonplace youth,* that sophisticated and talkative fellow, would
lay his hand over *the mouth of the demon* if he got the chance, throwing in his own phrases. It required years, in some cases, to discover
where he had interfered.

One of the most telling divergences between the everyday and
the demonic self, and one that Lawrence emphasizes, is their respective
outlooks on time. The ordinary man recognized a yesterday and a
tomorrow and preferred poetry in the frozen forms of the past or
the ethereal forms of the future. But to the demon all was timeless,
and all endured in the present. To the demon *the wild common* and
the gorse of one poem, the *virgin youth* of another, were *here and now*
in the later days just as much as they were in Lawrence's youth when
he wrote those poems. This demonic persona knew by nature the
mystic Now and the ever-living spirit of place.

In 1928 Lawrence still traced his first distinction of poetic selves to
CP, 851   "Bei Hennef," when he had *left England, and left many other things,*
and the demon had bolted out of captivity into *a new run for his
money,* to seek out the immediate simultaneously with untried manifestations of place.

To return to the spring of 1912, when Lawrence reached Waldbröl
from Trier, he stayed about two weeks with the Krenkows. He sat
through the mornings revising *Paul Morel,* impatient that Munich,
ML, 126   where he was to rejoin Frieda, was *15 hours' journey from this God-
forsaken little hole,* and that he could not head for there at once. The
Rhineland, under these circumstances, could never be more than *a
land of exile.*

Still, there was occasion to be lively, and Lawrence's response
came through the place as well as the most attractive person there.
One of the Krenkow family was a young woman he calls "Johanna,"
not long married to an older husband. Lawrence flirted with her, on a

walk to a village that ended in a hailstorm and their being thrown together alone in a closed carriage. Only the increasing fury of the hail, which drove the cabman inside for shelter, prevented flirtation from turning into serious involvement: at least according to the published sketch of the event, *a narrow escape* from going to another PH, 81 woman out of sheer loneliness for Frieda. This sketch, in tone like the one of Metz, portrays a boyish and exuberant Lawrence, eager to talk with the local population and observing his surroundings with a constant, bright curiosity. But the Lawrence who saw by a mythic sense is not totally absent even from this slight piece: the hailstorm left the roadway covered *with twigs, as green as spring,* which made him PH, 80 *think of the roads strewed for the Entry into Jerusalem.*

During these first weeks in Germany Lawrence the correspondent became one with Lawrence the traveler. Already an accomplished letter-writer, he filled his correspondence from now on with what are in themselves travel sketches, and the intimate glimpses of common life which these contain are woven with easy and consummate skill into Lawrence's endeavors to understand his own condition and refine his talents. The little sketches flow naturally into his outpourings on the relationship with Frieda, on his struggles with fiction and poetry, on his visions of time and place, on his very identity. Months before leaving England, when he was only in Bournemouth recuperating from his terrible illness, he seemed to have some inkling, while writing to a colleague at Croydon, that through descriptions of the country around him he could enter into deeper feelings: *How can I, in a far-off land,* ML, 95 *tell you interesting things — unless I become geographical.* Geography soon began to fill its large role in his life in the letters as well as in poetry and sketches, letters where echoes of escape frequently sound among the lively reportage: *I write on top of the Drachenfels, in the* ML, 124 *café under the trees. One can see miles and miles of Rhine — it twists and seems to climb upwards till some of it swims in the sky. We came here down the river from Bonn — that is a delicious town — masses of horse-chestnut trees in blossom. Germany is delightful. If I have to beg my bread I'll never teach again.*

As soon as Lawrence had joined Frieda in Munich, they went to Beuerberg, a short way up the Isar valley toward the Alps, for a brief honeymoon. This place, with the valley and the distant mountains around him, became a very Eden to Lawrence, and the sense of a primeval world recaptured flowed abundantly into the letters. Each day at the *gasthaus* in Beuerberg was perfection itself—almost. Villages *white and gay* spread all around, the river was of *green glacier water,* ML, 128 the *masses of Alpine flowers* could *make you dance.* Next, the lovers moved down a little way to Icking, to the borrowed upper floor of a

BEUERBERG, BAVARIA

We leaned in the bedroom window /
Of the old Bavarian Gasthaus (CP, 206)

cottage, to stay for a few months. Below their balcony was the *plain of dark woods — all in shadow, and* off there *the great blue wall of mountains, only their tops, all snowy, glittering in far-off sunshine against a pale blue sky.* Lawrence did his best to describe to Edward Garnett, one of his few confidants in the Frieda affair, what his happiness was like: *Frieda is awfully good-looking. You should see her sometimes. She is getting the breakfast. We are both a bit solemn this morning. It is our first morning at home. You needn't say things about her — or me. She is a million times better than ever you imagine — you don't know her, from literature, no, how can you? I don't. She is fond of you. I say she'd alarm you. She's got a figure like a fine Rubens woman, but her face is almost Greek. If you say a word about her, I hate you. I am awfully well — you should see me. I wish Weekley would divorce her, but he won't. I shall live abroad I think for ever.*

Although Frieda had not yet agreed to permanent union, for all Lawrence's high hopes and persuasion, and he was just beginning to see her as vital to his emotional stability, he already pictured in her the embodiment of freedom matched by the freedom of the Bavarian landscape. And even now he was convincd there could be no turning back to England.

Compared with the countryside he had known up to now, the Isar valley was vast and wild and primitive to Lawrence: his first restored world. Still, his days there with Frieda were not all rapture. Many vicissitudes blocked the way to firm happiness as a united couple. Lawrence was soon writing to Edward Garnett that it wasn't all *nibbling grapes and white sugar. Oh no — the great war is waged in this* ML, 132 *little flat on the Isarthal.* In the intensity of his great and honest emotions, Lawrence took these struggles to adjust to one another as a matter of life and death, and he chose to define them, by his current view of seeing the best emerge from all things, as *tragedy,* which he defined in this way: *I don't think the real tragedy is in dying, or in the perversity of affairs, like the woman one loves being the wife of another man — like the last act of Tristan. I think the real tragedy is in the inner war which is waged between people who love each other, a war out of which comes knowledge.*

Knowledge out of strife to overcome perversity of circumstances — tragedy had become that to him after his mother's death, bitterness and beauty combined as a weapon against despair. But now he could see regeneration in tragedy, and this turn of thought was to exert a great influence on *Sons and Lovers.*

One of the most glaring sources of contention between the lovers was Frieda's longing for her children, complicated by the demands Lawrence made on her maternal instincts. Other difficulties will be

WOLFRATSHAUSEN, BAVARIA

*A white, tiny village, with a great church, white-washed outside,
with a white minaret and a black small bulb — half renaissance,
half moorish* (CL, 418)

more apparent when we have gone further into Lawrence's self-examination in his writing.

Lawrence never saw his own problems as limited to himself. What he experienced he felt certain was a potential lesson for all men. He therefore undertook his writing task with a sense of mission, now as never before. This life in an exotic land was instructing him, he thought, in the shortcomings of English civilization. The way ahead must lie through the equivalent of a wonderful country, and he wanted to drag all England through it: *What the English can be if they are hauled by*   ML, 131
the neck into it, is something rather great. I should like to bludgeon them into realising their own selves. Curse you, my countrymen, you have put the halters round your necks, and pull tighter and tighter from day to day. You are strangling yourselves, you blasted fools. Oh my countrymen! — the prophet calls on Israel to repent and save itself.

With all the brightening of this land through the eyes of love, Lawrence hovered on the verge of a vast territory of self as yet undreamed of: *It is astonishing how barbaric one gets with love: one*   ML, 132
finds onself in the Hinterland der Seele, and — it's a rum place. I never knew I was like this. What Blasted Fools the English are, fencing off the big wild scope of their natures. Since I am in Germany, all my little pathetic sadness and softness goes, and I am often frightened at the thing I find myself.

The *bright doorway* of this woman and this mysterious wild country opened, it seemed, into a whole newness of life.

NOTES

[1] Michael Sharpe explores Lawrence's difficulties with "spiritual" women as a prime motive in writing *The Trespasser*. See "The Genesis of D. H. Lawrence's *The Trespasser*," *Essays in Criticism*, vol. 11, no. 1, January 1961, pp. 34–39. Jessie Chambers' account of the composition of *The Trespasser* offers an interesting perspective. See JC, 181–182.

[2] See ML, 1095, where Lawrence reports his growing dissatisfaction with the Île de Port-Cros, off the French Riviera, in 1928. The story "The Man Who Loved Islands," discussed in a later chapter, presents a significant late view (1926) of island symbolism in Lawrence.

[3] Jessie Chambers recalls the depth of Schopenhauer's influence on Lawrence: JC, 98,111. Some further comments of hers are recorded by Émile Delavanay, *D. H. Lawrence: L'Homme et la genèse de son oeuvre (1885–1919)* (Paris, 1969), pp. 694–695. See also Delavanay, "Sur un exemplaire de Schopenhauer annoté par D. H. Lawrence," *Revue Anglo-Américaine*, 1935, pp. 234–238. Lawrence sometimes stated his metaphysics in Schopenhauerian echoes, as in ML, 341. For a recent article, see Allan R. Zoll, "Vitalism and the Metaphysics of Love: D. H. Lawrence and Schopenhauer," *D. H. Lawrence Review*, vol. 11, no. 1, Spring 1978, pp. 1–21.

3

The Rover Vessel of Darkness

SM, 239   As indicated earlier, Lawrence was speaking as a puritan mystic when he wrote that the beauty of the greatest literature lies in *the identity of daily experience with profound mystic experience.* The probing of the depths to uncover this identity began with the fatal illness of the mother: the realization of mortality and the old question of immortality then came to haunt him in the form of darkness and space. While this was not the first time his imagination had approached the dark immensity, it was only now that he could begin to recognize the profound ambiguity of the message out of the vastness and blackness. He came abruptly up against the unending darkness of death, fearsome but fascinating, because from that domain his mother's shade called out to him. Now he must either perform the emotional severance he had shirked in her lifetime or be pulled into death after her. He hesitated for a time between obedience to her call by taking his own life and the half-severance of incorporating a fragment of her darkness into his ongoing life, giving her such immortality in himself as he could.

Staring into the obscurity peopled by departed souls, he sensed another darkness beyond that, most horrible of all, the utter darkness of annihilation. At intervals he could not help longing even for this. Yet, as if to offset this ultimate summons to extinction, his powerful hold on life began to insinuate the opposite, the creative form of darkness, with which he was later to concern himself almost exclusively — with significant exceptions — a darkness seen as the source of life and the power in the blood.

The quest for atonement with darkness at this period merges into the quest for atonement with time and space and for regeneration through love in distant lands. From the early summer of 1912 in Bavaria to the following spring at Lake Garda, darkness and space permeated Lawrence's writing under the double guise of destruction and creation, despair and hope, and for their meaning he relied heavily on the landscape and humanity that came under his scrutiny in Alpine Europe from Bavaria into Austria and northern Italy: the trees, the streams and lakes, the flowers, the rocks and snows and far reaches of mountain; the natives, too, especially the peasants and their crucifixes. This region was full of mystery and magic for Lawrence, who had never been among tall mountains before. That he absorbed it under the spell of passionate love, with vestiges of death still clinging, sharpened the sense of discovery instilled by the strangeness of this place alone, with its unearthly cleavage between light and dark. This sense of discovery is one of the foundations of *Look! We Have Come Through!* and of the final form of *Sons and Lovers,* which in this environment became Lawrence's first truly important novel.

But long before the influx of mountain shadows and the blackness of death, darkness had already granted him perceptions of the symbolic quality of common life. One of his earliest memories was of darkness as beneficent: *If I think of my childhood, it is always as if there was a* PH, 136 *lustrous sort of inner darkness, like the gloss of coal, in which we moved and had our real being.* Not that the other kind of darkness was absent from the infant years, the engulfing darkness of the nights when the father and the mother quarreled fiercely in the kitchen and the child listened in his bed upstairs, while the great ash tree across the street shrieked in the wind, at the edge of the enormous space opening out below Walker Street. At an early date Lawrence included such an episode in a long poem recounting the story of the troubled lives later to be molded into *Sons and Lovers.* He abandoned the poem, preserving only an eight-line fragment. But then he gave the event of the fragment a prominent place among Paul Morel's childhood impressions. Still another view of darkness and space prior to the mother's death is assigned to Cyril Beardsall in *The White Peacock,* Lawrence's first novel. For Cyril, darkness means the comforting night of his first home, and his love of it is simple nostalgia arising from contrast to an over-lighted city. But the passage is based on Lawrence's own feeling of exile in London when first away from his dark Midlands, and it suggests the inclination behind Lawrence's later affinity for the creative dark: *When* WP, 396 *does the night throw open her vastness for me, and send me the stars for company? There is no night in a city. How can I lose myself in the magnificent forest of darkness when night is only a thin scattering of the trees of shadow with barrenness of lights between!*

Darkness was conjoined from the beginning, then, with a certain cognizance of place: with the depth and mystery of the mines, with the remote reaches of night. Still, as anything other than pure description, images of darkness do not often occur in the earliest poems, and any emphasis on place is usually on the near and enclosing. But as soon as we come to poems composed in bereavement of the mother, darkness and shadow, space and distance appear all at once among the chief portals of discovery. Every shadow, partaking of the great darkness, is now personified and able to speak with the seeker. The mother has sent back the pentecostal gift of the tongues that shadows understand. Shadow now is at the heart of all things, in the candle flame of life itself

CP, 115   as the blue core, the *shadow inviolate* that controls the burning. In
CP, 110   other lines space and darkness are the all-pervasive *silence* that annuls every word spoken, every poem. But the son is content to listen to this *stillness* of the departed soul and drift therein with nothing more

CP, 115   audible than the far-off stars. In one poem, "Submergence," stars play a contrasting role of closeness, in a conjunction of space metaphors bringing comfort to grief: the constellation of the son's life has lost its chief star, but the little flickering stars in the people crowding the street momentarily warm his lonely sorrow.

Among the best of the poems plumbing the grief of the son is "The Shadow of Death." We might expect to find here a scene laid in the Biblical Valley of the Shadow of Death, but we come upon something

CP, 132   more subtle. The earth is a ship, a *rover vessel of darkness* just nosing out of the night into dawn. The voyager on deck cowers before the

CP, 133   light, for he has been transformed to *substance of shadow* by his mourning and resists belonging to the day. He is so nearly a wraith that even clouds may assert more material substance than he. But he will defy the whole world of matter in his knowledge of death's darkness. He will lift his portion of shadow to the wind as a sail and set out on the journey of life by that alone. Yet he will never be homeless, nor will his love, for although she is dead, he will always keep on deck a tent of *darkness* for *her perfect bed*. This image of Lawrence's soul roaming the world with the mother slumbering inside him is among the first of many in which the mother is not a parent but a lover. In none of the poems of this time is the darkness of death a ghastly horror. It is fearsome enough, but still, whether the sorrowing son thinks to join his mother there or to reach in for the wisdom she can hand over to his life, the darkness offers reconciliation with either choice. For one flicker of a way to rebirth, in the poem "Blueness," Lawrence seizes on an image that never left him, was with him still when his own death

CP, 697   was in the offing and he wove it into "Bavarian Gentians," one of his
CP, 136   best poems. "Blueness" invokes out of rain and flowers the *fountains of blue* that spurt upward from the *Darkness abundant* and flame into life. In "Bavarian Gentians" the image has come full circle: the blue

torch of a flower will guide the soul downward to the great dark source underground. "Blueness" is particularly noteworthy among the poems of grief in that it renders little grief, being almost purely dedicated to the wonder of life and the mystery of darkness behind it. It is a poem of reassertion against the near despair of others dating from the same time.

A few of these poems touch on the sacrificial aspect of darkness. The depth of the yew tree at night intimates the myth of death and resurrection, but as an argument to the woman to yield her dark mystery to the man. Under an oak tree the man senses druidic mystery seeping into him from the stars, as the darkness in him surges not only with the blood of passion but also the blood of sacrifice, bringing in a note of lusting cruelty that Lawrence was never wholly free of. Another poem treats destruction and creation as turned upon the poet, not reaching outward from him as before. In "Late at Night" trees again reveal their dark spirit. At the door of his bedroom the poet is confronted by dancing shadows of tree limbs thrown into the room by a street lamp. He stands arrested. Those shadows are like *tall strange women weeping* and treading back and forth across his bed. They beckon to him, and wring him with terror, as if he has broken in on a band of *Tall black Bacchae* performing *some female mystery*. A double restraint is suddenly injected into the son's devotion to the mother's memory. Deep down in him her shade forbids him to violate the laws of nature by crossing the boundary of life to meet her. Conversely, he dreads her devouring spirit. And the ghostly dances on the bed surely signify that the mother forbids the son the physical love of women, reserving such darkness in a distorted way to herself. [CP, 113; CP, 130–131; CP, 140; CP, 141]

All this turmoil of loss was subsiding when Lawrence reached Frieda and the intoxicating promise of release beyond the confines of England, a freedom like that glimpsed in the twilight at Hennef. But the darkness was still to be reckoned with, as became apparent when the lovers started their life alone together in Bavaria. In the previous chapter we saw bits of the glowing picture Lawrence painted in letters of those days in the Isarthal, with a few dark tones in references to the aggressive search for mutual acceptance. The verse of the time tells a complete and poignant story of this phase of the union, much of it centered on the dynamics of space and darkness.

In "Bei Hennef" and like poems the landscape retains some of a traditional use in poetry: as setting or storehouse of images. In the coming poems the self is thrust on nature and geography as if they had no existence outside it, as if their sole purpose were to appease and order the poet's violent emotions. The process is remarkably

clear in the poem on the lovers' reunion after the separation of "Bei
Hennef." On the first night of their honeymoon in Beuerberg, according
to "First Morning," Lawrence was impotent:

CP, 204

> *In the darkness*
>   *with the pale dawn seething at the window*
>   *through the black frame*
>   *I could not be free,*
>   *not free myself from the past, those others —*
>   *and our love was a confusion . . .*

The *bright doorway* of escape, gleaming ahead for some time now,
gave place this morning to a *black frame* opening on the past, and the
emotional constraint from which Lawrence could not find release could
hardly have been *those others* so much as the "purity" of his mother's
love, which had returned to plague the uninhibited love-making he had
found so gratifying with Frieda. To resolve the situation he has to call
on the landscape. He argues that the strength of his love is verified by
its power to embrace both the minuteness and the vastness of the land.
The argument evolves in the sunny morning, while the lovers are
outdoors gazing at the flowers beneath their feet and also at the
mountains far off. Because of their love, and only this, *the mountains
are balanced* and the flowers lift up from the earth:

> *Everything starts from us,*
> *We are the source.*

This all-embracing fruitfulness and vastness nullifies the impotence
of the night just past. The new face of nature and the bright distance
promise new access to power and virility, the inimical darkness dwindling behind.

    But the triumph was fleeting. A whole series of poems after this
one is tense with awareness that this is a woman the poet cannot live
without and that the attachment is tainted by a mother complex. This
realization is often frightful to contemplate, a never quite confessed
yet obvious reliving of the old anguish in a new form. The darkness of
the Isar valley countryside, with an outreach from here into hidden
extremities of geography and self, provides the focus for comprehending the experience. One agonized poem is called "Mutilation." The man
is walking away from the woman in the dark toward the vast unknown
CP, 212 of all northern and eastern Europe, holding *the night in horror* as he
goes, for she may decide to leave him, crippling him forever. Nothing
of the entire expanse of continent ahead could be of any significance
away from her. He might walk the length and breadth of Europe, but
his journey would only end in a circle, casting him back on this road

in Bavaria. No country can have a meaning if they are apart: England or France would be a mere place-name even if she were there — without him. Not only does the poem concern the meaninglessness of place without the newly essential presence of the woman but also the emptiness of certain directions. For Lawrence, from now on, east and north were ordinarily quarters of death or dying cultures. Hope lay south, and in due time, west. The reasons for shunning east are as yet unclear. The aversion to north is patently a facing away from the past.

At the close of this poem occurs what appears to be Lawrence's first invocation to the dark gods. They are not yet precisely the chthonic powers whose prime attribute is overflowing fertility. They are demonic, almost satanic, in the traditional sense, called up to charm the love of a desired woman. For a name they have that of the ancient Irish gods:

> Night folk, Tuatha De Danaan, dark Gods,   CP, 213
>   govern her sleep,
> Magnificent ghosts of the darkness, carry off
>   her decision in sleep,
> Leave her no choice, make her lapse me-ward,
>   make her,
> Oh Gods of the living Darkness, powers of Night.

Recalling the poem in which the Bacchic powers were in league with the dead mother to prevent normal sensuality, we note a measurable progress toward accommodation between the lover's soul and the fecund darkness.

What made Lawrence's present destiny even harder was to find himself subjected to a woman not yet committed to him. And the alliance could not have been troubled by anything worse than the torment she put him through for mother-love: her sometimes wild regret for having deserted her own children. This rift became visible during the honeymoon in Beuerberg. Here, in the marvellous darkness of night sprinkled with glow-worms, the woman holds the man and cries out her bliss in being with him: but always *that mother-love like*   CP, 206
a demon pulls her northward and abandons him to *the under-dusk of the Isar*. His solace must be drawn from the place itself, from the loveliness of night in Bavaria. His denunciation of her mother-longing is in part directed, as he knows, against his own mother. The mother in the mate is *fierce as a murderess* as she looks back to England, to   CP, 207
the place of the man's maternal captivity. The key analogy for this retrospection is one long established by tradition for disobedience of a divine command to renounce a condemned country and seek refuge in alien territory: the image of Lot's Wife — or, as the poet growls out,

Lot's Mother. The salt of her longing pierces and burns him, until he delivers a curse against this woman and against

CP, 208

> *. . . all mothers.*
> *All mothers who fortify themselves in*
>   *motherhood, devastating the vision.*
> *They are accursed, and the curse is not*
>   *taken off;*
> *It burns within me like a deep, old burn,*
> *And oh, I wish it was better.*

He has labored with this woman to cut the ties of the stale old land and escape to the life-giving darkness here, only to have her turn back in betrayal. It is important to notice here, in addition, that a feeling unknown in the poems of mourning now infuses the verse: open condemnation of the mother instinct. One of Frieda's contributions to *Sons and Lovers* may have been that she introduced Lawrence to Freud, but a much greater one was her re-enactment of a mother-love that shocked Lawrence into a painfully clear view of what his mother's hold on him had been.

CP, 205

If the poem just quoted finds Lawrence in deep dejection, another reveals a worse state of mind: "And Oh — That the Man I Am Might Cease to Be —." It rings with an annihilation wish beyond that of any grief poem, for extinction in darkness out of reach of all mothers living or dead. The words *black, dark* or *darkness* occur nine times in twenty lines, which beg for devastation of the physical world, the identical surroundings that at other moments release the sufferer — the Bavarian houses, the balconies filled with flowers, the distant mountains — and for utter engulfing of the soul. Never again was Lawrence to write so thoroughly hopeless a poem. This hair-raising form of darkness he made his peace with during the initial months with Frieda, and he was not to sink into it again, even at the lowest ebb of his spirits during the Great War or when he saw coming the end of life.

Two other closely related poems from the Bavarian interlude call for specific attention. Unlike most of the others, they take account of the woman's point of view. "In the Dark" is a dialogue between the lovers, and "A Young Wife" is a monologue spoken by the woman. Both poems take up variations on the themes of darkness and the extension of being into unknown space. Prominent in both are pine trees, whose darkness fascinated Lawrence from this time forward, from Europe to western America. "In the Dark" is a debate on the antithesis of darkness and light as representing the distinct views of love and life in male and female. As in "First Morning" the poem

CP, 210

opens with a *window of dark sky*. But here the man awakes to discover

his mistress weeping by the window. In reply to his questions, she
declares that he is destroying her, that he is throwing over her a shadow
that will take her life away. She claims to offer him an abundance of
light, only to have him turn on her *like ghosts, like a darkness upright.*   CP, 211
But he pleads that their love is like a *soft and eternal* night, and as she
still goes on inveighing against his pernicious darkness, he reminds her
that night is universal and that her *own small night goes with* her
everywhere, as with everyone else: the shadow that walks beneath her.
She protests again that she is purely a creature to dance in the sun,
while he fills the sunshine with shadows. He further defends his darkness as affirmative, as identified with the instincts and the senses. But
she will not hear of this impersonal unseen. She is herself, she will
not surrender her being to intuitive natural forces. The man talks on:

> *Hark at the river! It pants as it hurries through*   CP, 212
>
> *The pine-woods. How I love them so, in their*
> *mystery of not-to-be.*

Though the woman contends still that she must be herself, not a river
or a tree, the man coaxes her back into bed and quietens her, insisting
nevertheless that we must all *be gone in the dark* of the natural world
if our lives are to flow in wonder.

Apparently the woman comes to accept her lover's views of darkness, in what proves to be for her a painful stage of growth — unless
Lawrence was engaging in wishful thinking and not really stating
Frieda's experience. But Frieda did sooner or later profit from Lawrence's teaching in such matters: at least she often said so.

The poem "A Young Wife" phrases some of that teaching. It
begins and ends with *The pain of loving you/Is almost more than I can*   CP, 215
bear. The hurt is much like that which drove her from their bed in the
preceding poem. Her lover makes dark spring up everywhere, forces
her to recognize that as trees have shadows, *At the foot of each glowing
thing/A night lies looking up.* Clearly the shadow of death in nature
is what he has brought her to acknowledge — also, no doubt, the
shadow of cruelty in him. While she still shows no definite awareness
of the prolific darkness also infusing nature, a tone in her discourse,
her half-complaint, half-celebration, does indicate a deepening knowledge of existence beyond mere trust in momentary sunshine and love
unadulterated by conflict. The male in this pair of poems is therefore
fulfilling his natural function of communicating his superior vision to
the female.

When Lawrence and Frieda left the Isarthal in August of 1912,
they set out on a hike across the Alps to spend the winter in the Lake
Garda region of Italy. This turned out to be a month-long trek, with

a long pause at Mayrhofen in Austria. They stayed often in remote inns and sometimes slept in the log huts built for hay storage in the high meadows. They got lost more than once, stranded among the rocks, chilled and soaked. This climb over the great mountain barrier of western Europe sharpened to its keenest Lawrence's faculty for extracting from a briefly encountered scene components which in his writing acquire a doubly symbolic nature: they epitomize a time, a place, a people, and at the same time they project Lawrence's exploration of intricate states of thought and feeling through which he is passing at the given moment.

PX, 32

Late the second day on the trail to Austria, after much rain, the pair wandered lost until nearly dark searching for a path over the heights to Glashütte. At last they came upon a little chapel and opened the door with *a click of the latch in the cold, watchful silence of the upper mountains.* Inside, the walls were *covered close with naked little pictures* the peasants had drawn as votive offerings to the Virgin, some of them maybe a hundred and fifty years old. These crude little paintings were the first religious expression of the land to hold Lawrence's attention, making him feel *exalted in this rare, upper shadow* of the mountains. His response was to perform a little ritual

PX, 33

of lighting candle-ends left by worshippers and studying these *picture-writings,* which he found so eloquent they were like his *own soul talking,* as if they were written in God's own language. Some were portrayals of mountain accidents and of nearly fatal childbirth, with gratitude for being spared. Some were illustrated prayers, one imploring, for instance, the release of a loved one from prison. A whole group of the paintings offered thanks for the saving of property, usually animals. But much more than material loss was at stake, for Lawrence

PX, 35

could perceive *a symbolic power* in the animals of these pictures: *They did not merely represent property. They were the wonderful animal life which man must take for food.* In this chance discovery of the chapel, Lawrence felt all at once that he had approached the source of religious and artistic consciousness in these dark mountains: the spirit of the place.

PX, 33

The peasants became artists only under duress: *When their lives were threatened, then they had a fearful flash of self-consciousness, which haunted them till they had represented it:* till they had offered these little paintings to Mary. And yet their final purpose was not to thank a mild and compassionate Virgin. That was a subterfuge. The

PX, 36

real aim was to propitiate the dark deity of the mountains: *Deepest of all things, among the mountain darknesses, was the ever-felt fear. First of all gods was the unknown god who crushed life at any moment, and threatened it always. His shadow was over the valleys.*

NEAR ICKING, BAVARIA

The pine-woods.
How I love them so, in their mystery of not-to-be (CP, 212)

Although there is little hint of it in the sketch I am quoting, we may infer that Lawrence himself felt much of what he attributed to the peasant artists as he peered at their work by candlelight. Lost in the cold rain at nightfall, he and Frieda had barely escaped spending the night in the open. The chapel they had stumbled upon was the first sign of shelter. Of course, Lawrence's kinship with the folk painters was no simple parallel. Kinds and degrees of fear vary according to breadth of soul. Lawrence's respect for the dark powers of the region CP, 217 was the *glimmering fear* of the Isarthal poems, synonymous with the ancient "fear of God," not terror but awe.

While Lawrence pored over the votive offerings in the chapel, Frieda walked on a little way ahead and found a hay-hut. When she returned for Lawrence they decided to sleep in the hay-hut rather than the chapel — to their later regret, for the wind came in strong through the cracks, and the hay was damp.

Next morning they made their way over the ridge at last to Glashütte, where they put up at an inn to wait out the rain. Here, at once, Lawrence turned out a long sketch of the chapel and hay-hut experience, intended like the earlier "German Impressions" for the *Westminster Gazette,* but this time rejected and not published till after his death. In places the tone does resemble that of "German Impressions," but the treatment of the chapel incident is different, as already suggested: the first fragment of Lawrence's singular kind of travel writing. It belongs with a sketch soon to come, when Lawrence turned from the ex-voto pictures to the roadside crucifixes in the same area and instituted a much deeper analysis of the spirit of place in alpine Europe and of a religious awareness compatible with his own. We pick up here from the start a certain trend of Lawrence's thought. We see the folk art of the chapel catch his attention and we can link with this his interest in the crucifixes, already at work in his mind, surely, when he entered the chapel, though not mentioned in the sketch. The design unfolds in three versions of a crucifix piece, the last of which, over three years later, has a great share in the symbolism of *Twilight in Italy* and helps determine the tragic climax of *Women in Love.*

The journey south had scarcely begun at Glashütte, and as to weather it was a bad start. But from there on luck was better. Another thirty miles of hiking landed the couple in Mayrhofen, at the mouth of the Zemmtal, where they remained for over two weeks, living in a farm-house by a cold rushing stream. They were happy almost to delirium:
ML,   *We go out all day with our rucksacks — make fires, boil eggs, and eat*
139–140 *the lovely fresh gruyère cheese that they make here. We are almost pure*
vegetarians. We go quite long ways up the valleys. The peaks of the

mountains are covered with eternal snow. Water comes falling from a fearful height, and the cows, in the summer meadows, tinkle their bells. Sometimes F. undresses and lies in the sun — sometimes we bathe together — and we can be happy; nobody knows how happy.

David Garnett, son of Lawrence's editor and confidant, and Harold Hobson, a friend of his, joined the couple at Mayrhofen and went with them on mountain hikes to gather flowers for Garnett's study of botany. He was surprised at how much Lawrence had learned about the village in less than a week. He knew everyone's name and was well-informed on traits of character and love affairs. Lawrence had a wider scope now for taking in everything around him and sharing it with a willing listener.   GE, 245

Soon the whole party was on the road again, with Italy over the peaks ahead. They slept at Dominicshütte, high up in the Zemmtal towards the Pfitscherjoch. They crossed that pass with difficulty, through the cold and gloomy heights to the broad alpine meadows, with peasant crucifixes on every hand. At Sterzing they again joined *the highroad from Germany to Italy,* on which one had the opportunity, and Lawrence made the most of it, to see *all sorts of queer cuts, from Lords of England to Italian tramps.* Here at Sterzing the group broke up, Garnett and Hobson taking a train to Verona while Lawrence and Frieda continued on foot to Meran, eventually going on to Bozen, Trent, and finally to Lake Garda.   ML, 142 CL, 446

Lawrence mentions in a letter from Sterzing his intention to do articles for the *Westminster Gazette.* Three days later, newly arrived at the Lake Garda town of Riva, he sent in three, among them undoubtedly the already written chapel and hay-hut sketch, so lengthy it may have been considered as two, and probably a first version of "Christs in the Tirol." What preoccupied him most, though, was *Paul Morel,* which he had decided before leaving the Isar valley to redo. He seemed to question this decision when he spoke once now of the novel needing only a final glance. But he was prepared five days later to recast at least the first part, with the aid of notes furnished by his editor, Edward Garnett. After three months' labor he ended with a totally refashioned novel, *Sons and Lovers,* guided by the artistic assurance that had matured so rapidly in his short time abroad with Frieda. For this task they moved into the bottom floor of the Villa Igea in Gargnano, on the western shore of Lake Garda, a remote spot then accessible only by water.   ML, 142 SR, 31   ML, 141 & 143

It was good fortune for Lawrence, down to each material and social consideration, to find himself in Italy. In England he had been a poor schoolmaster sprung from a coal-miner's family. Here the Italians took him for *a howling gentleman and swell,* a deference that   ML, 152

went admirably with his pride in Frieda's gentility. He was overjoyed,
too, with the region: *The lake is dark blue, purple, and clear as a*
ML, 148
jewel, with swarms of fishes. He loved exploring the lakeside, with
its steep shores and mountains hemming close on both sides, with its
small lemon-orchards and olive ridges and pocket-size vineyards, and
the sharp green-black strokes of the cypress trees. Emancipation from
the burdens of England was spelt out everywhere across the face of
the land: *Yesterday F. and I went down along the lake towards Ma-*
ML, 151
derno. We climbed down from a little olive wood, and swam. It was
evening, so weird, and a great black cloud trailing over the lake. And
tiny little lights of villages came out, so low down, right across the
water. Then great lightnings split out — No, I don't believe England
need be so grubby.

Lawrence's wholehearted surrender to the life around him did
not alleviate the swing between harmony and discord going on with
Frieda, and he kept on recording this in the poems. But most of his
creative effort went into the novel. From this remove of time and place
he could see in sharp outline the life traveled over. More than ever
he was certain he could instruct not only himself, through the unified
act of living and writing, but the rest of the English nation as well.
Italy seemed the substantial proof of his conviction even more than
Germany had been. To free oneself from moral servitude and come
fully into manhood or womanhood: that was the only object of life.

On this score he found himself at odds with some of his chief
contemporaries. He now read a few books from home after several
months of seeing hardly a line of English, and the effect was to heighten
his already surging confidence. One of the books was a volume of Con-
ML, 152
rad stories, probably *'Twixt Land and Sea,* of which he wrote, *The*
Conrad, after months of Europe, makes me furious . . . . Why this giv-
ing in before you start, that pervades all Conrad and such folks —.
Another book he read was Arnold Bennett's *Anna of the Five Towns,*
a novel of his own region and much of it in almost his dialect. His
response to Bennett was even more devastating than that to Conrad:
ML, 150
I hate England and its hopelessness. I hate Bennett's resignation.
Tragedy ought really to be a great kick at misery.

Lawrence's use of the word "tragedy" calls for some further
clarification at this point. In the passage from a letter quoted in the
foregoing chapter, he spoke of the inner war between two people in
ML, 132
love as *tragedy,* not a maintaining of nobility in defeat but quite the
opposite: a *knowledge* leading to victory, a knowledge of each other
and the moral universe. The usage in reference to Bennett suggests a
greater prevailing over adversity than ever, a spurning of the outworn
conditions of personal and national life. A pertinent earlier use of the

term comes in a letter in which Lawrence was trying to console his
sister Ada for the loss of their mother. He said that the catharsis of ML, 77
tragedy, in all its pain and beauty, was the only way out of bereavement toward acceptance of life. Acting on the same conviction, he had
read tragedy with Helen Corke to comfort her after the death of her
lover. At the time of the mother's death he thought of *Oedipus* as *the* ML, 76
finest drama of all times,* and spoke of it in such a way as to recognize his emotional kinship with its hero.

In most of this Lawrence did not go much beyond the common
tradition of tragedy as purgation of pity and terror — with the important exception of holding battles between lovers to be a tragic progression. And this was a fresh meaning acquired since embarking on
his quest. Tragedy was no longer precisely victory by wringing beauty
and wisdom out of the stern conditions of life. It was a clash between
souls in which the death that came about was symbolic, and it ended
with resurrection into a new harmony, in a new self forged of essentials after the dross of bygone life had been reduced in conflict. Lawrence was still of this mind when contesting Arnold Bennett's outlook
on life. Why call it tragic to bemoan the hardness of fate? Why not
commit oneself to "tragic" regeneration in bursting the old shell and
rising to new heights of vitality?

The significance of defining the way to new experience as a
"tragic" way is highly evident in *Sons and Lovers*. Lawrence held firmly
to this view through the whole experience of composition. On finishing this novel he announced he had written *a great tragedy,* not only ML, 161
his own but that of *thousands of young men in England*. What he
said of the novel some time after its appearance echoes this sentiment:
One sheds one's sickness in books — repeats and presents again one's ML, 234
emotions, to be master of them. Once again it is the struggle for "tragic"
rebirth. And tragedy, like darkness, had a double face, of negation and
of affirmation. Through great effort a person could cross from the
negative state of stoical recognition and acceptance to the blessed condition of knowing that darkness and tragedy when wholly revealed
are forms of the highest good.

Another significant if unobtrusive gesture toward understanding
"tragedy" made at this time was Lawrence's first effort at serious
thought in a travel sketch. This was the first two versions of the
crucifix essay, in the second of which he brings up tragedy.

Perhaps on just reaching Lake Garda Lawrence made his initial
attempt to get at the significance of the wayside crucifixes planted thick
over the Alps from Bavaria to Italy. For some reason he was dissatisfied with the sketch in its first form and revised it before publication
in the *Westminster Gazette*. Apparently it was the first time he had

ever done such a thing, and this, especially since it coincides with the transforming of *Sons and Lovers,* adds to the importance of the revision. Along with a sharpening of language and the excision of extraneous passages, the revision marks a new awareness in the author that he can make descriptive and analytical prose about places as serious as the language of a love-poem sequence or a novel. On revision the sketch grows into a statement on the nature of the artist and of tragic art.

For Lawrence the only roadside crucifixes that still spoke of the earth from which they sprang were those of a dark region, the Tyrolese Alps with their gloomy skies, from south of Munich over the Brenner Pass to what was then a part of Austria. These crucifixes PH, 82 create an atmosphere of their own, he wrote, *an atmosphere of pain,* and, like the ex-voto paintings in the chapel, of fear and the hope of propitiating the dark powers of the mountains. Moreover, this discovery, like that of the mountain chapel, comes suddenly to the traveler as he passes through new and fascinating country. He is tramping along near the foot of the mountains at twilight, having known for some time that crucifixes stand by the wayside but hardly seeing them, since FR, 73 they are factory-made. All of a sudden he spies a carving that *startles* him *into awareness,* a Promethean Christ unyielding in his torment, looking much like a Bavarian peasant stretched on the cross of life. In the revision Lawrence recollects turning from this figure to watch a family of peasants doggedly carrying in hay out of the pouring rain, resisting the hardship of their environment just as the peasant Christ does his. That moment brings the traveler to understand how and why the nearby crucifix was created.

In a narrative interweaving action and realization more lucidly in the second than in the first version, Lawrence soon passes several figures recognizably carved by the same artist. Pursuing the thought broached on seeing the peasants in the field, he can now understand PH, 83 how the man *has whittled away in torment to see himself emerge out of the piece of timber,* with hint enough that the writer's artistic identity is involved. The best of this anonymous sculptor's work stands deep in a gorge, in the cold gloom, a *large, pale Christ* who is not at all stern and Prometheus-like but bitter that his youth and health have been torn from him by the mob. What makes pieces like these PH, 84 stand out so much, for Lawrence, is that *evidently the artist could not get beyond the tragedy that tormented him.* To probe and surpass the ML, 150 tragedy of life — to deliver *a great kick at misery* — this the peasant artist could not do, and it is the same fault Lawrence found with the fiction of Bennett and Conrad. In *Sons and Lovers* he meant to succeed

ITALIAN ALPS

Every now and again recurs the crucifix,
at the turning of an open, grassy road,
holding a shadow and a mystery under its pointed hood (**TI**, 4)

precisely where they had failed. Even so, in the sketch he falters, for the only definition of tragedy the crucifix suggests to him is far short of the great expansiveness of being we might anticipate. All Lawrence

PH, 84   can say here is that the purpose of all tragic art is *to get used to the idea of death and suffering, to rid* [oneself] *of some of the fear thereof.* The *kick at misery* never appears. But this is the sort of circumvention we must expect from Lawrence. It is common with him to veer and weave on the road to a better understanding of himself. The point for the moment is how far he has grown accustomed to phrasing his own condition out of what he gleans from his travels, even if the conclusion here is anti-climactic.

The last sentence of the revised sketch does touch on an issue central with Lawrence from now on, the figure of Christ, even though the manifest subject, at the moment, is the contrast between English and Italian life. Wondering why no such popular art as this of the Tyrol

PH, 86   exists in England, he writes: *And I suppose we have carved no Christs, afraid lest they should be too like men, too like ourselves. What we worship must have exotic form.* Surely Lawrence has in mind, for one thing, the protestant representations of Christ in his industrialized England: the Christ with long, fair hair and beard, and flowing oriental robes, as little like the average Englishman as possible, an *exotic form* indeed. What Lawrence implies by this he affirms often later on: that Englishmen in his time, in fact all men of the modern world, are afraid to face themselves in either the bitter or the joyful realities of life, would rather avoid risk by following sanitized convention, a sentimentalized exoticism. The peasant artists may never have gotten further toward the resurrection than the preparatory death, but at least they consent to personify their limitation in all its crudity. Again, to be sure, Lawrence has his own efforts at writing in view, his resolve to render the naked truth itself.

But the implications reach beyond these. The reference to the Englishman's demand for an exotic substitute, in fear of what resembles himself, may be derogatory. However, Lawrence is an Englishman, one who looks unblinkingly into his own heart as he draws moral conclusions and self-knowledge from an exotic form, the little crucifixes of the dark Alpine trails. If the average Englishman avoids what he dreads most, and the Tyrolese peasant carves it in wood, the wayfarer advances beyond both regional types in shaping through language his own awe of the supernatural.

To trace the growth of Lawrence's ideas about Christ, we must go back again to the period when he was grief-stricken over his mother. Then he looked upon Christ from a liberal non-conformist viewpoint

ML, 76   as the exemplary man: *Christ was infinitely good, but mortal as we.*

Once he had embarked on his search for a greater self in travels, his insular opinion was rapidly superseded. We have seen how in "Ballad of a Wilful Woman," the Biblical person or event is not a moral exemplar but a mythical basis of quest. What Lawrence perceived in the Alpine crucifixes led him further in the same direction, toward his mature conception of Christ, in which the Galilean ceases to be a historical figure at all: or at least the historical circumstances of his life cease to matter. He counts only as a mythical value in the formation of self: *The Crucifix, and Christ, are only symbols. They do not mean a* ML, 302 *man who suffered his life out as I suffer mine. They mean a moment in the history of my soul, if I must be personal.*

Lawrence's greatest accomplishment in the first three months at Lake Garda was of course *Sons and Lovers,* which emerged as a novel distinct from anything it could have been before. An enormous influence on the work, equal at least to that of Frieda, was Italy itself. This was largely an influence on the prevailing tone and not on narrative substance: the attainment of an esthetic and emotional distance owing to a literal distance from the scene of the book. Distance appears to lengthen the span of time since the events treated, with an attendant increase of nostalgia. The date when Lawrence finished the novel, November 1912, was less than two years after the death of his mother. Yet the episodes surrounding that excruciating event seem to belong to the far past. A regret for lost time and a depth of human understanding wanting in his first two novels were now available to Lawrence's spirit out of the way he had lived and traveled in the last few months and out of his presence in a world absolutely different from the England of Paul Morel's tragedy. Lawrence could now write with confidence, too, that his past was behind him. That the confidence turned out to be over-confidence does not for the moment signify.

While *Sons and Lovers* confines itself to a Lawrence surrogate of pre-questing days, a certain aura about the life of Paul Morel hints again and again that he will be an explorer beyond his immediate ken. At one point in Paul's babyhood Lawrence poses the question of how a child may be oriented in relation to the distant and magnificent vital powers. At this moment rival instincts vie for control in the mother: whether to offer the infant to his greater destiny or clutch him in maternal possession. She gives vent to the conflict in a little pagan ceremony: elevation of the infant. She is at once ashamed, the exclusive mother-love reasserting itself:

In her arms lay the delicate baby. Its deep blue eyes, always look- SL, 37 *ing up at her unblinking, seemed to draw her innermost thoughts out of her. She no longer loved her husband; she had not wanted this child to come, and there it lay in her arms and pulled at her heart. She felt*

*as if the navel string that had connected its frail little body with hers
had not been broken. A wave of hot love went over her to the infant. She
held it close to her face and breast. With all her force, with all her soul
she would make up to it for having brought it into the world unloved.
She would love it all the more now it was here; carry it in her love. Its
clear, knowing eyes gave her pain and fear. Did it know all about her?
When it lay under her heart, had it been listening then? Was there
a reproach in the look? She felt the marrow melt in her bones, with
fear and pain.*

*Once more she was aware of the sun lying red on the rim of the
hill opposite. She suddenly held up the child in her hands.*

"Look!" she said. "Look, my pretty!"

*She thrust the infant forward to the crimson, throbbing sun, almost
with relief. She saw him lift his little fist. Then she put him to her
bosom again, ashamed almost of her impulse to give him back again
whence he came.*

The mother has made her choice. She will wrap the child in her
motherhood. If she can prevent it he will not belong to the sun or the
orbit of life bounded by far horizons. Lawrence could not easily have
imagined this symbolic scene without the space and time interposed
by separation from his native land and his whole past. He was now
conscious that the alternative between constraint and release was
rooted in the beginning of life, envisaging a gesture of choice in even
the pre-mental infant. Out of this the eventual departure from England
had enlarged to a geographical, even a cosmic equivalent of the flight
from the mother.

In another important scene darkness as well as space leaves its
stamp on the child. This is the episode of the parents' quarrel on a
night when the wind howls through the giant ash tree across the street.
The difference of handling between this passage and the previously
mentioned fragment of a poem on the same event is remarkable. The
poem hardly gets beyond playing with a metaphor. In the novel space
and darkness stand out in stark relation to the slope on Walker Street
and the first two overpowering figures of Lawrence's life, the mother
SL,   and the father: *In front of the house was a huge old ash-tree. The west
59–60   wind, sweeping from Derbyshire, caught the houses with full force,
and the tree shrieked again. Morel liked it.*

"It's music," he said. "It sends me to sleep."

*But Paul and Arthur and Annie hated it. To Paul it became almost
a demoniacal noise. The winter of their first year in the new house their
father was very bad. The children played in the street, on the brim of
the wide, dark valley, until eight o'clock. Then they went to bed. Their
mother sat sewing below. Having such a great space in front of the*

*house gave the children a feeling of night, of vastness, and of terror.
This terror came in from the shrieking of the tree and the anguish of
the home discord. Often Paul would wake up, after he had been asleep
a long time, aware of thuds downstairs. Instantly he was wide awake.
Then he heard the booming shouts of his father, come home nearly
drunk, then the sharp replies of his mother, then the bang, bang of
his father's fist on the table, and the nasty snarling shout as the man's
voice got higher. And then the whole was drowned in a piercing medley
of shrieks and cries from the great, wind-swept ash-tree. The children
lay silent in suspense, waiting for a lull in the wind to hear what their
father was doing. He might hit their mother again. There was a feeling of horror, a kind of bristling in the darkness, and a sense of blood.
They lay with their hearts in the grip of an intense anguish. The wind
came through the tree fiercer and fiercer. All the cords of the great
harp hummed, whistled, and shrieked. And then came the horror of
the sudden silence, silence everywhere, outside and downstairs. What
was it? Was it a silence of blood? What had he done?*

The briefness of the scene may belie its significance. But it is one
of only two prominent incidents selected to objectify Paul's early childhood — the other is the doll sacrifice foreshadowing the mercy killing
of his mother, ultimately an act of will to break her stranglehold. In
the ash tree scene we find what underlies the whole structure of Paul's
experience: discord between the parents. Fundamental here are the
attitudes Lawrence establishes in the boy toward the two opponents,
the two opposing natures who came as close to being the determinants
of Lawrence's life as the influence of others on the self can be. Lawrence was always fleeing from this parental strife. Or in a more vital
sense he was constantly in search of psychological balance in some
ideal place between the two clashing natures, with the lost predomi-
nance restored to the father.

At the time he wrote *Sons and Lovers,* purportedly the tragedy of
a mother's boy, Lawrence was not yet conscious of the extent to which
he was his father's son. But the ash tree scene, in itself and in relation
to surrounding scenes, brings out attitudes in the perplexed, uneasy
child where the seeds of later awareness are evident, particularly if the
motifs of space and darkness are compared with those of the mother's
elevation scene.

The ash tree stands on the edge of vastness opening out before
the frightened infant soul, that *great scoop of darkness* that gives birth   SL, 76
to the wind and the voice of the tree. But this space is not only fearful,
it is also fascinating, in other scenes often appealing, as in *they all*   SL, 77
*loved the Scargill Street house for its openness, for the great scallop
of the world it had in view.* In the ash tree scene the soul is compelled,

to be sure, rather than attracted. With no shelter of parental love at home, the small soul is pushed out into space: but half in willingness nevertheless. The terrible and magnetic force of the tree and the wind summon it. And this force emphatically belongs to the father. Or rather it is the father. Only the father can hear music in the wind striking the tree. The mother is apparently indifferent to it. But she has already elected to draw back from the dark and distant unknown, whereas the father heartily greets strange experience from the realm of outer darkness and space. This facet of darkness is reminiscent of another belonging to the father in the novel: the darkness of the underground, of coal. The sentence quoted early in this chapter bears repeating here:

PH, 136   *If I think of my childhood, it is always as if there was a lustrous sort of inner darkness, like the gloss of coal, in which we moved and had our real being.* In maturity Lawrence can see that nether darkness as bringing men together in a world of their own, free of woman's

PH, 137   materialism — thus possessiveness — and creating for them an *intuitive and instinctive consciousness.*

But the mother's darkness in *Sons and Lovers* grows to be devouring altogether: in the end Paul nearly succumbs to the engulfing darkness of death, barely mustering the courage to recoil as his final action in the novel. The devastating solitude of this darkness makes

SL, 419   itself felt also in terms of distance: *When he turned away* from Miriam *he felt the last hold for him had gone. The town, as he sat upon the car, stretched away over the bay of railway, a level fume of lights. Beyond the town the country, little smouldering spots for more towns — the sea — the night — on and on! And he had no place in it! Whatever spot he stood on, there he stood alone. From his breast, from his mouth, sprang the endless space, and it was there behind him, everywhere.*

The tone of these final pages resembles that of the poems written just after the mother's death, except for a decisive new development.

SL, 420   *The vastness and terror of the immense night* is if anything more pronounced in the novel. The reaches of space in Paul are so enormous that they efface time: *There was no Time, only Space.* His mother's removal from the present sphere is no result of time's passage. It is totally an action of space. She has been here, she is now elsewhere: that is, *gone abroad into the night.* The distraught son may readily transfer his soul to her new sphere. He conceives this possibility under the figure of a constellation. Their two souls might spin through the void in each other's arms, terrified of the darkness but by their united motion maintaining an unquenchable rhythm of being. In the novel as in the poems the bereaved son overcomes his death wish, but in the

poems, save for a moment's comfort in the crowds, the absolute aloneness remains. That is, in a poem like "The Shadow of Death," the
soul of the son, wending its way on the *rover vessel of darkness,* is   CP, 132
intensely isolated. The envisioned contact with the beloved shade in
her deck tent is a desperate invention, precisely like the constellation
trope in the novel. But the novel does not stop here. Paul turns away
from his mother luring him into blackness. He faces the lights forming
a constellation of human activity in the simple darkness of night: *the*   SL, 420
faintly humming, glowing town. This about-face does not confirm
acceptance as such of the town Paul has just left: that is, any return
to the old life. We know from earlier on that beyond this town lie
others, and the sea, the night, and so on: a sphere of life where he has
recently felt he would be utterly alone. But he has now contemplated
the togetherness at his disposal through constellation with the mother
in outer space and rejected it. How he can gain togetherness in the
darkness of this earth, with its many constellations of towns, is the
concern of a future not germane to the story of *Sons and Lovers.*
Whether darkness is to be life-giving along this new path Lawrence
could not take up without violating the unity of his novel.

4

The Living of My Full Flame

The influence of Italy during his first stay figured large in the blazing forth of Lawrence's manhood and in the first profession of religious purpose in his art. From now through the second stay, ending June 1914, he awoke to one great reach of creative powers after another. Not till some while after the completion of *Sons and Lovers* did the real impact of Italy begin to make itself felt in his writing. But through the several false starts at fiction after this novel runs a counterpoint of the increasing effects of Italy against the always-evolving attitudes toward the abandoned homeland.

ML, 177   The pilgrimage he had already decided on: there was *nothing like keeping on the move,* and for now Italy was the ideal region of migrancy. For one thing he could maintain a real if skimpy independence as a writer in Italy, as he was doubtful of doing in more expensive England. As for his liaison with Frieda, the future held more promise here than it had in Germany even, while in England they were sure to be hedged about by countless problems. His satisfaction with *Sons and Lovers* proved Italy to be a place highly conducive to work. The Italians as a people he sometimes loved and sometimes detested, but in one respect at least they were always happily the opposite of Englishmen: *They haven't learnt not to be themselves yet.* In short, Italy provided the surroundings, human and natural, for Lawrence's boundless zest in life, love and work to expand to seemingly unlimited horizons.

Still the threat of being hauled back into the old life could loom. And the worst of it was that Frieda, the personification of his escape, might be the agent of return. Should Ernest Weekley agree to a divorce and a sharing of the children, she must be close enough to see them. So they talked for one thing of a cottage in England, and of Lawrence's going back to the classroom, an abhorrent thought. Even more, he shrank from being near Frieda's children, of whom he was jealous and in whom he feared new entanglement with the mother-love whose devastating effects were lessening at last.

Another question was that of class conflicts, which Lawrence addresses but cannot truly solve in an interesting letter. He might consent, he says, to a small country school, failing to mention that this would plunge Frieda into a far more provincial obscurity than she had fled to elope with him. Still she requires, as Lawrence puts it, association with *the intelligent, as it were, upper classes.* He cannot stand her   ML, 176 approach to anyone from a class beneath her own. By her very humility she makes the distinction felt — *even with my sister,* Lawrence adds. So the answer might be to rent a small house near London, where he could do some publisher's reading and where social intercourse would naturally be with a less class-conscious literary set.

Such statements evince in Lawrence not just a worry over the pitfalls in English society for an aristocrat and a miner's son setting up an illicit household, but probably more concern over rigidity of association imposed by the English class system. He was afraid he might lose his newfound freedom to mix with all classes, which in Italy was now proving its worth in his study of national temperaments. He lays breezy claim to the common touch himself, and to a social amenity he did possess, if not to the extent he asserts: *I could get along with anybody,* but *I find a servant maid more interesting as a rule than a Violet Hunt or a Grace Rhys.*[1] The statement is not quite candid. Lawrence assuredly sought out the company of literary women like these more than he did that of housemaids. But the craving to move at will among all classes is in the assertion, and he fears this may be thwarted in England. Sophisticated people from the British establishment could be largely avoided in Gargnano, while all around were examples of Italian character, ranging from the little aristocratic landlord to the old peasant woman spinning wool on the terrace of a church, all ready to respect and communicate with the agreeable foreign resident, who stood outside as a true observer must.

A month of suspension followed the completion of *Sons and Lovers.* The day after mailing the manuscript, Lawrence went for a long walk in the hills, came home with Christmas roses, declared that Italy was one of the most beautiful countries in the world and that living here apart made one *ex cathedra* in opinion. This half-jesting   ML, 162 presumption was a manifestation of Italy, an inflated after-effect of the assurance won in finishing *Sons and Lovers.* With writing in abeyance and the burden of the past dispatched to England, he could take more time for the study of Italian and Italians. He and Frieda took language lessons from the local school-mistress, and he practiced by talking with the peasants on his rambles. Local visitors came, too: their landlord, Pietro di Paoli, and the proprietress of the Hotel del Cervo. Before long these people, with many others, found their way into Lawrence's Italian sketches.

But he was all the while still musing over his provincial past. When he turned back to fiction in late December, he had settled on making use of the life of Robert Burns, though he intended to go wide of the facts: to bring his hero down to Derbyshire and take other license as he pleased. What is most illuminating is that in writing of Burns he

ML, 168   proposed to *do him almost like an autobiography.* Now this is a telling remark in light of the "autobiography" he had just hammered out

CB,   in *Sons and Lovers.* If he wished to continue that course, why did he
vol. 1,   not go on to the next phase of life in a hero already fashioned? The
184–195   reason he did not can be drawn from the few surviving pages of the Burns novel, which was soon abandoned. What was here passing through Lawrence's mind as a fictionalized identity of himself stands out in sharp contrast to Paul Morel. The consummated and the anticipated heroes do have a great deal in common: each in his way is a portrait of the artist, and they seek in comparable ways the love of woman. But more worth noting is their fundamental difference. In *Sons and Lovers* Lawrence had made conscious if not always convincing efforts to condemn his father. In the Burns novel he plainly meant

RC,   to set him up as a model to identify with. We know of his assertion in
254–255   later years that he had done his father wrong in *Sons and Lovers,* but the Burns fragment proves he already had misgivings in 1912. Jack Haseldine resembles the elder Lawrence in ways such as these: Jack is a fine singer, a lusty countryman alluring to women — the attraction between Jack Haseldine and Mary Renshaw, ostensibly based on that between Robert Burns and Highland Mary, is like the magnetism that brought Lawrence's father and mother together. The brief scene at the inn, with its enthronement of Jack among his elder cronies, recalls the pub life of the elder Lawrence: the opposite pole of existence from the home ruled over by the mother. The Haseldine home that we glimpse in the Burns fragment is a masculine stronghold.[2]

Lawrence took advantage of his breathing spell to theorize. On
ML, 171   just entering the Burns novel he stated his motto in a letter to be *'Art for my sake.'* The task was *to find exactly the form one's passion . . . wants to take.* That form promised temporarily to be a celebration of the natural man and artist in the Burns figure, a form of the father to contain his creative passion. Why this form fell quickly aside is ascer-
HL, 95   tainable, I think, from the so-called "foreword" to *Sons and Lovers,* which Lawrence turned out not long after giving up on the Burns

novel: prompted too, it seems, by exposure to Ibsen in seeing an Italian production of *Ghosts*. But it will be better to delay discussion of this "foreword" until we have taken up in order the other two novels Lawrence began in the months succeeding *Sons and Lovers*.

Right after leaving off on the Burns novel, Lawrence started *dishing* up a new one, in which he took *a curious pleasure—venomous, almost*: something he must get off his chest at once. As opposed to the preceding novel, this one would be from a woman's point of view: *The Insurrection of Miss Houghton*. Surely this was an effort to keep a vow made, oddly enough, just when he was commencing the Burns work: *I shall do a novel about Love Triumphant one day. I shall do my work for women, better than the Suffrage*. These colliding purposes show Lawrence in the process of making up his mind whether to write from a male or a female standpoint. For that matter, he may not have begun the two novels consecutively, but have gone through some overlap in composition before he came to a firm decision. In any case, the *one day* when he would do better for women than the vote was suddenly today.

ML, 174 & 176

ML, 170–171

But this second novel was also dropped, when half-written, though unlike the Burns novel taken up again afterwards: in 1920, to be wholly rewritten and published as *The Lost Girl*. No portion of the original manuscript appears to have survived. But judging from references in letters, the first like the definitive version was to be a probing of the shopkeeper middle class in Eastwood, and was to include a woman's rebellion against sexual restraints. The particulars of the revolt could not have carried over, for to the second version Lawrence brought people and places unknown to him before 1919. In the published work an Italian man and the Italian landscape emancipate "the lost girl" from England and set her face toward a new destiny. The bulk of this is modelled on Lawrence's post-war escape from England, not that of 1912. We cannot know for certain whether in the original novel Alvina Houghton flees from England to Italy, nor whether Lawrence pairs her with an Italian of the "primitive" type. Given his deep interest at the time in Italian character and surroundings, the chances are that he did lead her on some such journey to some such man. Ciccio also has traits in common with Jack Haseldine to satisfy the compulsion to fictionalize the father. Altogether, here would have been occasion to combine treatment of an uninhibited male spirit with the promise to do justice to women, with the added opportunity to satirize the lower middle class of Eastwood. One clue may warrant conjecture of a Ciccio-like protagonist in the initial version of *The Lost Girl*: one provisional title was *Mixed Marriage*. Of course, since

ML, 602

Lawrence did not mention this title until 1919 — though before he had done any work at all on the rewriting — he may have been thinking of what he would do instead of what he had done. If in fact a flight to a dark man took place in the original work, this was the first appearance in Lawrence's fiction of pilgrimage from a pale and dying land to a land of living dark fires, and it would exemplify perfectly the belief in blood over mind now first expressed in letters, a belief already entertained but now confirmed under the influence of Italy.

After some three months' labor, doubting at last that he could ever get such an "improper" work in print, Lawrence shelved this novel in favor of a "pot-boiler" safe to recommend to young girls — he hoped. This seemed the quickest way to replenish his dwindling funds. But the pot-boiler soon broke its bounds and went on its way to become eventually both *The Rainbow* and *Women in Love,* the surest foundations of Lawrence's fame as a novelist. The rejection of entertainment for truth came about simply because Lawrence could never write about anything but his own problems: he always said his books had to be lived out, not thought out. *The Sisters,* as he first called this latest novel, was like *The Insurrection of Miss Houghton* in theme, only more immediate, for it took up inevitably the love affair with

ML, 200   Frieda: *I can only write what I feel pretty strongly about: and that, at present, is the relation between men and women. After all, it is the problem of today, the establishment of a new relation, or the readjustment of the old one, between men and women.* In another letter Lawrence puts succinctly the course of experience which has come to overshadow all others in the quest for a new relation: how love flourishes through struggle in a location where strangeness is paramount and the

ML, 170   issue is never clouded by familiarity of surroundings: *It's not so easy for a man and a woman to live alone together in a foreign country for six months, and dig out a love deeper and deeper. But we've done it so far, and I'm glad* — it was the "tragic" pattern again.

At bottom the problem was how to transform the relation of mother and son, painfully analyzed in the work gone by, into the relation of husband and wife, to be lived and recorded in the work to come. This is perhaps why Lawrence gave up the first two projected novels in preference for the third. In the first a male self out of his father in the English countryside, and possibly in the second a dark male self in an Italian setting, with a heroine in quest born in part of a suppressed feminine instinct in himself, and even in part, as some of the poems tell us, of his mother freed and alive in him — these complex longings may well have given place to a direct approach, intricate in purpose though it remained, to the problem of himself and his chosen woman, the relationship that might do away with the old oedipal helplessness. In sum the new novel might render both man and woman their due in a direct progression from *Sons and Lovers* after all: with a hero immanent in Paul Morel and a heroine sufficiently like Alvina Houghton. The satirization of Eastwood could wait.

We are now in a better position to appreciate the bearing of the *Sons and Lovers* "foreword" on all this. This bit of symbolic confession tells us at once why Lawrence quit the Burns novel. He was still too much enthralled yet troubled by female ascendancy to do justice to a theme of male freedom and male volition. Not until 1917 and the undertaking of *Aaron's Rod* would he be ready for this move in the sense inferred by the Burns fragment. At the stage of the "foreword," he still could not stand clear of an oedipal connection between man and woman: no more between lovers than between mother and son. The male he glorifies as God's prime creature is yet confined to utter dependence on the female. But first a word about the form of the piece, which Lawrence sent to his editor as a "foreword" but asked him not to publish. The style and imagery are striking. It is a sort of general epistle, though addressed to one man, and it carries the Biblical imitation to the point of parody in language, echoing the Gospel of John and the letters of Paul. If he was not emulating Paul, at least he warned the recipient, like Paul in Second Corinthians, that he spoke as a "fool." This is Lawrence's first venture into the philosophy he was later to toil over at such length. But since none of it was ever philosophy in the technical, or at least the academic sense, we had better adopt a term to which Lawrence gives support later on and call it *symbology*.   SM, 141

The "foreword" puts Lawrence's doctrine in this way: Christianity has reversed the truth in declaring that the Word was made Flesh. Spirit is not primary but rather Flesh, Substance, which is the Father Himself. The Son is born of the Flesh and speaks the Word in his hour: so the Flesh is made Word. And the Word is not eternal: the Flesh is. The Word uttered will vanish, to be replaced by another. Only the unutterable and unsearchable Flesh abides forever. The same concept, we will see, informs "The Theatre" and the blood-religion, full-flame letter, all three of these given their final push into being by Lawrence's interpretation of Ibsen's *Ghosts*.

We see here a reflection of Schopenhauer, too, as so often in Lawrence's symbology: the eternal is not a spirit revealed to the mind but a will transmitted as form to the body only. A significant distinction between the two men is discernible, however: Lawrence prefers the amorphous term Substance to Form. Yet his Substance has the definite form of Father, Mother, Mate, Son and the like. The real basis of Lawrence's Substance, like Schopenhauer's Will, is that truth is perceived through the senses and an immortal disembodied spirit is impossible.

The crucial point for comprehending the "foreword" is how Lawrence fits the Mother into his scheme. About halfway through his "epistle" he declares that God the Father should rightly be called the Mother, and confusion is with us. But patience is essential with genius beating its way out of tangled emotions by symbols apocalyptically conceived: the affliction is not reducible to logic. The real trouble is with the abiding perplexity about the role of the Father as Begetter.

HL, 100   Lawrence wishes to set up a distinctly trinitarian pattern: *So there is the Father — which should be called Mother — then the Son, who is the Utterer, and then the Word.* The Word spoken by the Son is the Father expending himself in a moment of glory, a moment Lawrence equates with the Holy Ghost. For the Son this is a moment of utmost realization of the self, for he embodies the spontaneous and insouciant consciousness of the Father, his *infinitude and gloriousness.* Still, all

HL, 101   through his argument, Lawrence insists that the Mother *herself, whether she will have it or not,* is *God the Father.* His metaphor of a bee-hive reveals just how much he wishes for the ensphering protec-

HL, 100   tion of a maternal godhead: *And the bee, who is a Son, comes home to his Queen as to the Father, in service and humility, for suggestion, and renewal, and identification which is the height of his glory.* Now by this time Lawrence has left off calling the female Mother: she has become Woman, Wife included, the Eternal Feminine all in one, and yet the Father.

All this is perhaps best understood as vaguely Marian, with the Father maintaining his inscrutability except as man born of woman, who is then elevated to be the Mother of God. Or Woman may be regarded as the intermediary between Father and Son, the only possible channel between them, an intercessor. In any case, Lawrence was straining every resource of symbolism at his command to attribute everything to mystical and omnipotent maleness and yet satisfy his mother's coercive teaching that all he did was for her: that in serving woman man is serving God. He said in another contemporary letter that it was useless for him to attempt anything without a woman

ML, 179   behind him. Only she could keep him *in direct communication with the unknown.* And what she was to supply is plain in the same letter:

ML, 180   incarnate proof of his *belief in the blood, the flesh, as being wiser than the intellect.*

Under these shifting associations of the maternal, the paternal and the connubial, the central preoccupation remains the Son, who shines

HL, 101   forth brilliantly as *the exclamation of joy and astonishment at new self-revelation.* Some examples of the type are Galileo, Shakespeare, and Darwin. They carried out the urge to create anew which Lawrence came to see as the primary stimulus of all male activity, even beyond sex. Such men have great claims to sustenance and encouragement, being the pioneers and the natural leaders. Whatever his dependence on woman may be, this male has ultimate power over woman, showing the way to a new plane of civilization. Her appearance of dominance may be only her fixity as a kind of substance whose sole purpose is to nourish the male. We know that Frieda complained of just this, and so did Helen Corke: that Lawrence felt entitled to the whole being of a woman. He could not yet admit that Woman — Frieda, to be exact — would remain far from agreeing to such a role. And for that matter no woman could have adopted it without becoming very much what his mother had been. He was also blissfully unaware that in relegating the Father to remoteness inaccessible save through Woman, he was all but denying his own existence. The opening of Lawrence's eyes to the necessity of the Father descending directly to the Son was a later trauma.

Lawrence could never have formulated the *Sons and Lovers* "foreword" had he not fallen in love with Frieda and taken her to a new country to forge in isolation a whole relationship. He could not have written the novel itself, nor undertaken any of the other three novels conceived and begun at Lake Garda. The influence of travel here is all-pervasive. We catch this unmistakably in a precept of Lawrence's swiftly growing artistic creed: the artist goes forth to conquer a new territory and thus becomes a moment in the activity of the God who *expels him forth to waste himself in utterance, in work.*   HL, 101

All this while Lawrence kept a curious eye on the Italian scene, and the contrasts he observed between Italian and English character aided him in forming distinctions between the flesh and the mind that lasted him the rest of his life. His immediate outlet for these observations was more travel sketches, published in the *English Review*. In these, for the first time, Lawrence tries to understand a foreign place much as he would in a novel: through penetration of individual character, not principally through comment on the passing scene or the study of cultural artifacts like the *ex voto* pictures or the crucifixes. So both important forms of Lawrence's symbology stem from the Lake Garda residence. From the *Sons and Lovers* "foreword" sprang the study of Thomas Hardy, the Crown essays, and many other writings through the two books of psychology in the early 1920s. The travel sketches led to the travel book as symbology, from *Twilight in Italy* through *Etruscan Places*. And we will see how these two forms merge in a curious compound in *Studies in Classic American Literature*.

The *English Review* pieces are "The Spinner and the Monks," "The Lemon Gardens of Signor di P.," and "The Theatre." In their expanded form they comprise nearly half of *Twilight in Italy*. For the time being, we are concerned only with the initial versions.

In all three a buoyant expectancy prevails, the imminence of some momentous discovery. "The Spinner and the Monks," based on a walk Lawrence took alone in early February, is a sprightly account of searching through the dark alleys of Gargnano for a way to the church of San Tommaso on its light-struck terrace high above the village and the lake. The eager young man exults in this marvellous spot *above the obscure, jumbled tiles of square roofs, high enough over the pale blue lake, opposite the snow of the mountains beyond the water. And the snow glistened white, there was a blood-red sail like a butterfly breathing on the blue water, while the earth on my side gave off a green-silver smoke of olive trees, filming up and around the earth-coloured roofs. So I praised God.*

ER, An old peasant woman, he now discovers, is spinning on the terrace, with the old-fashioned distaff and bobbin. Unlike the dark Italians he has just escaped in the village below, she is light-complexioned, as if made of sun-stuff: sun-bleached leaves and stones, with her blue eyes alive in the present as flowers are, beyond recognition of past and future. All through this sketch runs a light-dark dichotomy, oddly — for Lawrence — of light to be sought and darkness to be shunned. But the blackness has little of the fearful in it, and little, either, of holiness or fecundity. It is the contrast that serves mainly as a source of joy for the young seeker.

For an instant, before the old spinner, he feels that he has belonged previously to the dark of the villagers below, and in his quest for the sunny church tower has come to the very genius of this upper level. He himself feels dark by comparison. He exchanges a few words with her, but is so discomfited by her indifference that he soon flees her, on the verge of fear, and climbs the ridge behind the church to hunt for snowdrops, which he has been told are commencing to bloom. He does not find any, but does come across primroses, crocuses, and a few remaining Christmas roses. As he descends into gullies to look for flowers, sunlight versus the shade reawakens in him momentarily the sensation of quest that sent him upward from the lower village to the church terrace. Uneasy in the shadow of a bank, he scrambles quickly back to sunlight, unreasoning gratitude welling up in him for the warm, bright, still beauty of the landscape. Now he sits down under the olive trees. And so pronounced is his communion with the audible and visible universe that when he spies two monks walking in

ER,
202 &
ML, 185

ER, 203

GARGNANO, ITALY

The thin old church standing above in the light . . . .
Its thin grey neck was held up stiffly . . . . It was like a vision,
a thing one does not expect to come close to. (TI, 19–20)

the deepening twilight around a monastery garden far below, he can almost feel them talking.

Now the little sketch changes into a sort of morality tableau. The monks, like the old spinning woman, become moral types for the edification of this consciousness in passage through the lakeside world with its mountains, water, flowers, trees and skies, the very description of which is a song of praise to the powers behind them. As opposites to the seeker the monks are oblivious of the natural world. They do not respond to the shining snow of the mountains across, nor to the sliver of moon glowing to life in the dusky sky. They can only know the past of the crucified Christ or the future of eternal life imagined in him. As pilgrims they belong to the abstract, in contrast to the pilgrim observer's immersion in the concrete. Like Bunyan's Christian he takes warning from the wicked. The vice of the monks is their blindness to the present moment, the acme of life. The old spinning woman is their contrary: an epitome of the present like the flowers the seeker has gathered to carry home.

The "Lemon Gardens" is another instance of a moral lesson proposed through creation of character and setting. In the decayed aristocracy of Signor di Pietro, his landlord, Lawrence expounds the questions of liveliness versus happiness, of the nature of passion, and of male and female being. He proceeds by direct contrast between the English and the Italian character.

Arriving at di Pietro's house to help install a door spring beyond the mechanical abilities of the genteel little man, Lawrence has a brief look into his private life. Darkness and light, again, first arouse the observer's curiosity. This Englishman from the dark Midlands, unfailingly enchanted by the sunlight of Italy, wonders why the Italians are so fond of gloomy interiors, concluding that what is true of the Italian's dwelling must extend to his personality: *The Italian is surrounded by sunshine: his very suppleness and ease and grace seem melted in sunshine. But he must be fairly dark inside, or his house could not be as it is.* An Italian newspaperman's opinion on the excess of passion in his race comes to mind: that the Italians are joyful but not happy — support for Lawrence's view that their brightness penetrates no deeper into their souls than sunlight into their houses. They mistake passion, a means to an end, for an end in itself.

ER, 212

So far the remarks are analogues to those of numerous English authors on Italians: E. M. Forster, for example. The next turn of thought is characteristic of Lawrence at the time, and it indicates how close to his moods his opinions ranged. Out of this geographical context for revitalization of the relationship between man and woman, he speaks with great optimism of northern — not to say personal —

ITALIAN WOOL-SPINNER

She felt again at the fleece as she drew it down,
and she gave a twist to the thread that issued,
and the bobbin spun swiftly (**TI**, 23)

potentialities: *The northern races are the really passionate people, because theirs is the passion that persists and achieves, achieves everything, including that intimacy between a man and a woman which is the fruit of passion, and which is rarely seen here: the love, the knowledge, the simplicity, and the absence of shame, that one sometimes sees in English eyes, and which is the flower of civilisation.*

Thus the diametric opposite of judgments delivered elsewhere: those lauding Italian spontaneity and cheerfulness over the narrow conventionality of the English. Such blank opposition without preparation can be disconcerting. But Lawrence understood, of course, that the character of a nation, taken by itself or in conjunction with another, is rife with contradictions, from which he could stress, at any given moment, what satisfied best his emotional and artistic needs. Often this meant proceeding by contraries, but through the whole range of these a consistent pattern and rhythm do emerge.

If Lawrence's first extensive conclusions on the superiority of body over mind find expression in these sketches, they do not come to any pure idealization of sensuality. The limitations of physicality as a way of life are fully set forth in the "Lemon Gardens" sketch. It is an essential complement to the blood-religion letter of approximately the same date. Southern fleshliness has the drawback of any unalloyed addiction. The Italian attachment to passion as an end in itself eclipses any godhead outside the flesh, whereas the ordinary Englishman, at the other extreme, is apt to be blind to any godhead outside of spirituality. What brings the Italian shortcoming home to Lawrence is the bitter disappointment of Signor di Pietro over being childless. An ER, 215 Italian *feels that his only real claim to being a man is that he has children. . . . [He] feels, no matter what he believes, that he is made in the image of God, and in this image of flesh is his godliness, and with its defacement and crumbling, crumbles himself.* His soul, as a spiritual entity, means nothing to him. The Englishman, on the contrary, *considers that in him is Almighty God, cumbered here in the flesh,* a spirit ashamed of its material prison.

If we are to reconcile the Englishman shrinking from his own body with the previous one as the only European capable of supreme passion, we might suppose them to represent the average and the extraordinary, the seeker in Lawrence identified with the second. Opposites then fall into place as the ordinary Italian and his English counterpart, as opposites did in the old spinning woman and the monks, typifying extremes the seeker of life must avoid.

A long description of di Pietro's lemon business follows, as guest and host walk through the little orchards: the grafting of trees, the setting up of temporary wooden shelters to protect them against freezing, the irrigation, the general economics of growing lemons here. Even these matters are of vivid interest in Lawrence's prose.

But his incomparable gift for making vital experience out of the simplest event comes out best in an excerpt like the following, which had to be changed very little for inclusion in *Twilight in Italy: In the* ER, 217 *morning I often lie in bed and watch the sunrise. The lake lies dim and milky, the mountains are dark blue at the back, while over them the sky gushes and glistens with light. At a certain place on the mountain ridge the light burns gold, seems to fuse a little groove on the hill's rim. It fuses and fuses at this point, till of a sudden it comes, the intense, molten, living light. The mountains melt suddenly, the light steps down, there is a glitter, a spangle, a clutch of spangles, a great unbearable sun-track flashing across the milky lake, and the light falls on my face.*

The sketch weakens at the conclusion, as if Lawrence did not quite know how to bring to a head the topics pondered. The questioning of why di Pietro is not content in the beautiful environment of the lake is commonplace. Not well-off but with enough to live on, yet this faded aristocrat envies the riches of England. After happiness and passion and national characters have been debated so expansively, this little picture of envious sadness is anti-climactic.

In late December 1912, a company of actors came to Gargnano and performed until mid-February. The first play the Lawrences saw was Ibsen's *Ghosts,* and after some others, on the evening before Lawrence wrote his famous blood-religion letter, they attended a performance of *Hamlet.* The resulting sketch, "The Theatre," is one of Lawrence's most amusing bits of travel writing, a marvellous depiction of Italian character in actors and audience, with conclusions on the intricacies of flesh and spirit touched upon but often left hanging in the sketches just discussed. Again the observation is self-involved, through a contrast of national types worked into Lawrence's response to the plays. In the process he finds ample confirmation of his apotheosis of the flesh, but he finds again reason to mistrust it also, because unqualified passion may erect obstacles to a plenitude of being.

Observing the segregation of men and women and the absence of flirting in the audience, Lawrence notes that passion and not love here rules the conduct of the sexes, with a certain shame of exhibiting intimacy. Unexpectedly, his reaction is tinged with nostalgia for England and his childhood. The children of Italian unions could never bask in the *wonderful warmth and cosy tenderness that makes life rich* ER, 223 *in an English home.* For a moment a distant harmony sounds that did now and then prevail in Lawrence's childhood home, as recreated in *Sons and Lovers* and *The Rainbow.*

But childish the Italians are, in a different sense, sparking further ambivalent feelings in Lawrence, since this immaturity also resembles that which he had relived in *Sons and Lovers*. The son in *Ghosts* is *childishly dependent on his mother. To hear him say "Grazia, mamma!" would have touched the mother-soul in any woman living.* But whatever reservations accompany this view, Lawrence can still *love this childish nation that lives by faith and wants no knowledge.* From this fullness of life in the spontaneous, Lawrence gets at his chief aim in the sketch: the paucity of being in the spirituality that has long since seized upon the northern soul. Of course the apprehension before spirituality has its source too in the rigors of overcoming "spiritual" intimacy with the mother. And in Ibsen Lawrence found the perfect scapegoat. All of Ibsen's people have the diseased northern mind. Though they cling to spirituality in desperation they realize at bottom

ER, 224   that it *is of no avail against the flesh.* So foreign to the Mediterranean actors is the North Sea playwright that only by strained re-interpretation can they create him on the stage. The Italian actor portraying the son in the play turns him, according to Lawrence, into a dangerous man-child, who dies the death the play calls for, but the flesh will not permit him the utter despair of the original, since the Italian always remains flesh and it is incapable of despair. This Italian version of Ibsen's character awakens sympathy in Lawrence, not the unqualified horror he felt seeing the play in Germany. In this fashion Lawrence sets up a contrast between traits of a land where he is and those of Ibsen's far-off land to help derive a terminology for his religion. Ibsen's flaw was that *he denied the universality of the blood, of which we are all cups.* Or in terms of the other sacramental substance he could not, even if he would, surrender to the rejuvenation of the flesh, confessing that *of the flesh all things are possible. It holds all things within itself, both the discovered and that which will be discovered.*

Still a question always looms: if the flesh is supremely good, why is the Italian wrong to put implicit trust in it? The crux is that Lawrence's perceptions outrun the discrimination of his language. "Flesh" may designate the Italian at his life of the body in the dark alleys of his village or the dark interior of his home, or his fixation on children as the sole immortality. "Flesh" may embrace as well the entire physical world as a manifestation of undying generative powers. The Italian may enjoy a greater breadth of life than the mental northerner, but the flesh that he takes to be the whole is but a small portion of the Father as Substance that the pilgrim narrator contemplates. The figurative language of the *Sons and Lovers* "foreword" may have given way to narrative in the sketches, but the implications of the symbology reverberate still.

By far the best part of this sketch concerns the performance of *Amleto,* a section later expanded to great thematic purpose for *Twilight in Italy.* The *maestra,* the Lawrences' tutor in Italian, brings word the play will be presented, only to meet with a blank look from Lawrence, who does not at once recognize the old familiar *Hamlet* in Italian. But he soon rises to the occasion, knowing that Enrico Persevalli, chief actor and manager of the troupe, has selected the play in honor of Gargnano's only English residents. Lawrence sits through the performance feeling like a prince called upon to witness an entertainment by rustics. The awkwardness of the actors, all peasants really, and the incongruity of Shakespeare in a foreign tongue are almost too much for him — this, for instance, when Persevalli swells with passion for the famous soliloquy: *I am sure, as he stepped forward whispering "Essere"* — ER, 230 *took another step* — *"o non essere"* — *plunged with his hand . . . the contadini thought he was stuck in the back, and they held their breath.* For all that, this naïveté of the actors, and especially that of the audience, recaptures for Lawrence momentarily a credibility of the ghost that he has not experienced since childhood, and he becomes as absorbed in the apparition as the peasants are. The audience is in all ways a source of joy, with its *warm feeling of life,* so different from ER, 232 an English audience, in which every person *keeps himself contracted* ER, 231 *as tight as he can, so as not to touch his neighbour.*

That the Italian *lives by the human ties which connect him with* ER, 229 *his neighbours* is what makes it impossible for Persevalli to play Hamlet, just as it was with the son in *Ghosts.* Hamlet's tragedy, says Lawrence, is that he can neither love nor hate. A cold diseased creature of mind and spirit, dead in flesh and blood, he only knows and pries to know, every particle of feeling gone. Watching the *decent Italian* actor strive to *put himself through the creepings and twistings of the unwholesome Dane,* with the Ibsen fiasco fresh in memory, Lawrence begins to specify in historical form his hatred of northern European mental life. We do not see the full effects until *Twilight in Italy.* The ideas are wayward and incomplete in the present sketches. They germinated when the Great War added impetus to the search for an adequate symbology.

The immediate consequence was the blood-religion, full-flame letter of the day after the Shakespeare performance, a letter in which Hamlet, and indirectly the Ibsen character, are the culprits. Again the parallels were personal: Hamlet and the son of *Ghosts* added to the Oedipus who overshadowed *Sons and Lovers.* At least the Renaissance and the modern examples had reacted to consuming mother-love by turning into mental monstrosities. The way out was the recovery of fleshly consciousness through spontaneous desire: *Instead of chasing* ML, 180 *the mystery in the fugitive, half-lighted things outside us, we ought to look at ourselves, and say, 'My God, I am myself!' That is why I like to live in Italy. The people are so unconscious. They only feel and want: they don't know. We know too much. No, we only **think** we know such a lot. A flame isn't a flame because it lights up two, or twenty objects on a table. It's a flame because it is itself. And we have forgotten ourselves. We are Hamlet without the Prince of Denmark. We cannot be. 'To be or not to be' — it is the question with us now, by Jove. And nearly every Englishman says 'Not to be.' So he goes in for Humanitarianism and suchlike forms of not-being. The real way of living is to answer to one's wants. Not 'I want to light up with my intelligence as many things as possible' but 'For the living of my full flame — I want that liberty, I want that woman.'*

Lawrence's astonishing enterprise at the start of 1913 extended to a play of his own, *The Daughter-in-Law,* inspired certainly by the dramatic performances at hand and related by antithesis to his travels. It is a variation on the same old theme: the stunting of a man's growth by a possessive mother. Now it is two sons: one capable of being a lover, the other not. The wife's fight to win her husband away from his mother is the central conflict, in which she is victorious, or ostensibly so, for the resolution of the plot is little more than a transfer of the man's childishness from mother to wife. More pertinent for our purpose is the fate of the younger son, so much under his mother's thumb that he can never be really a man. He admits it in sorrow:

CO, 257 *Tha knows tha's got me — an'll ha'e me till ter dies — an' after that —*
CO, 258 *yi.* Nowhere could he escape: *If I went t'r Australia, th' best part on me wouldna go wi' me.* The portraits stand out clear by the sharp flame of Italy. Lawrence might have followed this course himself if his mother had lived and never released him to travel. Perhaps with the other son he speculates on the alternative destiny of marriage to Jessie Chambers.

The nineteen or twenty poems added to the *Look! We Have Come Through!* sequence in these months, with two exceptions, probe the convolutions of harmony and friction in love. But these two have a special significance, since they revert to the son's memory of the lost mother, after the partial healing of time and of experience wrought by love and travel united. The earliest of the two, apparently the first poem written at Lake Garda, is an example of identification with the mother that would recur through the rest of Lawrence's life. Here it comes to a half-conscious resolve to dedicate his pilgrim's life to living out her frustrated and tragically shortened existence. The persona scarcely claims an identity for himself. Yet he controls their co-existence through a tender mastery he lacked in the earlier grief poetry, as shown by his willingness to allow her full possession of his consciousness. He asks who it is, in this strange land at dusk, watching the snowy mountaintops, the boat on the lake, the olive leaves dimming in the twilight. Does the Italian in the passing ox-wagon see two ghosts under the olives? The mother can never in body look upon these lovely foreign things the poet envisions gathering in his travels to bring to her: the mountaintops like flowers and the sailboat caught in the hands like a moth. But no matter. What he sees, she sees, for she is inside him:

I know you here in the darkness,   CP, 227
  How you sit in the throne of my eyes
At peace, and look out of the windows
  In glad surprise.

"All Souls," a poem from early November when the end of *Sons*   CP, 233
and Lovers was in sight, finds the poet watching villagers at the cemetery where the service for all the dead is being conducted. A few individuals who seem to strive with their dead stand apart by a candle on a grave, a candle that divides the mystery of life from the mystery of death. The son cannot so approach the mother. Her grave is far off in England and no candle, only weeds, thrust up from it. Yet the wayfaring son has not neglected her. By accepting the whole world as her grave he has reached accord with her departed soul. If the image is reminiscent of the world as a ship of darkness on which the ethereal son and the mother's ghost formerly sailed forbidden seas, a strong new note predominates before this poem is done. Not by darkness, now, but by unique light the son will carry on the life the mother bestowed. Instead of a candle he himself will stand on her grave as a naked flame, not just on some day set aside but every day of the year. He may do this half-consciously, maybe even forgetting her now and again as he goes forth to live. But still the candle of self will always blaze for her sake. But the phallic image, we note, separates as well as unites. It incorporates the intention to live by physical love with a mate, in defiance of the stigma imposed by the mother.

The last pages of *Sons and Lovers* come to mind, the candle replacing the constellation as containment against darkness. Likewise the candle of the blood-religion letter, alive for its own flame and not for the light it sheds on objects, and also the discussion in the theater sketch. A broadening cadence of symbols supports the denunciation of European mental consciousness, which has its source in a spiritual incest of mother and son. Yet Lawrence's compassion has by now so matured that he can transform filial intimacy even as he rejects it: the candle of passion can burn its brightest in free combustion and still rest on the maternal tomb.

The other Lake Garda poems pursue the quest for a whole and

CP, 228 binding love with Frieda. "Sunday Afternoon in Italy," like the passage in "The Theatre," depicts the nature of passion in Italy: still as a combat between men and women, with fleeting, infrequent moments of unison. If allusion to the warm and constant accord of the northern few is absent, that *flower of civilization* ideal, we do note that the resistance-sympathy cycle described in the poem is closer to the sex relationship ideal that Lawrence later arrived at.

But the poems lead into more problematic regions than this, bordering on a mythical dimension of the puritan conscience: not by a conviction of sin in the old sense, yet with the thought that the single human soul is a great battleground for impulses from beyond. In some poems a streak of cruelty erupting at times into violence wars with the tenderness of love. But the poet insists that passion must compre-

CP, 229 hend all emotions. "Winter Dawn" describes the purification that comes when a time of hatred between the lovers has concluded, leav-

CP, 230 ing the man chilled and empty but clean as if bathed in starlight. "A Bad Beginning" pounds home his stern demand for submission of a wife to her husband. He has bruised her throat in the night with love-making, but she bruises him through and through with her half-will-

CP, 234 ingness to fling away the old life and become entirely his. He orders this even more obdurately in "Lady Wife," a poem that exhibits two sides of the mythical sense controlling Lawrence's view of self. One is a condemnation of the metaphysical importance women assign to motherhood. The woman is not to think that in coming to her husband she is one of the angels who came to Abraham in disguise and stayed for a while in his house, and that like the angel ascending she may reclaim the holy sphere of motherhood when she will. No, she must put on sackcloth and learn submission to her husband, lending her strength to his serving of the *imminent Mystery*. Such insistence was naturally bound to cause periodically a violent antipathy in Frieda.

CP, 235 In "Both Sides of the Medal" the poet undertakes to resolve the issue of the love-hate cycle by appeal to the stars. The woman must realize that great passion is instinct with hatred as well as love. And great passion, like Balaam's ass, compels one willy-nilly to go the way of the Lord. To this supernal round of passional life they must submit:

CP, 236 *each of us to the balanced, eternal orbit/wherein we circle on our fate/in strange conjunction.* The image will reappear as a favorite of Lawrence's in one metamorphosis after another to signify the love of man and woman: two beings circling through space linked by emotional gravitation. Paul Morel contemplated his mother's spirit and his own so ensphered, and the same image had briefly served the lovers in *The Trespasser.*

The conjoining of love and hatred on a mythical level reaches its zenith in four poems revealing plainer than ever in the man a devastating cruelty that he makes every effort to bring into the whole account of his feelings and creative endeavors. "Rabbit Snared in the Night" may at first glance seem an intrusion in the series. The man holds the throbbing creature in his grasp. A spark of darkness in its eye makes the lust for sacrifice stir and mount in his veins. Fantasizing a reciprocal desire in the rabbit, he proceeds to throttle it as if in a ritual, his fingers *the black and monstrous fingers of Moloch*. Much CP, 242 of the vocabulary of "Rabbit Snared in the Night" echoes an incident in the Burns fragment where Jack Haseldine picks up a snared rabbit. Only there pity and not the lust to destroy triumphs.

"New Year's Night" is related directly to the rabbit poem: a strange concatenation of tenderness and torture with imagery recalling the Song of Songs. The cherished dove becomes, however, a temple offering: *You're a dove I have bought for sacrifice,/And to-night I* CP, 238 *slay it.* Sex and death are intertwined: *Here in my arms my naked sacrifice!/Death, do you hear.* The woman is offered *up to the ancient inexorable God.* Death swoops *like a falcon*, but *'Tis God has taken* CP, 239 *the victim;/I have won my renown.* One meaning from tradition is of course that of the little death in sexual intercourse. The *renown* the ensuing resurrection brings the man is the freedom to be and to create. Yet the kinship of cruelty and creative power remains to him undeniable.

The other two of the four poems elaborate more appealingly the mythic associations of journeys into new life. "Birth Night," a Christmas poem, transforms the season of the child born of woman into that of Eve's birth from Adam. The firelight of the night in which the lovers embrace is a womb. The man is a great conduit leading out of darkness into the woman and dissolving her spent life. Out of his veins and not his rib she is born: *You are born again of me./I, Adam,* CP, 240 *from the veins of me/The Eve that is to be.* A paradise awaits them. *The strait gate of passion,* in the poem "Paradise Re-Entered," will CP, 242 conduct them to regeneration. The act of love now becomes fully a journey. The couple approach the gate through the burning region of desire, passing also through *the darkened spaces/Of fear,* passing death too, piercing a space burned clean by angels. Then they besiege the gates from which God once drove them, retaking the Garden at last, these questing spirits who *travel/To Eden home.* This is the CP, 243 mythic homeland that Lawrence had always with him in his journeys, the other and symbolic plane of life accessible, as here, when the mythic otherness of the present moment has absorbed the past and the future.

Spring had now come to Lake Garda. At the end of March the lovers vacated the Villa Igea and went to spend a few days at San Gaudenzio, a farm on the cliffs above the lake. Here a deserted lemon garden offered Lawrence the sunny protection of its little hollow for his writing. He was making headway on *The Sisters,* and he may have jotted down in early form the sketches focusing on San Gaudenzio, but as no fragments are extant we cannot test the true importance of this place till he prepared the sketches for *Twilight in Italy* two and a half years later.

The couple could not avoid going to England that summer, but owing to Lawrence's persuasiveness against Frieda's wish to be near her children, to stay in England was no longer imperative. The first leg of the journey took them to Germany, to Irschenhausen again. At once Lawrence began longing to be back in Italy. In his habitual shifts and changes he felt cramped in the Bavaria he had found so wild and ML, free eight months before. He complained of suffering *from the tight-* 200–201 *ness, the domesticity of Germany.* This country might seem to liberate in comparison with England, but Italy far surpassed it. The North was now all tainted by what Italy had taught him in relation to *Ghosts* ML, and *Hamlet: Over these countries, Germany and England, like the* 203–204 *grey skies, lies the gloom of the dark moral judgment and condemna-tion and reservation of the people. Italy does not judge. I shall want to go back there.* Yet he was heart-struck over England, and his mis-sion was still clear: *I do write because I want folk — English folk — to alter, and have more sense.*

During the two months in Irschenhausen Lawrence worked hard on *The Sisters.* His about-face on Germany can be attributed also to the wringing out of his amorous conflicts on page after page of this work.

According to Mark Kinkead-Weekes, a six-page fragment of this abandoned manuscript survives.[3] Certainly nearly every twist of theme in the fragment leads to this conclusion: a strange mother who writes letters about her son's marriage as if addressing them *to some mythological place of her own creation,* a *miserable father,* a mur-dered brother perhaps suggested by Lawrence's preoccupation with *Hamlet,* a rivalry over Ella complete with an appeal from the victorious suitor that he love her more than their coming child.[4] The borrowing of national traits for the characters of this fragment is important. Loerke is here a "decent" German sculptor totally unlike the Loerke of *Women in Love.* Of course the rival also retains something of Law-rence's English opponent, Frieda's husband. Ella and Gudrun were at this stage largely Frieda and her sister Else. In support of the frag-ment's theme the letters suggest two strong-minded women coming

into their own through bringing a dominant type of male into balance
in love. Even though Frieda found these females *beastly,* for Lawrence   ML, 207
they were essential to incorporating into his emotional life the "continental" sort of woman who had all but overwhelmed him in the von
Richthofen sisters. Of course much of the effort still consisted of
attacking obstructions to harmony with Frieda, no doubt with some
vengeance for her maternal longings and vindication of himself. But
Lawrence appears unsure just now whether the obstacles to freedom
in love were decreasing or increasing, whether after the Italian sojourn
Germany could support his quest. Maybe this now-shrunken Germany
had been wild and free the year before because the momentary anticipation of life with Frieda had been wild and free.

The eventual trip to England kept them there from June into
August. Having appeared only in May, *Sons and Lovers* had not yet
attracted much attention. But Lawrence did meet and mingle with
people of distinction in such a way as to abolish his earlier fears of
class discomfort. He made the acquaintance of Edward Marsh, an
important man in the Admiralty and editor of the Georgian poetry
volumes; also of Herbert and Cynthia Asquith, son and daughter-in-
law of the Prime Minister. Cynthia was soon to become a sort of ideal
woman to Lawrence. Numerous other friendships also date from that
summer, one of which remained always influential: the friendship,
later interspersed with enmity, of John Middleton Murry and Katherine
Mansfield.

On returning to Irschenhausen in August, Lawrence again reconstituted the place according to present mood. After stuffy little England, Germany was once more a *great wide landscape where one can*   ML, 217
breathe. He had faced England with Frieda and scored victories.
Germany once more opened the path to the future.

Yet England was suddenly a source for sketch-writing, hinting
at another triumph over the past. Lawrence spoke of a book of "travel"
sketches on his hometown and went so far as to produce one, referred
to simply as *on Eastwood,* with two more in view: on the artists of   ML, 218
Eastwood and the Primitive Methodist chapel. Apparently nothing
more ever came of this project, and the sketch written has vanished.

The main thing in hand, however, was still *The Sisters,* which
after discussion with Edward Garnett Lawrence had just given *a new*   ML, 223
beginning — a new basis altogether. He was looking forward to a *glor-*   ML, 219
ious winter of work beside the Gulf of Spezia. While he now corrected
proofs of the *English Review* sketches of Lake Garda, other effects
of his geographical moods came into evidence. He cheerfully pro-
tested the mere "literary" quality of James Elroy Flecker's geography in his recently published poetic drama *The Golden Journey to*

ML, 220   *Samarkand: You knew it climbed Parnassus* **en route**? he inquired. For
Lawrence the journey *only took place on paper — no matter who went
to Asia Minor.* Just what he meant by his threat to write a book called
The Poet's Geographer one day is not entirely clear: except for his
aversion to the injection of "romance" into foreign places.

By September the Lawrences were on the move again, Frieda for
a short visit with her mother in Baden-Baden and Lawrence for a
hike across Switzerland to Italy. He probably had from the start the
notion of doing sketches based on his walk, but no evidence exists
that he did them any time soon. Switzerland proved disappointing in
ML,   any case: *banal.* Milan was no better, *with its imitation hedgehog of
231 & 232   a cathedral, and its hateful town Italians.* The journey assumed no
great importance for Lawrence till the grouping of all his sketches into
Twilight in Italy.

Fiascherino was to be home for Lawrence and Frieda from October 1913 through the next May. On the Gulf of Spezia near Shelley's
ML, 227   San Terenzo, this place made Lawrence nearly burst with delight: *I
am so happy with the place we have at last discovered, I must write
smack off to tell you. It is perfect. There is a little tiny bay half shut
in by rocks, and smothered by olive woods that slope down swiftly . . . .
Then there is the **villino** of Ettore Gambrosier, a four-roomed pink
cottage among vine gardens, just over the water and under the olive
woods . . . . You run out of the gate into the sea.* Here the immense
changes that had gotten underway in Lawrence during his first stay
in Italy continued at a heady pace, and the role of Italy as surroundings
if anything increased. He now enjoyed a steadier than usual balance in
the opposing forces of his nature, and though the friction with Frieda
went on, rebirth through interchange between man and woman still
glowed ahead like Eden recovered. Lawrence now and then spoke of
increasing closeness in love and the wonder of Fiascherino in the same
ML, 241   breath: *We are getting gradually nearer again, Frieda and I. It is very
beautiful here.* Italy was giving a new lease on what may have seemed in
danger of slipping away between visits.

Of Fiascherino Lawrence wrote no travel sketches as such, though
ML, 277   he spoke of having collected *some lovely matter* for them and his
letters abound in little gems of sketches, in which glimmers the pil-
ML, 255   grim's love of both the actual and the ideal place: *At this time of the
year all the women are out in the olive woods — you have no idea how
beautiful olives are, so grey, so delicately sad, reminding one constantly
of the New Testament. I am always expecting when I go to Tellaro
for the letters, to meet Jesus gossiping with his disciples as he goes
along above the sea, under the grey, light trees —* the Ligurian Sea was
all at once the Sea of Galilee.

TELLARO, ITALY

I have to go to Tellaro for the letters —
it is a little sea-robbers' nest still inaccessible (ML, 232)

That all this was like a rebirth in some special sphere of time and place is strikingly evident in Lawrence's exultation over what he could realize of life and love together in the writing of his novel. He turned out reams for *The Sisters,* starting over several times: though the seven times and eleven times mentioned are certainly hyperbolic. At all events he wrote it twice entire: *quite a thousand pages.* The occasional complaint that this place was too beautiful to work in was only the cup running over. He could affirm now that *Frieda and I are together, and the work is of me and her, and it is beautiful, I think.* He was writing in touch with a completely new body of thought and feeling that he was never wholly to lose sight of in his later work: *Something of the eternal stillness that lies under all movement, under all life, like a source, incorruptible and inexhaustible. It is deeper than change, and struggling. So long I have acknowledged only the struggle, the stream, the change. And now I begin to feel something of the source, the great impersonal which never changes and out of which all change comes.* The sense of discovery had indeed reached a high pitch, and with the magical and at the same time overweening gift of the artist, Lawrence saw his own life more than ever as the epitome of all experience: *The only history is a mere question of one's struggle inside oneself. But that is the joy of it. One need neither discover Americas nor conquer nations, and yet one has as great a work as Columbus or Alexander, to do.*

The "great work" of self-exploration called for increasing daring, and Lawrence thrilled to find himself equal to the task. The new path into the great impersonal sources from which all life and art sprang could only be staked out, he believed, by the joint effort of man and woman. But with the man leading, of course. We now begin to find less in Lawrence about the inspiring and sustaining powers of the female principle and more about the courage and vision of the male. Within that scope of vision, just now, Lawrence attempted to bring homosexuality. That this was a personal problem, a facet of *one's struggle inside oneself,* is plain enough, as stated previously, from the "prologue" to *Women in Love* written later on in England but not published with the novel. In Fiascherino Lawrence broached the question in a letter so relevant to the drift of his spirit that it will bear examining in detail.

Henry Savage, to whom the letter is addressed, had asked Lawrence about the work of Richard Middleton, a poet and friend of Savage's, dead by suicide two years before. Lawrence's answer runs as follows: *I think one has as it were to fuse ones physical and mental self right down, to produce good art. And there was some of him that wouldn't fuse — like some dross, that hindered him, that he couldn't*

ML, 264&267

ML, 269

ML, 270

ML, 241

ML, 270

ML, 251

grip and reduce with passion. And so again he hated himself. Perhaps if he could have found a woman to love, and who loved him, that would have done it. Lawrence then makes his own distinction between pure lyricism and what he terms *dramatic capabilities.* A pure lyricist, like Shelley, has no long-abiding passion, only intense moments. When these burn out he must die. Lawrence goes so far as to say that Shelley's drowning — not far from where he was writing — was no accident but the final seizure of the death-wish innate to the purely lyric poet. Middleton, on the other hand, showed signs of a talent more *enduring* and *dramatic,* but this talent *needed fertilising by some love* to which Middleton was never subjected and for want of which he killed himself. As to whom he should have sought, Lawrence amplifies his opinion to say that perhaps Middleton might have loved a man more than a woman. Then he pursues the matter in general: *I should like to know why nearly every man that approaches greatness tends to homosexuality, whether he admits it or not.* He touches immediately on the limits of homosexuality, which he feels is stymied for good at a sort of narcissism, and on the ultimate necessity of a male-female union as correlary to the greatest of human achievement: *I believe a man pro-* ML, *jects his own image on another man, like on a mirror. But from a* 251–252 *woman he wants himself re-born, re-constructed. So he can always get satisfaction from a man, but it is the hardest thing in life to get one's soul and body satisfied from a woman, so that one is free from oneself. And one is kept by all tradition and instinct from loving men, or a man — for it means just extinction of all the purposive influences.* The sole aim of the man who would attain and enjoy the greatest power in life must be *to find and to form the woman in whom one* ML, 252 *can be free.*

What Lawrence says about the artist and woman here repeats in essence the "foreword" to *Sons and Lovers,* but with far more emphasis on the initiative of the artist, the male, who must now paradoxically *form* the woman out of whom he is to be born: in short, he must take on a function of the Father. As for homosexuality in Lawrence's own inclinations, all this comes near to speaking for itself, and is put beyond question by the "prologue" to *Women in Love.* In this letter Lawrence patently saw himself as a parallel to Middleton, but as one of the victors and not one of the vanquished. His situation had been comparable to Middleton's in that before meeting Frieda he feared never to find the woman who could "fertilize" his "pure lyricism" and bring forth the *dramatic capabilities* leading to the *tragedy* of *Sons and Lovers.* Whether Lawrence was actively involved in a homosexual affair before or after the death of his mother, we do not know. But he was well aware that he might have taken that way in life and he

was sorely tempted by it. He now considers, looking back, that he is
out of danger. He is glad to have followed the *tradition and instinct*
that prevented his adopting the homosexual way of life, glad to have
come under the *purposive influences* Frieda offered. A resultant reborn
self had brought him not only to the magnificent triumph of *Sons and
Lovers,* but was in the process, at this moment, of bringing him to the
even more glorious conquest of *The Sisters.*

Naturally Lawrence's reading was always a significant factor in
his creative development, but of the certain periods when the effect
of books was especially telling, Fiascherino is one of the most outstanding. He saw no life, still, in what English and Irish writing had
to offer — always with the exception of Synge, whom he greatly
admired. Ernest Dowson, formerly a favorite, had proved a disappointment. So had James Stephens. Two English poets, Lascelles Aber-
crombie and W. W. Gibson, were among some people who dropped

ML, 252   in for a visit at Fiascherino. These might be *modern geniuses,* but they
would never face themselves as he was doing: such is the implication
of calling them *so tame, and so good, and so generous.* For the purposes of studying mankind, Italian peasants had more to offer. Lawrence and his guests attended a peasant wedding and after watching
one of the Italians get drunk, Lawrence could say, *Gibson wouldn't
interest me as much in twenty years, as Severino did that evening.*

One book from home did have a pronounced effect, Jane Harri-
ML, 234   son's *Ancient Art and Ritual.* And this is why: *It just fascinates me
to see art coming out of religious yearning — one's presentation of what
one wants to feel again, deeply.* Now the connection of this point with
his contemporary ideas of illuminating through art the divine ground
behind all movement is clear enough. But it seems to me significant
that a far more personal assocation between art and religion is implied
if we notice that in the same letter where he praises Jane Harrison's
thesis Lawrence makes his aforementioned claim for *Sons and Lovers:
One sheds one's sicknesses in books — repeats and presents again one's
emotions, to be master of them.* What is involved in both the repetition
of personal experience within a form and the re-awakening of old
religious sources is *presentation,* the bringing of the personal and the
universal together under the same endeavor.[6] But to work away from
limited personal therapy and into the regions of creation where the
spirits of time and place fuse with the artist's far-ranging self, we may
note what *presentation* meant to Lawrence when he wrote years later
about what he thought was the real subject of James Fenimore
SM, 100   Cooper's *The Prairie: The plot is nothing — a mere excuse for the
presentation. The presentation itself is marvellous, huge, vast, myth-*

ical, almost super-human in its import, like the story of the Sons of Anak.[5] All in all, Lawrence's great yen for books in Fiascherino may have been partly anticipation of the sort of journey into the distant and the ancient that American literature would later hold for him. At least he declared, *I love travels and rather raw philosophy and when* ML, 250
you can lend me books about Greek religions and rise of Greek Drama, or Egyptian influences — or things like that — I love them.

Unable to warm up, for the time being, to the literature of his own country, Lawrence found his thoughts best sharpened, at Fiascherino, by those of an Italian literary movement: Futurism. Although he thought their expression of it was made stupid by their childish worship of the machine and its age, the Futurists' disavowal of worn-out traditions was sound. Like himself they understood that *the old-fash-* ML, 281
ioned human element, the concentration of all artistic interest on the personal ego, was a dead letter. Study of the phenomena of the greater and inhuman will — that is, the *source, incorruptible and inexhaustible* ML, 241
— offered the only escape from the moribund present toward a resurgent future.

What is available in all this is sufficient to verify that the Fiascherino months were probably the greatest single period of growth in Lawrence's life, reaching a momentum that carried him through *The Rainbow* and *Women in Love.* What would tell us most on this score is all but lost: the *quite a thousand pages* of the successive onslaughts ML, 269
made on the novel then called *The Sisters.* The remaining fragment of an entirely scrapped section conveys little.[7] Lawrence accepted Edward Garnett's objections: *that the Templeman episode is wrong,* ML, 263
and that the character of Ella is incoherent, I agree. Ben Templeman, who appears at a distance in the fragment, was to be Ella's preparation for Birkin, whose declaration of love for Ella occupies most of the extant pages. For this love she is almost abjectly grateful: in contradistinction to the love scenes between Birkin and Ursula, Ella's later metamorphosis, in *Women in Love.* What this one clear point of the fragment really means is beyond the reach of any present evidence.

When Lawrence came at length to *preparing Twilight in Italy,* it ML, 364
is not surprising that he made no use of the Fiascherino experience, that he chose to end his first travel book with his arrival in Milan, just before going on to Fiascherino. These last prewar months in Italy were too near perfection, too near the idyllic living of the full flame, to carry any message of the disillusionment with Italy, the blight of mechanization and the decadence of the life of flesh and blood whose twilight Lawrence saw creeping over Italy when he looked back on it from England in the early years of the war. The war was the great

cleavage in his life, all the more so in striking just after the splendor of Fiascherino and preventing his return to that perfect spot for a magnificent continuation in the making of his own soul. But such spots as Fiascherino remained with him as being conducive to the resurrection. Far on in the future the Christ of *The Escaped Cock* walked the shores of just such a cove as that of Fiascherino and there won his resuscitation to physical life with the priestess of Isis, in a little temple set among the pines and the olives above the rocks and the swirling sea.

NOTES

[1] Violet Hunt (1866–1942) was the daughter of Alfred William Hunt, a Pre-Raphaelite painter. As a reader for *The English Review* she was in part responsible for Lawrence's first publication. For a number of years she and Ford Madox Ford, editor of the *Review* for a time, lived as man and wife. She was the author of a number of novels. *See* CB, vol. 1, 126–129. Grace Little Rhys wrote several books, the majority of them for children. She was the wife of Ernest Rhys, one of the founders of the Rhymer's Club. The Rhyses were members of the circle connected with *The English Review* in its early days. *See* CB, vol. 1, 129–132.

[2] Lawrence may have hit on the idea for this novel – or another *of the common people* entailing fictionalization of his father — as early as August 1912, a month before he began the final reshaping of *Sons and Lovers.* But any likelihood that the August reference is to the Burns work turns slim when the surviving mention in correspondence of a next novel after *Sons and Lovers* is studied in detail. For a clear arrangement of the evidence *see* SR, 30–37.

[3] "The Marble and the Statue," *Imagined Worlds: Essays on English Novels and Novelists,* edited by Maynard Mack and Ian Gregor (London, 1968), pp. 371–418.

[4] This and another fragment are at the Humanities Research Center, University of Texas at Austin. *See* "A Checklist of the Manuscripts of D. H. Lawrence," in SR, item #E441. The present quotations are from pages 291 and 293, respectively, of the first fragment.

[5] The descendants of Anak, the Anakim, were a semi-legendary people of great stature occupying parts of the Holy Land when the Israelites arrived. They struck fear in the hearts of Moses' spies, who felt *no bigger than grasshoppers* in their presence: Numbers 13:32–33.

[6] Lawrence in fact adopts the term *presentation* from Jane Harrison, who applies it to the *periodicity* of ritual. The source of ritual, for her, is *a desire of which the active satisfaction is blocked, and which runs over into a "presentation," Ancient Art and Ritual* (Oxford, 1913), p. 53.

[7] This is the second of the fragments mentioned in note 4, above.

5

The Island Shall Be England

When Lawrence and Frieda came back to England in the summer of 1914, they did not intend to stay long. Frieda now had her divorce, so they could make their liaison official by marriage: they did so, in July. They meant to visit here and there, maybe go to Ireland in August, where Lawrence planned to follow the suggestion of an editor and *write a little book on Hardy's people.* With all affairs personal and literary wound up by mid-October, they could return for the winter to the *beloved, beautiful little cottage* in Fiascherino.

ML, 287

ML, 267

As Lawrence knew before reaching home, his reputation was growing by leaps and bounds, to a great degree because the appearance of *Sons and Lovers* coincided with the spread of Freudian theory in England. Asked now for the first time to state his message, he put it in terms of a journey: *One must learn to love, and go through a good deal of suffering to get to it, like any knight of the grail, and the journey is always **towards** the other soul . . . . Your most vital necessity in this life is that you shall love your wife completely and implicitly and in entire nakedness of body and spirit.* This is the sort of quest into psychic regions his travels with Frieda had been so far, the rough going notwithstanding. Excellent work had come of it, for which the public as well as private rewards would rapidly accrue, not only in *Sons and Lovers* but in the short-story volume *The Prussian Officer,* whose fusion of form and content owed much to the confidence established at Fiascherino.[1]

ML, 285

But Fiascherino vanished like the dream it was. For in August came the Great War and untold complications to all journeys, some brought on by the conflict but many by changes in Lawrence himself and in his union with Frieda. Together these amounted to a partial

[91]

defeat of his great schemes, a setback well summed up under a geographical image: the condemned land of England was now doubly so, with the onus of the war added to a personal fate that refused after all to be sloughed off as readily as the Italian interlude had promised. For a variety of reasons Lawrence could not escape from England, either in spirit or in actuality, for the duration of the war. In these years he went through crisis after crisis: financial difficulties; illness brought on by the English climate; increased emotional strife; a deep concern over conflicts in the national consciousness that seemed to call for decisive action on his part; neglect and outright persecution by his own country, which had seemed on the verge of declaring him one of its greatest lights.

Each of these inflicted its own form of punishment. Simply to find money to live on, Lawrence must either return to Italy, where he could count on his writing to bring in the few pounds for necessities, or else risk being sucked back into the system he had fought to escape. As for his art, the new novel in which he had placed such hopes — that portion of *The Sisters* which evolved into *The Rainbow* — was sentenced to public burning as immoral shortly after its appearance in 1915: so that a fear of possible consequences made the big publishers shy away from his fiction. Also, soon after his marriage, which was supposed to settle so many problems, Lawrence was forced to recognize that he could never have the kind of harmonious union with Frieda that he had so much counted on. Yet the conviction that he could not live without it never lessened. He came also to a new realization on the perils of homosexual tendencies and expended great psychic and artistic energy to get beyond these. He put himself through the most harrowing processes of thought to visualize a physical but nonsexual intimacy between men, a blood-brotherhood. As to public affairs, in common with most English intellectuals he felt that civilization itself was threatened by the war, and that a concerted effort was essential to save the world from power wielded by the wrong people: from militarism and political blundering and economic greed. Lawrence's part in any of this was naturally rendered difficult by Frieda's German background and her divided loyalties. But most trying of all to Lawrence's new sense of community responsibility was that he must make a radical shift of direction to be effective. While out of England he had made great strides toward widening the horizons of being for himself and his fellow-countrymen. He had been just on the threshold of revealing as he felt no one ever had revealed the metaphysical sources of character. But the conquest of these realms truly did involve an expedition, geographical as well as metaphysical. It could not be effected in England. Yet in the face of all these unforeseen upheavals in English society, if he was to remain a pioneer in the diagnosis and cure of social and psychological ills, he must now find some way of driving home his message besides detaching himself from the national life and viewing it from overseas. He must participate in social and political action directed to the immediate transformation of England.

This was sometimes his outlook, but then he would go through violent and often rapidly alternating reactions. Even his detestation of the war was not constant: he sometimes thought it good for shaking Europe out of its complacency. And off and on, almost from the start of the war, he could still conceive of no way to save England except by leaving it, gathering the finest principles and people of the old land and heading for a place undreamed of before the war: Rananim, a colony in some remote region where the worthy few, like an apocalyptic saving remnant, could guard the best impulses of civilization through the coming debacle. Or, again, he took the view that only by cultivation of an isolate selfhood, turning his back on England as far as he could without setting out from its shores, could he save himself from mob contamination. This was tantamount to making his own little foreign land in England, and he went so far as to attempt it in Cornwall, nearly at Land's End. As conditions grew worse and worse in Europe, he turned to visionary escape, which now and again led to outright apocalyptic expectations, but which came to its most significant fruition in the American literature essays. Besides being penetrating and influential literary criticism, these essays are a remarkable fantasy of rebirth in a never-never land.[2]

All these agonies of the war years kept Lawrence in an almost continual state of shock, in which he sensed *the amazing, vivid, visionary beauty of everything, heightened by the immense pain everywhere.* ML, 310 His mystique of time and place underwent crucial changes never afterwards to be eradicated.

The return to England was instrumental in the delay of an essay on the Italian Futurists that Lawrence had meant to write for the purpose of orientation in shaping his theories on the impersonal, instinctive being of man. Once at home he took a different route to the same end through an English author: Thomas Hardy, one of the few contemporaries with whom he admitted kinship. If he undertook to write on Hardy at the request of an editor, this certainly coincided to perfection with a predisposition of his own. The Hardy-like opening of the Burns novel he had put aside suggests as much. What was to take shape in *The Rainbow* was the outgrowth of the thought begun in the *Son and Lovers* "foreword" and the letter discussing the Futurists, and then solidified in the Hardy piece. Lawrence therefore utilized Hardy just as he would have the Futurists: as a point of departure into dominions of

ML, 290   his own choosing. He had hardly set out on the book when he said, *It will be about anything but Thomas Hardy, I am afraid — queer stuff —*
ML, 298   *but not bad.* And not long afterwards it had *turned out as a sort of Story of My Heart, or a* **Confessio Fidei.** The association with Richard Jefferies' autobiography, which Lawrence saw as a painful but salutary exercise in self-revelation, shows how confessional he meant this piece of writing to be. Moreover, if we take into account the symbology of this essay expanded and contracted over the coming months and years, we cannot avoid concluding with Lawrence that "Study of Thomas Hardy" is a misnomer, and thus the oft-repeated critical assertion that it is an analysis of Hardy left unfinished is inaccurate. Lawrence's own title for the essay was *Le Gai Savaire.*[3] What Lawrence sought, using Hardy now and then as a touchstone, was a broad set of symbological concepts to serve as a metaphysic for his fiction. From now on he reworked the material time after time, never really giving it the final stamp. First publication became the "Crown" essays of 1915. Many other renditions follow: the lost *At The Gates* and *Goats and Compasses,* the "Reality of Peace" essays, climaxing for the wartime period in the above-mentioned American literature essays. The process then advances into the two books of psychology and through all the later network of writing to the final book of Lawrence's life, *Apocalypse.* This vast endeavor was a response, then, to a constant need: to fix in momentary form the endless unrolling of symbological thought. It is to Lawrence's metaphysic what the rewriting instead of revision is to
ML, 334   his fiction: even an "unfinished" work proceeds toward *a definite organic form,* and to go back and change it would be like cutting off a limb to alter the maturing process of a living thing.

    Le Gai Savaire was a call for mankind to take the road Lawrence had taken. Life must cease to be a getting of goods and a building up of safeguards for the individual gloating over his property. This growth
PH, 398   of a basic need into a vice had *brought to pass the whole frantic turmoil of modern industry,* and out of that the war. Life must exert the
PH, 408   *courage to let go the securities and to be —* which is just what Lawrence had discovered in Italy — to *risk* [oneself] *in a forward venture*
PH, 403   *of life,* for *the final aim of every living thing, creature, or being* must be *the full achievement of itself* in a journey into the unknown. Hardy's characters, according to Lawrence, typify but a part of this lesson.
PH, 410   None of them *care very much for money, or immediate self-preservation, and all of them are struggling hard to come into being,* but their
PH, 411   *tragedy* is that while they escape from security *to live outside in the precarious open,* they perish for want of the power to make *the wilderness* their own. Theirs is the *tragedy* of even the best among modern men, which is now defined at some length according to what Lawrence
PH, 420   terms the two moralities. First comes the lesser, *the established sys-*

tem of human government and morality, the creed of formal behavior. Then comes the greater, *the vast, unexplored morality of life itself,*   PH, 419 *what we call the immorality of nature.* It *surrounds us in its eternal incomprehensibility, and in its midst goes on the little human morality play, with its queer frame of morality and its mechanized movement.* In the end, the *real tragedy,* for Hardy's characters and for the over-   PH, 420 whelming majority of mankind, *is that they are unfaithful to the greater unwritten morality,* subjected in fear of convention to the more limited morality.

The truest insight of this comes to Hardy, Lawrence argues, in his molding of place: *The real sense of tragedy is got from the setting. . . .*   PH, 415 *It is Egdon Heath. . . . It is the primitive, primal earth, where the instinctive life heaves up. There, in the deep, rude stirring of the instincts, there was the reality that worked the tragedy.* All of Hardy's people are born *out of the body of this crude earth,* and all prove false to their origin: a Hardy character divorces his purpose in life *from the passionate purpose that issued him out of the earth into being.*

In this whole judgmental exercise Lawrence implies that where Hardy failed he will succeed. Hardy could put his characters in touch with the daimon of the English landscape but could not bring them to assimilate this energy: that is, bring them through from conventional into integral behavior. Plainly this is what Lawrence set out to do in *The Rainbow,* in a manner close to that initiated in the Burns fragment.

Le Gai Savaire was written out of a certain trust that the advice therein would be heeded and would lead to the betterment of England: if not in bringing about a quick end to the war, at least in building up a new and happy island afterwards. Lawrence still had hopes that England could be revived to human greatness through some means short of apocalyptic cataclysm. These hopes, born of necessity when Lawrence had to give up pleading with his compatriots from a foreign residence, were to fade in the course of the war. But they never quite vanished, even to the days of his last visit to England in 1926 and the fiction which grew out of that. What also remains constant from its first firm statement in the Hardy essay is the sense of the English earth as betrayed by those born out of it. All that Lawrence attributes to Hardy's grasp of *the greater unwritten morality of nature* and the tragic denial of human purpose conveyed by Egdon Heath can be said also of Lawrence's fictional vision, from *The Rainbow* through the last version of *Lady Chatterley's Lover.* Wragby Wood is in this sense a successor to Egdon Heath.

This perspective of Lawrence's native land arose by absence and return. The native land as one pole of experience was set in discoveries made abroad from *Son and Lovers* through the Hardy essay. As for reachievement of full accord with the English earth, which must consist largely in a reversal of the voracious industrial revolution, the first grand effort in that direction was to be *The Rainbow*.

Another of Lawrence's designs in *Le Gai Savaire* was the most inclusive elaboration yet of the cosmic interdependence of male and female as the ultimate source of all creativity. We recall that as far as the *Sons and Lovers* "foreword" went, the male who utters the word owes entirely to the female his access to the Father. *Le Gai Savaire* still equates the power to create with rebirth and sets up the mother-wife conjunction as a paramount need of the male. Man is born once of his parents — we may catch an echo now of Lawrence's declaration **PH, 433**   to Louie Burrows — but as Jesus said to Nicodemus, *"Ye must be born again."* The masculine soul has to be fertilized by the woman as lover between the ages of twenty and thirty, so that as men we may *be brought forth to ourselves, distinct.*

If the concept appears so far to have advanced little between versions of the symbology, the metaphors tell another story. Lawrence now adopts a more dynamic language of exploration in positing the centrality of the female. The mother-mate as hive to whom the foraging son brings home his accomplishments is superseded, for one thing, by the feminine principle as axle to the revolving onward and outward of the male principle as wheel. Even more significant are the figures of speech phrasing creativity as a venture to the periphery with little stress **PH,**   on the return as re-enclosure: *For a man who dares to look upon, and* **491–492**   *to venture within the unknown of the female, losing himself, like a man who gives himself to the sea, or a man who enters a primeval, virgin forest, feels, when he returns, the utmost gladness of singing.* He returns *rich with addition to his soul,* laden with *the inexhaustible riches lain under unknown skies over unknown seas.* This venture is like *landing on the shore of the undiscovered half of the world, where the wealth of the female lies before us.*

While *Le Gai Savaire* turned out to be the high point of Lawrence's exultation over what his marriage would do for him, such expressions already undermine the overt assurance. The male as adventurer sailing for new continents was already outreaching the bee magnetized by the hive. He would have to write his symbology over again, even though the manuscript was now of book length.

But a concerted effort at this would have to wait, for by this time Lawrence was well into *The Sisters* once more. Disagreements with Edward Garnett over the novel's method had eventuated in a change to another publisher, whose request for revisions ended in a recasting more extensive than any to date. Lawrence put off the task until late November, but when he began he forged ahead rapidly, trusting that when he delivered the manuscript the remainder of the substantial advance would take him and Frieda to Italy. Occupying a cottage in Buckinghamshire was a poor make-out after Fiascherino.

He soon gave his novel another name, *The Rainbow,* from an earlier suggestion by Frieda, and early in January, seeing that he had two separate though intertwined stories on his hands, he broke the work into two volumes. A bit later he decided to give up the house in Bucks, a depressing place, and move to a cottage the Meynell family had offered on their estate in Sussex. Once there, but due more to the England he was creating in *The Rainbow* than to the changed place, Lawrence declared that he had been dead since *the spear* of the war   ML, 309 was thrust *through the side of all sorrows and hopes,* and that only now was he rising from the tomb. Or again: *I was seedy in Bucks, and*   HL, 219 *so black in spirit. I can even hope beyond the War now.* When he was still not in a mood there to launch into *The Rainbow,* he took a significant action in growing a beard, again because he was *seedy,* and   ML, 293 because he craved something *warm and complete* to cover his *nakedness.* But surely the beard was as much an attack as a retreat, for his beard from now on was to Lawrence the grand assertion of male dauntlessness. And perhaps all of this was a way of saying that the symbology had failed but the contemplated emergence of *The Rainbow* out of the welter of manuscript pages was reawakening hopes of a new life. Although *Le Gai Savaire* was positive in tenor, no matter how low in spirits Lawrence may have been in Bucks, it had not pounded out for him an identity for the next phase after the incomplete and now outmoded victory of *Sons and Lovers.*

One further point before passing on to *The Rainbow.* In his attention to fashioning a symbology to complement his fiction, Lawrence often reflected on the lack of such coordination in other authors. What he says of Hardy in *Le Gai Savaire* prefigures his whole theory on the rift between moral and passional intention in early American authors: *His sensuous understanding . . . apart from his metaphysic is very great*   PH, 480 *and deep. . . . Putting aside his metaphysic, which must always obtrude when he thinks of people, and turning to the earth, to landscape, then he is true to himself.* The vital reversion of *The Rainbow* to the English landscape was by no means a turning away from the people but on the contrary a turning toward their primal bond with the earth. Still the distinctions pursued in his analysis of Hardy's novels cleared the way for setting forth — to repeat — on what Lawrence believed Hardy had failed to do: to reunite spirit of place in England with the spirit of the race, to construct a cycle of landscape change from a near Eden of the past to a projected Eden of the future.

To appreciate *The Rainbow* as the shaping of a new land at home in lieu of an exotic land from which the author was cut off by the war, we had best examine the novel along with the contemplation of action that engrossed Lawrence while he was writing it. His prophetic convictions are contained in a three-fold pronouncement made when he was momentarily engaged in all three efforts: *I write my novels, & I write my book of philosophy, & I must also see the social revolution set going.* In the same letter he sets forth the partial and deathward nature of *lyrical* experience as opposed to the life-giving force of *collective experience.* He drew a comparable distinction at Fiascherino in 1913, when the greater talent beyond the *lyric* was the *dramatic.* But the basis is the same, the "impersonal" or "instinctive" being, with the national now more emphasized than the universal. In the self, he declares, lies the whole *living organic English nation. It is not politics — it is religion.* One *must give expression to the great collective experience, not to the individual,* and thus instigate the revolution. However, *it is not a political revolution I want, but a shifting of the racial system of values from the old morality & personal salvation through a Mediator to the larger morality and salvation through the knowledge that ones neighbor is oneself:* which is of course the lesser-greater morality issue of *Le Gai Savaire* translated into social terms.

DR, vol. 6, 7

DR, vol. 6, 5
ML, 251

DR, vol. 6, 4
DR, vol. 6, 4 & 5

This letter of February 1915 came at the height of recasting *The Rainbow* and just after Lawrence's plans for social action had taken a sharp turn at the urging of Bertrand Russell and Lady Ottoline Morrell. Almost since the war began Lawrence had spoken off and on of leading a group to an island to set up an ideal community. But as he had not yet given up on England, his two recent associates gave a boost to his wavering hopes and so contributed to the formation of *The Rainbow.* Lady Ottoline was bringing Lord Russell down to Greatham, Lawrence announced, when they would try to come to grips with some of the complications of his island dream: *But they say, the island shall be England, that we shall start our new community in the midst of this old one, as a seed falls among the roots of the parent. Only wait, and we will remove mountains and set them in the midst of the sea.* He had more reason than ever now to think that *The Rainbow,* with its promise of great things, was the only title for his novel.

ML, 314

The novel looked back from this imminent change of ages to the Eden of England's green and pleasant land before the Industrial Revolution. It was a journey in time combining escape to an ideal past with the expectation of national rebirth. The narrative opens around the turn of the nineteenth century with the rich cadences of rural English life among the Brangwen family of Marsh Farm. They live suspended in the blood-being springing up between heaven and earth, with an additional equilibrium to complete the fullness of life: a notion of the beyond to temper their immersion in the surging natural life. The men and the women hold to this balance in different forms. For the men,

who are more nearly content in the *drowse of blood-intimacy* with RA, 2
the land, the barest form of geographical contrast suffices: *Whenever* RA, 1
one of the Brangwens in the fields lifted his head from his work, he
saw the church-tower at Ilkeston in the empty sky. So that as he turned
again to the horizontal land, he was aware of something standing above
him and beyond him in the distance. But he has no vertical aspirations.
The women, on the other hand, are drawn not merely by the seen but
by the spoken world beyond, and by its verticality. They perceive there
a certain superiority to their own life, and they covet it for their children. The vicar, the curate, the squire and his lady belong to that
finer, more vivid circle of life, not so much by virtue of money or birth, RA, 4
but by virtue of knowledge, which the Brangwen women take to be
merely a question of education.

Yet while the Brangwen women envy the upper classes and dream
of circumstances to promote their children to that level, they have a
present reward of which they are scarcely conscious: a vicarious gratification of outward-reaching instincts to relieve their involvement with
farm life. The "heroic" life of the upper classes comforts them in their
own commonness and sets the whole distant world flowing into everyday proximity. In Mrs. Hardy of the manor house *the Brangwen wife* RA, 5–6
of the Marsh aspired beyond herself, towards the further life of the
finer woman, towards the extended being she revealed, as a traveller
in his self-contained manner reveals far-off countries present in him-
self. . . . So long as the wonder of the beyond was before them, [the
Brangwen women] *could get along, whatever their lot. And Mrs.*
Hardy, and the vicar, and Lord William, these moved in the wonder of
the beyond.

Then a canal slashes this little world in two. Then the railway
arrives, and the mines with their colliers multiply. So that when a
Brangwen eyes the distance now he is more likely to see a spinning
headstock than a still church tower. The trains that announce the far-
off coming near give a certain pleasure but they also arouse fear and
foreboding. As the old world slips away, what brings the distance
into proximity is mechanical.

The great question of *The Rainbow* is how to realize the passionate
potential of life in the self through mating with the other while the
world deteriorates from rural to industrial. This marriage is a unifica-
tion of the near and the far that grows progressively more difficult with
the advancing decay of the technological world, a struggle portrayed
by three generations of lovers. Tom Brangwen, of the first generation,
cannot have even in his time the old harmony of remoteness and closeness that his ancestors enjoyed. Strongly attached to Marsh Farm, yet
he is restless to visit foreign parts. Luckily he meets in the widow of

a Polish exile a woman who can restore, as Frieda did at first to
RA, 27   Lawrence, his flawed sense of well-being: *She was strange, from far off,
yet so intimate. She was from far away, a presence, so close to his soul.
Adjusting his existence to these opposites in the woman he loves and
RA, 43   marries constitutes the great adventure for Tom Brangwen: *Such a
wonderful remoteness there was about her, and then something in
touch with him, that made his heart knock in his chest.*

But her foreignness is not always just magnetic. It repels too, as
when she talks at length about her aristocratic childhood in Poland
RA, 57   and he feels in her *a curious superiority.* He may then grow resentful
and hostile, but still she is such an exotic wonder that he cannot help
being fascinated, even as he draws back. Through this strange and
marvellous woman from above and beyond him Tom Brangwen
obtains at length a restorative vision from the near at hand to the
remote in time and space. When she is in labor with their first child,
RA, 76   he comes to know *a great, scalding peace* which can of itself pass *off
into the infinite.* He testifies to the revelation by a simple action: *He
went downstairs, and to the door, outside, lifted his face to the rain,
and felt the darkness striking unseen and steadily upon him.*

*The swift, unseen threshing of the night upon him silenced him
and he was overcome. He turned away indoors, humbly. There was
the infinite world, eternal, unchanging, as well as the world of life.*

If we turn to the experience of Lydia Lensky, the woman of this
couple, we meet with another of the forms by which Lawrence so often
represented mediation between far and near: a sequence of death and
resurrection, this time in a total projection of self upon landscape.
Interestingly enough, this crisis of Lydia's in the second chapter of
The Rainbow is closely analogous to one Lawrence underwent while
reforging his novel. A comparison between a passage from the novel
and one from a letter will show the extent of the transformation of
experience into fiction: Lawrence as the returned native striving to
get in touch with the English spirit of place as never before, through
a woman to whom England is an alien land. She has just arrived in
Yorkshire. For Lawrence it was his first week in Sussex. The woman
seeks resurrection after the death of her husband. Lawrence was just
stepping from the tomb to which the war had consigned him. The
wording of the two experiences is often similar. The letter reads,
ML, 310   *And I saw the sea lifted up and shining like a blade with the sun on it;*
RA, 47   the novel reads, *very strange was the constant glitter of the sea
unsheathed in heaven.*

A crucial juncture in the lives of many of the characters may find
them in an England reshaped as mythic landscape. In each of the
three marital histories such visions find a form appropriate to the

character. The second marriage, between Anna, daughter of Lydia by her first husband, and Will Brangwen, her cousin by marriage, never attains the equilibrium that exists between Tom and Lydia. Will, though endowed with artistic talent and the desire to unfold to a greater existence, is all too ready to make do with conventional religious symbolism and too much inclined to dependence on his wife. He suffers from the limitations of the *lyrical* artist, powerless in the long run to throw himself into the *collective* matrix of the universal consciousness. Principally, he cannot fashion the woman he needs for the great voyage into the unknown. In admission of this failure he RA, 171 finally burns a carving of Eve that he had struggled with for a long time. In the absence of male initiative in Will, Anna takes over the dominant role, while Will sinks more and more to a secondary position.

Near the culmination of Anna's victory the roles of husband and wife are skilfully envisaged through mythical landscape blended with an intricate pattern of association demonstrating well what Lawrence meant by getting behind personal to cosmic consciousness. At this point Will knows that Anna has won, but he seeks to conceal her victory by classing it as his own, by a vision of time and place which is obscurely self-defeating. He sees his wife and himself alone on a wilderness island, which is clearly England, from which the ugly and awful works of man have vanished. He feels a *new, strange certainty* RA, 190 *in his soul,* imagining how he would provide for her in the wilderness. The confidence of this fantasy bears him to further illusion, to an immortality attending his daily life: *It was as if now he existed in Eternity, let Time be what it might.* All of this seems potent enough till we discover, as Will never consciously does, that his vision is dogged underneath by a *vague, haunting uncertainty*: because he cannot leave RA, 191 off being *unsure* of his wife, which signifies that his need for her is clinging and immature, precluding a marital reliance that would ultimately leave him responsible to himself.

Anna's climaxing view of the world is likewise determined by the mythic faculty. Like the Brangwen women of old, she lives in two worlds at once, but her imaginary topography differs greatly. Vicarious experience for her is in the myth of Moses rather than in identification with the landed gentry and the clergy. In one way her stand is an expansion of being that compensates amply for the loss of the stable world of former days: *Here she was, safe and still in Cossethay. But* RA, *she felt as if she were not in Cossethay at all. She was straining her* 192–193 *eyes to something beyond. And from her Pisgah mount, which she had attained, what could she see? A faint, gleaming horizon, a long way off, and a rainbow like an archway. . . . There was something beyond her. But why must she start on the journey? She stood so safely on*

*the Pisgah mountain. . . . Dawn and sunset were the feet of the rainbow
that spanned the day, and she saw the hope, the promise. Why should
she travel any further? . . . Sun and moon travelled on, and left her,
passed her by, a rich woman enjoying her riches. She should go also.
But she could not go, when they called, because she must stay at home
now. With satisfaction she relinquished the adventure to the unknown.*

Of the many symbolic aspects the rainbow assumes in the novel,
one of the most arresting is its dual nature of far and near: a protective
arch but conversely a beckoning curve into greater glory. The symbol
can be temporal or geographical, and may inhibit or liberate, or both,
depending on context and outlook. During her childhood Anna played
beneath an arch in the heavens anchored in the pillars of her parents'
love, a rainbow figure for the near-perfect curve of her existence. In
the passage quoted above, this perfection may appear simply to have
matured. But if we compare Anna with her daughter Ursula we
discover another potentiality measured against time and place. To
an extent unheard-of since the condition of the early Brangwen men,
Anna has lapsed into the rhythm of the flesh. But in her it has become
slothful, at least beside the striving of Ursula against the bounds of
existence. Anna is too ready to substitute contemplation of the Promised Land for possession of it, and thus like Moses will never enter it.

Ursula's distaste for her mother's total immersion in breeding
only increases as the girl grows up — nine pregnancies through the
years — until the *herded domesticity* drives Ursula to strenuous efforts
of escape. In one respect at least this judgment is inherent to the
whole thematic structure of the novel: a drift into utter physicality is
as stultifying as the opposite drift into utter mentality. The fulfillment
of Ursula's *strange, passionate knowledge of religion and living* lies
somewhere between the extremes. The first opportunity to break the
subjugation of home presents itself in a prospective lover. But she
rejects him out of a growing conviction that her destiny is to be a
sojourner, a destiny demanding movement through time and space
unconfined by the cyclical gratification of sensual desires that controls
her mother. This suitor could only lead her along her mother's
pathway. He becomes an object lesson: *All her life, at intervals, she
returned to the thought of him and of that which he offered. But she
was a traveller, she was a traveller on the face of the earth, and he
was an isolated creature living in the fulfilment of his own senses.*

As Ursula struggles toward maturity, she emerges as the finer
spirit of mankind entrapped by the modern world. She toils through
a period of school-teaching, discovering along the way that she has
joined an *evil system where she must brutalise herself to live.* It is
a *dry, tyrannical man-world* of patriarchal *enclosedness* typified by her
first suitor as well as her working environment. With this system she

RA, 92

RA, 353

RA, 406

RA, 417

RA, 405

RA,
410&412

must relinquish all connection if she is to grow. The social theme of the novel is by now fully expanded: a progressive shrinking of circles of existence and the possible circumscribing of new ones through other rainbows. We note that a woman is the principal rebel here, against male-imposed restrictions, and is the one most capable of new vistas. Lawrence's faith in what woman could do by "fertilizing" the male imagination may have been on the wane by this time, still *The Rainbow* is a forceful statement of her independent abilities in which we are reminded again of Lawrence's pre-war promise to do his *work for women, better than the Suffrage,* to portray *woman becoming individual, self-responsible, taking her own initiative.* ML, 171&273

But if this seems to refute the necessity for male leadership, we have only to notice that Ursula's present initiative stops short at last because no male in her world has the greatness to take her life and destiny in hand. She must be satisfied with a vision of the future only. The appearance of the right male scheduled for the original *Sisters* was now to be delayed for a sequel to *The Rainbow.*

Ursula's crowning experience here is the love affair with Anton Skrebensky, with whom marriage is unthinkable because he also is cut to the measure of the patriarchal social system. In the acute stages of their involvement she all but consumes him in the throes of her desire to smash old forms of awareness, to slough off the traditional identity of the human being, who is in truth a *primeval darkness falsi-* RA, 448 *fied to a social mechanism.*

In this fashion, from a first to a third generation, the adventure of consciousness in marriage seen as a quest for the opposite shore of another's being comes finally to the brink of an unbridgeable chasm between pioneering woman and mass male. This crisis of being plunges Ursula into sickness near death, with a climax in the realization of pregnancy and a subsequent miscarriage. In this fearful episode she crosses into a mythical domain where the deepest instinctive being erupts as a herd of horses: those creatures that Lawrence saw as roaming *the dark underworld meadows of the soul.* AP, 61

First Ursula leaves a house in detestation of enveloping walls. She goes to a wood, among trees that fill her with awe as they come alive like ancient warriors ranked around and shaken by the wind. Without sensing what she is about she draws on legend far back in the Anglo-Saxon past, reliving a moment from Bede's story of how her pagan ancestors greeted Christianity, a creed which at that time opened a new realm of being to the pilgrim through time and distance: *She felt* RA, 486 *like a bird that has flown in through the window of a hall where vast warriors sit at the board. Between their grave, booming ranks she was hastening, assuming she was unnoticed, till she emerged, with beating heart, through the far window and out into the open, upon the vivid green, marshy meadow.* But Lawrence has departed from Bede in one respect, imposing upon this symbolic flight a new purpose. Bede's sparrow winging from the darkness outside one wall to that beyond the next is lost and bewildered in either darkness. The only true moment of well-being is presence in the lighted room itself. But Ursula's fleeing soul has renounced walls, so that the openness and greenness of the meadow beyond give promise of restored health by atonement with the natural world the soul travels through.

Soon the herd of horses appears out of the rain, and Ursula must get around them to continue her way. Her attempts at circumvention become hallucinatory: maddening and helpless like actions in a nightmare. She manages to escape in the end by climbing an old oak tree and falling in a heap across a hedge, barely ahead of the turmoil of horses with their crushing hooves. The trees at the start were living, mysterious columns beckoning onward. Their function is now concentrated in a single tree.

But the psychological potencies unleashed in the horses continue to harrow Ursula through two delirious weeks of illness, while her being struggles free of Skrebensky and his aborted child. If we call to mind that according to Lawrence the deepest of psychological forces cannot really lead the individual astray, then the essence of the scene comes clear. Ursula had decided before setting out on the walk to the wood to submit to the falsity of marriage and Army life in India with Skrebensky, largely because of the child. She had written saying she would come out to him at once: not knowing he had already married another woman. This submission would have meant surrender of the quest for greater being that had motivated her all along. But her subliminal being would not let her go back on herself, would see her destroyed rather than sacrificed. In bringing on the miscarriage and purging her of a debased purpose, the horses serve a profound creative function.

With all this behind her, Ursula can approach a true new birth:

RA, 493 *When she looked ahead, into the undiscovered land before her, what was there she could recognise but a fresh glow of light and inscrutable trees going up from the earth like smoke. It was the unknown, the unexplored, the undiscovered upon whose shore she had landed, alone, after crossing the void, the darkness which washed the New World and the Old.* She has covered the worst of her pilgrim's passage, through the hinterlands incarnate in creatures and in nature. She has not yet recovered Eden. She cannot recover it alone. It is not for her to create Adam, as she tried to her sorrow to create Skrebensky. The true man will *come from the Infinite,* created by God, and she will have only to hail him.

But Lawrence must be more explicit about the land they will possess: the England to come. Over the ugliness and deathliness of the coal-mining world around her Ursula sees superimposed a vision of a rainbow, by which she knows that on this island will come to pass *the creation of the living God*. We almost expect such phrases as "Lo! RA, 494 a new heaven and a new earth" or "When this mortal shall have put on immortality" — as though the author may have gone too far. As an equal and opposite reaction to her recent ordeal, Ursula's transcendent confidence may be credible enough, but Lawrence's eager acceptance of his character's mood as a resolution to the story is too sudden and insistent to be wholly convincing. This development in Ursula carries with it too many vestiges of convalescent delirium.

But while this ending may have its flaws, it catches perfectly Lawrence's ephemeral faith in the individual Englishman and in the nation as a whole. The island of the reborn will not be some far Rananim but England itself, on which Lawrence nevertheless brings to bear his revitalizing experience with time and distance. As a high point in the testament of search the ending of *The Rainbow* makes a superb impression. Its merit stems in part from the apocalyptic pattern followed by the novel as a whole: a pattern that has long ruled the imagination of western man, particularly the puritan imagination.

On completion of *The Rainbow* early in 1915, Lawrence was prepared to set in motion his crusade for national renewal, with which he was active into the summer and fall. Most of his effort he divided between planning action with collaborators — like a series of lectures in cooperation with Bertrand Russell — and the rewriting and further rewriting of his symbology. Through the tangle of many drafts destroyed, the important outlines are still traceable. In the early stages Lawrence held to a faith in the goodness of man and his eventual malleability according to innate virtues. He also kept fairly close to monotheism as a metaphysical base. But his growing disillusion with the course of national and international events, and his reading of early Greek philosophers, brought changes of mind. At one new beginning of the symbology in April he swore, *I will not tell them, the* ML, 331 *people, this time that they are angels in disguise. Curse them, I will tell them they are dogs and swine, bloodsuckers*. The *great and happy* ML, 328 *revolution* was all of a sudden far off. By July another self-assignment to recast brought this remark: *These early Greeks have clarified my* ML, 352 *soul. I must drop all about God*.

Then the lecture plans with Russell ended in violent quarrels. For one thing Lawrence wanted an aristocracy and Russell a democracy. Lawrence still clung to the remains of his belief, though doubts eroded it by the day, that some *spirit of unanimity in truth* could prevail *among* ML, 362 *mankind,* and that this instinct must be reached as the source of action. Russell expected to remake the world by systematic and logical reform. It was the gap between the mystical and the practical idealist, and the current of feeling in each man was so strong that complete rupture was inevitable. This break with Russell contributed much to Lawrence's eventual disgusted withdrawal from any campaign to reform his country.

Only one attempt did he make to deliver his symbology as a public manifesto. With John Middleton Murry, an ever-pliable follower, he undertook to publish a little periodical, *The Signature,* which lasted for three issues. By this time, the fall of 1915, the Lawrences had left Sussex and rented a place in Hampstead. The reformers issued their periodical from London, and Lawrence's contribution consisted of his symbological essays in the form to which he had brought them by the last quarter of 1915. Only half of these "Crown" essays were published in *The Signature,* but the rest are preserved with few changes in a volume from after the war, *Reflections on the Death of a Porcupine.* These essays, although they are far from transmitting the optimism of *The Rainbow*'s ending, still belong with the writings that hold out a hope of reviving the dormant spirit of good in England.

The "Crown" essays are thick-sown with travel imagery reflecting Lawrence's search to blend his two present streams of feeling: the disposition to run away and the disposition to stay and fight it out. This search for equilibrium between opposing impulses manifests itself not only in "The Crown," but, as we might expect, in other outpourings such as the letters, where the language of the voyage appears as the principal and at times the only means of expressing the powerful concerns that moved their writer: *I shall see Russell and we shall talk about the scheme of lectures,* Lawrence wrote in July 1915. *But as yet he stands too much on the shore of this existing world. He must get into a boat and preach from out of the waters of eternity, if he is going to do any good.* Behind this picture of Russell we glimpse Lawrence self-portrayed as Jesus standing off from the shore of the Sea of Galilee and preaching to the great throngs, challenging them to follow him to a new life on a far strand. In this same letter Lawrence's reference to *The Rainbow,* of which he was just correcting the proofs, is in full agreement with this picture of himself as leader of a great migration, but one that would take place right at home: *Whatever else it is,* [*The Rainbow*] *is the voyage of discovery towards the real and eternal and unknown land. We are like Columbus, we have our backs upon Europe, till we come to the new world.*

For symbolism in "The Crown" Lawrence drew on a specifically English source: the royal arms, the lion and the unicorn opposed

HL, 240

beneath the crown. What better way to renew England than by a reawakening to its own heraldic symbols?

The lion Lawrence takes to be the flesh, the senses, the darkness, the power of the self. The unicorn is the spirit, the mind, the light, altruistic love. The crown is the transcendent prize, the heavenly vision for which the lion and the unicorn are locked in eternal combat. Being, according to Lawrence, is the struggle itself. If the purpose of either force were ever completely achieved, this *would of necessity entail* PX, 366 *the cessation from existence of both opponents.* But modern man has forgotten this fact: that he lives not by the victory of either half of his soul but by the tension of the ongoing quest. Men today waste themselves in flying from one extreme to the other. This message unrolls in reach after reach of imagery such as this: *Now the unicorn of* PX, 371 *virtue and virgin spontaneity has got the Crown slipped over the eyes, like a circle of utter light, and has gone mad with the extremity of light: whilst the lion of power and splendour, its own Crown of supreme night settled down upon it, roars in an agony of imprisoned darkness.* The proper condition, as against this dwelling in either totality, is a traveling back and forth between them, a concept elaborated by set after set of images right through the essays.

Taking up the universal opposites further as light and darkness, Lawrence sees conception as a ray of light piercing the darkness of the womb, from which we come forth in uninterrupted growth. *And when* PX, 368 *we have come to the fulness of our strength, like lions which have been fed till they are full grown, then the strange necessity comes upon us, we must travel away, roam like falling fruit, fall from the initial darkness of the tree, of the cave which has reared us, into the eternal light of germination and begetting, the eternal light, shedding our darkness like the fruit that rots on the ground.*

We travel across between the two great opposites of the Beginning and the End, the eternal night and everlasting day.

The many convolutions of such language in "The Crown" are often reminiscent of the speech of the Old Testament prophets: where redundancy was never taken as a crime against clarity but as an opportunity through one more twist of repetition to illuminate another obscure facet of the symbolism. In "The Crown" the soul in its transit through life is presented under one variation after another of this travel symbolism. In one passage it is the flesh reaching the heroic proportions of a David, dancing *naked in glory of itself, before the* PX, 369 *Ark, naked in glory of itself in the procession of heroes travelling towards the wise goddess, the white light, the Mind.* Elsewhere we come upon the figure of the great progress as a gratuitous action issuing in some unforeseeable advancement: *Life is a travelling to the edge of* PX, 374 *knowledge, then a leap taken. We cannot know beforehand. We are driven from behind, always as over the edge of the precipice.* Such flights of language portend, besides, the discovery in the American literature essays of how great spirits of place function, how one polarity of place in subsiding propels mankind unawares to answer the call of another polarity of place. Or, in another nuance of "Crown" symbolism, that moves near to the thought of *The Rainbow,* Lawrence PX, 378 depicts the link between diametrical eternities in this way: *My source and issue is in two eternities, I am founded in the two infinites. But absolute is the rainbow that goes between; the iris of my very being.* In this passage, the rainbow itself is an emblem of travel, a road by which the two eternities are united, the way of the pilgrim. The rainbow is the highest visionary form as well as the holy inspiration to the soul in transit.

But in this particular passage Lawrence offers wider ramifications under closely related images. We have already noticed how the physical events of birth and growth are made to stand for ethereal concepts. Equally comprehensive of the puritan uniting of common experience with heavenly realities is the recourse in this passage to sex as an ordinary experience with extraordinary implications. The symbolism of sex in Lawrence, to emphasize the point, is puritan in that he insists on finding in the literal rendering of sexual details a mystical experience: a procedure forbidden to most former puritan mystics by social inhibitions that Lawrence was instrumental in removing. In "The Crown" the going in of man to woman is the rhythmic repetition of new birth, the motion back and forth between eternal opposites: PX, 377 *She is the doorway, she is the gate to the dark eternity of power.* Sexual congress proceeds as the blood traveling forth in daring toward oblivion, the little death consummated. The flame of light enters into the flame of darkness and is absorbed. Having touched the immortal PX, 378 source the lover is *thrown forth again on the shore of creation, warm and lustrous, goodly, new-born from the darkness out of which all time has issued.*

Much of the substance of "The Crown" does approach that of *Le Gai Savaire,* but significant omissions and modifications are noticeable. The periodic reforging of personality in sex does not lead here to the veneration of woman. Neither is man born again of his wife in adulthood, as he was once born of his mother in infancy, nor does the woman participate equally in the work of the life-transforming male.

If "The Crown" adheres chiefly to interweaving an obscure imagery having national overtones, it does on occasion engage in more overt prophetic statement. For instance, Lawrence sums up the meaning of England's devastation by the Industrial Revolution in terms that stand as prescient to the ecological disasters of today and the spurious triumphs of exploration in space. He sees man as perverting his life aim by going forth on material conquest in denial of spiritual conquest: *The supreme little ego in man hates an unconquered uni-* PX, 391 *verse. We shall never rest till we have heaped tin cans on the North Pole and the South Pole, and put up barb-wire fences on the moon.* We kill the mysteries and devour the secrets, and when our rampant materialism is done we are left in a void like the second death, from which no resurrection is possible. Again the problem is one of demolishing one of the great opposites of the universe and coveting the other. Lawrence does not here call this proclivity in man a "tragic flaw," but what is left to implication resembles the statement in *Le Gai Savaire* of man's *real tragedy* as blind defiance of the great PH, 420 *unwritten morality* of nature.

Off and on through "The Crown" Lawrence also touches on the question of immortality, at least once in definite terms. He might almost have used as a starting point John Bunyan's assertion on having received the grace to acknowledge election, how immortality came at once into his grasp: *Now I could see myself in Heaven and Earth at* GA, 75 *once.* For Lawrence, immortality could be such a state of being, awareness of the fleeting moment as eternal, not translation into a future life. It was a fullness of being here and now: *I am not immortal till I* PX, 410 *have achieved immortality. And immortality is not a question of time, of everlasting life. It is a question of consummate being,* of spanning the two eternities as the rainbow.

But perhaps the most expressive intimations of immortality in "The Crown" depend upon the symbolic expansion of a concrete incident, some of which also finds its way into a letter. In February 1915, when Lawrence was emerging from the tomb of months of war, he saw a soldier who had lost a leg go struggling along on crutches against an ocean background, *like a babe just born, new to begin life.* Men looked PX, 401 at him in fascination, women desired him: he was the infant England just crept from the womb of time's disaster. Lawrence identified with him too, and the feeling as he endeavored to communicate it in writing was a dual one of faith in the tender new shape of life and the terror of death that still clings to the newly risen. Then immortality takes control of the outlook. We have met with Lawrence's view that the dead enter the living and dwell there, donating their vividness to a soul present in time. But in war this could become a fearful thing, for the number of the dead, many of them unfulfilled in life and therefore devouring instead of solacing to their living hosts, could be overpowering. Lawrence symbolizes his acute consciousness of this peril in the sea beyond the crippled soldier: *I felt as if legions were marching* HL, 223 *in the mist* of the ocean, *legions of white ghosts tramping.* He fears *the ghosts of the dead.* But the feeling is ambivalent, for in the same letter he proclaims, *Did I not tell you my revolution would come? It will come, God help us. The ghosts will bring it.*

We may liken the cumulative effect here to the agonizing discipline that Ursula's soul undergoes in *The Rainbow*. The ghosts will bring about the revolution by entering the living and spurring them on. What is demanded of the living is the courage to participate in death by accepting the energy of the departed for the rebuilding: *In truth, we proceed to die because the whole frame of our life is a falsity, and we know that, if we die sufficiently, the whole frame and form and edifice will collapse upon itself. But it were much better to pull it down and have a great clear space, than to have it collapse on top of us.* A Samson-like suicide to achieve the destruction of the old temple is useless. Better demolition and reconstruction from the foundations up, inspired by the presence of the martyrs within us.

PX, 415

Lawrence now moves into imagery resembling that of the last pages of *The Rainbow*: the bursting of the old shell and the bringing forth of a shining new mankind. In this manner "The Crown" reverts to the tone of exuberance sounded in the novel earlier in the year. On this wave of enthusiasm as he finished the novel, Lawrence had stated his purpose in the projected series of essays: *I am going to begin a book about Life — more rainbows, but in different skies — which I want to publish in pamphlet form week by week — my initiation of the great and happy revolution.* Getting his revolution into prose form and publishing half of this in *The Signature* was as far as Lawrence advanced into political action. Practical politics was not one of his talents.

ML, 328

NOTES

[1] For a thorough discussion of the development of these stories and their importance to this phase of Lawrence's career, see Keith Cushman, *D. H. Lawrence at Work: The Emergence of* The Prussian Officer *Stories* (Charlottesville, Va., 1978).

[2] For all its personal orientation, Lawrence's analysis of American authors has become highly influential in modern criticism of American literature. In *American Renaissance* (1941), F. O. Matthiessen gives Lawrence considerable credit for penetrating remarks on Hawthorne, Melville and Whitman. Leslie Fiedler, in *Love and Death in the American Novel* (1960), makes the flat assertion that Lawrence comes closer than any other critic he knows of to grasping the real nature of American literature.

[3] The word form *savaire* is puzzling. It does not occur in any of the Romance languages, as far as I can determine. Clearly Lawrence was

alluding to Nietzsche's *Joyful Wisdom,* which in the original is *Die Fröh-liche Wissenschaft,* with *La Gaya Scienza* as a sub-title. If Nietzsche meant the latter phrase to be Italian he misspelled *gaia.* The term goes back to the troubadors of Provence, or at least to the fourteenth century, when a Consistoire du Gay Savoir flourished in Toulouse. A poetic work issued by this society was entitled *Flors del Gay Saber.* Apparently Lawrence meant to adopt the original term — which still survives in the dialect litera-ture of southern France — and gallicized the spelling to facilitate pronun-ciation.

6

One Must Travel West
or South

Lawrence never committed himself unreservedly to staying in England to help reform the country. The Rananim to be founded under his and Bertrand Russell's guidance at Garsington, Lady Ottoline Morrell's estate, suffered its inevitable fate. The individualists, Lawrence prominently among them, could not subordinate their wills to a group purpose.[1] Two possible avenues of escape from the holocaust come up repeatedly in Lawrence's letters. Rananim might be planted elsewhere through migration with a saving remnant to some far-off spot. But transference of the ideal to a new country would do little to improve the stubbornness of strong wills. The other alternative was to return to Italy for a life with Frieda as sole companion: the condition on which Lawrence had staked so much before the war. Neither of these journeys was taken at the time but both are of great consequence in the next developments of the travel instinct in Lawrence.

In his daydreams Rananim grew to be the opposite pole to a metamorphosis of England. And although practical steps for a colony went hardly further than the abortive beginnings of political action at home, what happened to Rananim in the fascinating territory of Lawrence's spirit is another story. Eventually, like a latter-day Pilgrim Father, he set out through American literature on an imaginary voyage to the New World which in effect sublimated Rananim. But this took place later in the war. The first excursion toward enlightenment by invention of a foreign land carried him not west but south, to Italy: a mental substitute for the physical presence the war continued to deny him.

While the earlier travel sketches aided in orientation to a country and provided a channel for self-analysis, *Twilight in Italy* was Lawrence's first conscious and sustained exploitation of travel writing as symbology. He could not have adopted a more congenial form, as the four books from this one to the posthumously published *Etruscan Places* well demonstrate. In fact they transmit Lawrence's genius to the reader as effectively as any of the novels do.

A long enchantment with the potential of travel writing lay behind *Twilight in Italy*. An important early attitude comes out in the young Lawrence's reaction to Samuel Butler's *Erewhon*, which he praised highly to Jessie Chambers: *It begins like a book of travel.... You'd* JC, 120 *never dream it was satire. It's so fresh, so romantic, such a sense of a new country. And then he just turns all our ideas of society upside down, but with the greatest seriousness.* The seed of later commentary of his own in similar form was already sown. A love of travel works capable of statement on universals continues unabated into the fertile Fiascherino period, when two of Lawrence's avid interests in reading, we remember, were *travels* and *raw philosophy,* precisely the two areas ML, 250 of thought he was soon to bring together.

We have seen how Lawrence's first off-hand sketches were largely subsistence writing, but how with the mountain chapel sketch came a new tone, to be sounded further in the *English Review* pieces and the crucifix sketch. But now, in July 1915, came the most significant turn of all. Lawrence had several times begun, scrapped, and rebegun his symbology. *The Signature* was planned, with most of the moment's rendering of the symbology to go into that. With the stress on spiritual progress as a sort of "travel" in his native place so prominent from *Le Gai Savaire* to the "Crown" essays, it was only fitting that another step should be taken to give the widest symbolic scope to travel in a foreign setting: to turn to Italy, with some of Germany incorporated, proposing how the world might be remade through appraisal of national character. It was a highly personal appraisal, and figuring large therein were the nostalgia and regret for places that the gyrations of fortune had made unattainable to the writer. But, as we will see, the book goes far beyond the limits of meditative reminiscence.

Lawrence stated his purpose in the midst of work on *Twilight in Italy,* an assertion already quoted in part: *I am writing a book of* ML, 364 *sketches, or preparing a book of sketches, about the nations, Italian, German and English, full of philosophising and struggling to show things real.* The book is a gathering and a rewriting, but with the bulk of the later sketches perhaps composed for the first time. There are ten sketches in all. The first one in the book is a third version of the crucifix piece, the title changed from "Christs in the Tirol" to "The Crucifix Across the Mountains" — plainly a piece of great importance to Lawrence now, the one which finally sets the pattern for what he wanted his travel writing to express. The next three sections of the volume are the *English Review* sketches, much deepened by revision.

The last six pieces are all original to the volume, and the dating of their composition poses problems. Outside of some thin circumstantial evidence, there is no reason to believe that they had come in any form from Lawrence's pen until he set himself the task of producing the book. Even if earlier versions did exist, what is of ultimate importance in *Twilight in Italy* must date from 1915, for it reflects what preoccupied Lawrence at the time.

The fundamental premise of *Twilight in Italy* is that given regions of the globe, specifically North but also East by implication, are regions of death, and that reaffirmation of life comes about in purposeful travel in one of the creative directions, West or South, with completion of an ideal pattern through accompanying passional movement between Above and Below.

For a brave beginning of his avowed intention to evaluate the three national characters best known to him, Lawrence postulates a source TI, 3 for the *imperial vanity* still adhering to the German soul. It originated in the southward pilgrimages of the medieval emperors, who passed into Italy to imbibe of the old Roman spirit of which they counted themselves the inheritors. The wayside crucifixes dotting the old imperial way across the Alps are the enduring vestiges of that vanished world, Lawrence continues. Yet he does not for long maintain the apparent thesis of these remarks: that the modern German character might have its roots in the spirit behind these artifacts. The real point pursued is how the crucifix, implanted in the mountain world by the north German emperors, *multiplied and grew according to the soil, and the race that received it,* a type of crucifix markedly different from the sentimentalized commercial varieties that predominate both to the north and south of this isolated section of Germanic Europe: the mountains from southernmost Bavaria to just over the Brenner Pass. It is not an imperial arrogance or any other political tendency that Lawrence is drawn to follow home in the Teutonic alpine soul. It is rather the dilemma of sensual versus spiritual reality and of life and death experienced in close conjunction, a dilemma intensified in this elevated atmosphere by the inescapable juxtaposition of strong light and strong darkness, of deathly snow and fertile green. This dilemma determines the character of man in the region.

The crucifixes turn out to be as multiform as Lawrence's present concerns. The enigma of sensuality and death was on its way in his mind to the wondrous proportions it reached in *Women in Love*. But even this theme is subsidiary to the real subject of *Twilight in Italy,* which is how the test of orientation toward some new quarter of the earth or sky is always paramount in the mobile individual. The chief person here is the narrator-traveler, no matter what typical national individual may fill the foreground of the action. This foot-traveler's amazement in discovery is a surpassing experience, even more so three years after the event than in the earlier renderings. But it is not now so much an awareness of pain-worship into which the narrator is jolted by the sight of the peasant on the cross and the peasants at work. It is rather discovery of a whole mystique of the senses which rules the peasants here. In description recalling the famous harvest scene of *The Rainbow,* only with reverse effect, Lawrence follows the in-and-out movement of the toiling peasants from field to shed and back, the *hot welter of physical sensation* revealed by the way in which they walk   TI, 5 with their armfuls of hay under the rain. They absorb so much sensual experience in life that it *becomes at length a bondage, at last a crucifixion.* It does so because of the stark contrast in the spirit of place in which the mountain peasant has his being: *The ice and the upper radiance of snow are brilliant with timeless immunity from the flux and the warmth of life. Overhead they transcend all life, all the soft, moist fire of the blood. So that a man must needs live under the radiance of his own negation.*

Lawrence's weighing of this eternal issue between flesh and spirit too much revealed comes to ambiguous conclusions. The struggle gives these people the souls of artists, compels them to constant expression of the contradiction before their eyes in folk plays and songs. Yet the crucifixes show how tormented they are in their knowledge. They live in the mystic Now, beautiful and complete, yet they are without the "flow" that must pervade the living moment to make it the most desirable of states. *Finality* is in the long run the condition of the mountain   TI, 7 peasant. He cannot go beyond himself in any creative direction, caught in his impasse between Above and Below, zenith and nadir, farseeing into both but forming of them only a cross on which to rack his being. This conclusion is far more subtilized than those Lawrence arrived at on first assessing the chapel ex-voto pictures and the crucifixes, and far more comprehensive of the landscape, but it has changed little in essentials.

Far more is at stake, however, than delineation of the regional character. The peasant incorporates the narrator-traveler's concerns, and through him the plight of all mankind. For Lawrence now puts the question he has mulled over in various contexts since his blood-religion letter, his own form of Shakespeare's "to be or not to be." He places it now in the mind of a *little brooding Christ* who sits and   TI, 8 reflects in his *glass case beside the road,* just after his resurrection. Instead of penetrating the Below by harrowing Hell, he has ascended to the snows of death above, the region of not-to-be. But nothing in that realm was transformed, or even touched, by his passage. Now he has come back to the region of to-be in the valleys, but to his sorrow and mystification a knowledge of life and death does not add up to a unified knowledge of Above and Below. He must go on asking what is likewise the narrator's unresolved question, to wit: *What, then, is being?*

This question subsumes for the first time the principal theme of the book. Its ramifications characterize the seeker as well as the quest. He is the male spirit extricating himself from the native spirit of place gone dead in order to find atonement with a new spirit of place to the south. To achieve this end the author finds himself compelled to look back from forced reconfinement in the native place to the experience of having borne the crucifix of himself across the mountains from northern to southern Europe.

A greater contrast than ever now divides the carvings of the decadent lowlands from those higher up. North of the Alps the crucifix TI, 4 is seldom more than *a factory-made piece of sentimentalism.* To the south of the mountains it has more variety but is degenerate still. In lower Austria the Christs are self-conscious in their introspection, or TI, 11 often merely *crude and sinister,* purely death-worshipping, and lower TI, in Italy they tend to be more and more *vulgar or sensational. . . . Only* 12–13 *high up, where the crucifix becomes smaller and smaller, is there left any of the old beauty and religion.* This ancient glorious hardship is the encounter with the question of being that is glossed over in the valleys below.

The intense utterance of this sketch was beyond Lawrence in the two earlier forms. Knowing this to be the revision with which he set out to shape *Twilight in Italy* permits verification of an exact starting point for his decision to elevate travel writing to philosophy. But still the process goes back to the Lake Garda residence in one respect. At that time Lawrence could put into poetry if not into prose the full challenge of the mountain crucifixes. A comparison is in order.

The poem in question is "Meeting Among the Mountains," in which we witness specific identification of a fearful but fascinated mind with the crucifixes. Lawrence the traveler is caught in a moment of sharp guilt at having stolen another man's wife. He stands looking at a Christ slumped forward full-weight on the nails, while the new-CP, 225 fallen snow on the mountain tops is *like transcendent/Clean pain.* Down the mountain road comes an oxcart, whose driver rocks along as if in a dream, a peasant who by chance resembles Frieda's first husband. Immediately the hatred and misery of the nearby Christ is transferred to the wronged husband, who to Lawrence's stricken con-CP, 226 science now goes his way *With a pale, dead Christ on the crucifix of his heart.* Almost instantly the lover identifies with the husband by entering himself into the Christ image. The stigmata might suddenly break out in his hands; the dead Christ might suddenly hang on his bone structure. This remote place has become, unexpectedly, the place of ultimate discovery about the self. The prose texture of the *Twilight in Italy* sketch may convey its meaning at more leisure, but the point is the same.

More emblems in the scheme of Lawrence's symbology evolve in the next revisions for *Twilight in Italy*. "The Spinner and the Monks" has a new beginning. Still absorbed in the potential of creative movement from lower to higher areas, Lawrence clarifies more fully than before his moral landscape of lake shore and village overtopped by slopes and mountains. The two churches now typify a new set of the opposites — in the periodical version no contrast between churches had occurred to him. But he now requires symbols for the opposite but complementary natures of the Holy Ghost: The Dove versus the Eagle embodying love and hate, pride and humility, and other such antinomies. Lawrence here draws on a book he had read late in 1914, ML, 304 Mrs. Henry Jenner's *Christian Symbolism*. She had said that the Holy CS, Ghost was most often represented as a dove, but infrequently as an 40–42 eagle when shown inspiring the holy men of the Old Law. Lawrence takes over the distinction to specify the traveler's discovery of two churches in a foreign country, a discovery like that of the crucifixes and the ex-voto pictures in the wayside chapel. The suddenness of the discovery is significant here, too. Knowledge springs directly out of the traveler's progress through the world around him. Wandering around the village he has gone by the Church of San Francesco many times without noting its existence, for it is set back among a cluster of buildings around it. He has seen vaguely, like a distant vision, the Church of San Tommaso towering out of a hillside that rises sharply over the rooftops above the lakefront streets. But what these churches may mean, or even that the clanging of often-heard bells has been coming from San Tommaso, does not occur to him till one day when at last his *everyday trance* [is] *broken in upon* and San Tommaso becomes TI, 20 for him *a living connection*. This jolt establishes for the perceiver that the world's two kinds of churches stand for the two natures of the Holy Ghost. The Church of the Eagle, San Tommaso, is the Old Testament church of pride and imperiousness, letting the command of its bells fall on the world beneath. The Church of San Francesco, unobtrusive and huddled among other structures, permitting any intrusion but nevertheless unmoved, is the New Testament Church of the Dove.

Now the traveler ascends to the terrace of San Tommaso, and his journey up from the village streets is more emphatically a spiritual progress than in the 1913 version. The Eagle-Dove image sustains a more intricate opposition of light and darkness, whose reconciliation the rambler ponders as he climbs. Identification with either realm is not absolute. As long as he was down in the village, he felt *pale, and clear, and evanescent, like the light,* while the Italians winding through the warren of alleys around him *were dark, and close, and constant, like the shadow.* But when he reaches the terrace of San Tommaso to discover the old woman spinning, she emerges as an incarnation of sun and stone and the Eagle world, against whose essential nature he grows obscure and diminished, an emissary from the dark world below. By this transfer of roles the narrator is testing the different orders of reality to discover the one most congenial to himself. Like every other manifestation of person or place, the old spinner is highly symbolic. Fiercely subjective and self-contained, she is like the morning and the Creation, but she goes to the extreme. In her denial of any exterior reality at all, she is cut off from examination of the self as opposed to the not-self: *Her world was clear and absolute, without consciousness of self. . . . She was not aware that there was anything in the universe except **her** universe. . . . The lands she had not seen were corporate parts of her own living body.* She is therefore dangerous to the questing traveler, for whom the act of seeing new lands provides access to the mystery of being. But escape from her turns out to be easy, as she refuses in any case to grant him existence. So the pilgrim flees from her up the mountainside, further into the world of the Eagle.

TI,
24–25

On the upper slopes, looking for snowdrops that turn out not yet to be in bloom, he is still sharply aware of light and dark and wary of an overplus of either. Simply going down into a gully to pick other sorts of flowers becomes a descent into darkness which makes him uneasy and sends him scrambling back up into the light: in repetition of the urge that sent him up from the village to San Tommaso in the first place. More and more on this *Saturday afternoon, when a strange suspension comes over the world,* all things conspire to produce a symbolic atmosphere.

TI, 28

This and the other rewritten sketches are controlled by that expectancy of discovery so heightened in Lawrence during the war years, when he lived on the verge of the miraculous and the terrible. In such a light he looks back on his pilgrim self as witness to an emblematic scene: the two monks pacing a monastery garden near the church he has left. These figures epitomize and climax the metaphysical problem of light versus dark, this final statement given in expository as well as narrative terms. His adventure has engendered such sensitivity in the traveler that even far up on his hillside he is capable of *attending with* [his] *dark soul to their inaudible undertone.* And he turns the little scene into an allegory in which he sharply distinguishes between the twilight of the monks and that which is now falling over the

TI, 29

world outside their garden. He sees them as creatures of *neutral regularity* strolling oblivious and pale, never knowing how to look at the mountains across the lake: at that other twilight, where *the wonderful faint, ethereal flush of the long range of snow in the heavens, at evening, began to kindle.* But while it would mean nothing to them, to the pilgrim that snowy ridge is *like heaven breaking into blossom.* Sud- TI, 30 denly that vexing question of being versus not-being, uttered first in the crucifix sketch, finds its response in the symbol of the greater twilight: *After all, eternal not-being and eternal being are the same. In the rosy snow that shone in heaven over a darkened earth was the ecstasy of consummation.* In that twilight is the reconciliation of opposites, a revelation all the more profound in that the twilight of the monks below — *the flesh neutralising the spirit, the spirit neutralising the flesh, the law of the average asserted* — stands out in such contrast to the true twilight. The technique of shifting symbols reaches now beyond the limits of this sketch. The snows above in "The Crucifix Across the Mountains," according to the Bavarian peasant's defiant assertion of the senses, were a pure *radiance of his own negation.* But now, trans- TI, 5 fused with the two illuminations of the universe, of the night and the day, the snows are transformed into a great synthesis: *the supreme* TI, 31 *transcendence of the afterglow* that reveals *day hovering in the embrace of the coming night like two angels embracing in the heavens.*

And yet, after all, the question is not settled. For how is man to draw this garment of perfect illumination down to his own shoulders? *The two in consummation are perfect, beyond the range of loneliness or solitude,* but *where in mankind is the ecstasy of light and dark together, the supreme transcendence of the afterglow?* The dark-skinned Italians can be ecstatic by night, the blue-eyed old spinning woman by day, and the monks, who by rights should unite the two, amble along in their twilight of neither here nor there. The traveler is light to the Italians of the village and dark to the old spinner, but whether he can join the two opposites in himself remains a question. At least he apprehends a symbolism by which the question may be posed, and the exultant tone of the prose itself is a sort of consummation between counterforces. The pilgrim has met with salvation and damnation objectified in people and place, and the situation has resolved itself by a glimpse of the Delectable Mountains.

A brief inquiry into how the question of being has been symbolically extended since the crucifix essay will bring a better understanding of Lawrence's strategy. We would do well to relate this symbolic extension to the meaning of the Holy Ghost, not here specified by name as the great reconciler but nonetheless implicit, given the Dove-Eagle dichotomy of the chapter opening and the elaboration of the symbol in coming pages. Also, the Holy Ghost has figured in some manner as the transcendent encounter of opposites in all symbology since the *Sons and Lovers* "foreword": the supreme if momentary unifying impulse of the counterforces eternally impinging on the human soul in passage through the world.[2] But what are we to make of the dual nature of the Holy Ghost in the present instance, and how does this agree with a like duality of the twilight? If we concentrate on this quadrilateral pattern an ascending order emerges. The first two concretions of the Holy Ghost, the two churches, are each in itself a consolidation of qualities, but their reconciliation with each other remains an open question. The narrator's inspiration evolves then to the old spinner and the monks as opposite physical forms of spiritual realities, again combinations within themselves but incapable of mutual harmony. The rhythm then grows to incorporate the two twilights, to reveal as the climactic point their utter incompatibility. Now identification with a "holy ghost" is conceivable with any one of these entities: from the lower church as Dove to the monks as Dove, from the upper church as Eagle to the old spinner as Eagle. But the symbolic transformation proceeds without ceasing. As we have seen, the monks come to stand largely for inadequate synthesis of the great Light and the great Dark, for an unacceptable "holy ghost" of twilight. The authentic Holy Ghost is in the clasping and sundering of Night and Day on the eternal snows. The Holy Ghost of this Twilight in Italy is prophetic of how pilgrim man may re-create himself in greatness on earth. The symbol will accompany Lawrence in all the years to come: to the American wilderness, to a prospective future of Europe foreseen as a reign of the Holy Ghost. Surely if he had ever himself experienced that Dispensation of the Holy Ghost, he would have completed his Trinity by adding to the Churches of the Eagle and the Dove, somewhere in Italy, a Church of the Phoenix.

If the first two segments of *Twilight in Italy* have unity in that philosophic conclusions stem directly from physical symbols, the same cannot be said of "The Lemon Gardens." For Lawrence attempts here to insert his symbology in wedges into a narrative little changed from the *English Review* version. The darkness of the landlord's villa, his disappointment at having no child by his young wife, and his weariness with the old Italian way of life cannot support the symbolic weight Lawrence places on them in superimposing all-inclusive theories of European cultural movements upon simple narrative.

Lawrence now drops the glowing claim that only a few English couples can ever achieve in passionate attachment the acme of civilization. He retains the distinction between the brilliance of Italian exteriors and the shadows in the Italian soul given to passion as an end in itself, and he launches from this into a long historical and philosophical disquisition that makes little sense as history and is philosophical only as a cloud of symbols may be. The history is largely that of Italian art as Lawrence understands it. Curious and arbitrary though his observations may be in a technical sense, yet they mean a great deal in the study of Lawrence's sensibility. They do not appear unprecedented in this volume, but have a background whose outlines we should take into account before proceeding.

The first important hint appears in the correspondence of mid-1914, where Lawrence drew parallels between his experiments in reaching universal consciousness through fiction and the abstractions of the Italian Futurists. The earliest full exposition of views comes in Chapter VII of *Le Gai Savaire* and lays the foundation for the "Lemon Gardens" argument. *Le Gai Savaire* begins, we remember, with the familiar insistence that all creation springs from the interaction of male and female elements. Man is the striver, the dissatisfied quester after new frames of being. Woman is permanence and rest from striving, centripetal as man is centrifugal. Soon after advancing this premise, Lawrence turns to the sources of religion in the Western world as seen in the light of this duality. The Jews were a "female" race, living in direct physical worship of the Father. But a change had to come, and it did come, when *Christ rose from the suppressed male spirit of* PH, 452 *Judea,* bringing Love, which is of the Spirit, to replace Law, which is of the Body. Since then the two impulses, both inhering to some degree in Christianity, have been in stress, now one predominating, now the other, with the great goal of balance as the ideal: the true Holy Ghost.

Yet, when it comes to applying this dualism to the great artists of Italy, who serve as chief examples of the argument, Lawrence is no model of clarity. He generalizes with great abandon and takes little care to be consistent. Still, he presents a valuable study of contrasts within self and society, those obscurely functioning contradictions which we do not and cannot understand, but which determine the course of our history. And often the confusion of thought is only on the surface, where terminology may become a tangle. For instance, when Lawrence asserts that medieval Christianity was *predominantly* PH, 454 *female,* and then speaks of its most constant activity as a fight against the body, whereas the ancient Jews, professing also a "female" form of worship, were secret voluptuaries, then one may well wonder where the real distinctions lie. If this passage is placed beside a corresponding one in "The Lemon Gardens," however, it becomes plain that Lawrence has clarified the point between writings, that what he really saw in medieval Christianity was a fruitful opposition between the two natures of man: *In the middle Ages Christian Europe seems to have* TI, 34 *been striving, out of a strong, primitive, animal nature* [female to Lawrence], *towards the self-abnegation and the abstraction of Christ* [male to Lawrence]. *This brought about by itself a great sense of completeness. The two halves were joined by the effort towards the one as yet unrealised. There was a triumphant joy in the Whole.*

While the appraisal of history emerges clearly enough in this paragraph, inconsistencies still crop up in other areas of either text. In *Le Gai Savaire* the *triumphant joy in the Whole* is a phenomenon of the Renaissance, not of the Middle Ages. And when we come to individual artists and the movements springing out of their work, in either essay, we enter a dense thicket indeed. The way out, in *Le Gai Savaire,* runs something like this. Botticelli's *Nativity of the Saviour* was the height of Christianity's blissful and short-lived balance between male and female religion: between male child and virgin mother, as Lawrence's matriarchal mystique led him to claim. Then with Correggio the male began to predominate, the great mystery of the female to fade, and art became increasingly secular as the male sought to know his own experience rather than exult in the mystery. Male momentum steadily conquered female stability until finally, in contemporary art, everything has turned to motion, to male abstractions of line and form. Raphael was the great forerunner of modern art. On the other hand, Michelangelo went against this whole trend. He was man and woman within himself, complete, though he asserted female flesh against male spirit.

PH, 455

And so the great strife of male and female runs through our history, and Lawrence makes a beginning toward classifying the great men of the past by the proportion of male and female they incorporated. The pure males tended to be bodiless: Shelley, St. John the Evangelist, and Spenser, for example. A preponderance of the female nature, of the flesh, held sway in men like Shakespeare, St. Paul, and Lord Byron. Among the personalities more or less in balance were such men as Victor Hugo, Schiller, and Tennyson. But too much balance is undesirable, for it is disproportion between masculine and feminine that sends the soul forth to struggle for its own articulation. Hence an androgynous imbalance is the most creative of all states of being.

According to the symbolic pattern of *Le Gai Savaire* Michelangelo, who though in equilibrium favored a femaleness of expression, should be the true ancestor of modern Italians, a distinctly female race to Lawrence. But inconsistently this is not the case. On the contrary, Lawrence here sees Italian fleshliness as subdued in a *Raphaelesque conception of the ultimate geometric basis of life* to marriage and child worship. His fear of abnormal attachment to offspring urges him to

PH, 463

pronounce such a marriage an *absolute static combination* from which there is no escape and which *has arrested the Italian race for three centuries*. If we put these statements of *Le Gai Savaire* beside those of "The Lemon Gardens," we discover a reassignment of symbols characteristic of Lawrence's search for philosophical terms. The *Twilight in Italy* conclusions are not fundamentally different from those of the earlier piece, for all that, but the arguments are nevertheless reliant on a shifted symbolism. In *Twilight in Italy* Michelangelo, and not Raphael after all, is the forerunner of present-day Italian phallic worship, with its utter subjugation to the senses and its decree that the only immortality is in begetting children. Raphael is in fact not even mentioned. But to take Lawrence to task for this sort of ubiquity would be to no purpose. He is not dealing in logic. He may at various times see opposite attributes in the same symbol. Out of the perpetual re-examination of symbols the point does come forth clearly — that since the Renaissance the Italians, or to be exact, the whole Mediterranean world, has gone the way of the flesh, while northern Europe has gone the way of the spirit. As for apparent contradiction, Lawrence often admitted that inconsistency was one of his great obstacles in stating his metaphysics, an inconsistency which by parallel study of pieces of writing we can trace more easily than he could to contradictions in the lessons of place.

The manner of discovery in "The Lemon Gardens," as in the preceding segments of the book, is still a sudden awareness of a hitherto overlooked facet of native life. The procedure now leads the traveler into the future of man, the question of quantity versus quality of life. As the childless landlord watches his young wife play with her infant nephew, Lawrence all at once realizes the physical basis of immortality in the phallus-worshipping Italians. This richness of the flesh is why the spiritual Englishman finds the Italian attractive. Yet he feels more mature, for he has gone beyond the phallic in quest of the godhead. At this point, Lawrence begins to go far beyond anything in the *English Review* sketches, into a comparison of England and Italy in terms of the industrial age. He moves toward condemnation of modern technological society, an attitude brought on by the war, since it is absent from the *English Review* sketch.

What has the Englishman discovered? Lawrence asks. He has discovered the power of science and industry. This power has to do with "charity," in Lawrence's mind, for its ideals posit love of mankind as a whole rather than man as single self, generating a passion for social reform. But now with all the treasures of the world in his grasp, the Englishman does not know what to do with them. It is his present tendency, Lawrence thinks, to reject them and deliberately revert to the Italian position. But going back is impossible, and the mistaken attempt to do so can only lead to one or the other of two equally destructive alternatives. If the Englishman undertakes to serve the future through his children, aping the Italian, then in his present state of social evolution he will see that future simply in terms of numbers, not of some mystical immortality. Lawrence now touches on a world overcrowded with inwardly empty people, a problem that bothered him long before it did most: *Fifty million children growing up purposeless, with no purpose save the attainment of their own individual desires, these are not the future, they are only a disintegration of the past. The future is in living, growing truth, in advancing fulfilment.* The other alternative is the one that Lawrence feels Europe has taken in the Great War, hurling itself into the annihilation of human flesh long made uneasy by domination of the spirit: *We turn perverse and destructive, give ourselves joy in the destruction of the flesh.*

TI, 45

As to which future is preferable, the Italian or the English, a continuation of the study of Pietro di Paoli brings the traveler to an answer. The analysis is more successful here than in the foregoing attempt to comprehend the history of Italian painting by a like analysis. The *padrone* leads his visitor on a tour of his lemon gardens. Through these, as before, we see economic decline and the breaking up of an ancient way of life on the lakeshore. Therefore the Italian must make a choice for the future. In fact he has already made it. He is quite ready to renounce the sun of the lemon-garden world for the machines and smoke of industrial England. In sum, as the Englishman longs for the Italian's disappearing way of life, so the Italian longs for the present condition of the Englishman. The traveler too must choose, and this choice forms the conclusion of the essay.

The direction of this conclusion is significant, requiring also a thorough understanding of how it is reached. Lawrence is not yet ready to condemn the modern world out of hand, for all his grave reservations about it. And we see in this instance exactly how and why Lawrence hoped to get at *things real* through a travel work. It is a question of putting things in perspective. He can look back through these pages of speculation to a now remote and for the present unattainable place which had probably been the most vital of all places to the flowering of his talent. To the beauty of that past is now added the nostalgia for what the war has made an even more ancient and rapidly vanishing world. From this juxtaposition of emotions he can grasp the meaning of past, present and future: *I sat on the roof of the lemon-house, with the lake below and the snowy mountain opposite, and looked at the ruins on the old, olive-fuming shores, at all the*

TI, 53

LAKE GARDA, ITALY

All summer long, upon the mountain slopes steep by the lake,
stand the rows of naked pillars
rising out of the green foliage like ruins of temples (TI, 48)

*peace of the ancient world still covered in sunshine, and the past
seemed to me so lovely that one must look towards it, backwards, only
backwards, where there is peace and beauty and no more dissonance.*
Against this double sense of the past the great looming present is
*England, the great mass of London, and the black, fuming, laborious
Midlands* — those Midlands of Lawrence's glory and misery. The
choice between Italy and England is not easy, obviously, but Lawrence
does not hesitate, in this instance, to choose England. We note, then,
that Lawrence still exhibits some of the hopefulness of *The Rainbow*'s
ending: *It is better to go forward into error than to stay fixed inextric-
ably in the past* — or to put it another way, to lapse back into the past.
If England survives the war she may after all put to use what the
TI, 54   industrial revolution has brought, the *vast masses of rough-hewn
knowledge.* Out of this, England may yet be able to raise up *a great
structure of truth.*

What this structure may be Lawrence does not say. Obviously
he had no clear idea of it. It was not to play any outstanding role in
his wartime thinking, in any case, although similar hopes did reappear
from time to time throughout his life. The significant point, at the
moment, is that hints now appear in the text which modify to some
degree the scheme of creative directions Lawrence had envisaged into
the future. The traveler has gone south to reconstitute his life, but his
dreams cannot be said to have materialized in Italy. The emperors, we
are reminded, always took their way back to Germany with what they
had gained in spirit from a sojourn in Italy. The traveler envisions a
similar construct of experience: escape, release, and return, as though
by prolonged contact with the South the North may learn that its
greatest resources for renewal lie within its own spirit. As we will see,
however, this theme is not pursued to any great extent. What is pursued is the idea that Italy, like the rest of Europe, is suffering through
the latter stages of a dying culture, and must itself be left behind when
the soul turns to face the west, the most creative of all directions later
in the book.

"The Theatre" continues to explore the duality of spirit in Europe.
A perfect case study of being versus not-being and flesh versus spirit
has presented itself in an Italian playing the role of Hamlet. To a point
TI, 69   the part suits him, for to Lawrence *the whole drama* of *Hamlet* is a
convulsed reaction of the mind from the flesh. A loathing of the body
has begun to assert itself in the modern Italian, as he rebels against the
old bondage of phallicism, and the actor is caught up in this revolt. He
worships the Northern way while still in subjection to the Southern way.
TI, 74   Consequently, he can only be *a maudlin compromise* between the two.
Representative of a neuter zone, another twilight in the Italian char-

acter, *he is as equivocal as the monks*. Lawrence's estimate of Shakespeare's play has not changed in any important respect since the first version of this sketch, but his opinion of the actor's character has: he was formerly just *a decent Italian* trying to contort himself into Hamlet's disembodied travesty of life. Surely Lawrence is guilty here of reconstructing the example to fit his theme, though the distortion may have been unconscious, so intent was he on making his point convincing. At all events, the theme derives principally from discussion of the play itself, not the performance.   ER, 229

Hamlet is the pivot, as Lawrence has it, of the great upheaval in the European character at the Renaissance: the movement to put down the Flesh, the Father, the Self, and set up in its place the Spirit, the Christ-like Son, the Not-Self. The Father and King must die, at the instigation of the Mother, we find, if we look into the murder of Hamlet's father. Whatever application this theory may have to a general understanding of the play, it is of prime significance to characterizing Lawrence at this pass. No breath of such an opinion occurs in the first version of the sketch. In *Twilight in Italy* it comes as an unmistakable sign of Lawrence's suspicion that he may be in danger of cancelling out his male being by allowing too much scope to female influence. This theme assumes an importance above any other as the book progresses, arriving at escape and migration as a means to founding a new order of manhood. In this endeavor Italy ceases to be the land to seek and becomes the land to flee. Not only the dead hand of the mother holds the writhing soul captive now, but the hand of all women. The shape of America looms far away as the great goal of masculine self-sufficiency. Through the grip of marriage and child worship the women have set up their rule in Italy, refusing the male spirit a natural growth. By definition the male is *the soul that goes forth and builds up a new*   TI, 60
world out of the void. Denied their proper function at home, the men of Italy often sail to America to work for several years: *It is the pro-*   TI, 59
found desire to rehabilitate themselves, to recover some dignity as men, . . . as creators from the spirit.

If nothing of this is visible in the initial form of the sketch, Lawrence may have begun to sense it during his budding interest in the Italian Futurists. At least, by the time he wrote *Le Gai Savaire* he made this point of the male spirit rising in rebellion against the reigning female spirit of Italy. He there interprets a piece of Futurist sculpture by Boccioni, *Development of a Bottle Through Space,* as an attempt to withdraw from the embrace that has locked in the Italian male for so long. But still Lawrence finds in the mechanical abstraction of the Futurists an equal and confusing insistence on the centripetal female as against the centrifugal male. Boccioni, then, got no further than the twilight zone where most of the Italians of *Twilight in Italy* stand suspended.

But against this moral twilight of Italy Lawrence again and again holds up the magic light of the Lake Garda landscape. Looking back now on the spring of 1913, when he and Frieda went up the lakeshore to the clifftop farm of San Gaudenzio to stay for a few days, he is car-
TI, 81   ried away into a visionary prose where the flowers *are little living myths* and *the cypress trees poise like flames of forgotten darkness.* Also, the family with whom he became acquainted at San Gaudenzio offered him in further form the contrasts that occupied most of his thinking about Italy. Paolo Fiori was like the old spinning woman, blue-eyed, belonging to the mountains and to space, and as if by natural association he believed in an aristocratic world. His wife, Maria, was a dark native of the plain. She believed in no social distinction except that imposed by democracy: money. Lawrence was on Paolo's side, of course, even though the actual facts of social structure might be sacrilege before Paolo's purity of spirit. But of equal significance with this betrayed sense of aristocratic order, indeed inseparable from it, was this living example of marriage between light and dark, another relation of opposites such as informs the book from the start.

Paolo and Maria had suffered a strong friction in the early stages
TI, 85   of marriage, he could see that. Her passion *was the primitive, crude, violent flux of the blood, emotional and undiscriminating. . . . His was the hard, clear, invulnerable passion of the bones, finely tempered and unchangeable.* In the long run they have attained a state now and
TI,   then touching physical fulfillment: *Their souls were silent and detached,*
84–85   *completely apart, and silent, quite silent. They shared the physical relationship of marriage as if it were something beyond them, a third*
TI, 92   *thing.* But on the negative side, *instead of having united with each other, they had made each other more terribly distinct and separate.* In a moment of perfect fusion they begot the older son, Giovanni. Then followed a son of their withdrawn opposition, Marco. Just after the birth of the latter, Paolo went to America to work for five years. The bearing of this departure and return on their whole situation comes to be the central thread of the sketch.

Paolo went to America for money to pay off the mortgage on San Gaudenzio, which in his soul he never left for an instant. His was no quest for revitalization but one to maintain the circumstances in which his permanent being was rooted. Maria, like the women early in *The Rainbow* and Mrs. Morel, wanted to see her sons rise above this peasant life. So she had admitted the necessity of Paolo's going to America. Yet she felt abandoned, and according to talk misbehaved in his absence. Since his return they have lived together in negative mutual acceptance, with no more than an occasional glimmer of consummation. What stands out in Lawrence's conclusions is that while the voyage to America has saved the ground on which the finished spirit of Paolo ought to flourish, he has in fact died at the quick and his voice is like a voice from the past. It is not only that his individual past has perished and the coalescence of opposites between him and Maria has failed, the ancient aristocratic system into which he was born has collapsed also. In that order the male was the *doer, the instrument of* TI, 89 *God,* and the simple Paolo might then have had his being and purpose in *a man of further vision,* an aristocrat of the sort to whom he longs to owe fealty. Maria's adherence to the ethic of a money society contributes much, naturally, to the annulment of Paolo's ideal. Their situation brings us at length to something near Lawrence's conclusions at the end of "The Lemon Gardens": *The old order, the order of Paolo* TI, 94 *and of Pietro di Paoli . . . was passing away from the beautiful little territory* of San Gaudenzio. It all seems in the distant past now, for the war has made abnormally long the few years since the traveler used to sit and write in the deserted lemon garden of San Gaudenzio, a spot now as silent as Pompeii, suspended in the regret of the past, with the writer's own past overlapping that of Italy.

But again we must recognize that Lawrence is inconsistent. The old aristocratic order of the *padrone* and the peasant did not appear so masculine in previous analysis. In fact, with its devotion to the immortality of the flesh through passion and offspring, with the consequent opportunity for women to dominate, Italian life was portrayed as just the opposite. As with all the symbology, if we are to be satisfied at all it cannot be by isolation of any rational argument. It must be with whatever insights unfold in spite of a confusing welter of symbols.

So an uncertain future overshadows San Gaudenzio, along with the rest of Italy. Like the *padrone,* the Fiori sons will insist on adopting the industrial economy that England has already found false. Yet the traveler still condones that goal, still allowing for a future that may after all exceed the short-sightedness of a money-technology society. At least such is implied by the departure of Giovanni, the child of an instant of fusion between parents, for America, an alternative recalling Lawrence's earlier assertion that it is better to go ahead in half-envisioned hope than cling to a dying past. The traveler cannot forget how, when he left Lake Garda, he and Giovanni said good-bye to one another. It was as if Giovanni were imploring him for a soul. But Giovanni will put up a good fight for that soul himself, in America or back in Italy — if only the war does not destroy him.

The next segment, "The Dance," concentrates on a specific aspect of the contrast between northern and southern Europe: the sensuality innate to the Italians bursting into physical activity. In a dance two English women visiting at San Gaudenzio are drawn into a passionate swirl where the woman is like a boat lifted over the powerful exquisite waves of the man. Both peasants and middle-class Italians are dancing, but the lustiness of the peasant men most dazzles the women. At one time when the dance stops, the men sing bawdy songs TI, 101   with a *malicious, suggestive mockery* that penetrates the understanding of the women, however foreign the language. But Maria Fiori at length stops the singing, and the dancing resumes. But by now the English women have recovered their reserve and do not surrender to the surging of the dance as before.

While "The Dance" conforms to the overall thematic structure of *Twilight in Italy,* and may anticipate something of Birkin's satyr-like dance in *Women in Love,* the sketch is too limited in scope to add significantly to the evolution of the book as a whole.

The sketch "Il Duro" is another matter. A detailed appraisal of the man called by this name returns us to the identity quest by comparison and contrast delineated earlier in the book, to revelation that comes from matching the selfhood in the traveler with that of a foreigner.

Il Duro has been to America, has gone abroad like the traveler-narrator, and has remained unchanged by his experience just as Paolo has. But his was no quest paralleling that of either Lawrence or Giovanni Fiori. Il Duro came home with what is locally considered a for-TI, 104   tune. He lives alone, his exceptional good looks tinged by *the slightly malignant, suffering look of a satyr,* and pursues a life of amorous sensation. He is a creature comparable to the Bavarian peasants of the crucifix sketch in having gone to the limit of the senses and become TI, 107   *too complete, too final, too defined.* That which endows the Bavarian peasant with a talent for religious mummery binds Il Duro directly to TI, 108   the earth in the art of vine-grafting, at which he works *like some strange animal god, doubled on his haunches, before the young vines, . . . grafting the life of man upon the body of the earth.*

Lawrence now devises a set of relationships between himself and Il Duro of the kind he has previously experimented with in travel prose: a mixture of envy, admiration, distaste and final disclaimer of any vital analogy between the character of the other and his own — a disclaimer to be taken nevertheless with reservations. Il Duro has much that Lawrence wishes for. He is not mental but physical, and his physicality differs from that which Lawrence has condemned in other Italians in that, for one thing, Il Duro has learned the secret of being alone, to the degree of refusing any permanent communion with a woman. It is a condition Lawrence cannot help craving. From this point on in *Twilight in Italy,* this so far subdued wish of the lover — to know the secret of isolate and independent integrity — steadily gains ground against the much-pondered yearning for equilibrium with the mate. We observe a hesitant but inescapable identification with Il Duro the outsider, first as sympathy with a man who has placed himself beyond the ken of Italian "immortality" in woman-child adulation, but equally because of the process by which Il Duro effected his liberation. He did not acquire his new frame of being in America, as such, but he discovered there the means of keeping himself economically free to follow his own bent. He is to be envied, therefore, for having traveled far and wide and profited greatly from it in fostering the kind of truth that serves him well.

Yet while he fascinates he also repels, and in describing the negative side of the matter Lawrence appears to realize that he is close to betraying a dearly held conviction, for it is precisely in Il Duro's repudiation of marriage — again a sudden discovery to the traveler — that he notes the distinction in kind between himself and Il Duro. The familiar Laurentian concept of marriage is repeated: true wedding takes place in the spirit beyond the flesh, where marital conjoining gives rise to *an absolute, a Word,* a sort of Holy Ghost. But for Il Duro, one   TI, 109 of *the ministers of Pan,* sensation itself is absolute. And while he seems attracted to Lawrence, in homage to a finer spirit, Lawrence asserts that he cannot return the feeling. He takes the same way out of involving himself too deeply in a strange nature that he took in his flight up to San Tommaso from the lakeside alleys of Gargnano. He momentarily identifies himself with light: *There was nothing between us except our complete difference. It was like night and day flowing together.* Obviously the statement is far too pat, but what Lawrence implies is that no rewarding twilight comes of this juxtaposition. Still he brings forth an image of Il Duro that reveals just how much he himself did incorporate of darkness, how much the pure isolation of the satyr-like creature does appeal to him. It is an image announcing similar images in *The Lost Girl: I can always see him crouched before the vines on his haunches, . . . his face seeming in its strange golden pallor and its hardness of line, with the gleaming black of the fine hair on the brow and temples, like something reflective, like the reflecting surface of a stone that gleams out of the depths of night. It was like darkness revealed in its steady, unchanging pallor.*

This passage brings out, as nearly formed as such a feeling can be, an obscure and yet potent motive behind the writing of *Twilight in Italy.* This is the imperative to create in language a self occupying two points in time. In the fluidity of the present the traveler is highly sensitized to himself as remembering. Then there is what he remembers as having absorbed into the self, concretely realized in Il Duro, a contradictory incarnation half accepted and half rejected. This image from the magical past flows into the present from the twilight zone of a country visited as a seeker and remains with the seeker as a moment's experience of great value in the molding of the future self.

The last individual in whom Lawrence chooses to embody his preoccupations in this section of *Twilight in Italy* is John — a Giovanni whose Americanized name has come home with him to Italy. A three-way contrast between him and Paolo and Il Duro at times serves to accentuate his character. But he has self-completeness too, and when all points are set forth he is the man most like the traveler himself.

TI, 116   While Paolo and Il Duro *had passed through the foreign world and been quite untouched,* . . . [John] *had come more into contact with his new surroundings,* had learned English well and become considerably involved in American life. His projected future has an intimate connection with Lawrence's too. John has come home, fulfilled his military obligation, married, and fathered a child. He is as well prepared financially to stay in Italy as Il Duro is. And yet he has a longing to return to America that amounts to obsession. Lawrence's perception of John's

TI, 117   motives is full of implied comparison-contrast with his own. A *pure elemental flame* in John's soul has sustained him in going out to face the world. On the other hand, he cannot conceive of what the traveler

TI, 115   feels a male must build: *a coherent purposive life.* In spite of John's compulsion to go, to stay or go does not appear to be a moral choice: *Either one stayed in the village, like a lodged stone, or one made random excursions into the world. . . . It was all aimless and purposeless.*

But Lawrence does after all turn John into a figure of destiny. All these Italian men, in their flight from woman's oppression, represent a wave of the future. A near approach to identifying with his subject now prompts Lawrence to use language anticipating that of the Ameri-

TI, 118   can literature essay "The Spirit of Place": *There was a strange, almost frightening destiny upon him, which seemed to take him away, always away from home, from the past, to that great, raw America. He seemed scarcely like a person with individual choice, more like a creature under the influence of fate which was disintegrating the old life and precipitating him, a fragment inconclusive, into the new chaos.* Lawrence was in one of his alternating periods of planning to migrate to America when he wrote this sketch, so the note of self-projection is not surprising. It is particularly clear in the valedictory image of John

TI, 119   that closes the sketch: *His father was the continent behind him; his wife and child the foreshore of the past; but his face was set outwards, away from it all — whither, neither he nor anybody knew, but he called it America.*

The two final sketches of *Twilight in Italy,* "Italians in Exile" and "The Return Journey," are characterized by the recurrence of moments suspended in time, moments again of instantaneous discovery, and here marked by a now blissful and now painful awareness of places: strange places that still convey a sense of deep familiarity. The mood established is sometimes elegiac, sometimes frightened, sometimes bored. Because these two sketches grew out of Lawrence's journey across Switzerland in September 1913, largely on foot and alone, the air of pilgrimage is much in evidence, and much strengthened by having receded now into the past. A world under sentence of doom lies behind. The traveler forges ahead uneasily, as if pursued, on his "return" to Italy. On the mundane level, this was Lawrence's return for a second stay in that country. Woven into the creative direction theme are many vague but never realized hopes of a better world ahead.

Without transition from the San Gaudenzio portion of the book, the traveler is suddenly on his way from Konstanz to Schaffhausen by steamer, from the western end of Lake Constance into the Rhine. The new scenes around him, the quaint villages and the natural beauty, fill him with an overwhelming *poignancy of the past.* All that takes place TI, 123 near him seems fraught with symbolic import, even to the fighting of two rooks and a hawk in the sky, which is like some omen from a classical legend. From Schaffhausen the traveler sets off to the south, in that area of twisting borders crossing a bit of Germany again, and then coming at sunset to Eglisau, Switzerland, a *village of tall, quaint houses* TI, 124 *flickering its lights on to the deep-flowing river.* So much in quest of the mysterious is the traveler that in this village, trying the extent of his German on the landlady of The Golden Stag, he pretends to be *a* TI, 126 *sort of romantic, wandering character,* and maintains this happy fiction in his own mind as he goes to sleep that night, *listening to the running* TI, 127 *and whispering of the mediæval Rhine.*[3]

Seldom do we find Lawrence so much the carefree traveler excited mainly by the "romantic" and "picturesque." That he is alone, a wandering male untroubled by the toils of women, undoubtedly contributes to this lightness of mood. However, he does not lose contact with what is remote and mysterious. And given the unfailing contradiction in which Lawrence's imagination always revolved, we should remind ourselves that this walk took place at a period when he was most hopeful and joyful concerning his love affair: he was on his way to Italy in full possession of the triumph of *Sons and Lovers* and of having won what seemed a rebirth in love that Italy had bestowed upon him during his first sojourn there. He was anticipating what truly became the best of his Italian days, those at Fiascherino. But all this was memory when he wrote the sketch, and thereby a new dimension is added to the journey. He knew full well, by now, that the journey had brought

EGLISAU, SWITZERLAND

*Down here was a small, forgotten, wonderful world
that belonged to the date of isolated village communities
and wandering minstrels.* (TI, 124)

only a modicum of the promised rewards, even though he plainly felt it to be a model of experience for building a really victorious future.

While the romantic wanderer filled with a poignant nostalgia never fades altogether, other masks before long pre-empt it. One is the already familiar role of the traveler as fugitive from the settled average. The further he goes into Switzerland the more the deadness of the country strikes him, especially in the cities: Zurich, for instance, where he pauses for only two hours before resuming his trip. He travels on driven by the dissatisfaction that dogs him all the way: *That is how I always feel in Switzerland: the only possible living sensation is the sensation of relief in going away, always going away* — going away to the South, to be sure, to Italy.　　TI, 128

Then a group of Italians, silk-factory workers "in exile" in Switzerland, enter to relieve this dejection. He first comes across them in an inn in either Kilchberg or Langnau, where he stopped for a night on the road. Their warm talk at a nearby table lights *a bonfire of life in the callousness* of Swiss materialism. When a number of these Italians collect in a room of the inn to rehearse a play, he goes to join them and accomplishes a momentary escape from Switzerland by entering into a sort of make-believe, much aided by the atmosphere of the melodrama the Italians are rehearsing. He enters into *a tiny, pathetic magicland far away from the barrenness of Switzerland*. Much more comes out, however, than the sensual warmth of the south as contrasted with the spiritual coldness of the north. Here is a body of Italians engaged in a quest, like those of the Garda region who go to America. And again they represent in one sense a parallel, in another a divergence, in relation to the quest of the traveler himself: a much clearer association than ever, since these men have forsaken the southern country to which the wanderer is returning in his own search. We have already assumed that to the wartime Lawrence Italy could no longer have represented a land of rebirth but was rather the regretted past of great hopes disappointed. The former self on which the traveler looks is a forerunner, however, of that self who still entertains hopes in a changed form, and by this dual stance the text is imbued with poignancy.　　TI, 130 ... TI, 133

The extent of Lawrence's affinity with the group varies. He responds strongly to the knowledge that they are thrown together by a common destiny and that they acknowledge the leadership of Giuseppino, the most perceptive of their number. He reiterates the theme of how the modern Italian is breaking away from the old sensuous past to lay hold of a spiritual future, just when northern Europe is bent on reversing the process, the first and destructive stage being the war. In a sense these Italians afford the best opportunity yet to observe the experiment of so many of their countrymen in surpassing the old form of life: the environment is like America in that Switzerland is an industrial country with a northern European ethic.

The purposes of this company of exiles come clear when the traveler challenges them with the question of ever returning to Italy themselves. Their reply is affirmative but deluded. Yes, one day they will go home. But the traveler knows they never will, and he can sympathize TI, 136 with their positive-negative conflicts, for these are like his own: *They laughed with the slight pain and contempt and fondness which every man feels towards his past, when he has struggled away from that past.* They have lighted the flame of the spirit and muted that of the flesh, and Giuseppino will lead them on the new path.

But the wayfarer cannot trust the reforming spirit that infuses them, not when he finds out more of its nature from Giuseppino. This is an anarchist group, he learns, and his response to the naïve idea of living without a government is full of fear tempered by fascination, informative of the motive forces inside Lawrence in late 1915. He per-
TI, 138 ceives the new spirit in Giuseppino as *something strange and pure and slightly frightening.* He feels guilty as well, his soul *somewhere in tears* that he cannot grant Giuseppino the verification of his utopian theories. When he finally parts company with the group, they give him literature of their movement and seem to look upon him, Giuseppino with
TI, 139 the rest, with some *implicit belief . . . as representative of some further knowledge.* These mixed emotions have only strengthened with time. Lawrence is still strangely torn between their trust in him and his inability to accept a higher leadership and thereby affirm their faith in anarchist society. It is not a mere political question. Lawrence indeed had almost ceased to believe in political solutions when he wrote *Twilight in Italy.* The question concerns the psychological future of mankind. We recollect the statement earlier on, that it is better to push ahead in error than clutch at a dying past. In their fashion the anarchists are doing just this. They have in a sense formed the nucleus of a Rananim. Their society would base itself on the assumption of goodness in man, not evil: Lawrence's own assumption early in 1915, and though often repeated much weakened by now, except for a brief recrudescence in the "Crown" essays. When Lawrence was putting the finishing touches on *Twilight in Italy* in late 1915 and early 1916, his own plans for a new society and the basis of those plans were beginning to look, no doubt, as naïve as those of the Italian anarchists in Switzerland. Maybe he harbored a guilt, too, at not having realized a rosy future through united action. Nor had he recovered, either, from his anger over the "betrayal" by Russell and Lady Ottoline and others, Frieda included, who refused to embrace his utopian schemes. Most significant of all,

he had failed to convince himself. And what comes out at the close of "Italians in Exile" as commitment to any ideal is what has already in effect replaced any vision of corporate action toward a better future. The attitude of the wanderer to the Italian anarchists is a subconscious rejection of Rananim. It is by now firmly fixed that the future lies in travel dominated by personal concerns nonetheless conceived as universal. The alternative modes of life are not belonging to a group or remaining aloof: they are a choice between absolute aloneness and the relative isolation of making a better life with the beloved. For the time being — and this rounds out the whole thematic compass of the book — the decision is in favor of individual separateness, and of the momentaneity that goes with it. When the anarchists press the traveler too closely to join with them in spirit, he flees from any promise of commitment to an outward trajectory of the soul: *I wanted to arrest my activity, to keep it confined to the moment, to the adventure.* When he is ready to leave the village next morning, though it means traveling through the stiffness and morality of a Swiss Sunday — altogether too much like an English Sunday — he cannot bring himself to a further goodbye to the Italians. He clings to one purpose, that of simple on-going, *thanking God for the blessing of a road that belongs to no man,* TI, 141 *and travels away from all men.*

To open the last section, "The Return Journey," Lawrence augments his vagabond mood by a historical enlargement that betrays how much his spirit was America-bound beyond Italy. He would soon be taking refuge in Cornwall, the westward edge of a crumbling Europe. South for the moment was in danger of being overridden by West: *When one walks, one must travel west or south. If one turns northward* TI, 145 *or eastward it is like walking down a **cul-de-sac**, to the blind end.*

So it has been since the Crusaders came home satiated, and the Renaissance saw the western sky as an archway into the future. So it is still. We must go westwards and southwards.

It is a sad and gloomy thing to travel even from Italy into France. But it is a joyful thing to walk south to Italy, south and west. It is so. And there is a certain exaltation in the thought of going west, even to Cornwall, to Ireland. It is as if the magnetic poles were south-west and north-east, for our spirits, with the south-west, under the sunset, as the positive pole. So whilst I walk through Switzerland, though it is a valley of gloom and depression, a light seems to flash out under every footstep, with the joy of progression.

The Switzerland through which the pilgrim to a better land is traveling recalls this morning a fantasy of last night, when the sight of the Italians was like a look into a bewitching domain under the surface of the everyday world. Looking down on the Swiss landscape from a height, the traveler sees it as a weird sort of *relief-map* which *seemed to intervene between me and some reality. I could not believe that that was the real world.*

One way of coping with this unreal landscape is to take up again the romantic masquerade of the first day in Switzerland, but now the role played suggests much more than romantic escapism. In one lakeside village, Lawrence enters a little teashop kept in their residence by two fluttery old ladies. They ask him if he is Austrian, and he instantly

TI, 147   enters into the spirit of the question: *I said I was from Graz; that my father was a doctor in Graz, and that I was walking for my pleasure through the countries of Europe.*

I said this because I knew a doctor from Graz who was always wandering about, and because I did not want to be myself, an English-
RS, 60   *man, to these two old ladies. I wanted to be something else.* When one realizes that Lawrence here has in mind Otto Gross, an apostle of eroticism, a former lover of Frieda's and the first one to offer her liberation from her provincial marriage, a new vista opens into Lawrence's psychological make-up. The identification may, of course, have been hardly more than a convenient coincidence of circumstances. But without the risk of reading too much into the association, we may say that it probably goes this far: Gross was a wanderer of the same cast as Lawrence, many of his ideas Lawrence had had the opportunity of considering through Frieda, and Lawrence may have felt a certain triumph in putting those ideas into practice by winning Frieda over to a wandering life where Otto Gross had failed. However, Lawrence did not carry the masquerade into any moments of great importance. All he did under his disguise as the son of Otto Gross was to exchange some commonplace talk with the two old ladies, and shed a few half-sincere tears — or so he says — over the death of their sister.

And then he went on his way again, feeling he had made a close if ephemeral friendship with the two women. This attitude toward chance acquaintances of the road holds throughout this section, and always it provides the traveler with some advantage in his resolution of escape and search. He meets a young Frenchman about to go to Algiers for his military service. Immediately Lawrence feels the call of Africa, and makes such extensive plans to visit his new friend in faraway Algiers that it comes to seem more real than the Switzerland where they sit on a mountainside and talk. And then comes an evening passed at an inn with a young Englishman, when the contrast in spirit between the two travelers brings into question the demands made on the individual by the modern world and the alternatives of acquiescence or revolt. This young man, caught up in the machine of London business all year, is on a two-week vacation during which he has flung himself into travel, walking and walking, having covered over a hundred miles of Switzerland in the four days just previous to the meeting. He is exhausted in body but his will drives him on at this frantic pace. Our traveler is appalled at his grinding determination, yet is ready to admire his courage while he pities his plight. But he places himself at the opposite pole from his fellow-countryman, who is also soon to be on a "return journey," not, like Lawrence, to a country where liberty invites, but to the crushing round of the English metropolis. *All he had* TI, 151 *courage for was to go back.* So that Lawrence is not long in beginning to detest his doggedness: his courage is a sort of cowardice, after all, a submission to being trodden on. With this thought, Lawrence sets off next morning in the opposite direction from his trapped countryman.

Now comes the stage of the journey when the wayfarer climbs to the highest point of his walk, up over the Gotthard Pass, stopping to spend the night at Hospenthal, and then descending through Italian Switzerland toward his immediate destination, Milan. All through these two days and one night a heightened sense of reality permeates the narrative, as though a kind of death and rebirth were really taking place. Once again, climbing toward the snowy peaks, the traveler is conscious of *the very quick of cold death* that reigns above, imposing TI, 153 again that contrast between warm life and cold non-life that so affects the Bavarian peasant. Only now the constant companionship of death in the overhanging threat of the peaks does not rouse the inhabitants to expression. It leaves them dark in spirit, *almost sordid, brutal.* However, their degradation may be due to commercialism and tourism, for the *parasitism* of hotels and foreigners has sapped away much of the native spirit of place. At any rate, what this passage most reflects is Lawrence's dislike of nearly everything Swiss. When the mountain defiles broaden now and again and he might feel happier, the blight of the industrial age offends his eyes in some ugly factory or quarry encroaching on the world of nature. The sense of unreality increases with the rarity of the atmosphere. At his meal in the evening, in a little hut-like house where he finds lodging, he might be severed from the whole world. He sinks into uneasy self-questioning as to why he should be up here, anyhow, on the ridge of the universe. Yet, underneath, a certain content soothes his troubling in that he is detached from any given place and any personal entanglement whatever. All Europe seems to withdraw into another reality with which he has nothing to do: *I was* TI, 157 *free, in this heavy, ice-cold air, this upper world, alone. . . . It was a sort of grief that this continent all beneath was so unreal, false,*

HOSPENTHAL, SWITZERLAND

The little village with the broken castle
that stands forever frozen at the point where the track parts (TI, 155)

non-existent in its activity. Out of the silence one looked down on it,
and it seemed to have lost all importance, all significance. It was so big,
yet it had no significance: what could one do but wander about?

This is a key passage for confirmation that *Twilight in Italy* is
primarily concerned with the growth of a free male spirit. It finds
Lawrence, during the first journey he ever made alone, on the threshold of complete escape into a new self. He achieves for a moment an
Olympian superiority to the whole man-made world. He is the wayfarer
personified, with no allegiance except to the road itself. Geographically
as well as spiritually, he stands at one of the furthest possible points
from contact with civilization in the mass. The setting is of considerable importance to the theme, because mountains figure as they have
from the start: as the borderline between the lower world and the
world beyond. They may be to the alpine peasant the frigid non-being
of eternity horrible to the flesh. Conversely, they are the region that
receives the Twilight of the Holy Ghost above the monks strolling in
the garden. In a like capacity they are now the region of final break-
away from the past and over the border to male independence and
integrity.

Leaving Hospenthal next morning, the traveler falls in with another companion of the road, a youth from Basel who reminds him
somewhat of the English clerk, for he too has pressured plans for a
long ramble, except that this youth, Emil, is a seasoned hiker. Together
the two men go over the crest of the Gotthard Pass, *crossing in silence* TI, 159
from the northern world to the southern. The mood of the traveler is
suddenly gladness. It is wonderful to go down the slopes *so sunny,* TI, 162
with feathery trees and deep black shadows, through a country that
looks as though *Pan really had his home* here. The lure of Italy is TI, 163
fragmenting the gloom of Switzerland.

Again the traveler parts company with one who must drag himself
back north, and this time he feels worse about it, for unlike the English
clerk, Emil truly has the venturing spirit.

Unhappily, the rebirth so much hinted at before, and now brought
to pass, is a disappointment. But this turn of events is most truly in
keeping with the dominant tone of disillusion and the need to escape
even from Italy, whether it be the Italian men fleeing the country or
the traveler with his glimpse of analogous freedom in the heights. The
concluding disappointment first comes along the roads of Italian Switzerland, where *great blind cubes of dwellings rise stark from the de-* TI, 164
stroyed earth, destroyed, that is to say, by the suburbs creeping over
the country. Instead of avenues to adventure such as the traveler longs
for, these roads are the diseased veins of modern industry. All this is
part and parcel of the *sordidness* that has now entered into Italian life,

HOSPENTHAL, SWITZERLAND

Here, away from the world,
the villages were quiet and obscure — left behind (TI, 152)

much of it just since the traveler's first visit to Italy. This reaction is typical of Lawrence. A place that thrilled him the first time and retained its bright hues in retrospect nearly always failed on being revisited to live up to expectations.

Although Lawrence's journey led him eventually to the happy time in Fiascherino, he chose to end *Twilight in Italy* in Milan, the industrial center of Italy, and on a low note admitting of no rebirth for Italy, or the self in Italy. In describing Milan, Lawrence could easily set forth the things incorporating his repudiation of the current world. Around the cathedral with its *glow of the great past,* life still seemed vivid, TI, 168 but it was only a vigorous *process of disintegration.* Here as everywhere else *was the same purpose stinking in it all, the mechanising, the perfect mechanising of human life.*

A few days after finishing the proofs of *Twilight in Italy,* Lawrence wrote Cynthia Asquith that the message of his travel book was the same as that of *The Rainbow:* that the old world was *toppling* and a ML, 422 new one must be made to rise out of the debris. He went on to say that Cornwall, where he was, was like the beginning of that world, with Europe now hardly more than a memory. But he was already looking much further off than Italy, wishing he *could go on a long voyage, into* ML, 423 *the South Pacific.* Admitting as he did periodically that he was frightened by America, he would pass the western continent by and sail on to the very ultimate of southern climes. But soon enough he would begin to amalgamate the South of Melville's Pacific with the West of Cooper's American wilderness.

NOTES

[1] Lawrence's plans and frustrations in relation to Rananim are taken up in even-handed detail in DN. The evidence offered in that book still seems to me to point to the self-defeating nature of all Lawrence's utopian schemes. When the showdown came, whatever the emphatic verbal commitment, Lawrence always chose the independent search for a new life — always including Frieda — over group action.

[2] *Compare* HL, 96; PH, 454 & 467; PX, 396.

[3] Armin Arnold has closely traced this walk of Lawrence's through Switzerland. *See Texas Studies in Language and Literature,* vol. 3, no. 2, Summer 1961, pp. 184–188.

7

The Quest of Rupert's Blessed Isles

Late in July 1915, with finances improved by an advance on *The Rainbow,* the Lawrences had left the cottage in Sussex lent by the Meynell family and were soon established in a flat in Hampstead. This move to the vicinity of London had meant to Lawrence going *back into the world to fight,* which turned out to be largely an offensive by the printed word: *The Rainbow,* the *Signature* essays, *Twilight in Italy.* But the latter, as we have seen, was already a resolve to carry the battle with the world to other latitudes. It was not long before Lawrence was talking seriously of going to America. After giving up on *The Signature,* he went so far as to start recruiting for a Rananim in Florida. Something might have come of this, at least the Lawrences themselves had already arranged passage, if the banning of *The Rainbow* in early November had not caused him to put off sailing to fight the suppression. Resistance unfortunately never amounted to much, due partly to the failure of supporters to rally and partly to Lawrence's own recurrent half-heartedness in the matter, not to mention the complete and abject surrender of his publisher. Other complications followed, all of which added up to indefinite delay. Having already given up their Hampstead apartment in preparation for leaving the country, the Lawrences went instead to Cornwall in December, first to a borrowed cottage in Porthcothan, then in March to one they rented in Zennor.

Save for a few reconsiderations in proof, *Twilight in Italy* was now behind Lawrence, as was the sputter of *The Signature* and most of the tempestuous controversy with Lady Ottoline and Russell. Once more he and Frieda were in a remote spot, and the hope still glowed that they might conquer the realm of mutual peace and love. But this was not all that Cornwall sparked. In brief flare-ups of zeal Lawrence continued to feel that he might unite his first program for a new life with

ML, 357

DN,
167–176

his communal ambitions, that in the West Country he might hope to save a corner of his native island, that here Rananim might flourish. *When I looked down at Zennor, I knew it was the Promised Land, and* ML, 436 *that a new heaven and a new earth would take place.* He wrote this in an outburst of millennial ardor to John Middleton Murry and Katherine Mansfield, and soon succeeded in coaxing them to come and take a nearby cottage as the first members of the new society. *I have crossed* ML, 437 *the ridge,* he cried, *the new world lies before us.* Attempts were made to charm others to the incipient colony, but as always the scheme collapsed, with even the Murrys moving to another part of Cornwall after much friction with their utopian leader. Anyway, the impulse simply to be with Frieda was always stronger in Lawrence than the opposite one to surround himself with followers: *We are going to do all our* ML, *own work. I am going to cover the spring on the hillside, and clean it,* 443–444 *and we can live so cheaply and I love it. The situation is perfect, with a moor-slope coming down to the back door, and the sea beyond in the front.*

It isn't scenery one lives by, but the freedom of moving about alone.

It was almost a reflex, by now, for a heady perception of liberty to spring from first exposure to new surroundings.

For much of the time during the coming months in Cornwall, Lawrence was busy still with writing and rewriting his symbology. But what absorbed most of his attention during 1916 was one of his most esteemed pieces of fiction, *Women in Love.* Of the many elements of Lawrence's thought incorporated into this magnificent novel, among the most significant are those of time, place and pilgrimage working as undercurrents to the presentation of human character and the whole of the human condition.

When Lawrence made up his mind to begin another novel, feeling well enough after bouts with colds and much gloom, he first thought of continuing with *The Lost Girl,* the manuscript of which he had left in Germany but hoped to recover in spite of the state of hostilities. When he found he could not, and hence could not go on with what was probably an Italian quest, he turned his hand to *the second half of The* ML, 449 *Rainbow,* which almost at once went far beyond being a sequel. *The Rainbow* had envisaged a promised land in England. *Women in Love* could not envisage one anywhere. It could, however, make of flight to the mountains of a strange country a preparatory act essential to the founding of any redeemed society. This geographical break with the past and the theme of wayfaring beyond the British Isles is slowly prepared for in the earlier parts of the novel. Once the action begins to draw us in that direction, it builds up to an almost intolerably vivid experience with place and time. All the resolutions that Lawrence was able to bring to the intricacies of this novel come, at last, through the relationship of the seekers with place and movement seen as inseparable from their relationship with each other.

One of the earliest distinctions made between the two sisters of the novel, Ursula and Gudrun Brangwen, has to do with traits brought out in each by place and travel. Ursula has been a stay-at-home. Gudrun has traveled enough to bring her to disillusionment and to land her at home again. We may recall, incidentally, that in *The Rainbow* Ursula rejected the voyage to India as a false way out of life's dilemmas, choosing rather to suffer through the apocalyptic travail of England. Ursula is still, in the new novel, the true seeker. Though she has not budged from home, she is not passive but wears always a look of WL, 2 *sensitive expectancy,* in contrast with the disillusion and cynicism that going away has stimulated in Gudrun. Ursula, we see, will not consider a change of place unless it brings in its wake a change of soul. Gudrun has clutched at changes of place as if that action in itself would issue in a change of soul.

A similar distinction is soon apparent between the two men of the novel, Gerald Crich and Rupert Birkin. Birkin, though he has spent time abroad, has not up to this period looked upon ranging the world as a way to transformation of the self. Gerald, on the contrary, once expected just this result. In his boyhood he dreamed of spending WL, 213 *his years in wonderful Odyssey.* Later on, when he went into the wilds as an explorer, he met only with disenchantment, and like Gudrun he returned home. But he came with the ambitious delusion of creating an "ideal society" through a new kind of mechanized exploitation of the mines, a technological "revolution" at first successful but doomed not to fill the void at the core of himself and the world.

The utter nullity of life in modern England and the destructiveness of personal relationships patterned on that life are thoroughly illustrated as background to the emergence of the pilgrim theme in *Women in Love.* The crying need is for a new kind of marriage and friendship, a new way of consciousness altogether. Both men and women and all the places the narrative touches in the British Isles are caught up in this slowly revolving madness of civilization, under the impact of which the two couples, Ursula and Birkin, Gudrun and Gerald, work out their destiny of redemption or damnation. On another plane, the possible rebirth of friendship between men is equally explored. Speculation on how the world must end and what may come to pass in its stead also streams through the pages in thought and image.

The prison of Rupert Birkin's days is his liaison with Hermione WL, 11 Roddice, a tortured soul of *no natural sufficiency* who possesses him

by will alone, by a passion directed from the head, under which he
writhes but is spellbound. The growing strain between them at length
comes to a climax with Hermione attacking him in a *voluptuous ec-*   WL, 98
stasy to kill, striking him on the head with a stone paper weight. He
escapes from her, but in a half-conscious state that amounts to the
death he must go through to strive beyond the world of the old relationship. The direction of this struggle, following a consistent symbolic
scheme of motion in the book, is outward to a new kind of environment.
Birkin wanders off from his encounter in a dazed condition and enters
the woods where he becomes the first of the characters really to enter
a new world: by thrusting his naked body into the *lovely, subtle, re-*   WL, 100
sponsive vegetation, rolling in the hyacinths, covering himself with
fine moist grass, embracing a birch tree. He comes back to life, then,
in what he willingly accepts as a world of madness far preferable to
the madness of society which has always passed for sanity: a new world
of pure aloneness and remoteness that we readily recognize as Lawrence's ideal sphere. Thinking in the vein of remarks made by Lawrence himself in his Cornish seclusion, Birkin wishes *he were on an*   WL, 101
island, like Alexander Selkirk, with only the creatures and the trees,
in his own little world of gladness and freedom.[1]

    To go back a little, Ursula was present at the first warning of the
mounting storm between Birkin and Hermione and became conscious
of *a sense of richness and of liberty* in him. But the attraction evolves WL, 38
slowly. Not long after Birkin's rupture with Hermione, a real island
becomes the scene of the first true communication between Ursula
and Birkin. This island is in the pond of a mill, an out-of-the-way place
where Birkin has sought sanctuary as the first stage of a new life, intend-
ing to give up his position as school inspector and live withdrawn from
society on a modest private income. In an old boat the couple push
out to the little island, and the making of a new world of union between
man and woman in solitude is under way. Their talk centers upon
whether or not love, of humanity or of individuals, is dead as an ideal.
From this time on, grappling with the definition and significance of
love is one of the agonizing problems of the novel. Birkin here contends that love is dead, Ursula contends that it is not. He recommends
the complete annihilation of humanity and a new start, and she dis-
likes him for his violent preachiness. Challenged as to what he does
believe in if not in love, he can only answer, *in the unseen hosts,* and   WL, 121
feel foolish that he has nothing more explicit to offer. But they do
achieve *a beam of understanding,* when she can agree with him that   WL, 122
the trouble lies in the vulgarization of the word "love": though they
soon enough fall into discord over this point too. Birkin clearly per-
ceives this little island as the epitome of a world free of humanity, a

surviving place where man and woman can begin anew. But Ursula refuses this image. As she watches him absently setting daisies afloat

WL, 123   on the pond, *the brilliant little discs of the daisies veering slowly in travel on the dark, lustrous water,* she pleads that they follow the flowers to the shore, *afraid of being any longer imprisoned on the island.* Partly she fears domination by Birkin in this momentary Eden, partly she fears the new breach of consciousness to which his invitation to a new life compels her — we may interpret all this, to be sure, as a despairing admission that Lawrence's hammering out of his relation with Frieda apart from the rest of the world was not proceeding as he might wish.

Gerald Crich, the other principal male in *Women in Love,* is identified from the outset with the north, the quarter of death, and geographical analogies keep this correspondence steadily before us all through the novel. He is the fictional personification of the directional symbolism the traveler of *Twilight in Italy* imparts by other means. The first attraction between Gerald and Gudrun introduces an instinctive association with the north into the very atmosphere when

WL, 9   she asks herself: *"Am I **really** singled out for him in some way, is there really some pale gold, arctic light that envelopes only us two?"* This suspicion presages the fate toward which they are finally compelled.

All through its early stages, however, the link between Gerald and Gudrun remains unattached to any geographical locale. It is much too involuted for such expansion, their real presence being in a mental place only, in an ugly psychological isolation: as when Gerald spurs his Arabian mare until she bleeds to make her stand facing a passing locomotive, while Gudrun watches from nearby, satiating herself in

WL, 104   the sight, caught up in a sado-masochistic rapture as if by *a vision isolated in eternity.* When not carried away by such fantasies, Gudrun

WL, 112   goes about sunk in *the heavy slough of the pale, underworld* life of the colliers into which her return home has plunged her, convinced however that Gerald will be her escape from this region, though no hint comes yet that the escape will bear them to any definite place. The eventual locating of their destined climax in geographical surroundings that embody it thoroughly, the eternal mountain snows, is a development that requires long and careful preparation. The desolation in which their last struggle unfolds envelops them in a dim arctic light indeed, where the psychological and geographical isolation have at last become one and the same thing.

The loose and episodic structure of *Women in Love* may leave an impression on the unwary reader that the book runs on much like Birkin's description of a life one might well choose to lead, drifting

on in a series of accidents — like a picaresque novel. And even when   WL, 294
we recognize that each episode is laid out according to a recurring pattern, we may still fail to grasp how the action builds progressively
toward a culmination. But a rising action and a dénouement do appear,
in a thoroughly traditional sense, if we observe first what the basic
repeated construction of the episodes is, how these slowly gather momentum, how they break from a turgid and discursive course into a
swift rush turning upon the departure from a moribund England in
search of a better land on the Continent.

In the episodes alluded to so far, and in most that concern us, the
repetitive structure depends upon a tension between two conditions of
existence, the actual and the projected. The actual circumstances of
life in England are always a frightening conglomeration of failures, on
every level from that of the individual to that of society at large. The
projected circumstances are always posited in some form of escape,
largely through a new variety of instinctual personal relationships
which at length take on geographical equivalents. The sisters at the
start find life in Beldover empty and appalling, though for different
reasons, and each sees a prospect of escape through joining with one
of the two men. In the fruitless round of life at Shortlands, the family
seat of the Criches but a larger social entity as well, a travesty of escape
from the narrowness of modern society obtains in that most of the
family members subscribe to *a strange freedom, that almost amounted*   WL, 22
to anarchy. . . . It was rather a resistance to authority, than liberty.
Birkin offers in discussion what is meant to be a truer release from the
trammels of convention: *"It's the hardest thing in the world to act*   WL, 27
*spontaneously on one's impulses — and it's the only really gentlemanly
thing to do — provided you're fit to do it."* The only criterion is rightness of instinct, and this the anarchic Criches lack, as do most other
unconventional people in the novel.

Another of the proposed escapes from the stultifying life enmesh-
ing the main characters takes a form complementary to the chief quest
of the book. Rather than toward transformed relations between man
and woman, this is the opposite solution of flight from sexual involvement altogether, as well as from involvement in a degraded social system. The two sisters take this course on one occasion, in search of
distance and detachment, and through this scene we are led back to
the main theme with a greatly reinforced grasp of thematic design.
Invited to a huge, almost public lake-party at Shortlands — given every
year by Gerald's father as a paternalistic show of solidarity among all
the classes of local society — the Brangwen sisters, aghast at the whole
affair, approach Gerald with a curious request: they wish a boat so
that just the two of them may go off and picnic alone. *"Can't we go up*   WL, 153

there, and explore that coast?" Gudrun asks. *She pointed to a grove on the hillock of the meadow-side, near the shore, half-way down the lake. "That looks perfectly lovely. . . . Really, it's like one of the reaches of the Nile — as one imagines the Nile."*

Gerald smiled at her factitious enthusiasm for the distant spot.

Avoidance of the crowd and the society it represents is but one of Gudrun's motives in instigating this adventure. She wants to run from Gerald, too, even while she is drawn irresistibly to him, as he is to her. Her response to the always opposing calls to creation or destruction comes down in all cases to a change of place which ends as a desperate trek into nowhere. This present "voyage" sets a pattern for the greater climactic journey later on. The sisters paddle to the chosen spot and land there to enjoy a remoteness more symbolic than actual. The thicket of a little stream mouth and a grove of beeches furnish them with *a little wild world of their own,* where they swim nude in reversion to a half-savage or childhood freedom, beyond men, beyond mankind. And then, after they have dressed again, Ursula sings while Gudrun dances, motivated in part by a wish to recapture pristine being in this secluded place. But Gudrun cannot help being tormented, as always, by a fear that she is outside life while her sister is one of its partakers. Through contact with Ursula in this place apart, a ritual contact, Gudrun struggles for some measure of contentment, which has always evaded her.

WL, 156

Then comes an accidental development that reveals her as incapable of withstanding her own fundamental hollowness. A little herd of Highland cattle come near the dancing woman in animal curiosity. Gudrun dances toward them, daring to approach their dangerous horns, with *a terrible shiver of fear and pleasure,* responding involuntarily to the risk of pain and mutilation given or received by herself. This is the second instance in the book when animal life becomes for her the means to human cruelty and violence — the first was the Arabian mare episode. As this scene with the cattle looks back to that with the mare, so it looks forward to the chapter "Rabbit": in all three scenes Gudrun is thrilled that animal instincts can be made instrumental in human brutality. This pretended reach of the Nile where she performs her dance before the cattle has granted none of the freedom it promised, only the same old encounter with the dangerous and annihilative self over which she cannot prevail. The remoteness here is postulated as psychic as well as geographic. In the mare and the rabbit scenes, the "distance" is in both cases purely psychic, far off only in the exotic depths of perverted consciousness in Gudrun and Gerald.

WL, 159

Roused as she is to this pitch of madness, Gudrun cannot leave off when Gerald and Birkin suddenly arrive. Gerald runs up and chases away the cattle. Gudrun is furious at his interference. She flies off in pursuit of the herd, and on the hilltop where they have paused she again runs back and forth in dangerous proximity to their horns, till they take fright and race away for good. Gerald has followed her. She now turns to mock him, and to slap him in the face: hers is the first blow, she declares, as hers will be the last, and she feels *an un-* WL, 162 *conquerable desire for deep violence against him.* He responds to her hostility by declaring that he is in love with her, even as his face smarts from the blow.

And so this little quest for a place where primal innocence might assert itself in the sisters comes to a sort of reverse consummation, with a pair of soon-to-be-lovers immersed deeply in primal guilt.

The continuation of this scene adds immensely to the already powerful depiction of how space symbolizes the relation between Gudrun and Gerald. Just as they are rowing back toward the main gathering of the water-party, a younger sister of Gerald's falls from a boat into the lake, and Gerald dives repeatedly in attempt to rescue her. It cannot be done. Another young man has also leaped in after her. She has clutched him in panic, drowning them both. But the concentration of the scene is on the horror and fascination that Gerald and Gudrun experience from the shock of knowing two worlds: the world above water, and the terrible and totally alien world under water. When he dives, Gerald vanishes from Gudrun as if gone into the boundless. It is all she can do not to follow him into that *insidious reality.* He ceases WL, 174 to be a man. Each time he surfaces, he is like a vision of some amphibious beast. Horse, cattle, rabbit, and here another order of creature all affect her with the same wish for a violence unto death and for chaos beyond earthly bounds. When Gerald finally ceases diving in hopeless defeat, they exchange a few telling remarks. Gerald cannot get over how far away and how endless the domain under water appears. His conversation with Gudrun is a little death rite. He says, *"There's room* WL, 176 *under that water there for thousands."*

"Two is enough," she murmurs in reply.

"It's . . . a whole universe under there," he goes on as if in a trance, *"and as cold as hell."*

After the lake-party both Gudrun and Birkin contemplate going abroad in search of a finer existence. Temporarily indifferent to Gerald Crich, Gudrun is seized with the idea that a new form of life might await her in St. Petersburg, or in Munich, among the set to which she as an artist might belong. As for Birkin, he suffers a bout of illness and on recovery goes off to the south of France alone. But soon he is back, and in the much-admired scene where he throws rocks into the mill pond to smash the moon's image, he refutes the notion that travel, at least alone, can cure anything: *"You can't go away. . . . There is no* WL, 238 *away. You only withdraw upon yourself,"* he says to the night and the moon. This is one of Lawrence's best expositions of what he held to be the male dilemma of reliance-independence in regard to woman. The feminine principle has kept Birkin in bondage to Hermione and now refuses to submit to his vision of the world in Ursula. Yet he has just realized the futility of seeking a promised land without a woman. The image of the moon mirrored in the water spurs him to action as only an archetype can, a ritualistic response to the feminine which is at one and the same time a defiance of its potency and a recognition of its inevitability. Birkin may intone *"Cybele — curse her! The accursed Syria Dea!"* till he is out of breath and fling stones at her lunar image till his arm is limp, but the pieces of her shattered reflection reknit at once, forever beyond his reach.[2]

   Yet his senseless action is not without effect. Ursula has happened by and is watching him from hiding. She suffers in full knowledge that he is doing violence to an image of her, and at last she cannot resist coming out and pleading with him to stop. The ensuing conversation finds them still at odds over whether or not "love" should be the cohesive force in marriage. But the moon-shattering and with it the recent experience of each with place add urgency to their need to come to agreement. When questioned as to what she has done in his absence, Ursula confesses that she too has been in the throes of emotional torment, and has seen this native land of theirs as the chief contributor to it: *"I looked at England, and thought I'd done with it."* To which Birkin replies, *"It isn't a question of nations. . . . France is far worse."* And so they must set about defining what they want without reference to place, if possible, knowing that for the time being they have been betrayed by any trust whatever in place. What the scene comes to is a brief harmony between them, until the inevitable opposition reappears and remains for the rest of the chapter. Birkin does not succeed in clarifying, either to himself or to Ursula, quite what he wishes of her, but at least, for the first time perhaps, the reader may separate the principal strands of Birkin's conflicts. Although in rebellion against the influence of the moon, he wishes for the *golden light* in Ursula. But he wants it to come down to him, not shine over him. He wishes her to serve him, and he will likewise *serve* her, but *in another way — not through yourself.* He will, it is apparent, serve the higher powers. But the manner by which she will aid him in contacting those powers is remarkably different from Lawrence's description of it a couple of years before. It is now her service to him that is stressed, not his to her. To talk of love is inescapable. His chief affirmation now is that they must not live together by surrendering to each other's love — however, **the only real fear** appears to be that he will surrender to hers.

WL, 241

WL, 242

Their marriage must be carried on in *proud indifference* to one another. This, Birkin's fear of yielding what he has won of isolate male being, is the real point of contention in the seemingly fruitless arguments they are always falling into when she demands to know whether he loves her and he refuses to make so simple a declaration. He gives in here, nevertheless, at her insistence, and does say that he loves her. This brings a few moments of quiet in each other's arms before they part for the evening.

Here again, as with Gerald and Gudrun at the water-party, water symbolizes two orders of time and space. The water is the perfectly fluid but unbreachable boundary between Birkin and that far-off but infinitely desirable entity, moon-woman. The key to his feeling, as we have seen, is that Ursula must descend and be subject to him. That he cannot finally encompass this wish is clear from his inability to shatter for good the surface that brings the moon near, true enough, but at the same time keeps it remote.

What happens next brings us another stage toward exposure of the full thematic texture of the novel. Next day Birkin, yearning for Ursula, faces his own confusion. Is it only an *idea* of his, he asks himself, to demand something beyond the mere sensual merging of love, or is *it the interpretation of a profound yearning?* If it is the second, and therefore truly sincere, why does he find himself perpetually *talking about sensual fulfilment?* He confesses to himself that the two impulses disagree. And then, in a state of heightened attention brought about by his ongoing struggle within, Birkin has a sort of prophetic vision. He sees two incarnations of the totally sensual understanding. The first is an African statuette belonging to a friend, the effigy of a woman. He recalls her astonishing cultured elegance, her diminished beetle face, the astounding long elegant body on short, ugly legs, with such protuberant buttocks. That she represents some of his deepest concerns is obvious from his thinking of her as *one of his soul's intimates.* She is mystically dead, he reasons, for in her *the relation between the senses and the outspoken mind* has been severed. Her race has traveled very far since it died to the wholeness of life, into a *mystic knowledge* of *disintegration and dissolution,* into *dreadful mysteries, far beyond the phallic cult.* Where one goes *beyond the phallic cult* will require investigation later in another context. For the present, we confine ourselves to Birkin's contrast of races. It begins to seem to him that all races must pass beyond, must take a journey into utter reduction, and this thought leads him to his second incarnation of dissolution: Gerald Crich. As the African went through the burning sun-annihilation, so the European will go through the frigid snow-annihilation, *death by perfect cold.* Gerald is one of those demons of the

WL, 245

WL, 246

WL, 247

frost-mystery. Birkin foresees the perishing of Gerald according to the genius of his race, and he envisions all of Europe following him, who is their omen of *universal dissolution into whiteness and snow.* Now this is exactly what happens, of course: Gerald dies at last in the not-being of the snow, and symbolically all of Europe dies with him, for he is the exemplary man of the age, the industrial magnate and the organization man.

Birkin and Lawrence would have us believe, then, that the dynamics of race history consists of going to the utter limit of the race genius and then traveling even beyond that limit to an absolute smelting down of a race consciousness, which began in balance but tilted over into either the way of the spirit or the way of the flesh. Faraway Africa is the domain of the unalloyed flesh. High tundra is the domain of the unadulterated spirit.

Also, in the present scene, we have a working out of affairs that reflects in large measure how thematic resolution on the good side of existence will be achieved when the novel is brought to a close. There are several scenes such as this, which repeat and reweave until they culminate in the final thematic statements. What Birkin deliberates next is the alternative to those opposite ways of destruction he has just clarified for himself. For a choice still seems possible, at least in certain fortunate individuals: *There was another way, the way of freedom. There was the paradisal entry into pure, single being, the individual soul taking precedence over love and desire for union, stronger than any pangs of emotion, a lovely state of free proud singleness, which accepted the obligation of the permanent connection with others, and with the other, submits to the yoke and leash of love, but never forfeits its own proud individual singleness, even while it loves and yields.* In other words, life conceived in terms of "love" in the worst sense — which is, as we plainly see, the capitulation of a man to a life constructed on woman's emotions — is the first step toward the dissolution of mind and body. But curiously — and this is sign enough that Birkin is still not clear on just what he wants — he decides on the instant that Ursula is precisely the being who can enter with him into this way of life, despite her demands for "love," and he sets off at once to ask her to marry him. Quite characteristically, also, he envisions their future happiness by making over in a vision the world before his eyes. He heads for Beldover, for Ursula's home, and as he goes the ugly town before him is transmuted by his joy. The town on the hill all of a sudden looks *like Jerusalem to his fancy. The world was all strange and transcendent.* This is an image from Lawrence's childhood, and it recurs several times, notably in a very late fragment in which his native Eastwood is made over through a futuristic fantasy that will have much to tell us about the latter stages of Lawrence's wayfaring soul.

PH, 829

That the rest of this chapter is anti-climactic is important to Lawrence's manner of handling his themes. Birkin's proposal does not come off. He muddles first into asking Ursula's father for her hand and receives an easy consent. But when both men confront her, she stubbornly refuses to give any answer at all. All at once we wonder what has happened to Birkin's resolution that she is the right woman to fill his needs, and why he came to this decision at all, for he sees her now merely as he saw her before his great self-searching: *She* WL, 258 *believed that love far surpassed the individual. He said the individual was more than love, or than any relationship. For him, the bright, single soul accepted love as one of its conditions, a condition of its own equilibrium.*

We can only conclude that they are still a great way from union, and that the conditions for any whole relationship are little likely to be found in England, despite the "holy land" vision Birkin has just had of it.

For all that Rupert's first venture abroad is a failure, one of his chief traits is assuredly "mobility," as Gerald admits with some envy: *"You can go away and change as easily as if you had no soul."* This WL, 198 virtue of mobility is certainly meant to indicate not an absence of soul but a capability of meaningful change in the self, to a considerable degree through recognition of the deep power obtainable from place and change of place. From midway in the book, that is from about the "moony" episode, conviction builds in chapters denoting movement, such as "Excurse" and "Flitting," that abandonment of England for the Continent is after all the pathway to a new life. But naturally this time the flight will not be solitary.

In "Excurse," touching at first on one of his periodic reversals, Birkin wonders whether it might not be ideal to drift through life without any deep attachments at all, even to Ursula. But a bit later, when he and she set off in his car along autumn roads, he begins to approach a view that eventually accommodates most of the thematic strands of the novel. Where are they headed? Ursula wants to know. *"Anywhere,"* WL, 295 Birkin answers, in a real access of mobility. And Ursula likes his reply. This "excurse" brings them first to a lovers' quarrel before they are physically lovers, and also to their first love-making. A new initiative born of sexual union seizes Birkin. They cannot, he declares, continue to engage in the activities of this condemned land. *" We must get out,"* WL, 307 *he said. "There's nothing for it but to get out, quick."*

She looked at him doubtfully across the table.

"But where?" she said.

"I don't know," he said. "We'll just wander about for a bit."

When she insists on knowing something of a destination, he still refuses to be definite, suggesting instead a simply itinerant marriage as an ideal. The timing of his declaration carries the significance of their first physical union as the threshold of a new life. *"I don't know,"* he says. *"I feel as if I would just meet you and we'd set off — just towards the distance."*

Now that other ideal, of a sort of Rananim, creeps into the conversation. Insisting on the metamorphosis of travel, but failing to convince Ursula that it could be anything more than travel, Birkin makes WL, 308 a stab at defining their destination in this way: *"To be free, in a free place, with a few other people!"* But in further explanation he says, *"It isn't really a locality, though. . . . It's a perfected relation between you and me, and others — the perfect relation — so that we are free together."*

But for the moment, with the discovery of each other in passion as uppermost, they take flight only as far as Sherwood Forest, a sort of prelude to the grand flight to come.

How far the hope of achieving freedom with a select few falls short of reality becomes apparent in time, for the other people with whom Birkin and Ursula go seeking a free place, Gerald and Gudrun, come to disaster. Why Birkin should ever have believed that Gerald and Gudrun were the right companions seems curious enough, in light of his supposed penetration. But the choice is certainly representative of two elements that give much force to the novel: first, of the irony that attends any effort to found a new social order in the nearly hopeless world the book paints; and maybe even more representative, of the fine line that Lawrence draws between salvation and damnation, so fine indeed that the reader may lose sight of it at times when entangled in Birkin's devious reasoning and in Lawrence's own antithetical assertions in the text.

Perhaps one of the best ways to elucidate these obscurities is a fuller exploration of the ideal of "mobility" that reigns supreme in the novel's chief character. It is this as a moral commitment, this refusal of fixity, which underlies Birkin's inclination toward geographical seeking, toward transience as the only conceivable goal for one who would embrace newness of life. This conviction of mobility is radical in Birkin. It informs his views of love and friendship, of all aspects of existence touching singleness and togetherness, of life and death, of all change ruling in universal process, in which being and becoming take on a complex rhythm that is not in the end confusing or contradictory, although plenty of confusions and contradictions come and go along the way, and doubts remain, even in the end, as to the feasibility of anyone ever attaining to what Birkin asserts as a faith.

Much of what Lawrence puts into Birkin's mind of "mobility" came to him from the early Greek philosophers, who had so much ML, 352 clarified [his] *soul* about ten months before he started *Women in Love,* and who figured large after that in all his attempts at symbology. Lawrence accepted from Heraclitus, and from John Burnet's explication of him, the tenet that the strife of opposites is the basis of all things, that harmony is only a temporary stasis of conflicting elements forever in flux in opposing directions. What seems to be permanence or rest is simply the resultant state of the tension between warring opposites. Hence all that exists has its cause in mobility. A good passage to take up for a closer understanding of Birkin's philosophical views is a conversation between him and Ursula in the "Water-Party" chapter — a conversation placed for thematic equilibrium beside the contest between Gudrun and Gerald in which their reactions to the Highland cattle bring blows and a protestation of love. Birkin here quotes Heraclitus only once, but his dark-river-of-dissolution/silver-river-of-life antithesis is fundamentally indebted to the Greek philosopher all the way through. It is hardly necessary to do more than change Heraclitus's fire-versus-water terminology into Lawrence's terminology of two varieties of water. Birkin says of the small marsh he and Ursula are sitting near that it is *a river of darkness . . . putting forth lilies and* WL, 164 *snakes, and the ignis fatuus, and rolling all the time onward.* We like, he says, to take account only of *the silver river of life, rolling on and quickening all the world to a brightness,* but to ignore what *rolls in us just as the other rolls — the black river of corruption.* The two diametrically flowing streams, then, the two mobilities ever in progress — this is fundamental to Birkin's way of knowing the universe. All people follow both processes, the corruptive bringing all to the end of the world, which is just as good as the beginning, ultimately, for it means the start of a new creative cycle.[3]

But this is not to say that no values prevail within the universal round, for Birkin makes it plain that he thinks they do. They are achieved by "knowledge," that is, by experiencing and surpassing all the stages of both the creative and the destructive, but experiencing them only so far as to comprehend their nature. Turning to an image, he asserts that there are flowers belonging to the putrefying stream, such as lilies: love as *sensuous perfection* or as Aphrodite, love which belongs to *the first spasm of universal dissolution.* Gerald and Gudrun fit into this cycle, according to Birkin. The dark river, Birkin proclaims, is *our real reality* today. But when pressed by Ursula as to whether he and she likewise belong to this, his answer is both yes and no. They may be lilies of corruption in part, yes, but they also have the potentiality of *warm and flamy* roses which belong to the contrary process. Through this distinction of flowers Birkin arrives at Heraclitus's view of "wisdom": *"You know Herakleitos says 'a dry soul is best.'"* EG, The fiery rose is "dry," the lily is only phosphorescent. The soul as rose 138 & can manifest itself through the upward and creative process while the WL, 164 soul as lily can only sink downward. But best of all, as Birkin goes on to assert, is to know that one belongs somewhat to both processes and acting on such enlightenment to choose the *dry soul* wisdom: *"I only want us to **know** what we are,"* he insists. Those who can only slenderly know themselves are lost.

WL, 165

This passage is one of the several heavily drawn presentations of the central theme of the novel, the focus upon the two flowings, the parallel opposing channels reaching into mystical remoteness, the inextricable sources of life and death beyond the ken of common vision. Though both streams exist at once within the individual, and within the world too, the individual is ultimately responsible to some power in himself beyond a simple giving up to the flow. The "responsibility" and the "knowledge" work together. One must take his own direction and fare forth to search out the dictates of that responsibility, with many pitfalls in the way. The two couples are two pairs of pilgrims toward this goal, and the evolution of their destinies is the ultimately clear contrast which carries the message of the book. Gudrun and Gerald surrender to the stream of corruption. Ursula and Birkin learn their way to the best that can be had at a time when the whole world is set in the direction of dissolution. They accomplish their task in the teeth of history.

That Birkin's beliefs concerning friendship and marriage are also founded on his "mobility" of soul is evident everywhere, and no more so than in the very changeability of the language he employs in asserting his views, particularly on marriage. Again, let us take the question of "love." Sometimes he pronounces it desirable to a union, but again the most objectionable of deterrents to true marriage. The reader may find himself at times inclined to accept Gudrun's estimate, when Gerald asks her what Birkin's ideas of marriage are, exactly: *I can't make out — neither can he nor anybody.* Gudrun and Gerald are, to be sure, quite definite about what they believe in: *in love, in a real **abandon**, if you're capable of it.* How ironic this is and how pertinent to Birkin's argument that "love" is the foreshore of degradation, the fate of Gudrun and Gerald amply illustrates. And Birkin's ideas are not after all vague, if one takes into consideration the whole of what he has to say and allows for the clash of feelings and gropings bound to figure in the search for any sort of new relationship. The kind and proportion of love essential to the right kind of marriage may be often in question, but the end in view is never in doubt, and this end is founded upon stability within mobility, a condition whose nature is clearly stated by Birkin on a number of occasions. These statements, plus the outcome of his efforts at convincing Ursula to found a union more or less in agreement with what he teaches, far outweigh the contradictions that

WL, 282

WL, 283

Birkin utters often in the heat of the moment. Marriage is to be a permanent commitment, he always maintains, and when called upon to define it exactly, he turns most often to an astronomical figure: marriage must be *an equilibrium, a pure balance of two single beings: — as*   WL, 139
the stars balance each other. This is the *maintaining of the self in mystic*   WL, 144
balance and integrity. You can achieve this state *if you accept the*   WL, 283
unison, and still leave yourself separate, don't try to fuse. Or again,
in marriage the couple *give each other this star-equilibrium which alone*   WL, 312
is freedom.

Therefore, each soul must have its own way to travel in this universe, like a star in orbit, enjoying a freedom within its own being. But this freedom could not exist — no orbiting would be possible — without the pull of the other star. The system of intertwined orbits itself images a third sort of freedom, which is the consummate freedom, Lawrence's Holy Ghost. We see before us, then, a magnification of imagery introduced as early as *Sons and Lovers.*

These symbols, like all symbols, must of course at last find their expression in individual acts, if they are to become meaningful as fictional substance, and as such they are most clearly set forth through the journey of the two couples, through a moral quest created in terms of a geographical quest. We have seen how much care Lawrence has expended on preparing for this journey, the climactic statement of the novel's vital message. *Twilight in Italy* had been the turning point, the firm acceptance of the journey abroad as the primary means to the discovery of new being. *Women in Love* is the first of the novels to adopt the principle wholeheartedly. Lawrence would never again produce a work of the first importance on any other principle — except for *Lady Chatterley's Lover* — and even this has its own special symbolism of journeys.

Birkin and Ursula do at length marry, and almost from that moment they decide irrevocably to go away, to set off into the distance: to *wander about on the face of the earth.* It must be so if they   WL, 354
are to have a world that is sunny and spacious. So the flight prepares, and it is to be a double flight of the two couples. Even before Ursula and Birkin have taken decisive steps to depart, Gerald proposes that all four of them go away together at Christmas, to a mountain resort near Innsbruck. Both he and Gudrun envy the state of happiness that Birkin and Ursula have wrought for themselves in marriage. This going away is to be a sort of trial marriage for Gerald and Gudrun. They attach themselves to the happiness of Ursula and Birkin, all but desperate to share in the anticipated release of flight. All four agree, in rejection of England for the Continent, that one should repudiate *this*   WL, 344
home instinct. The prospect of sloughing off the problems of home

overjoys Ursula, who, we remember, has never traveled much, though she has always been a seeker, so that the quest for love and a new land will be simultaneous for her. Gudrun enters into the spirit of the quest with her usual exaggeration concealing insincerity. She shrinks from

WL, 366 the very thought of *life fixed in one place* with an ordinary man. A woman must cast her lot with a *Glücksritter,* a soldier of fortune, and ride off after joy. Yet through all the surface talk it is patent that neither she nor Gerald could ever lay hold of such freedom. And if they were to commit themselves to marriage, they would after all lapse back into

WL, 345 the common round, *in acceptance of the established world, . . . the established order,* and with that make a secret and hypocritical retreat into an underworld life of perverted thrills. Integration of the personal and the impersonal, in Laurentian terms, could never take place in them. To refer their situation to the language of *Le Gai Savaire,* they could never break with the narrowly impersonal order of society and go into the wilderness to seek harmony with the greater impersonal order of the unconscious natural world.

At every move now, the four characters prepare for a drifting life. That Gerald is the one to choose the time and place of their first getting away is a curious but wholly consistent development of events. He belongs by nature to winter and the snowy mountains, this purely arctic man, and fittingly it is the season of birth, or rebirth. This explorer of years before, who returned in disenchantment to become the conqueror of material forces at home, is now ready to leave his hollow triumph behind and seek the conquest of the woman he cannot do without in the snow of the Alps, where his soul will be in its element. So Gerald the great arranger has planned the great exodus. He and Gudrun do not look beyond the immediate destination, but already Birkin and Ursula

WL, 371 are making ready for *whatever country and whatever place they might choose at last.*

The true condition of Gudrun is pointed up in climactic fashion in an incident just before the journey gets underway. She and Gerald go to the Pompadour Cafe, to what might be called the cesspool of the degradation from which the homeland suffers. The flat opposition of impulses in Gudrun reaches a fervid state. She loathes the atmosphere in the cafe *of petty vice and petty jealousy and petty art,* but she always has to return to it as her real native element, when all is said and done, *this small, slow central whirlpool of disintegration and dissolution.* A pearls-before-swine scene develops as a group of acquaintances at a neighboring table begin ridiculing Birkin's views, which one of the number intones aloud from a letter Birkin has written him. The letter takes up the opposing streams of corruption and creation treated pre-

WL, 374–375 viously in the "Water-Party" chapter: *There is a phase in every race . . . when the desire for destruction overcomes every other desire.*

In the individual, this desire is ultimately a desire for destruction in the self, . . . a reducing back to the origin, a return along the Flux of Corruption, to the original rudimentary conditions of being. But if one follows the process to the end, then he comes at last to *the living desire for positive creation, relationships in ultimate faith, when all this process of active corruption, with all its flowers of mud, is transcended, and more or less finished.*

Gudrun's response to this mockery is a cold and savage fury. She resents the insult to Birkin, of course, but most of all she feels the message strike home. She is deeply involved in the *process of active corruption,* as is Gerald, though he manages to ignore for now the implications. Gudrun, however, unable to endure the revelation, asks to look at Birkin's letter and then walks out with it. As she and Gerald return to their hotel she all but raves against the *canaille* of the cafe, WL, 377 and the *thing that cannot be borne,* ostensibly the ridicule of Birkin, is still the laying bare of her own soul by Birkin's words. The event provides her with a way of denying her true element and delivering a malediction against it: *I feel as if I could never see this foul town again — I couldn't bear to come back to it.*

The climactic chapter in *Women in Love* is the one entitled "Continental." The first feeling it builds is the joyous mystery of escape, which as I have pointed out elsewhere is modeled on Lawrence and Frieda's first journey out of England. The scene contains what never changed for Lawrence: the belief that vision into ultimate reality, a knowledge of past and future and space as the soul's dwelling place, within the two great opposing streams of the universe, never comes so near to realization as when the world is witnessed from the eternity of the present moment by the pilgrim traveler. The soul of Ursula begins *stirring to awake* on the channel ship, after its long dormancy. Birkin, WL, 378 wanting to be at the *tip of their projection* into space, leads her to the prow to look with him into the *black, unpierced space ahead.* The differences in their response to this long-awaited thrust into the unknown are complementary and not conflicting, rooted in the divergent responses of the male and the female. To Ursula it is a place, the destination, that beckons, *the sense of the unrealised world ahead.* To WL, 379 Birkin the voyage, the mobility, is all: *the wonder of this transit* is to him *overwhelming.*

They are to meet Gudrun and Gerald in Innsbruck. The sundering between the old world and the new does not really come till they reach the snow-covered mountains past Zurich. Two spheres of climate and geography now occupy the present and the past, two worlds of nature at work within the other elements of the novel. Behind lies the spring and summer world of England in which most of the action up to now has transpired, a world which was only a realm of death in spite of the seasons. The winter world of the Austrian mountains, conversely, may offer resuscitation. The characters have taken as their first step the great stride from the world of "being" — following the universal distinction drawn in *Twilight in Italy* — to the world of "not-being."

The initial effect on the two couples is of sheer exhilaration in the cold, white, rarified atmosphere, but with great elemental forces in play underneath. Gudrun declares that she feels super-human, in effusions similar to those which made of the lake cove of the sisters' picnic a reach of the Nile. The escape from England is the foremost topic of conversation. In one light they see the native land they have forsaken as on the verge of apocalyptic explosion, but Birkin has a second view, recalling Lawrence's flight from the clinging spirit of the dead mother. WL, 386 England is like *an aged parent who suffers horribly from a complication of diseases, for which there is no hope.*

The first response of the two couples together to the great white mountains comes when, after a night in an Innsbruck hotel, they go up the next afternoon to Hohenhausen to emerge on the stage that Lawrence has set for rebirth or the failure of rebirth. To the proper season WL, is added the proper shape of the locality: *It was snow everywhere, a* 387–388 *white, perfect cradle of snow, new and frozen, sweeping up on either side, black crags, and white sweeps of silver towards the blue pale heavens.*

Lawrence had three intimate past encounters with the mountain scenery of this region to stimulate his creative powers: the trek with Frieda and partway with David Garnett and Harold Hobson in 1912, his largely solitary walk through Switzerland in 1913, and a third hike of which little record remains: a climb through the greater Saint Bernard Pass in June 1914 with a man named Lewis. This last mountain excursion may be of more importance than presently available evidence can testify to, considering the scenic details of the rejected "prologue" to *Women in Love:* a point to which I will return. What is most pertinent at this juncture is the easy transposition of symbolism that Lawrence is able to make from *Twilight in Italy* to *Women in Love.* We recollect how acutely aware the traveler was in the earlier work of the frosty mountaintops as the very cusp of the boundary between the flow of being and not-being. The streams of destruction and creation amplified by rivers and other images in the novel can be brought to meet presently at this mountain borderline where the final alternatives to the future are in question. This region now enspheres all the human types that Lawrence has involved in the crisis of civilization. The identification of the region with Gerald Crich, modern man on the edge of distintegration, is direct, as the torrid sunland of Africa was with the race of man that created the statuette. By another configuration of theme the same limits circumscribe Birkin's choices. Of the two extremes formerly threatening his advance to proud single being in marital unison, one at least was familiar: the mental fetishism of his native land. The two extremes are now fully set in exotic form, the utter sensuality of tropical Africa as against the utter spirituality of the arctic zone of alpine peaks.

Interpretations of feeling in the two couples run parallel to begin with, as in the first joint look they take at the snow. Gudrun breaks into uncontrolled thrill-language. In *sudden intimacy* with Gerald she cries   WL, 388
out that this is their world, in a sort of iniquitous triumph. But Ursula declares to Birkin that this vastness makes one feel small and alone, as though only by drawing near to each other can two people conquer this world of the above. Again the reverberation of theme reaches back to *Sons and Lovers*. Soon the foreground of the narrative is filled with the impending disaster between Gerald and Gudrun, and remains so for most of the two next-to-last chapters. These two people dare fate with their powers of exploration and discovery: *They felt powerful*   WL, 389
enough to leap over the confines of life into the forbidden places and back again. Gerald is confirmed in his element in every way from the sportsmanship of the robust skier to the deepest affinities of soul, *strong*   WL, 391
as winter . . . invincible. As for Gudrun, *she had reached her place. Here at last she folded her venture and settled down like a crystal in the navel of snow and was gone.* The arctic light which Gudrun has always felt would enfold her and Gerald has begun to wrap their lives. They have arrived at the ultimate deathly North.

But if the concentration of theme through these pages is on Gerald and Gudrun, this by no means indicates that Lawrence has relegated to a secondary position his primary technique of character: comparison and contrast of two couples who are at last opposed in nature and who yet share both halves of the interlocked opposites that comprise the universe. If in this latter stage of more and more divergence until the final severance the human success is accorded less space than the human failure, still the author is never remiss in pointing up the specific and equal significance of scenes dealing with each couple.

During their first hours in Hohenhausen the final stage of the Gerald-Gudrun affair commences, with the doom of place settling upon them. They are alone together for the first time in their room at the inn. Crouched by a window Gudrun takes in all the frozen loveliness of the peaks. But her conviction of belonging is no longer there. Alienation has taken possession of her: *She could see it, she knew it, but she was*   WL, 393
not of it. She was divorced, debarred, a soul shut out. The reversals of feeling to which Gudrun has always been subject are from now on so erratic and violent that her sanity is often suspect. Even so, the feeling

of estrangement from this place might offer her an incentive to escape. But for Gerald, looking over her shoulder at the snowscape, nothing is visible except *the blind alley, the great cul-de-sac of snow and mountain peaks under the heaven. And there was no way out.* The only recourse to desperation is a frantic sexual desire for Gudrun, to the limit of rape if necessary: *He would destroy her rather than be denied.*

WL, 391

WL, 392

Not only this demand, but all those that each makes on the other are born of the separate fates they sense in this locality. For the first few days Gudrun is only watchful. But it is not long before she comes to see their whole affair as a deadly combat for the upper hand. And once she knows she can win, and how to win, she acts out of boundless cynicism in tossing away both her advantage and her lover. Just at the time of this realization, one evening when the fourteen guests of the hotel gather socially in the Reunionsaal, her first meeting with Loerke occurs, the rat-like little sculptor who will lead her down the dark sewer of corruption.

Just before we come to the heart of this scene the two couples go out briefly into the frigid night. As in nearly every confrontation with the polar world, the contrast between the two sisters is marked. The key sensation is that of ranging, of committing the self to motion through the mysterious, terrifying, but yet gratifying reaches of space. Ursula feels like a bird flying far into space, in such harmony with the universe as to *hear the celestial, musical motion of the stars.* But she confesses the need for Birkin's nearness in her far-ranging. She must know where he is ranging, too. This thought of the two souls winging through a universe, the perpetual travelers, brings them together in a very simply enacted moment of unison in agreement with what Birkin has many times said is the orbital nature of love. He confesses he would die in this extremity of the snowy world without her. That they are *warm and together* is their bulwark against the *frozen eternality.*

WL, 398

WL, 399

So far the scene is almost point by point like the first encounter with arctic reality some pages earlier, but as with most of the repeated scenes, this one implants further nuances. Here a differing sense of time enters to reveal what is taking place in Ursula. Her mind catches glimpses of childhood life. Seeing a peasant walk to a nearby barn with a lantern in his hand takes her back to Marsh Farm — it is one of the few reminders in *Women in Love* that Ursula had an existence in *The Rainbow.* She drifts back over the whole journey of her soul since those early days. And slowly she relinquishes her entire past, rising *on the wings of her new condition* to take the journey of new life with her star-balanced lover.

WL, 400

Gudrun's responses in the snowy night are completely the opposite, as we might imagine. She too desires *to plunge on and on,* seeking her consummation in the beyond. But she must be *alone,* she stresses, to come to that oneness with the All. Already it begins to seem like the sealed-up isolation of the damned.

On coming back into the Reunionsaal, the two couples join in the merry-making of the German guests. Sexuality becomes the dominant chord. The men lustily swing the women about in a Tyrolese dance, while animality takes control of the scene. Gudrun finds distasteful the *well-seasoned bull* of a professor she dances with. The magnetism of **WL, 401** Loerke, who has been described as a mouse, begins to exercise its power. But the creature that emerges triumphant is in Birkin, a mythological half-beast, a satyr. The first purpose of this scene is to prepare for the one that follows between Birkin and Ursula. This is one of the crucial episodes for interpretation of the novel, and it therefore requires a thorough context.

Once before in the presence of Hermione, then his lover, and of Ursula, Birkin had danced in a manner which Hermione saw as less than human, which seemed to dissolve her very soul and which contributed to her attack on him with the stone paperweight. The effect of that dance on Hermione was unnerving: *her soul writhed in the black* **WL, 85** *subjugation to him, because of his power to escape, to exist, other than she did.* In short, Hermione could never go where Birkin was capable of leading her, and she was murderously envious of any state of being he might reach without her. In a scene some time after this one, we learned through the excited accusations of Ursula against Birkin something of his sexual life with Hermione. These revelations touch on the knotty problem of spirituality versus sensuality in Lawrence. Vociferously jealous of her rival, Ursula holds forth on how Hermione has been one of those *spiritual brides* to Birkin but was not *common and fleshy* **WL, 298** *enough* for him. Still, we soon learn that her allusions are to no platonic **WL, 299** alliance, for she continues thus: *You love the sham spirituality, it's your food. And why? Because of the dirt underneath. Do you think I don't know the foulness of your sex life — and hers? — I do. And it's that foulness you want, you liar.*

Strangely enough, Birkin is ready to agree: *He knew she was in the* **WL, 300** *main right. He knew he was perverse, so spiritual on the one hand, and in some strange way, degraded on the other. But was she herself any better? Was anybody any better?* And then, for what is most significant as preparation for the culmination of the novel in the mountains, he takes this line: *He knew that his spirituality was concomitant of a* **WL, 301** *process of depravity.*

A few other foregoing scenes are relevant to the alpine climax, for instance the one where Birkin pictures life going on *after the death* **WL, 246** *of the creative spirit* in the African statuette, postulating *dreadful mysteries, far beyond the phallic cult,* in which the protruding buttocks of the figure play so dominant a role. Or again, we might think of Birkin's bright-river/dark-river discourse, of his contention that everyone belongs to corruption as well as to creation. But most of all, there is the scene at the inn in England, the first intimate love scene between Birkin and Ursula, which follows close upon Ursula's spiritual-bestial accusations. This scene contains a brilliant rendering of emotions extremely difficult to translate into language without going too far in any one of several directions. Ursula kneels before Birkin, *her arms round his loins, . . . her face against his thighs.* With her fingers she traces *the back of his thighs, . . . down the flanks,* finding the reality of his being *in the straight downflow of the thighs. It was here she discovered him one of the sons of God such as were in the beginning of the world.* A near worship of these dark and divine forces in the male releases in her the *golden light* of lunar origin that Birkin has craved since the hour by the pond when Ursula was the moon-goddess to him. The passional exchange goes on building, as *a dark fire of electricity* flashes between the lower centers of the body. This interchange brings deeper and deeper physical intensity, Ursula stroking *the full, rounded body of his loins* until she arrives at a source of mystery *deeper than the phallic source,* epitomized in *the smitten rock of the man's body, from the strange marvellous flanks and thighs.*

WL, 305

WL, 306

In this scene Lawrence touches on a number of emotional reflexes, some well nigh indefinable. We may read it as a rush of language decorating if not disguising oral and anal gratifications. We may see a fetishistic preference for male hinderparts over the female as the latter are represented by the bulbous extrusions of the African carving. We may follow a common interpretation that buttocks in any sense are a displacement reference to the genitals. But none of these opinions tells the entire story: certainly not the last opinion, for the language does succeed in its prime purpose of outreaching genital associations. And to some extent this success is due to what may be mistaken for deliberate obscurity. Limiting the description of specific physical contact to Ursula's stroking serves a purpose that might be lost in more explicit treatment. What actually takes place is subordinate to communicating intuitions centering on the buttocks that go beyond any of those suggested. I can best illustrate these by blunt popular expressions such as Lawrence himself turned to in *Lady Chatterley's Lover* to convey similar meanings centered this time on the genitals. These expressions are built on the word "ass." My examples are those current in America. If the word is "arse" in Lawrence's dialect and the idiom of his day differed, the gist is nevertheless the same. Such popular locutions have the virtue of being direct yet capable of subtlety. To fire his ass, to lose his ass, or the invocation, my ass! as a witness to falsehood — these and many more suggest that the ass can stand for individual integrity, even the very identity: for what is unique yet vulnerable. And like most intensely individual concepts, this one hints at a mysterious link between the human being as finite and universal being as infinite: it suggests a "soul." This bond between the particular and the universal is by no means spiritual but inescapably physical, gross yet precious. The ass communicates perfectly, with delicacy and disgust, our participation in the flesh that perishes as well as in the life force that never dies.

These nuances contribute to the high degree of physical expressiveness in the ass — which again goes beyond simple displacement for the genitals. Verbal usage again bears out the point, if we contrast the popular expressions referred to with those based on the genitals. Synecdoche of the latter is far less inclusive than that of the posterior and ordinarily confined to single qualities or to negative analogies: like "balls" for virile strength or "prick" for an overbearing fool.

A little thought on these common discriminations will help us to understand, I think, what Lawrence wishes to invoke from *deeper than the phallic source,* the mystery that suffuses Ursula's awareness. The Old Testament images by which he embodies this — the sons of God uniting with the daughters of men, the rock cleft by Moses' rod — may at first seem a far cry from those just offered in comparison. But doubts may lessen if we remember that in the cultures Lawrence desired to reawaken, mythic and religious parallels were often discovered in crudities of language.

And so up here in the mountains — to pick up where we left off — in the mountains where all forms of experience must be confronted together, Birkin and Ursula submit to the extremities of physical experimentation, to know that everyone belongs to corruption as well as creation. During the night after all the animal energy of the Reunionsaal, Birkin leads a fearful but numbly willing Ursula beyond forbidden limits of sexual experience. The specific sexual acts accomplished again are not named, but their nature is quite clear from Ursula's thoughts afterwards: *How could anything that gave one satisfaction be ex-* WL, 403 *cluded? . . . Degrading things were real, with a different reality. . . . Why not be bestial, and go the whole round of experience?* Oral and anal sex are clearly admitted to approval here, though of course these must be understood in the whole context of the book and of Lawrence's general views on the subject. The first thing we should note is what Lawrence thought these practices led to, and under what circumstances they are acceptable. This he makes evident also from Ursula's thoughts. She gives in to Birkin's licentiousness because he is *self-responsible,* and through responsibility the experience brings freedom: *She was free, when she knew everything, and no dark shameful things were denied her.*

Since, as we know, the contrast between the two couples carries the burden of theme in this novel, we must immediately match these revelations with the experiences of Gerald and Gudrun, and when we do we begin to see the final complications of the problem. The earlier "Rabbit" chapter comes to mind, a sexual scene in fantasy alone. First Gudrun and then Gerald handle a wildly kicking big rabbit that brings blood on their forearms with his clawing. Gerald gets him under control by a blow that brings a rabbit scream and by twisting the panic-stricken beast to catch him under his arm. Gudrun is enthralled by all WL, 232 this in a *sullen passion of cruelty*, implicated with Gerald *in abhorrent* WL, *mysteries,* in *obscene recognition*. It is as if he *had knowledge of her* 234–235 *in the long red rent of her forearm, so silken and soft*. As in the Arabian mare scene, the obscenity takes place in the spirit, founded upon a blood-lust and a depraved cruelty. The entry of the man and woman into the *unthinkable red ether of the beyond* in pursuit of this degenerate knowledge gives us a perverted search into space as moral discovery. For another variation of the depravity this couple lusts after, we might consider Gudrun's readiness for anything with Gerald when WL, he learns that his father will die and suggests to her that they *dance* 279–280 *while Rome burns:*

> They both felt the subterranean desire to let go, to fling away everything, and lapse into a sheer unrestraint, brutal and licentious. A strange black passion surged up pure in Gudrun. She felt strong. She felt her hands so strong, as if she could tear the world asunder with them. She remembered the abandonments of Roman licence, and her heart grew hot.

But the fact is that in *Women in Love* all the sort of experience suggested here apparently takes place only in the minds of Gerald and Gudrun, and no physical "bestiality" — that is, extragenital sex — is directly attributed to anyone except first to Birkin and Hermione and then to Birkin and Ursula. When Gudrun at length throws over Gerald for Loerke, the ultimate little beast that leads the human spirit over the edge of the last gutters of corruption, she only plays mental games WL, 439 with him: they go into their *inner mysteries of sensation* through the *subtle lust* they find in primitive art: Egyptian, ancient Mexican, and the African wood sculpture which Birkin has also found deeply instructive on the last throes of sensuality. All this may seem odd, but it is perfectly consistent with Lawrence's view that the mind is the source of obscenity and not the body, a firm conviction from which he never lapses. Nearer the heart of the matter, however, are still the concepts of "responsibility" and of "freedom." The bright river of life and the dark river of disintegration must be united through an acceptance of the highest responsibility if a meaningful freedom is ever to be reconstituted for modern man. No such meaningful purpose is to be attributed to either Gudrun, Gerald, or Loerke. The fatal division in Gudrun's character, verging on madness, inclines her to utter cynicism. Gerald's former mission in life was undertaken with a sense of responsibility, but on the disastrous principle that society must cease altogether to be an organism and reconstruct itself according to the mechanical lifelessness of industry. But he is a divided soul too, in that he surrenders himself to an emotional life of abandon and violence, all responsibility gone and no real freedom gained. Loerke's assertions of supposed principles are schizoid to the degree of doubling back one on the other. He holds the decadent art for art's sake view that the world of art and the world of everyday life have no connection. He scorns the idea that a piece of sculpture he did of a girl he had mistreated embodies his cruelty. It is purely a "form" he has produced. Yet he professes to believe that art should express industry as it once expressed religion. It is only emotional life, then, which he would like to keep alien to his art, a perversion indeed. The mechanical activity of modern society he is more than willing to interpret. Clearly, he is the artist perfectly complementary to the capitalist like Gerald, and his view of the world is thus primarily the same as Gerald's, except that he exults to the end in the degradation inherent in such a view. None of these three characters, then, is "responsible" to the truly vital self or the vital society, and it is impossible that "freedom" should mean anything to any one of them beyond self-abandonment to the will to consume and annihilate.

But the anomaly remains, no matter how deep the mental corruption of these three, that the novel appears to suggest some viable and creative order of experience for those who engage in the physical practice of sodomy, while it condemns those whose licentiousness and cynicism are focused in the mind.

I will not attempt to settle this question just now. We must first take account of some later developments in the action. It might be well to mention, nevertheless, at least one possible influence on Lawrence's thought, a bit from one of the Heraclitean fragments that meant so much to him at the time. In modern days we have perhaps lost the distinction between the shame or shamelessness of a thing depending on when and how it is performed. Heraclitus says: *For if it were not* EG, 141 *to Dionysos that they made a procession and sang the shameful phallic hymn, they would be acting most shamelessly. But Hades is the same as Dionysos in whose honour they go mad and rave.* Ritual aberration in almost every conceivable form was practiced in ancient temples, and one can still see in certain American Indian ceremonies ritual obscenities which the participants would not dream of repeating outside the ceremonies. All of this sort of ceremonial reasoning had the deepest influence on Lawrence, and may well have suggested the order of experience he is endeavoring to construct for Birkin and Ursula.

Now comes a scene whose placement after the foregoing complications of love brings about a further clarity in the demarcation between souls. Ursula is engaged in drawing out Loerke on what he claims is the irreconcilability between the world of art and the world of living. Gudrun comes to join the conversation, agrees with him, and rouses Ursula to hot disagreement. In reaction against their callousness and in growing recognition of the estrangement between herself and WL, 425 her sister, Ursula goes out of the inn *alone into the world of pure, new snow,* where seeing the distance it occurs to her, *like a miracle, that she might go away into another world.* In her revulsion she wants to have done with this world of snow, with *the unnaturalness of it, the unnatural light it throws on everybody, the ghastly glamour, the unnatural feelings it makes everybody have.*

This passage brings a sudden veering in narrative direction and bears us forward a certain degree, though not the whole way, toward resolving some thematic difficulties. The keynote is: *One might go away.* It is to be the second going away in the novel, this time out of the *utterly silent, frozen world* of ideality and deviation joined, to the *dark fruitful earth* of the south, where all as seen from up here is more "natural." The hint is unmistakable that the freedom and responsibility achieved by exposure to all physical experience has brought about a further exercise of freedom and responsibility in the choice to go away, again, to a new land, a new life. The hint is strengthened by a description, on the next page, of what sexual relations between Ursula and WL, 427 Birkin are now like, where such phrases as *they were never **quite** together, at the same moment, one was always a little left out* point only to genital coition, as if other practices have been surpassed. However, it cannot be said that the matter is absolutely settled. One cannot say, emphatically, that Lawrence intended, with this, to see his chief characters through a whole Blake-like arrangement of experience, in which knowledge and the passage to a higher innocence come only by experiencing the forbidden and transcending it. For Lawrence does not by any sign rule out repetition by his exemplary pair of lovers of the *shameful things* so emphatically presented as essential to growth and yet so roundly condemned, in another sense, as licentious and disintegrative. And it does not seem enough, at least not at this point in the novel, to hint at a transcendence of the extragenital and to show the new stage of achieved "innocence" through a geographical image only, with Italy as the "natural" world and the Austrian Alps as the "unnatural," but without any suggestion that once the lovers are in

Italy "natural" sexual relations will be fully restored. Anything like an answer to this, and to other questions, cannot be had without watching the unfolding, in order, of the final portion of the narrative.

While Ursula and Birkin — who takes little convincing of the desirability of leaving here — begin to see the new world beyond the polar extremity of the peaks, the absolute reverse begins to transpire in the souls of the other couple. Neither Gudrun nor Gerald can stop short of final propulsion into the void, and while togetherness grows between their opposite number, total apartness proceeds between them. The penultimate battle is joined in their bedroom on the same night when Ursula and Birkin are engaging in their reckoning with licentiousness, with significant contrast as the obvious purpose. Gerald has a frightening will that comes close to overmastering Gudrun at the outset, but before it is all over, Gudrun has gained the upper hand and knows full well how to keep it, how to control and manipulate her lover. She might be the woman behind him, she thinks as she watches him sleep the morning after. She might direct his *faculty of making order out of con-* WL, 407 *fusion* and turn him into a leader *more dauntless than Bismarck*. But WL, 408 with Gudrun all fine schemes turn to ashes, and she is soon mocking herself for considering worthwhile any effort to change the world. She has come to know Gerald through and through as *the ne plus ultra* WL, 443 *of the world of man*. And what can be the next spiral of consciousness for her? Simply this: *Knowing him finally she was the Alexander seeking new worlds. But there were no new worlds, there were no more men, there were only creatures, little, ultimate creatures like Loerke*. There in the bedroom, in annihilative cruelty followed by an access of tenderness with all the discontinuity of the deranged personality, Gudrun begins to ache with pity that such a beautiful man as Gerald should be wasted on the poor show of the world. She wakes him, but her real purpose is desperately selfish, to make him *convince* [her] *of* WL, 409 *the perfect moments* of life. In embrace they come as close as they ever will to touching the quick of one another. But Gudrun's greatest profit from their love-making, which she thinks of as one of the high points of her life, is the *supreme pangs of her nervous gratification,* which WL, 410 is always the wrong form of sexual satisfaction in a woman, as far as Lawrence is concerned. There can be no rest for this devouring lust.[4]

Lawrence now proceeds to demonstrate the nihilism of Gerald and Gudrun in relation to alpine space, in a climax of the mountain-quest theme. They go out on a toboggan and fling away down the slopes destruction-bent, in unison, Gudrun consciously sharing the identity of Gerald as conqueror, fusing with him in their trajectory in an ironic parallel to the conquest of the world to which she has just thought to inspire him. Together they become *one molten, dancing globule, rushed* WL, 411 *through a white intensity.* This is one of the arctic moments she has always known to be reserved for her and Gerald together. She is trans-figured in *a terrible merriment,* and cries out, *"It was the complete moment of my life."* Her glee is like a knife into Gerald, but he loves the sensation. Once again they climb and descend the slope. Steering to perfection, he strains to *pierce into the air and right into the very heart of the sky,* a quest into time and space for ultimate being corresponding on another plane to the triumphs Gerald has long since achieved in industry and to those which Gudrun knows to be within their concerted reach in politics. But it is all perverted into a quest for annihilation, in a love of the great risk for itself alone: it is the death-courage that Law-rence condemned, not the life-courage of carrying the best through the debacle. Not content even yet, Gerald and Gudrun seek out the most dangerous slope they can find and carry their venture to the brink, arriving at the point which in this book as in *Twilight in Italy* Lawrence presents as the sheering off into not-being. For days afterwards, the feeling instilled on the slopes prevails between Gerald and Gudrun: *an intensity of speed and white light that surpassed life itself, and car-ried the souls of the human beings beyond into an inhuman abstraction of velocity and weight and eternal, frozen snow* — abstraction or ob-scenity: the two have merged.

WL, 460 And then, as the deathly thrill begins to break apart between them, Gudrun turns to Loerke as a tobogganing partner, who performs with a gaiety and mockery quite unlike Gerald's *gripped intensity of phy-sical motion.* At the time of her climactic ride with Gerald, Gudrun was still undecided about her future, but she knew even then that it was all up with Gerald. Seeing her go over to Loerke, he begins to know that he can have no experience beyond her, and the knowledge leads inevitably to a compulsion to kill her.

WL, 461 Out in the snow with Loerke on the day before she must make her decision about leaving, in answer to his question *wohin?* she can only wonder where indeed? And they go on to speak of wayfaring as a thing without direction, not only geographical direction but moral direction as well. Gudrun and Loerke play with the idea as they play with his-tory, art and everything else. Wayfaring need not be either a quest or
WL, 462 a flight: nor a matter of destinations at all. *One might take a ticket, so as not to travel to the destination it indicated.* One might drift as a puff of wind. Loerke purses his lips and blows toward Germany. This is his invitation for her to abandon Gerald and come with him, and she is clearly willing. At this moment Gerald appears out of the snow and knocks Loerke aside. Gudrun attacks him, and the pleasure of the pain of her blows arouses in him the desire for fulfillment in
WL, 463 murder. He chokes her and exults in her struggling, in the *reciprocal lustful passion in this embrace,* for which we have long been prepared.

From this moment of mental orgasm he turns in revulsion, however, and soon enough that Gudrun's life is spared. Even this ecstasy he did not desire. A disgust with life to the bottom is all that is left him. He wanders off into the snow to his death.

We know that Gerald has been a Cain figure from the beginning — he killed his brother, ostensibly by accident, when a child — but Birkin and even Gudrun have called the accidental nature of the killing into question. Cain is the wanderer, we also remember, rejected yet singled out by God for distinction. But as Lawrence reads the myth, the race of Cain is self-destructive in its ultimate quest, belonging to the not-being of the mountains above. Gerald's climb to self-destruction becomes, then, a quest for ultimate denial as against the quest of Birkin for ultimate affirmation. As he goes along Gerald sinks into a near-void of consciousness in which his only urge is to walk on and on: a frightful turning inside out of all quest motives. He loses all sense of place, he simply drifts upward toward the crest of the pass. In a mountain hollow like one of the first Lawrence ever saw, Gerald comes upon a crucifix like the one that Lawrence mentions on page 14 of *Twilight in Italy,* the last crucifix below the pass. The little figure of Christ turns into the condemner, the projection of self that will murder Gerald, and as such gives the incident great power, with even this final image of blessing turned into the curse of Cain. Cain has wandered many lands in Gerald, drawn on to the place that is no place, where his goal of new being meets him in the utter loss of all being. Gerald lies down to die in the snow, the denier to the end.

Before long Gudrun goes off to Dresden with Loerke, to a life in the art world, to final spiritual death in the north. We hear nothing more of her, but it is hard to see how the bohemian world of Dresden could be different in any important respect from the life centered on the Cafe Pompadour in London: save that now she is led by the rat of the dark river instead of the wolf of the snows.

The path for Birkin and Ursula is precisely the opposite. Just when Gudrun and Gerald were having their physical-spiritual climax in the tobogganning runs, Birkin began to fear that up here they will all cease to be human and turn into snow creatures. We have also seen how WL, 412 Ursula imagined a new world to the south just after Gudrun started to feel the sympathy with Loerke that sends her off eventually to a "new world" in the north. The going away of Birkin and Ursula quickly follows their first proposals to leave, and in the discussion between the two sisters nearing their farewell, the whole quest theme of *Women in Love* emerges in concepts of space and geography in which the physical world stands for moral place.

As to any fixed destination, the affirmative is as indefinite as the negative. But there is a right direction. Where will they go? Gudrun

WL, 428   asks Ursula. *I only know we are going somewhere,* is Ursula's reply: not "nowhere," as would fit Gudrun's impulses. Won't they want the old world of England, after all? Gudrun inquires. No. Ursula thinks rather *that Rupert is right — one wants a new space to be in, and one falls away from the old.* It's an illusion, Gudrun declares, to think that one can escape the world: one must see it through. We know quite well, of course, that she is truly attached in her own corruption to the decayed and dying body of the old world. But Ursula, following her husband's philosophy, describes a sort of inner apocalypse in which one labors through the destruction of the world before it comes about in actuality,

WL, 429   and she puts this in terms of travel through interstellar space: *One has a sort of other self, that belongs to a new planet, not to this. You've got to hop off.* She goes on to state, or to try to, how she and Birkin have got beyond "love" to welcoming something more than human that comes out of the unknown. Gudrun ends the scene by bestowing

WL, 430   her false blessing on the quest of her sister: *"Go and find your new world, dear,"* she cries. *"After all, the happiest voyage is the quest of Rupert's Blessed Isles."*

Ursula and Birkin do go to Italy, but they have not been there long before they are called back to Austria by the news of Gerald's death.

As a summation of what he meant to incorporate into his novel, Lawrence gives Birkin the foreground in the closing narrative. He stands just where Gerald's body was found and thinks of north and south in both senses, as real and as imaginative direction. If Gerald had only heard the dogs of the Marienhütte a little above him, he would perhaps have survived to go over the pass and descend to the south.

WL, 469   But *the south? Italy? What then? Was it a way out?*

Now Birkin's response to himself, having just been to Italy, is that strictly speaking it is not a way out, not for anyone. But from this level of thought he surrenders himself to the non-human mystery that his vision of the south has led him to. If humanity, like Gerald, should prove a blind alley of creation and die out, then what comes after mankind from the incorruptible source may outshine our species. Birkin thus transcends any earthly direction and reaches imaginative entry into the direction in time of the life-potency, beyond either the rejected world of the north or the accepted, but itself ultimately rejected, world of the south. A crucial progression is now evident away from the strong misanthropy from which Birkin has suffered now and again. He no longer takes a grim satisfaction in the possible annihilation of the species. He can now contemplate such an eventuality with a reverent equanimity before the will of the universal creative mystery.

But an even larger or at least a more complex question raised by the concept of journeys in a creative direction awaits resolution as the novel draws to a close: this is the question of any final distinction to be drawn in sexual relations between *degrading things* that liberate and irredeemable depravity. It was to escape *unnatural feelings* that Ursula and Birkin followed her inspiration to go south from snow to sun. They went to Verona — a place of romance near the Lake Garda of Lawrence's victories in love — and, in association with that place, the text has pointed to a sexual accord between them in purely genital terms.

If Lawrence intended that the "bestiality" of the night after the Reunionsaal dance should be confined to the weird regions of snow and engaged in there as a limit to be transcended and forgotten in a greater physical union to the south below, then there is a great flaw in the structure of his novel, for he never affirms by any unmistakable sign that the affirmative structure of sexual experience is such a linear movement. In fact, everything coheres toward a quite different conclusion. That the redeemed of the novel engage in physical "bestiality" and the damned engage only in mental depravity makes the point that physical practices as such are not of crucial importance. Depravity is of the mind and not of the body. The figure who confirms this theme beyond question is Loerke. Out of his brutality he has *loved and tortured* a WL, 422 girl, and made a statue of her on the claim that nothing matters but art. He is one of the *little, ultimate* **creatures** *of sensation within the* WL, 443 *ego, the obscene religious mystery of ultimate reduction.* The little sculptor has his own direction to travel, his own sort of "mobility," down *the river of corruption, just where it falls over into the bottomless* WL, *pit.* In stating exactly what it is in which Loerke has gone so many 418–419 stages farther than anyone else toward dissolution, Birkin could only specify *stages . . . in social hatred.*

If we join this evaluation of utterly misanthropic nihilism with Birkin's modified view of humanity, based on the surrender of the will to the vast creative mystery and its unseen purposes, and add this in turn to the amorous harmony between Birkin and Ursula, we begin to grasp that *Women in Love* is a compelling indictment of mental depravity, of spiritual obscenity, of a cerebral hatred of mankind which Lawrence felt was not only destroying the world — a death that must come about in any case — but was wresting from the world any hope of rebirth. These intellectual agents of disaster such as Loerke and Gudrun and Gerald represent far worse forms of perversion than any nonviolent sexual aberrations.

But this is not all, for Lawrence did not choose to end *Women in Love* with the limited success of a new relationship achieved by Birkin and Ursula and the social hopes that this might comprehend. He chose to end it with Birkin deploring the failure of a new relationship to develop between himself and Gerald as an additional hope for the future. We have seen how a new meaning of love between man and woman was sought throughout the novel, and it may be said that this theme culminates in a final association between male and female under a new form of love and place: Rupert's Blessed Isles, whose location is unfixed but appears to subsist in migration from a northerly to a southerly direction, a migration that creates a moral climate in the participants where the Blessed Isles really lie. But also, throughout the novel, the need recurs for a "blood-brotherhood" between men, a necessary adjunct to the new love between man and woman. What Lawrence meant by this is not easy to define. It is easy enough, of course, to say that he was simply recommending homosexuality implicitly without daring to recommend it openly. But both the intention and the expression in the novel clearly reach for something more, and the argument is strengthened by the unearthing, a few years back, of a rejected "prologue" which verifies that Lawrence once had in mind making the original attraction between Gerald and Birkin openly homosexual, if not in practice plainly in emotional affinity. What Lawrence wanted to do, as stated earlier, was to enjoin a physical but non-sexual intimacy between men. We may not consider this possible, as he describes it, but we still must endeavor to understand what he meant to say and to what extent he succeeded in saying it, in efforts whose high points are as follows.

From early in the novel as published we know that a powerful attraction exists between Birkin and Gerald, but as they do not believe WL, 28 in *deep relationship* between men their *suppressed friendliness* has never developed. But it does grow in the novel. Their talk enters more and more into confidences: on life, on women, on all the things around which close friendships revolve. They speak, or largely it is Birkin who speaks, of declaring a blood-brotherhood. The crucial and revelatory scene comes in the "Gladitorial" chapter. A "fight," according to Birkin, is an effective way of breaking old worn-out forms of being. WL, 260 So they then decide to do *some Japanese wrestling.* This must be done nude, says Birkin, or so he was taught by the Japanese who instructed WL, 261 him in the art. When that man was *hot and roused,* he had a *definite attraction.* The description of the bout which now takes place between the two men — with the penetration into Gerald of Birgin's *fine, sub-* WL, *limated energy,* with *the physical junction of two bodies clinched into* 262 & 263 *oneness,* with the lapsing into unconsciousness of the two men, Birkin on top of Gerald — all this may be taken as mere side-stepping language for a thoroughly homosexual encounter. They go so far as to think of each other as beautiful after the wrestle, and Birkin's pronouncement is, WL, 265 *We are mentally, spiritually intimate, therefore we should be more or less physically intimate too — it is more whole.* As we move on towards the close of the book, with the blood-brotherhood never materializing into a definite declaration, Birkin says bitterly that he as well as Gudrun loved Gerald. He says this just when he is about to depart with Ursula for their new world to the south, as a sort of protest to Gerald's assertion that Gudrun is *something final* in the way of experience. In other words, Gerald cannot rise to the further friendship that Birkin recommends. At the novel's end Birkin explains to Ursula, as best he can, what that intimacy with Gerald would have meant, had it not failed. He says that Ursula is all women to him, but that he *wanted eternal union with a man too: another kind of love.* And he hints that if Gerald had truly accepted their blood-brotherhood, he need never have died. Ursula is clearly jealous and suspicious, declaring that Birkin's wish is a *perversity . . . false, impossible.* Birkin's refusal to believe that such a union between men is impossible closes the book. WL, 431 WL, 472 WL, 473

The rejected "prologue" of *Women in Love* obviously has a bearing on the whole course of the preceding ideas. Not that we would be justified in reading it as a part of the novel, but we may at least take it as evidence of how the novel might have gone.

In this "prologue," not long after meeting, Birkin and Gerald go mountain-climbing in the Tyrol, just where the actual *Women in Love* ends, and curiously enough, the environment of the upper world is wholly creative in the "prologue," the opposite of its final nature in the novel. The three men — Hosken, who introduced Birkin and Gerald, is along — are *enkindled in the upper silences into a rare, unspoken intimacy, an intimacy that took no expression, but which was between them like a transfiguration.* (One thinks, no matter if the association was probably unconscious, of Christ's transfiguration on the mountain in the presence of his two disciples.) And when they come down from the mountain, this *transcendent intimacy* remains as a deep and covert influence on their lives, especially on Birkin and Gerald, although they do not even see each other for a long time to come. The high mountains have produced an almost translunar purity of emotion, reminiscent of the mountain heights at the end of "The Spinner and the Monks." To leave this region is a *sudden falling down to earth* with all the deterioration that this implies. The "prologue" then goes on weaving through the life of Birkin both before and after this episode, finally stopping at the wedding with which the published novel opens. Birkin has had a spiritual relationship of long standing with Hermione, much like that which Lawrence had with Jessie Chambers. He is incapable of a physical relationship except with low women. He is hounded, at times obsessed, by a secret love for men of one of two types: the men of Gerald Crich's sort, *with eyes like blue-flashing ice,* or men of a *strange Cornish type,* with eyes like *liquid darkness.* He can suppress PX, 92 PX, 93 PX, 92 PX, 105 & 106 his desire for months at a time, then it will burst forth in him almost beyond control. He knows that it is impossible to *slay a living desire,* but he knows that this desire is the cause of his being divided against himself. The only hope implied for righting his imbalance is in some metamorphosis of the desire, another transfiguration.

It is next to useless to speculate on what Lawrence might have done with his novel if he had retained the "prologue." How, for instance, would he have reconciled the opposing symbolism of the same region: in one instance a Mount of the Transfiguration, in the other something resembling the core of Dante's Hell? But as to how his own mountain experiences helped to shape his vision of place, this we can pursue with profit for a little way.

It seems likely, though admittedly there is little definite evidence to go on, that in those years of the quest for love with Frieda back and forth across the Alps, some crucial experience or experiences worked great changes in Lawrence's homosexual cravings. The "prologue" may be pure extension into fantasy of some days with male companions in the Tyrol, either with male companions alone, or, for that matter, with Frieda present. All these excursions except one have been taken up in earlier pages. I do not wish to make conjectures, given the paucity of evidence, upon any of them. I do wish, however, to make a brief mention of Lawrence's trans-Alpine trip before the war, in June 1914. This was a hike across part of Switzerland and maybe part of France YL, too, with a man named Lewis, an engineer. The two postcards Law- 113–114 rence wrote to his sister Ada from Switzerland make it obvious that much of the scene of Gerald's death is based on that place where Lawrence and his fellow-climber struggled up to the *Hospice du Grand St. Bernard.* And the mountain-climbing described as a *transfiguration* on the first page of the "prologue" to *Women in Love* is apparently modeled on the same experience. We cannot say for sure when Lawrence wrote this "prologue," but most evidence suggests that it was not part PX, 106 of the earliest versions of *The Sisters.* The attraction to the *strange Cornish type of man* brings in another possible association: Lawrence's fervent friendship with William Henry Hocking in Cornwall, which could not have begun much before Lawrence had set himself to write *Women in Love.*[5]

We can proceed on the premise, then, that the "prologue" to *Women in Love* summarizes Lawrence's major conflicts with homosexual urges up to 1916. These opposing inner forces no doubt counted heavily, along with the falling short of hopes for liberation through Frieda and the catastrophe of the war in cutting off the paths of pilgrimage to foreign lands, in Lawrence's wartime dejection.

Insistence on the psychic disturbances of the author to any great length, however, may lead us to overlook what is infinitely more important: the powerful artistic conviction of a Lawrence text. Whether it is the presentation of a mother-son love nearing incest, or of sodomy as a sort of mystic experience toward rebirth, or the attempted transformation of homosexual impulses into some new bond between men, Lawrence always comes near to convincing his reader that he truly can take some of his characters beyond the old experiences of the race and envision for them a new world in which the distortions wrought by the disintegrating of man's soul in its present state may be reshaped to express in their original purity the impulses from which these distortions come. It was in reference to *Women in Love* that Lawrence said: *Nothing that comes from the deep, passional soul is bad, or can be bad*. With his trust in this, he can imagine a new life under conditions that we can scarcely conceive. This imagining is the essence of his art and the secret of his unfailing appeal. WL, VIII

NOTES

[1] While on a privateering expedition in 1704, Alexander Selkirk quarreled with the captain of his ship and asked to be put ashore on a Pacific island. He remained there alone for over four years. His experience was apparently the basis for Defoe's *Robinson Crusoe*.

[2] A work attributed to the second-century writer Lucian, *De Syria Dea*, describes the temple and rites of a Canaanite mother goddess at Hierapolis. Her particular name seems to have been Atargatis, but Astarte, Cybele and several other such deities had many attributes in common with her. Lawrence may have read about her in Frazer's *The Golden Bough*.

[3] For a full analysis of this "Romantic" aspect of Lawrence's thought, with differing conclusions, *see* Colin Clarke, *River of Dissolution: D. H. Lawrence and English Romanticism* (New York, 1969).

[4] Lawrence's descriptions of female sexual climax here and in *The Plumed Serpent* and *Lady Chatterley's Lover* rely on the distinction made by Freud between clitoral and vaginal orgasm, a distinction whose validity is still debated. Lawrence plainly agrees with Freud that "vaginal" orgasm is more "feminine" than "clitoral": the latter being "masculine" because the clitoris is a vestigial penis. For Lawrence a woman who responds as Gudrun does here is usurping a masculine role. This "corruption" of nature is completed by Loerke's womanish traits, as revealed in the homosexual liaison in which he is involved when Gudrun meets him.

[5] Besides Hocking, some verbal associations may possibly be involved in the similarity between Hosken and Hobson. Harold Hobson was the friend of David Garnett's who hiked with him and the Lawrences over part of the trans-Alpine trail in the fall of 1912.

8

He Called It America

Few experiences of any writer with place and the sense of time encompassed by that place have been as strange as those which Lawrence went through with America during the Great War. We might state it as a paradox: he wrote a book about himself and called it a treatise on American literature. Such a statement would go at least halfway toward the truth of the matter. But if the truth ended there, so would much of the interest. What goes beyond the paradox holds the best of the truth. Out of the great tension produced between Lawrence's refusal of the actual world and his vision of a new world across the ocean came a great perspicacity in isolating and arranging real strands of American spiritual history from its earlier literature.

A phantasmagoric combination of places overshadowed Lawrence when he went to Cornwall in the last days of 1915. For many internal and external reasons, sailing to America had been postponed. Cornwall presently and at scattered intervals for most of two years served as a substitute for America as a place of renascence, but more often than not it was a way-station westward in the soul of a Lawrence who felt *like a Columbus who can see a shadowy America before him*. This Lawrence was in a sense re-enacting the drama he had formerly thought to be over and done with: the drama of his initial flight from England in 1912. Though now, for merely one aggravation of the problem, it was the whole of Europe, and not England alone, that loomed at his back as the possessive ghost of his mother. What most intensified the struggle, however, was the realization that up to now he had based his symbology of existence on a fundamental mistake: Frieda, the beloved through whom he was to issue forth into newness of life — the second birth so confidently aspired to in *Le Gai Savaire* — was now discovered to be despairingly close to the old mother image made over

ML, 437

as wife. And how could he break free of her, seeing that he depended on her all but absolutely for emotional stability?

Conflicting attitudes toward Frieda and Cornwall are strongly in evidence at this period. Sometimes Lawrence thought of the place AL, 370 half-nostalgically as a truly achieved Fiascherino, a real Blessed Isles of love, a feeling made concrete by *Women in Love.* Sometimes Cornwall was a jumping-off place into the unknown, even the last shore where he would have to bear the burden of female power as abrogated by Frieda. For another contradiction, which we need only mention now but which will come up for discussion in the chapters on Lawrence's actual stay in America: if Europe was dying of idealism, a male attribute, how could it represent to the fugitive soul the maternal monster expanded to include the whole feminine principle? Anything like a sufficient answer to this question demands much weighing of Lawrence's internal stresses and their issuance into his writing over a long period of time to come.

For the moment we are concerned mainly with the Lawrence who had come fully to connect this present crisis of his life with the crisis of the war and who felt he possessed incontrovertible proof that in his own person he was living out the last days of the old world and catching the first dark glimmerings of the new. In the working out of these intimations of a high destiny, a peculiar twist of the travel or pilgrim instinct turned Lawrence almost wholly from the actual to the imaginary. He conjured up a fantasy land out of his reading of American authors, as about the same time he conjured up another in the writing of *Women in Love,* and in his America unfolded the most curious and determined quest of all for recovery of the primordial male identity. Under this impulse Lawrence wrote a series of essays on early American authors which constitutes a remarkable addition to the literature of enchantment with the New World, where the genius of an unknown, unexplored and yet ancient continent has always promised to the seeker setting out West from Europe vast new reaches of the human spirit. At the same time as these essays are fantasies of escape, they are also highly original and penetrating literary criticism. Finally, all things taken together, they stand as the best rendering of the principle that Lawrence had firmly established for himself in *Twilight in Italy*: that a symbology of being is best anchored in the deepest perceptions of place.

It was February 1916. Cornwall was *like the beginning of the* ML, 423 *world.* Lawrence, though undergoing one of his periodically recurring aversions to America, read *Moby Dick* for the first time, a copy of which happened to be in the house where he and Frieda were staying temporarily. A kindred spirit was suddenly there before him, with an

amazing correspondence of vision into time and place. The significance of his discovery fairly bursts out of a letter to Lady Ottoline Morrell.
ML, 424   Of the novel he said only that it was *a very odd, interesting book.* What it suggested to him was another matter. In one paragraph of the letter Europe is a doomed ship, a *Pequod.* One must go down with it or consent to live like a castaway. From the headlands of Cornwall, a sea as mysterious as Melville's called: *And the sea came in great long waves thundering splendidly from the unknown.* The urge to follow Melville
ML, 425   was all but irresistible: *I wish I were going on a long voyage, far into the Pacific. I wish that very much.*

Although he had not read *Moby Dick* before, Lawrence had been well acquainted with other American adventure stories in his boyhood. In this present dismal time of adulthood, one of his motives, perhaps the initial impetus, was the hope pure and simple of recapturing his adolescent spirit of voyaging. But he soon conceived a profound admiration for Melville and a far more complex attraction to his novel:
SM, 250   *Moby Dick* became *one of the strangest and most wonderful books in the world.* And out of this grew a thirst even to bypass America altogether and carry the expedition for a new life to the remotest of the South Seas, though it was of great significance that an American had shown the way. Here was an author who confirmed the rightness of Lawrence's searchings for the wellsprings of impersonal consciousness by turning to a mystical concept of place far beyond the Futurists' Italy or Hardy's England. Melville's far-off ocean of miraculous elemental life seemed identical, by occult correspondence, to the human unconscious. It did not matter that Melville had been only dimly aware of what he was creating, nor that he had covered his accomplishment by clumsy attempts at metaphysical speculation and a too-deliberate symbolism. One had only to look underneath these to see what Lawrence himself wanted to uncover in fiction: the flow of cosmic forces into particular persons and situations. The true essence of Melville was
SM, 245   in his *magnificent records of actual happening,* by which Lawrence meant those passages of the novel purportedly describing just the everyday events at sea but concerning at another depth the impact of elemental sea-life on the soul of man, with a mystic identity of the two. In both the earlier and the later version of his essay on *Moby Dick,*
SM, 237   Lawrence is carried away in the quotation of these passages, this *sheer movement of substance in its own paths, free from all human postulation or control.* Lawrence called this true symbolism and went on to define it further in a statement I have quoted in a preceding chapter, as
SM, 239   the *identity of daily experience with profound mystic experience.* Here
SM, 240   was how *actuality, of itself, in deep issues, becomes symbolic.* The chief example was the fight with Moby Dick himself, a piece of report-
SM, 249   ing that edged over into a *wonderful* and *awful* symbolism.

In the phrasing of some of his ideas on symbolism, Lawrence may have borrowed from the Imagists with whom he was associated before and during the war. One of their guiding principles was that *symbolic*   IP, 34
meaning must have its source in the literal meaning, and not be imposed upon it. But we should call to mind what a thoroughly puritan view of symbolism this is: an allegorical view obtaining in such works as *Pilgrim's Progress,* in which the heavenly is no more than an intensification of the natural. But most of all, the apocalyptic potency of Lawrence's imagination kept him constant to the double view that all that happened to him was actual and symbolic together. For the time, the Pacific, those *utmost waters,* represented the quarter of the globe   SM, 247
where salvation lay: to reach and to colonize an island in the midst of those waters was tantamount to recapturing the magnanimity of the primal masculine nature. However, the fear of corrupting the great quest always accompanied the hope of its attainment. And what was Ahab's quest but a perversion of Lawrence's shimmering hopes? Ahab was the puritan imagination in extremity, driven by a cold insanity of will to reach *the last attainment of extended consciousness.* To do this,   SM, 249
Ahab must slay the *deep, free sacral consciousness in man,* that is,   SM, 235
the great white whale, in the *last home of its existence,* the furthest waters or the deepest reaches of man's soul. This conquest of the lower centers of consciousness is the great mistake of our world, for out of it self-destruction flows at last: man cannot sever himself from half his being and survive. When the *Pequod,* the vessel of the spiritual monomaniac born of American civilization, is destroyed by Moby Dick, it is the lower consciousness rising up to smite the mental consciousness for its presumption and pride. Lawrence could well have said, in other terminology of his, that Ahab was guilty of the sin against the Holy Ghost: to destroy a vital part of oneself is unforgivable by its very nature, for that which is destroyed by an utter act of will can never be restored. But conversely, and in other terminology still, Lawrence might have pointed out that the voyage to the outer limits and the perishing of Ahab is essential to the birth of the new age. Under differing conditions the same destiny, with most of the same implications, overtakes Gerald Crich in *Women in Love.* How Lawrence tried to resolve the contradictions of such a fate is matter for later discussion.

As he gleaned such thoughts out of Melville but was apparently not yet setting them down, Lawrence was having another bout with writing his symbology in discursive form. Judging from such phrases in his letters as *bursting into new seas* and *shadowy America,* he looked   ML, 437
upon his reading of *Moby Dick* as integral to his achievement in writing this first, *the destructive half,* of his newest philosophy: which was probably the elusive *Goats and Compasses,* a work that has perished,

from all accounts. At the same time he was moving to another part of Cornwall and seeing this move as the dividing line between the old world and the new. In saying that he had crossed the ridge he certainly meant that in Melville he had seen the first of a new infusion of hope for the future.

But for the time being Lawrence could go no further with American things. *Women in Love* intervened of itself. He must be present at the last writings of the old world. No more talk of philosophy appears in the letters, of the creative half remaining, until he had done the novel, which also, as he looked back on it and thought up ML, 477 apocalyptic titles such as *The Latter Days,* was *purely destructive.* ML, 519 For another task he also put together his love poems since 1912 for ML, 500 the volume *Look! We Have Come Through! My final book of poems,* Lawrence called it, *my last work for the old world. The next must be for something new.*

Through the preparation of both of these books, the reading of American literature continued. As for the idea of going to America, it was the same situation of approach and withdrawal which had prevailed and would prevail for years, none of the longings any nearer to reality than this one expressed in a letter to Amy Lowell, which finds AL, 370 Lawrence reveling in the *non-human elements* of the *great rollers coming from the west. . . . Your remoter America must be splendid. One day, I hope to come to see it.* But what he truly desired now was to ML, 454 absorb this magnificence in books. In May 1916, about a month after launching into *Women in Love,* he read *Two Years Before the Mast,* with which he was overjoyed, and he looked forward with great anticipation to *Typee* and *Omoo,* though he did not get around to reading them until late in the year, after the completion of his novel. The pull of the Pacific was strong and increasing, but watery remoteness was only one of the two western magnetisms of place at work in his heart. AL, 371 The other was the wilderness of the American continent. This was active at least by August 1916, when he read Crevecoeur's *Letters of an American Farmer* and liked it immensely. But the truly overwhelming discovery of the wilderness came with the rediscovery of James Fenimore Cooper, who took his place with Melville as a great spellbinder. Lawrence read *The Deerslayer* in November and looked upon ML, 488 it as *pure and exquisite art.* He then went on to delight in others of the Leatherstocking series.

It was now early winter, and a kind of hibernation stole over KL, 98 Lawrence, with little work but with *the intimation of other worlds* from America arriving all along from the prophet of the sea and the prophet of the wilderness. At the beginning of 1917 Lawrence went through a revulsion against England more acute than ever, with an equal and opposite pull toward America. All that he had feared seemed on the point of coming to pass in the new government of Lloyd George, whom Lawrence detested as *sterile, barren, capable only of rapid and acute*   IH, 226 *mechanical movements* — those traits which Lawrence had seen as the end of England in Gerald Crich. Lawrence asked for passports to America, to *set off in quest of our **Rananim**.* On this occasion his   KL, 107 inevitable drawing back from commitment to America did not have time to develop: he was bluntly refused permission to leave the country. But by now, after an incubation of a year, he had a fairly definite plan in mind for all the enthusiasms gathered out of American authors: *a set of essays, or lectures, on Classic American Literature,* by which   HL, 394 he had meant to earn his living on arriving in America. So strong was the urge to produce these, now, that he went on eventually to do what he had said he could not do, *write for America* in England.

But not for a while yet. He took another route, at first, back to the long-postponed creative half of his symbology. In March, coming out of the winter lull, he wrote the articles "The Reality of Peace." He completed seven in all, four of which came out in the *English Review* the following May through August, and one of which has since turned out to be "The Whistling of Birds," first published in *Athenaeum* in   CE, 37 & 1919. The other two are lost somewhere. Much of these articles is in   ML, 584 the vein of the "Crown" essays, but at least some of the renascence urge anticipates that of "The Spirit of Place," the introduction to the American literature essays, in phrases such as this: *We are lifted to be*   PH, 6 *cast away into the new beginning. Under our hearts the fountain surges, to toss us forth. Who can thwart the impulse that comes upon us? It comes from the unknown upon us, and it behooves us to pass delicately and exquisitely upon the subtle new wind from heaven, conveyed like birds in unreasoning migration from death to life.*

Next, in June or July, Lawrence began a symbological work which he finished by the end of August and which has also disappeared. He gave it the title *At the Gates* and based it, he said, *upon the more*   HL, 414 *superficial* Reality of Peace. In the same letter he reports that he has finally embarked upon his *set of essays on* The Transcendental Element in American Literature. Or, as he titled them a month later,   ML, 526 *The Mystic Import of American Literature.* When not writing he went out in the field with farmer friends to help with the grain harvest: *Heaven and earth have passed away; apocalyptically I bind corn in*   HL, 416 *the fields above the sea, and know the distance. There is no more England, only a beyond.* The essays in their first stage occupied Lawrence off and on for the next two years, until September 1919; and then again in mid-1920, in what may be referred to as the second stage, he rewrote at least 'some of them in Sicily. There was a third stage as well, for the essays were wholly rewritten later on in America.

I have not been able to determine in just what order Lawrence worked on the essays in the first stage. In any case the progress of his responses to the separate authors, as the revelations of American literature opened before him, are of much greater moment. Fortunately, this progress can be outlined for at least four of the authors: Melville, Dana, Crevecoeur, and Cooper.

Dana, we remember, is the second American author Lawrence mentions reading at this time. Even though the only version currently available of Lawrence's essay on him is the third and last, that of 1922, the reasons why he originally thought the book so astonishingly good are still traceable, both in the Dana essay itself and in the first lines of the "Two Principles" essay, written at the time of the early versions as transition from authors concerned with the land to the sea-as-unconscious theme in Dana and Melville. In reading *Moby Dick,* Lawrence had met in Ahab with the idealist run amok, set on taking the realm of the senses by force and annihilating it. Melville in that novel was more often "ideal" observer than participant. But in *Two Years Before the Mast* Lawrence came across a centrally involved narrator whose purpose, though it operated in far different fashion, was closely allied to that of Ahab: to establish the sovereignty of the mind over the blood. That is, Dana's was a search for greater knowing, not for greater being, and thus it stood opposite to Lawrence's own allegiance to the quest. But Dana too, like Melville in ignorance of his own powers, was endowed with the mystical sense that transforms straightforward narrative into profound symbolism, though Dana was a more limited man and kept the strictest control over himself always, inflexible in reducing being to knowing all the way to the outer peripheries of existence.

In Dana, however, the greater clarity of the narrator's position brings into play the moral enigma that Lawrence felt is submerged in *Moby Dick* by the intense concentration on obliterating the blood psyche, a moral enigma with deep affinities to the nexus of themes in *Women in Love*. At the time he read Dana he had done two-thirds of a draft of the novel. What he saw in Dana is how man is fated to be caught in a great universal antagonism between being and knowing:

SM, 196   *This is the great cross of man, his dualism. The blood-self, and the nerve-brain self.* Mankind cannot avoid going now to one extreme, now to the other, either in himself or in the ages of his civilization. Some men, like Dana, must be the precursors to a given way of life, at the beginning and the end of ages, and Lawrence in consequence sets him down in his column of heroes. Most who go to sea never confront the great elemental force but merely lapse from consciousness altogether and become as creatures of the sea. This even Melville frequently does, becoming less than a man. But Dana remains unblink-ingly himself. We find him sailing up the California coast *on the brink* SM, 204 *of the unknown,* reaching the limit of his *glamour-world.* Yet once SM, 206 there all he can do is hamletize as the self-conscious actor until he borders on a *scientific indifference to self.* But he is drawn back invol- SM, 205 untarily to the East Coast, his world of actuality, passing the extreme verge of his life on the homeward voyage. The dark waters of Cape Horn seem to *almost swallow him up.* The icebergs, the fog and the SM, 207 gales come to a truly ancient mariner atmosphere. But Lawrence emphasizes that Dana *has carried his consciousness open-eyed through* SM, it all. He has won through. The ideal being.* 208–209

And from his book, we know too. He has lived this great experience for us, we owe him homage.

Lawrence speaks of the passage around Cape Horn as weathering the *polar death-mystery,* and we think at once of the mountain topog-raphy objectifying the same mystery, the last ridge of the ideal world, in *Women in Love.* A moment's comparison of Dana with Gerald Crich is highly informative, particularly if we call to mind also the parallel already suggested between Captain Ahab and Gerald Crich. All three are under the spell of a mechanical, ideal principle. But Dana differs from the other two in that his ruling purpose, when all is said and done, is to submit his integral self to the primitive forces and to have knowledge of them: only this, and not to bend them to his devouring will. His thirst for knowledge is *a new phase of dissolution,* SM, 196 true enough, and he has surrendered much of his humanity in relin-quishing being for knowing, but Lawrence stresses his integrity and therefore his responsibility. He thus escapes the scathing condemnation Lawrence so often heaped upon idealists.

If we now think back over Lawrence's psychological journey from the time of *The Rainbow,* though it is only about a year, we realize that the former questing surrogate in Ursula is a bygone figure indeed. A new ambiguity toward idealism has intervened. The ideal world was purely antagonistic before. To achieve her rebirth Ursula did not have to enter into the ideal state herself and suffer through metamorphosis therein as the only means to a sublime future of balance between the instincts and the rational faculty. Quite the opposite. As she was about to consent to the ideal world through acceptance of life with Skre-bensky, her instincts rebelled to prevent her surrender to these forces of evil. But at least since the "Crown" essays and *Twilight in Italy,* Lawrence has moved away from that simple dualism. He must see pioneers setting forth into areas of experience where profound ambiguities prevail. The ideal destiny and the intuitive destiny are now an amalgam, not forever opposed antitheses. Not that Lawrence has lost faith in the triumph of equilibrium in the uncharted distance, but the ranges of experience between are not so easily overleaped, and across some of those dangerous divides the very territory of hell must be traversed, or a purgatory maybe, but in any case a condition not to be bypassed in any progress of the human soul toward a high destiny.

But Lawrence did not quite know what to do with the inescapable stage of deathly mentality until he had added the wilderness to the sea in his penetration of imaginary regions westward. Dana, however much Lawrence felt like thanking him, had lapsed back into mundane civilization. Lawrence suspected there were further reaches of spiritual biography at sea that he must look into, and for that purpose he wished to read Melville's *Typee* and *Omoo* — with a preference for *Typee*. But he did not have the opportunity to do so until late in the year. Whether by accident or design, the next book after Dana that he read, or at least the next to have a telling effect on him, brought him ashore where he had the primeval spirit of place of the savage continent to contend with, and this new dimension enthralled him equally with that of the sea. The book was Crevecoeur's *Letters of an American Farmer,* the work of a son of the Enlightenment who went to till the soil on the frontier, who parades much eighteenth-century cant on the benignity of nature and the nobility of the savage, but who yet according to Lawrence had the soul of an artist beneath the exterior of the convention-bound man and could see now and then into the true daimonic nature of his environment. Lawrence had read him before August 23, 1916, for in a letter of this date to Amy Lowell he mentions him. More than that, he sets down his most specific response yet to AL, 371 American literature as a whole: *I liked Crevecoeur's* Letters of an American Farmer *so much. And how splendid Herman Melville's* Moby Dick *is, & Dana's* Two Years Before the Mast. *But your classic American literature, I find to my surprise, is* older *than our English. The tree did not become new, which was transplanted. It only ran more swiftly into age, impersonal, non-human almost. But how good these books are! Is the* **English** *tree in America almost dead? By the literature, I think it is.*

The hypothesis that the European psyche had aged rapidly in America, which Lawrence could have borrowed from de Tocqueville, helped to bolster his belief in the affinity of that psyche with the *impersonal, non-human.* Clearly the germ of the American literature essays was alive and growing a good year before Lawrence did any serious work on them. He had probably formed the nucleus of this assertion out of *Moby Dick* and *Two Years Before the Mast* alone. The effect of Crevecoeur was a more immediate longing for direct contact with a wild spirit of place: *Often I have longed to go to a country which has new, quite unknown flowers & birds. It would be such a joy to make their acquaintance. Have you still got humming birds, as in Crevecoeur?* With Melville and Dana, Lawrence had been to the outer verges of experience, but it was not, except by pure fantasy, a journey that he held in prospect for himself. He could relate more closely to Crevecoeur's tiny, improbable creature of the air than to Dana's albatross or Melville's whale, though as vision the substance is virtually the same. He liked the particular way in which Crevecoeur saw beyond the stylized categories of civilization into the *dark, primitive, weapon-like* SM, 64 soul of the hummingbird, so small but so fiercely its own isolate self. Such creatures must have arisen from *the breath of the first creation.* They preceded even the flowers they feed on, Lawrence felt, and he was so captivated that he eventually wrote a poem about them from descriptions like Crevecoeur's.[1] They were the first dazzling animation out of the turgidity of matter, but monsters back then, piercing *the slow vegetable veins* of creation.   CP, 372

Crevecoeur not only helped Lawrence to communicate with ancient life forms in the American wilderness, but since he stood almost at the beginning of American literature, he was indisputable proof that *some little salt of the aboriginal America* had seeped into immigrant SM, 61 veins almost on arrival.

Lawrence now moved forward in history and gave his attention to an author with whom his mind had clearly been preparing a reacquaintance for some time and who soon held a place of equal esteem with Melville: James Fenimore Cooper. Where his reading of this author falls in the chronology of the 1916 study of American literature is difficult to fix, but there is sufficient indication that Lawrence recalled reading some of his books in boyhood and came back to them with a new sense of their greatness. Jessie Chambers records that Lawrence and she read in their youth *Last of the Mohicans* and *The Pathfinder,* JC, 96 *with its impression of the expanse of level lake and silence.*

On June 12, 1916, Lawrence wrote Koteliansky of how he was finding in Cooper and others *a beautiful literature for boys, adven-* KL, *turous and romantic. I can read it now, when all other books seem* 80–81 *rather tiresome.* He praises *Moby Dick* and *Two Years Before the Mast* and calls *The Last of the Mohicans* and *Deerslayer lovely beyond words.* He may at this time have been recalling the excellence of Cooper from childhood, for he mentions both books some five months later almost as if newly acquainted with them. When he wrote asking ML, 485 for these two, he also requested *The Pathfinder* — the other Cooper we know he read in his youth. He became possessed with the idea that the

ML, 488 art of such writers as Cooper was *the subtlest and loveliest and most perfect in the world.* This particular passion was ablaze for most of the time he worked on *Women in Love,* and under its spell he moved forward into the most curious and self-absorbing phase of his imaginary travels in America.

The magnificence of Melville, for Lawrence, rested on his easy ability to transform common activity into the mystical workings of the universe. With this assessment many can agree. No such heightened realism informs the work of Cooper for most people, but rather a romanticism at best improbable and at worst preposterous. But Lawrence is not out to make discriminations between the two authors. He goes to Cooper for the same thing he had sought so diligently in Melville: the dispatching of the psyche to the limits of geographical and spiritual experience. With Cooper, however, he felt no necessity to read abstruse symbolism into common activity. The unreality of Cooper's sentiment and language, simply as they are, abetted the search. Lawrence went to Cooper for what looks like the same satisfaction that a boy has in reading him: pure uncritical wish-fulfillment. But since Lawrence to a great extent realized what he was doing, the wish-fulfillment takes on a complex turn of dynamic psychology. He was conforming to a universal pattern. People, especially males, dream of impossible acts of heroism from adolescence on. We have in current times the forceful example of the world-wide thirst for American western movies and books — which are more and more discussed, particularly in Europe, under a sophisticated terminology of myth. Cooper too has in later times enjoyed on the grounds of myth a greater reputation in Europe than in America. If we need to look into history for examples of wish-fulfillment, we might take the incredible exploits of medieval romances, and further back, the same exaggerations in the classical epics: Lawrence in fact with good reason compares the novels of Cooper with the Odyssey. The old romantic epic as resurrected in Cooper was just the sort of literature to appeal to a strong side of Lawrence's nature in his wartime plight: a need for new country attainable only by active fantasy-making, and an urgent part of that need the acquisition of a strong male identity.

Of the two kinds of Cooper novels, Lawrence took up the Anglo-American tales concentrating on refined whites as a springboard to his real absorption, the frontier adventures of Leatherstocking and the Indians. Implicitly he identified with Cooper and with all that Cooper in these novels assumed as a fictional self. He goes out with Cooper

SM, 93 into *another world of reality,* of *mystery and passion, . . . the mystical*

"next step": in the shape, of course, of Natty Bumppo. It is *the Odyssey*   SM, 94
of the white soul, as it vanishes into the unknown. Homer's Odyssey
was *the unfolding of the pristine soul of a race.* Cooper's "Odyssey"
spins out *the passing of the final race-soul,* at this end of that great
span of time since Homer. Lawrence goes on to call the adventures of
Natty a *consummation on the brink of oblivion, . . . the mystery of
conjunction in finality, when at last the soul in the conqueror embraces
and is at one with the ghost of the conquered.*

What is this *myth of the atonement* that prompts Lawrence to call   SM, 81
Cooper a great visionary of the future of America? And, in due course,
another question: How much of it is truly Cooper's vision, and how
much Lawrence's sophisticated invention?

Lawrence had before him the only undeniable example in modern
times of the absolute subjugation, and as far as he could see, annihilation, of a culture as ancient as any in the world by an invading race
which in a short time produced the most advanced culture on earth
in territory wrested from the stone-age possessors. That the conquered
were a dark race and therefore equated with the passional self, while
the conquerors were white and therefore equated with the rational self,
made the case complete: this was the history of the world in little,
and from it the future could most likely be extrapolated. If in the vast
movement through the era of the brain toward an end bordering on
the era of blood, Melville and Dana had encountered blood-being in
the seas, and Crevecoeur in the animal life of the land, it was Cooper
who had confronted the same elements in human form, and who must
therefore have gone further than the others in foreknowledge of the
new race of man, when the *myth of the atonement* would be consummated in full. As the life-history of an alter-ego, Natty Bumppo, unfolds
across *the aboriginal American landscape* with a magnificence that   SM, 98
Lawrence cannot find words sufficient to praise, he detects also an
internal chronology to support his opinion that Natty endures the final   SM, 99
days of the white race pressing to the limits of the known world and
touching the western mountains where the Pacific and the continental
influences coalesce to form the first shores of the new epoch. The
chronology demands that we begin with Natty as an old man and
accompany him by regular steps back to his youth in the last of the
Leatherstocking series, for his story is a *biography in futurity, . . . the*   SM, 101
return of the aged Ithacus and of his rejuvenation. The two novels that
most move Lawrence to prophetic heights of criticism are the last and
the first of Natty's career, *The Prairie* and *The Deerslayer,* and Lawrence exhibits in his comment on these some of his most imaginative
skill in what makes his criticism of American literature great: the

analysis of psychological motives in others which may be applied equally to himself.

SM, 99   *The Prairie,* as Lawrence reads it, is *the story of the recoil and death of the white element in the force of the native daimon.* It takes place under *great wings of vengeful doom* out there on the western prairie which *is the last stronghold of the aboriginal Daimon.* The plot

SM, 100 of this novel is of little consequence, says Lawrence: the *presentation* is everything. Incidentally, this terminology, like that which Lawrence offers in defining symbolism, has the ring of Imagism. One of F. S.

IP, 18 Flint's rules for the writing of imagistic poems was *to use absolutely no word that does not contribute to the presentation.* But what is acute in Lawrence's view here is that he sees the westward movement in America as it is more and more looked upon today: as a laying waste to nature, not as a taming of savage hinterlands. This aspect of colonization Lawrence emphasizes throughout his treatment of Cooper, from the first movement of settlers into upper New York State in *The Pio-*

SM, 99 *neers: How long will such a civilisation sterilise the creative world? Not long. The Spirits of Place take a slow, implacable revenge.*

    Besides the aged Natty, the other men on the prairie are certain orders of whites and Indians also magnified by Lawrence to a mythic scale. This being the region that his mind conjoined with the imagined Pacific, Lawrence's Plains Indians, if not Cooper's, manifest the effects

SM, 100 of a watery realm. That they are nearly *one flesh* with their horses gives them a sensuousness completely oriented to life, to its *voluptuousness* and its *sudden ferocity.* Curiously, Lawrence thinks of this quality as *Polynesian.* As we will note later, he saw a likeness between their life-ways and those of the natives of Melville's *Typee.* Both sorts of natives inhabit the very borders of existence. As for the horse and its total lack of connection with Polynesia, the stallion in the later *St. Mawr* has sometimes been seen as traceable to Moby Dick. As regards primitive life orientation on their own continent, the Plains Indians for Lawrence are opposite in tendency to those of eastern America, whom he classifies as death-directed. This rounds out the symbolical pattern, becoming consistent again with Lawrence's usual symbolism of direction: the east as death, the west as life. Natty may have gone west to die, fleeing in his old age from civilization, but that his quest is for rebirth makes all the difference: to die in the region of life assures resuscitation.

    These Plains Indians exhibit another trait which is vital to their compatibility with the spirit of Natty Bumppo. They inhabit the prairie but they are not of it, any more than Natty is. That they are in transit explains why Natty joins and subsequently identifies with them. In an unusual assignment of roles, Lawrence makes of the westward-moving

whites of this novel those who truly belong: that is, the whites who
contrast with Natty. These people are *Ishmael and his huge sons and*   SM, 99
his great werewolf of a wife, who *roll lonely and inevitably forward*
from the frontiers of Kentucky into the vast, void prairie. The outcasts
are the inheritors here. We learn from Cooper's text what Lawrence
continually suggests, that these conquerors of the empty spaces leave
a path of ruin behind them, felling sometimes the only grove of trees
for miles around to make a breastworks for a few days use. And yet,
in Lawrence's scheme, they belong. Their power of motion will not
bear them beyond the prairie. They halt, they entrench themselves on
a rise and stubbornly resist all efforts of the Indians and the elements
to dislodge them: *The brutal spirit of the prairie, the brutal recoil of*   SM, 100
Ishmael, these are the place-reality. They will withdraw into their own
place and devour it.

The contrasting and dominant theme with which Lawrence is concerned in *The Prairie* is the Great Plains as a zone of psychological
testing in Natty's pilgrimage. This prairie is the great void to be traversed, and Natty is equal to it. Once across, the aged hunter comes
to the *hills of the Far West,* which Lawrence imagines to be the home   SM, 99
of Pacific-influenced Indians and to give almost directly, in the topography of his fantasy, on the Pacific Ocean. This is *a region of sus-*   SM, 100
pended abstraction for Natty. In these hills he dies, having *gone beyond*
himself. But Lawrence is careful to make a cycle of his destiny, and
in so doing he takes the seemingly contradictory course of reversing
his usual symbolic directions. He has Natty at last looking eastward
for rebirth — even to the point of misreading Cooper, who really has
Natty die looking westward.[2] For Lawrence the action unfolds thus:
Natty expires at *the limits of the world, looking far eastward, where*
his soul's land lies, among the forests and darkness of the trees and the
great sweet waters. In countering Cooper's symbolism with his own,
Lawrence was stretching a point to read himself into Natty. Natty's
east lay west to Lawrence, from where he was in Cornwall, the sort of
"east" he found not only in Cooper but in Crevecoeur and in Hawthorne. In this particular period of envisaging an accomplished rebirth
in America, though he may have talked much of the Far West, Lawrence focused on the lakes and forests he had first encountered in
American literature as a boy.

While he devoted some discussion to each of the Leatherstocking
series, it is in his views on the last volume, *The Deerslayer,* that
we grasp the finished design of Lawrence's symbological reading of
Cooper. A reversal of biography, Lawrence called the series, a map-
ping-out from age back to pristine youth. It is a journey in which Natty
bears the whole white consciousness to the brink of extinction. In even

vaster symbolic terms the journey points to a new amalgamate race that will recapture youth and institute a new era. Small wonder, in view of the ultimate prophecy he then thought it to contain, that Lawrence SM, 106   called *The Deerslayer one of the most beautiful and most perfect books in the world.*

One of the secrets of its beauty is the symbolism, which, as mentioned earlier, was not the same to Lawrence as Melville's. That symbolism dealt in the underlying significance of events related as common narrative, without intimations of profundity interfering with the concrete surface. With Cooper the symbolism functioned by a sense of escape into a magical narrative that left any realism of the actual scene behind. The difference between Cooper and Melville here was grounded in differing perceptions of time. Melville's prose is a revelation of the past deeply ingrained in the soul of man, a past that merely edges over into the present and the future. But the lake scene of *The Deerslayer,* for instance, casts a spell that *must lie in the luminous futurity which glimmers as a plasm in all the landscape.* From the first words of the novel the language carries the reader straight into the luminescent future of Lake Glimmerglass and an American race reborn.

Deerslayer is Natty as virgin youth, though race-old as only the reborn can be and as only the aging Cooper could conceive of him. As he is quite plainly a projection of Lawrence's concept of his own deepest self at the time, what Lawrence thinks he is and does requires close scrutiny. First, Deerslayer is proof against any hint of domination SM, 109   by woman. And why is this so desirable? Because *a race falls when men begin to worship the Great Mother, when they are enveloped within the woman, as a child in the womb. And Deerslayer represents the heroic spirit of his race passing in singleness and perfection beyond his own race, into the pure unknown of the future.* All sexual love spurned, Natty *goes his way into the woods with the young Indians.*

If this seems altogether like the adolescent hero disappearing womanless into the sunset, we soon find that Lawrence's view is more intricate than this. Despite his rebirth, Natty is a "slayer," we remember, and deathward set through that range of experience from which the new American will evolve out of the extinct soul of Natty's own race and that of the Red Men, for whose destruction he will be responsible, paradoxically, though he loves them. Natty understands instinctively that all this is to come to pass, and that he acts for his race as a SM, 110   whole. In the beyond *he sees the Red Man, the sensual being which for ages he has been destroying or fleeing from. And that which he has most perfectly destroyed he now most perfectly accepts across the gulf.* He cannot pass across the gulf to unite with the other race. He must remain true to *his own mystery,* the white man's, while still acknowledging that of the Red Man to perfection. This view of Natty Bumppo as an archetype of future humanity gave Lawrence emotional authority to predict what the world beyond catastrophe would be like, and this he finds symbolized and foreshadowed by Cooper's setting as much as by the character: *The lovely American landscape is the pure land-* SM, 111 *scape of futurity: not of our present factory-smoked futurity, but of the true future of the as yet unborn, or scarcely born, race of Americans.*

One might infer that Lawrence was forecasting a race of mixed blood, with an outward swarthy appearance as a sign of the inward blend of the pale soul of the mind and the dark soul of the blood. But any such supposition is cancelled out by Lawrence's assertion that the Red Man is to be wiped out and his influence to be exerted only by the entrance of his soul into the conquering soul of the white man. As far as Lawrence was depending on actual conditions for his symbology, and this was slight, he thought in common with most Europeans that the number of Indians left in the United States was infinitesimal and that their disappearance was imminent. As for the specific nature of the future America, we can gain some idea of it from *The Plumed Serpent,* or more succinctly from an even later work, the fragmentary dream-vision printed in *Phoenix* as "Autobiographical Fragment" — henceforth referred to by Keith Sagar's more appropriate title, "A Dream of Life." In this the narrator wakes a thousand years hence in a land of gentle, bearded agrarians who live in mystic harmony with the earth and sky, keeping a ritual cadence with the cosmos in dance. But we find here a people more like ancient Egyptians or Minoans or Etruscans than American Indians, for Lawrence consistently refused to see American Indians or any other race of dark blood alive today as anything other than deteriorated remnants of the ancient mystic-sensual way of life, as much in need of an infusion of spirit as the white race was of an infusion of blood.

But for the moment the main inquiry must be into the individual attributes of the free and creative self in the future, as far as Lawrence can see this in Natty. First and foremost, it is a male self upon whom devolve the grave responsibilities of leadership: to show the way, in the case of Natty, by what can only be the sacrifice of self to the future. The renunciation of mating means death. But the choice is not what we might expect, between a "normal" and desirable marriage and a sacrificial celibacy. The acceptance of sex, for Natty, would mean falling into the hands of the passionate and overpowering Judith Hutter. If he chose her, *he would be gone, merged, consumed into the woman,* SM, *having no being of his own apart from her.* Between his soul of pure 108–109 spirit and hers of complete sensuality there can be no fusion, no balance. The male spirit, then, is at a desperate pass: either to submit to female sovereignty or to go its way alone toward a future whose realization is impossible short of several generations. In this present world, no true marriage is possible.

Now this may seem a curious conclusion for Lawrence to allow himself to be driven to so soon after he had tussled with the problem in *Women in Love* and won through to a marriage between Birkin and Ursula that is one of the most successful he ever imagined. We are accustomed, of course, to oscillations in his attitude to women. What is of interest in a comparison of the novel with the essays is how the investigation of marriage in conjunction with symbolic landscapes having a temporal dimension brings two such opposite results. The polar heights of *Women in Love* precede another terrain which may not yet be mapped but which promises to hold a true marriage of days to come. In the landscape of *The Deerslayer* as Lawrence construes it, no revitalized marriage of the future seems inherent at all. Union between the sexes is presented as impossible in the setting which is considered a foretaste of the new age. However, if we delve a little further into the troubled sources of Lawrence's inspiration, and take full account that we are dealing with a lake, we see implications for sex relationships ahead that do not at first meet the eye. For most of his life Lawrence had faith in lakes as places of rebirth. To go back to a basic setting, one reason is surely that Lake Garda was the scene of high hopes and some realization of them. In this connection, during his
ML, 500   absorption with American literature, Lawrence *got together* his book of poems *Look! We Have Come Through!,* the record of a husband and wife journey toward unison culminating in what is hesitantly de-
CP, 191   scribed as *some condition of blessedness.* These blissful associations may offset to some degree the urge to flee the woman altogether.

But another significant lake association tends precisely in the direction of female repudiation, one that goes a long way to explain the togetherness of Deerslayer and the Indian braves. Lawrence was on a walking trip with Koteliansky and other friends in the Lake District of England when the war broke out — soon after his hike through France and Switzerland with one or more other men in June 1914, the hike on which he may have drawn in constructing the relationship between Rupert Birkin and Gerald Crich. In the Lake District excursion Lawrence experienced something of the kind of male camaraderie that he often felt must be the basis of civilization in the age to come. This is how he described the occasion some six months afterwards:
ML, 309   *The War finished me: it was the spear through the side of all sorrows*

*and hopes. I had been walking in Westmorland, rather happy, with water-lilies twisted round my hat — big, heavy, white and gold water-lilies that we found in a pool high up — and girls who had come out on a spree and who were having tea in the upper room of an inn, shrieked with laughter. And I remember also we crouched under the loose wall on the moors and the rain flew by in streams, and the wind came rushing through the chinks in the wall behind one's head, and we shouted songs, and I imitated music-hall turns, whilst the other men crouched under the wall and I pranked in the rain on the turf in the gorse, and Koteliansky groaned Hebrew music — **Ranani Sadekim Badanoi.***

It seems like another life — we were happy — four men. Then we came down to Barrow-in-Furness, and saw that war was declared.

It is a clear picture of Lawrence's ideal of a male community, a brotherhood living in freedom from civilized restraint, like Natty and the warriors. The experience took place in about the closest thing England has to a lake and forest wilderness, and so near did it remain to the realization of his hopes that Lawrence took the name of his Utopia, Rananim, from the song Koteliansky sang at the time. Upon this idyllic season, as upon the idyllic season originating at Lake Garda, fell the blight of the Great War.

The male bond in these American literature essays is what we have already taken it to be in *Women in Love,* a redirecting of homosexual proclivities toward a new scale of spiritual and physical intimacy in a world made over. The matter has an important place also in the essays on Melville and Dana. Ishmael's closeness to Queequeg, the Polynesian harpooner, is an intimation of friendship in the age to come — as it is also, of course, symbolic of the unity of opposites, light and dark, blood and mind, in that future age. Dana has an analogous experience with Hope, a South Sea islander who was for a brief spell his *hearts-* SM, 206 *brother,* and *full of the mystery-being of that great sea,* the Pacific. But Lawrence's supreme opportunity to speak of racial sympathy between males as presaging a new world still came with the bond between Natty and the American Indians, a womanless confraternity of warriors with Natty representing the last state of the white soul, and Chingachgook, his Indian heart's brother, the last state of the red soul, with not only love for the Indian as soul-mate involved, but also the passion which is in death, for Natty is a slayer: *No woman could give* SM, 110 *him the sheer flame of sensation he feels when the hand of a hostile Indian is laid on him as he lies in his canoe believing himself to be far out on the water.* But when death is past in the catastrophic process of killing and bringing to life, the glorious hope of the future remains. It is all prophecy to Lawrence, pure prophecy rooted in place and in the spirit of place: prophecy in Natty Bumppo and in Cooper who created him, prophecy in himself, obscurely at work on a grand design, summed up in what Lawrence said of Cooper: *The great demon, the vast Spirit of Place in the New World, drew him, polarised the whole of his living psyche. . . . And he dreamed his true marriage with the aboriginal psyche.*

SM, 96

The question was posed a few pages back as to how much if any of this prophetic vision really coheres in the novels of Cooper, with their worse than operatic artificiality of situation and emotion, and how much is due to pure invention out of Lawrence's overwrought imagination. In answer we may say that at least the points of departure for Lawrence's projections of Cooper into apocalyptic realms are truly in the works themselves. Cooper was one of the first to admit some understanding of the Indian to his pages, no matter if this is overlaid with the cant of his day. He truly exhibits what Lawrence saw in all American writers: a flat contradiction between the straitened morality to which they confess allegiance and the workings of the unconscious beneath. Through the vague awareness of Natty Bumppo, Cooper caught a fineness of spirit that was being extinguished by the white devastation of Indian cultures, even as in the same character he repeated the stock claims of the superiority of civilization over savagery. And Cooper does convey the feeling that the future may lie in some mystical mingling of the spirit of Natty with the spirit of Chingachgook, though this is very imperfectly prefigured. For a further aspect of Cooper's underlying prophetic tone, even as he spoke of what he roundly called the *advancement of civilization,* he let slip his strong suspicion that the results of settlement westward might be disastrous to American life and not to its glorious benefit. He expressed what we would now refer to as a concern for the environment. Lawrence only carried Cooper's fears to their last implication, to the working out of a whole cycle of exploitation and exhaustion in ideal, mechanical civilization — until the new time returns, the new world that Cooper presents in the lake setting of *Deerslayer.*

PA, vi

As for historical prophecy, at least this may be said also for Lawrence's essays: they point directly to what many have been forced to face since his time. The *advancement of civilization,* or to use its current name, development, is a hell-bent course in the impoverishment of nature and a suppressing of the spirit of the continent by material greed. Further, there are stirrings, confused, obscure and simply barbaric though they often are, towards some sort of reshaping of a "primitive" ideal in America, which in one of its aspects encompasses a new awakening of what might be called the spirit of the continent: in the demand of Indians, for instance, for a greater part in the national life and the national soul. Lawrence's "prophecies" thus make a degree of sense sixty years afterwards that most prophecies never live to achieve.

Lawrence's perusal of American literature took him on into several more authors than those discussed: Franklin, Poe, Hawthorne and Whitman, on all of whom he wrote essays. He applies his revolutionary theories to these authors also with thoroughness and finesse. Franklin comes out to be a complete example of the automatizing of life, a *very* SM, 45 *Frankenstein of virtue.* He is the only American discussed in whom Lawrence found not one saving tinge of free spontaneity, but a man absolutely and totally blind to the mystery of spirit of place. In Hawthorne, Lawrence discovered one of the firmest supports for his theories and in *The Scarlet Letter* one of the greatest books. Hawthorne's art proceeded on a downright duplicity, he said, pious and spiritual on the surface and yet lustful underneath to demolish all spiritual creeds. It was Hawthorne's skill in symbology that carried him through to a great triumph, almost if not entirely in spite of himself. In the writers with whom he had challenged his imagination up to Hawthorne, Lawrence had sensed various stages approaching a climax in the coming fall of the spiritual consciousness, or as in Cooper a prophecy of the event. But in Hawthorne alone did he see a dramatization of the actual fall. The Reverend Dimmesdale is the very flame of ethereal purity. Hester, the sensual soul in revolt, overthrows him in seduction. She is exposed to mockery when found out, but in the exaltation of her scarlet emblem a sacred heart of shame is worshipped, a subtle reversal of purpose deceiving even Hawthorne in his conscious self.

This reading of *The Scarlet Letter* puts Lawrence in a position to expatiate again on the facet of his theories closest to his heart and to his personal problems at the time: the resurgence of male mastery and a concomitant reawakening of instinctive submission in woman. The role of woman in Lawrence's scheme has now grown more complex, since in Hawthorne's novel the tension between upper and lower consciousness exists in the direct embodiment and the direct involvement of man and woman, not in the adventure of the male soul with the impersonal in the shape of the sea, the wilderness or a native race. Woman derives from the passionate cosmic substance, much as in *Le Gai Savaire,* and yet man is responsible for the form in which she appears, for man is the creator and he inevitably creates woman in his own image, so that he may if so inclined pervert the natural being of woman: which complicates *Le Gai Savaire.* To explain his stand, Lawrence goes back to the Biblical myth of creation. For him *the Eve* SM, 139 *myth symbolises the birth of the upper mind, the upper consciousness.* Perhaps the apparent contradiction that woman is the instinctive half of being and yet that her birth signifies the birth of the mind can be resolved by assuming that it was the "idea" of woman that was born out of Adam — a perversion — and not the female creature herself. For a while, in any case, a natural balance existed between the upper and the lower consciousness of mankind. But under a misdirected male leadership came a day when idealism had gone to insufferable lengths, as in Dimmesdale. The primal sensuality in woman rebels. But woman, Lawrence insists, cannot take the lead. She can only sustain, and if her role as sustainer is denied her, she will turn destroyer. Lawrence SM, 143 is categorical about this: *Man must either lead or be destroyed,* and his destruction is accomplished by the woman whose spirit he has betrayed. With her natural bent for imitation, woman may become more spiritual than man and dominate in the affairs of life. In this she is abetted by another natural tendency of hers, possessiveness. Yet, all the while, she will remain the sensual psyche waiting for the male principle to resume control and show the way to a new flowering.

An ominous change has worked itself out in Lawrence's symbology since the days when he could assure a woman friend that his *Sis-* ML, 273 *ters* would be the story of woman becoming *self-responsible.* As he sees it now, indeed she does become so, but the difference is formi- SM, 143 dable: *When man falls before woman, and she must become alone and self-responsible, she goes on and on in destruction, till all is death or till man can rise anew and take his place.*

Up to now all representations of the male self have been of the purely mental variety, culminating in Natty Bumppo. In *The Scarlet Letter* a primordial male self appears as well, set off in opposition to the spiritual Dimmesdale and as bent on destroying him, deliberately, SM, 150 as Hester is by unconscious compulsion. This is Chillingworth, the *sensual male being in complete subordination, as we have him in modern life,* a vestige too contorted and stigmatized for Lawrence to feel any real identification with him. Under present conditions, allied as he is with *the aboriginal spirit of the primary, sensual psyche* of the American continent, Chillingworth has had no choice but to turn sorcerer and bring down by demonic means the reign of the spirit. He proves, if only by negative act, that the instinctive self cannot be for much longer confined, in space and time, to the small compass assigned it in American society. And even in malignity he is an exemplar of Lawrence's hunt for maleness, intimate with the spirit of place with which the male must recover kinship and through which he will regain the sceptre over the universal forces that issue forth through man: will recover the *splendid vivid loneliness* of essential male selfhood.

Poe furnished Lawrence with many instances of a state beyond anything in Hawthorne or Cooper. If *in the last conjunction between* *Leatherstocking and Chingachgook we see the passing out into the* *darkness of the interim, as a seed falls into the dark interval of winter,* then in Poe we see *the first vivid, seething reduction of the psyche, the* *first convulsive spasm that sets-in in the human soul, when the last im-* *pulse of creative love, creative conjunction, is finished.* This is the decomposition, the inevitable. Lawrence does not fail to follow, here as elsewhere, the established parabola of his thought on the adventure of the soul in America. He reminds us that Poe leads on to *that crisis of* *perfect quiescence which* **must** *intervene between life-cycle and life-* *cycle.* SM,
116–117

SM, 116

Two of the essays in the series as Lawrence planned it do not concern particular authors. The more important of the two is the one published as an introduction to the whole group in the *English Review* and plainly incorporating conclusions that Lawrence did not arrive at until after his thorough study of all the authors involved. Most likely Lawrence went over this essay, "The Spirit of Place," a number of times before sending it in to his agent on August 3, 1918, three months before it was published. ML, 562

"The Spirit of Place" is jubilant with the assurance of discovery. Lawrence felt that he had at last fulfilled two of the crying needs of his pilgrim spirit: to phrase a symbology, and to bind it to a particular place, here an imaginary America which served the purpose better than actuality could have. The sense of actual place as a restorative Lawrence had for the time being all but lost, through the war and all the aggravated effects that went with it: clinging as he was in Cornwall to the last saving shred of Europe and then bereft of that when sent inland by the authorities for fear he might be spying and contacting German submarines. He was evicted from his cottage on the coast in October 1917, in the midst of composing his American essays. The hard-won beliefs molded into this fantasy-grasp at spirit of place consoled him for the virtual loss of a native region or of any actual sojourning place, keeping aflame in him what he described in a letter as *another world of reality, actual and mystical at once, not the world* *of the Whole, but the world of the essential now, here, immediate; a* *strange actual whereabouts:* a direct model of the world he had seen in Melville. ML, 526

"The Spirit of Place" puts into explicit language the duality of soul that Lawrence sees as the dynamic of American character: how spirit of place operates as the primary cause of this division, and how spirit of place has given American literature its particular stamp. He discovers in American writing an *alien quality* that *belongs to the* SM, 16

American continent itself, for *all art partakes of the Spirit of Place in which it is produced.* It is this spirit which marks off American literature from English. The qualities of this literature are not only those of a newly settled continent but *the incipient realities of a whole new era of experience.* Almost the entirety of American literature, in Lawrence's opinion, is the endeavor of spirit of place to enter into the formation of American character. But the spirit acts in strange ways. The authors are hardly conscious that they are its instruments. They make overt claim to one set of ideas, humane, idealistic European ideas, which run in diametric contradiction to what the true artist says in the undertone of the text. In explaining how this state of affairs came about, Lawrence asks us to open our understanding to *the greater inhuman forces that control us,* the propulsive power of the migratory instinct in all mankind. Our species goes here or there at the bidding of spirit of place. Choice does little to determine our wayfaring: *We cannot see that invisible great winds carry us unwitting, as they carry the locust swarms, and direct us before our knowledge, as they direct the migrating birds. A place attracts its own human element, and the race drifts inevitably to its own psychic geographical pole.* The reason why America happened to be discovered by white men, to begin with, was that a circuit of place influence in Europe fell apart. First there had been a Roman-African circuit, then in the Middle Ages a Rome-Germany circuit — like that described in *Twilight in Italy.* When the latter broke apart, a new America-Europe circuit connected and Europeans sailed there willy-nilly. What was it exactly, then, that brought the Pilgrim Fathers, those puritan ancestors of American authors, to American shores? Not what they said, not the quest for religious freedom, for they at once established their own religious tyranny. Actually, they were the extremists of the European crusade to kill the mystery of the body and deify the mind: and so it went, all through early American literature.

But the spirit of place that drew the Pilgrims to American shores was the absolute opposite of the ideal they imported. It was dark, sensual, demonic, issuing from heavy forests and vast stretches of plain and the mighty uplift of mountains, as well as from the native race of America. While the early American authors worked assiduously at extending the idealist ethic over the unconscious, the blood-consciousness went on exerting itself through their fine words by symbolic means. One day, out of all this clashing, but only by the agency of apocalypse, would come a great synthesis, the right blend of races, at least in spirit, of the native Indian and the invading white, to manifest itself in a new golden age.

The other essay that gives us a clue to the overall structure that Lawrence had worked out for his essays — which does not emerge in

SM, 19

SM, 19–20

their partial publication in the *English Review* — is "The Two Principles," with which the published series broke off. In this piece Lawrence's design was to extend the theoretical foundation of thought outward from the mystique of the continent to the mystique of the sea: reversing the order in which he had made his discoveries in American literature. He felt that he had demonstrated, by a more or less chronological treatment of authors, a likewise chronological arc of experience in the transferred European soul caught in the toils of the new world. The encompassing of the sea was the second and last great stage in the geographical and simultaneously spiritual extension of the questing soul as it neared the boundaries of collapse. In this phase, the individual human character is so near dissolution that it is overshadowed in narrative importance by the vast impersonality of the sea. But there exists always the *true correspondence between the material cosmos and the* SM, 176 *human soul,* and this conviction gives Lawrence the opportunity to formulate his theories of the unconscious. This was the *new science* ML, 596 *of psychology* — though very old, he said, for the great distant ancients had known it — by which Lawrence meant to convert the world to a better way of life. He had gone into occult literature by this time, to add to what the pre-Socratic Greeks had taught him. But he still sticks to a framework of Biblical myth, putting the moment of creation at the point when the eternal substance of God, which always was, divided itself and yet remained whole in both halves: this was the separation of Fire (or Light) from the other elements. Afterwards, the waters were parted by a firmament and there came about the four-fold division of the universe which may be expressed in a variety of ways, as in the four elements or in the four arms of the cross as a symbol. Lawrence calls it *a four-fold travelling,* a going back and forth between the waters SM, 177 above and the waters below, and a going back and forth between the fire on the left and the fire on the right. His terminology often approaches that of Heraclitus. However, Lawrence stresses in all this that creation does not derive from some particular moment in the past. It is an eternally recurring cycle and God is as much present in the world today, and as much at work making it, as he ever was, ever is, ever will be. Always and forever the energy glances back and forth between the great living halves of the universe: Fire and Water, Male and Female, Earth and Air, Spirituality and Sensuality, and all the other opposing principles. A breaking asunder is as natural as a uniting. Cycles run inexorably from creation to destruction to creation again. In the arc back and forth we have the moments of perfect consummation, of consummate equilibrium between the two extremes. All of which, as we readily see, is what Lawrence found confirmed in American literature, a confirmation going on near the same time when he was giving voice to equivalent feelings in *Women in Love*. His own theory of fiction seemed to shine out of transatlantic literature: *In a story the movement depends on the sudden appearance of spontaneous emotion or gesture, causeless, arising out of the living self.* It was a kind of mysterious mobility.

If Lawrence's theories brought him to classify character as dependent on cosmological forces and historical cycles kept in motion by these forces, a sort of determinism may seem to lie at the conclusion of his train of thought. If so, a clash ensues between the high degree of individuality associated with his system and the rigid rule of a cosmic unconscious. If a key exists to this dilemma, it is to be found in careful examination of two conceptions of existence, one of which Lawrence openly espoused, and the other of which he denied consciously but could not escape. These opposing stresses put him in much the same position, in fact, as the American authors he was investigating. Something may now be added to previous discussion of the tragic view of life and the puritan view of life.

Reference to tragedy in the first version of the American literature essays is not prominent, except in the case of Poe. Lawrence finds no sense of tragedy in him because he creates no living self to be involved, which brings Lawrence to reiterate his view of tragedy: *In tragedy self meets self in supreme conjunction, a communion of passionate or creative death. But in Poe the self is finished, already stark.* A fuller and closely comparable definition occurs not in the essays but in Lawrence's preface to his play *Touch and Go,* written in the summer of 1919 between periods of work on the essays: *Tragedy is the working out of some immediate passional problem within the soul of man, ... a creative activity in which death is a climax in the progression towards new being.* How all-inclusive the concept may be Lawrence states in this way: *The whole business of life, at the great critical periods of mankind, is that men should accept and be one with their tragedy.* Such figures he does identify, certainly, in American literature: some of Melville's protagonists, and, pre-eminently, Natty Bumppo. But with the latter at least, tragedy goes well beyond traditional limits of definition: with him the tragic process no longer completes itself in one and the same individual. Natty accepts his part in the tragedy of the race as a whole, though in his single self he can never see rebirth but only foreshadow it in others.

To rectify any injustice that might seem to attach to his cosmic scheme, Lawrence would presumably have his belief in immortality to fall back on: some triumph for the sacrificial being in uniting after death with the souls of the passionate living. We know how important

SM, 118

SM, 117

PX,
291–293

such a conception of immortality was to Lawrence's theories in general. It suggests on occasion a Job-like wonder and thankfulness simply to be implicated in a power and a glory of such cosmic magnitude, without the solace of individual immortality. Even so, that the whole duty of men should be to *accept and be one with their tragedy* continues to give pause when the injunction must be extended to cover Dimmesdale as well as Leatherstocking, or in *Women in Love* Gerald Crich and Gudrun Brangwen. In that they cannot help belonging to the phase of the tragic process in which they are fixed, such figures may have to be viewed simply as victims of an overriding fate, whatever Lawrence's attempts to generate sympathy for them.

The crux of the problem abides in the contradictions of the puritan nature. What could be more puritan than Lawrence's definition of tragedy in the preface to *Touch and Go*? The *passional problem,* or the working out of salvation, proceeds in light of the knowledge that resurrection is ahead when one has overcome and cast off the lesser self, has been reborn out of sin through grace. The statement reflects Lawrence's puritan optimism and his trust in the magnitude of the individual soul in the eyes of the divine. Yet the correlative foreordination of the puritan creeps in: some are fated to be saved and some to be damned. Then the Job-like consent to the universal will begins to show its eerie side. All works together for good in the end. But the premise dictates the conclusion that even the damned ought to accept their torment as essential to the greater good. Where to go for an answer to this dilemma is difficult to say.

But these essays on American literature from which so much flowed besides a fantasy solution to Lawrence's most pressing problems are still best comprehended if linked to those problems. The urgent question for Lawrence near the end of the war was how to achieve a great rebirth in the male without succumbing to the agency of rebirth, the woman. He began his first novel on this theme, *Aaron's Rod,* shortly after he was forced out of Cornwall, though he delayed completion of it for some time, until among other things he had finished the first two versions of the American literature essays. But he confessed to his condition, and suggested how his work might go on in the upcoming years, in a letter to Katherine Mansfield in November 1918: *Beware* ML, 565 *of it — this mother-incest idea can become an obsession. But it seems to me there is this much truth in it: that at certain periods the man has a desire and a tendency to return into the woman, make her his goal and end, find his justification in her. In this way he casts himself as it were into her womb, and she, the Magna Mater, receives him with gratification. This is a kind of incest. It seems to me it is what Jack*

[John Middleton Murry] *does to you, and what repels and fascinates you. I have done it, and now struggle all my might to get out. In a way, Frieda is the devouring mother. It is awfully hard, once the sex relation has gone this way, to recover. If we don't recover, we die. But Frieda says I am antediluvian in my positive attitude. I do think a woman must yield some sort of precedence to a man, and he must take this precedence. I do think men must go ahead absolutely in front of their women. . . . Consequently the women must follow as it were unquestioningly. I can't help it, I believe this. Frieda doesn't. Hence our fight.*

NOTES

[1] Lawrence mentions **W. H. Hudson,** who described hummingbirds in several works, as one source of his impressions, and Henry Bates as another (SC, 33). He read Bates's *The Naturalist on the Amazon* in 1919. That same year he read Thomas Belt's *The Naturalist in Nicaragua,* which also contains descriptions of hummingbirds.

[2] *See* James Fenimore Cooper, *The Prairie* (New York, 1954), p. 452.

9

The Tremble of Space

Even though commissioned as a school text, *Movements in European History* seems to follow inevitably upon the American literature essays. The book dates from the last months of the war and the first few after the Armistice. The thesis Lawrence explores is like that of the "Spirit of Place" essay: that history is a matter of *great, surging movements* welling up spontaneously in portions of the human race and bearing them forth to overcome or to mingle with other men, to establish also a bond with a new spirit of place that will in time make of them a new race. While the Romans, for instance, had been able to adapt to vastly different lands and peoples in their advance over the known world, they were eventually modified by the contact. As stated in "The Spirit of Place," the *mysterious religious passion* of Africa, *seething in Roman veins,* spawned the whole Christian experience. But mysterious limits arise. The pagan Romans could not push far beyond the Rhine, not because of the German warriors, for they defeated these again and again, but because of their inability to adjust to spirit of place. They were *filled with mysterious fear when they found themselves in the dark, cold gloom of Germany, the northern savage land. They felt they had gone beyond their natural limits.*

    Still, if the Romans could not penetrate the German spirit of place, the Germans at length did penetrate theirs, and modern Europe arose from the fusion of the two races — the men of the icy north and the men of the warm south. This parallels Lawrence's view that the true future of America lay in the fusion of the native Indian spirit and the encroaching spirit of the European, when the coming amalgamation should at length reach its communion with the daimon of the American land.

MH, xxvi

SM, 16

MH, 44

This sweeping of races across great stretches of the world and the centuries in *Movements* was for one thing an outlet to Lawrence's pent-up imagination, just as the American essays had been. For he was all but frantic to resume his migrations after four years of restless confinement in England. But all he could do, just now, having completed his fantasy flight through space to America, was to take up an analogous flight into the past. For his own solace, he wished to demonstrate how the greatest good may be extracted from history as a means to living in the past and the future from the present moment of one's own day. In his introduction to *Movements,* Lawrence rejects a scientific view of history: *It is all beyond reasonable cause and effect, though these may be deduced later.* He rejects graphic history as well, that is, stories of great men and women made vivid and personal: *It is all outside personality, though it makes personality. . . . All that real history can do is to note with wonder and reverence the tides which have surged out from the innermost heart of man, watch the incalculable flood and ebb of such tides.* He who learns to appreciate history in this way can experience a wonderful *fulfilment in the past* as a greater dimension to his own life.

MH, xxviii

But while history is far *greater than any one man,* men are nonetheless the *substance* through which *life makes its own great gestures,* and therefore *in individual men the power is at its greatest.* The embodiment of great impersonal forces in a single man, another ramification of theories which for Lawrence began in fictional practice, was of prime significance in his view of the future.

In contradiction with his belief in the gratuitous as the motive force of history, Lawrence held that ages succeed one another according to a universal law, which if not exactly founded on cause and effect does perforce imply a logic and a teleology. The pattern does not allow for a future extrapolated from the marvelous events of the recorded past, but it verges on theoretical rigidity in another direction. It posits a future repeating the conditions of pre-history: that "Minoan" past which had antedated either the need or the faculty for producing written records. That future in fact might be almost upon us, when intuition and mentality should be in harmony as they had not been since the dim aeons of the early world.

While in his American literature essays Lawrence had confined himself to general prophecies on the inevitability of the soul's entrance into a new historical epoch, in *Movements* he comes to speak of that millennium as such. His vision of history had of course always been apocalyptic. Some of the wartime letters evince a tendency to outright belief in intervention from heaven to bring about the destruction of the old world and the advent of the new. But in his history book Lawrence

heeds another and different strain of eschatology, which he clearly
endorses, though he avoids the theological and mystical terminology
of his source. This was the eschatology of Joachim of Flora, a monk
of the twelfth century who through allegorical interpretation of Biblical
texts had declared that three ages must constitute the history of the
world. The first had been the Dispensation of the Father, superseded
with the coming of Christ by the Dispensation of the Son, which in turn
must give place (about the year 1260, by Joachim's calculations) to
the Dispensation of the Holy Ghost.

Now this was just the current of thought to appeal to Lawrence,
for he had been moving in this direction at least since *Le Gai Savaire.*
Probably he never read Joachim's work itself. Only the fundamental
three divisions of history and a few of the accompanying prophecies
were of interest to him, and his source for these was G. G. Coulton's SD,
From St. Francis to Dante, a partial translation, with much supporting 150ff.
material, of the autobiographical writings of Salimbene, a thirteenth-
century Franciscan who for a time was an ardent Joachite. Lawrence HL, 322
read this book in early 1916, when he was making his discoveries in
American literature, and the ideas of Joachim lay in his mind and
exerted their strong if silent influence all through his approach to new
ages in *Women in Love* and the American essays.

For Joachim it was inconceivable that the history of the world
could be complete without the coming to pass of a third age, since the
whole mystery of God's plan must be three-fold. In each of the ages
God necessarily dealt with his people according to the spirit of that
age. Under the Law he had acted through faith, that of the patriarchs
and the prophets; under the Gospel he acted through love, in the
apostles and the clergy as their successors. In the impending age of
the Holy Ghost, that is, under the Eternal Gospel mentioned in Revelations 14:6–7, he would act through wisdom, to some extent directly
in the hearts of men, but also in certain holy men outside the established
clergy. Many Franciscans, whose founder had promoted this latter
ideal of holiness, looked upon Joachim as their John the Baptist, and
when his works began to have their real if short-lived effect fifty years
after his death, in the middle of the turbulent thirteenth century, the
propagators of Joachim's doctrine were accused of blasphemy, of
plotting to set up St. Francis as the Christ of the Third Age.

Both the chief precept of Joachim, that of the Three Ages, and the
implication that a great figure would overshadow the coming epoch
held fertile suggestions for Lawrence. In his history he translates these
into political terms. Up to the Renaissance in Europe an age of glory
in war had prevailed, under kings and popes. Then had begun the age
when production and discovery became the ideals. These two ages

correspond to what Lawrence had seen in *Twilight in Italy* as the age of the Flesh and the Father through the Middle Ages, and the change to the creed of the Spirit and the Son with the Renaissance. The most succinct statement of the whole pattern, in the history book, reads thus: *Kings, tyrants, dukes have had their turn; commerce has taken full power in the world. There still remains the last reign of wisdom, of pure understanding, the reign which we have never seen in the world, but which we must see.* The hopes for a new age which Lawrence had kept alive during the war by a distant vision of a new America now glowed afresh in the prospect of a European millennium. A chief hope of these was for a great man to usher in the age, a hope coordinated with Lawrence's quest for a new male ascendancy and growing and changing for several years after the war in the leadership novels. He had decided long since that mankind could only be led as it would consent to be led. Heretofore it had too often consented to the worst. As proof of this, Lawrence had the long line of bad emperors from Gibbon as his main source for the history of the ancient world, and his own low opinion of Lloyd George and Woodrow Wilson. As he saw it, the only salvation for Europe, and it must be a united Europe, was that men should strive for the wisdom to recognize and then to submit wholly to the greatest and wisest man among them. Europe must unite *round one great chosen figure, some hero who can lead a great war, as well as administer a wide peace. It all depends on the will of the people. But the will of the people must concentrate in one figure, who is also supreme over the will of the people. He must be chosen, but at the same time responsible to God alone. Here is a problem of which a stormy future will have to evolve the solution.*

    Limited by his audience of schoolboys, Lawrence could not here throw himself into the symbolic reaches of prophecy. But he was anything but hampered by his readers in the exercise of another gift, a narrative power deriving from his love of time and space and distance: in this case of the vastness of the past which he insisted must be perceptible above all things in the writing of history. The best examples of this come in the chapter "The Germans," when Lawrence is recreating the battle of centuries between the fair races of northern Europe and the dark men of the Mediterranean. That this conflict unfolded in a largely unknown land made it all the better to describe. Passage after passage like the following conveys the excitement and the color with which Lawrence writes when he has in hand the meeting between races and spirit of place: *In the north of Germany were huge flat lands, often wet, swampy, impassable, through which wandered the great rivers Rhine or Rhenus Flux, Weser or Visurgis, and Elbe or Albis. To the south, however, the whole country was covered by a vast forest of*

MH, 198

MH, 306

MH,
45–46

dark fir and pine trees, tracts of which still remain. This Hercynian
forest created the greatest impression on the Roman imagination. No
one knew how far it stretched. German natives who had travelled
through it had gone on for sixty days without coming to the end of it.
In the illimitable shadow the pine-trunks rose up bare, the ground was
brown with pine-needles, there was no undergrowth. A great silence
pervaded everywhere, not broken by the dense whisper of the wind
above. Between these shadowy trunks flitted deer, reindeer with
branching horns ran in groups, or the great elk, with his massive
antlers, stood darkly alone and pawed the ground, before he trotted
away into the deepening shadow of trunks.[1]

Such enthrallment is reminiscent of that which the lakes and forests
of America had thrown over Lawrence's imagination. It approximates
also the first indelible impressions that Bavaria made on him when the
fugitive pair of lovers had thrilled in the search for the untrammeled
spirit of life during their first months in Germany. The accumulation of
experience in Lawrence never failed to keep to a rhythm which magnified the happenings of his own life to the dimension of history and a
symbolic geography of the world, and by equal effort reproportioned
all the history and geography that he knew to fit within the compass of
the self.

Still, for all its imaginative reach, *Movements in European History*
remains a lesser work, partly because it was not directed to an adult
audience with whom Lawrence could be completely open, and partly
because any such reconstruction of historical events must inevitably
emphasize the political movements of the past, and Lawrence was never
at his best when dealing with actual politics. Such events, no matter
how sweeping, did not suggest the great scope of man's progress
through the earth in such a way as to fire his highest vision.

At long last, in mid-November of 1919, Lawrence was able to
scrape together enough money to leave England, but not for America,
even yet, and largely because of the same complicated impasse of
combined eagerness and hesitation that had always characterized his
attitude to America. Instead of sailing west, he went south again to
Italy, and was elated to be heading in that direction. He spent a while in
Florence, waiting for Frieda to end her first post-war visit to Germany.
While in Florence he met Maurice Magnus and began with him a half-
willing and sporadic association which in a couple of years led to a
piece of writing, to be considered in due course, in which Lawrence
makes important revelations on the spirit of pilgrimage by which he
lived.

When Frieda joined him in Florence, they went briefly to Rome,
then sought out an isolated place in the Abruzzi region: Picinisco,

where they endured the cold and discomfort of a farmhouse for only a week, but the effects of that week were sufficient to make this spot the setting for the end of *The Lost Girl*. From Picinisco the Lawrences went to Capri, and even from this island tamed and much modified by hosts of foreign artistic residents, he felt a strong surge of the primal

ML, 617 self: *To look down the Salernian Gulf, southeast, on a blue day, and see the dim, sheer rocky coast, the clear rock mountains, is so beautiful, so like Ulysses, that one sheds one's avatars, and recovers a lost self, Mediterranean, anterior to us.* There was talk off and on, in Capri, of sailing to the South Seas with Compton Mackenzie, whose project for buying a boat and heading out for adventure Lawrence shared in discussion now and again. But he did not really agree with Compton Mackenzie's concept of travel, as we will amply see in "The Man Who Loved Islands," a story satirizing this acquaintance.

Several people in Capri took notice of Lawrence's craving to burst into new seas and land on mysterious shores. Francis Brett Young saw this yen to depart as always under the surface of Lawrence's every

RE, 95 mood: *He strains after some new continent in which his thoughts and passions are more elemental. Africa is his latest nirvana.* He never did go to Africa, but he never entirely left off talking about it either, right up to his last days.

Capri could not hold Lawrence for long, for even as he glimpsed

ML, 617 the ancient being there, he called it *a gossipy, villa-stricken, two-humped chunk of limestone.* By early March he had rented the Fontana Vecchia in Taormina, Sicily, and settled in for what was to become a two-year stay, with a few trips in and out. The Fontana Vecchia was

ML, 624 *a lovely villa on the green slope high above the sea, looking east over the blueness.* Here, on the dawn coast of Sicily, with Etna at his back,

ML, 628 Lawrence still fretted, as we might guess, *to go to the ends of the earth,* and kept his plans to go always simmering. Even an eastern direction, in this setting, had its appeal. Material hindrances to his departure lessened as time went on. The long squeeze of dire poverty was soon at an end. A small but increasing trickle of money began to arrive, some from England and more from America. What kept Lawrence in Europe was of another order. The equal portions of fear and longing to test his dream, a condition which had been instrumental in bringing about last-minute reversals of decision when he was on the verge of going to America during the war, acted now with far greater power, for it was now Italy and the fascination of the Mediterranean against which the craving for America or the Pacific must struggle, and not against England. The two years in Sicily became one long hesitation over going away. From time to time Lawrence was seized with a potent urge to leave, yet nearly all his important imaginative work of the time

TAORMINA, SICILY

The ancient fountain still runs, in a sort of little cave-place
down the garden — the Fontana Vecchia —
and still supplies us (ML, 624)

centers on the meaning of escape from England to Italy, upon the complexity of contradictions which Italy as landscape and as human culture exercises upon the refugee. While constantly playing about the edges of perception was an aura of mysterious being perfectly evident to Lawrence's consciousness but impossible to lay firm hold of. The strongest of this feeling is concentrated in the sea, the Mediterranean, as though that lost world of Minoans and Greeks and their ancient gods were truly on the brink of reappearance, along with the coming of the cataclysm essential to their return. Desire for these events, and a considerable fear of them, joined with disgust with the present world, were all active in Lawrence, and they add up to revealing one of his strongest rages, so far, to know and yet to realize as forever unattainable the distance in time and space where the greater existence beckons and yet forever eludes.

Aside from the imaginative work, this vision inheres in many of the letters, as in the following passage, which finds Lawrence at the concert RE, 98 of a famous cellist in Taormina: *Imagine sitting there and looking through the broken windows at this coast swerving and swerving south, silvery in the gold of evening, swerving away into God knows what dawn of our world. That coast rouses a nostalgia that is half ecstasy and half torture in me, swooping in the great dim lines to Syracuse and beyond. — And then the snore of that sententious cello, and the Italian crowd in its ever-so-Sunday clothes! Is it to be borne? Will Etna not erupt, out of shame of its modern fleas. Suppose I'm one of 'em.*

The concession made in the last sentence speaks of influential if not decisive changes in Lawrence. Some of the bitter vulnerability of the war years is gone, and the bit of detachment and self-criticism that he never quite lost again has lightened some of his attitudes. In a good many assertions of this period, from time to time a firm and self-contained amusement with the world also appears, as when he spoke ML, 620 of Capri as a *stewpot of semi-literary cats,* or of mailing manuscripts to ML, 625 America as dropping them *down the bottomless pit.* This side of Lawrence is still principally confined to his letters, but it was soon to bulk larger in his travel writings as well.

The first significant work of this new release from England, equal in its effects to the pre-war release, was the novel finally published as *The Lost Girl,* the piece of work originally meant to succeed *Sons and Lovers.* The half-done manuscript had lain in Germany throughout the war and had never ceased to concern Lawrence. If his attempt to have this manuscript sent to him through neutral channels in 1916 had succeeded, this might have become his next-completed novel after *The Rainbow,* rather than *Women in Love.* Now he finally did retrieve his manuscript, went to work on it during his last weeks on Capri, in

TAORMINA, SICILY

This coast swerving and swerving away
into God knows what dawn of our world (RE, 98)

TAORMINA, SICILY

Oh painted carts of Sicily,
with all history on your panels (SS, 24)

February 1920, and with a total rewriting of the earlier version, finished the novel in less than three months.

While Lawrence had expressly declined to write satire on the foreign colony of Capri, satire did continue to form the basis of the earlier portions of *The Lost Girl,* satire on the provincial society of Eastwood much in the same vein of his original conception of the novel. From statements in letters in late 1912 we know that he meant ML, 150 the novel to achieve what he felt Arnold Bennett's novels of the Midlands had signally failed to achieve: to defy and defeat the conditions which made life in that region barely endurable. But the escape of Alvina Houghton, the "lost girl," from the Midlands to Italy is now cast in terms that Lawrence did not have at his command until after the harrowing experience of the war.

The Lost Girl may not stand with the best of Lawrence's work, but it is a document of vital significance in arriving at the deeper currents of Lawrence's battle with the world and himself as he went forth to roam after that Babylonian captivity in England during wartime. The habit of putting himself into more than one character, operative to some extent since his long struggle with *The Rainbow* and *Women in Love,* gains a new prominence in *The Lost Girl,* with further significant developments in most of the later novels. In *The Lost Girl* both Alvina Houghton and her lover Ciccio take on identities which Lawrence sought earnestly to extract from interaction between himself and places that appeared capable of bestowing newness of life. In this novel the principal bearer of Lawrence's aspiration appears to be the heroine, but a great deal of indirection is at work: Ciccio marks the appearance in Lawrence's fiction of the dark lover who personifies his ideal of maleness and therefore enacts his creator's deepest participation.

Alvina Houghton's rebellion against the stultifying life of the industrial Midlands can never carry her to freedom so long as she has nowhere to turn except the alternatives available in England. What it takes to liberate her — or rather to set the process of her liberation going, for it is a long way from accomplishment at the novel's close — Lawrence attempted to compound out of his currently most prominent ideal regions of escape: Italy and America, with Italy as an intermediate stage of actuality which is in fact as terrifying as it is liberating. Although Lawrence insisted that Alvina is not morally lost, she is certainly in the process of "losing" her soul in order to find it, and still in this condition when we take fictional leave of her in the mountains of Italy.

If Lawrence wished to deliver Alvina to her salvation, it is curious that he did not convey her — nor any other protagonist during these years — to Sicily, the part of Italy that he himself now looked upon as something close to a satisfactory haven. Alvina gets no further than the cold, dark mountains of the central peninsula, that region from which Lawrence fled to Capri after a week's stay. Alvina's only real hope for a new life is America, where she does not expect to go until the war is over and her Italian husband comes back to her from military service. How Lawrence's own state at the time is reflected in Alvina's temporarily arrested progress toward rebirth will only be evident when we have taken into account in some detail the substance of *The Lost Girl* in conjunction with two other works: to a limited degree *Aaron's Rod,* but primarily the "Introduction" Lawrence wrote for Maurice Magnus's *Memoirs of the Foreign Legion.* Lawrence did not write this piece until about two years after the events, when he was on the point of deserting Europe, and made of these pages a kind of farewell to the old continent of the soul. Of less apparent but equal importance is the fact that the crucial stage of Lawrence's brief but revealing association with Magnus took place in the same area where *The Lost Girl* ends and at almost precisely the same time when he was beginning to rewrite that novel.

What concerns us most in *The Lost Girl* is the compelling problem which is never more than obscurely transferred from Lawrence's consciousness to his fictional creation: how to get past the emotional actuality of Italy to America, where a true male flowering may lie. This novel is Lawrence's first endeavor to take up in fiction the vision of America which had occupied his efforts for so long in the American literature essays — and still occupied him in this period, for he revised these essays to some extent on finishing *The Lost Girl*. He had a great longing, now, to do in full what he believed Cooper and Melville had done in part: to unite the dark and light spirits of humanity in an all-inclusive passional and ritual relation. This was absolutely necessary if he was to conquer any new continent of the soul. As Lawrence put

CM, 178 it in a letter, *Alvina, in whom the questing soul is lodged, moves towards reunion with the dark half of humanity.* The white spirit of Alvina is to cross over to meet the dark spirit of Ciccio. And this man who arrives in the Eastwood-like town in England and captivates her

LG, 149 spirit is not only Italian. He is a member of *a strictly Red Indian troupe* of circus people — who call themselves the Natcha-Kee-Tawaras — whose performances are meant to create an enchanted atmosphere in which the attraction between the pale woman and the swarthy, exotic man can proceed on both a physical and a mystical level. Or it all comes to the same thing if the sexes are reversed, as in the principal act of the troupe, a skit which dramatizes the growth of sympathy between a white male prisoner of the Indians and a squaw. It climaxes in a fight with a bear that leaves all the braves dead and the prisoner, cut free of his bonds by the squaw, victorious over the bear and ready to claim his mate. It is a scene to out-Cooper Cooper.

A much better scene, whose effect is nearer to what the whole book suggests, is one in which Ciccio, *extraordinarily velvety and alive on* LG, 173 *horseback,* makes the blood of the inhabitants of Woodhouse (Eastwood) run cold as he trots and wheels along the street of the town like an Indian out of the Wild West. This is a moment of realization for Alvina of the sort that plagues her throughout the book and reaches an uneasy climax at the end: that cruelty lies under the civilized veneer of mankind. Lawrence was doing his best, but without much connection, to transmute into fiction the savage suavity of the horseback Indians from Cooper.

In this Indian masquerading intended to be highly symbolic, Lawrence finally goes all out to transform the powerful attraction between Alvina and Ciccio into the ritual terms he has set up. Alvina prepares for the consummation of her love by being initiated into the Natcha-Kee-Tawara band, with such ceremonial bits as this: *"Tonight* LG, *. . . the Natcha-Kee-Tawaras make their feast of affiliation. The white* 238–239 *daughter has entered the tribe of the Hirondelles, swallows that pass from land to land, and build their nests between roof and wall. A new swallow, a new Huron from the tents of the pale-face, from the lodges of the north, from the tribe of the Yenghees."*

None of this, unfortunately, ever rises above a travesty of Cooper heavily tinged with Longfellow. And when Ciccio is acting in the capacity thrust upon him by these scenes, he remains a caricature half-Chingachgook and half-Luigi.

A change for the better comes about as we move into the last four chapters of *The Lost Girl,* into something that displays real substance of vision. Lawrence now concentrates on Alvina to portray his own post-war flight from England, a land she looks back on from the Channel boat as like a coffin sinking: the burial of the dead self again, along with the land that held it. As she travels on and nears the Alps, space, past and future invade her consciousness in all their splendor. *And it all seemed bigger, nobler than in England. She felt vaster influ-* LG, 351 *ences spreading around, the Past was greater, more magnificent in these regions. For the first time the nostalgia of the vast Roman and classic world took possession of her.* This great world, indeed the whole world, is on the brink of apocalypse, *in one of its convulsions,* LG, 352 and *the event elated her.* Within this tremble of the coming disaster, however, she senses a pure wonder beyond danger, thinking, *whatever* LG, 353 *life may be, and whatever horror men have made of it, the world is a lovely place, a magic place, something to marvel over.*

This simple wonder is an aspect of Lawrence's travel impulse in danger of being overlooked in the post-war writing, for the pure compulsion to leave behind some place found wanting and to seek out a better place is likely to be powerfully wrought on the surface and the less complicated curiosity and delight submerged. Moreover, even this compulsion to run away can be deceptive. For during the war, as we have seen, the whole matter of flight and search, the condemned land versus the promised land, became the pursuit of emotional states the real topography of which lay in Lawrence's soul, and not in any such real geographical opposites as Italy and England. But still the outer place sustains the inner search, partly by the compulsion to move on and partly by the marvel of travel for its own sake, the marvel such as strikes the eyes of Alvina Houghton as she penetrates Italy. The two impulses create a marvelous visionary tension, for example when Alvina arrives at her last place of sojourn in the novel, Pescocalascio — Picinisco in real life — and goes through her own and Lawrence's

LG, 361   experience of being "lost": *On the cart rattled and bumped, in the cold night, down the high-way in the valley. Alvina could make out the darkness of the slopes. Overhead she saw the brilliance of Orion. She felt she was quite, quite lost. She had gone out of the world, over the border, into some place of mystery. She was lost to Woodhouse, to Lancaster, to England — all lost.*

If we think back on Lawrence's great desire to fulfill his mother's unconsummated life, so powerfully influential during his first stay in Italy, we find him haunted still in Alvina by this desire, though he is not at this juncture openly aware of the presence of that lingering spirit: it is only by viewing the whole span of his journeys that we can identify the various elements of any one moment's search. At the same time the "lost" girl reaches out yearningly for the male being with which this mysterious landscape is instinct.

As Alvina ends her journey for the time being in the cold Italian valley, we see that Lawrence is struggling to take up where he left off in *Women in Love.* In that novel the snow-covered mountains were a region of the last negation through which the soul must pass to enter the greater existence within itself and the greater union in equilibrium with the mate. The eternal snows had symbolized an utter denial of the blood-consciousness since the rewriting of the *Twilight in Italy* essays in the latter part of 1915. In *The Lost Girl,* however, the mountain spirit of place has undergone important alterations. While it remains hostile and destructive and must apparently be overriden before Alvina can set sail for her America, it is now also a dwelling place of Lawrence's aboriginal gods. The struggle with them and the meaning of the outcome glimmers obscurely through the final pages. Like those faring west in Cooper's *The Prairie,* Alvina has struck in the Abruzzi

LG,   one of those *places which resist us, which have the power to overthrow*
370–371   *our psychic being. It seems as if every country has its potent negative centres, localities which savagely and triumphantly refuse our living*

NEAR PICINISCO, ITALY

The white, wide streambed, and the scrub and lower hills became dark,
and in heaven, oh, almost unbearably lovely,
the snow of the near mountains (LG, 351)

cultures. But how will she ever be capable of overcoming this spirit of place, or of circumventing it, if the terrible gods resident here sap her energy and absorb even her sense of the mere wonder of the world?

LG, 371–372 *How unspeakably lovely it was, no one could ever tell, the grand, pagan twilight of the valleys, savage, cold, with a sense of ancient gods who knew the right for human sacrifice. It stole away the soul of Alvina. She felt transfigured in it, clairvoyant in another mystery of life. A savage hardness came in her heart. The gods who had demanded human sacrifice were quite right, immutably right. The fierce, savage gods who dipped their lips in blood, these were the true gods.*

Like Kate in *The Plumed Serpent* later on, Alvina has moments of revulsion from such states as these, when she can seriously think of retreating to the "sanity" of England. Nevertheless, the prime mover in her is just these dark thoughts, which keep her in "Suspense," as the novel's final chapter is called, and which stems from a parallel condition in Lawrence: the dark gods he had fashioned during the war, so much from the idea of America, were exercising an influence of increasing power over him, and some of that power was fearful, putting in question, eventually, even his seldom faltering trust in the "rightness" of the unconscious.

That which stems from Lawrence in Ciccio remains halfway in the background through the novel. This character's effect on the whole pattern of meaning is nevertheless most powerful. Lawrence as the dark stranger we caught an initial glimpse of when he first lured Frieda out of England. The role grows from *The Lost Girl* till the end of his life. I have pointed out the original source of this figure as Lawrence's father and the dark being the son absorbed through him from the mines. All the peasantry of southern Europe has since contributed a great share to the creation, and Lawrence's own imagining during the war of dark Celts and, most of all, American Indians and Pacific Islanders, has now brought forth a character who is Italian, at the same time Indian, and altogether, in the end, that "dark soul" of Lawrence that must claim mastery over the female soul within him and over the so often antagonistic but potentially complementary soul of the mate.

The next major unfolding of Lawrence's fictional quest in Italy and beyond is *Aaron's Rod,* a work that revolves upon two male surrogates: Aaron Sisson and Rawdon Lilly. Lawrence began this novel, we recall, in the autumn of 1917, just after being forced out of Cornwall and just when his ongoing battles with Frieda brought the need for male assertion to a crisis. Though he spent considerable time on the

LS, 31 novel in 1919, he referred to it as only ⅓ *done* just after finishing *The Lost Girl,* said that he was *awaiting events* to take it up once more, and

WINTER SCENE, ALPINE REGION

The grand, pagan twilight of the valleys,
savage, cold, with a sense of ancient gods
who knew the right for human sacrifice (LG, 351)

promised that *once it starts again it will steam ahead*. These *events* somewhere in the offing were another expected turning in the constant readjustment of Lawrence's psyche. *The Lost Girl* is witness to his efforts both to do justice to the woman's soul in him, and at the same time to make her subject to a male ascendancy with which he could identify. But the forging of a new male wanderer for his post-war condition, a natural leader and aristocrat — to the point of doubling this character — became a far more elaborate undertaking. The forging had already extended through the revision of the American literature essays during the summer of 1920, and now went on into the quickly written book that sprang out of a junket with Frieda to Sardinia in January, 1921 — but *Sea and Sardinia* is a special case reserved for discussion later in this chapter. In March 1921 the idea of the male in search of himself appeared ready to take a definitive form in *Mr. Noon,* the first half of which was written immediately on completion of *The Lost Girl.* Clearly it was meant to stand in counterbalance to the female adventure just treated. Lawrence never completed this novel. Part One, published in *Phoenix II,* ends with Gilbert Noon still in England, the Emmie he PX, 191 has pursued about to marry his rival. But a *scandalous* elopement is LS, 42 hinted at in the next *volume*. In a letter to his English publisher Lawrence outlines an action in three parts, coming to a close in 1919. Apparently he wrote nothing more than about half of Part Two. I have not seen the unpublished text but I understand that the elopement does take place and that it is based directly on the Lawrence-Frieda elopement of 1912.[2]

But by early April 1921, just before leaving Taormina for points north, eventually to reach Germany on his first post-war visit, Lawrence had decided to make *Aaron's Rod* his next novel. Stopping off at Capri and making the acquaintance of Earl and Achsah Brewster, he discussed with them what steps Aaron should take toward a new life. RC, 243 One interesting alternative that Lawrence had in view, to which we will return later, was to send Aaron to the Abbey of Montecassino for a period of contemplation. Like all the novels from *Women in Love* through *The Plumed Serpent, Aaron's Rod* was to entail a journey toward regeneration from the British Isles to a distant land that might embody a new life principle. And like all of these novels after *The Lost Girl,* the transformation of life into fiction demanded a few months or more for the events of Lawrence's discovery of self in travel to mature into fictional material.

LS, 41   When Lawrence began to concentrate on *Aaron's Rod* in Baden-Baden, it truly did all pour out as predicted, in a month of concentrated work inspired directly by his presence in Germany. Each day found ML, 655 him *sitting away in the woods* to write — in his later years he often did his best writing outdoors, where the rhythm of space and of nature gave freedom to his racing pen. He felt himself called upon to attend to another depth of freedom now as well. From the day of the Burns fragment in 1912, Lawrence had in some manner thought of male freedom in the shape of his father. It was about a year after finishing *Aaron's Rod* that he confessed having been blind to his father's virtues in *Sons and Lovers*. But by then he had already made some recompense in *Aaron's Rod,* indirect though it may have been, for Aaron is a hero modeled in many respects on the elder Lawrence and on qualities in Lawrence himself attributable to being his father's son.   RC, 254

The ideal held out before Aaron Sisson is to travel away from any fixed place and to live in a sort of naked liberty, to learn to be alone and integral, and as an essential complement to this singleness, to learn how to recognize and submit to some *more heroic soul*. The series of transformations to which Aaron is exposed takes a long and erratic course. He is an obstinate seeker, yet a dependent and often a passive one as well. Ultimately he becomes convinced that he must rely on Lawrence's other half of a protagonist, Rawdon Lilly, though in the end their relationship takes a curious turn that promises little in the way of a unified or stable future.   AR, 346

A miner with a talent for playing the flute, Aaron walks out on his wife and family in the Midlands only half-conscious of where he is headed. He picks up a living by playing in an orchestra in London, but nothing very decisive happens until he comes in contact with the foreign and the aboriginal, though in a much sophisticated form, in an American woman with Indian blood: Josephine Ford, who seduces him. But this was a wrong turning, bringing to pass the collapse of his small freedom, followed by drunken regret and illness. In this state he wanders into Lilly's neighborhood, and Lilly takes him in and nurses him back to health. Here Lawrence makes a first attempt to achieve some sort of harmony out of distinct male facets of himself. A scene of physical contact between males occurs, analogous to that in *Women in Love* and more so to the one further back, in *The White Peacock*. When Aaron has sunk to his lowest ebb, Lilly massages all of his lower body with oil, and life appears at once in his eyes. He goes off into a restorative sleep and is soon on his way to recovery.

Now our first impulse here, as with all such scenes, is to read the episode as an elaborate disguise for repressed homosexuality, but it is difficult to be content with this limited exercise in clinical diagnosis, though no doubt it is correct as far as it goes. But we must not fail to appreciate the extraordinary extent to which Lawrence was able to transform his perverse impulses — which hold no more important a place in his complicated make-up, for that matter, than numerous other impulses constructive and destructive — into concepts which in his imaginative rendering of them often come near to producing a millennial sort of human relations beyond the restrictions of present-day sexual complexes, relations in which life-giving fleshly contact outside sexual bounds seems possible. We should not forget, either, that here as all through the novel Lawrence is dealing with two fictional constructions of himself and using every means to bring them together: Lilly who in the larger sense is the mind — or better, the spirit — while Aaron is the flesh — or better, the soul. The musing that Lilly engages in while his patient sleeps, which carries him far afield, will not seem to lose connection with the situation at hand if we bear this relation of the two men in mind. Lilly first characterizes Aaron's acceptance of

AR, 119   his ministrations as submission *to a bit of healthy individual authority.* This submission Lilly opposes to that demanded by present-day community authority, a *mob power* that brings on such catastrophes as

AR, 120   wars. Mobs of *Europeans, Asiatics, Africans* have inherited the earth. He longs for a few of the vanished races who had *living pride,* American Indians or South Sea Islanders, to conspire with him against teeming mankind. The point appears to be that he despairs of ever bringing a man like Aaron up to his own level of self-reliance, and thus instituting a brotherhood of a superior few. But the question goes much deeper than this, we see, when we remember that both these men are Lawrence. His true purpose, psychologically speaking, is to bring together in himself the spontaneous but darkly working soul whose origin is in the coal lustre of the Midlands, and the roving, inquisitive spirit that separates him forever from that source, and to fashion of this blend an aristocratic male who can regain control of the human condition. Lilly is the active principle here, who has gained some measure of independence and mobility, and such as it is he keeps it viable by travel. He can cross space to attain his ends to some degree, even if he cannot abrogate time to find accomplices and entirely heal the inner breaches of the individual.

Heart-to-heart confidences between Lilly and Aaron now reveal a common rebellion against the possessiveness and maternal blindness of women, which in fact Lilly holds partially responsible for the teeming instinct of humanity and the consequent loss of living pride and male integrity. This conclusion perhaps contributes to Aaron's education, eventually, but what it brings us to for the moment is important information on what the novel holds to be a successful man-woman relationship: the marriage of Lilly and Tanny — that is, of Lawrence and Frieda. Their union is sustained, clearly, by frequent change of

AR, 126   place, for this gives scope to the personality. *"There's a doom for me,"*
AR, 127   Lilly remarks, a doom to travel plainly. *"But there are lots of me's,"*

he adds. *"I'm not only just one proposition. A new place brings out a new thing in a man."* His life with Tanny has always been a life of living alone with her in different countries, and of enjoying the unfolding of the various *me's*.

Soon after his stay with Lilly, Aaron is likewise prepared to set out to foreign parts. Lilly has escaped him, but he decides to go to Italy in the hope of rejoining his benefactor. On the way he relives for Lawrence a good part of the journey from England to Florence in late 1919. There is the stop in Novara (Turin) at the villa of Sir William Franks (Sir Walter Becker). Aaron is here ushered into the plushest of bedrooms, and Lawrence takes the opportunity to deplore how the technology of the modern world has taken the marvel out of traveling. This coal-miner suddenly admitted to the most opulent circles would have opened his eyes in wonder in a former age, but now we all have our vicarious discovery of the world through the cinema, and everything is *Connu! Connu!* to us all.   AR, 163

Of more vital significance to the unfolding of theme is a confrontation between Aaron and his elderly and wealthy host. Men like Lilly and Aaron represent a challenge to this "self-made" individual. It may look wonderful to be *a man for crossing frontiers,* as Lilly is, but AR, 167 by Sir William's philosophy, he who puts his trust in providence without a bank account is simply improvident and will end by begging. Sir William gives his puzzled report on what Lilly has earlier described to him as his motive for keeping on the move, and the elderly knight's incomprehension of that motive achieves an important emphasis by contrast. Lilly has called the belief to which he subscribes, and into which he has drawn Aaron, as a covenant with the *Invisible,* by which AR, 174 a man works as he wanders, all right, but never to make provision, rather for the work itself, and that alone. Sir William has long been a resident of Italy, a bearer of England's overseas economic domination, a seeker in absolute contrast to Lilly, a ruler of the modern world of just the sort Lilly hopes to supplant.

As it was night-time when Aaron arrived in Novara, no visible estimate of his new surroundings is possible until next morning, when on awaking and looking out his bedroom window, he has his first real view of the Alps. From this point on we see Aaron following essentially the same curve of self-examination in relation to place as Alvina Houghton does in *The Lost Girl,* and as Lawrence in real life, but never reaching as Alvina does a decisive pass where grappling with place-reality promises a real transmuting of self. Alvina plunges into the heart of the mountains. Aaron only advances toward them and then retreats, remaining always outside the center of metamorphosis that the mountains offer. The mountains are alive to him, all right,

AR, 180   standing beyond the city like *marvellous striped sky-panthers circling round a great camp,* and in their presence he can feel *himself changing inside his skin.* When he goes out to walk in the city and thinks back on his trip down from England, he knows that he has passed a crucial

AR, 183   barrier in the Alps, those *tigers prowling between the north and the south,* and must *enter on the responsibility of a new self.* But he is simply not yet prepared to confront a change so radical. He always turns back when the perspective along any street appears to be bringing the fierce mountains too near. All he is capable of receiving yet is what

AR, 184   Lawrence characterizes as *a feeling of bravado and almost swaggering carelessness which is Italy's best gift to an Englishman*: at least to an Englishman of Aaron's sort. This is, however, far short of what Aaron has set out to find. But in any event the employment here of wild animal imagery to denote the Alps is a clear witness to Lawrence's conviction, on setting out after the war, that he must challenge the encircling heights of the world as he would a ring of beasts in order to reach his goal: like Christian braving the lions of the path to gain the shelter of House Beautiful.

Aaron does soon claim, in Italy, to have taken a new lease on his refusal to surrender the core of his being to the possessive grip of his

AR, 201   wife. Having now crossed *a certain border-line* and found *himself alone completely,* he accepts *his loneliness or singleness as a fulfilment.* But only to a point, it seems, and that point is not yet thoroughly identifiable. In fact he never truly displays any such certainty in the challenge to achievement and therefore does not demonstrate the psychic wholeness that Lawrence is sometimes tempted to attribute to him.

In time Aaron goes on to Florence, just as Lawrence did in 1919,

AR, 254   to that *town of men* which exemplifies a new vista of male freedom. This new feeling is all well and good until Aaron's flute and his further charms involve him in a brief love affair with a second American woman, and the point is thus doubly made that Aaron's fulfillment lies somewhere in the exotic distance, but probably not through women, and the nature of that distance he is still far from comprehending. Not that this affair is identical to the first, the one with Josephine Ford, the other American woman. Aaron here wins through to a momentary triumph. This second woman too would devour him, would strip him of his singleness and his liberty. But he has grown, for in the last analysis he can resist her spiritual clutches, even while in the depths of physical love with her. He never loses hold on the male isolation at the center of himself, though at times this isolate stance is plainly taken on the verge of despair, for he can grow horrified at how near he comes to being the victim in these embraces, even as he maintains a godly aloofness. He will not go on with this woman, he decides in the end, for he knows that she may sap his innermost vitality and toss him aside like a rind.

Aaron's maleness, then, is no more than a precarious foothold that may give way at any time and tumble him back into subjection to a woman. This is not much to show for all his seeking so far. The next chapter after this realization may well be entitled "The Broken Rod" and concern itself with phallic and musical failure. But Lawrence makes the mistake of allowing accident to decide this next turn of affairs, an accident that advances the theme not at all. Aaron is sitting in a cafe with Lilly and some others when a bomb is thrown in from the street by an unknown hand. The explosion wreaks no injuries on the principals of the story but it smashes Aaron's flute so badly that Lilly advises him to throw it in the Arno, which he does. And all that Lilly can advise him further, just now, is that he will have to live without a rod for a while, that one will grow again.

The fact is that Lawrence hardly seems to know where to turn next. That the ending of the novel may be indecisive will be nothing new: *Aaron's Rod* will simply share the fate of all the later novels. Lawrence has by now made of his novels a form so instinct with the immediate struggles of the author that the structure comes to depend altogether on the sheer exercise of the novelist's rare skill with words. Often no conclusion appears possible in lives perpetually at the mercy of conflicting personalities. What Lawrence is forced to do finally, in this novel, is to face up to the fact that Aaron — that fleshly and spontaneously expressive side of himself going back to an identity he shared with his father and all dark emanations therefrom — must fail to coalesce in any real sense with the world-roving and self-reliant intelligent self in the shape of Lilly. Lawrence's ultimate picture of his failure reaches far back into his past and conjures up in dream terms a mysterious future. Aaron dreams that he is in an underworld with miners, a *vast country* that he must go on exploring in spite of himself. AR, 332 The miners there are going to eat a naked man, or rather a sausage the size and shape of a man, but the dream acceptability of this food does not diminish in Aaron the terrors of homosexuality and cannibalism. As he proceeds on his dream way, he passes in endless rooms the children, then the wives, of the miners, who have abandoned them to attend their fearful rites. Obviously Aaron has his own desertion of his family in mind. And he is two selves here, in this nightmare sequence that points up the split-self imbalance on which the book is founded. One of these selves is like his more ordinary personality, the other one is similar to Lilly. A long voyage on a boat commences. Stakes rising out of the water strike the fleshly Aaron as he passes, a suffering to be endured for the sake of the voyage, and all that the other Aaron can do to warn him fails for a long time to arouse him. After a while, however, the more ordinary Aaron shifts in the boat out of reach of the stakes, the two Aarons become as one, and the boat AR, 334 sails on into deep, serene water. At last they near *a lake-city, like Mexico.* And then Aaron wakes, but with a few fragmentary recollections of having seen as a last vision a *roadside Astarte* with eggs in her *open lap.*

No clearer representation is needed of Lawrence's imagined America, nor of the whole content of current dilemmas hinging upon a pilgrim theme. We encounter the underworld of the mines and a form of the self Lawrence wished to inherit from his father, here and elsewhere a form of the dark self he sought in time or in place, a free self nonetheless haunted by homosexuality. And then a voyage over a lake, another recurring feature of Lawrence's obsessive geography. The painful journey leads to a mythical city where a goddess of rebirth holds sway, offering the emblems of immortality out of her body, as she sits by the roadside like a temple prostitute.

Aaron resolves, next, to do what his experience points to as neces-
AR, 337 sity, to go to Lilly and to yield *to the peculiar mastery of one man's nature rather than to the quicksands of woman or the stinking bog of society.* But the submission is not so easy to effect, for Lilly simply will not give him the chance to make it. Lilly is about to follow his migrant bent further, before long to go to another continent, but only with Tanny, his wife, again escaping his willing disciple. Aaron must be satisfied with observing in Lilly what he would like to be able to
AR, 340 copy: the *alert enjoyment of being central, life-central in one's own little circumambient world.* In their last interview Lilly preaches to Aaron this integral destiny of the unique self, and yet strangely enough he ends by preaching also that this self must submit, when it feels the inevitability of such a course, to a man of greater self. Aaron's "soul" will tell him to whom he must submit. Since this sort of homage is precisely what Aaron has come to offer Lilly, we have every right to be puzzled as to why this relation of leader and follower cannot now be established between the two men.

No answer to this question comes through the action of the novel, but a great many implications are inescapable, the simplest of which is that the potential leader in Lawrence personified by Lilly is as far from feeling ready to assume his position as ever, and must pass on through the world in search of himself. Furthermore, the balance and decisiveness sought is not to be had in Europe. No way lies open here to the uniting of the dark impulsive blood-self with the ubiquitous and resourceful intelligence. Aaron's dream does signify the possibility of such a coherent self, but solely through a voyage over far waters to a mythical place. And if we take this dream to be substantially one of Lawrence's own, as I think we can, it provides us with a clue that will assist in interpreting *Kangaroo* and *The Plumed Serpent,* soon to be written. Lawrence plainly associates homosexual desires, the eating of the sausage, with his failure to connect within himself the two types of male represented by Lilly and Aaron: the leader and the follower, the man of intuition and intelligence with the man of the right blood passion who nonetheless requires the direction of the greater man. This concept is of importance to understanding the next two leadership novels, where Lawrence goes much further in his efforts to transmute homosexual emotion into non-erotic loyalties and political allegiance. By this line of thought we are soon led back to Lawrence's insistence that the depths of the psyche are by nature good, that a division imposed by modern society and current views of human intimacy are responsible for such aberrations as homoeroticism, and that these divisions can be cured by linking together again the sources of the blood and the sources of the mind.

During this same period Lawrence quickly molded a waking quest into one of his most interesting works: the seven-day excursion he and Frieda made through Sardinia in January 1921, from which *Sea and Sardinia* was derived, written in February and March. It is a work that Lilly might have created. For once, and squarely between the two trials of *The Lost Girl* and *Aaron's Rod,* Lawrence emerges as a free and integral male. He glories in the journey for its own sake. The woman with him on this adventure he may call the *queen bee,* but she is   SS, 4 amenable and controllable and the supremacy clearly belongs to the male narrator. This is but one aspect of the equilibrium between male and female forces which accounts in great part for the artistic success of the work.

In the first few pages the essential Lawrence stands out boldly: his restlessness, his fascination with distance, yet his conviction that places are not to be run away from except to plunge into other places for access to the secrets of being. He evokes the mystery and awe of having lived for about a year between the sea and Mt. Etna: the volcano that has done much to reveal to him the early voyaging Greeks and their *sense of the magic truth of things.* But she is terrible, this Etna,   SS, 2 a goddess whom few *men can really stand . . . without losing their souls.* At some loss to know just why he feels the necessity now to travel, the narrator suspects that it is Etna he is fleeing from. On the other hand she bids him go, and so partakes of the dual nature inevitable in the maternal: the great demonic mother to escape from and simultaneously the mother goddess who sends the male forth to conquer: a double personification of place by whose tension the traveler can live.

The spirit that permeates the book, once the two travelers are on their way toward Sardinia, is that of the exuberant setting forth of a traveler with a sprightly interest in everything, a readiness to endure discomfort, even a preference for it, since it seems to bring a heightening of experience. *Andiamo!*, an injunction repeated early and late in the narrative of the trip, voices the soul of the book. And never did Lawrence better embody his belief that the present moment, with the soul in transit, is the all-inclusive unit of time, the *terra incognita* of constant discovery. Two Lawrences accompany us, then, through this prose exploration, the adventurer into fearful regions and the simply observant and able writer with a consuming curiosity, in a constant state of delight with the world. The seemingly incongruous juxtaposition of these two masks of the traveler is in fact one of the secrets of the book's success.

SS, 3 & 202

On the disturbing side of the traveler's quest the encounter with the goddess continues, now in the shape of Mount Eryx, once he has sailed from the eastern around to the western end of Sicily. Eryx is the successor to Etna, with a magic perhaps greater and more ancient, thrusting up from that distant past which Lawrence had the extraordinary faculty for seeing in places: *From the darkest recesses of my blood comes a terrible echo at the name of Mount Eryx . . . . Eryx, looking west into Africa's sunset. Erycina ridens.*[3] She is an Astarte like the one Aaron glimpses in his dream of sailing outward to male freedom. She guards the west, the direction of renewal, and the west, *be it Africa or be it America,* must have its *Erycina Venus,* the west which *is strange and unfamiliar and a little fearful.*

SS, 34

SS, 42

But most of all, in the early part of *Sea and Sardinia,* comes the sense of freedom bestowed by the sea, the westward-leading sea. Except for short crossings here and there, mainly of the Channel, this was Lawrence's first encounter with the sea, and though the passage from Palermo to Trapani to Cagliari took only a night and less than two days, to the narrator's high state of expectancy it is like the fulfillment of some long-awaited voyage into the remotest oceans. As soon as the sail begins, just outside the harbor of Palermo, he falls under this spell: *There is something in the long, slow lift of the ship, and her long, slow slide forwards which makes my heart beat with joy. It is the motion of freedom. . . . I wished in my soul the voyage might last forever, that the sea had no end, that one might float in this wavering, tremulous, yet long and surging pulsation while ever time lasted: space never exhausted, and no turning back, no looking back,*

SS, 26–27

even. The pilgrim is caught up in realms of feeling where two voyages, the mundane and the heavenly, coincide as they seldom can. This exultance in sheer motion outward over the waters begins, of course, before the sighting of Mt. Eryx, but the surge of liberty is reinforced by the outward-beckoning female presence of the western Sicilian mountain, which poses no real threat to male freedom but rather offers a mystery for exploration, a mystery that borders on the imaginary land situated in time and space outside the closely circumscribed human soul of today and founded in the intuitive way of life of the ancients. The true explorer into these realms is the male soul, the soul that alone has the power and the duty of forging on into new territory.

Night passes on board the Cagliari-bound ship, and not so comfortably. Morning finds the traveler still in that buoyant condition of skimming along the waves of the sea on the verge of bursting the ties of the old world altogether. He would like to be an explorer indeed, *to find three masculine, world-lost souls, and, world-lost, saunter and*   SS, 46 *saunter on along with them, across the dithering space, as long as life lasts!* It would be sweet *sometimes to come to the opaque earth,*   SS, 45 *to block oneself against the stiff land, to annul the vibration of one's flight against the inertia of our terra firma! but life itself would be in the flight, the tremble of space.* This sense of *the tremble of space* between the old world he had repudiated, the dying Mother Europe, and the new world yet to come, dark with female mysteries but subject to a rejuvenated male principle, was the controlling power of Lawrence's imagination all through the period between his post-war departure from England and his sailing for America by way of the East.

The tremble of space around the wayfaring male soul is the vibration of many things, but largely as an anticipation of the novel Lawrence was to resume writing on finishing *Sea and Sardinia,* the travel book serving as impetus to further endeavor. The *tremble of space* adventure became the breaking forth from a stymied womanless quest like Aaron's toward the completion of that search in seas beyond time. But still the chief identification in *Sea and Sardinia* is not with a figure like Aaron but rather one like Lilly, because the far-sailing Lawrence persona encountered here would unquestionably be master of the ship, as Lilly controls Aaron in their time alone together early in *Aaron's Rod.* But the never-ending expedition, insofar as Lawrence sees himself in both a Lilly and an Aaron figure, would lead to an almost angelic, or demonic state of union in conflicting selves. As an association of male self and male otherness, it would produce an analogous state uniting self and other in never-ending motion altogether beyond the sphere of physical sex. Hence the sea, in Lawrence's first real venture over its depths, gave back to him temporarily a wholeness of male identity independent of any reliance on woman and at the same time unimperiled by homosexuality.

In a more pervasive sense this sweeping far out across the waters signified by the Sardinia trip brought to a culmination an ideal exemplified by the only successful travel to be undertaken in *Aaron's Rod*: the wayfaring of Lilly and Tanny. It brings distinct manifestations of joy expressed simultaneously with Lawrence's "tragic" sense of quest. The feelings involved blend on the page with natural ease. Much of the joy springs from the sense of immediate involvement with the people brushing the life of the two travelers in passage, the procession of other travelers on boats and trains and buses, the passersby on city and village streets. The narrator sees them all in various shades of the comic, and while seldom refusing communication yet remains the individual on his guard: shrewd, good-humored, able to select and present a brilliant and balanced picture of his environment, participat-
SS, 49   ing but never forgetting that *I am no more than a single human man wandering my lonely way across these years.* All the same, the presence of the *queen bee* is essential, a living extension of the context provided by Mt. Etna and Mt. Eryx.

This kind of self-view in the traveler inches over easily into the
SS, 52   one that sees Cagliari from the approaching ship as a Jerusalem, *like some vision, some memory, something that has passed away*: which
PH, 829   we are justified in taking both as that city of *golden flesh* which Lawrence the child had sometimes seen when looking at Eastwood from
SS, 93   a distance, and as a New Jerusalem outside time altogether. Inland and two days later on the Sardinian journey, the village of Tonara on its heights calls up the same image. Not so many elements dominate a great imagination, after all. It is the astonishing variety of forms they can take in creation that matters.

SS, 55   The city of Cagliari seems like *this world's end, . . . left outside of time and history,* and the doorway to this seeker's promised land,
SS, 62   where the last *sparks* glow of *the old, hardy, indomitable male* spirit nearly vanished from the world, the spirit which in Lawrence's flight from female Sicily this "travel book" briefly recaptures for him. And so it continues, as a little train carries him from Cagliari to Mandas,
SS, 72   a *running away into the distance, . . . lovely space about one, and travelling distances* that keep bringing a former and comparable leaping-off place to mind: Cornwall with its male Celtic past. Never had Lawrence come upon a better opportunity than this juncture of time and place to express his impassioned belief in the possibility of rebirth
SS, 92   *into separation and sharp distinction.* Over and over he observes the vestiges of this parturition, from the distant past and in the Sardinians

CAGLIARI, SARDINIA

*The cathedral must have been
a fine old pagan stone fortress once* (SS, 57)

SS, 134   he is traveling among: *They knew that in the beginning and in the end a man stands alone, his soul is alone in itself, and all attributes are nothing — and this curious final knowledge preserved them in simplicity.* Perhaps this knowledge can expand from the personal to the

SS, 91   social sphere and bring the present era of ideal *love and oneness* to an end. Everything that surges into the traveler's mind in conjunction with observation of the passing scene falls readily into the now familiar pattern: intimations of the faraway past, the "New Jerusalem" of childhood, the recent years in Cornwall, the seeker's earlier days in

SS, 122   Italy. It all flows out of the country itself: *Whenever one is in Italy, either one is conscious of the present, or of the mediæval influences, or of the far, mysterious gods of the early Mediterranean. . . . Italy is like a most fascinating act of self-discovery — back, back down the old ways of time.*

Then comes what must always follow in the progression of Lawrence's beliefs: the future emerging out of the past in a cyclical movement. The past becomes Italy, the future we recognize as America:

SS, 123   *Apart from the great rediscovery backwards, which one must make before one can be whole at all, there is a move forwards. There are unknown, unworked lands where the salt has not lost its savour. But one must have perfected oneself in the great past first.* The "Minoan distance" lies in both directions, and this trip through Sardinia is the means to recapturing a sense of the one in the past and foreseeing the one in the future.

One of the most distinguished portions of *Sea and Sardinia* is the evening in Sorgono, in the heart of the mountainous interior. It is cold in the grimy room the traveler and the queen bee must take, and cold walking in the lonely fields with the sun sinking. They at last find their way to a fire in the public room of the inn, a dazzling great fire on which an old man, one of the indomitable male Sardinians, is roasting a kid for their supper, using one of the leaning spits characteristic

SS, 102   of Sardinia. This patriarch seems to the traveler like *time immemorial . . . toasting itself another meal.*

Into this glowing scene another male presence obtrudes. As we look on, it is difficult not to see in the course of events a projection of

SS, 104   authorial hopes and fears. A traveling peddler comes in. He is *breezy* and *boisterous,* impudent and tipsy. The circle of local inhabitants around the fire treat him with good-humored contempt. He talks constantly, worming all he can out of the traveler and the queen bee about their affairs, suspicious that they must be selling something and not just on a trip to see this country. He has a companion, this man, to whom he refers in a gesture of outrageous humor as a woman and as

SS, 109   his *wife.* These remarks fall on *a sudden dead silence* all around.

SARDINIA

It is wonderful in them that at this time of day
they still wear their long stocking-caps
as part of their inevitable selves . . . .
They are not going into the world's common clothes (SS, 90)

SARDINIA

Lovely space about one,
and travelling distances — nothing finished, nothing final (SS, 72)

NEAR MANDAS, SARDINIA

The old nostalgia for the Celtic regions began to spring up in me.
Ah, those old, drystone walls
dividing the fields — pale and granite-blenched (SS, 82)

SARDINIA

*The wistfulness and the far-off feeling
of loneliness and evening* (SS, 97)

This is the sort of character to whom Lawrence cannot help feeling drawn, in a dimly realized ramification of his bid for severance of the male from a female atmosphere. This man's independence he can admire. His wandering is one equivalent to that which Lawrence called for earlier in this book: those male souls on board a ship heading into *the tremble of space*. Of this man's possible homosexuality Lawrence says nothing directly, but clearly in his estimate of the peddler's degradation he includes some hint of what he has long held to be true: that homosexuality as such means the *extinction of all the purposive in-* ML, *fluences*. It is precisely this which separates the traveler from the 251–252 peddler. The traveler may see in the other *a kindred soul*, but *fate,* SS, 111 *in the guise of that mysterious division between a respectable life and a scamp's life, divided us*. He may express a preference for this man over the dull citizen, but still *it is a pity the untamable, lone-wolf souls should always become pariahs, almost of choice.*

A parallel situation came Lawrence's way some time before the Sardinia trip in his association with Maurice Magnus, but with effects that spin out, as we will see, for a year beyond the Sardinian phase.

The bus ride to the north coast of Sardinia at Olbia, the boat over to Cività Vecchia and the eventual return from there by train and boat to Sicily — all these events suited Lawrence's creative needs perfectly. The last happening comes as an unforeseen but ideal capping off of the whole voyage. This is a marionette show in Palermo that the traveler attends just after his return to Sicily, in the company of the queen bee and another woman. His entry into the spirit of the play is instantaneous: *A serpent-dragon was just having a tussle with a* SS, 198 *knight in brilliant brass armour, and my heart came into my mouth.* He is enthralled by the puppet figures: *How much better they fit the* SS, 202 *old legend-tales than living people do. . . . For in fact drama is enacted by symbolic creatures formed out of human consciousness.*

Now it happens that the legend of this puppet-play reflects in symbolic form the just-completed quest of the traveler through the Mediterranean and further reflects the imagined expedition of the band of male seekers through *the tremble of space*. On stage, Orlando and another knight are prisoners in a witch's castle, as the traveler was held by Etna in Sicily. The other knights come to their rescue, save them, and burn the witch. The audience here is mostly men and boys: *It was an affair for males,* as Lawrence comments, and all of them SS, 200 thrill to the great adventure, which is of course the liberation of themselves from female dominance by breaking out of prison and pushing off for the ends of the earth. This great deed is summed up in the word by which the knights set out: *Is there not the massive, brilliant, out-* SS, 202 *flinging recklessness in the male soul, summed up in the sudden word:*

SARDINIA

*Ahead we saw the big hump of the island of Tavolara,
a magnificent mass of rock which fascinated me
by its splendid, weighty form* (SS, 169)

Andiamo! Andiamo! Let us go on. Andiamo! — let us go hell knows where, but let us go on.

Now the witch looms high in the traveler's imagination, and he lives through a dramatic purgation which is one of the best examples in Lawrence's work of the equilibrium he always sought and sometimes attained among conflicting forces. She is to him the principle of evil, *this old, ghastly woman-spirit,* and he hates her bitterly. This is the very stuff for a Freudian analysis, Lawrence himself recognizes, and how he enjoys seeing it enacted before his eyes: *This white, submerged idea of woman which rules from the deeps of the unconscious* is overcome by *the surging hot urgency* of the knights, and up she goes in flames. **SS, 203**

Then, even as the victory flares up before him, the traveler realizes it is temporary: *Would God the symbolic act were really achieved. It is only little boys who yell. Men merely smile at the trick. They know well enough the white image endures.*

But it would be a narrow view to conclude from this admission of the impossibility of complete victory that defeat is the only alternative. The whole of the book demonstrates otherwise. A never-ending rededication to the quest is in itself a victory, especially with such periods of success as that which is so beautifully recorded in *Sea and Sardinia,* those periods when all the warring elements of the quest fall into a meaningful rhythm and pattern.

In spite of the unexorcised female nemesis in the traveler's conscience, harmony has for the most part prevailed throughout the book between him and his queen bee. This concord, as I say, is akin to that which Lawrence was to summon up in *Aaron's Rod* between Rawdon Lilly and his wife Tanny. But the equilibrium of the relationship is greater in the travel book than in the novel. *Sea and Sardinia* in fact records the nearest approach to Lawrence's ideal of life since the days at Fiascherino: to be on a journey with the mother nemesis receding into the background, to be in command of his own destiny and enjoying a husband's authority in a marriage of love. He might from this firm relationship fantasize a further voyage of pure male adventure, but it is obvious that what counts most is the stability in mobility attained with his queen bee.

Other manifestations of this variety of male volition belong to *the tremble of space* between Europe and America, notably some of the short fiction of the fall of 1921. For one, Lawrence took up *a bobbed short story* written in 1918 and gave it *a strange and fiery brush* to turn it into the novella *The Fox.* As he said, this piece shows how he was pulled westward. The youth Henry, who ran away when young and grew up in western Canada, now goes about in the old country **ML, 678**

SARDINIA

The full-gathered shirt fastened at the throat
with the two gold filigree globes, a little dark, braided, stiff bolero
just fastened at the waist (SS, 135)

again like a real untamed male seeking his own. He breaks into an uneasy semi-lesbian relationship between two women at an isolated farm, falls in love with one of them, Ellen March, persuades her to think of marrying him and migrating to Canada. But while Henry is away for a time, Ellen falls again under the strong influence of Jill Banford, her companion, and changes her mind. The ensuing rivalry between Henry and Jill is deadly. The climax comes when he is chopping down a tree with the girls looking on. He wills that the tree shall fall on his rival, for while he tells Jill to move out of the way, he steadily exerts a silent force to keep her in the path of the tree's fall. Jill knows his solicitude is pretended, that he merely wishes to command her to move. So she refuses to budge, thereby sealing her own doom: the tree kills her. Later, Henry and Ellen marry and at the close of the story look forward to a new life in western Canada.

But this is far from a "happy" ending. Happiness is, in fact, rejected as an ideal. That was what Ellen had bent every effort to achieve for Jill and herself, always seeing happiness *a little way beyond, in the* TF, 67 *blue distance.* But that distance always proved to be *a void pit* swal- TF, 68 lowing all exertions, bringing *an agony, an insanity at last.* The problem Lawrence poses at his story's end is in terms of the essential battle between man and woman. Henry is an extreme case of the male who wishes to possess his wife to her very soul: *He wanted to take away her consciousness, and make her just his woman. Just his woman.* But Jill refuses to fall quiescent under his will, though she hovers on the verge of this. An impasse then, at least for as long as they remain in England. Reliving a phase of his wartime experience, Lawrence spirits the couple away to the coast of Cornwall. As they stare out over the sea to America, the intricate contrast of their views centers upon the westward urge. Henry believes that once they have crossed the ocean, she will totally yield to him, and he will then *have all his own* TF, 69 *life as a young man and a male.* She agrees that this submission may well come to pass, but her own thoughts tend to belie what she says: she still retains a determination to experience life for herself *over the* TF, 68 *westward sea,* and Henry is in such torment to be gone that the reader senses a strong doubt in his unconscious as to the outcome he so desperately craves.

The imbalance between opposing forces in *The Fox* is clearly envisioned and forcefully rendered. It is a marvelous example of how purely analytical Lawrence was trying to be, and of how he could bring the struggles within himself, as well as between him and Frieda, into the shape of a fine piece of fiction.

The Captain's Doll dates also from the fall of 1921. It is another battle between the sexes, this time of a man to prevent his woman from "losing" him in the image of a doll, to force her to "honor" him instead. It is a battle he never quite wins, though there is promise of equilibrium in tension between them. One of the chief symbolic representations of the battle is that the man, Captain Hepburn, must climb a glacier, must face himself in the awful frigid regions that spelled doom for Gerald Crich. But the captain overcomes that frightful spirit of place. When he descends to the lowlands he plans to travel, to go to East Africa and help with founding a plantation. He will also write a book about the moon. He persuades the woman, Hannele, to accompany him as his wife, though she is far from subdued, much less so than Ellen March.

A third tale of this time, though less successful as a story than either of the foregoing, is a fascinating example of how far Lawrence attempted to proceed into the hinterlands of the unconscious to envision an exalted being for himself. *The Ladybird* tells of a strange relationship between Count Dionys and Lady Daphne, with their sym-
LB, 68   bolic names.[4] The count will be *king in Hades* when he is dead, and Daphne will be his queen. The afterlife of this couple is so pure a fantasy that Lawrence is able to bring together in it both the Lilly and Aaron sides of himself, with room for the dark femininity in his nature as well, besides producing a perfect imaginary balance of sexes between his masculine self and woman as the other. The woman here has little of Frieda in her make-up. She is a dream lover of Lawrence's, Lady Cynthia Asquith, and this story is one of the nearest Lawrence ever wrote to pure sexual fantasy, with its wholeness of male identity relegated to the perfection of eternity. *The Ladybird* is the peak of the struggle evident in all three of the short novels in question. While *Sea and Sardinia* is the quest for a stable self in the past as undergirding to the tentative future selves of *Aaron's Rod,* the three short novels are projections of the conflict into a *tremble of space* smacking of dream and nightmare.

One other ramification of the problem suggests itself from what I have been able to learn of the unpublished portion of *Mr. Noon.* Since the elopement here turned out to be so faithfully autobiographical, Lawrence's intention was probably to continue a literal rendering of his and Frieda's experience up through the war and their leaving England in 1919. Putting *Mr. Noon* in context with other works written between the post-war departure from England and the sailing for America, we may reasonably suppose that Lawrence here saw no way to resolve the man-woman relationship with the partial success of *Aaron's Rod* or the greater success of *Sea and Sardinia.* Maybe the characters of *Mr. Noon* had become altogether too life-like for the author to conquer their destiny.

A year after the Sardinian experience the further reaches of space and time still quivered and beckoned, but with much uncertainty of direction. Lawrence's travel impulse now darted back and forth between the East and West. The East was Ceylon, where some of his inclinations and the urging of his friends the Brewsters pulled at him: the East as region of contemplation. The West was America, toward which other inclinations and the persistence of Mabel Dodge Luhan's invitations exerted an equal force: America as region of action. East had for the time lost its deathly nature, perhaps because Lawrence felt so much under the spell of the dawn, of the Greeks as coming from the east to Sicily, a preoccupation he mentions over and over in the letters. Be that as it may, just as Lawrence was at last coming to an end of his vacillation by making a firm decision to go east, and within weeks of his actual departure, he wrote a piece that stands as his real farewell to Europe. In fact the writing of this piece may well have aided in his decision. I refer to the "Introduction" to Maurice Magnus's *Memoirs of the Foreign Legion.* The experience related therein dates from roughly the first half of Lawrence's now more than two years out of England since the war, and it bears the particular stamp of states of mind undergone during that time as reshaped by the feelings peculiar to Lawrence's abandonment of Europe.

Next to Lawrence himself the principal figure of the introduction is Magnus, a man in some ways like the peddler in *Sea and Sardinia,* for whom Lawrence had felt a simultaneous aversion and attraction. Magnus is likewise a wanderer, one who flouts the restrictions of society to live like a scamp and a pretentious sponger. His irresponsibility is so flagrant that it has at last brought on rejection by nearly everyone. With these vices in Magnus and the peddler we may contrast Lawrence's frugal independence and his ready acceptance by those he wished to cultivate. An even more important distinction is Lawrence's faith in his own wandering as a pioneering venture that would in time contribute to the solidarity and mutual trust of mankind. Lawrence could readily enough separate himself from his opposite number here. The sympathy with Magnus's type springs from deeper sources. For one thing Magnus is devoted to the memory of his mother, though in a theatrical sort of way. In this but not only this, Magnus has qualities like some of Lawrence's own, but with distortions by which they have proved fatal to the personality rather than providing through stress the opportunity for renewal. One of these distortions is homosexuality, which Lawrence is at great pains to denounce, virulently in some passages deleted in revision. We know that any strong repulsion suggests a fascinated attraction, the strongest impulse of which in this case is to see Magnus as a kind of degraded self. Lawrence could not refuse, nor did he entirely wish to, an empathy with this self. When he arrives at expressing the admiration that he does feel for Magnus, he employs PX, 358 terms like those often applied to himself: *Humanity can only finally conquer by realizing.* And though Magnus may in the end have betrayed human after human, in the spirit he was always right, for it was his aim to realize existence through the utter depths of experience — as in the Foreign Legion — and he never quite lost sight of his aim, eternal failure though he was in achievement. Lawrence makes it plain that by realization, by knowledge, he means first sexual knowledge, and beyond that a knowledge of the ghastliness of war. That these two sorts of experience overlap in his mind need not surprise us. He had said long before that violence stems from repressed sex, and he always saw the Great War as having come about ultimately because of the denial of growth in sexual being. He comes close here to saying what other opponents of war have said in our day, that war is the ultimate obscenity. With Magnus, Lawrence's esteem is centered on this: that his object was always to enlarge the boundaries of existence by subjecting himself to the bitterness of conditions. *He carried the human consciousness unbroken through circumstances I could not have borne.* He has therefore contributed by example, both positive and negative, to Lawrence's own life-values.

Magnus's great hope, when Lawrence makes his acquaintance, is to become a monk at the Benedictine monastery of Montecassino, and while Lawrence knows at once that Magnus can never realize this ambition, again Magnus appears to reflect, almost to parody, impulses of Lawrence's own. The place of their most important encounter is Montecassino, and this setting is of great significance to what Lawrence gleaned from their acquaintance. Moreover, the location of Montecassino in relation to Picinisco, another place revealing Lawrence's state at this time, is of vital importance.

The hill of Montecassino is one of the oldest religious centers in Europe. St. Benedict himself, in the sixth century, did away with ancient pagan shrines there and founded a Christian sanctuary. The monastery of Lawrence's time dated from the sixteenth and seventeenth centuries — unhappily, it was demolished by Allied bombs in the Second World War. But it has since been rebuilt in a similar style. Montecassino lies some ninety miles south of Rome, and, what is more important for our purposes, it lies near the road Lawrence took in and out of the valleys leading to nearby Picinisco. He could see it from almost anywhere on PX, 311 the way in or out, *the big, noble monastery . . . crouching there above.* On his way down here to Picinisco, in Florence, he had first met Magnus, who was often at the monastery and who was eager to show Lawrence this place that Lawrence had long wanted to see. During his brief sojourn in Picinisco, Lawrence had in mind that he would before long pay a visit to the monastery. He may already have considered the monastery as a possible stopping-off place for Aaron on his way forward. At least, Lawrence had discovered, almost within sight of one another, the two places that soon became the first conceived objectives after the war for the male and the female demons of himself. Further, these two places set up for us the fundamental pattern of all the fiction, plus most of the other writing, up through *The Plumed Serpent*. The woman must always go to the wilds, whether the cold mountains of Picinisco, as Alvina Houghton does, or to the forests of the American West like one of Lawrence's fictional women in America. This woman is in part Lawrence himself, and the dark male who must be her salvation in most cases is the primal male self to whom he longed to subject his anima. On the other hand, this woman is also the female counterpart, mother then wife, over whom his belief in male forcefulness demanded that he establish dominion. The mountains of the Abruzzi in *The Lost Girl* are the realm of atonement with death for Alvina, imperative to following the dark male to America, the Italian mountains representing the threshold of rebirth.

With the male quester a different order prevails. A simple thrust into freedom, a wandering band of men free from all ties: this sort of ongoing as an end in itself held great attraction for Lawrence, as *Sea and Sardinia* amply proves. But Lawrence actually experienced little of that kind of journey, and as *Sea and Sardinia* also reveals, Lawrence the traveler at his best was the one who traveled with Frieda, when in command, and who held to the ideal of an itinerant male camaraderie as a dream.

But there was always, at bottom, the male with the sense of community, the male of Rananim in its dozens of imaginary forms. This is the male who fixed on Montecassino as a possible example of a corporate life, and by a fortunate concord of place and person Lawrence could identify to some degree with Magnus, to the point of contemplating putting a fictional hero through a Magnus-like ordeal toward finding a new life in Montecassino. That Lawrence decided against this course is even more significant, and his reason for doing so emerges with all clarity in his introduction to Magnus's book.

Lawrence had given up on Picinisco and had been a few weeks in Capri when he carried out his plan to visit Montecassino, in February 1920. He could sense little there of a viable community life among the monks, nothing beyond a feeling of being *with one's college mates*. **PX, 314** In really coming to know Magnus, in the couple of days spent at the abbey, Lawrence had to go deep inside himself, and into the distant past. He and Magnus agreed on many things, only to be strongly opposed on others, and the agreement itself was painful to Lawrence:

PX, 323   *It is terrible to be agreed with, especially by a man like M—. All that one says, and means, turns to nothing.* Still, all this discord leaves Lawrence broken-hearted, and causes him to shorten his stay. He simply cannot bear being near this misshapen image of himself, who

PX, 324   in disappointment at having failed to make this one of his *mental friendships,* walks along beside Lawrence in fear of himself and of

PX, 326   life: *He seemed to walk close to me, very close. And we had neither of us anything more to say.*

It is the place, however, and not the man, on which Lawrence sketches out his state of soul. And the topography could not be more to his purpose. From the hill of the abbey he can see the mountains where Alvina Houghton is to be "lost" and to suffer the death of the old European female self on the way to resurrection in America. Down below, in full view from Montecassino, lies the ugly present world of

PX, 325   industrialism, all of it busy and *barren like the black cinder-track of the railway* he can see from the abbey. And busy too with political

PX, 324   factionalism. Up here is the monastery on its own *mountain top, the last foothold of the old world.* Which old world? A terrible composite.

PX, 326   This *hill-top must have been one of man's intense sacred places for three thousand years.* It reaches back into the Minoan distance, this place. But looming between Lawrence and this homeland of his soul is the Christian accretion, the Middle Ages living on in the monastery. A violent discord between this medieval world, with its monastic ideal, the viability of which Lawrence is here to test, and the industrial

PX, 319   world below is the conflict Lawrence recognizes most: *To see trains stop in the station and tiny people swarming like flies! To see all this from the monastery, where the Middle Ages live on in a sort of agony, like Tithonus, and cannot die, this was almost a violation to my soul, made almost a wound.*

The final disillusionment is the shattering of two hopes we can see behind all the assertion, though these are never plainly stated themselves. A certain quickness from the days of instinctive pre-history has flowed into the Christian monastic life, but such as remains of it is too faint ever to revive. The monastic ideal, the narrator had somehow hoped, might have been a means to that end. The other, the concomitant disappointment, is more vaguely conceived: with the possible reawakening of an intuitive bond between men that would go beyond the repellent intimacy of homosexuality and still not be simply *mental* in Magnus's terms. In his persistent self-examination, exposing himself to conditions and penetrating to strange places to objectify his search, Lawrence has honestly seized the opportunity to observe Magnus as a self-projection under circumstances he had thought of as possible to self-renewal. He is vastly disappointed in the individual. As for the corporate condition, the brotherhood of the abbey, Lawrence never discovers more than the schoolboy camaraderie of his first impression.

All this we must see in conjunction: the male self faced by three worlds here, and the female self suffering near at hand. It is a total recognition of the futility of expecting a way out in these regions. Only one direction of movement, after all, is possible. The traveler is a *child* PX, 318 *of the present* and must carry the present into the future to find any reinfusion from the past. He goes away on a train, and on a steamer, knowing all the region he is leaving to be *the old world, that had come* PX, 328 *to another end in me.*

For the time being, Lawrence could hold Sicily to be a form of escape. On the way there he associated himself *with Odysseus pushing his ship out of the shadows into the blue. Whatever had died for me, Sicily had then not died.* Much of Lawrence's life in Sicily we have encountered in *Sea and Sardinia.* But he wrote his "Introduction" nearly a year after that book, and by now Sicily had given way to the call of those truly far-off places which had for years stuck in his imagination, first America, but, as if he must try yet another experiment in perfecting a knowledge of the past before pushing on into the real future, Lawrence felt impelled to take a roundabout way to the West and experience first a place of far more recent attraction, the East: if we can call it attraction. Perhaps it was more nearly compulsion, from that direction so lately the quarter of death. Lawrence must have known, truly, from his clearly put failure to find any potential in the meditative life at Montecassino, that contemplation in Asia as opposed to action in America could never be the way of life for him.

NOTES

[1] One reason for Lawrence's interest in European history just now was that he had been reading Gibbon: *I found a great satisfaction in reading Gibbon's* Decline and Fall of the Roman Empire — *the emperors are all so indiscriminately bad* (ML, 551). Lawrence is often indebted to Gibbon for phraseology, though the styles of the twentieth-century animist and the eighteenth-century rationalist emerge quite differently on the page. Compare with Lawrence's text these borrowings from Gibbon: *In the time of Caesar, the reindeer, as well as the elk and the wild bull, was a native of the Hercynian forest, which then overshadowed a great part of Germany and Poland . . . . The most inquisitive of the Germans were ignorant of its utmost limits, although some of them had travelled in it more than sixty days' journey.* The History of the Decline and Fall of the Roman Empire (London, 1909), p. 215.

[2] The full text of the *Mr. Noon* fragment, edited by Lindeth Vasey, will be published in due course in the Cambridge Edition of Lawrence's works.

For pertinent references to the history of composition, *see* SR, especially page 110. As late as October 1922 (unpublished letter, Charles Smith collection), Robert Mountsier, then Lawrence's American agent, was still urging him to finish the novel. Lawrence doubted that he ever would, though he did not rule out the possibility.

[3] *The smiling Astarte, Ashtaroth, Venus of the aborigines* and *Aphrodite* are all names that Lawrence uses to identify this goddess (SS,33,34,42). In calling her *Erycina ridens* he was alluding to the "archaic smile" seen on the statues of so many ancient Mediterranean goddesses. The cult of Venus on Mount Eryx was certainly ancient, carried on by Carthaginians and probably earlier peoples before the Romans adopted her as Venus Erycina. The mountain bears the name of King Eryx, a son of Aphrodite either by Poseidon or one of the Argonauts. That Aphrodite was born of the sea and that she was a mother-goddess before she became a goddess of erotic love had their own significance to Lawrence at this time.

[4] Lawrence's choice of a name for the heroine of *The Ladybird* has only a general relation to classical mythology. One story has it that Daphne was mortal, and a god, not Dionysus but Apollo, fell in love with her. Dionysus as the ancient model for Count Dionys offered richer material to Lawrence's ways of invention. In the version of the myth where Dionysus had to be torn prematurely from his mother's womb, he spent the rest of his gestation period sewn up in the thigh of his father, Zeus. He traveled widely around the Mediterranean before he won his way to full godhood, descending into Hades near the end of this time to rescue the shade of his mother. Another form of the myth identifies him not as the son of a mortal woman but of Persephone herself. His fertility-god attributes and the especially passionate rites that women devoted to him are well known.

10

A Subtle Layering
of Distances

Decision had been a long time in coming, and hesitation still dogged him from Italy to Ceylon, but late in February 1922, Lawrence took the irretrievable step and boarded ship in Naples for the East. As he left, the towering female influence of the past tugged at him exactly as it had on his first and by now less important sea voyage, from Sicily to Sardinia the previous year. Now he wrote: *We came through the* ML, 694 *Straits of Messina and then for hours we saw our Etna like a white queen or a white witch there standing in the sky so magic-lovely. She said to me, "You come back here," but I only said, "No," but I wept inside with grief, grief of separation.* It was no accident, surely, that Lawrence in a letter was addressing these words to his mother-in-law, whom he liked and to whom the erring son in him could sometimes appeal.

He dispatched an even more interesting message to her from the Gulf of Aden, with the Red Sea behind and the waters of the Indian Ocean opening straight ahead into the East. This letter of March 7 is remarkable for its description of the deserts almost to be touched as the ship went through the Suez Canal. It is remarkable too for its evocation of the rebirth that Lawrence imagined for himself, both cultural and personal, as he slid through these narrow waterways away from his Judeo-Christian heritage and out into the first vast ocean he had ever ventured upon: *Next morning we were in the Red Sea.* NW, *There stands Mount Sinai, red like old dried blood, naked like a knife* 110–111 *and so sharp, so unnaturally sharp, like a dagger that has been dipped in blood and has dried long ago and is a bit rusty and is always there like something dreadful between man and his lost Paradise. . . . It is a strange exit through this Red Sea — bitter. Behind lie finally Jeru-salem, Greece, Rome and Europe, fulfilled and past — a great dreadful*

[253]

dream. . . . And God be praised Sinai and the Red Sea are past and consummated. The waters had parted and closed. The captivity was past. Now for the leading of the pillar of cloud and the pillar of fire.

In Lawrence's symbolic geography, now prepared to encompass the whole world, the East had grown through months of indecision to

ML, 685 be *the source*: by which he meant that he hoped it would nurture a soul newborn out of the old Judeo-Christian past into the blood-knowledge he must possess in strength before proceeding to America, that *extreme periphery*. And then, from that utmost limit, one must come back, whether this meant coming back to Europe or merely advancing into a new state of life symbolized by some other location. Altogether Lawrence perceived far more gradations to recovering the pristine self in the pristine space and time than he had previously taken account of. The traveler labors under such a need for the whole pattern of rebirth that the deathly region of the East has to be traversed as a way-station which is like a tomb between crucifixion and resurrection.

What Lawrence had pictured in Ceylon was another variant of his old ideal: to live in company with a few like-minded individuals and cultivate one's soul in simplicity. Ceylon was to be something approaching an interim Rananim. With him and Frieda would be only the Brewsters and their young daughter: though Lawrence went so far as to suggest, unsuccessfully, that Mabel Dodge meet them in Ceylon

LT, 17 so they could all prepare for *the later Onslaught on to that Land of Promise of yours.*

The Brewsters, it turned out, were just as good company as Lawrence could have wished for, unlike most of his prospective Rananimers. But he was, of course, full of contraries as to the place

ML, 698 itself, and it is the sum of these that tells us most. He felt like Jonah having run away from his responsibility to save England as Nineveh, and he might soon return. Yet he spoke also of holding to his purpose of sailing on to America. The dark people of the East and the pre-mental consciousness perhaps still latent in them produced other contraries. He found them on the one hand *picturesque* if rather *silly,* yet

ML, 701 on the other hand one could sense in them *the vastness of the blood stream.* Even that primitivism at close quarters, however, had something mudlike and faintly nauseating about it. In nearly the only bit of writing Lawrence did in Ceylon, besides letters — the long poem "Elephant" — he asserts that what the people here need is a new sacred authority, a real king, not the sickly Prince of Wales whom Lawrence saw on a state visit, riding above the multitudes on an elephant.

The upshot of it all was that after five weeks, Lawrence was through with Ceylon.

But he would not take on America yet. First, Australia. And as soon as he was on board ship with the sea carrying him in that direction, he revived from his tropical semi-torpor and became the Lawrence who loved travel just for its infinite variety and its never-ending challenge to the spirit. *The world of idea may be all alike, but the world* ML, 702 *of physical feeling is very different — one suffers getting adjusted — but that is part of the adventure.* And what did he care now about the salvation of England, in this world where it was *strange and fascinating to wander like Virgil in the shades.* And then Ceylon itself went through the never-failing magic of Laurentian place-alchemy to become already something *wonderful to have known.* If the present was keen in its ML, 701 immediacy to this Lawrence, the past, from the most recent to the remotest, brought the intoxication of nostalgia, with the future, dreaded but profoundly desired, completing the rhythm.

Lawrence spent about three months in Australia, altogether, two weeks in west Australia and except for his days on the ship enroute, the remainder of the time in Thirroul, on the coast south of Sydney. Here he wrote the novel *Kangaroo,* set in his immediate surroundings, and if we add to this the fact that he drew on his impressions of Australia for the novel he later wrote in collaboration with Molly Skinner, *The Boy in the Bush,* we recognize that Australia, and not the "East" in the form of Ceylon, was the real prelude to America. Yet the Australia experience came about almost by accident. True enough, Lawrence and Frieda had at least once considered migrating there during the war, but no further attraction presented itself until they met some friendly Australians on the ship to Ceylon who urged them to come for a visit. It is still not likely, on fleeing there from Ceylon, that Lawrence would have remained long — for he said he would like to go on rolling with the momentum gathered — if Frieda had not put her foot down against any more immediate travel. Which led to renting a bungalow on the ocean front, and once again, as in the early days, in a spot out of reach of people: the sort of "exile" that Lawrence was always prepared to like and soon did like in this its latest form.

Accident or not, the Australian sojourn brought together for Lawrence in an ideally situated spot all the major concerns that he was accustomed to making manifest through place. The people were to some extent comparable to Americans as he had prepared himself to take Americans. The Australians lived by a materialism, inseparable from their democracy, which kept all life on the surface. They were always on the go, but without a purpose, a trait to which Lawrence was acutely sensitive, seeing that he too was always on the go, though with him the whole purpose of life was bound up with roving. They also displayed, to a greater degree even than the Americans, the free and casual ways born of democracy which in reality he found agreeable, for all his carping: if only because this gave him free rein in alternating between his outgoing nature and that other nature of withdrawing into those dark and isolate moods where he acted through something of a cross between British reserve and a holy-man self-containment. In these moments his own people were foreigners to him: they had always been so at home, and so were they now in Australia. Lawrence always reached his best expression about a place when he could feel that its inhabitants were a breed strange to him. But if in all these ways the Australians with their right proportion of the British temper incorporated also many attributes of the Americans, they did not suffer to any extent from what Lawrence saw as an American disease: a gripped idealism and a will to dominate. Australia was, in short, for all these reasons, the perfect land through which to explore by fictional application the political sphere in which Lawrence's mind had been feeling its way for some time.

Another and more vital sphere which underlies any politics was also eminently visible in Australia — the spirit of place and the connection between this and the resident human spirit. Here, to a greater degree perhaps than in America, the life of the population was carried on entirely on the surface and no joining of human spirit and spirit of place had ever occurred. In a sense, then, it was virgin territory for that redeeming society which Lawrence's imagination was always devising. Rananim, he thought, might be constructed here, in this *weird, unawakened country, . . . if one could have a dozen people, perhaps, and a big piece of land of one's own.* But he added ruefully, and flatly, that it couldn't be done. What truly engrossed him was to receive and translate the vibrations of the landscape, to match them with his own instincts. The rhythm of these two forces he was soon transferring to Richard Somers of *Kangaroo*, a rhythm of fascination and wonder counterbalanced by a fear and an expectation unsure of their object. The agoraphile in Lawrence responded keenly. This continent was new and young, yet *so hoary and lost, so unapproachable. The sky was pure, crystal pure and blue, of a lovely pale blue colour: the air was wonderful, new and unbreathed: and there were great distances.* It was all so remote as to be at times *invisible,* as if European *eyes hadn't the vision in them to correspond with the outside landscape.* But then he caught an almost indefinable delicacy, and a European painter came to his rescue. He saw Puvis de Chavannes' *Winter* in Melbourne and found in the continent around him the same *subtle layering of distances* that this painter had created as background in his paintings of the Old World.[1] The phrase well sums up the process

ML, 708

KA, 9

KA, 85

of vision that had been going on in Lawrence since he had set out for America by way of Ceylon and Australia.

The source of the fear and anxiety, for Lawrence as for Somers, was the bush, its emptiness and incipient but never tangible life, along with its intermingling of death: *The bush, the grey, charred bush. It* KA, 9 *scared him. . . . It was so phantom-like, so ghostly, with its tall pale trees and many dead trees, like corpses, partly charred by bush fires: and then the foliage so dark, like grey-green iron. And then it was so deathly still. Even the few birds seemed to be swamped in silence. Waiting, waiting — the bush seemed to be hoarily waiting.* The fear and the anticipation culminate for Richard Somers one night of full moon when he is walking alone in the bush. He feels stirring about him *something big and aware and hidden! He walked on, had walked a* KA, *mile or so into the bush, and had just come to a clump of tall, nude,* 9–10 *dead trees, shining almost phosphorescent with the moon, when the terror of the bush overcame him. He had looked so long at the vivid moon, without thinking. And now, there was something among the trees, and his hair began to stir with terror on his head. There was a presence. He looked at the weird, white, dead trees, and into the hollow distances of the bush. Nothing! Nothing at all. He turned to go home. And then immediately the hair on his scalp stirred and went icy cold with terror. What of? He knew quite well it was nothing. He knew quite well. But with his spine cold like ice, and the roots of his hair seeming to freeze, he walked on home, walked firmly and without haste. For he told himself he refused to be afraid, though he admitted the icy sensation of terror. But then to experience terror is not the same thing as to admit fear into the conscious soul. Therefore he refused to be afraid.*

Lawrence's complex love of distance incorporated another stratum of feeling that figures to a lesser but significant degree in his outlook: the accompanying opposite, the fear of distance, an agoraphobia coupled with a determination to turn such fear to account, to know terror but to deny its power admittance to the deepest soul. Behind the revealing passage just quoted lie comparable experiences echoing their way back to childhood: the ash-tree scene in *Sons and Lovers,* poems such as "Song of a Man Who is Not Loved," the impact of mountain distances in *Women in Love* and *The Lost Girl.* Distance has many faces, many layers, many lessons for the traveler. At the present juncture, with the first great expanses of land and water both behind him, we may note in Lawrence that any fear of distance nearly always runs through experience with land masses and not with the sea. The fear of the Australian bush stands in contrast with the almost unadulterated sense of liberation awakened by the vastness of the waters in *Sea and*

Sardinia, and also with the intense excitement of pressing on into watery strongholds vibrating in the early essays on Melville and Dana.

Another distance Lawrence also never lost sight of in Australia was that of time. From this distance was missing just the age that he ML, 711   wished to think of as a model for the future, the *Semite-Egyptian-Indo-European vast era of history.* The *coal age, the age of great ferns and mosses,* was all he could conjure up in Australia to fill his need for a mythic history, and as that was pre-human it served little purpose. Consequently his considered opinion was that Australia could not ML, 712   be reached — not yet — as a source of new life. If he had no *fighting Conscience* left, and desired to withdraw from the world entirely, Australia would be the place to stay. And when he had rounded the world to here once more, he might remain. What lay ahead, and what could not be shirked, was of course America.

Yet, to repeat, Lawrence wrote one novel on Australia and helped to write another. In these we find embodied something akin to Somers' reaction to the bush, threaded into those views Lawrence already held of the world. But we do not find much of the sense of unreachability expressed in the letters.

Kangaroo came into being in about seven weeks: one of those concentrated spells of composition in which most of Lawrence's later novels were produced — though recent availability of manuscripts and letters has shown that he made significant revisions in America. It was, all the same, one of those sudden outpourings of a brimful consciousness like *Sea and Sardinia.* Australia demanded of Lawrence, as his first touch with a virgin continent, what his first embarking on great waters had demanded. Both ventures had been held in prospect for years: largely, in his writings, through the American literature essays. Just as he had taken his exposure to the breadth and agelessness of the Mediterranean as a prelude to the rebirth he experienced in sailing through the Red Sea past Mount Sinai into the Eastern oceans, so he took his Australian sojourn as a prelude to encountering the ancient yet virgin spirit of America. *Kangaroo* was intended from the start LT, 24 &   as a forerunner to *an American novel.* Lawrence wrote to say so both TS, 35   to Mabel Dodge and to his American publisher, Thomas Seltzer. With *Kangaroo* Lawrence set out on what was to prove one of the most trying experiments of his life: to put his vision and his mission into political form. It was an experiment that failed from any practical point of view and was always informed by a radical skepticism toward political solutions to anything, in entities from the size of Rananim to the size of a nation. The significance of Lawrence's two political novels, *Kangaroo* and *The Plumed Serpent,* can only be appreciated by taking the politics they contain as metaphors connoting psychological quest and the two continents involved as hinterlands of the soul where concentrated attempts are made to embody the manifestations peculiar to each continent — the kangaroo for Australia, the eagle-serpent pairing for America. Each novel seeks to give shape to these spirits of place in men of heroic stature who command allegiance through a mystique of the senses.

Through all this quest the problem of identity is acute. The ubiquitous seeking spirit of Lawrence appears now in one character, now in another, a placing of the self in the proposition or questioning of the moment in the constantly unfolding inquiry into the formation of self with respect to place, in all the myriad and perpetually shifting forms encountered in travel. We have observed how Lawrence divided himself in *Aaron's Rod,* a leadership but hardly a political novel. In *The Plumed Serpent* we will encounter him in three fairly well-defined forms. In *Kangaroo,* the distribution of traits in the author-seeker is more indirectly carried out. One character in the novel has merely borrowed ideas in reading Somers' work and applies them without imagination. The man Kangaroo, on the other hand, brings into visible form the "dark lordship" of Lawrence's predilections, in a form like those found in a poem of two years before, "The Revolutionary," and in the poem just written in Ceylon, "Elephant."

But the identification with the man Kangaroo, in agreement with Lawrence's attitude to Australia, is a remote and tentative one. The prime burden of his questing spirit is imposed on Richard Lovat Somers, a self-possessed *smallish man, pale-faced, with a dark beard* KA, 1 who when the novel begins has just come to Sydney with his wife Harriet on a ship from west Australia. The hopes he bears for a new life on this new continent are already dwindling. Maybe Europe is not moribund after all, he feels, and maybe after a three months' trial residence here he will sail for home. Following a brief stay in the city — but long enough to make the acquaintance of Jack Callcott — Somers and Harriet move to a cottage on the sea, just as Lawrence and Frieda did. Throughout Lawrence's writing of the novel everyday experience flowed into fiction by a transference more immediate than he had ever before employed. This kind of direct transformation was to function in much the same fashion in *The Plumed Serpent* as well.

With Jack Callcott, and with four other men, Somers tests the feasibility of a new sort of male relationship as the foundation for a new society. This is the gist of his hopes for a new world in Australia and the thematic core of the novel. Jack Callcott is an intelligent working man and in his way a leader. Through the relationship that grows between Callcott and Somers, Lawrence can investigate the possibility of a social concord between the artist and thinker in Somers and the

KA, 36   sturdy common man in Callcott — it is pointed out that *the intuitive response* between them is due to Somers' own derivation from the lower classes. The fellowship that Callcott wants with Somers is "matehood," a blood brotherhood extending to the laying down of their lives for each other, a fighting pair who together could accomplish any feat, an allegiance in which Callcott's declared need is for submission to a man superior to himself. This fellowship would be part and parcel of a secret political group that Callcott now invites Somers to join, a group hoping to seize power in Australia under absolute obedience to their top leader when the anticipated political disaster of a socialist uprising comes to pass. On both of these levels, the personal and the political, Somers feels a certain temptation. He has often expressed the wish to participate in really effective political action, and he has

KA, 120   always *half wanted to commit himself to this whole affection with a friend, a comrade, a mate.* And yet, on the other side of a dividing line in his creator, Somers realizes when faced with the actual offer of

KA, 121   sacred brotherhood *that in his innermost soul he had never wanted it.* He does want, nevertheless, *some living fellowship,* and what is now phrased by Somers is an idea that has flourished since *Aaron's Rod* and has been confirmed by Lawrence's travels in the East: *the thing that the dark races know: that one can still feel in India: the mystery of lordship.* We cannot fail to recognize at once, however, that a sort of lordship is just what Callcott has appealed to Somers for: to accept his allegiance to the death — only to be met with a refusal like that of Rawdon Lilly to Aaron Sisson at the close of *Aaron's Rod.* A reluctance to assume the authority for which they seem naturally fitted is common among Lawrence's heroes. But something more is involved in this instance, and that is the source of the desire for lordship, which in this case Somers mistrusts, and rightly so, as his experience with Kangaroo, the supreme leader of Callcott's group, soon begins to make manifest.

This ponderous, swarthy and charismatic lawyer looks and acts his totemistic part fully. He speaks quite a few of Somers' own ideas — from Lawrence's essays on education and democracy — right back to

KA, 129   him. Somers is drawn to him: *"Why, the man is like a god, I love him,"* he says to himself. Still, his heart falters to hear his own beliefs rendered back to him, and his will to implicit faith is constantly countermanded by his will to resist. Before long we begin to see that the duality of Lawrence's thought and the insistent dialectic to which it gave rise will never permit him, and by extension his characters, the luxury of political solutions. The source of the reservations and objections concerning his own published ideas Somers does not at once articulate. But before long, and with the aid of Harriet's insight —

she being the first to state the accusation objectively — Somers discovers that the lordship expounded by Kangaroo is founded on the same impulse as Callcott's matehood: love. Unable to accept such a foundation, Somers is left still in pursuit of that dark instinct which he knows to be the binding force of the universe, but which is emphatically not "love." Love can only mean a false harmony, a possessiveness of some sort, and ultimately the loss of singleness in merging.

In Somers' creator, at least, the binding force of the search is a condition of stress, of tension. In a confrontation between Kangaroo and Somers the issues involved take shape with a wholeness that Lawrence could only fully achieve in a piece of fiction. The scene takes place in Kangaroo's rooms in Sydney. He and Somers are alone. Longing to make of Somers his greatest adherent, and working on what he senses to be a corresponding desire in Somers to be transported into pure faith, Kangaroo all but chants: *"I believe in the one* KA, 152 *fire of love. I believe it is the one inspiration of all creative activity. I trust myself entirely to the fire of love."* In this manner he offers to Somers a comrade-leader alliance which is at least a mystical homosexuality. Somers protests that love — in all its forms, he plainly means — is not *the only inspiration of creative activity.* The answer he re- KA, 153 ceives might almost have come from the mouth of Birkin: talk of an equilibrium of separate natures as between heavenly bodies and the potentiality of a new age through human imitation of such cosmic gravitation. The words are so near to Somers' beliefs that he can only reply to Kangaroo's challenge by conceding that all he says is true. But Somers is soon bringing forward an all-important distinction between their views, one couched in the terms of Lawrence's old dichotomy: the love of Kangaroo is conceived in the spirit, not in the flesh. The mystery of the flesh Somers attempts to put into words in this fashion: *the great God* must enter us again, through *the lower* KA, 155 *self, the dark self, the phallic self, . . . the unspoken God: who is just beyond the dark threshold, . . . whom I fear while he is my glory.*

Kangaroo now declares that Somers is possessed by a demon that prevents him from accepting love and vows to exorcise that demon. On the contrary, Somers argues, *my demon is what I identify myself* KA, 157 *with.* The demon is in touch with the dark God, and while he lives largely by a fierce solitude, he still swings back at times into communion with other men. He alone knows how to accomplish this difficult feat of contact, to be realized only *at the lower threshold, . . . in the sacred dark* where *men meet and touch, and it is a great communion.* This disagreement on the nature of communion is the point of severance between Somers and Kangaroo. It is on this account that Somers rejects Australia, in all its political and personal manifestations, and sails away to America retaining only what the remote, dark spirit of place has to offer as sustenance in his coming battle to know the spirit of America.

This interview between Somers and Kangaroo naturally brings to mind the preceding fictional occasions when the question of man-to-man relationship came up. Lawrence's answer now is what it has always been, but his determined effort to put it in terms as yet untried adds new interest. The perplexity is this: since the love that Kangaroo offers Somers is in essence homosexual, how can Somers reject it as "spiritual" and then dare, himself, to speak of a relationship founded on the *phallic self?* A bit of thought will supply us with Lawrence's consistent answer. What is conceived in the spirit and imposed on the life of the body turns obscene or perverted. In the purity of the unconscious resides another potential of close male relationship untainted by sex. What is interesting here is that this is Lawrence's first unhesitating attempt, in fiction, to put this relationship wholly in terms of the dark gods, to define the great conflict of what constitutes an acceptable intimacy and a normal integrity in the most primitive depths of the unconscious.

The interview with Kangaroo must, however, be taken in conjunction with a later encounter to yield a full example of how Australia clarified for Lawrence some of the obscure regions of his religious quest. The scene in question is one of a transitory temptation to lovemaking between Somers and Victoria, Jack Callcott's wife. He easily

KA, 164   arouses in her *a glow of offering.* He is filled with desire, *weapon-like desire* like the visitation of a god. But he declines to go further, and his reasoning as to why calls up Lawrence's puritan mysticism. It may be, Somers thinks, a fear of committing himself, in other words mere

KA, 165   impotence. Why, he inquires, should one refuse these *great moments, these sacred moments?* And Somers' inclusion in his thoughts of both Leda and Ganymede suggests that he has homosexual as well as heterosexual moments in mind. His answer to himself is this: he is *puritanical.* And while this word may, on the face of it, be interpreted as simply referring to the sexual austerity of the puritan, the succeeding thought proves that much more is involved. These moments of the gods are ultimately only *flashes of desire for a visual object,* and this visual impetus to emotion in action no longer satisfies Somers. Once again, as when before Kangaroo, he retreats to another plane of awareness than that on which a mentally directed contact between individuals is grounded; he retreats to a plane of consciousness which refuses relationship on the basis of sudden and powerful urges that strike and depart like the visitation of a god, because in effect they deprive the human of his own soul for a time, its place usurped by the possessing god.

What is curious is that just such metaphors as these serve Lawrence off and on to embrace the very feeling that here they stand opposed to. For instance, in the revision of the American literature SC, 22 essays a few months later, in a passage quoted in an earlier chapter, the soul of man is described as an obscure region where gods from the unknown come and go and embody for the moment what the soul may be. But here in *Kangaroo* the true passional state is delineated as one in which the single self is never lost, either to the other being with whom a temporary contact is established or to the great darkness where they meet. Somers makes his distinction in this way as he resists the temptation to make love to Victoria: god-like flashes of desire, no, *he had no use for them. There was a downslope into Orcus, and a* KA, 165 *vast, phallic, sacred darkness, where one was enveloped into the greater god as in an Egyptian darkness. He would meet there or nowhere. To the visual travesty he would lend himself no more.* If the choice so far seems to lie between gods from above and a god from below, and this appears to be a mere confusion of terms, then the matter is clarified to some extent by thoughts which occur to Somers just previous to his moment with Victoria, between that moment and his former interview with Kangaroo: *If I am to have a meeting it shall* KA, 159 *be down, down in the invisible, and the moment I re-emerge it shall be alone. In the visible world I am alone, an isolate instance.* And so, out of all the repetition which was Lawrence's way of holding some tough problem in his thought, the vital factor emerges: the right of the single being to inviolable integrity, freedom from any possession with which all love is tainted, and the preservation of this integrity even in the presence of the dark gods ruling life through the unconscious. It is no difficult matter to see how this creed is "puritan": the puritan always meets God as an individual. He is not possessed and merged into an all-absorbing godhead, not at least in this present sphere. In a communion of saints enveloped by his God, he still maintains the strictest individuality.

The prominent geographical symbol for the surging passional forces in *Kangaroo* is the sea, which rolls just below the steep bank where the cottage stood in which Lawrence wrote the book and watched himself and Frieda come and go as Somers and Harriet. In this element of the novel Harriet eventually becomes almost as implicated as her husband, when she emerges as a precursor to the women in search who predominate in the fiction of Lawrence's American period.

Since the trip to Sardinia the sea had been the element of discovery. Or further yet in the past, it was the great beckoner to realization in KA, 264 Cornwall, to that *west lost in the sea* that Somers is aware of while KA, 248 remembering here in Australia the *nightmare* of his spiritual break with England in the wartime days. In Australia it is the eastern and not the western distance that vanishes into the ocean. But of course in the end, as Lawrence was taking his pilgrim way around the world, LT, 18 the directions merge: Lawrence had spoken, even, of deliberately heading east to go west. In the Australian cottage on a cliff above the eternally crashing Pacific, Richard and Harriet Somers each one from time to time sends out the self in spirit to breast the waves toward KA, 22 America, to be caught up in that *heavy, earth-despising swell* of the Pacific, a swell which appears to them as a *part of its pacific nature.* ML, 706 Lawrence could now and again say, in a letter, *we live mostly with the sea — not much with the land.* The ocean granted him a counter rhythm to the surface-scurrying population and the unreachable Australian spirit of place. Somers' first real challenge to involve himself deeply in the politics of Australia comes to him on the shore, with Jack Callcott delivering his invitation to join the Kangaroo brotherhood and Somers replying over the noise of the waves. Other serious talks occur to this same accompaniment. Somers gives physical expression to his revulsion from Kangaroo's offer of "bosom" love by suddenly stripping KA, 169 and plunging briefly into the *green ripples of the broken swell* along the beach near his house.

Toward the end of the novel the imagery of the sea builds to make it finally the avenue of escape from the entanglements of Australia into continuation of the pilgrimage. Somers has realized that he must reject Kangaroo's new society, founded on the leader's embrace of his fol-KA, 357 lowers, a sort of eternal confinement in a *marsupial belly*. This is the KA, 385 total *collapse of the love-ideal* for Somers, of whatever vestiges of that old Christian way he may have retained. He voices his final decision at the time of Kangaroo's death from shots fired in a political disturbance. Somers is then left alone with Harriet to profess his fidelity to KA, 384 *the God of fear, of darkness, of passion, and of silence, the God that made a man realise his own sacred aloneness.* This God now leads over the sea, after this creative or at least nourishing pause on the remotest of continents. Instructing his hero on the next step, Lawrence defines with exactness his motivation for writing *Kangaroo* and with KA, this his current theory of the novel: *Man is a thought-adventurer.* 327–328 *Man is more, he is a life-adventurer. Which means he is a thought-adventurer, an emotion-adventurer, and a discoverer of himself and of the outer universe. . . . We insist that a novel is, or should be, also a thought-adventure.* In that vein he has Somers commanding himself

to *draw your ring round the world, the ring of your consciousness,*   KA, 408
tracing the arc now toward America.

If the sea in *Kangaroo* is the great expanse of earth where atonement is sought with time and being, it is not so for Somers alone but for Harriet too. She has the greater part in the original decision of choosing the cottage on the low cliff over the sea. And she feels in her own search for being in conjunction with Somers that *the Lord*   KA, 90
had sent her here. She has brought with her the ideal of *a land with a*   KA, 412
new atmosphere, untainted by authority, and, in contrast to her husband, *in the first months she had found this in Australia, in the silent, silvery-blue days, and the unbreathed air, and strange, remote forms of tree and creature.... In the silvery pure air of this undominated continent she could swim like a fish that is just born, alone in a crystal ocean. Woman that she was, she exulted, she delighted.... And she just could not understand that Richard was so tense, so resistant.* In such a spirit she maintains, throughout most of the novel, a background position of importance. This is where Somers wants and needs her: Lawrence's old idea of the woman sustaining the man in his battle with the world. Somers feels *that he could never take the*   KA, 110
move into activity unless Harriet and his dead mother believed in him. In practice, besides encouragement, this role of sustainer includes that of ego-puncturing now and then, not only in Somers but even in Kangaroo.

Then Harriet's role expands, notably in the last chapter of the novel, which Lawrence wrote in its definitive form in America. Her elation dwindles. The land turns sombre, then gruesome, and Harriet begins to anticipate Kate in those moments of revulsion from Mexico. At her side Somers preaches that the freedom she felt in her first days down here was illusory. He lays down the law to her that she cannot *escape the dark hand of the Lord, not even in free Australia.* In this   KA, 413
last chapter Harriet can be easily linked not only with Kate of *The Plumed Serpent* but with Alvina Houghton at the close of *The Lost Girl:* America is the next fearful and awesome terrain to cross toward the celestial city of recovered being. The subtle layers of distance are ready to melt into seascape and then into the conifer-dark and snow-glistening mountains of the long-awaited continent.

NOTES

[1]The phrase is from a letter to a painter: Earl Brewster, the American friend with whom Lawrence had stayed in Ceylon. Elsewhere in the paragraph (ML, 709), Lawrence speaks of being reminded of Puvis in the *pale, pure silver* of Australian trees, in the *blue sky* and *very blue hills,* all

these having *exquisite forms.* Then he denounces Puvis for his *foolish human figures — Classical remains.* This letter is interesting as a document in Lawrence's developing views of landscape art, especially since a few years later he allied himself completely with Cézanne's approach, and Puvis and Cézanne are now discussed as forerunners to opposing styles in modern art. *See* Richard J. Wattenmaker, *Puvis de Chavannes and the Modern Tradition* (Toronto, 1975).

11

The Continent of the Afterwards

The ship on which the Lawrences sailed from Australia to America put in at Wellington, New Zealand, then at Rarotonga and Tahiti. If any desire to live in the tropics remained with Lawrence after his stay in Ceylon, his visits to the Pacific islands erased it. They were lovely enough to look at, but they aroused a sort of *reptile nausea* by their ML, 713 tainted smell, which was made all the worse by their reputation as earthly paradises. Lawrence's geographical outlook had evolved a great deal since the time when he used to fabricate dreams of the Pacific through Rananim and the voyages of Dana and Melville, or even since he had pipe-dreamed with Compton Mackenzie on Capri in 1920 about seafaring in the Pacific on their own sailing ship. He now wrote Compton Mackenzie from Rarotonga never to come to this place, for the people were only *brown and soft,* and he felt the same aversion CM, 235 to them that he had felt to the Singhalese. If Lawrence had never fully expected a realization of primitive fulfillment in the South Seas, still he could formerly cherish the dream as dream. Now that too had vanished.

Landing in San Francisco in early September, after a few days the Lawrences continued by train to Lamy, New Mexico, and finally by car to Mabel Dodge's place in Taos, where they arrived on his thirty-seventh birthday, September 11, 1922. Their determined and possessive hostess assigned the Lawrences a new house in her compound of artists and writers, real and would-be, at the edge of Taos Indian land and in sight of the pueblo, on which Lawrence gazed as if *looking from the top of a hill way back down to a village one has* ML, 717 *left and forgotten.* In most of his contacts with American Indians, he felt a tingle of kinship in the involuntary region of memory.

[267]

In no time Mabel Dodge had Lawrence on his way to a ceremony of the Jicarilla Apaches on their reservation a good many miles from Taos.[1] Here he came face to face for the first time with Indians in a "wild" setting, after long anticipation through the pages of Cooper and other writers such as Prescott. Lawrence wrote a sketch of his first evening at the ceremonial ground, "Indians and an Englishman," which sets at once the ambivalent tone characteristic of his whole experience with America. He fell readily into mockery of the tri-cultural society of the Southwest, accusing Anglo, Hispanic, and aboriginal of living life as a performance, as a series of movie-set stunts half-inspired by animosity between the groups. But the gibing obviously turns back on the author, too, on his half-serious, half-romantic expectations of America. Easily perceived also is the fear of the overwhelming experience that he had long anticipated America to be. This fear is itself full of a curious opposition, already visible to some extent in his response to Ceylon and the Pacific islands: he feared the loss of PH, 96   his whiteness, aware of *a jeering, malevolent vibration* against it in the primitive peoples of America, even as he desired at the same time to surrender his consciousness to the Indian's darker tide of blood. This dual voice of craving and defensiveness led him straight into his other controlling emotion toward America. He might assert that the modern ML, 721   Indians were *up against a dead wall* and that the modern dominant race could expect no more than to *pick up some threads* from them PH, 99   while following *the great devious onward-flowing stream of conscious human blood,* but what really attracted and perplexed and tormented him was what he called in the new revision of the American literature SC, 51   essays a great *yearning myth.* In the Apache sketch this comes out for him through the voice of the aged shaman at his ritual singing by a PH, 99   ceremonial fire, a *voice out of the far-off time* which sent through PH, 95   Lawrence *a nostalgia, unbearably yearning for something, and a sickness of the soul.* The wall was far from dead, at that.

It was all this that must be wrought into the many shapes of lan-ML, 736   guage at Lawrence's command, at this high point in the *savage enough pilgrimage* of his post-war years. And through all the hesitations and fears attending this effort, the conviction still flows strong in the writing of the period and afterwards that Native American ritual is a form of religion as religion should be. The most poignant expression of this conviction came several years afterwards, when Lawrence was back in Europe, too ill ever to see America again. This expression is from the article "New Mexico," an expression vivified by a nostalgia for the Southwest both as landscape and as the seat of Indian religion. In the American Indian, Lawrence confirms again, he glimpsed a surviving example of the oldest religion in the world, far off in racial distance beyond *Greeks, or Hindus or any Europeans or even Egyptians,* some pure religion now corrupted almost out of existence.   PH, 144

Now it may seem odd, at first, to think that a man of puritan imagination should find the nearest equivalent to his own religious faith in what remained of aboriginal American cults. What similarity could there be, at bottom, between the drumming, dancing, chanting Indian and the apocalyptic puritan? On the surface not much, but on more fundamental levels a great deal: in attitudes on the presence of deity, for example. If we go back to the apostle Paul, an ancestor of the puritans, we find that his concept of the nature of deity owed much to the mystery religions whose animism was but a later growth of that on which all the tribal primitivism of man is based. Here direct participation in the actuality of the god, in the very person of the god, comes about as a result of the proper initiation. For Paul, Christ had come to create a new world within the present world by his sacrifice, and to admit his chosen to that world. Once Christ had entered the soul and transformed it, it was "dead to sin" — to the old world of the former life. This translation to a higher realm, this identification, was not an act to take place in a future world after a sufficient period of discipline and good works here below. It took place with conversion. Nothing could have been less acceptable to the mystical side of a Christian like Paul than the later popularized idea that the two worlds exist in chronological order: this corruptible state of trial and preparation followed by the next, the incorruptible state of the future. In the soul of the true puritan Christian, the two worlds coexist. Bunyan felt the indwelling of eternity, as did Blake, for whom eternity and deity were always present in the imagination. Emily Dickinson, another great puritan poet, made her life-long refusal of the moralistic church of her father and sister rest on just this premise: that immortality is always present in daily life for the one who chooses to adopt it as a way of vision.

All this belief in the immanence of deity and eternity was there in his tradition to back up Lawrence and to encourage him to a deep affinity with similar tendencies in Native American religion: the conviction that deity is present and active in everything. This further step from a mystically oriented puritanism to feeling perfectly at home with Indian religion was not a long one. Lawrence asserts that in Indian cosmology *there is no God looking on. The only god there is, is involved all the time in the dramatic wonder and inconsistency of creation.* While this may seem to violate the puritan tenet of a separate and transcendent godhead, it holds perfectly to the equally puritan and far   MM, 52 more important tenet that the godhead is involved, and in the most dramatic and intimate fashion, in the doings of his universe. The supernatural, whether the God of puritanism or the divine power of American indigenous belief, pervades every fiber of life. For the finest heirs of the puritan tradition, this belief brings into being on the plane of the supreme imagination a mythic domain which is "primitive" in most senses of the word that animistic religion is "primitive" — or better say "primal" — the fundamental imagination linking a powerful sense of the earthly with a powerful sense of the divine.

In like manner, no great abrogation of principle was involved in making the Indian practices of access to divine power conform to the best of puritan vision. Given the immanence of the power sought, why need it be addressed through plea or prayer? Why not through imitation, through enactment in ceremony of its mysteries, which was for Lawrence the key activity of Indian rites? The Indian's nearness to his gods permits him this approach, and the nearness of the puritan to his makes for a great sympathy between the two in a puritan imagination as deeply engrossed in a consciousness of divine potency as Lawrence was.

While Lawrence's first responses to America came readily to hand in sketches and letters, the piece of work uppermost in his mind was more difficult to achieve: the writing of an American novel, the project he had had in mind at least since June, when he wrote from Australia to Mabel Dodge, in reference to Taos, *I shall be so glad if I can write an American novel from that centre.* She reports that he approached her the first evening after his return from the Apache ceremony about writing a novel based on her life. The description of the plan that she attributes to Lawrence may be in part fashioned on what Lawrence did later on — seeing that she wrote the account after his death — but it is all certainly in the spirit of what must have been Lawrence's intention: *He said he wanted to write an American novel that would express the life, the spirit, of America and he wanted to write it around me — my life from the time I left New York to come out to New Mexico; my life, from civilization to the bright, strange world of Taos; my renunciation of the sick old world of art and artists, for the pristine valley and the upland Indian lakes.*

This plan of collaboration with Mabel Dodge never advanced past the writing of a few pages and some sketchy outlining, but it sounds very much like a picking up of threads from *The Lost Girl,* some hints of which we saw also in parts of *Kangaroo.* No one could miss, either, the implied contradiction between these plans and the skepticism Lawrence gave vent to in the Apache sketch. From one

LT, 24

LT, 52

point of view, Lawrence took the experience of whites like that of Mabel Dodge to be largely masquerade, but paradoxically he could treat it also as a serious quest. It was a cleavage of views which along with several others was never quite bridged in the American writing.

In Mabel Dodge's experience there was in any case a remarkable parallel with the questing prepossessions I have been outlining from the start of Lawrence's journeys. An "upper world" similar to that of Taos has recurred again and again as the crucial region of rebirth, largely the mountains of the several pieces of fiction we have looked at. Lakes have not been so much in evidence thus far, but they come to be of great significance in the American period. We do not forget, of course, Jessie Chambers' report of how Lawrence loved the American lakes in Cooper, nor his fixation on Lake Glimmerglass as Eden in the first versions of the American literature essays — not to mention his first breaking of the trammels of early life in the lake region of Garda. Lawrence may already have seized, then, upon the lake as a particular locality of redemption in his American symbolic geography. But this cannot be stated for certain, for Mabel Dodge is not the most reliable of recorders, and, as I have said, her summary of what Lawrence wished to present in his fiction pertaining to her bears a suspiciously close resemblance to what she could have read in "The Princess" and "The Woman Who Rode Away."

An absorbing matter that has its real inception here is the prominence of woman as protagonist in Lawrence's fictions of passional regeneration in America. Again we must go back to *The Lost Girl* to retrieve the clues. Men are of apparent secondary importance in all of the American fiction, including *The Plumed Serpent*. What takes place in America may be said to represent the penultimate stage of the conflict between male and female elements in Lawrence's character. America had always been a principal battleground for the struggle, as our reading of the American literature essays has shown, in particular through analysis of the soul of Natty Bumppo and the strong feminine quality of his quest for atonement with the native American and the American spirit of place. The course of Lawrence's imagination in the actual America, as we will see, flows directly out of that initial imagined experience of his wartime fantasy.

The first real indication we have of the attitudes Lawrence would adopt toward the male and female modes of being in America is not in fiction, however, but in a poem he wrote shortly after coming to New Mexico — perhaps the first bit of writing in America — a poem in response to the recent death of Sally Hopkin, a lifelong friend and early confidant. In both a letter of condolence to her husband and in AC, 293

the first line of the poem, Lawrence sees England as principally the
CP, 410   grave of the women he has *loved and cherished.* He alludes to the
women as several, but foremost in his thoughts is his mother. Beyond
the long-held identification of England with the grave, a change has
come about, or rather Lawrence assumes that a change is coming over
him, an imaginative anticipation of what he hopes to attain in America.
It is first of all a reconciliation with the spirit of the mother. He had
told her to die, he says: which reminds the reader that Paul Morel,
and very probably Lawrence himself, administered an overdose of
drugs to a suffering mother, an act painted in *Sons and Lovers* as of
double significance: a mercy killing but at the same time a bid for freedom by the dominated son. Lawrence now plainly feels that his mother
would understand his action, but he also calls for a completely transformed relationship. The emotionally enslaved, devoted but resentful son is for the time absent. A large and sheltering masculine spirit
has taken his place. The spirit of the woman he now summons out of
the grave of England to assume her niche in his heart, which appears
CP, 410   to contain all the room of the *dark-wrapped Rocky Mountains motion-
less squatting around in a ring,* is the docile and grateful object of
tender possession. In the world of the poem, for the time being at
least a realm of triumph, the problem of mother-wife is easily resolved.
The masculine soul here stands beyond sex, and knows how to introduce the woman into his realm. She is as if virgin once more, made so
by death, freed in perpetuity from the physical burden of man. This
CP, 411   *delicate, overlooked virgin* can reside in his heart forever. Wives may
CP, 412   be *exclusive* and mothers *jealous,* but the eternal virgin and the eternal
hero who know love beyond sex can dwell free of any strife in the
region of pure feeling.

The germ of all the American fiction is here, no matter how many
changes it may undergo, several of which will convulse from a
quiet and gentle mastery into violent demands for complete female
subjection.

It was a good while, after all, before Lawrence could summon his
powers to the writing of fiction. Frieda's objections put a quick end
to his collaboration with Mabel Dodge. The origin of his delay in
finding another fictional subject is not so easy to categorize, but we
can trace its course and glimpse some of its workings in other poems
of the first couple of months in New Mexico, and in the revision of
the American literature essays.

"Spirits Summoned West" Lawrence put in the ending section of
Birds, Beasts and Flowers, whose earliest poems date from two years
before the landing in America. At least two of the other poems of this

final section strongly convey the same haunting from the distant past and the faraway land that the "Spirits" poem does, a haunting that exerted such a powerful influence on Lawrence in New Mexico. He entitled this last section of the book "Ghosts," and devised an epigraph that speaks volumes. This is in part a quotation from Empedocles, which Lawrence extends to describe a mystic expedition of the living in search of atonement with the dead. The living soul must *follow the* CP, 406 *trail of the dead, across great spaces. For the journey is a far one, to sleep and a forgetting, and often the dead look back, and linger, for now they realise all that is lost. Then the living soul comes up with them, and great is the pain of greeting, and deadly the parting again.* The suggestion is that with some of the spectres Lawrence could not so easily come to terms as he gives the appearance of doing with his mother's ghost in the "Spirits" poem. "Men in New Mexico" is about the failure so far of human rebirth in America, and of course refers all but directly to the poet's rebirth. The landscape refuses to come awake from *the last twilight/Of Indian gods.* The inhabitants, Anglo, CP, 407 Hispanic, and Indian are all deeply asleep, with *A dark membrane over the will,* helpless among the *Mountains blanket-wrapped/Round* CP, 408 *the ash-white hearth of the desert.* By implication the traveler to a new-created land stands on the threshold as if drugged.

The "ghostliness" of the next poem, "Autumn at Taos," is not overt but is hinted at by the rhythm of experience in Lawrence. The metaphoric structure presents the Rocky Mountain landscape in the image of a hawk and various beasts: tigress, wolf, otter, bear, jaguar, puma, leopard. The horseman of the poem rides out of a canyon thick with aspen yellow as a tigress's hair or the feathers of a golden Horus, crosses foothills mottled like an otter, and then, with relief, enters a desert as gray as a wolf. He fears and at the same time is breathlessly fascinated with the mountain heights he can now look back on: those *Jaguar-splashed, puma-yellow, leopard-livid slopes* CP, 409 *of America.* Such beast associations will arise again in the wildcat at the heart of the mountains in "The Princess," and in the wolf as a symbol of escape in other pieces of writing.

Once more we meet the familiar theme of passage through high country as issuance from a dangerous encounter with the self. A kind of "ghostliness" has always attended this passage, a reminder of lost or unattainable being and awareness of a vestige of that remote being in the landscape. But the embodiment of that quality here in an almost exclusively animal imagery is new, a strategy for conveying that fierce and untamable quality which Southwestern mountains always held for Lawrence. It is a "ghostly" spirit of place that edges over into a trans-human savageness, and while Lawrence has no great difficulty translating it into poetry, it is just this quality that he was a great while giving voice to in fiction.

We can see a comparable crisis of expression building in the first poems destined for *Birds, Beasts and Flowers,* poems written in the fall of 1920. Even further back we can pick up some anticipation of the problem in the earliest form of the American literature essays. There Lawrence first epitomized what was already an established attitude of his, which was to play an increasing role as time went on. The traveler must commit himself to harmonizing his quest with the living nature he newly encounters from spot to spot. In a sentence expressing this requirement Lawrence made use of words later chosen

SM, 30   as title of the book of poems climaxing in America: *Every great locality expresses itself perfectly, in its own flowers, its own birds and beasts, lastly its own men, with their perfected works.* Such an affirmation is the poem "Autumn at Taos," with its connection of bird and beast to the region. Another is "Men in New Mexico," with its perception of lethargy in the advance toward human greatness in the same region.

The foregoing quotation is from the early form of Lawrence's essay on Crevecoeur, a piece of prose with a special relation to the spirit prevailing in the poems of *Birds, Beasts and Flowers.* In a way the French-born American author was a predecessor for Lawrence. An adorer of noble savagery in the Enlightenment sense, Crevecoeur had come over to America to brave the wilderness. He failed, in Lawrence's eyes, for after a while on the frontier, a few glimpses of the

SC, 34   *primal, dark veracity* of the wilderness, he ran back to Europe to cultivate his taste for wildness in Paris drawing rooms. Yet Crevecoeur had vision. Lawrence quotes his fascinated description of the hummingbird and finds it a demonstration of *beautiful, barbaric tenderness of the blood:* the right spirit for penetrating the savageness of America. The special connection here is that Lawrence wrote a poem called "Humming-Bird," published in the *New Republic* in May 1921. Since hummingbirds do not exist in Europe, Lawrence had at that time not seen one alive and was depending on Crevecoeur for his imagery, with assistance from W. H. Hudson and others.[2] The poem therefore belongs with those inspired by the idea of America and written in the fall of 1920. These poems represent Lawrence's first concentrated effort at verse in a few years. The stimulus of a distant America was reinforced by that of the Etruscans, whose lingering presence he could still perceive around Florence. The long curve of feeling that finally brought him to the portals of America flared so brightly at this time, that it opened vistas through human antiquity into the remote spaces of far earlier creatures.

Lawrence's absorption with the hummingbird displays for one thing that empathy with the otherness of creatures that informs most of his poems about animal life. But the imaginative force of this poem goes beyond that to a fear tempered by the willingness to face it, a fear of vastness in almost inconceivable reaches of time. It is a much intensified instance of the feeling found in the Crevecoeur essay. In the poem Lawrence seeks out a retrogression to the ages when *life* CP, 372 *was a heave of Matter,* before flowers existed, when plant life flowed in *slow vegetable veins* and the hummingbird that pierced them was a monster, just as the ancestors of today's tiny lizards were monsters. The distance back to that age was infinitely beyond the Etruscan or the Minoan, the pilgrim self extended in time and space to the ultimate.

This was what Lawrence had expected from America. The task of comprehension, taken up in poems like "Humming-Bird" and continued in "Autumn at Taos" and others, was to get an imaginative grasp of nature to connect him with the stream of time and the succession of creatures in time and space in order that he might develop his substitute for Darwinian evolution and move forward from that into a new conception of consciousness. From long before he saw them his outlook on the American earth and its creatures was what he took Crevecoeur's to be. But in rehearsing his predecessor's feat of understanding a savage otherness, he was shaping another purpose also. He was bolstering his courage to face the darkness where souls are reduced and reborn through unison with the spirit of place. And he did not intend to retreat, as he accused Crevecoeur of doing.

The same strains of fear and magnetism and meditation on alien life forms runs through all the America-directed poems of 1920 and 1921. One of the first poems to picture an as yet unvisited America in this way is "Turkey-Cock," which attributes to that native American bird an *aboriginality/Deep, unexplained.* To the poet this creature CP, 369 expresses the very soul of the Indian and his continent, the Aztec specifically. This is *the bird of the next dawn* perhaps, the creature CP, 371 by whose aid one may *Take up the trail of the vanished American/ Where it disappeared at the foot of the crucifix.*

On coming to America, however, Lawrence shifted over to the eagle as the bird of the continent and tried in two versions of a poem called "Eagle in New Mexico" to capture the power to nourish another element of his response to America: the challenge-surrender contradiction that ran parallel to the fear of the new land. The two versions of the poem render plainly the two sides of the attitude. In both, the eagle is a solar priest, in one offering the hearts of his prey to the sun, in the other capable of flying up under command from the father of life to strike out the heart of the present sun and initiate a new age. In the latter version Lawrence is drawn to accept the lead of the

CP, 783   American eagle, though he knows him to be *vindictive* and *sinister.* Yet in the other version he refuses to yield his blood to the eagle, lest he be left a husk of nerves, as Americans seem to him to be. He here puts forward another kind of life to drive the eagle-priest

CP, 374   out of office, a suggestion of his own potential as sun-priest: *Even the sun in heaven can be curbed and chastened at last/By the life in the hearts of men.*

But the present interest is not the contradiction in the two versions of the poem — a thing almost to be taken for granted in Lawrence — but rather the extent to which he finds the right elements for questing in his contemplation of American wildlife. The same process is discernible in the poems "The Blue Jay" and "Mountain Lion," and to a far greater extent in "The Red Wolf." In this last poem Lawrence is clearly pleased, in a face-to-face meeting with an old Indian in Taos Pueblo, that the man sees him with his red beard as

CP, 405   a *thin red wolf of a pale-face.* The poet elaborates this figure into a
CP, 404   "questing beast" indeed, one who *has followed the sun from the dawn through the east,/Trotting east and east and east till the sun himself went home,/And left me homeless here in the dark at your door.* The lone wolf traveler has lost the sun here in the east become west, an arc of wayfaring begun on the dawn coast of Sicily and traced around through Ceylon and Australia to this spot. Here the traveler

CP, 405   will wait for the sun *to come back with a new story,* a myth in which he will learn how to be the *red-dawn-wolf* to supplant the aged Indian and his way.

Fully as absorbing as the poems of *Birds, Beasts and Flowers* but representative also of a number of differing attitudes is the version of the American literature essays produced at this time: another preparation, in their way, for the fiction.

Relations between the Lawrences and Mabel Dodge deteriorated in less than three months to the point of their moving out of her house, leaving the town of Taos altogether, and settling for the winter in a mountain cabin on the Hawk family's Del Monte Ranch several miles north of Taos. Beginning in mid-November before the move and finishing the work at Del Monte, Lawrence took up a thorough recasting of his American literature studies. While these helped as the poetry did to sharpen his vision of the new continent, he also made them the occasion to work out of his system what he disliked about America.

As if to match his tone with that of American culture, Lawrence adopted a racy prose style, flippant and exclamatory, an exaggerated twist to the kind of showiness he had displayed in his psychology books a couple of years before.[3] Gone now are the long cadences of the earlier rendition of the essays, the prose that endeavored to summon up in wonder the vastness of history and a mystical transubstantiation of time and place to create a future land. The earlier prose sought a level like that of the initial sections of *The Rainbow*. It sprang from — one might almost say it created — the expectancy on which Lawrence lived through the black days of the war. Place, whether the England of the novel or the America of the essays, was seen as a slowly unfolding miracle of words in which every progression of nature or of history tingled in deep accord with the vibrant feelers of the human soul, a *great mystic passion* of history or of landscape.   SM, 16

With the mountains of New Mexico about him and exposed, through the Taos colony of artists, to one of the more curious results of the westward movement, Lawrence turned abrupt and colloquial. He seized his subject by the throat. The authentic clue to understanding why he launched into such a radical reworking of what really remained essentially the same ideas is to be found in this drastic change of style. Through this he was carrying out what he had formerly seen as happening to American authors in their striving for contact with the spirit of their land: *They have felt that they were trespassing,*   SM, 254 *transgressing, or going very far, and this has given a certain stridency, or portentousness, or luridness to their manner.* He gives every indication of being just where he affirmed American culture to be in his foreword to *Studies in Classic American Literature:* at *the pitch of*   SC, Fwd. *extreme consciousness* just prior to *shifting over from the old psyche*   SC, 7–8 *to something new.* And again Lawrence turned as if by compulsion to beast imagery like that of the poems to picture the exigency under which he labored. He spoke of his *strange and fugitive self shut out*   SC, 15 *and howling like a wolf or a coyote under the ideal windows.*

Consequently, there is a strong shift of emphasis in some of the revisions, for instance in the "Spirit of Place" essay designed to introduce the whole set. Earlier the stress was on the *vital magnetism* of   SM, 23 the western continent. In this reworking it is on the agony of escape and the revulsion against Europe. Previously Lawrence had spoken much of early twentieth-century American society as an interim preceding an imminent unanimity with spirit of place, and he had done so in a tone of celebration paired with a sometimes elegiac note for a vanishing Europe. The "Spirit of Place" essay in the published book takes Americans sharply to task for not having progressed further in the creation of *a living homeland,* for having instead been   SC, 12 mastered and turned into mechanical little egos by their machines, after having largely succeeded in flinging off the European past. Even from the beginning the American character had run to type in a *dry,*   SC, 27

moral, utilitarian little democrat like Benjamin Franklin. And Law-
SC, 12   rence had already castigated the Taos set for their way of *escaping to some wild west.* It was what he had earlier berated as a comic-opera bid for freedom by Americans. An occasionally sour strain of disen-chantment with his own expedition to America also surfaces at times:
SC, 28   *Lucky Coleridge, who got no farther than Bristol. Some of us have gone all the way.*

The Cooper essays stand as the best examples of fundamental continuity in Lawrence's search over the years. We do find differences between versions, though, some resulting merely from the change in angle of view, now that Lawrence had gazed on America with his own eyes, and some from the new stridency of style. But some go consider-ably deeper than these. Formerly Lawrence had been enraptured by Cooper. Now we might say he was only entranced — but always with the scoffing, at times jeering, to which he subjected all of American culture, and indirectly certain of his own illusions. Still his fundamental view of Cooper has not changed. As for social realities concerning Indian and white, Lawrence finds that what he sees bears out what he asserted during the war. He now knows that the Red Men have
SC, 41   not all died off, nor are they likely to. But he sees *the last nuclei of Red life* near the breaking point — the Bursum Bill, designed to do away with Indian rights to tribal lands, was all the talk in Taos circles
PX, 238   at the time. Lawrence contributed his bit to its defeat in an article for the *New York Times.* He still held that soon all central Indian culture
SC, 41   would vanish and that then *the demon of the continent* would demand to be incorporated into the soul of the new American race. If not, it would destroy any hope of a vivid national life. The belief that this force would remain latent in the American unconscious until Indian society effectively ceased to exist Lawrence now based on his own
SC, 42   observation, which convinced him that there could never be *any real reconciliation, in the flesh,* between the races. The Indian jeers and undermines, the white man is torn between annihilating and senti-mentalizing the Red Man. The fusion must await a time when the daimon of the continent will instill in its own way the retained spirit of the Red Man in the future American race. But as yet there is a
SC,61   *slightly devilish resistance in the American landscape,* as well as in the indigenous population, to the white immigrants. Of all except this last view, there is plenty of the same substance of thought in the ear-lier essays. And again the *resistance,* like the penchant for scoffing, has much of its source in Lawrence's struggles with himself.

Doubtless the scoffing tone is traceable to another reason as well: a desire to offset the rhapsodic admiration Lawrence had formerly entertained for Cooper. Yet in spite of the toning down not much is
SC, 43   changed. He may decry Cooper's *presentment* of the Indian as *popu-*

lar wish-fulfilment stuff that *makes it so hard for the real thing to come through,* but then he shows himself quite willing to accept these wish-fulfillments as myth, *as presentations of a deep subjective desire, real in their way, and almost prophetic.* He is still convinced that Cooper envisioned the beginning of a new American humanity in the comradeship of Natty Bumppo and Chingachgook, and he declares still that *probably, one day America will be as beautiful in actuality as it is in Cooper.* The Edenic hope may have lost a great deal of its headiness, but underneath it is still there. And whereas formerly Lawrence relied much on "symbolic meaning" as a term for all this, he now relies on the not very different *myth-meaning.* At this juncture, when he states what myth means to him, it turns out to concern his own journeys into the unknown: *True myth concerns itself centrally with the onward adventure of the integral soul.* SC, 56 SC, 64 SC, 69

To this point in *Studies in Classic American Literature,* Lawrence had concerned himself almost exclusively with the male soul in relation to the native spirit of place. The rewritten Poe and Hawthorne essays involved him to an inordinate degree in his other perennial problems, the nature of woman in her relation to man and the nature of human will as it bears upon this relationship. What we meet with is a change indeed from the assured male mastery of the poem "Spirits Summoned West." In this prose we find a determined yet fearful insistence on restoring a lost male dominance. The situation wished for is not a submission of rebellious woman to the male as he currently is, but a rebirth of purpose in the man along with a renewed willingness in woman to follow the male lead. Lawrence could not have found two authors more fitted to his arguments than Poe and Hawthorne, and the truculent certainty of his approach reveals a crisis in a long succession of self-probings.

In "Ligeia" and "The Fall of the House of Usher" Lawrence discovers his old enemy spiritual love flourishing unchecked. Both Ligeia and her husband are driven by mental volition to frightful extremes. The husband must "know" his wife purely out of the mind, which by itself can only dissect and destroy. But to this horror Ligeia submits. This is the "love" that Lawrence of course finds in the ascendant nowadays, and it is nearly the whole cause of modern neurosis: even, he thinks, of tuberculosis. We are back to the nemesis of a loving will severed from a loving body — to the old mother image — and also to the recurrent sense of failure to eradicate that legacy of the mother in the marriage with Frieda. In the urgency forced by America a weakness of the chest appears categorically to have psychological origins.

In Lawrence's reading of Poe the male is fully as ghoulish as the female. In fact it is he who is first of all *the vampire of . . . consciousness.* The will of the woman is no less powerful however. By his SC, 74 obsession with analyzing her spirit the husband kills the wife. But she has her own back: in the action of the will from beyond the grave. But not in vengeance against the husband precisely. He remarries, deliberately it seems in order to destroy another woman. The thwarted and devouring ghost of Ligeia overshadows her, and in compact with the husband, who remembering the "purity" of his first wife soon comes to loathe his second, Ligeia annihilates her rival.

In the first version of the American literature essays, Lawrence made much of immortality through the atonement of the living with the dead. For the time being, he has lost touch with that assurance, so lately reiterated in "Spirits Summoned West." All that he can sense SC, 81   about him as he delves into Poe is the *terrible spirits, ghosts, in the air of America* — the dead will not be appeased, either in himself or America. It is like a recurrence of the same fear toward the war dead.

A great deal of this essay on Poe follows the wording of the early version almost exactly. But still paragraphs are thrust in, or sentences into existing paragraphs, that show how acute Lawrence's need was to put into forthright language the hope that the male soul can prevail in its spiritual-geographical quest. The best opportunity of all to voice this wish comes in the two rewritten essays on Hawthorne, particularly SC, 89   the one on *The Scarlet Letter*. Lawrence calls this novel a *parable, an* SC, 106   *earthly story with a hellish meaning* and *one of the greatest allegories in all literature.*

The allegory dramatizes for Lawrence a key phase in the apocalypse of western humanity, the terrible effect of disregard for the SC, 100   hierarchy of male and female in the universal order. *It is man's business to bear the responsibility of belief,* he argues in Milton's puritanic tradition, and woman must find her true belief through man. If man fails SC, 99   to establish this belief for her, disaster ensues: *Unless he fiercely obeys his own Holy Ghost, his woman will destroy him.* She cannot help doing this. It is simply her nature. Now the Renaissance, according SC, 105   to Lawrence, saw *the downfall of the true male authority, the ithyphallic authority and masterhood.* But that force can never die. It reappears in Hawthorne's vision of America as Roger Chillingworth: SC, 106   *the black, vengeful soul of the crippled, masterful male, still dark in his authority.* But his natural role has been wrested from him by the saintly Dimmesdale, the paragon of mental-spiritual consciousness. The triangle is completed by Hester, who is compelled to seduce and destroy this pure and bloodless travesty of a male. She destroys as a "loving" woman, diabolical in spite of herself, in conspiracy with the old outcast blood-being in Chillingworth. It is all an allegory prophetic of the coming destruction of the modern psyche, Lawrence claims, and this destruction appears certain to take place in the New World, as will also the rebirth of phallic consciousness, a description of which Lawrence emphatically lays down in these terms:

It is probable that the Mormons are the forerunners of the coming   SC, 101
real America. It is probable that men will have more than one wife, in the coming America. That you will have again a half-oriental womanhood, and a polygamy. . . .

*But it takes time. Generation after generation of nurses and political women and salvationists. And in the end, the dark erection of the images of sex-worship once more, and the newly submissive women. That kind of depth. Deep women in that respect. When we have at last broken this insanity of mental-spiritual consciousness. And the women **choose** to experience again the great submission.*

If a like opinion of male dominance pervades most of the American fiction, and even *The Boy in the Bush,* with the theme transported to Australia, what is missing in the essays is the strong female criticism, the skepticism of male mastery forthcoming in most of the works, notably *The Plumed Serpent.*

In the *Scarlet Letter* essay Lawrence makes no attempt to conceal the extent of his personal involvement in the issues. When he rages against spiritual women for deploring the hard physical labor of men, he admits he has in mind his mother's distaste for his father's work. And he plainly associates his father's dislike of books, just here, with the true old male authority. He even lashes out at his mother's memory, far indeed from the tenderness of "Spirits Summoned West," suggesting that what killed her was her unrelenting assault on the blood-consciousness. And then he unleashes a vicious attack on Jessie Chambers, his *first lover,* as one of those *leprous-white, seducing, spiritual*   SC,
women. The connection in which the thought of her arises is another   102-103
memory, a glimpse of Lawrence himself as the phallic male, with a
reversion to the animal imagery of the poems. He recollects *meeting*   SC, 102
the eyes of a gipsy woman, for one moment, in a crowd, in England. She knew, and I knew. What did we know? I was not able to make out. But we knew.

Probably the same fathomless hate of this spiritual-conscious society in which the outcast woman and I both roamed like meek-looking wolves.

In preparing *Studies in Classic American Literature* Lawrence omitted an essay called "The Two Principles" in its *English Review* publication. Like lengthy sections of the earlier pieces on Cooper and Hawthorne, which he omitted as well, this essay took up theories of psychology which he had in the meantime expanded in his two books

on the unconscious. What this essay was meant to prepare the reader
SM, 175   for is *the relation between the sea and the human psyche,* specifically,
as it turns out in the 1923 essay on Dana, the American psyche. After
SC, 120   Cooper, says Lawrence, *the next great move of imaginative conquest*
was to the sea, and Lawrence pursues the voyages of Dana and of
Melville with utter absorption, just as he had done in the initial essays
on Melville. In these authors he continues of course to find the great
psychic split of all American authors, the attachment to an ideal
morality on the surface and an almost unrealized mystic vision into
SC, 131   elemental forces beneath. Dana is a *subtle explorer* who has set out
SC, 122   to *conquer the sea in his consciousness,* but alas to do so intellectually.
SC, 138   By his voyage Dana is borne into *a great extreme of knowledge, knowledge of the great element.* We all have to know this extreme, Lawrence goes on to say, *before we can know that knowing is nothing,*
before we are prepared for true being. Dana's book does indeed create
just such an effect, as even Lawrence's few quotations from it are made
to witness. Dana goes around the Horn to California and back again.
SC, 131   With him we *pass into another world, another life, not of this
earth. There is first the sense of apprehension, then the passing right
into the black deeps. Then the waters almost swallow him up, with
his triumphant consciousness.* And one excerpt after another bears
out this perception of reality.

What Lawrence has to say about Dana he has in effect to say about
Melville. He is perhaps more directly self-implicated with Melville's
quest at this time than with Dana's. His talk of going to sea in the *Typee*
and *Omoo* article recalls more explicitly his paean to traveling the
SC, 140   oceans in *Sea and Sardinia*: *Love and home are a deadly illusion. Woman, what have I to do with thee? It is finished.* **Consummatum est.** *The
crucifixion into humanity is over. Let us go back to the fierce, uncanny
elements: the corrosive vast sea.* He had now experienced the Pacific
himself. Likewise, his reading of Melville's ultimate inability to live
among the primitive people of the islands is a reinforcement to his own
directly acquired view, and his comments on Melville bring out in as
exact words as he could choose what he wishes to infuse into his writing
about America. A new note has crept in since the war years, when the
romance of exploration was a far more vital need than now, a note
stemming in part from disappointment with the dark races east of Suez.
SM, 226   Lawrence speaks less now of the Pacific natives' life as a *sacred reality*
of *mindless, naked spontaneity* and more of their *uncreate* being. He
SC, 145   forces himself to confess, now, that *through all our bitter centuries of
civilization, we have still been living onwards, forwards,* beyond the
reach of the Pacific primitive. He goes so far, even, as to assert that we
have accomplished *a great life-development* since the ancient setting

out from Egypt. As a bald assertion this is contradictory enough. But Lawrence is only following his common procedure: to set up a kind of dialectic within himself and work it out on the page. He continues, in the present instance, in this fashion. He denounces those *who glorify* **SC, 146** *the savages in America*: this would include for him nearly all the whites whose acquaintance he had made in Taos. His way, he insists, will be no such reversion, no such betrayal of his own soul. He may seem to recommend a *retrogression,* but what he really has in mind is *a great* **SC,** *swerve in our onward-going life-course now, to gather up again the* **145&146** *savage mysteries. But this does not mean going back on ourselves.*

So the battle goes on, obscured by many cross-currents: how to recapture the spirit of animism in an over-mental world without surrendering to what may not be even a debased survival of glorious ancient ways among today's primitives, what may be the failure of their ancestors ever to have achieved a fully created spirit at all.

In the second essay on Melville, on *Moby Dick,* Lawrence is as exasperated as ever with Melville's sententiousness but pronounces him still the greatest of all writers about the sea. As before, the *Pequod* is the *ship of the American soul* and the voyage under the monomanic **SC, 157** Ahab is the tracking down and destruction of *the deepest blood-being* **SC, 169** *of the white race.* Lawrence had by this time read Raymond Weaver's *Herman Melville, Mariner and Mystic,* but it had no pronounced effect on what he had long since decided and stated about Melville. But he added a page and a half of apocalyptic thundering beyond what he previously saw as the reach of the allegory. *Doom! Doom! Doom!* he **SC, 168** preaches. In hounding to death his blood-being, man has sunk his own soul. Lawrence can now read the Great War into this fable and place the years afterward in a *post-mortem* world. What next? what next? **SC, 170** he seems to ask.

The only conceivable answer is a resurrection in some guise. The troubled dream of an ending and a fresh beginning in America comes to its penultimate stage in the Melville essay. For his last grapple with the problem Lawrence turns to Whitman, whose spirit in some ways is nearest to his own.

The Whitman essay is extant in two forms. The first is not that of 1918 but the revision of 1920 in Sicily. I have not as yet discussed the earlier version, since it does not belong specifically to the war period but rather to the preparation afterwards for America.

Lawrence was generous with the word "great" in all his American literature essays, but in 1920 he declared Whitman *the greatest of the* **SM, 254** *Americans* and *one of the greatest poets of the world.* His pre-eminence arises from his stance in the perpetual contest between blood and mind in the Western world. Whitman went beyond all other men in *subjecting* **SM, 256**

the deepest centres of the lower self and attaining *the maximum consciousness in the higher self.* In both versions of his essay Lawrence
credits Whitman with this sort of voyage to the limits. We might have
thought that Poe had also reached these, but we recollect that in Lawrence's reading he portrays only the utter reduction by spirit, nothing
after. Melville and Dana too were said to have made forays into the
furthest parts of the unknown to conceive the blood through the mind.
But Lawrence makes a significant distinction in the first writing of his
Whitman essay: Melville and Dana still came to rest at one remove
short of Whitman's exploration in that they symbolized the soul by the
external world — the sea — while Whitman plunged inward to *the quick
of quicks,* into the soul itself. Still, this distinction does not quite carry
the conclusiveness that Lawrence claims for it, because he does not
put forward a telling contrast of terms between symbolic and actual
"plunging."

SM, 257

Nevertheless his analytical intent is clear, as is the inherent association of his own art with that of Whitman, a proceeding which resolves itself into multiple problems: how to be a pure self in *spontaneous* outflow and still not to *affect* oneself, as Whitman so often does in
flamboyant expression; how to experience the infinite while remaining
oneself; and greatest of all concerns, how to attain without homosexuality the male comradeship vital to the regeneration of mankind. The
first of these quandaries — how to control and to release the self without
affectation — was settled to some extent by Lawrence's choice of style
for revision of his essays: the unleashing of language. But still, is not
this style itself an affectation? In the 1920 essay — to consider now the
interaction of self and infinity — Lawrence cannot but tacitly approve
of Whitman's becoming *in his own person the whole world,* but he
strenuously objects to his *merging* with everything and everyone in
boundless love, a continuous giving of the self without that opposite
of *retraction into isolation and pride* which alone can save the self
from breaking apart. Yet Lawrence is not consistent in his estimate
of Whitman's empathy with the Other: in one place in the revision he
asserts that Whitman does in fact remain himself in spite of his eagerness to unite, and suggests that much of Whitman's greatness resides
in his grasp of this *maximum truth.*

SM, 256

SM, 258

SM, 259

SM, 258

It is the last of the three questions proposed above, that of male
comradeship as the key to the future of humanity, which offers the most
comprehensive view of Lawrence's inner landscape and points to a
change as real as the overturning of style between versions. The 1920
essay extols the Whitman of "Calamus," *the deepest, finest Whitman,*
who recognizes that in the final analysis *man acts womanless,* that
manly love . . . alone can create a new era of life. As always Lawrence

SM, 262
SM, 260
SM, 263

summons up the thought of death, just as Whitman did, when the thought of homosexuality enters. In 1920 Lawrence could reconcile the two in this way: Whitman *has come near now to death, in his cre-* SM, 262 *ative life. But creative life must come near to death, to link up the mystic circuit.* From this point on to the end of the first essay, Lawrence glorifies Whitman's vision, laments that no one has been capable of taking up where he left off, and finishes with a pealing *Ave America!* SM, 264 to hail his own anticipated arrival there to work out Whitman's quest.

In effect Lawrence stops short in the early essay of elaborating the death process as inseparable from the attainment of balance between perfected males. In the late version he faces it squarely, in a new concluding section to the essay and to the book. He now comes up with firm doubts that male comradeship is truly *the new cohering principle* SC, 177 *of the world.* If the new Democracy is to be founded on love of comrades, *it will slip so soon into death.* All this reasoning leads on to what SC, 178 really amounts to a reassessment of Whitman, who *is a very great poet* SC, 179 still, but *of the end of life.* Now Lawrence turns to the imagery of travel as the only way out of the impasse. Whitman remains as if camped at the brink of a cliff, at *a dead end,* and what Lawrence envisages beyond he draws from an idealized American landscape, a *wilderness of unopened life.* He senses, *over the precipice, blue distances, and the blue hollow of the future.* To circumvent this end, to get down the cliff, Lawrence reconstitutes Whitman's road imagery. *The high-road of* SC, 183 *Love* is in actuality not the *Open Road* that Whitman sings: *It is a narrow, tight way, where the soul walks hemmed in between compul-* *sions.* For Lawrence as for Whitman the soul is not *above,* but then SC, 181 to go beyond Whitman, neither is it *within.* It is in the form of one's life, in the form of ongoing pilgrimage: *It is a wayfarer down the open road.* As regards the moral form of this road, in place of Whitman's Love, Lawrence posits Sympathy. Love forces one's own soul *into* SC, 183 *other people's circumstances,* makes it bleed of their wounds. Sympathy, or compassion, always sees to it that the responsibility for advancing along the way devolves upon the other soul for whom the compassion is felt. Lawrence uses Whitman's attitude about slavery to make his point. Whitman should not have cried out his willingness to assume the wounds of the slave, but offered him a hand in climbing out of oppression and setting forth on the road, in full awareness that *the soul has a long journey . . . down the open road, before it is a free* SC, 184 *soul.* The issue of Love versus Sympathy was to come out in approximately the same terms as this in *The Plumed Serpent.*

The greatest exigency evident in Lawrence's quest to make America and his own soul conform to some common imaginative standard, as he finished his American literature essays for the last time, was the

SC, 186   need to press on: the *great soul . . . travels on foot among the rest, down the common way of the living.* This is Lawrence's picture of perfect Democracy, of what America through Whitman had to contribute to the philosophy of human society. But for a spell of several months — from January to May 1923 — he did little substantial writing on shaping a new society in a new world. For about the first three of these months he did no traveling to speak of either, though he had in mind during most of the winter a trip to Mexico in the spring — when he was not saying he would come back to Europe, or go to Russia, or to Greenland. At these times he greatly desired to escape America

ML, 740   altogether, even though he could claim to see beyond *a vast death-happening* to how the *quick* would survive on American soil.

He carried out his project of visiting Mexico, leaving the Taos area in the latter part of March, arriving in Mexico City a few days later. But he did not yet propose to write a novel in that country, was even on the verge of giving up the thought of an American novel anywhere. For the time being he was plainly unable to get beyond the obstacles which the American literature essays had been designed to ease but had only succeeded in making more obvious. Let him speak as he might of the undying *quick* in the American soul, and of his assurance of reaching it, his feeling all during his first stay in the United States is in the main summed up by this remark in a letter: *I feel bitter in America — it makes one suffer, this continent, a nasty, too-much suffering.*

But Mexico released a certain amount of this tension. Aside from the usual grumblings and flinchings in contact with a new environment, Lawrence liked Mexico. He compared it with southern Italy, generally

HL, 565   a compliment to a place, coming from him. He observed *a good natural feeling* among the Indians. In spite of the many qualifications he was always making in his estimate of them, he felt they had potential for

ML, 744   becoming *a new, young, beautiful people.* Their principal attraction was that they appeared still a long way from the surrender to the white psyche which had all but engulfed the Indians north of the border.

In short order Lawrence absorbed a great deal of central Mexico. He went to a bullfight and walked out on it. He visited the Museo Nacional only to find the Aztec carvings distasteful. He saw Cuernavaca, then took a trip to Puebla, Tehuacán, and Orizaba. On this tour he almost threw over any further schemes for Mexico in favor of returning to New York. But he ended by going back to Mexico City and was soon expressing a desire to stay for the summer in Mexico and write some fiction. At first he thought he would remain near the Capital.

IH, 312   He was offered a house in the suburb of Coyoacán, but that was too near. Finally, in what he declared a last effort before throwing up his hands and heading back to the States, he set out for the Guadalajara

TEOTIHUACÁN, MEXICO

Snakes fanged and feathered beyond all dreams of dread (PS, 75)

area. Almost at once he came upon a house he wanted in the lakeside village of Chapala south of Guadalajara. He moved in right away and settled down to writing the novel I will call *The First Quetzalcoatl,* later to become *The Plumed Serpent.*

The fundamental design that Lawrence had in view for his novel was firmly linked to the overwhelming sense of place he was experiencing in Mexico. The Capital was to represent the present degenerate form of life thrust upon Mexico by invading Europeans. The lake region was to incorporate the rebirth of a native culture. And at least as far as setting goes, Lawrence had quickly mastered his material. The first chapter, which saw no great change through all the rewriting to come, recreates the city as the later chapters do the lake: with all the effectiveness that characterizes the best of Lawrence's travel writing. But there is much more here than a lively composition of place for anyone who would understand Lawrence. In *The First Quetzalcoatl* he did not succeed in writing a good novel but he did establish a symbolism of place and create a fictional religion that vivify one another admirably, and he did reveal his involvement with America as an extension of himself in a more transparent way than in the American literature essays or in the eventually published *Plumed Serpent.*

In *The First Quetzalcoatl* Kate looks back on her dead husband, killed in the Irish rebellion, much as Mrs. Bolton does on hers in *Lady Chatterley's Lover*: she still feels connected with him as if he were alive. Kate is not an active seeker: she wanders only to keep out of reach of England. That land and that past are a grave to her. But a significant motive is in part responsible for this avoidance. She has renounced mother love for her children and something in the western continent strengthens her against returning to it. Hence she is fulfilling for Lawrence what he craved both from Frieda and from the memory of his mother.

As a corollary Lawrence set about creating in Kate a woman to acknowledge the male power of Cipriano and Ramón, the two men who body forth his vision of masculine splendor. She at once realizes, on knowing them, that both have eyes for hidden things she could never see, and when those eyes turn away from her *a strong black light* goes out. She has been drawn toward Mexico almost unawares ever since leaving England, for she admits to herself now that she came because *she had imagined Mexico* to be *a pure pastoral patriarchal land*. The key to her condition in this novel, beyond the conscious avoidance, is in fact her sense of movement from one male dominion to another. The main motive in her reluctance to undergo rebirth is that she still feels connected in spirit with her dead husband. But she stands in awe before Ramón's variety of male lordship: *That which rises up out of the blood, like a tree with its roots in the dark water*

HT, 27

HT, 80

HT, 60

which is below the earth, that is manhood. But Lawrence undertakes a race identification and not simply an individual one. The Indians can be recalled to manhood as a people. They may suffer now just what Lawrence always has in one deep corner of his soul: *The misery of* HT, 134 *a man who has never been able to come into himself, never able to accomplish his own manhood.* But they only await the appearance of the proper hero, now incarnate in Ramón, to step forth into their sacred destiny, to profess a religion of men, not of priests and women. Lawrence had on his side the fact that Pueblo Indian ceremonies are often practiced largely by men in the isolation of the kiva.

Ramón's experience with place is analogous to Lawrence's own up to this time, except that Ramón started from the other side of the world, from Mexico. Both men set out early from home and traveled much. Ramón could entertain no hope, finally, of a way out of the modern dilemma in either Europe or the United States. The sole hope seemed to lie in Mexico, to which he returned to make his connection firm by writing a history of his country — just as Lawrence had written a history of Europe. Ramón's task is now to reawaken the lost gods of Mexico, though he affirms, following Lawrence's recommendation in a late Melville essay, that he is only swerving to pick up the clues of these gods before advancing into the future along wholly new lines. This turning aside out of the path includes a burning of the present gods, the Christian images. Lawrence retained this action in *The Plumed Serpent,* indeed expanded it, but there Ramón goes about his task with the assurance of a decision long since made. In *The First Quetzalcoatl* he trembles at his own daring and looks upon the deed as objectifying *the crisis of my life, and the life of my soul.* HT, 203

The core of life in Ramón's new world will be a religiously ordered association of man and woman, of man and man, a contact with divine mystery amplified from hints going back through *Kangaroo* and *The Lost Girl.* Perhaps to soften a little the militant *machismo* found in some sections of *The First Quetzalcoatl,* Lawrence's myth stresses to a greater degree than in *The Plumed Serpent* that during the god's long absence from Mexico *he has been looking for a wife in the watery* HT, 70 *countries.* For existence requires *a goddess and mother of gentle rain* HT, 241 as well as a father of *heavy, breaking Tlaloc rain.*[4] This journey of the deity in quest of a consort, and all other mythical elements of the novel, Lawrence refabricated out of Indian lore, Southwestern and Mexican, with special twists of his own. He recalls the legend that Quetzalcoatl took flight into the ocean realms of eternity from the snowy volcano of Mt. Orizaba, and then adds as his own invention the god's rebirth from the lake. The virtual birth of the Aztec nation from the Lake of Tenochtitlan no doubt suggested the parallel, but echoes of Cooper's symbolic lakes and Lawrence's sea voyages in quest of self resound also, together with his view of snowy mountains as the last brink jutting into death and eventual rebirth: with of course the added resemblance to the phoenix myth. Even more specifically, Lawrence now and then picks up imagery from his experience in sailing from Europe to the East, with the Red Sea as a channel past the obstacle of Mt. Sinai into a fresh world.

All through *The First Quetzalcoatl* the links between imagined situations and Lawrence's own are more direct than in *The Plumed Serpent,* often enough in Cipriano's character but more so in Ramón's. In addition to conflicts wrought in geographical terms, the author and his creation share the entanglements of maternal love, not spun in Ramón's case by his mother but by his wife, Carlota. She holds their

HT, 128   two sons by the *deadly egotism* of mother love, vitiating their lives and insuring that they will one day turn on her. Ramón is too proud to appeal for their sympathy, but this is not the only way in which he is caught up in the struggle. Carlota outdoes herself in trying to cast the same maternal spell over her husband.

Although victory in this battle is vital to Ramón's venture in consciousness, the issue remains subordinate till late in the novel. The primary bid for male freedom lies in the reaching out between Ramón and Cipriano for a new sort of harmony. The fealty scenes in *The First Quetzalcoatl* are set forth in physical manifestations as in *The Plumed Serpent.* Through a laying on of hands about the head, Ramón causes the old gods to stir in Cipriano's blood, so that he kneels to kiss his master's feet. This rousing of ancient deities within brings Cipriano to brood heavily over the restoration of dark male supremacy. All his life these gods in his veins have nurtured a burning desire for revenge against the pale and bloodless modern world. Upon being invited to become Ramón's disciple, he begins to speak at once of revolutions and other violence to exalt his gods once again. And then, as always in Lawrence, comes the talk of where marriage must stand in complement to eternal male friendship. Cipriano is violently emphatic about it: he must have Kate for a wife to complete the presence of the dark gods and his submission to Ramón. If necessary he will force her to marry

HT, 145   him. She must *come into this death and oblivion* with him. The end to be gained is that male friendship and marriage will be of inseparable

HT, 146   value to life. "*When I really enter into her presence, I shall be perfect for you,*" Cipriano declares to Ramón. This and other scenes touch on themes less emphatically developed in *The Plumed Serpent* but worked out in extreme form in such stories as "The Woman Who Rode Away."

Most of Cipriano's early insistence on vengeance and having his way through force disappears, even in the course of *The First Quet-*

zalcoatl. Watching Kate wade out to her boat in the lake, he becomes aware that she may not answer his call and that he cannot compel her to do so. Receiving the touch of Ramón again in another ritual, on the eyelids and at the base of the spine, he feels that revenge against the modern world would be only personal vindictiveness after all, and that all he really wants is to enter into *his divine, dark self.*   HT, 280

Toward the end of the book, when Ramón is setting up new images in the rededicated church and proclaiming himself the Living Quetzalcoatl, the conflict with the mother figure surges up. Both in family relations and in religion Carlota is the nemesis, for in religion, crawling in on her knees during the apotheosis ceremony and calling on Jesus to forgive the blasphemy in which her husband is engaged, she represents the religion of priests and women: the Christianity in which real men can no longer have a part. As in *The Plumed Serpent,* she collapses during her frantic pleas, seemingly of a stroke. Kate sits with her much of the night in a nearby house, as the new ceremonies of the ancient religion take their course outside. Carlota dies at dawn, as the revived Indian spirit in the people overpowers all other awareness. This scene is better handled in *The First Queztalcoatl* than it is in *The Plumed Serpent,* even though it reflects more plainly Lawrence's own attempts at exorcism of maternal tyranny. Kate, in full acknowledgment for the time being of the new male greatness come to rule the world, is carried away by *the deep, magnificent male courage* of the singing in the plaza,   HT, 262 while Carlota withers before her eyes.

Ramón soon takes another wife, a situation more profitable to discuss in the context of *The Plumed Serpent.* But her purpose in both versions is this: to play the part of the *old, powerful female will which*   HT, 311 *could call up the blood in a man and glorify it, and by glorifying hold it to herself.*

A few other significant points distinguish *The First Quetzalcoatl* from *The Plumed Serpent.* Lawrence's Joachitism is more emphasized by the earlier Ramón in his discourses. For example, he announces that his religion is *the religion of the redeemed Adam, in whom dwells the*   HT, 331 *Holy Spirit, the Holy Ghost:* a phrase remarkably in agreement, surely, with Paul's understanding of Christianity as well as with the doctrines of Joachim of Flora. A more important distinction, and the one that must have had a great deal to do with Lawrence's decision to rewrite the novel, is the place of American Indian materials and themes. Lawrence had not fully made up his mind on what to do with these by the summer of 1923. There is far less ceremonialism in *The First Quetzalcoatl,* and much of it is drawn from Lawrence's hurried observation of half-Hispanicized folkways in the more accessible parts of Mexico, not of the purer native survivals in more remote places. He had not yet determined, either, how to assimilate into fiction what he had seen of Southwestern Indian ritualism. He had yet to witness the Hopi and Santo Domingo ceremonies that he employed so extensively in *The Plumed Serpent*. For another thing, as suggested above, Kate gives us glimpses of stresses involved in the reconstitution of the feminine principle in relation to the spirit of the continent that Lawrence later discovered he could best fictionalize in the three short novels he turned out in the summer of 1924. Most vital of all, Lawrence had not yet achieved a consistent view of how white spirit as opposed to red spirit was to count in his resuscitated culture. When we first meet Cipriano, in *The First Queztalcoatl*, he looks more Italian than Indian, and acts so too, while later on he is progressively more Indian, in looks as well as actions. Ramón at the outset reminds Kate of an Indian chief and he hates the white world to the extent of declaring that the white man has no place at all on the American continent. But then in later pages he is described as largely white himself. In *The Plumed Serpent* he is almost purely white, with a trace of Tlaxcalan blood, and the true heir of ancient animistic Europe.

From time to time in *The First Quetzalcoatl*, Kate feels a great homesickness for Europe, as she does later in *The Plumed Serpent*, but now she prepares to leave for Europe with no convincing counterforce to the magnetism binding her to Mexico. This was another conflict that Lawrence had not even begun to work out fictionally on first writing the novel. During his few months' residence in Mexico he had turned it into a sort of dreamland, and the two men of his invention, while they may owe a little to what he could glean from the most superficial observation of Mexican revolutionary figures, were almost wholly creatures of his fancy. One can imagine that he might ask himself the question that Kate puts to herself, looking about from the lakeshore: *"What am I doing here? . . . What does this place exist for, anyhow?"*

HT, 234

Lawrence turned out the more than 450 holograph pages of *The First Quetzalcoatl* in about two months. He then put the manuscript aside, went on a half-hearted search for a hacienda for a little while, going by boat around Lake Chapala, then made up his mind to head for New York and from there back to England, to give Europe another try. He simply dropped Mexico as Kate had done in his novel.

Lawrence was in the New York area for around a month, in July and August, correcting proofs a great deal of the time. Not for long did he continue with the idea of going to England, which seems to have been mainly Frieda's wish anyhow. She wanted to see her children — Kate may have renounced motherhood but Frieda had not. The Lawrences disagreed radically. Frieda herself sailed for England, while

Lawrence set out for Los Angeles, by way of Buffalo and Chicago. He and the two Danish artists who had lived in a cabin near his the previous winter thought of acquiring a sailboat and heading out over the Pacific. His *revulsion* from New York, as he later called it, had made him *want to go to the uttermost ends of the earth.*   RC, 74

Another plan was that he and his companions might travel down into the western part of Mexico and look for a ranch on which to begin the long-delayed Rananim. This trip was the one Lawrence finally undertook, with only one of the artists: Kai Götzsche. In late September they left Los Angeles by train and made their way down the west coast of Mexico, stopping to visit at Alamos, near Navajoa, and again to consider taking a boat, this time from Mazatlán to Manzanillo. They went on by train, however, arriving in Guadalajara in mid-October, after making part of the journey by muleback to span a gap in the railway.

Lawrence had left the holograph manuscript of *The First Quetzalcoatl* with his New York publisher, Thomas Seltzer, to be typed. During his month in the Los Angeles area, and another month later on in Guadalajara, Lawrence was at work on another novel, one that holds a curious position in the Lawrence canon, *The Boy in the Bush.* Though it is set in Australia, that Lawrence revised it in California and Mexico gives it a special affinity to all that was occurring in relation to travel and to place at the time.

During his brief stay in western Australia, Lawrence had become acquainted with an Australian writer, Mollie Skinner, who at his suggestion undertook to write a novel about the early days of white settlement in the region. His interest, according to a conversation reported years later by Miss Skinner, was comparable to that which we know had drawn him to American literature. Awed and fascinated by the lonely bush just beyond the town, he said to her: *Tell us what drew*   CB,
these early Settlers. Tell us what kept them here. Fifteen months later   vol. 2, 137
her manuscript caught up with him in Los Angeles. He found *real*   ML, 751
quality in these scenes. But without form, like the world before creation.
He offered to *recast* the work and publish it as a joint effort. Then without waiting for Miss Skinner's consent he went ahead with the task, which with interruptions occupied him for over two months, approximately the time he had put into *Kangaroo* and *The First Quetzalcoatl.*

The original manuscript from which he worked has apparently not survived, but there is no reason to doubt that Lawrence did precisely what he said he had done in a letter to Miss Skinner: *The only*   ML, 760
thing was to write it all out again, following your MS. almost exactly,

but giving a unity, a rhythm, and a little more psychic development than you had done: a psychic development which he was soon describing however as *rather daring*. It seems probable, from various reports, that the foundation material of the novel — the adventures of Jack Grant in Western Australia in the 1880s — was in page after page left nearly intact by Lawrence's revising, and that in mere number of words Miss Skinner's contribution to the novel bulks far larger than Lawrence's. But Lawrence did not have to change much to alter the whole nature of the narrative. Jack Grant, under his touch, becomes a completely Laurentian hero. Event after event bears the distinctive Lawrence stamp, sometimes by no more than the addition of a few words recognizable as Lawrence's own. *The Boy in the Bush,* the novel that took form and rhythm out of Mollie Skinner's "House of Ellis" manuscript, is unquestionably a Lawrence novel.

It is especially a novel that must be read as Lawrence novels so often are not: in direct relation not only to the setting but to the surrounding places impinging upon Lawrence's alert mind as he wrote. By the fall of 1923, Lawrence was still grappling in his soul to bring into his personal mythos two regions that bore a direct relation to Australia: Mexico and the American Southwest. He had not so far achieved much with either. *The First Quetzalcoatl* hung in suspense, and he was far from satisfied with it. A part of Australia had found its form in *Kangaroo,* but that was southeastern Australia, the most settled and tamed portion of the continent. Here at hand now was material which he had in effect commissioned through his charge to Mollie Skinner. This was a rough bulk of life presented to him by a woman, just what he had always loved to take and mold. A bit of the Australian continent had caught up with him from the past, that region where, like Somers in *Kangaroo,* he had had a glimpse of immensity from which he never KA, 9 recovered: a *vast, uninhabited land* that *frightened* and compelled him, a land of air *new and unbreathed,* where *there were great distances* of landscape that seemed to be waiting, waiting. Mexico had brought him a comparable fear, and so had the American Rockies. If at the moment he could still do nothing in fiction with either of these, he might do something with Western Australia. Jack Grant might be made to BB, 251 bend that awesome country to the shape of his own being: *He loved the earth, the wild country, the bush, the scent. He wanted to go on for ever. Beyond the settlements — beyond the ploughed land — beyond all fences. That was it — beyond all fences. Beyond all fences, where a man was alone with himself and the untouched earth.* And he goes, when he matures enough to know his purpose, with one steadfast aim: BB, 252 *to find another, more terrible, but also more deeply-fulfilling god stirring subtly in the uncontaminated air about one.*

The destiny inherent in the puritan mythos had discovered a perfect ground upon which to evolve, a virgin continent for the experience Lawrence had identified with in Cooper and other American authors, when the virgin continent with its dark god intact was America, not Australia. Down under, by recall from California and Mexico, Lawrence could send forth *the splendid, powerful, wild old English blood*   BB, 341 not to play *wild,* as he had seen English blood several generations removed doing in New Mexico, but to recover the wildness he had engendered in the New Mexico poems, *the wildness of a wolf or a fox.*

In his quest to re-enter the oldest of human time and know the oldest of gods, Jack Grant is one of the most successful of Lawrence pilgrims, and one good reason for this is no doubt the fact that Jack is able to pursue his destiny without being vexed by politics, that force which Lawrence was having such difficulty assimilating into his ideal scheme of existence: the difficulty which at times had put such a strain on *Aaron's Rod* and *Kangaroo* and would continue to do so on the still unrealized *Plumed Serpent.* It was another advantage that for the time being Lawrence was womanless, separated from Frieda by the Atlantic and the width of the North American continent: but even so, he was determined eventually to bring her back to Mexico to submit to his needs. Further, his travel down the west coast of Mexico between the two halves of his rewriting task gave him extended direct exposure to a region like the Australian bush. This reinforced his sense of the untamed land still ahead, of which some great thing might be made: even to the founding of Rananim. But typically, when he was offered free land near Guaymas on which to establish his commune, Lawrence declined — because, he said, it would be *like living on Mars.*   ML, 754

The *daring development* in Jack Grant and the *rhythm* and *unity*   ML, 760 of his experience constitute an almost perfect example of what Lawrence wanted to make of the male soul's adventure in consciousness, the presentation controlled by a sure touch through the whole novel. The story opens with an "innocent" young Jack arriving in Freemantle. Son of an English father and an Australian mother, he has inherited from her a knowledge of the difference between *tame innocence* and   BB, 7 *wild innocence,* along with her inclination of the latter. He is soon swept up in *the magic clarity of this new world,* though with revulsions now   BB, 20 and then, and is soon acquainted with two girls, the light Mary and the dark Monica — the same pairing of womanly being that Lawrence had found fascinating in Hawthorne and Cooper. In fact the dark Mary might almost have aboriginal blood: another feature in a familiar pattern. But Jack mistrusts women, though he feels their power, and for a long time avoids any entanglement with them, dreading the thought of being yoked to one woman. All this while he is becoming a true part of the Ellis family on their solitary farm: nearly all of this comprehensive introduction to a new way of life must belong to Mollie Skinner's pen. On the other hand, Jack Grant's brief contact with the BB, 81 old *lone wolf* of a grandmother, whose advice is to *watch the glow inside you,* and who delivers an enigmatic summation of life, *in Yourself is God!* — all this puts the boy on an undeniable course of Laurentian search. The book goes on to present one of the most puritanic of pilgrimages. The fierce male soul regains an ideal condition of the old Miltonic ascendancy, along with a Bunyanesque capability of avoiding BB, 341 this *great trap* of a world *set wide for the unwary.* This double state of grace is shown to be possible only to the wanderer, the wayfarer, BB, 154 and only by coming to a full knowledge of *Jehovah the great and dark.*

Jack advances from boyhood into manhood through several years of determined effort both to harmonize with and to master the conditions of the new land, human and natural. He spends a long time in wild regions seeking his fortune with Tom, who becomes the kind of companion and follower that Lawrence wished for his heroes. Jack and BB, 326 his travel mate defy the wilderness: *Man for man, they were up against the great dilemma of white men, on the edge of the white man's world, looking into the vaster, alien world of the undawned era.* Jack discovers a rival too, in Easu, a coarse and arrogant man from another branch of the Ellis family. The rivalry centers on Monica but not only on her. BB, 341 Easu is an imposing figure but a *mongrel* playing *wolf.* Jack at last kills him in self-defense.

The Jacob-Esau parallel is obvious and significant. The brutal and essentially false heir to the world is supplanted by the less physically powerful but wily and farseeing man of imagination. Jack's search for his god is like Jacob's in that he also carries it out by going off to remoteness, to the strange land of the bush, there to wrestle with and to know his god. The mythic experience of Biblical characters, always close to the heart of Lawrence's writing, saw a strong upsurge in America, from *The Boy in the Bush* into *The Plumed Serpent* and the play *David,* which was Lawrence's visionary farewell to America. In the Australian novel that he reworked in America, he was much assisted in this natural bent for scriptural symbolism by a like inclination in Mollie Skinner. But it is to Lawrence's own ends that the principal allusions are molded, with land as well as with humans. For instance, in putting a geographical interpretation upon Paul's BB, natural body/spiritual body argument. *The natural body was like in* 191–192 *England, where the sun rises naturally to make day, . . . all the cosmos* BB, *just a natural fact.* But in Australia Jack knows *another sun,* which 192–193 gives him *a great passional reaction in himself, in his own body. And as the strange new passion of fear, and the sense of gloriousness burned through him, like a new intoxication, he knew that this was his real spiritual body.*

The killing of Easu is not the last of Jack's initiations into manhood. Soon after that event he gets lost in the bush and nearly dies of thirst. He loses all sense of intimacy with the outer world, either with place or with people. But inside himself he comes near to his *Creator moving around unrealised.* He is saved, to keep the thematic pattern complete, by his soul-mate Tom, and Lawrence stresses this restoration to the world as the moment of Jack's rebirth: that is, his first real attainment of male wholeness. He is now *dark-anointed,* which means as well death anointed: the dark Christ in him arises. Lawrence continues in close adherence to his most deeply rooted symbology, really to the point of being simplistic. Jack the man, having returned from over the border of life, is henceforth a lord among men, but *the eternal stranger* too, with a tragic bearing, in that he is one of the few who know that life and death are one. Like Lawrence, Jack Grant is haunted by the immortal self beyond the immediate ego. He embodies fully Lawrence's sense of the tragic, of triumph that comes about through death and looking back on death, when a man never wishes to act again without the knowledge of death. All this implies not only a knowledge of the whole of time and space but bestows as well a great measure of control even over immortality and the coming life of the world.

Jack Grant now occupies much the same position in Lawrence's visionary construct as Count Dionys of *The Ladybird*. If we bring these two extensions of their creator into juxtaposition we see how far-reaching Lawrence's imaginative grasp of places like America and Australia could be. Two years after *The Boy in the Bush,* writing at night on the Mediterranean coast of Italy, Lawrence set down his momentary feeling for the eternal youth of Italy: youthful, that is, when conceived against the faraway America he was now remembering, a continent of *wonderful, hoary age.* The spirit of that place as he recalled it from Italy resided chiefly in ghosts inhabiting the timber around the New Mexico ranch. All of which speaks of the past, near and far. But Lawrence employed another phrase in the same breath to define the spirit of America: *the continent of the afterwards.* What he meant by this is obscure when confined to the little sketch of 1925. The manner in which he used the word *afterwards* in *The Boy in the Bush* offers some clarification. The mature Jack Grant is like Count Dionys in knowing himself to be one of the lords of death, of *the vast dark kingdom of afterwards.* As Count Dionys lays future claim to Lady Daphne in the underworld, so Jack intends to take Monica with him as *a quiet, fearless bride in the dark chambers of the dead.* In this train of thought he contemplates what his function and that of his few equals will be in the hereafter: what is *the*

BB, 322

BB, 324

BB, 334

MM, 81

BB, 329

BB, 342

goal of the afterwards? It will be to *order the goings of the next living.* The spirits of the noble dead will determine the future of mankind and will lead it, we may know, back to the lost life of the blood. The *afterwards* of Australia and the *afterwards* of America embody then two realms of experience. First, the absorption in death of the aristocratic soul that has journeyed far in search of consummation. Second, a perfected future society that will enjoy a natural congress between death and life such as Lawrence was later to describe as characteristic of Etruscan civilization. That living on of the dead through their presence in the heart of the living we recognize as Lawrence's credo of immortality going far back and voiced with such extended assurance in the first version of the American literature essays.

But Jack Grant goes much further towards assuming his lordly power here and now than any other Lawrence character. He resolves to discover gold, to become wealthy, convinced that such a conquest will be a natural foretaste of his afterlife: *"I must start the river of the wealth of the world rolling in a new course, down the sombre, quiet, proud valleys of the lords of death and the ladies of the dark, the aristocrats of the afterwards."* It has the Calvinistic ring, but it means more to Jack than the pursuit of material good to prove his election. It is also the conquest now of the dark under-earth and the wresting of treasure from it. To accomplish this feat Jack wanders for a long time alone. The imagery Lawrence employs to render the search recalls the association with mines that has helped to direct the course of his spirit since childhood.

Jack finds his gold. He takes possession of Monica, too. But wealth and one woman are not enough. He wants Mary also, the other girl he has known from the start. As he understands the sexes, no woman can be complete unless she is joined to the man for whom she is meant, no matter if he has other wives, and Jack is convinced that Mary is,
BB, 372 *by the mystery of fate . . . linked to him.*

But Mary refuses to participate in this plural marriage. As Jack sees it, she knows that she belongs to him, but she cannot break the slavish bonds of convention. Jack is not to be deterred, however, from fostering a patriarchal ideal stemming from the Old Testament and those early Mormons Lawrence had called the real precursors of a new
BB, 371 American race. Jack *wanted to go like Abraham under the wild sky, speaking to a fierce wild Lord, . . . a perpetual travelling,* and to take
BB, 368 such wives as he needed for his *own completeness.* He also desires, in fulfillment of the ancient ideal, a few faithful male companions, a sort of tribe. All these goals Jack Grant may not have achieved when the novel ends, but he is on the point at least of arranging for a second woman, one who is only too eager to join him. This last scene takes

place on the road, with Jack's red stallion headed inland in a *quick,*   BB, 388
strong, rhythmic movement. His next significant goal, we are informed,
is some wild part of Australia where he can set up as a patriarch.

Just how strongly Lawrence felt all this in his pilgrim bones is
evident from a letter he wrote his mother-in-law a few days before he
completed reshaping Mollie Skinner's manuscript. Mexico, *this black*   ML, 763
country where he was, was *full of man's strength.* He complained that
Frieda, in her refusal to accompany him a second time to Mexico,
failed to *understand that a man must be a hero these days. . . . I must*
go up and down through the world, he declared, balancing the potentiality of one country against that of another. In this mission a man does
not *ask for love from his wife, but for strength, strength, strength.*
Lawrence's appeal to his mother-in-law plainly arises from the momentarily most powerful side of his dual attitude to a magna mater figure.
He cries out that she understands him, while Frieda does not, comparing her sympathy for his struggles to that which he declares he used
to have from his own mother.

The Boy in the Bush ends the first phase of Lawrence's search for
himself in America. He sailed from Veracruz for England in late
November 1923, fully resolved to return to America, nevertheless, as
soon as he could persuade Frieda to come with him. Next time he
meant to go deeper into some more primitive part of Mexico: to
Oaxaca, he had decided by mid-December, while counting the weeks
in a damp and wintry London that he could scarcely bear.

It was no doubt at Frieda's instigation that they spent the winter in
Europe. They went to Baden-Baden for a short time to visit her mother,
with brief stays in Paris going and coming. Lawrence spoke of going to
Spain, where he had never been, before heading back to America: an
interest prompted maybe by his fascination with the Spanish elements
of the New World. The flame of Rananim sputtered in alcohol that
winter, too. Having drunk a great deal of wine at a dinner in the Cafe
Royal, a rare thing for him, Lawrence called on those present to join
him in a commune, in Mexico if conditions permitted. Only John
Middleton Murry and Dorothy Brett answered the summons, and in
the end only Dorothy Brett came west with the Lawrences, in March
1924.

During the little more than three months he was in Europe on this
occasion, Lawrence found the Old World as dreary and hopeless as
ever, but still he put his keen observation to work to apprehend in the
crosscurrents between places and his own state of mind a more than
personal significance. He made himself a sort of foreign correspondent
for *The Laughing Horse,* a little magazine that Spud Johnson brought
out from time to time in New Mexico. Johnson published two of the

three letters Lawrence got off to him that winter. These were a "London Letter," a "Paris Letter" and a "Letter from Germany." The "London Letter" was sparked by Lawrence's receiving the latest issue of John-son's periodical, a special Southwest number full of Indian lore. One piece concerned the mythical Navajo Turquoise Horse. Another was a story in which the noise the sun makes is a laugh. In London the whole

ML, 768   spirit of place seemed to Lawrence to be *mouldering,* its air breathed
ML, 769   to death, while in New Mexico the Turquoise Horse was *waving snow out of his tail* and heading for *the blue mountains of the far distance.* In Mexico his mane would be the sun, his body the sky, while his lash-ing hooves would shatter the old world. Lawrence was gasping to be

ML, 770   riding west *on a blue stallion.* It was the first hint of Lou Witt striking out for the New World with her stallion St. Mawr.

The "Paris Letter" was also suggested to Lawrence by the sight of a horse: a piece of sculpture in the Tuileries depicting Hercules slay-ing the Centaur. Lawrence begins by wishing the slaughter had been the other way around. The spirit of place of Paris is not so much moldy as it is simply exhausted: by the pursuit of sex and food as pleasure, but also by the enormous burden of monumental buildings that seem the only vestige left of a regal quality. Material civilization, even the best of it in works of art, has heaped itself up on the human spirit until

PH, 121   it hardly has the strength to budge. Lawrence rejects it all: *What I believe in is the old Homeric aristocracy, when the grandeur was inside the man, and he lived in a simple wooden house.*

The last of these letters is the best, the "Letter from Germany," written February 19, 1924, from Baden-Baden. Besides being of great interest in itself, the letter has close and revealing ties with a story, "The Border Line," probably written in Baden-Baden also, with which it shares some descriptive passages. But more than this, the two to-gether form within easily perceivable scope the interdependence in Lawrence between personal conflicts and the power of prophecy in larger human events.

The letter was not published until 1934, four years after Law-rence's death, at which time it was rightly hailed as an early forecast of what was taking place in the German spirit to lead it to Nazism. It

PH, 109   was not so much in the people that Lawrence saw *the old, bristling, savage spirit* — though he did note that the *queer gangs of* **Young Socialists** with *their half-mystic assertions* were like *broken, scattered tribes.* More than all else, he sensed a coming to life in the spirit of

PH, 107   place beyond that *great divider,* the Rhine, a stirring of something in
PH, 109   the *inky blackness of Germanic trees* in the *still-unconquered Black Forest.* It was that attribute of place, now perceptible as never before, which had struck him and so much helped to shape his experience on first coming to Germany in 1912, and which had lured him into the

depths of the past in *Movements in European History*. He connected
it now also with what he had conjectured in the "Spirit of Place" essay
introducing his critique of American literature. The polarity of place
that kept Europe together periodically during certain ages was now
falling asunder again, and Germany was inclining eastward under *the*   PH, 108
fascination of a destructive East, that produced Attila. Lawrence was
of two minds as to this *old fierceness coming back.* To be *dangerous in*   ML, 777
a manly way was good, but a fear of possible consequences never ceased
to lurk behind this profession, especially in connection with any influence from that deathly direction, East.

Lawrence's penetration of spirit of place in this instance owes
much to a personal crisis, a crisis of manhood. He had seen immediately, on arriving in England from Mexico, that Frieda and John
Middleton Murry were on far too intimate terms for his comfort —
later admissions have established that they came close to having an
affair at this time. Lawrence's story "The Border Line" puts all his
suspicions into a perspective that suited his needs.

Alan Anstruther, based on Lawrence, a Celt with a *dauntless,*   SH, 588
overbearing manliness of his own, was killed in the Great War. His
widow, Katherine, indisputably Frieda, has since married Philip Far-
quhar, John Middleton Murry to be sure, a friend of Alan's whom she
came to admire years ago and even to think more manly than Alan:
in the sense that he seemed to know better how to treat a woman. But
by the time of present action in the story, she is beginning to realize
that Philip's power is *in his weakness, his appeal, his clinging depen-*   SH, 601
dence. Still she goes to Germany to meet him.

But she has hardly set out from England when she experiences
the first of her psychic progressions that correspond to geographic
movement: *It came to her on the boat crossing the Channel. Suddenly*   SH, 592
she seemed to feel Alan at her side again, as if Philip had never existed.
Which is only the beginning. As she journeys on toward Strasbourg,
she travels under the influence of warring impulses, remembering how
movement toward Alan across any stretch of earth was always like
a motion with wings. But she goes toward Philip *with a strange disin-*   SH, 593
tegrating reluctance. In the Marne country, still devastated by the war,
she begins to live in absolute conjunction with the landscape. Going
home to Germany, a manly country, begins to feel vaguely like the
equivalent of going home to Alan, and the passing landscape commences to penetrate her consciousness as the region of death to be
crossed on the way. One of the Lords of Death, to revert to the terms
of *The Boy in the Bush,* is calling her.

The climactic region is the Rhineland, specifically Strasbourg,
where Katherine must spend the night waiting for a train to Germany.
This is the true border line of the story, running between the Latin and

Germanic races, between the extremity of the old life and the potentiality of the new. Katherine walks out in the dark night, crosses the
river of the town — a tributary of the Rhine — and seeks out the cathedral. While she stands looking at it, life begins to rouse in its stones,

SH, 596   not a Christian spirit but *the great blood-creature waiting, implacable,*
under a crumbling world. It is the spirit from the east of the Rhine that
Lawrence senses with fear and wonder in his "Letter from Germany."
In these surroundings Katherine catches sight of her dead husband
awaiting her. He lays a hand on her arm, they stroll in peace under his
strange, silent authority as far as the river bridge, where he must
leave her.

Next morning she continues east by train across the Rhine, to the

SH, 600   *Germany of the pine forests . . . and the old barbaric undertone,* all
SH, 599   *wild and unsubdued, pre-Roman.* Here she rejoins Philip, only to
realize how inadequate he is and to watch with relief as he wanes under
some strange illness that Germany has subjected him to. He is so far
out of his element here that his survival may be at stake. As Katherine

SH, 602   watches him degenerate to a *whimpering little beast, who claimed*
reality only through a woman, she feels the presence of Alan more and
more, especially on her walks around Baden-Baden among the *bristling*
and *wolfish* fir trees. The sense of his presence grows until one day
Alan is able to make love to her in the forest, and shortly after, to the
point where he can enter the room in which Philip lies dying. In this
last scene the immortality of the "real" man in Alan permeates
Katherine's existence to the core. He pulls the arms of the gasping
Philip from around her neck and lets him sink into death. Then he

SH, 604   leads her to another bed *in the silent passion of a husband come back*
from a very long journey.

"The Border Line" does not for most readers fall among Lawrence's best stories, remarkable as it is in disclosing Lawrence's talent
for laying out regions of Europe as symbolic of the quest for true
masculinity and true possession between man and woman. Any effort
at appreciation of the story is bound to be hampered by that perennial
difficulty with Lawrence: the frequent transparency of fictional surface
covering personal insufficiency and personal vindictiveness. Even so,
in this tale Lawrence came close, by a sheer power of making symbolism of place overcome most odds, to creating a situation and a
series of actions that carry over into the realm where personalities
cease to matter and sub-conscious mythic forms take over.

The Lawrences were back in London before the end of February
1924, and by early March on the *Aquitania* headed for New York.
They soon went on to New Mexico, and Lawrence hoped that shortly
they would be on their way to Oaxaca. On the ship Lawrence could

say again what the westward impulse always brought out: *I like to feel*   ML, 784
myself travelling. And it's good to get away from the doom of Europe.

NOTES

[1] The ceremony that Lawrence attended at Stone Lake, New Mexico, is an autumn dance connected both with harvest and a sort of dedication of seed for next year's corn. The main event is a relay race between the two clans of the tribe. The winner is the ruling clan for the coming year. Lawrence gives his impressions of one night of the ritual in "Indians and an Englishman" (PH, 92–99).

[2] In the Seltzer edition of *Birds, Beasts and Flowers* (1923), this poem bears "Española," presumably Española, New Mexico, as the place of composition. Why this is so remains a mystery, since the poem was first published in *The New Republic* in May 1921, sixteen months before Lawrence ever saw New Mexico. However, he revised and added to the collection while he was making ready to leave the Taos area in March 1923. He mailed the manuscript to Seltzer between March 14 and 21. On the latter date he crossed from the U.S. into Mexico at El Paso (TS, 77–78, 87). Slight substantive changes were made in "Humming-Bird" at some time: for instance *telescope* in the *New Republic* text becomes *long telescope* in *Birds, Beasts and Flowers*. I have not been able to examine all the manuscript material of the volume (*see* SR, 199–200), but possibly "Española" as the place of composition really means that Lawrence made the small changes in the poem there, or even simply mailed the manuscript from there with a resulting confusion of postmark for place of composition, since he went through the town on his way from Taos to Sante Fe.

[3] Lawrence considered his writings on the unconscious to be an extension of the earlier versions of the American literature essays. The two efforts were so deeply intertwined that he could assert the following in an early form of an "epilogue" to *Fantasia of the Unconscious: I reckon this book of mine is a real American book. If there had been no America I should never have written it* (PL, 338).

[4] Nahuatl mythology made no such distinction between male and female rain. The Athabascans, the Navajo especially, made much of it. Rain accompanied by thunder and lightning was male, while more gentle rainfall was classified as female. *See* Washington Matthews, *Navaho Legends* (New York, 1897), p. 235. Lawrence read either this book or some other on Navajo mythology, making use of information as he pleased in his "Aztec" mythology. He did not read Lewis Spence's *Gods of Mexico*, his chief source, until he was ready to rewrite his Mexican novel.

12

The Dark Gods Are at the Gates

Once he was back in the States, Lawrence postponed his trip to Mexico until the fall. On friendly terms once more with Mabel Dodge Luhan, he and Frieda stayed for a little while in one of her houses, during which time Frieda acquired from Mabel a small ranch high up in the mountains beyond Del Monte Ranch. One of the names of the new place was Kiowa Ranch — because it was said that the Kiowa Indians had formerly camped there — and this was the name that Lawrence adopted. On May 5, 1924, when most of the snow had melted in the high country, the Lawrences and Dorothy Brett went up to Kiowa with some Taos Indians and a Mexican carpenter to assist in making the disused cabins ready for occupancy. For a month they were all busy at the hard work of repairing and cleaning up, of building a chimney and an outdoor Indian-style oven. All this put Lawrence back into rhythm with the Southwest. England now seemed *as unreal as a book one read long ago*. This mountain territory he now wanted to plumb to the depths: *The sun is setting, the pines are red, the Indians are just starting drumming* — his helpers from Taos Pueblo drummed and sang by their campfire under the trees at night, just as the Kiowas perhaps had done long in the past. The dark gods, hesitant up to now to emerge in America, almost at once appear in Lawrence's prose.

ML, 789

For the whole of this spring, summer and early fall of 1924, Lawrence was absorbed in a singular way by the spirit of place centered on Kiowa Ranch and its surrounding mountains — that this was the first piece of land he could call his own assisted his fascination — and by close observation and analysis of Indian ceremony: the rites themselves and what he thought to be behind them. Above all else, perhaps, he was making ready for the final onslaught on the dark gods of Mexico in the fall.

The first piece in which Lawrence had his say about this new spot and what Indians might make of it was "Pan in America," which he found time to write even as repairs on the cabins went forward. He fixed on *a big pine tree* which *rises like a guardian spirit in front of the* PH, 24 *cabin where we live.* Its mystery, its darkness, its trunk as a column of life — this tree was *still within the allness of Pan.* The thousands of such trees all around him — those *vast trees* that *hummed with energy* PH, 23 from Pan — were a portion of the great American wilderness which had long enchanted him and which now became the basic component of the fiction he wrote during the next few months. All of this concerns a woman who enters the forest and encounters there for better or worse the male spirit who is the sole access to the dark gods. The shift of roles from the days of *Le Gai Savaire* is now complete.

Linking up his thought between continents, Lawrence comments on how in the Old World, Pan became the Christian devil. For the immigrant Europeans he inhabited the forest of America in such a guise too, we remember. For as Lawrence mentions in his essay on *The Scarlet Letter,* Hester is fearful of the demon of the forest westward. At Kiowa Ranch the surroundings brought it powerfully home to Lawrence that in this western forest and in the local Indians, Pan was still Pan if unhappily fading away. The blaze the Indians had left on his giant pine long before, like the drumming and chanting of the present Indians under the trees nearby, was a sign of the *vivid relatedness* still PH, 27 stirring. In the hunting societies of former times the potency of Pan had maintained the *living stealth* and the *subtle, hypnotic, following spell* PH, 28 that the Indian had cast over his quarry. This male affinity with the stuff of life, Lawrence does not forget, had gained man the reverence of woman. Pan was still at work too in the pueblo dances, represented especially by the spruce twigs tied on the dancers' arms. Knowing that most Indian rituals are in some manner directed to bringing rain, Lawrence saw these bits of evergreen as tokens offered to the Pan-power by which *the wheat sprouted like green rain returning out of* PH, 23 *the ground.*

During this same period Lawrence wrote a short story centered on Pan in Europe, on his apparition in a London park during a snow storm. The principal worth of the story is not as fiction but in what it shows of Lawrence's transition from Old World to New at this time. Possibly he wrote this story just before "Pan in America." He said on TS, 131 April 4 that he was writing stories out of his stay in Europe, we know that this story was written and accepted for publication by June 3, and what happens in the story has parallels in both language and action to what is said on the first page of "Pan in America." This story, "The Last Laugh," is a typical bit of Lawrence fantasizing in that it brings

forth the drama of his sexual conflicts in a geographical setting com-
pounded of the familiar old-world/new-world dichotomy. As in other
analogous efforts around this time, personal preoccupation fails to
realize itself in an absorbing piece of fiction. Lorenzo himself is here,
by name, setting the action in motion by observing ironically that
Hampstead freshly covered with snow is a "new world." He then drops
out of the story, but Lawrence's vengeful purpose is only too obvious
in what happens to the two principals of the piece, the woman modeled
on Dorothy Brett, the man on John Middleton Murry again: Miss
James and Marchbanks. The pair leave Lorenzo and soon thereafter

SH, 634   enter a park where *big black holly trees tufted with snow, and old,
ribbed, silent English elms* invite comparison with Lawrence's American conifers as incarnations of Pan. Here Marchbanks is all at once
compelled several times to break into animal-like laughter, contending
that he hears such laughter from among the trees. Miss James can hear
none of it just now, being partially deaf. But she is soon aware of the
presence of Pan, for she catches sight of his form, and before the story
is over his nearness has cured her deafness — with the obvious sexual
suggestion of ears — so that she can eventually hear both his laughter
and the voices in the air welcoming him back to the world. Only she,
in fact, is adequate to life next morning, when in a vision reminiscent
of the ending of *The Rainbow* she sees the old sky peeled away and a
new one gleaming over London, fulfilling Lorenzo's half-conscious
prophecy. Marchbanks does not remain with her on this night of Pan's
return. Just the opposite of what was promised by his receptivity to
panic laughter comes to pass. He goes off in the park with a dark
woman, deserting the only woman capable of true response. Another
male appears, a young policeman, who escorts Miss James home, but
he can get no further than the sofa of her living room, where he is
found next morning lame in one foot. Marchbanks comes on the scene
again, only now to get a glimpse of Pan — a fatal glimpse, since this is
daylight, when any sight of Pan may be fatal, and he is in any case false
to the vision of Pan. He drops dead as if lightning struck.

Like "The Borderline" this story envisages a supernatural triumph
of male spirit to compensate for the frustration of Lawrence's current
situation and it projects the triumph on place and change of place. The
London policeman falls impotent, John Middleton Murry as Marchbanks tempts Pan by refusing to recognize the right woman and dies
for his inadequacy. Dorothy Brett as Miss James is a forerunner to
Lou Witt of *St. Mawr*. No man is worthy of her, for none has the pure
contact with Pan: the laming of the policeman foreshadows that of
Rico, Lou's husband. It was of course Lorenzo who in real life led

Brett to America and she was the right woman to appreciate *his* sensitivity to Pan.

On this last voyage to America Lawrence did not fail to describe himself as *a wandering soul.* He was more convinced than ever of the ML, 793 utter diversity of the world, a quality in which he exulted. It was typical of him that when he began to concentrate heavily on one place, as he did now on New Mexico, he stressed the uniqueness of each and every place. There could never be, he declared, a universal unity among men. *Great racial differences* were *insuperable,* because *the spirit of* ML, 796 *place ultimately always triumphs* to make for such distinctions. This was one of his prime lessons from travel: *I have known many things, that may never be unified: Ceylon, the Buddha temples, Australian bush, Mexico and Teotihuacán, Sicily, London, New York, Paris, Munich.*

One reason for saying this was that New Mexico was coming into focus toward the ultimate comprehension that Lawrence could achieve of any place: comprehension through fiction and travel sketches. Between May and October of 1924 he brought together all that had failed to coalesce in the southern Rockies in 1922 and 1923 as place and as ground of ancient human culture. The upshot was that he produced in this period of less than five months a series of writings which constitutes one of his most outstanding achievements in response to place: three sketches on Indians that belong with "Pan in America" — "Indians and Entertainment," "Dance of the Sprouting Corn" and "The Hopi Snake Dance"; and then three of his finest shorter pieces of fiction: "The Woman Who Rode Away," *St. Mawr,* and "The Princess."

"Indians and Entertainment" and "Dance of the Sprouting Corn" were the first of these writings, both done not long after Lawrence had attended a Santo Domingo spring corn dance on April 23, and both influenced not only by that event but by the same Indian dancing at the ranch that had inspired "Pan in America." Also, he had been reading Adolf Bandelier's *Delight Makers,* a novel set among ancient cliff-dwelling Indians. Lawrence was determined to get a much better grasp of Indian ceremonialism before returning to his Quetzalcoatl novel. The chief point of "Indians and Entertainment" is that imitative art, with the Indian, is not directed to observation of himself in action as an individual, like white imitative art, but is a participation in the creative forces of the universe. The white man's idea of sitting apart in a theatre and watching a comic or a tragic image of himself and feeling edified thereby comes from his belief in a God who has created the world in his own image by a preconceived plan and whom man seeks to ape by mimesis. But the Indian sees only a *shimmer of creation* in MM, 51 everything, *never the distinction between God and God's creation.* As he is deeply imbedded in this creation, the Indian can assert himself as a single being only under certain special circumstances, or else he may offend the order of nature. He must always seek identification with universal being that is hardly even a god as such, if he is to draw strength from it. If he dances a bear-hunt, he is pitting the demon of manhood against the demon of bears, in a generic sense. He may, how-

MM, 49   ever, in something like a spear dance, measure out *the peril of his own isolation, in the overweening of his own singleness. The glory in power of the man of single existence. The peril of the man whose heart is suspended, like a single red star, in a great and complex universe, following its own lone course round the invisible sun of our own being, amid the strange wandering array of other hearts.* But this wayfaring heart is not observing the movement of its own ego, as the white man

MM, 50   in a theatre does. The Indian here is *not representing something. . . . It is a soft, subtle **being** something.* This is the Indian's action in the deer dance too. He becomes the animal in order to draw it into his village for food. Woman is the key force in this instance. The maidens lead the dancers, dressed as different animals, luring the deer and the

MM, 51   others in to supply food for the tribe, through *the magical wistfulness of women, the wonderful power of her seeking, her yearning, which can draw forth even the bear from his den.* Beyond her admiring but essentially passive role in "Pan in America," woman now acts accord-ing to her nature as a provider. And so it is with the ceremonial races

MM, 54   which the Indians run. It is *the effort to gather into their souls more and more of the creative fire, the creative energy which shall carry their tribe through the year.*

In the end Lawrence brings all this movement home to his own seeking, for he relates himself to the Indian spirit, and not to the white. The races are like his own running through the world, a running *with the changeless god who will give us nothing unless we overtake him.*

In this sketch Lawrence alludes to dances he had seen in Taos as far back as Christmas of 1922, and to the races of the San Gerónimo festival shortly after his first arrival in the area. His most recent expe-rience with ritual, the Santo Domingo spring corn dance mentioned above, called for longer treatment. The result was "Dance of the Sprouting Corn." Later on, he borrowed directly from this dance a good many of the costumes and the movements that went into Ramón's ceremonies in *The Plumed Serpent,* and much later still, reverted to the same dance for details of ritual in "A Dream of Life," in which he foresaw a distant future for an England restored to primitive grandeur. In "Dance of the Sprouting Corn" the minutest attention is paid to the unfolding of the dance, bit by bit, before the observer's eyes, and the

reasoning follows closely that which is already established in "Indians
and Entertainment." In the rhythmic energy of the dance, man *partakes*   MM, 61
in the springing of the corn, in the rising and budding and earing of
the corn. And when he eats his bread at last, he recovers all he once
sent forth, and partakes again of the energies he called to the corn, from
out of the wide universe.

If Lawrence was storing impressions for a return to his Mexican
novel, he was also soon thinking of an immediate metamorphosis of
Indian ceremonialism and the spirit of the mountains around Kiowa
Ranch into the most extreme expression he ever attempted of that
terrible and catastrophic process which he felt essential to a new unity
between the light spirit and the dark spirit in America and the reconstitution of male glory. This is the fable, though presented as bald
realism, called "The Woman Who Rode Away." It is one of Lawrence's
most powerful creations. The woman lives in subjection to the mechanical male power of her husband, a male like Gerald Crich, a man who
has built a successful career out of silver mining and ranching. Man
and wife live in an isolated part of Mexico, walled in by their adobe
house and overshadowed by the machinery of the mine up a slope,
with the wild and unknown mountains beyond. The woman has never
been awakened to any further life than this until, pulled on by strange
urges, she rides off into the mountains to know the gods of some remote
and mysterious Indians she has heard about. Into wilder and wilder
country she rides, until the Indians meet her, take her to their village,
imprison her for some months while in ritual they remove from her
all taint of white civilization, until she loses all her will and submits
voluntarily to being sacrificed at the winter solstice. Through this sacrifice the Indians, this lost tribe whose line of kings has kept the flame of
the old religion alive, hope to regain the universal potency they have
lost to the white man and his science.

The personal implication of the author in this tale is too obvious
to require much comment. Wish fulfillment renders. submissive an
overwhelming female power, not to the mechanical male of the present
age but to the suppressed male of the blood. But "The Woman Who
Rode Away" carries an artistic conviction beyond any such self-drama-
tization, through Lawrence's creation of fantastic place from real
place and his compelling exposure of reaches of the human psyche in
mythic terms. In short, "The Woman Who Rode Away" utilizes with
greater power resources tapped in a story like "The Borderline" with
some success, and with less, as we will see, in "The Overtone." That
America which Lawrence had been preparing since his early interpretation of Cooper is now truly realized in his fiction for the first time.
It is the merging of the red soul and the white soul which in Lawrence's

scheme is fated to occur. The configuration formerly sketched in Natty Bumppo and Chingachgook has now evolved into an apocalypse of sacrifice and transformation centered on the woman and the Chilchui Indians. Only here the roles are reversed. It is not the white race that absorbs and appeases the soul of the annihilated Indian, but the Indian that absorbs and redirects the soul of the sacrificed white woman, representative of all her race. The setting in which this occurs is a powerful fantasy of a restored wilderness such as Lawrence had predicted since witnessing the destruction of a wilderness through his reading of Cooper. This wilderness he creates from a coalescence of scenes visited since landing in America. It edges away from what is plainly the west coast of Mexico around Alamos, Sonora, where Lawrence had visited the previous fall. It stretches into higher mountains like those above Kiowa Ranch, with a lake resembling the sacred Blue Lake of the Taos Indians, with cottonwood valleys and aspens and bare rocks above the timberline, and over in the hidden valley a Taos Pueblo transposed and rearranged to suit Lawrence's convenience. For rituals Lawrence now had an accumulation to work with, using chiefly the Santo Domingo dance fresh in mind, the Taos winter dances too, and all with an added primitive splendor imagined from his reading about Aztec and other Indian ceremonials.

In this tale the prose is marvelously cadenced for the situation. The woman enters into a visionary pilgrimage almost from the moment she leaves the confinement of her hacienda-like home. The landscape takes on quickly the dimension of dream. Never for a moment does the presentation falter, but maintains a power which makes of the region traversed a real and a dream region together. When the Indians appear they too are both true to life and phantasmagorical. In the village the ceremonies come alive with the potency of Aztec ceremonies materializing out of the depths of the past. When the woman is given potions, when her clothing is cut away as if in a flaying of the skin of civilization, when the priests handle her as a sacred creature beyond any ordinary sexual contact whatever — all this conveys her slowly into a mindless harmony with the physical world where she can hear the blooming of the flowers and the turning of the spheres. This story is one of the most perfectly realized of those which Lawrence wrote with an American setting because here he chose to remain within the artistic boundaries set by his theme. He produced a mythical-realistic conjoining in allegorical form and left aside actual social and political questions.

Since "The Woman Who Rode Away" is a story that many deplore as after all an outrage, however vivid as a performance in prose, any defense of its artistic merit must take up the question of what significance it can possibly have for twentieth-century man. That the life-urge of the present technological age — exemplified in the story by the husband — is well on its way to exhaustion is certainly no fiction to any observant human today. That the frustrated instincts of mankind incarnate in the woman must seek some way out of its dilemma is equally obvious. That the power of renewal may be latent in some region of the soul under the surface of the present age, symbolized by the Indians of the fable, is beyond no one's acceptance. Where the modern humane mind balks is at Lawrence's insistence that human sacrifice is the only means to the end desired, that mankind itself must undergo a death and rebirth, or a sacrifice of some that others may live — which amounts to the same thing on the level of the race. It is a future terrible to contemplate, but distinctly not beyond the bounds of probability. We can imagine easily enough, in our time, a population at last desperate, when the comfort and confinement of plenty such as the woman enjoyed ceases to be enough to give life a value. Or we can perhaps better imagine the exhaustion of those material resources on which the millions of lives like that of the woman rely, and the terrible exigency to follow, when the survival of the race itself depends on some re-establishment of bonds with instinctive life in the self, the earth, the moon and the sun, the disregard of which has landed humanity in its present fix. "The Woman Who Rode Away" bears with ease the interpretation that the husband and the wife are the two unfoldings of human consciousness in a super-technological age. When renewal of the race is imperative — if such is even possible — then both the exploiting mind (the husband) and the mind rocked to sleep by the rewards of exploitation (the wife) must be superseded.

As to the sacrificial offering of the victim's heart, the modern mind is all but incapable of understanding its efficacy. Indians like Lawrence's fictional Chilchuis believed implicitly, of course, that they must feed the sun the blood of a few in order to maintain the life of the many. Curiously enough, though we generally refuse to face the fact, we apply by another line of reasoning the same principle. For instance when pressed to a final defense of atomic powerplants, proponents will argue often enough that the death of a few by radiation is simply the price of maintaining an acceptable standard of living for the majority. The reasoning is the same. Only the terms are different. Sacrifice by obsidian knife bloodies the hands. Sacrifice by radiation leaves them unsoiled.

By mid-July Lawrence had finished "The Woman Who Rode Away" and begun a second and more ambitious tale, *St. Mawr*. The writing of this went on for about two months, with interruptions — one was a trip to Hotevilla on the Hopi Reservation in August to attend the Hopi Snake Dance, and the writing of a sketch on that event. The theme of *St. Mawr* is like that of "The Woman Who Rode Away": the recapture of intuitive life through discovery of a primordial America which is simultaneously a place and a symbol of a deep plane of existence. The ramifications of this tale give it a greater range of complexity than "The Woman Who Rode Away," but a complexity whose texture begins to show flaws near the close.

The discovery of America in *St. Mawr* is a rediscovery. Lou Witt is American by birth. We first meet her in voluntary exile in England, married to a fashionable portrait painter, Sir Henry Carrington or Rico, spiritually intimate and "loving" with him and going through the motions of fun as a substitute for real life. Still she has never lost SA, 3   *the lurking sense of being an outsider everywhere, like a sort of gipsy, who is at home anywhere and nowhere.* Lou's mother, Rachel Witt, is even more of an outsider than her daughter. She shares the story to the extent of dominating it at times, although in the long run her purpose is to serve as foil to Lou's search. More than any other piece of fiction so far taken up, *St. Mawr* endeavors through the experience of both women to pinpoint the problem of male identity, only to have it escape real detection in the end.

Since the working out of the mother's destiny is one of Lawrence's real triumphs in the story, we may well consider her first. Her relationship to the symbolic center of the tale, the golden bay stallion St. Mawr, is never as close as her daughter's, but the analogy between her emotional condition and America as a symbolic place parallels that of Lou and is more a thematic whole. We find her living her embittered life only for the sake of the acid sarcasm she can pour over the world. The source of her great disappointment is that, now in her early fifties, she has found that she can make all males knuckle to her. Her one compelling desire is to be mastered, and as no real men exist anymore to carry this out, she goes on living in England simply to thrust herself SA, 7   as the *grimness of the big, dangerous America, into the safe, finicky drawing-rooms of London.* However, she is at last fascinated by Lewis, a Welshman, groom to St. Mawr, with whom she first comes in close contact on a ride several people take from her cottage in Shropshire to some rock formations in the hills overlooking Wales, a ride that introduces the journey and geographical motifs fundamental to the destiny of both women. Later on comes another journey that brings Mrs. Witt as close to understanding true maleness as she is capable of after all her conditioning. St. Mawr at this point is threatened with castration for having seriously injured Lou's husband. Mrs. Witt volunteers to save him by going on a horseback journey, accompanied by Lewis riding the stallion, halfway across England. On setting out, she considers this ride as the first leg of a return to America. This she equates with possible renewal by surrender to a real male, to Lewis, to whom she proposes on the ride. But he refuses. He is the isolate, inviolate male especially dear to Lawrence just now, one who cannot mate with modern woman because she has lost the faculty of respecting true masculinity. Lewis is modeled on the image of Lawrence that he was to celebrate most fully — and to bring out of isolation — in *Lady Chatterley's Lover*. The keeper of something wild in *St. Mawr* prefers to spend his time ministering to the stallion, as a priest of perhaps the only truly male being left alive. The stallion likewise will not mate in England. Even mares, as the story has it, are infected by the malady that the eclipse of male power has brought upon the world. Rachel Witt goes on to America anyway, and St. Mawr and Lewis go with her and her daughter. She all but exhausts herself to locate a freighter that can carry them all to New Orleans. But then, once at sea, she collapses inwardly and she never truly revives, except to a feeble superciliousness which is the only response she can summon up to the New Mexico ranch where her daughter Lou leads her in hope of a new life. But America cannot bring rebirth to the elder woman. She is too far gone. "Wit" is truly all that is left her, and she has lost the surroundings even to practice much of this by leaving England, where she could use her wit to heap scorn on that moribund nation.

Lou is not just her mother at an earlier age. She has lulled herself into a half-hearted belief in life with her husband. The stallion changes all that, almost from the moment she first sees him: *that mysterious fire* SA, 13 *of the horse's body had split some rock in her*. She wants to hide from her husband afterwards, no longer able to *bear the triviality and super-* SA, 14 *ficiality of her human relationships*. With Rico and all his kind these days there is *no mystery in being a man*. But she sees *a terrible mystery* SA, 45 *in St. Mawr*. Right away, as if through the horse, she begins to long for America, and for the opportunity of taking the stallion with her. It begins to seem at this point, and the connection is long maintained, that Lawrence has hit upon a near-perfect symbol of the maleness that must save the world if it is to be saved: that sacred power that he must bear out of England and establish for growth in the new soil of the New Continent. Phoenix, a half-Navajo, half-Mexican war veteran who has attached himself to Mrs. Witt as a servant, comes to the fore as a human counterpart, with all the suggestion at first of rebirth in the great spaces of the Southwest. He is never quite a prospective lover for Lou, but he reflects and partially embodies the right sort of maleness.

Now the first critical occurrence toward changing Lou's circumstances is the same geography-as-revealer scene that initiates the relationship between the mother and Lewis: that ride to the borderline hills above Wales. This trip is based on a visit Lawrence made to the area shortly before setting out for America on the voyage that he was to project through his fictional women. To Lawrence a trip west, in this case from London to Shropshire, was generally a first step toward America, as going to Cornwall had been in wartime. On this outing to the hills Rico rides St. Mawr. Among the rocks up here, Lou senses something of *the old savage England* and finds herself almost convinced thereby that humanity does not even exist anymore. It is just after this, on the way home, that St. Mawr acts up on seeing a dead adder. Rico, in trying to quiet the rearing stallion, only succeeds in pulling him over backwards and falling under him, a mishap from which Rico emerges with a bad ankle for life.

SA, 59

Of great interest here are the subliminal impulses involved. In attempting to assert his false maleness over truly sacred maleness, Rico brings on himself the same sort of injury that the young policeman suffered in "The Last Laugh" when Pan brushed through his existence. Moreover, Lou and her mother have all but willed Rico's crippling in having forced him as a matter of pride to mount St. Mawr. After the accident their sympathy is all with the horse, whom they must rescue by transporting him to America, to get him beyond the reach of Rico's pettily vengeful plan to emasculate him. The two women, consistent with Lawrence's belief, have turned destructive because they have no glorious males to show them how to live: destructive, that is, toward such a contemptible specimen of a man as Rico. The pattern remains faithful to that which Lawrence drew from his investigation of American literature, notably from his reading of *The Scarlet Letter*.

The thematic movement toward America as symbol and actuality builds with gathering force. At almost any point where masculinity is in the foreground we are never very far from a figurative geography to express it, a kingdom of maleness, another country beyond the immediate, a remoteness, a distance, an inaccessibility, whether Lewis or Phoenix or St. Mawr holds present attention. As is usual for Lawrence, the direction east is bad: Lou feels as if the evil that is smothering the world rises up *from the core of Asia*. South and West are the truly metaphysical quarters of the world. The action turns in that direction with the outbound freighter on which Lou, her mother, Phoenix, Lewis and St. Mawr head first for Santander and subsequently for the Gulf of Mexico.

SA, 65

The repudiation of England is now accomplished. The last vestige of maleness has departed with St. Mawr, and the unreality of that immediate past at once prevails in the story just as it does in Lawrence's letters. But the momentum of the tale, wonderfully paced up to this time, unhappily begins to falter. Excitement still attends the quest for a country of aloneness and self-sufficiency that is still god-infused. But an uncertainty of transition enters the picture and loose ends begin to appear. The Texans whom the travelers meet on a cattle ranch, their first real stop, have a degree of what they seek, even if it is cinema-like on the order of what Lawrence first surmised in New Mexico. The curious thing is that Lawrence drops St. Mawr at this point, and Lewis stays in Texas with him. Even though the horse is *too beautiful, too*   SA, 120 *perfected, in this great open country,* he appears to belong. At any rate, he recovers enough interest in mares to follow one out of the story. Lou never even thinks of him later on, after all the significance attached to getting him to America. As for Lewis, who sticks by his symbolic lord, it is hard to imagine what he can find to sustain his aloofness among the over-friendly cowhands of Texas. He too is dropped, apparently to do the best he can as a sort of Lawrence in a movie-set Southwest, with insufficient maleness after all to bear him on to the truly male region of the New Mexico Rockies.

St. Mawr's suddenly changed behavior does have one effect on Lou, apparently the one Lawrence meant to bridge the gap between the stallion as a symbol of supreme maleness and the ranch landscape, which soon comes to take the place of St. Mawr. The sight of the stallion in Texas makes England feel momentarily real again, in retro-spect. But no, Lou's sensibility will not have this. Instead, it forces on her the question of what place is ultimately real at all. Then the author moves his characters quickly to the ranch — Kiowa, of course, but called Las Chivas (the goats) in the story. Lou finds the place for sale on arrival in Taos. She goes up with Phoenix to look at it. He is the last illusion of human maleness to be stripped away, in the decision that Lou makes about him on the way up the mountain: he is by nature a servant, and out here he displays that quality of the modern Indian not visible in England, a faint repulsiveness and furtiveness.

On seeing the ranch, Lou at once feels the sacredness, the blessed-ness, of the place, and knows she must find a replacement for virility here: *I can never, never mate with any man, since the mystic new man*   SA, 129 *will never come to me.* She is convinced that the place itself, *a wild*   SA, 146 *spirit more than men,* wants her and that she can live in intimacy with it, immersed in a transcendent sexual emotion in which no individual man ever need be involved — in short, a perfected relation with place according to the principles the story has laid down.

Whether she can truly achieve this aim may be questioned when we compare her enthsuiasm with that of an otherwise unidentified *New*   SA, 134 *England woman,* who started out with a similar elation some time ago and was defeated by the spirit of place at the ranch, having at last to retreat to the village below. Yet we cannot feel the two women are alike. Really we do not know much about what sort the *New England woman* was, for she remains a dim figure, even though Lawrence adopts her point of view to relate the most impressive portion of the ranch's history. The reason for the failure of viewpoint here is that Lawrence chooses to represent in so shadowy a character his own gripping experience with spirit of place at the ranch that summer, his own breathless absorption with making *the nearness as perfect as the distance*. It was an ambivalent experience, as we might guess. The eternal "presence" of place is both menacing and reassuring, and with it Lawrence runs the whole gamut of awed fascination inevitable for him in any American spirit of place. Since it is impossible for this *New England woman*, barely alive at all, to receive all the experience her creator has thrust upon her, we do not know how to find her comparable to Lou Witt, who is so remarkably alive. The result, as to any bearing on Lou's future in union or disunion with place, is simply ambiguous. Lawrence could portray in memorable prose the magnificent landscape with its undercurrent of cruelty, but he could not do what he had set out to do: to put the supreme male symbol in a setting instinct with the same maleness. St. Mawr, in a word, is still in Texas.

SA, 137

Whatever these flaws may amount to, *St. Mawr* stands by itself in one respect. In no other piece of fiction does Lawrence succeed so well in representing the symbolic opposites of place that ruled his wandering: a deathly England against a life-giving virgin land. He might well feel what he wrote to Martin Secker: *Yes, the novelette* St. Mawr *is finished, . . . some beautiful creation of this locale and landscape here. But thank God I don't have to write it again. It took it out of me.*

LS, 60

Lawrence perhaps did a little work on *St. Mawr* after he came back from the Hopi snake dance on August 25, but his next great effort was to write on the ceremony he had just seen: first a flippant little piece and then, almost at once, a far longer essay which he felt *rather deeply about.* And with good reason, for it was his amplest statement yet on animism, and in a responsiveness complementary to the tales it anticipates the uncompleted task of re-creating the snake and eagle symbol in Mexico.

HL, 613

It was *a parched, grey country of snakes and eagles* into which he went to attend the dance, on Third Mesa, Arizona, to which in those days the road was hardly more than a rough trail. He found in the ceremony *none of the impressive beauty of the Corn Dance at Santo Domingo,* which we recall he had seen the preceding April and then written about. The Hopi dance was *uncouth rather than beautiful, and rather uncouth in its touch of horror.* But it was the best Indian

MM, 62

MM, 63

MM, 64

ceremony yet out of which Lawrence could weave through place and event what all three of the Indian articles written that summer set out to do: to define animistic religion as it still prevailed in America.

The dryness and sternness of the Hopi country had put man to the test, driven by some inward fate *to the top of these parched mesas,* MM, 67 as to how he might *get himself into relation with the vast living* MM, 65 *convulsions of rain and thunder and sun, . . . the vastest of cosmic beasts.* In short, here was a race like the individual women of this summer's fiction. Hopi culture recognized what Lawrence was finding so vital to fully realized being, that the *law of isolation is heavy on* MM, 64 *every creature.* By the tenets of Hopi religion it was not an individual but a species isolation. Therefore the Hopi's turning to snake and eagle as messengers to the greater potencies, the *cosmic beasts,* was no MM, 65 brotherhood appeal and the approach was always sure to be dangerous. Man has no means of drawing on these powers save by his *living will,* MM, 66 in exploitation of the one advantage in his favor, that everything in the universe works by analogy. The cosmos is greatly like a dragon, so that snakes are best able *to carry the message and thanks to the* MM, 76 *dragon-gods who can give and withhold,* serving as messengers to where *the earth's dark centre holds its dark sun, our source of isolated being,* MM, 68 *round which our world coils its folds like a great snake.* Often in this essay Lawrence comes close to the language of the poetry in *The Plumed Serpent.* That he had his coming endeavor in mind and that he hoped to carry over some of this spirit of the peaceful Hopis into it — a hope never realized — is plain from this important assertion in the middle of the article: *This is the religion of all aboriginal America.* MM, 66 *Peruvian, Aztec, Athabascan: perhaps the aboriginal religion of all the world. In Mexico, men fell into horror of the crude, pristine gods, the dragons. But to the pueblo Indian, the most terrible dragon is still somewhat gentle-hearted.*

The Mexican spirit of place was still what Lawrence had most to fear and yet to seek in America. He could not even maintain this softened view of the Indian throughout the sketch. Even with the Hopi, he later thinks, *cruelty is coiled in the very beginnings of all* MM, 78 *things.*

In late September and early October, his final weeks at Kiowa Ranch in 1924, Lawrence wrote "The Princess," another tale involved with the horse as a bearer toward the living core of things — all three of the tales from this time are a climax to Lawrence's own horseback riding, which he did only in America — and another of the attempts to recall masculinity to a position of greatness. "The Princess" does not come up to the other two tales in scope, but for all that it is a fine story, with modifications of the pilgrim and place themes that bring about a special equilibrium between it and *St. Mawr,* and to a lesser degree between it and "The Woman Who Rode Away."

Dollie Urquhart, a "princess" because her eccentric father always calls her that, is brought up to believe that he and she are the last of a royal race. Colin Urquhart sounds quite like Lawrence himself when he says that a "demon" rules at the core of everyone, and that a certain few of these demons form a natural nobility. The aloneness that Urquhart cultivates in the midst of a busy and much traveled life, and teaches his daughter to cultivate, on the surface appears Laurentian enough. But it is all sham, in fact, for Colin Urquhart does not draw his isola-

SH, 474   tion from a profound inner source. He is simply vague and *absent* and draws only on a vain pride.

While her father lives, till she is thirty-eight, the Princess grows into an exquisite, scentless virgin flower, father and daughter sufficient to themselves. Sensuality for her remains a grotesqueness to be smiled at. However, the wilderness of the American West, to which she is exposed when she goes off camping and canoeing with her outdoor-loving father, secretly plants in her soul what will in time undermine her false integrity. The force begins to work as soon as her father dies. Travel she must, now more than ever. But whereas Europe was formerly the magnet and the United States an uncouth hinterland, at present the Southwest lures her. She is soon installed at a guest ranch with much the air of Mabel Dodge Luhan's compound for artists about it. She is back now at the edge of this wilderness into which her father so often led her, and like Lou Witt she is drawn to it as the access to male power — except that with the Princess the impulse at first is purely unconscious.

And so, once in New Mexico, the Princess entertains the idea of marriage, an obscure longing for a prince to complete her ego. The man who attracts her is soon at hand, and a familiar dark-man/light-woman Laurentian pair emerge. Domingo Romero, now a guide at the ranch, is also, like the Princess, the last of an aristocratic line, an old Spanish-American family — though as described he seems more Indian, and like Phoenix owes much to Lawrence's view of Tony Luhan, the Taos Indian whom Mabel Dodge eventually married. Member of a superseded race, Romero is almost gone in what Lawrence classifies as Penitente death worship, and this in the Spanish colonists he attrib-

SH,   utes to the influence of place: *Unable to wrest a positive significance*
482–483   *for themselves from the vast, beautiful, but vindictive landscape they were born into, they turned on their own selves, and worshipped death through self-torture.* The Spanish of the Southwest, then, as Lawrence

would have it, have never reached the oneness with the land that the Hopis enjoy.

The Princess does recognize in Romero's eye, however, a glint of dauntlessness beyond despair. This means to her that he is a fellow natural aristocrat and hence fated to intimacy with her — all of which develops still in a Laurentian pattern promising success. But the Princess does not know, cannot know, what marriage is. She welcomes from Romero's heart to hers *a dark beam of succour and sustaining,*   SH, 485 even though his smile often suggests a savage grotesquerie. Consciously she experiences no need to marry him. Their *two 'dœmons'* are mar-   SH, 486 ried already. Their *selves,* body and all, she cannot picture as ever being together.

And yet she cannot prevent herself from subconsciously casting their attraction upon this mountain landscape and resolving to go with him, ostensibly only as her guide, high up *to look over the mountains*   SH, *into their secret heart, . . . to see the wild animals move about in their*   487–488 *wild unconsciousness.* We have regressed, then, to the atmosphere of the first poetry written in America, the search for conjunction with both land and fauna. The rest of the story unfolds in what is one of Lawrence's best pieces of conjoining between landscape and psychic desire — the link that he failed to forge in *St. Mawr,* for all the magnificence of that tale.

It is early October — just when Lawrence finished the story — when the Princess and Romero and her friend and companion, Miss Cummins, set off for an abandoned shack way up among the peaks, where Romero says there is *a little round pond* that wild animals come   SH, 487 to. They climb on horseback among the blue shadow and dark green bulks towering overhead, and the red of oak scrub and the yellow of aspen. The quest is marvelously visualized, the Princess following Romero as initiator into an unconscious realm. *With that black, un-*   SH, 489 *heeding figure always travelling away from her* she *felt strangely help-* *less, withal elated.* How close to herself she is she really knows when a chill enters her heart on realizing that *a tangle of decay and despair*   SH, 490 *lay in the virgin forests.* Miss Cummins, an obvious symbol of self-control, is soon eliminated: her horse injures itself, not badly, but out of a timorous kindness to animals she refuses to proceed.

But the Princess will not turn back. Once Romero has seen Miss Cummins part of the way down, he must come back to where the Princess waits and continue with her alone, for *there will never be*   SH, 493 *another day* to carry out her desire. Lawrence never allows us to forget the duality of all this, spacing expertly such phrases as the *fierce, heavy*   SH, 494 *cruel mountains, with their moments of tenderness.*

SH, 497   As they go on, Romero becomes to the Princess thoroughly *strange and ominous, only the demon of himself,* and she grows more perturbed, compelled to look into *the massive, gruesome, repellent core of the Rockies.* At one place the horses have to slide and scramble down, at another the ride is against a knifing wind. But they finally do arrive at the cabin, with its spruce grove and its pond close by.

The action of "The Princess" follows a similar structure to that of "The Woman Who Rode Away," but it is even more reminiscent of all the previous pilgrimages undertaken partially or totally against the pilgrim's will: in *Women in Love,* in *The Lost Girl,* in *The Captain's Doll,* all of them into mountain country, sometimes to triumph and sometimes to be destroyed by the utterly naked core of the self encountered there. The simultaneously geographical and metaphysical journey of the puritan seeker is nowhere better exemplified in Lawrence than in the three tales he spun out so rapidly in mid-1924 and, with the exception of the later stages of *St. Mawr,* with such assurance of theme and execution.

The Princess sees her wild animals, all right, particularly a bobcat SH, 501 that watches her *demonish and conscienceless* across the pond: the body of water that so consistently recurs in the quest topography of Lawrence's America. In the night, now, her struggle becomes always SH, 503 more intense. She wants *to be taken away from herself* and at the same time *to keep herself intact, intact, untouched.* She at last invites Ro- SH, 504 mero to her bed and submits to his *terrible animal warmth that seemed to annihilate her.* Her all but unbreakable virginity is at last ruptured, at any rate in her body.

Then comes the revulsion. Her virginity of soul is after all impenetrable. Her cold repudiation of her night with Romero plunges him into despair and cruelty. He takes away her clothes, tosses them into the pond in a perfectly symbolic gesture, along with her saddle and his. They are beyond where even horses can carry them. They are indeed two demons facing one another now, and with Romero love and death are too closely allied for him to lose love except by death. Her calling him to her in the night is unretractable mating to him. He will not take her out of the mountains till she consents either to marry or to live with him. She continues to refuse, yet she does not hate him. She knows full well that he is her doom. The tragic and the fatalistic in the last male stronghold of Romero's character can only take over now. Nothing can come of this contest but death. The Princess reaches the point where she might agree to stay with him to escape this deadlock, but she will never confess to liking the idea.

Knowing in time that he will likely be sent to jail for kidnapping if he goes back to the lower world, Romero fires on the two horsemen who come in search of them, killing one of the horses. Even in the last stages of the ensuing gun battle, after a moment of thinking she might love him, the utter enclosedness of the Princess reasserts itself. No, she will never love a man. One of the rescuers kills Romero. The Princess is "freed," and now protects her inner fixity by the pretense that Romero went mad.

But she does at length marry an elderly father substitute. An important element of her self-delusion henceforth is that a madman up there in the mountains had shot her horse from under her. He had indeed.

The best way to appreciate the brilliant accomplishment of the three tales just discussed is to read them together in order of composition — Lawrence intended that they be published as a separate volume, but as yet they never have been — and with these to read "Pan in America" and the three Indian sketches. At no other period of his life since *The Rainbow* and *Women in Love* had Lawrence achieved such a concentration of power and poured it forth on the page in such prose.

That Lawrence completed "The Princess" just as he was about to head for Mexico and the resumption of his Quetzalcoatl novel has its own significance. The magnificent male, the Pan-presence, could not come to exist in human form and possess the true female in the New Mexico Rockies. So Lawrence killed off the last near-embodiment of Pan in Romero. Five days before he perpetrated this act, he was *look-* ML, 811 *ing out of the kitchen door* of his cabin *at the far blue mountains, and the gap, the tiny gate that leads down into the canyon and away to Santa Fe. And in ten days' time we shall be going south — to Mexico.* He could hope for further creation in that always creative direction, the South.

The move was soon accomplished. The Lawrences and Brett were in Mexico City by October 23, and by November 9 in Oaxaca, a place he had long desired to see. Dorothy Brett reports that once the Law- LA, 181 rences had rented a house and moved in, he looked over the *Quetzalcoatl* manuscript and declared that he would write the book all over again, being now in a more *untouched* part of Mexico than Lake Chapala and finding here an easier access to the spirit of the country.

The novel that Lawrence now embarked on turned out to be the most daring and baffling of all his experiments in long fiction. It was no less than an attempt, elaborated through a largely invented myth and ritual, to resuscitate and to establish in the people and institutions of a Mexico of his own imagining the ancient Aztec gods — or rather Toltec, since he felt that the Aztec gods were already degenerate descendants of the glorious old deities of earlier American culture.

MITLA, OAXACA

Mitla under its hills,
in the parched valley where a wind blows the dust and
the dead souls of the vanished race in terrible gusts (PS, 75)

In the New Mexico tales he might conceive of the spirit of the continent operating on the level of the isolated psyche, but in Mexico, a country of revolution at that time, he would not let himself escape facing all the implications — individual, social, political and religious — of the deepest connections between dark self and primeval place.

All of this task Lawrence had already set for himself in *The First Quetzalcoatl*. His realization that he had not succeeded is not only verified but characterized by his remark to Dorothy Brett. It was not the specific place Oaxaca on which the matter centered: he retained Lake Chapala as the setting. It was that the spirit of Mexico, like that of New Mexico, had taken a long time to work its complete magic in him. For the second time now the American Southwest had served as a threshold to what must be the ultimate meeting ground between Lawrence's spirit and that of the continent, the most Indian of North American places, Mexico. The control he had wrought out of the struggle with his material at the ranch in the Southwest carried him great strides forward in his renewed engagement with the Mexican spirit of place and enabled him to put together the intimations of primitivism in the Valley of Oaxaca and the aura of the lake, both absolutely necessary to his purpose.

Whatever Lawrence may have failed to accomplish in *The Plumed Serpent,* he succeeded magnificently in extrapolating from the actual country of tumult and bloodshed a fictional Mexico where events do often glimmer with the magic of myth. The responses of the three principal characters to their situation are often powerfully convincing, even when those responses are by ordinary standards bizarre, and what contributes most to this conviction is their efforts to put themselves in harmony with the intensely created place. When spirit of place and spirit of person do reach accord, then the subconscious self that was always Lawrence's true subject fuses into a mythic self to a degree unexcelled in any other novel of his.

This mythic dimension of search is set forth from the beginning, when Kate's subliminal self is repelled by the bullfight in the first chapter, where the bullring represents the little circle of degeneration and despair ruling this land where the most ancient of cultures, in a form still able to stir, meets with the worst of the modern industrial materialism. The rebellious, seeking self in Kate, who would re-establish vital contact with the deep blood surge in the cosmos and simultaneously with the center of her own being, finds itself thrown into conflict, in all the first four chapters of the novel, with the many and ubiquitous manifestations of modern degeneracy: in the sensational and decadent rites of the bullring; in the omnivorous and indiscriminate sensationalism of the tourist mentality in her American companions, Rhys and

Villiers; in the clash going on at the political and economic level between socialism and a brutal paternalism subservient to foreign business interests; in the mural art sponsored by the progressive government, with its political and social message along Marxist lines. Kate resists all these overpowering influences. In the puritan scheme of throwing off the yoke of evil and going in quest of eternal good, Mexico City exemplifies the whole modern world as City of Destruction. Given all the stresses at work here, Lawrence could hardly have found a better place to draw the battle line between the two worlds whose clashing was the main impetus of his art and life.

Mexico offered, besides, an ideal culmination of place for reconciling male and female being with each other and with the cosmos. While confronting Mexico City, Kate must also meet the realization of her fortieth birthday — Lawrence himself was in his fortieth year, though several months short of that birthday, when he wrote of Kate's dilemma. She must now come to know what it means to be a fully mature woman, one having a right relation with real masculinity, which of course she must identify before she can relate to it. Standing on the rooftop of her hotel within the toils of this city of the damned, she can still look away across the distance to the two mountains dominating the Valley of Mexico. The expansion of topographical symbolism that begins with these peaks functions by a careful coordination of male-female universality and death-rebirth complexity. The proximity of themes is not new, but it evolves more naturally here in death-ridden Mexico than in some other parts of the world. The two volcanoes have carried a male and female identity since pre-Columbian times and carry still their Nahuatl names: Ixtaccihuatl, the White Woman, and the male Popocatepetl, the Smoking Mountain.[1] And the mountains seem to reveal also how gripped this landscape is by the old indigenous death-worship, which brings Kate to ask herself the most difficult of

PS, 44   questions: *Why had she come to this high plateau of death?*

The unravelling of this question will, of course, require the action of the whole novel. At the moment her self-examination before spirit of place tells her chiefly that whereas in pre-Conquest times *Mexico had had an elaborate ritual of death,* it now has only what she has seen epitomized in the bullfight and all the lifelessness of modern society in this valley: *death ragged, squalid, vulgar, without even the passion of its own mystery.*

A recapitulation is again in order. The situation of Kate Leslie before the Mexican mountains picks up a theme that goes winding back through the New Mexico tales to *The Lost Girl* and Alvina Houghton's presence before deathly yet ultimately life-giving mountains in the cold Abruzzi, to her surrender to a maleness in Ciccio that holds the promise of America after the war. Another former expression of the theme is the emphatic assertion of masculinity in the mountains formulated in *The Captain's Doll*. But here in *The Plumed Serpent* some further affirmation of place is essential, beyond mountains. To repeat a point made in discussing *The First Quetzalcoatl,* Lawrence now had recourse to a lake as the matrix of rebirth, the sort of lake for which he had been preparing his themes since meeting with Glimmerglass in Cooper. In *The Plumed Serpent* the newspaper item that reports the rising of a golden man from Lake Sayula — west of Mexico City in the quarter of creation — is much expanded and mythologized over the simple "factual" paragraph given in the first form of the novel. The *Plumed Serpent* account brings the lake to Kate's imagination in *a strange beam of wonder and mystery.*   PS, 53

All of this comes to solving the mystery of self through solving the mystery of place. Ramón Carrasco, the leader of the Quetzalcoatl religious movement, has been engaged in a similar effort much longer than Kate, for most of his adult life. He has in *The Plumed Serpent* almost none of the Indian blood attributed to him in *The First Quetzalcoatl,* being now nearly pure Spanish and French. He brings to mind Lawrence's thought on the movement of peoples in the "Spirit of Place" essay. Ramón is the long since transplanted European who has come to the point at last of doing what Lawrence insisted all white culture in America must do to flourish: to admit into his life venture the soul of the vanquished Indian. Ramón has completely embraced the aboriginal and is determined to make it flower again in a pagan revival centered on the Lake of Sayula as navel of the earth.

This total change in the racial character of Ramón between versions of *The Plumed Serpent* puts the matter more in conformity with the author's own identity expedition into the New World. Not only does a new form of the old male splendor seem still attainable in America, but the reawakening is now made possible in a hero like his creator. Of great significance also, the relationship between males which can be established between the new Ramón and the new Cipriano is more in keeping with Lawrence's concepts of long standing on a brotherhood in the wilderness: a Natty Bumppo-Chingachgook brotherhood prophetic of a new humanity. For whereas Ramón has become almost pure white, Cipriano has been transformed into a full-blood Indian, a Zapotec and therefore closer to the earliest antiquity of the native American than the Aztecs were.

Yet while he is of blood indigenous to Mexico, Cipriano's role in the novel is more enigmatic than that of Ramón or of Kate. For one thing, he is Oxford-educated, with all the contradictions that this crossing of cultures implies. Beyond a vague identification with Mexican darkness, he stood for a long time arrested between worlds. He renounced any thought of the Catholic priesthood he was being educated for to become a general among the men of the Mexican Revolution. But he seems to have had no firm convictions on what he might make of Mexico, or Mexico of him, till he came under the influence of Ramón and adopted his beliefs. So that for all the fierceness and activity he soon displays, Cipriano is powerless to fulfill himself in relation to Mexico without the support and direction of the white race. His necessity extends not only to Ramón but to Kate. A priest-like celibacy is all that Cipriano has retained of his former religion, and we soon learn why. He must be a lover on the level of deified senses. He can fall in love with Kate because in his eyes she replaces the Virgin Mary of his youth. Kate is not long in sensing *the intense masculine yearning, coupled with a certain male ferocity, in the man's breast.* The situation goes beyond Christian analogies, of course, for before long Kate will play Ixtaccihuatl to Cipriano's Popocatepetl and be deified with him in the pantheon of the new religion. As to the fundamental role of Cipriano, all this produces a curious development in *The Plumed Serpent.* The religion deep in the soul of Mexico may be his, but his access to it must come through Ramón as hierophant and Kate as white goddess, counterpart to that other imported fair goddess, the Virgin Mary.

PS, 65

Lawrence proposes to make of Cipriano an authentic incarnation of Mexico, to fashion at last a reality out of the long dream of true maledom. The character's endeavor to define his religion through the other two chief figures is one approach to clarifying his nature. On a broader plane we are presented with Cipriano as Mexico through two interwoven but often opposed sets of attitudes, neither simple in itself: the set of attitudes centered in Ramón and that centered in Kate. On this interplay the structure of the novel depends. Without close attention to what each view represents and the radical shifts in direction Lawrence takes in reconciling if not resolving these two points of view, one may conclude that *The Plumed Serpent* is obscure and confused if not some sort of excursion into madness. Many implications attach to the dichotomy, but all of them hinge upon a central dual question: What is essential manhood, and what will Mexico be when this sort of manhood is brought back to it?

It will be best to deal with Ramón's side of these matters to begin with, for, as we will see, Kate's is the last word on all that the novel builds up, as far as Lawrence could reach one.

The Plumed Serpent does not enter into Ramón's past to the extent that *The First Quetzalcoatl* does. But here too Ramón is plainly a

man who has gone in quest of life's meaning, gone out to free himself
from the past of his country and from his own, a quest that led him
through a college education in the United States. But having seen what
modern intellectualism has to offer towards the making of a true man,
he has repudiated it as sham and come home to complete the circle of
his pilgrimage and seek under the burdensome immediate past of
Mexico the oldest stratum of national being where true maleness lies.
"There is no liberty for a man, apart from the God of his manhood," PS, 68
he tells Kate, and when pressed to explain, he can only speak in such
terms as Lawrence's surrogates perennially employ: *"One is driven,
at last, back to the far distance, to look for God."* But this remoteness,
to Ramón, is extremely close to home: it is at the center of himself
and at the center of his native land. He is thus a new experiment for
Lawrence, whose fictional protagonists up to now have always sought
on foreign soil the proper geography for reuniting with older godhead,
as indeed Kate Leslie does in this novel. Lawrence's invention of
Ramón Carrasco as the prophet to remake America in its original
image, instead of choosing an English spiritual explorer in a far land
according to his usual pattern, shows a determination to confront the
duality of America as near to the source as possible. That is, as we
have seen, Lawrence felt in frustrating proportions both a death-deal-
ing and a life-giving quality in America more powerfully than he felt
them anywhere else in the world, and he could not always see the
deathly quality as that which is preparatory to resurrection. America
held a dangerous potential of reversion to ways that would sink any
post-technological culture into the morass of bloodshed which had
suffocated the Aztecs. It is in the cruelty and death which creeps into
The Plumed Serpent that we discover Lawrence flinching away from
his own vision and caught up in the fear that after all not every tremor
of the unconscious is good at the source. Sheer evil does exist, and it
makes itself felt in the pattern of this novel almost in spite of the writer.
But there is a route past this disastrous region of the American soul,
Lawrence is convinced, and it lies a great way back in the spirit of place.
This is the quest that Ramón is intent on, sometimes with clear vision,
sometimes not: the regression to pick up the true thread of instinctive
being, to retrieve the oldest and best of symbols in the concept of
Quetzalcoatl and proceed bravely to the future. As Ramón puts it,
"Quetzalcoatl is to me only the symbol of the best a man may be, in PS, 270
the next days."

     Lawrence's claim had always been that myth and ceremony must
concretely express the best of human conditions. Ramón puts this
belief into effect with his elaborate rituals of drum and dance and song
done in costumes based on native Mexican garb. A new mythology
is propounded, mostly written by Ramón and influenced by the Indian

and the esoteric literature Lawrence had read. It is a mythology of cycles, of gods growing old and returning to the bath of renewed life far off behind the sun, their departure bringing about the opening of a new cycle with restored gods. As Quetzalcoatl once had to give way to Jesus, now Jesus must give way to him. For one of his ceremonies Ramón devises a farewell to Christianity by removing all Christian images from the village church next to the lake and burning them on a nearby island. Next comes the welcoming of the new gods, the installation of their images. Then eventually come deification ceremonies in which Ramón and Cipriano are themselves invested with godhood as Quetzalcoatl and Huitzilopochtli. The rhythm of life that the novel brings to pass around the lake, navel of the new world, moves in renewed awareness of the universal mystery in a communal pattern. Rananim is here, and much more than Rananim.

But it would be a great mistake to see in *The Plumed Serpent* a whole-hearted affirmation on Lawrence's part of what Ramón is doing.[2] Getting near the heart of the duality of Mexico does not lead to a resolution of the dilemma but only to a brilliant revelation of its nature. The crux of the matter is again Cipriano, the complete embodiment of Mexico in the final version of the novel as he never was in the first draft. In spite of his aim to get back to the most primitive and beneficent god in Mexico, Ramón chooses as his chief disciple a man who represents in almost equal degrees both the earliest and most creative pulse of the native American and the Aztec blood-lust. General Viedma develops a thirst for an all-out holy war that Ramón must keep in check. Cipriano can even act like the prototype of a Mexican revolutionary general, whose crusade is for himself and for no principle. Yet, curiously enough, Ramón is already endangering the future of his Mexico when he agrees to make a ritual sacrifice of the execution of some men who made an attempt on his life, even allowing Cipriano to wield the knife. Ramón is not capable here, nor does he ever become so, of wholly dissipating from his vision of the future the possible reversal to blood-lust.

Kate embodies Lawrence's primary examination of his own attitudes toward America, that is to say, of Mexico as a place for a new quickening of true maledom. For her as well the chief problem is adjustment to a life of which Cipriano is the key. She enters with him by degrees into a sexual relation which has all the divine sense of mystery that Lawrence's theme demands. It is from the start a marriage partaking of the new impulse to mystical knowledge. It leads in time to ceremonial intercourse in the newly dedicated temple, an act which carries Kate so far as to recognize Cipriano as a true god. Whether he kills people as Cipriano Viedma or not is immaterial. He is a god who can make her virginal again each time he takes her, and who teaches her that real contact for a woman with the divine regions of physical love is not in clitoral orgasm but in something deeper, darker, more passive and vaginal.

We must pause for a while over this extreme development in Kate's search for regeneration, not for the purpose of dwelling on the obvious point that the novelist as lordly male is pressing for the submission of woman at any cost, but for the purpose of inquiring whether he achieves any authentic fictional semblance of unconscious experience. What first comes to mind is that Cipriano condenses and personifies the whole male energy of America, fragments of which we have met with in Lou Witt's *wild spirit more than men* of the mountains, in Romero of "The Princess," in the young *cacique* of "The Woman Who Rode Away." The rejuvenation of woman here personified in Kate comes about by total contact with this potency. America the place has at last found its precise boundaries in male form, and the questing European soul has had its ultimate fructifying union with that spirit of place.

SA, 146

This, at least, was Lawrence's plain intention, consistent with the purpose of the whole novel to restore demi-gods to the earth. Kate must see her dark lover as of divine origin. Let her be, says Lawrence's attempted fictional logic, a kind of Leda to Cipriano's swan. Certainly, if Lawrence could transfer such a conviction to the reader, Kate would enter as a consequence into the mythical frame of mind that refuses human moral standards, the frame of mind that allows Zeus to take virginities and slay thousands without submitting to human judgment as brutal or bloodthirsty. To descend the scale a bit, if Cipriano exists at the level of some classical or Biblical hero, he can belong to a class of worthies who in legend help themselves to virgins and slaughter indiscriminately without losing, to this day, their heroic stature. We would do well to remember that these stories of old are no working off of some peripheral violence at the edges of an otherwise "healthy" human consciousness. They embody the tangle of love and violent death which lies near the center of the human soul and which is fed there by nature itself. We realize, though we can seldom afford to face the fact and hope for gods to save us from it, that all we really know of the life force is that it seems to be composed equally of the will to create and the will to destroy: to create in order to destroy, to destroy in order to create again — the cycle of virginity and death. The ancient myths take account of this inexplicable course of existence, which goes its way oblivious to any morality we can devise. The modern story knows no way to encompass it.

In this respect, as in all others, *The Plumed Serpent* is Lawrence's bid to re-create a mythic consciousness out of America and a story form to contain it. He fails, of course, for he is attempting a feat probably beyond the grasp of any modern writer. Still there is good reason to admire his boldness in striving for a form to reach a plane of experience that we know to be real enough still, even if we have lost the faculty for incorporating it into our conscious lives. A remarkable failure is a great thing in itself, particularly if the author recognizes his failure and manages to assimilate it into his work. This Lawrence did, as the whole course of Kate's experience discloses.

Immediately after Kate's apparently utter surrender to the glorified male, Lawrence puts the whole matter of her experience to a further test. Ramón's first wife has brought on her own destruction by violent opposition to her husband's cause, collapsing at last in a frenzy. He later takes a second wife, Teresa, who is at last the truly submissive woman in a world of perfected male authority. In this definitive version of Lawrence's American novel, Kate faces squarely, by comparing herself with Teresa, the choice she has already gone a long way toward making. Is she to remain in Mexico as the new woman this land now requires, to the extent of becoming altogether a goddess in the pantheon, or, when the problem at last issues in a choice of places, is she to return to England to a catty middle-age in London drawing rooms? The Mexico of the novel is the future, the England the past: two selves, two times, two places.

The dilemma is never entirely solved, and Lawrence tacitly admits his inability to solve it. Kate — and Lawrence with her — can never quite bring herself to trust this rampant maleness. She rejects becoming like Teresa, when all is said and done. Back and forth her mind goes, as the novel approaches its end, between Mexico and England. Her

PS, 438 conclusion is that she *must have both,* and although she veers around considerably before her last words, she does not essentially alter this decisive indecision. She goes back to Ramón and Cipriano near the

PS, 442 end *to make a sort of submission.* Seeing them immersed in the ceremonial male chanting, she feels an intruder, however, and also questions again whether she really wishes to commit herself wholly to their movement. Her way out of the dilemma, if it can be called a way out, is to resort to the feminine alternative of tears and a plea that she is not loved and appreciated. When Cipriano breaks into hot protestations to the contrary, her reply, which ends the novel, is to the effect that he and what he stands for are irresistible, hence inescapable: her

PS, 443 culminating words are *"You won't let me go!"*

No Lawrence novel enjoys a truly decisive ending, and this one is perhaps the most indecisive of all. The hesitancy begins some time before Kate's final unconsenting consent, in what Lawrence had ultimately to make of the religio-political issues he had aroused. The

Quetzalcoatl crusade succeeds, ousts Christianity as the state religion, and at the same time brings about a reawakening of the blood, with baptisms in the sea and *a great sense of release, almost of exuberance.* **PS, 419** Still, Lawrence never fails to mention the sense of violence, the touch of horror underneath. If the Minoan distance of time and place might seem in resurgence at last, to sweep away the moribund civilization of the spirit, Lawrence still could not set aside the old question of America, especially of Mexico: was the spirit of place here ultimately malevolent after all? The issue is not settled. Lawrence goes on, in leading up to Kate's final endeavor to grasp the enigma, by limiting the scope of the novel from the unsolved public themes to the private themes, eventually down to the dimensions simply of the basic feeling between Kate and Cipriano: and even here, to repeat, no final resolution offers.

The inescapable difficulty in appreciating *The Plumed Serpent* may result, then, in the reader believing that Lawrence is shirking the issue. And if the crushing events of bloodshed and barbaric apotheosis from earlier in the book are seen to overshadow this ending, and to demolish Kate's always weakening and reviving skepticism of the world the book makes, then the reader may conclude that Lawrence created, before the fact and with implied approval, a totalitarian horror of a society. But it seems to me that the interplay of forces in *The Plumed Serpent* goes much deeper than these overtones of Lawrence's probing so easily lead the reader to suspect. At best he was only partly aware of what he was doing. But if we set the Mexico of the novel among the places which brought him to the pass of writing his American novel, we catch sight of other forces at work within the novel that epitomize the extremity of his search, an extremity that led him not only to the limits of what he had conceived to be the restorative powers of the dark gods but over the border into profound contradictions concealed beyond the gates of entry into this new world. He had spoken of *a vast* **HL, 565** *death-happening* that must take place before *the next real thing* **HL, 564** might come about in America. But when his novel led him over the frontier into the next America, the *death-happening* clung to it still: he could not disentangle his critical intelligence from the new dark land, but he could not force approval of that dark way on this intelligence either. The progression of places, and with that the ever-changing, never-changing search for pure manhood, lays out a clear path to this climax of Mexico in Lawrence's pilgrimage: the grave of England, the temporary breath of life in Aaron's Florence, the fatalistic attraction of Europe's mountains to Alvina Houghton, the outreach for divinity and manhood in the Australian bush, the firm but awe-struck hold on these twin realities finally taken in the novellas of New Mexico

— all this culminated in the Mexico of *The Plumed Serpent*. In this place created to actualize at last the reign of the Holy Ghost, from the lowest practical level of Rananim to the highest point of direct incarnation of the gods in men, Lawrence was forced to recognize in spite of himself the ambiguity of his vision: the dark self and its gods encompass not only the pure and spontaneous being but the frightful alternative of atavistic destruction. Kate is alert to this alternative early PS, 133 in the novel, to a possible new burgeoning of *old, evil forms of consciousness* more easily in Mexico than elsewhere. The clear intention of her creator is to make of Ramón's revival of earlier lifeways a dividing force between the old forms of evil and of good, the evil repressed and the good flowering forth. The triumph is never reached and the implications threaded together in the final course of the novel tell us conclusively that it is never to be reached.

The clearest of these implications are to be sought in how Mexico as the world reborn finally stands in the sensibilities of the three main characters. Ramón continues idealistic and confident, through the submissiveness of his new wife and his political activities, which are now curiously but revealingly remote from the center of this political novel. Cipriano is the glorious conqueror, sexually dominant and capable of engaging in bloodshed as the gods must hold human bloodshed to be. But the telling discrepancy continues between all that Cipriano is or may be and the limitations of Ramón's view of him. As for Kate, we have already seen how Lawrence brings about in her a fully realized dilemma in relation to Cipriano and to Mexico — maleness and place conjoined — which is an unblinking portrait of Lawrence's own divided condition and in no way a shirking of the issues.

In my view, this impassioned inconclusiveness does not detract from the novel if we read it as all Lawrence novels must in the last analysis be read, not as isolated triumphs or failures as works of art in themselves alone, but as stages in Lawrence's odyssey of the blood, the deeply puritan investigation of the heretofore, the here and now, and the hereafter, an odyssey that must always be seen within the context of places existing as both created and creating in relation to the questing soul.

For a whole view of what Lawrence's art was grappling with in the era of *The Plumed Serpent,* we must set the novel into a framework with three other works dating from his final months of writing it. First, those travel sketches which alone can truly stand under the heading "Mornings in Mexico" — those written in Oaxaca in December 1924, just before he finished the novel provisionally in January. Next, the "Flying Fish" fragment he partially dictated to Frieda when he lay ill to the point of death. Then the play *David,* written largely after

Lawrence's return to Kiowa Ranch in the significant interval when he was holding off from putting the final revisions to *The Plumed Serpent*. "The Flying Fish" and *David* will fall more naturally into the following chapter. The "Mornings in Mexico" sketches will give us a crowning view of what Lawrence felt as most compelling about the place from which he was drawing his inspiration as he tackled the final stages of his novel.

Doubtless Lawrence was acting under the influence of the impasse he saw *The Plumed Serpent* to be when he whipped off the four "Mornings in Mexico" pieces. For one thing they served as relief from the intense struggle with the fiction. They are filled with Lawrence's customary delighted observations of the world about him, but he takes the agile leap from this to cosmology in the manner employed since *Twilight in Italy*. The fascinating surface of Mexico has led him to a cosmology endemic to the land and in accord with his own inclinations. In the first sketch, the parrot and the little dog in his patio, and the Indian who works for him, suggest an interpretation of indigenous beliefs about time and space. The Aztecs did not view the ongoing of the universe as a process of evolution, which is simply a modern mistake, but as a series of annihilations and new creations. That they were right is evident from looking at the parrot, the dog, and man — or the monkey, so near in many ways to man and yet of another order entirely. Lawrence puts his estimate of the monkey like this: *He's got length*   MM, 7 *and breadth and height all right, and he's in the same universe of Space and Time as you are. But there's another dimension. He's different. There's no rope of evolution linking him to you, like a navel string. No! Between you and him there's a cataclysm and another dimension.* Apocalypse, the wiping out of the old cosmos and the ushering in of a new Sun, a new Age — evidence of this universal scheme that Lawrence gathered from the place where he was gave him imaginative support for his novel: for the wiping out of one set of gods in favor of another.

This first of the Mexico sketches finds Lawrence attempting, then, to state some imaginative correspondence between himself and his location, and to state it as he had attempted to do in *Twilight in Italy*: to see ultimate reality through observation of a locality. At the start of this sketch he places himself exactly: *One says Mexico: one means,*   MM, 1 *after all, one little town.* He sits there in his sunny patio writing, *one little individual looking at a bit of sky and trees, then looking down at the page of his exercise book.* He warns us that one such confined consciousness can hardly expect to issue authoritative estimates of large subjects. Yet this is just what he proceeds to do.

This day was Friday, December 19, 1924. Lawrence also turned out a sketch for Saturday, but apparently for thematic reasons he put

it last among the four. The next one in the published order takes place
on Sunday, and is called "Walk to Huayapa" (strictly, Huayapam), a
small village in the hills near Oaxaca. The acute observer, the man on
the road, here comes forth at his best, studying the fierce shyness of his
young Indian servant, Rosalino, and along with that the isolation, the
MM,   *lurking,* the *unwillingness* of this valley *wild and exalted with sunshine*
10 & 15 below *the stiffly pleated mountains,* with the distant village on the
MM, 11 slopes *magical, alone,* as though *a few white tiny buildings had been
lowered from heaven and left.* It was one of Lawrence's favorite points
of perspective, the drawing of his thought from places seen far off, in
time or space or both. The isolation of Mexico, of its human life, of
its spirit of place where contact at most is a touching and a swerving
away, and yet all the while the fascinating richness of the country:
this is the theme of Lawrence the pilgrim on seeking out the Mexican
village.

In the next piece, "The Mozo," Lawrence goes on with his impres-
sionistic analysis of the Mexican spirit by reporting how Rosalino's
actions in the week following the walk to Huayapam characterize him,
and by working outward from this individual who is so appealing to
MM, 23 him because Rosalino has *a certain sensitiveness and aloneness, as if
he were a mother's boy.* In this respect he stands in stark contrast to
the majority of Indian men, who seem to Lawrence in their tautness
and keenness to fulfill a mythical birth story that Lawrence calls to
mind in this Christmas season: the myth in which the Aztec goddess
of love brings forth the obsidian knife of sacrifice. But the contrast
is not far-reaching, in some ways, for in the depths of his heart Rosalino
too has the obsidian knife: he reacts into a black and fatalistic gloom
after the visit to Huayapam, which has brought on a profound homesickness for his own village in the hills. And here at the center of the
feelings he shares with the rest of his race lies the Indian sense of time
MM, 32 and place. *The Indians of the hills have a heavy, intense sort of attachment to their villages.* They have a gloom at their core that has long
prompted them to feed the sun as the only means of sustaining life. As
for distance, they know only the near and the far, and no such exact
measurements as miles. Out of this same inability to grasp anything
other than what the blood can sense comes their feeling for time,
which in its crudest form is the Mexican's *mañanismo.* This adhesion
to the present as the only reality had become a truly fascinating concept to Lawrence, the same one that he was trying to make fictionally
MM, 26 concrete in *The Plumed Serpent:* a return to living in *the naked moment
of the present disentangled* from past and future.

This sketch shows Lawrence to be ambivalent, inevitably, about
the native Mexican character and the spirit of the continent which it

HUAYAPAM, OAXACA

The ragged semi-squalor of a half-tropical lane (MM, 14)

reflected. He had long since declared the present moment to be the terrain of his own consciousness, and what we have seen as his sense of the near and the far would correspond to his estimate of the Indian feeling for distance. But a fear as well as a deep awe emerges in the phraseology of description at various points in the sketch, in such sentences as *the instant moment is forever keen with a razor-edge of oblivion, like the knife of sacrifice.*

The sketch placed last in this group of four takes up events of December 20, the day before the visit to Huayapam. But it rightly stands last because in it is concentrated that response to place and time from which Lawrence was spinning out these fundamental realities in his novel. The writer-discoverer sits in his patio as in the first sketch.

MM, 37   It is market day in Oaxaca: *From the valley villages and from the mountains the peasants and the Indians are coming in with supplies, the road is like a pilgrimage, with the dust in greatest haste, dashing for town.* This pilgrim motion and the setting in which it takes place, from close by to far away, yields a wealth of meaning to the observer. The Indian is essentially alone, as a person should be, but he does require contact now and then, and the trajectory of his movement to seek it, only to veer off again into his isolated hills or corner of valley, is to Lawrence the precise image of cosmic as well as social circularity.

MM, 42   The curve the Indian follows, like every curve, *plunges into the vortex and is lost, re-emerges with a certain relief and takes to the open, and there is lost again.* This same adherence to circles and cycles is per-

MM, 35   ceivable everywhere. The branches above the patio have a *reeling, roundward motion* in the wind. The clouds follow suit. In this swoop

MM,   around *the bend of the inevitable. . . . There is no goal, and no abiding-*

36 & 42 *place, and nothing is fixed.* There is *nothing but the touch, the spark of contact.* It is Lawrence's world of the imagination established in harmonious analogy with the place where he happened at the time to be in his pilgrimage, and the sketch discovers a congruent order between the vision he strove for in *The Plumed Serpent* and the actual land that was the novel's source. He ends the piece with the same kind of star imagery that the novel employs: the spark of contact in both

MM, 43   instances is *the flashing intermediary, the evening star that is seen only at the dividing of the day and night, but then is more wonderful than either.*

This discovery of perfection in the inward and outward flow of Indian culture plainly contradicts the assertion in the preceding sketch that in its knife-like isolation the Indian heart touches another largely in blood and violence. No doubt the effort of writing the sketches was in part dictated by the need to put into additional form the struggle with the same contradictions in the novel.

This inward battle to find the imaginative proportions of America as the most vital place to remaking the world ended in Lawrence's falling desperately ill around the first of February 1925, on the same day that he wrote the last page of *The Plumed Serpent*. Malaria may AL, 697 have been involved, certainly tuberculosis was. The halting journey north from Oaxaca, which at last brought Lawrence shattered but recovering to Kiowa Ranch in early April, was a pilgrimage indeed, a life-or-death quest. This journey taken under the conviction that it might well be his last wrought appreciable changes in Lawrence's outlook, changes that brought him to the threshold of his last period of existence.

NOTES

[1] According to an Aztec legend of which several versions survive in modern times, the two mountains personify a pair of lovers. An Aztec princess fell in love with a prince she could not marry because he was a foreigner. They met by stealth and suffered many tribulations that vary according to the version, but all agree that the princess died and left the prince in such sorrow that he swore to keep eternal vigil over her body. The gods were touched by such fidelity. In time the lovers either became the two mountains or were absorbed by the two mountains. The volcanic fire of Popocatepetl is the torch of the vigilant prince. The form of Ixtaccihuatl is that of the princess, who is only in a long deep sleep after all. Some versions have it that she will awake when the day comes for the European invaders to be driven out and Indian culture to be re-established. Lawrence may not have known the story but for him also the two mountains bide their time till the day of the Indian returns.

[2] There is no good reason to be misled by what Lawrence said in a letter: *I do mean what Ramón means — for all of us* (ML, 859). To do so is to set aside the first principle of literary criticism: that a work of fiction must be permitted to speak for itself.

13

The Only Thing Is To Build an Ark

When Lawrence was strong enough to travel, he and Frieda undertook the first stage of a return from outer limits, though it consisted only of taking a train from Oaxaca to Mexico City. Lawrence was still far from well, and as he fought to recover, having arrived in the Valley of Mex-

PS, 44 ico that Kate had prophetically thought of as a *high plateau of death,* he held for a while to the hope that a sea voyage, and strangely enough a return to England, would save him: even though he meant after a while to come back to Taos. But one doctor forbade this voyage to England and recommended instead that the patient go straight back to the New Mexican mountains. He did so, and there he did regain some semblance of health.

Lawrence left two significant imaginative records of this sickness nearly to death and the recuperation that followed. One of these propels the seeking soul into the sea voyage Lawrence was contemplating as a rebirth. This is the fragment called "The Flying Fish." The other is the play *David,* whose special qualities, almost unique among Lawrence's work, belong to the time of convalescence at Kiowa Ranch, although he had the idea of writing such a play from as early as the fall of 1924, maybe even before he went down to Mexico.

From the calamity of his Mexican illness to the end of his life five years later, Lawrence sought a differently circumscribed male reality, one enclosing itself against social and political spheres and boarding a vessel often real, often symbolic, sometimes both: a vessel occupied in isolation, or with a woman or a few kindred spirits only, heading into the final outreach of the pilgrim's traveling. The vessel was in many ways an ark, during this period which opens with "The Flying Fish" and closes with "The Ship of Death." Two parallel courses of imaginative outpouring run through the period, each determined by response to distinct sorts of place but sometimes swerving to merge. One course hints at or even finds its Ararat in England, the other in lands beyond seas or beyond centuries past or future.

"The Flying Fish" dates from this last stay of Lawrence in Mexico City, from the time he was first able to give dictation to Frieda, when he still thought he would be able to sail to England and in his mind was already on the way. He said years later that he had begun the story *so near the borderline of death* that he did not feel like going on   RC, 288
with it when he grew better, and so left it a fragment.

The story finds Gethin Day longing in his illness to leave Mexico and go home to tight little England, to his ancestral home of Daybrook, to end his many years' quest for the significance of life in world travel, the latest phase of which has landed him in *big wild countries* like   PH, 783
Mexico. He knows that death transports all men from this little day of our life to the Greater Day, which can be like a resurrection. But he is at last sure that he can never accomplish rebirth on foreign soil but only in his native country. So this fragment of fiction reduces the scope of pilgrimage to the bounds of England, and it does so through the symbolism of a book, a family relic that Gethin Day now calls to mind, the *Book of Days,* written by a kind of Sir Thomas Browne ancestor of his, Sir Gilbert Day. In the sixteenth century Sir Gilbert was himself a traveler, an adventurer on the Spanish Main who came home to build his symbology of life into his country house, Daybrook. The true quester, according to Sir Gilbert, must come to the greater reality while borne by the vessel of his ancestral home. Daybrook *rides within the*   PH, 781
Vale as an ark, he wrote, and *though I say that Daybrook is the ark of the Vale, I mean not the house itself, but He that Day, that lives in the house in his day. While Day there be in Daybrook, the floods shall not cover the Vale nor shall they ride over England completely.*

The symbolism of this book, with its insistence on home as the true place of spiritual expansion, Gethin Day has carried in his mind since childhood. The truth of it does not light up, however, except on the touch of death. Although not as ill as Lawrence was at the time of writing the story, Day has an attack of malaria and extensive contact with the deathliness of Mexico which create around him an overwhelming aura of death. What jars him most is a cablegram from his sister Lydia: *Come home else no Day in Daybrook,* by which he understands   PH, 780
that she is seriously ill if not, by now, dead. Lydia is twenty years his senior and has always remained the essential resident of the family seat, always putting to him the question, on any return to England: *"Are you still wandering? . . . You would find far more room for*   PH, 781
yourself in Daybrook than in these foreign parts, if you knew how to come into your own." To come into his own in the ark of Daybrook,

breasting the seas of modern society in England itself, is what Gethin Day sets out from Mexico to accomplish, as soon as he is able to travel.

It is scarcely necessary to point out at any length how this piece of fiction conforms to the pattern of experience we have traced from the beginning. The older sister is the mother figure, England if personified as place, from whom the traveler has always fled. News that his sister has died does reach Day before he leaves Mexico for England, prompting the dual response we associate with the mother, of release and a new

PH, 785   glimmer of sympathy. Now he can *think of her as quite near and comforting and real, whereas while she was alive, she was so utterly alien.* Close to the end of his stay on the western continent, and at the extremity of experience, Lawrence again found himself reaching out to unite two opposites of place and time through the image of his mother. At the start of his westernmost experience, he had assumed in the poem "Spirits Summoned West" that her ghost could be invoked out of the grave of England and unite with the wild spirit of the western continent as a feminine being capable of supporting in him a masculine wholeness. "The Flying Fish" refutes that possibility but offers a better alternative. America has brought to pass a key crisis of place

PH, 788   and time, *a gap in* [Day's] *time-space continuum,* to use Lawrence's phrase, which accomplishes the appeasement of the mother nemesis and sends the voyager back to man his ark in home waters. A network of experience appears with reverberations going back to the idea of a world-wide voyage in the early poem "The Shadow of Death."

Mexico and England are in this way brought into tragic juxtaposition as the near and the far lands, the two poles of significance between which Lawrence had moved within a magnetism of variable strength and direction since the start of his traveling days. What had been the near country is now the far country, and the far country he so eagerly sought has revealed by its nearness its absolute strangeness to his spirit. Between Mexico and England lie two regions to be traversed, both of them oceans. The first is restorative and strengthening, the Gulf of Mexico. We should not forget the actual experience Lawrence transformed here, which was his sailing from Vera Cruz to Southampton in November 1923, more than a year before his illness in Oaxaca. Nor should we forget the gist of that experience. He was going back to Frieda then, and to England for the first time since his post-war departure. He was returning to meet a willful woman and hoping to conquer her, which is precisely the conquest Lawrence

RC, 288   had in mind for Gethin Day on his way to becoming the *regenerate man* that he was meant ultimately to be.

In the Gulf, the initial segment of his journey toward the ancestral ark, Gethin Day makes two mystical discoveries. First, he sees confirmed the assertion of the visionary Sir Gilbert that life in our common day is like the twinkling of a flying fish rising from the water through the air, a momentary course of existence sustained *in a terror that was* PH, 793 *brilliant as joy, in a joy brilliant with terror,* before descending in willing subjection to the universal will back into the deeps, into the Greater Day. The figure of speech is analogous to that of Bede's sparrow, a symbol of traveling which occurs to Ursula as comfort in *The Rainbow.* And then comes the second revelation in the Gulf of Mexico, another symbol of voyage: a school of porpoises that Day watches in fascination for hours as they glide under the clear surface of the water almost touching the bow of the ship, in a *perfect balance* PH, 794 *of speed underneath, mingling among themselves in some strange single laughter of multiple consciousness.* This togetherness in ongoing, this joy of separateness in unison while propelling one's soul through the deep seas of the unknown, is the perfect emblem of Lawrence's desire for wholeness, and it is no wonder that he develops it here in two pages of beautiful prose. The concept is also a prefiguring of changes taking place during his illness leading him forward to what would discover its best form in *Lady Chatterley's Lover.*

Next intervenes the region of death, the other ocean, the Atlantic with England at its far shore, the waters *like a cemetery, an endless,* PH, 797 *infinite cemetery of greyness, where the bright, lost world of Atlantis is buried.* The kind of life conveyed by the porpoises has now sunk deep indeed. The ark which has before found its significance in a link with pure animation, through the animal life accompanying it on its way, is now a death-ship. We remember, however, that Lawrence meant to bring about a resurrected England, a New Jerusalem, once Gethin Day has regained the ark of his native vale.

The fragment ends here, in a *horribly travelling grey silence.* PH, 798 Gethin Day has not yet come close to regeneration. But his creator was reviving after deathly sickness and looking for another expansion of horizons. He wrote from Mexico City to Dorothy Brett at Kiowa Ranch, to which she had preceded the Lawrences by a few weeks, that he envied her *the great space and loneliness* of the mountains. At this DR, time he still expected to go to England, but he earnestly hoped that in a vol. 9, few months he would be back at the ranch. As we have seen, he was to 44 go there much sooner than he expected, when the sea voyage was forbidden, undertaking a long ordeal of a journey that almost terminated at the border because Lawrence's health was barely good enough to get him past American immigration officials.

His mood for the first few weeks at Kiowa Ranch, in the spring of 1925, was intimately bound up with his need to write something to get his spirit out of Mexico. He was in bed a great deal with relapses. He

ML, 834 watched the late flurries of snow, saw the first of *the hairy, pale mauve anemones that the Indians call owl flowers,* and contemplated the receding of the immediate past: *Lying on the porch this warm afternoon, with the pine-trees round, and the desert away below, and the Sangre de Cristo mountains with their snow pale and bluish blocking the way beyond, it seems already far to Coyoacán.* He read too, for instance, Charles Doughty's famous travel work, making his way, as

ML, 838 he put it, *through the sandy wastes of Doughty's* Arabia Deserta . . . *without quite knowing why.*

One task awaited completion that he shuddered to take up again.

ML, 840 He must *prune and correct, in typescript, The Plumed Serpent.* Against Mexico itself he felt a great revulsion, so deeply was that country implicated in his sickness. Still he announced to several that *The Plumed Serpent* was his most important novel to date, that it was worth the great cost to his health and emotions.

And so, much of his essential self was still in Mexico and panting for escape. To help accomplish this end, Lawrence turned his attention to imaginary places, to the Bible lands where he had never been but which had always expanded his mythic sense, lands he once identified in this way when speaking of their presence in the hymns that had

PX, 600 vivified his youth: *Galilee and Canaan, Moab and Kedron, those places that never existed on earth.* For equilibrium after the great expense of spirit in creating from native American legend, Lawrence turned to legend of the Old World and wrote his play *David,* which even so retains some mingling of New World elements.

For some time he had pondered trying his hand again at drama, the immediate impetus being his friendship with the actress Ida Rauh and his desire to create a role for her. He had thought at first of working on a play in Oaxaca, instead of rewriting his Quetzalcoatl manuscript. He wrote Ida Rauh to this effect on November 17, 1924 — two days before he decided to revise the novel after all. He told her that he would

RL, make the play *either Aztec or Jewish — King David or Moses: or else*
11/17/24 *Montezuma.* And then when *The Plumed Serpent* was close to being finished, in January, he toyed with the idea of dramatizing it too:

RL, *I could take a wonderful & terrible play out of it.* In any event, as he
1/16/25 went on to say — this also to Ida Rauh: *I shall not forget that play. It's rankling somewhere.*

Then the illness flattened him. Yet, by the time he had been in Mexico City a few days — having arrived on February 26 — weak as he

still was, he had *a very attractive scheme worked out for a play.* He   RL,
proceeded then to outline at least most of *Noah's Flood* and asked   3/3/25
himself whether he would be strong enough to write it. He soon was,
for about two weeks later he had begun. In fact, he may already have
written the only fragment he ever did of *Noah's Flood,* and abandoned
it — perhaps because he could not create in it a suitable role for Ida
Rauh — and have gone ahead to *David.* At least this conclusion is
possible from what he wrote to Ida Rauh on March 19: *I began a*   RL,
play which, poco a poco, will, I think, come to what I want: & you   3/19/25
want. Lawrence still does not mention a title when he next refers to
the play on April 6, the day after he had come home to Kiowa Ranch.
He says he will go on with it *when the spirit moves* him and speaks of   RL,
it as *a real thing to me, in a world of unrealities.* The spirit was not   4/6/25
long in moving him, for within a week or so he was forging ahead with
a play now identifiable as *David,* and he had finished it by May 7.

As their proximity of composition suggests, *Noah's Flood* is an
essential part of the inspiration for *David.* In the former Lawrence goes
back to long before the time of the great king, to the opening of the
cycle when lordship first passed from demi-gods to men. Lawrence
identifies Noah and his sons with the Sons of God who loved the
daughters of men. But the contest in the play is over the demand of
mortals for fire, so as to control the sun and the rest of the cosmos.
Noah warns them that they will not thereby bring about the ages of
happiness they expect, for they will soon drown fire *in blood, and*   TB, 126
quench it in tears. They are not to be trusted with the holy element.
Yet there seems no way to keep it from them, their time having come.
Lawrence meant to follow the contest of wills through the building of
the Ark at least, and if he meant to continue the story through the
Flood itself, as no doubt he did, we can foresee men bringing on their
own destruction. Presumably it would have been Noah and his sons
who would bear onward after the Flood the sacred flame of life. Lawrence is thus brooding over the age of degeneration after Noah's fated
surrender to the will of mere men, facing up in this manner to the loss
of the heroic. Whether he would have found elements to mistrust in the
heroic itself, as he had done in *The Plumed Serpent* and would do in
David, we cannot say from the fragment. Neither can we know just
how Lawrence would have conceived and carried out the progress of
the Flood and the destiny of the Ark. But this much is certain: the
instinct for escape by water that he had begun to spin out here is
consistent with the other promptings to which he listened more and
more at this time, starting with "The Flying Fish." This was the intuition of escape by sea and arrival at some place of containment which

was in essence a return to beginnings, a reversal of the instincts that had controlled his American experience. He turned away now from primitivism unleashed to seek its own apocalypse. He turned away from *The Plumed Serpent.*

What he was veering toward is spelled out in *David,* Lawrence's most thorough rendering of the transition now sought between New World and Old, a transition looking back on *The Plumed Serpent* and forward to that season of wayfaring culminating in *Lady Chatterley's Lover* and "A Dream of Life." He chose for this bridging his own Biblical story, the hero with his own name, and he wrote in a style that echoes the King James Bible and Elizabethan drama, but with enough admixture of a harmonious modern idiom to avoid stiltedness. Woven into this texture is chanting and dance whose rhythms are indebted to the Psalms and Koteliansky's Rananim chant and the singing and drumming of Southwestern Indians.[1] Like *The Plumed Serpent* the play takes up the mystery of power as a strength coming from the inscrutable beyond, appearing where it is least expected, as in David the shepherd boy, and disappearing in like fashion, as from Saul the king. Another theme is that perennial concern of Lawrence's, blood-brotherhood, here touching David and Jonathan, the Biblical friendship to which Lawrence so often alluded.

But most to be noted in *David* is Lawrence's speculation on the progression of ages and the cyclical flow of divine energy into man. In *The Plumed Serpent* we stand at the end of the present era, when the civilization of the mind is ready to give way to a future civilization of blood consciousness. *David* takes us back to the dawn of the now waning civilization of the mind. The anointing of Saul from the Great Source takes place in the ancient manner, through the instincts, while that of David comes about through his wits. Their separate ways of seeing the Source and the ambitions of each thus stand in direct CO, 145   contrast. Samuel says to David: *"Saul hath seen a tall and rushing flame and hath gone mad, for the flame rushed over him. Thou seest thy God in thine own likeness, afar off, or as a brother beyond thee, who fulfils thy desire. Saul yearneth for the flame: thou for thy to-morrow's glory."* Saul is the soul of blood. David is the ego. But Saul has lost the flame of God through disobedience to its promptings, like the Indian kings of "The Woman Who Rode Away." In his case a madness, but a clairvoyant madness, has come to fill the void. Lawrence makes use of this madness to issue a prophecy. In the throes of CO, 150   his black hallucinations Saul foresees a whole cycle of man, *the days of the seed of David,* the technological age, when *by cunning shall Israel prosper.* And he envisions the end of that age, with a population explosion and the extinction of every creature except man, with the

death of God and a final manmade calamity: *Only men there shall be,*   CO, 117
in myriads, like locusts, clicking and grating upon one another, and
crawling over one another. The smell of them shall be as smoke, but
it shall rise up into the air, without finding the nostrils of God. For
God shall be gone! gone! gone! And men shall inherit the earth! . . .
They thicken and thicken, till the world's air grates and clicks as with
the wings of locusts. And man is his own devourer, and the Deep turns
away, without wish to look on him further. So the earth is a desert,
and manless, yet covered with houses and iron.

Saul is of the dark races: this Lawrence emphasizes. And in Saul,
in one sense, he gives the first hint of his coming preoccupation with
the Etruscans. Seeing that even in his decline Saul is one of Lawrence's
ancient instinctive heroes, we may be surprised to find the upstart
David, of the lighter races, wearing Lawrence's red beard. But this
seeming contradiction is, in fact, one of the clues to what Lawrence
was attempting in the play, an endeavor finely tuned to his psychological condition at the time. He could not bring himself to put the
finishing touches on *The Plumed Serpent* because he realized how
profound were the destructive urges of that novel, though all the while
protesting that it was his most significant work yet. In writing *David*
during this same time, he chose to turn away from complete identification with the blood power of Saul, who is something of a Ramón and
Cipriano combined, and to see his reflection as well in the great forerunner of the age of intelligence. Lawrence was doing his best to make
an epic drama of his own struggles, to project a spirit into *David* that
could look with equanimity on all ages, instinctive or mental, and
identify with a forever questing human consciousness personified in the
representative men of both types of ages, in Saul and in David. For that
matter, he created Samuel in one of his own images, too, the image
of the prophet. It is Samuel's function in the play to raise the mythical
cry as to the ways of God in the progression of ages: *"The heart of*   CO, 77
man cannot wander among the years like a wild ass in the wilderness,
running hither and thither. The heart at last stands still, crying:
Whither? Whither? . . . *Then comes the prophet with the other vision*
in his eyes, and the inner hearing in his ears, and he uncovers the secret
path of the Lord." This changeover of ages is reminiscent of Ramón's
call for a new era, except that we are now back at the dawn of the one
whose end Ramón announces.

So Lawrence weighs with great care what he must now conceive as
a far-reaching interplay of opposites in human greatness. He looks back
with regret but equally with mistrust on the magnanimous but dangerous leadership of Saul. And he looks with a somewhat smaller
measure of faith and doubt combined on the leadership of David, that

which is rooted in shrewdness rather than magnificence. To reconcile these ambiguities Lawrence works into the play the roles of Jonathan and of Michal, a daughter of Saul's and the great love of David. Between David and Michal there exists a powerful blood togetherness that almost comes up to Lawrence's ideal. They must separate as David flees from the wrath of her father. They are still apart and David is still in flight at the final curtain, but that David will come into his own on the death of Saul, to possess the kingdom and the princess, is assured by forecast in the closing scene. David and the type of David will inherit the earth, to see greatness for a time.

It is through Jonathan, however, that the final summation is delivered on the two sorts of hierarchy and their two sorts of world exampled by the play. Jonathan is the most sensitive of men to the blood response that imposes love and obedience. Therefore he adores his father. But he has sworn an equal blood love with David, with the Lord as witness, and so it is he on whom the final conflict of the two ways centers. Jonathan becomes a tragic figure, in the Laurentian sense, in that he must see his way through to the end, even though it means his death, and even though his love for his friend causes him to renounce the way of his father. He embraces David and sends him on his way to greatness. He understands that an age of David must come. Like the Natty Bumppo of Lawrence's estimate or the heroine of "The Woman Who Rode Away," Jonathan gives himself to death so that the kind of life-mystery to which he belongs may have a rebirth in the future far beyond his own life span. His benediction of David CO, 154 runs, in part: *"Take it! Take thou the kingdom, and the days to come. In the flames of death where Strength is, I will wait and watch till the day of David at last shall be finished, and wisdom no more be fox-faced, and the blood gets back its flame."*

It was a fictional vision of the Holy Land, then, that extracted Lawrence at last from Mexico, a vision to compensate by a certain idealization of his namesake for the perils of the blood in his vision of aboriginal America.

We might almost omit saying that during his convalescent summer ML, 832 at Kiowa Ranch, Lawrence had *a lurking hankering for Europe* and ML, 847 spoke of sailing by the end of summer. Or he could say, *I feel very much drawn to the Mediterranean again,* as we saw he was drawn in *David.* Still, in September, on the deck of a ship headed for England, ML, 855 he was already regretting his departure from America: *I lie and think of the ranch: it seems so far far away: — these beastly journeys, how I hate them! I'm going to stop it, though, this continual shifting.*

The journeys went on, of course: a month in England, with the Mediterranean in mind for the winter, and another new place in that direction full of attraction — this time Ragusa, or Dubrovnik as it is now called, on the Adriatic in Yugoslavia. It was supposed to be inhabited still by "real peasants." Another recurrent temptation of place again appears in the letters: *I have a sort of feeling I should* ML, 873 *like to go to Russia, later in the spring. Nobody encourages me in the idea.* The middle of November found the Lawrences settling for the winter in Spotorno, Italy, in the Villa Bernarda standing high above the village and commanding a long sweep of Mediterranean shore-line. There was, even so, a call from further south, *to see spring once* ML, 868 *more in Sicily* and go on a walking trip there.

Having that curve of Mediterranean coast before his eyes had as strong an effect on Lawrence as always: *After a while, it's always set me longing to wander. . . . I still wish my old wish, that I had a* ML, 876 *little ship to sail this sea, and visit the Isles of Greece, and pass through the Bosphorus. That Rananim of ours, it has sunk out of sight.* This ship to sail for islands of the classical world, a vessel of which Lawrence talked off and on for the rest of his life, would in truth have meant boarding an ark.

If the man himself did not sail away just now, his pen was at least wayfaring true to form, and still searching out a balance of forces between the worlds of Europe and America. Lawrence wrote the story "Sun" shortly after moving into the Villa Bernarda, a story in which the questing woman he had carried in his spirit to America as Lou Witt and Kate Leslie retraces Lawrence's voyage back from the gray waters of the Hudson to the Mediterranean south. Juliet's ark carries her further than Lawrence went just now, to Sicily, to the Island of the Sun itself, as sacred to the solar orb here as in the *Odyssey.* In this story all of Lawrence's old haunting love of the Mediterranean, as well as his craving for a ruddy and sun-fed life to enter his pale and dwindling body, comes out in powerful prose. The doctors in New York say Juliet needs the sun, and with her small boy to the sun she goes, her husband staying behind to conduct business in the sunless city of destruction. As Juliet lies naked outdoors day after day in Sicily, and teaches her child to do the same, in the presence of a cypress like *a low, silvery candle whose huge flame was darkness* SH, 530 *against light,* she is *put into connection with the sun* through *some* SH, 535 *mysterious power inside her,* and her *conscious self* becomes *second-ary: the true Juliet was this dark flow from her deep body to the sun.* She has been in the past guilty of over-mothering her child: the old hurt so much in need of being set right by cosmic powers. Under the solar influence her enveloping fear to let the child go turns into encouragement of cultivating aloneness with the universe as a first demand on the human soul, and into a balanced accord between

SH, 534

SH, 544

SH, 545

mother and child that can only exist through this knowledge of the beyond. Even Juliet's husband, who has never been out of *a damp, cold crevice inside himself,* profits a little from his wife's rebirth when he arrives unexpectedly on the scene. With *a desperate kind of courage of his desire . . . not entirely quenched* by the world of death in the modern city, he will *dare to walk in the sun, even ridiculously.* Soon after the entrance of the husband we are told of a strong and proud peasant with whom Juliet has rarely spoken but by whom it would be glorious to bear another child. This will not come about, however. She alone cannot liberate herself entirely from the world to which her husband is still bound and which to some extent holds her. Her next child will be her husband's, for, as the author decides, *the fatal chain of continuity would cause it.*

While "Sun" may not rank with the finest of Lawrence's stories, it merits attention because it comes at another important juncture of his life. It announces the shift of interest back to the Old World and new hope in its restorative powers, and it also initiates a further stage in the sequence of fiction leading up to *Lady Chatterley's Lover.* The woman is not quite freed from a husband who is not quite impotent, and the natural aristocrat from the earth-bound class remains in the background merely as a desirable alternative. But plainly all this is but a step or two away from the triangle of the Chatterleys and the gamekeeper.

The spurt of activity just after the Lawrences had located in Spotorno also brought forth *The Virgin and the Gipsy,* when for the second time just after a visit to England Lawrence aimed a blow at his native land and grappled once more with the problem of vanishing or vanished manhood. On the first occasion, with *St. Mawr,* he had come no nearer to seeing the resurgence of living maleness, or to defining it westward, than Lou's vision of the spirit of the Rockies as replacement for any man at all. In this second effort, Lawrence went back to a former — and to a future — favorite: the outcast, the wanderer who lives by his intrinsic superiority while circumventing the mass of men. From yet another angle *The Virgin and the Gipsy* asks the old questions of what is masculinity, what is femininity, and how are these qualities to survive and prosper in a world of unnatural morality and lifeless conformity.

Renewed contact with England had made these questions native again, so to speak, and he molded them this time into figures on a north of England landscape. It was a new ordering of the griefs and convictions around which Lawrence's life revolved, a scathing attack on the family as it existed in middle-class England, especially virulent in its exorcising of a ghoulish mother tyrant. The broken home over which she rules in this story clearly reflects the circumstances of the Weekley household that Lawrence broke up, though the hollow clergyman whose wife has run away and the repulsive mother who rules him bear only the remotest similarity to the Weekley mother and son.

Not so the daughters, who are based on Frieda's children: especially on Barbara, who was now twenty-one and had felt the spell of Lawrence's magnetic personality. She came to visit the Lawrences in Spotorno at Christmastime, 1925, and stayed a long while. *The Virgin and the Gipsy* was an immediate result of this visit. Barbara was already from previous meetings well on the way to becoming another of the many women with whom Lawrence cultivated a close and sympathetic bond but no love affair except as fantasized in his fiction. Echoes of youth awakened in him at this time, recollections of an old stone quarry near home in Eastwood. Other writings — notably "A Dream of Life" the following year — also demonstrate that he associated this quarry with youth and early love. The gipsy of the story, who lives in the stone quarry, is another of the many incarnations of Lawrence's dark self, of the image of maleness he had inherited from his father. Like the son the gipsy is a rover, a man of the earth belonging to no one corner of the earth. Lithe and sensual, a coppersmith whose wares bring him a sufficient income from the well-off, he lives with his wife and children in a caravan, disdainful of the modern world, whose men are of no more account than housedogs. Yvette, younger daughter of the rector, is fresh and pretty, with *some of the vague, careless blitheness* of her unconventional mother,   VG, 6 a quality that her father and grandmother fear and hate, for they are not merely slaves of convention, they are the makers of the outwardly respectable world. The mother is *like some awful idol of old flesh,*   VG, 12 and her rector son, Yvette's father, is an anguished hypocrite, because *he knew his heart's core was a fat, awful worm,* and *his dread was*   VG, 27 *lest anyone else should know.*

We recognize, then, that Yvette is a sleeping beauty, a potentially free soul held prisoner by the monsters of family and society. To effect her freedom, Lawrence sends her forth to encounter the dark stranger in a symbolic landscape whose elements are familiar. Like all three of the women of the American short fiction: the "princess," Lou Witt, and "the woman who rode away," Yvette goes to a high place to establish connection with the spirit of release. Only now it is a Hardy-like landscape: an upland of England *veined with a net-*   VG, 18 *work of old stone walls, dividing the fields, and broken here and there with ruins of old lead-mines and works. A sparse stone farm bristled with six naked sharp trees. In the distance was a patch of smoky grey stone, a hamlet. In some fields grey, dark sheep fed silently, sombrely.*

But there was not a sound nor a movement. It was the roof of England.
VG, 20   Up here the gipsies live, in *a disused quarry, cut into the slope of the road-side, a sudden lair, almost like a cave.* Here Yvette sees for the
VG, 19   first time the gipsy man, *one of the black, loose-bodied handsome sort,* dark as are the American liberators. It is altogether likely that Lawrence's fictional use of this quarry was partly inspired, at the time, by recollections he was calling up in a letter to Rolf Gardiner. He men-
HL, 675   tions that his *father was born in the cottage in the quarry hole just by Brinsley level-crossing.* It was a spot that he associated with *The Widowing of Mrs. Holroyd* and "Odour of Chrysanthemums," and the tragedy of maleness in those works.

Lawrence develops his story by alternation and contrast between
VG, 28   the world of the *moral believer,* who yet keeps the other sanctity of the *sensitive, clean flesh and blood* — that is, the gipsy and his kind — and the world of *the life unbelievers* at the rectory, whose morality defiles the natural flesh. The satire on the mother-centered family of hypocrites is as good as the best of its kind. And although the balancing off of the life outside the conventions has flaws, the only one detracting seriously from the force of the tale is the over-neat pattern of the symbolism in some places.

Still, to bring the story to its conclusion, Lawrence provides one of his best sequences of events relying on natural forces as symbolic counterparts to human motives and human action. He makes a convincing fictional case for the rebellion of the earth itself, specifically the river, against the unnatural race of human creatures clinging to its banks. The rectory stands very near the water, on a bend. When the story has advanced through many confrontations between Yvette and her stifling environment, but not yet to any consummation of the great attraction between her and the gipsy, a spring day arrives when the river seems to flow abnormally full and swift. Yvette sits in the garden close to the bank, but in spirit she is at the gipsy camp, saying goodbye as she has half-promised to do, this being the day when the caravan breaks winter camp and takes to the road. As with Lawrence
VG, 71   himself, *it was part of her nature, to get these fits of yearning for some place she knew,* almost to the point of conjuring up the place around
VG, 29   her, and she feels as she often has: she has *wished she were a gipsy. To live in a camp, in a caravan, and never set foot in a house, not know the existence of a parish, never look at a church.*

Granny is alone in the house at the moment. Yvette, alone also in the garden, takes a last stroll next to the full-flowing river before going in for the evening. All at once comes a huge roaring. At the same instant she sees the gipsy running toward her and a great hump of water rushing down. The gipsy reaches her in time, when the first wave overflowing the garden swirls about her legs, and terror prevents her from moving. Under his control they struggle on to the house and into it, in their sole hope of climbing above the flood, if only the house will stand the shock of wave after wave of the deluge. Granny, trapped on the ground floor and too obese to move well, struggles also to reach the stairs, clutches at the bannister a moment, but then is swept away in another onslaught of water. Reaching the top floor at last, drenched and chilled to the bone, Yvette and the gipsy take refuge in a bedroom near the main chimney, which may be strong enough to withstand the crashing waters. The wind rises, and numbed with cold, they take off their dripping clothes and go to the only place where warmth is possible: the bed. All night they stay there wound in each other's arms, while the flood waters subside below. Next morning the gipsy steals away before the rescuers come. The rectory is all but destroyed, Granny is drowned and her stranglehold on the family is gone. Yvette has passed the terrible but beautiful storm of emotions ushering her into womanhood, so initiated by a real male. The flood was caused, we learn, by the bursting of a dam upriver, with the obvious analogy between the pent-up river and the pent-up life in Yvette that has finally smashed free.

Reducing the story to its symbolic framework reveals that the pattern is too neat, and this together with the half-inert character of Yvette hinders the movement of the story. Yet it is well worth reading, all the more so in that it makes manifest the psychological preparation going on in Lawrence to create the England and the English of *Lady Chatterly's Lover*. The bedroom that "sails" through the flood in the story is another ark, a point we may miss if we read it apart from the other concurrent fiction.

The geographical forces pulling at Lawrence were as always in a constant process of realignment. Some days the call of America came weakly and excited no response other than a vague nostalgia. But never was the dream of a ship to roam the Mediterranean on his own odyssey far from Lawrence's mind. He read things about life on a yacht as he dreamed. Now and then, too, he went the whole way toward putting such a voyage over the waters into the symbolic light which alone could satisfy his craving, for example in a letter to Dorothy Brett. As to where he might go next, his only anticipation was this: *I feel it's the Flood, the only thing is to build an Ark*. But there is ML, 887
more than this in the letter, an opening into unconscious as well as conscious emotional processes. He recounts a recent dream in which Aaron, a favorite horse at the ranch, plays a prominent role: *I* ML, 888
dreamed there had been a flood at San Cristóbal and Aaron lay drowned and I could only find alive a bunch of weird, rather horrible

pintos. As we know that the horse always symbolized the deepest self to Lawrence, and as we know Aaron the man to have been one of his fictional surrogates, we can see in this dream the fear and the hope for the survival of the instincts in wholeness after the crucial experience of America. But the disillusionment is at this instant strong. The dream implies an impossibility of associating any such magnificent horse as St. Mawr with New Mexico, or even such a lesser horse as Aaron. The weird pintos, the only results of the dreamer's quest, are a horrifying fragmentation of all exalted hopes. This dream suggests as well the tugging of opposite shores, the compulsion to conquer a flood to reach what arises beyond it. Later this same spring, Lawrence described how the sense of a great gulf between the two present geographical poles of his spirit affected him: *Europe is very unreal, in America. And in Europe, America becomes like a sort of tormented dream to one.* The vessel to link the realities was not to be found.

ML, 910

Early in 1926 relations between Lawrence and Frieda reached one of those periodic points of intolerable stress, partly because her daughters were visiting them. At the same time Lawrence's sister Ada, with her deep dislike of Frieda, was there to crown it all. He fled with Ada to Monte Carlo to stay a few days, and then having seen her off from there to England, he veered back to Capri, where the ever-devoted Dorothy Brett was waiting to see him. From her account of their few days together, it appears that Lawrence was all but prepared to desert Frieda and come to Brett. She reports that he came to her bedroom one night and spent a little while in bed with her but found it impossible to go beyond a kiss and left in dejection. According to Frieda, Lawrence became impotent sometime in the mid-twenties. She herself was probably already having an affair with Angelo Ravagli, their landlord at the Villa Bernarda.

LA, III

If Lawrence could not actually leave Frieda for Brett, he could find a substitute for another elopement in talking with Brett of his dream ship and of how he longed to wander off to freedom in it: *"In the old days, Brett, the sailing ships had sails of crimson silk. Think of that in the sunlight: crimson silk on a blue sea, with the sunlight and the white waves."* It would have been the scarlet of the heroes hoisted to carry them through the world.

CB, vol. 3, 41

Lawrence left Frieda alone with her daughters in Spotorno from late February to early April. From Capri, leaving Brett and the Brewsters, with whom he had stayed, he continued for a few days in nearby Ravello, visiting two more women friends, Millicent Beveridge and Mabel Harrison, and then in their company wound north through the peninsula, taking in various cities before making his way back to

Spotorno, feeling somewhat restored by the solicitude of several women who suffered his domination gladly.

This brief drifting about Italy away from Frieda reawoke in Lawrence an imaginative range of time and place which had been dormant since before he left Europe the first time for America: a fascination with the ancient Etruscans. One of the places he went through was Perugia, with its collections of Etruscan artifacts in the university museum. No sooner had he arrived back in Spotorno than he began to speak of doing *a book, half travel and half study, on Umbria and*   ML, 895 *the Etruscans.*

He and Frieda had already decided not to stay in Spotorno past the end of April: Lawrence had found the Riviera distasteful. Anyhow, they had only alighted there so that they could do well by visitors from England, and the visitors had come and gone. Lawrence now wanted to locate in Perugia, to gather materials on the Etruscans. Frieda had a strong hankering for the ranch in New Mexico, or might go to Germany with her daughters. The outcome of it all was that the Lawrences saw Elsa and Barbara off to Germany from Florence, and soon afterwards rented the Villa Mirenda, a few miles outside the city near Scandicci, from which Lawrence felt he could range out to look at Etruscan tombs and art works: *the Etruscan things*   ML, 901 *appeal very much to my imagination. They are so curiously natural.* But once he was fairly settled in the Villa Mirenda, though he read much on the Etruscans and continued to bring them up in his letters, he felt little inclination to work on a book of any kind: *I get such a*   ML, 927 *distaste for committing myself any further into "solid print."* The hesitancy extended to writing another novel as well, even though Alfred Knopf and Martin Secker were both trying to persuade him to write one. He sat much on the terrace, between frequent spells of bad weather, typed out Frieda's German translation of *David,* and wrote *an occasional scrap of an article.*   ML, 923

In the circle of daily life Lawrence had located the "real peasants" he had thought of looking for on the coast of Yugoslavia: in the families that worked the land of the Villa Mirenda. It was the closest thing yet to one of his ideals: to live in the midst of a life centered on the soil and the countryside among active and simple people, but attached to them only as the uncommon and visionary man who draws sustenance from the natural order. Not that he found the peasants idyllic, either, as we will see from the effect of the Villa Mirenda experience on *The Man Who Died.* But as to nature itself here, it had remained harmonious with human population. Tuscany here was unspoilt, near as it was to Florence, and when Lawrence did eventually

get back to writing, he took great delight in working outdoors in these
surroundings. But all that the renewed contact with the Mediterranean
world had planted in his mind — the odyssey-like voyages, the Etruscan way of life, the peasant life around him at the Villa Mirenda —
all this belongs to a strain of writing that for the moment falls into
a place secondary to what England soon called on Lawrence to attempt.

The Lawrences followed through now with plans they had made
in early summer: to go to Baden-Baden for a visit with the *Schwieger-
mutter* of a couple of weeks, then on to England for the month of
August, to return to Sandicci in September. Then, Lawrence hoped,
he would be up to making his tour of the Etruscan hill-towns.

This was Lawrence's last visit to England, and coming as it did
at a time when his creative energy was dormant but ready for resurgence, it opened up to him new and unexpected vistas of his native
land which we can see taking immediate effect in his work: to such
a degree as to determine the character of one stream of creation in the
last phase of his life. It was as if the long spells of absence over the
years had suddenly given him new eyes for home, a new if wavering
faith in the potentialities of the English people, and a new grasp of
the mysteries beneath the face of England. He had brought to England
with him his maturing absorption in the Etruscans. This helped to
make him sensitive as he had not been since the days of the war to
the most ancient stirrings of spirit of place in Britain.

During the two months in his own country Lawrence spent some
time in his native Midlands. What he saw there gave rise to *Lady
Chatterley's Lover* and "A Dream of Life." Beyond the Midlands, in
August, he made an excursion that really opened to him a new region
of Britain, far as he had traveled in distant climes. He went to Scotland, to Inverness and on west to Fort William, to Mallaig, and for
one day to the Isle of Skye. Compton Mackenzie, with whom many
voyages had been planned and few ever taken, had invited him *to go
to an isle off Lewis, in the Outer Hebrides,* but apparently he did not
go. It was probably nothing more than the first day or two of elation
Lawrence often experienced in new places that led him to write, *I
am much better since I am here in Scotland.* What he meant with
more conviction is that it was *most refreshing to get outside the made
world. . . . It restores the old Adam in one.* This reawakened balance
could not have lasted in the mist and darkness of the north, of this
we may be sure. But the magic of the landscape kept hold of Lawrence long enough to bring through a momentary vision of the pure
beings of ancient times who had sailed these seas. Here as well as
in the Mediterranean, at the other pole of Europe, was escape from
the corrupt world, and one might sail to it in an ark: *There is still*

ML, 918

ML, 931

NEAR FLORENCE, ITALY

Man can live on the earth and by the earth
without disfiguring the earth (PH, 46)

something of an Odyssey up there, in among the islands and the silent lochs: like the twilight morning of the world, the herons fishing undisturbed by the water, and the sea running far in, for miles, between the wet, trickling hills, where the cottages are low and almost invisible, built into the earth. It is still out of the world, and like the very beginning of Europe. Whether or not this trip provided a setting for the end of "The Man Who Loved Islands," it assisted in bringing Lawrence to a brief imaginative realization of Britain as the sort of pristine land he had so often glimpsed in the Minoan distance of the Mediterranean.[2]

ML, 933

The other aid to the realization was the Midlands and the uncommon view Lawrence took of the area at the moment: *Curiously, I like England again, now I am up in my own regions. It braces me up: and there seems a queer, odd sort of potentiality in the people, especially the common people. One feels in them some odd, unaccustomed sort of plasm twinkling and nascent. They are not finished. And they have a funny sort of purity and gentleness, and at the same time, unbreakableness, that attracts one.* He was at a Lincolnshire beach when he wrote this, and in another letter we see that he was still in the same frame of mind as when he had felt the presence of ancient

ML, 934

mariners two weeks before in Scotland: *Queer and forlorn this country is, this shore, as if still expecting the Vikings and sea-roving Danes.*

By early October Lawrence and Frieda were back in Italy at the Villa Mirenda. It took him a few weeks yet to get down to serious and sustained writing once more. Even though he may not have revised "The Man Who Loved Islands" now, its elaboration of the island as ark makes it appropriate for discussion at this time.

The protagonist, Cathcart, is one of Lawrence's most curious and subtle combinations of himself and another man — though Compton Mackenzie, the other man, saw no Lawrence in Cathcart, only

IH, 187

an ectoplasm presented under the facts of his life. And while, like Compton Mackenzie, Cathcart does acquire an island near England — or rather two, in the fiction — and yet another island in Scotland, the fictional hero actually goes far beyond his initial role: that of a

SH, 725

man who plays at being absolute lord of his own island domain, *to regain Paradise, by spending money.* This hero enters two other reaches of human character that only Lawrence himself could have access to: the sphere where the question of isolation against commitment is decided and the sphere where death is contemplated in all its splendor and dread. It seems advisable to examine these three aspects of Cathcart separately; how they coalesce can best be appreciated by reading the story.

Cathcart as the romantic materialist, born on an island crowded with people — presumably Great Britain — leases an island he will not have to share with anyone and goes there to enjoy his solitude. But he is frightened to discover that out here on the water, space and time are reversed: *When, in the city, you wear your white spats and dodge* SH, 724 *the traffic with the fear of death down your spine, then you are quite safe from the terrors of infinite time. The moment is your little islet in time. . . .*

But once isolate yourself on a little island in the sea of space, and the moment begins to heave and expand in great circles, the solid earth is gone, and your slippery, naked dark soul finds herself out in the timeless world.

What happens is that the souls of all the men who ever knew this island come thronging in to upset Cathcart's claims to sole proprietorship. To save his illusion he compounds it. He brings in a few common people to form a little economy and directs it as a benevolent despot: the Master, his subjects call him. He anticipates, in due time, a little utopia. But the inhabitants fall out with each other and appropriate funds entrusted to them, and Cathcart's dream vanishes with much of his capital. The island will never serve as the ground for Cathcart's invented world. Another variation of Rananim has failed: or, to put it differently, another ark has sunk.

Cathcart has two more islands to go in the course of the story, each one smaller than the last, but from the second one on he almost ceases to be anything that Lawrence might have had in view of Compton Mackenzie as a successful author pretending to stand outside it all. His protagonist now becomes something of a Lawrence renouncing a vile world and yet something of a figure set up to criticize Lawrence's own measurement of civilization and selfhood: he becomes victim and culprit in one. From the beginning of the story Cathcart possesses Lawrence's perceptivity to time and place. In the night on the first island, there comes to pass *an infinite dark world where all the souls* SH, 723 *from all the other bygone nights lived on, and the infinite distance was near.* Cathcart experiences *strange awarenesses of old, far-gone* SH, 724 *men, and other influences; men of Gaul, with big moustaches, who had been on his island, and had vanished from the face of it, but not out of the air of night.*

On the second island there are no ancient ghosts, but the feeling which now prevails is still Lawrence's: Lawrence the traveler, who in Cathcart occupies the island as a migratory soul: *The island was* SH, 734 *no longer a "world." It was a sort of refuge. . . . It was as if he and his few dependents were a small flock of sea-birds alighted on this rock, as they travelled through space.*

From the start Cathcart has been writing a book, a reference work on flowers mentioned in classical authors, and like Lawrence at the time, he is indifferent to publication. He lives in a state of release

from all desire for contact, which is no more than a distortion of Lawrence's ideal of isolation and self-containment. But Cathcart allows
himself to fail. The soft but willful submission of his housekeeper's
daughter brings him down, and at this point we learn that he contains
SH, 737   much indeed of Lawrence: *It was the automatism of sex that had
caught him again. Not that he hated sex. He deemed it, as the Chinese
do, one of the great life-mysteries. But it had become mechanical,
automatic, and he wanted to escape that. Automatic sex shattered
him, and filled him with a sort of death. He thought he had come
through, to a new stillness of desirelessness. Perhaps beyond that there
was a new fresh delicacy of desire, an unentered frail communion of
two people meeting on untrodden ground.*

By more ordinary standards of character motivation, this development is intrusive, since no hint has been given to this point that a
revulsion from sex was instrumental in driving Cathcart into hermitage.
But the development must be taken along with Cathcart's inability to
reconcile himself at the outset with all the living, and next, with all the
dead. Now, even though he professes the purest of Laurentian sexual
doctrine, he is incapable of seeking out a way to put that doctrine
into practice, to arrive at reconciliation with the great creative mystery of sex. Still, he is incapable likewise of maintaining his isolation:
he simply yields to the nearest temptation.

Now while some doubts are implied in the story as to Lawrence's
ideal of isolation, none is intended, I think, as to the sexual doctrine.
In fact, the certainty of this belief furnishes the touchstone of the
story. Somewhere inside, Cathcart has the right impulses. The efforts
that he makes to escape the world are epic in their misanthropy, and
while they lead to his doom, we cannot but admire his attempts to
create his own reality. If he had been capable of exerting his strength
in another direction, he would have kept his integrity remote in the
midst of the world and waited, like the gamekeeper in *Lady Chatterley's Lover,* for the right relationship to come his way, and it is evident that he knows the nature of a right relationship. Evident too,
then, is the underlying reason for his flight from the world, and it is
one for which we can feel some sympathy: Cathcart detests the mob
life of the earth, but he cannot hold himself aloof in the midst of it,
so he becomes a recluse as the only way of being true to his real self.

Yet he simply cannot surround himself with enough safeguards
to keep out of the world, even on this second island. When the housekeeper's daughter proves to be pregnant, he marries her, settles on
her most of the remainder of his income, and moves to his third and
last island, in Scotland, where Lawrence had perceived some kind of
SH, 738   northern odyssey, to *a few acres of rock away in the north, on the outer*

fringe of the isles, truly the last hope of an ark. Up here he can have the utmost of silence and unapproachability, sometimes asking *what repulsive god invented animals and evil-smelling men,* deriving *his single satisfaction from being alone, absolutely alone.* He writes no more on his book, even effaces all lettering on the things in his hut to destroy any vestigial power of the word.   SH, 742   SH, 742–743

On the one hand, this is Lawrence's secret of being alone turned into the horror of being cut off from any unison whatever with other humans: it is the last throes of misanthropy. In another domain, it is certainly a metaphoric structure for the contemplation of death, of the death facing Cathcart's creator, and a revulsion against the writing that has sustained his life. The imagery Lawrence chooses, winter and endless snow in this arctic place, is that which has long been congenial to him as death utterly annihilative and unending, in a "north" beyond all touch of life: a condition like the death of the eternal mountain snows in *Twilight in Italy* and *Women in Love.* This story marks the end of that sort of stark white death in Lawrence's writing. From *Etruscan Places* to the end of his life, he recovered almost fully the imagery of death as creative darkness and as some kind of absorption through harmony into the allness of the universe, utilizing some place turned symbol as an anchor to this world. Actually, this counter movement originates in *Lady Chatterley's Lover,* and began not long after the time when Lawrence was elaborating the extremity of death as an arctic land in "The Man Who Loved Islands."

Cathcart's life, in this last phase, becomes a combat with the engulfing snow. Life has shrunk away to the south, withdrawing from the north. The snow piles up day by day, and each time Cathcart digs out a path to his boat as a gesture towards freedom, the snow falls deep again. He fights it all through the winter, only to lose when spring is about to appear, though he is hardly by this time in a mental condition to recognize the seasons. One day when the sun turns bright, he is simply overcome to recognize how distorted and fantastic his island has become, with hills of snow where no hills should be, sending off fumes of snow in the wind like so many volcanoes. The last he feels is a darkening of the sky, the calling of thunder that heralds more snow, and the breath of the snow itself, which for the last time he turns to face. Neither an island riding the flood nor the boat of his last pitiful outreach can be the vessel of salvation to save Cathcart from himself or the world.

For Lawrence this protagonist, insofar as he is based on the successful Compton Mackenzie, was the very emblem of damnation in the pseudo-artist and his island, his England. But at around this same time, less than a month after his final visit to England from July to September of 1926, Lawrence set out to write what was to have been a short tale but which rapidly turned into his last massive fictional venture, *Lady Chatterley's Lover*. In this work the hope of a different England emerged from the surprising last turns in Lawrence's long

IH, 357   despair with his homeland. He spoke now *of good stayers at home* as superior to good travelers, and he toyed even with coming back

LS, 76   to the Midlands *to do an English novel*. It would be wrong, however, to think of these glimmerings of adventurous joy alone as responsible for Lawrence's feeling a new lease on life for England. The inevitable opposite seeped in as well, the overwhelming pain of going over the old home territory. With a tortured look on his face, he had told

IH, 357   William Hopkin that he hated *the damned place*.

It was in Tuscany, however, and just after declaring that he would never write another novel — apparently in another phase of reaction against *The Plumed Serpent* — that Lawrence actually did begin his *English novel*. Between October 1926 and January 1928 he wrote three versions of it, all of them now in print: *The First Lady Chatterley, John Thomas and Lady Jane* and *Lady Chatterley's Lover*. These three, or at least the second and third versions, are unquestionably among Lawrence's greatest fictional achievements. They arise from an attempt at total readjustment of place and identity, the place being home regained after long wayfaring, the identity being a reassessment of the male Lawrence as a stay-at-home self might have been, or that his father conceivably might also have been. That this concern was Lawrence's prime motivation is plain on recognizing that, whatever else may have grown and changed from version to version of the novel, the most far-reaching development of all is that of the gamekeeper from the first to the third version of the book. The original Parkin is a fairly simple form of what Lawrence's father might have been together with the image of what Lawrence had lately seen as potential in the common people of the Midlands. One potential of this man takes the same basic form as that of his two fictional successors: that of restoring some of the quick of life to English womanhood in the person of Connie. But Lawrence had not yet given up entirely on political solutions. The first Parkin ends up as a Communist leader among the workers of a plant where he has gone to work after being forced out of his gamekeeper's job. A definite hope attaches to a Communist future, aside from the function of smashing the old system to leave room for new growth.

In *John Thomas and Lady Jane,* Parkin is still Parkin; that is, strictly a working-class man who must still find his fulfillment as a male within limits imposed by his class and his sort of nature — and limitations are quite as much in question as positive potential in both Parkins. There is still a political level in the second novel, too, but a rather dim one. Parkin has become politically indifferent. He only wishes to be free from all extremes. The political talk is largely between Connie and a close friend of Parkin's, and only to the effect that real and revitalizing contact between the classes is impossible.

In the third and last form of the novel the gamekeeper has advanced to such a being in the author's mind that a change of name is necessary, to Mellors, and a whole new identity shapes up. Mellors is closer than ever to being Lawrence himself. He knows how to preserve and defend the best of both worlds, both the instinctive life of the working man and the natural nobility of English culture already largely drained out of the upper classes by the industrial blight. Mellors is educated, too. He can and does pass for a gentleman. There is hardly any thought of politics in *Lady Chatterley's Lover*. And, incidentally, it was shortly after completing the third version of his novel that Lawrence wrote his well-known letter to Witter Bynner, rejecting the leadership principles of *The Plumed Serpent* and consequently any politics whatever. Man must lead in another fashion.

While the pivot of the three-stage novel is thus the familiar campaign to create a viable and as far as possible impregnable male soul, the emphasis on the feminine point of view, together with the quest for a new space in the homeland where man and woman may weather the engulfing flood of current society toward a future replenishing of the earth — that is to say, the ark motif — brings about a climax to the new perspective of Lawrence's geographical symbolism that we found first broached in the hopes of resuscitating the vales of England in "The Flying Fish."

The ark is the wood at Wragby, the estate in whose manor house Connie carries on her half-life with her husband, Clifford, whose lower body has been left paralyzed by a war wound. It is to the wood and to the gamekeeper there that Connie must go to escape the impotent intellectualization of Clifford, and not only that, but also the welter of mines and industrial plants surrounding Wragby. In *The First Lady Chatterley,* while Lawrence may fail to give ample breadth and depth to his characters before he projects them into action, he does provide, as in all three versions of the novel, an admirable creation of the wood as symbolic place, a creation springing from the English countryside as he knew it in boyhood and as he still found it breathing under the wasted surface on his last visit to England. Connie's first stirring to a new life comes when she glimpses Parkin washing himself, stripped to the waist, behind his cottage deep in the wood. She cannot help returning there later, *to escape, to escape the level* FL, 25 *monotony of doom, to break through into magic once more! To pass into the life of the woods!* It is her sudden empathy with the newly hatched pheasant chicks that brings her first surrender to Parkin, and afterwards not only does it seem that he is the very spirit of the FL, 36   woods but that she herself has become the woods: *All her body felt like the dark interlacing of the boughs of an oak wood.* Or at another moment she envisions the wood, ark-like, as a little sacred sphere surrounded by a howling and barbarous world of Cliffords and their society.

Into this little world of the wood versus devastated country ruled over by the arid mind, Lawrence injects the last great fictional elaborations of his lifelong concerns. To take the central one, a man must FL, 68   be *the living clue to all the world to a woman* — we are at the opposite pole, now, from the conviction of Lawrence's first days of travel, when woman was man's only link with the godhead. The gamekeeper is Connie's resurrection. Mrs. Bolton, the nurse who comes to live at Wragby and tend Clifford, lost her husband twenty-three years ago, but he has never left her, because death cannot break true marriage. Connie and Clifford have in truth never been married, even before FL, 69   his crippling. He never possessed that miracle of male life *which can wake a woman's heart once and for all.* And so, *his terrible accident, his paralysis or whatever it was, was really symbolical in him.* He wants to be half a man. Plainly Clifford's mutilation is not, then, some sort of cruel joke Lawrence is playing on a character, but an essential element in the novel's design. As with Rico in *St. Mawr,* Clifford's injury comes from within himself, only here, with even more force than in the novella, the point is made that Clifford represents nearly the whole of post-war maledom in Europe, the whole of a civilization. Modern woman certainly comes in for scathing criticism in several of Lawrence's works. The three forms of *Lady Chatterley's Lover* deliver an equally powerful indictment against the male.

The two men between whom Connie is now thrust provide her with a situation from which she can draw overwhelming conclusions on another Lawrence prepossession: immortality. In religious terms, FL, 83   the flaw in Clifford and his kind, she decides, is that they have *always believed in the mortality of the body and the immortality of the spirit.* It was that fatal breakdown in males, in modern times, on which all of the distressed condition of mankind was to be blamed, including that most monstrous event of Lawrence's lifetime, the Great War: *If men had believed in the immortality of the body they would never have made that war, or any such war.* What immortality comes to mean to Connie, through her physical unison with Parkin, is something FL, 64   *more imminent* than *the long-drawn-out kind* of *immortality after death*. It is a harmony here and now with the whole physical process of the cosmos rather than some ghostly eternity, a surrender to the will of life itself as eternal. Life apart from the body, whether the body of the human or the body of the world, is now inconceivable to her. And by implication she discounts that tradition of Christianity which the Greeks found so difficult to believe, the resurrection of the body in a spiritual realm. Or rather she reinterprets it entirely, to mean the rejuvenation of the sensual body through physical love, just as we will see the process transpire in *The Man Who Died*.

On one occasion when Connie is in deep thought concerning this immortality, she thinks of a corollary which troubles her a little and which troubled Lawrence a great deal more. If immortality is, as she has defined it, the unthinking and therefore timeless participation of the body in *the soft glowing loveliness, loveliness of the flesh*, then FL, 48 Parkin is the perfect example of immortality. And so he is. But Connie must add that someone, though not Parkin, ought to *think* about this sort of immortality. Clifford is of little help, of course, and she is left stranded in her state of feeling without logic. But much more disturbing is the realization that while Parkin may be an all but divine creature when nude and making love, he has an everyday personality that is common and static and totally uncultivated. At times he cuts a ridiculous figure. He cannot even speak standard English, but only the local dialect, with all the social stigma that this implies, even though paradoxically it is said to be the true blood speech. Try as she may, Connie cannot ever truly consent to overlook all these failings, to give up the life of culture and live simply as a working man's wife, though there is no material reason, since she has money of her own, why she could not divorce Clifford and buy a little farm where presumably the ideal from the wood of her love-making with Parkin might be made unassailable. From this dilemma, this impossibility of reconciling the body and the soul of life, Connie never emerges in *The First Lady Chatterley*. The parallel dilemma in Lawrence is that he has not succeeded, in this first shaping of his novel, in achieving the manly ideal of a figure perfectly in accord with all facets of life. The immortality of the body is there, in Parkin, but only the man who can also realize this ideal in mind as well as body can truly be said to be the whole male. This is of course a conclusion that runs entirely counter to Lawrence's often scornful denigration of the mind.

After doing his utmost to make the dilemma manifest, Lawrence makes strong gestures at resolving it. The course of the affair between Parkin and Connie in *The First Lady Chatterley* follows the general outline that it does in the later versions, but with crucial differences. Connie thinks she may be pregnant. When she mentions the subject in general to Clifford, he readily agrees to claim any child she may have as his own, while Parkin would like her to go to Canada with him but will not insist. The geographical theme here begins to take a new turn, such a turn as it has never taken before in Lawrence's fiction, if we discount a remotely similar turn in *The Rainbow*. Connie does leave England, to stay a little while in Paris and longer in a villa at Biarritz. For one thing, this is a ruse to make Clifford believe she will have a lover abroad to father her child. But the trip is equally a chance to arrive at some firm regional perspective as to what place might sustain her instinctual love with Parkin. While in France, Connie gives this matter of place much thought in conjunction with the males that pass within her ken. The real spark of maleness is missing in Parisian men. Among the peasants further south, the spark is still there but on the verge of being extinguished by contact with the town. The place is not here. As for escape from England to the colonies, so often a real alternative to Lawrence characters before, Connie balks FL, 120   because of the *amorphousness* of life in those colonies. As she is on the point of going back to England to face whatever comes, certain FL, 119   now that she is pregnant, the thought of place is fixed: *with intense tenacity she stuck to England.* For the time being, Lawrence was resolute in his attempt to reawaken in England itself the ancient spirits of time and place as the right environment for the blood-consciousness lovers.

In the meantime Parkin's estranged wife has tried to make him take her back and raised a terrific row when he refused. He gives up his gamekeeper's job, to circumvent the scandal, and takes one in a steelworks. Unhappily, he is going the way of all men: that is, in terms of thematic texture up to now, his fate would seem to be unfortunate. But Lawrence tries to bend the novel in another direction. Parkin institutes divorce proceedings against his wife. Connie is hesitant about divorcing Clifford but would take that step, then buy a small farm for Parkin and herself to live on. But Parkin refuses to live on her money. She brings in a childhood friend, Duncan Forbes, to help her talk with Parkin. Forbes is not successful in convincing him how to bow to Connie, but in the final interview the prime wish of this particular Parkin seems to have reversed most of his earlier feelings. He now sees his former position of gamekeeper as that of a servant. He is secretary of the Communist league at his factory. It is not merely suggested, now, that Communism may be the necessary destroying force to precede renewal of society, but that it may be the renewal itself. Duncan Forbes suddenly feels in Parkin's presence the power of a charismatic leader, a sort of leftover from Lawrence's FL, 219   intensely political period: *There came forth from* [Parkin] *a sort of power: a glow of soft, human power which made Duncan suddenly see democracy in a new light, men kindled to this glow of human beauty and awareness, opened glowing to another sort of contact.*

It is strange indeed to find Lawrence's long-cherished flame of male authority reasserting itself under the aegis of democracy and/or communism in a factory, and certainly so in a novel where the hero began as a wood spirit in seclusion from industrial society. To complete his new role, and to put himself well on the way to being a sort of Don Ramón yet, Parkin will agree to live with Connie only if she as a sort of Teresa will sustain him in his political activities.

But this never comes about. Connie now decides to tell Clifford of her pregnancy and to carry out their half-agreement to bring up the child as their own. Clifford's response to his wife's revelation is all but to kneel and worship her as the virgin mother of his heir-to-be. Connie is so horrified and repelled that she begins to see Wragby and all it stands for as putrescent, and to move strongly in the direction of accepting Parkin as he wishes to be accepted. Even so, the ending does not take her to him, only to the half-formed resolve that in the near future she may go and submit: again remotely echoing *The Plumed Serpent.*

It would have been frustrating for Lawrence to leave the situation at that, an ending too inconclusive even for him.

Something had gone wrong, then. Lawrence had failed to get the imaginative hold he wanted on the essence of the male spirit he wished to create, and also on the England which was that man's country. Both of these interwoven shortcomings he sought to remedy in *John Thomas and Lady Jane.* To take the landscape first, a great deal of the now considerably longer novel is concerned with a more intense creation of place. A new brilliance, both terrifying and wonderful, is injected into the natural scenes. The wood at Wragby is a haunting place to Connie to a far greater degree than it was in *The First Lady Chatterley.* Even what might pass for mere description, of seasons and weather and flowers and trees, often takes on a glow and a rhythm reminiscent of the best such passages in *The Rainbow,* that quality of enchantment in landscape for which Lawrence is justly famous and which he elicits with such natural ease. The scenes of love in the wood of course partake of this intensity. For instance, there is the lovemaking in the little grove of firs — it is as though Lawrence's Bavarian or American evergreen forests of discovery had been reduced and transported to a hoped-for England. In this fir grove Parkin looms all of a sudden before Connie, and she soon experiences with this woodland apparition the deepest of all abandon in sex, a true metamorphosis. Here she is awakened to the many potentialities of *the vivid* JL, 130 *dream of passion* that must control the life of mankind if that life is to know the greatest reality.

As a counterpoise to this deepened beauty of landscape in *John Thomas and Lady Jane,* the ugliness of industrial growth across the surface of the Midlands is heightened in proportion. A remarkably revealing tension evolves between what we constantly glimpse as the submerged spirit of English place and the spreading usurpation of industry, which has by now all but blotted out the true features of this piece of earth and seeped in to poison much of its depths. Out of this juxtaposition the several ambiguities with which Lawrence is struggling also unfold, those aspects of his novel which make it far more than a clear-cut opposition between the pastoral and the industrial. These are the complexities of relation between the people and the place. An excellent example of these strivings within the novelist's imagination is found in Chapter IX of the book, in a drive Connie takes through the countryside. She takes the same drive in *The First Lady Chatterley,* but little emerges there except the simple spoiling of beauty by development. In the second version of the work, the situation is otherwise. We accompany Connie *through the long, sordid straggle of Tevershall village,* nominally attached to Wragby but now given over largely to miners. The Midlands spreading away around her give Connie, who in other parts of the nation has felt connected still to the ancient England, the impression that she has left England now, and *entered some weird and unnatural country where everything came from underground.* She passes many of the stately halls of England, some of them in rolling uplands, where a vestige of the old England does linger, thinking what it must have been like to be *a lord of such a country.* Most of the houses are in disrepair when not ready for demolition, to make way for this new civilization that lives not in harmony with all levels of the natural spirit of place but by tearing the bowels out of the earth.

JL, 149

JL, 150

JL, 152

All through this presentation, as a further reach of theme, we have the perhaps insoluble but perfectly revealed dilemma of what man and place bode for the future. The spirit of place is, after all, *not cowed nor broken,* and so it may contain yet a survival of meaning for the future, after some *awful necessity for transition.* This thought brings us at once to the men of the place and to Lawrence's ambivalence toward miners. *The very ugliness* of place has *preserved a manly relentlessness in the men. . . . It was still a country of men, men with weird, incomprehensible underground natures, like trolls. . . . Below, down pit, they were womanless, and partook of the elementality of the minerals.* If we call to mind Lawrence's enthrallment with coal as profoundly linked to the most vital of male being and the human unconscious generally, we can see that he is still toying with the thought that the miners in their

JL, 150

JL, 157

JL, 150
JL, 151

brotherhood may indeed be the precursors of a glorified future society
and not at all a dehumanized horde forced to gouge the earth apart.
But still, on a nearby page, Lawrence does paint them as *not quite*   JL, 157
men. No no! Ghoulish and uncanny. The contrary views of his father's
way of life remained, the question of whether in the mines the father
had exemplified a male life to be envied and emulated, or whether he
had been brutalized by mine labor. The question persists by Lawrence's
asking, but never answering, whether the children of the miners can
ever achieve what Ursula of *The Rainbow* had trusted they could:
ever *make a new world, with mystery and sumptuousness in it.*

Parkin is the figure set up to resolve all this, and in one sense he
is a celebration of Lawrence's father, a celebration urged to some
extent, no doubt, by the death of the elder Lawrence in 1924, but
delayed until Lawrence could undertake to fashion an England resting
on hopes in his father's kind. But Lawrence has further reservations
still. Parkin must go beyond the collier mentality. Connie is certain
that he does. *Even he was limited by some of the weird, mineral
elementality of the colliers,* but she concludes, simply, that he is *a man.*
This is not in itself an enlightening definition, of course, given the
inexactness of the term all through these pages. But Connie does assign
one definite trait to Parkin as a *man.* That he is *solitary, fighting for
his own solitude,* places him as the opposite of the intercommuning
miners underground and extols his position as the aloof possessor and
protector of true spirit of place and spirit of the future.

And so the fundamental difficulty with the hero remains. Woodland integrity of spirit and woodland love are destroyed by forces in
the modern world beyond any power of Parkin or Connie to halt the
catastrophe, the same forces as those operative in the first version. The
difficulty is that the Parkin of *John Thomas and Lady Jane* is a figure
of helplessness still, just as the first Parkin was, now even more helpless
perhaps, for he chooses not to turn political and work to transform by
that means the very industrial system from which he had formerly lived
withdrawn. The present Parkin leaves his industrial job, and can only
protest to Connie: *"I shouldn't care if the bolshevists blew up one half*   JL, 365
*of the world, and the capitalists blew up the other half, to spite them,
so long as they left me and you a rabbit-hole apiece to creep in, and
meet underground like the rabbits do."* In answer to this enduring
desire of her lover to find an isolated place of love in the midst of
holocaust, Connie pointedly remarks, to contrast this second Parkin
with the first, that she is glad he has left the factory, lest he *deteriorate
into a socialist or a fascist, or something dreary and political.*

Still we are left with the question of what Connie and Parkin are
to do. In this second version also they reject the colonies. Connie
had an unconquerable aversion from leaving Europe. She had been   JL, 369

overseas. In search of an ending Lawrence leads his couple to the church at Hucknall Torkard, where the heart of the passionate Byron

JL, 368   is buried. Here a *sense of the greatness of human mistakes* makes Connie *want to cry.* On they go, later, to a wood and to some semblance of the old idyllic love-making in natural surroundings. But then, ironically, a gamekeeper comes to drive them out, and they wander half-lost across the dead countryside. They speak of alternatives. Connie suggests that they go to Italy, on her money of course. Parkin halfway consents but then interposes a suggestion of his own that he will look for some farm work in England. The only positive promise he will make is that if Connie cannot bear to be alone, he will come and live with her. And so the book ends.

These half-hearted choices are inconclusive enough, but what has happened to the chief male character is worse. Instead of creating in this second version a stronger man to balance the heightened conflict between the industrial and natural ways of life forced upon spirit of place, Lawrence had actually weakened his former concept of the man by taking away his political verve and substituting nothing for it. The only solution, then, was yet another rewriting, in order to focus upon a quite different male protagonist. Parkin was to become Mellors in *Lady Chatterley's Lover,* a gamekeeper in deliberate exile from modern society still, but now, through a scholarship, a grammar school product who could have escaped his class except that he came to despise worldly success. One of his principal masks to protect himself from his social superiors, and one through which at the same time he can express his scorn, is to speak to them only in the local dialect. But Connie sees through this mask, on taking her first real notice of

LC, 64   him, and recognizes that *he might almost be a gentleman.* The protagonist's history, especially in education but in sexual experience too, it soon appears, is now close to Lawrence's own.

Only *Lady Chatterley's Lover* completes the design that Lawrence set out to trace. This design was to be a study of the depletion of English manhood, to discover also what might be left of it still in contact with the true underlying spirit of place, and whether its resurgence was conceivable. We should note, as a contrast to Lawrence's fears in *The Plumed Serpent* that the indwelling genius of America might be malign, that his trust in the soul of the English land was all but perfect, and that his task as he saw it was confined to recalling the proper spirit of man to England. The original procedure was magnified to bring a greater number of widely different men within range of Connie's experience and to study their capabilities for carrying her, and a vividness of life with her, through the present deluge toward some replenishing of the earth. Lawrence could never have carried out this design without forging a new character for his gamekeeper, one that would get around his ambivalent feeling toward the manhood of the colliers. All attempts to make Parkin distinct from those denizens of the Midlands, in the two previous tries, had come to nothing decisive. But now the novelist can easily leave the miners almost out of account, for he has removed his hero from their level. The significant contrasts between Mellors and several upper-class men can be pursued unobstructed, for Mellors can now be put on a footing with them.

We now pick up Connie's relationships with men from her girlhood, from her affairs with German boys where the deepest intimacy was in clever and passionate discussions, with sex as an almost perfunctory adjunct. Then comes her marriage with Clifford, the aristocratic intellectual who lives by irony and the privilege of his class but is by no means master of himself nor of any living power. Their relation, too, is far more mental than physical. After Clifford is lamed and made impotent in the war, he fastens onto Connie as if by this to prove his own existence, and she drifts along with him at Wragby in a sort of trance, a married nunhood. Several other men appear on the scene before Connie meets the gamekeeper. Tommy Dukes, for one. As in the second version of the novel, where he made his first appearance, he is the articulate observer who serves as an *oracle* to   LC, 52 Connie. He realizes the deadness of present civilization and talks brilliantly about it, but is impotent to do anything. His celibate life, in which he maintains a number of friendships with women, as with Connie, is due partly to an overdevelopment of the brain at the expense of the blood, and partly to his scorn of the artificial ways of love in current practice. He does cultivate a form, though a very unsatisfactory form, of one male ideal that Lawrence is deeply involved in investigating: aloneness. In this he is a badly framed parallel to Mellors.

At Wragby we are now ushered into a society of words without substance. Clifford and Tommy Dukes and other men have many sessions of scintillating conversation. Connie's role at these sessions is that of listener, a silent support that is absolutely necessary to this display of male wit. To build up the image of this world further than he had yet gone, Lawrence now introduces a character new to his growing theme, Michaelis, an Irish playwright from the lower classes who has made a name and a fortune writing society plays, but who is now being snubbed by high society because they have discovered that his plays really satirize them.[3] Clifford has invited Michaelis down to Wragby because Michaelis has influence in the literary world, and

Clifford himself is scheming to become a successful author. All male accomplishment so far achieved or attempted is through the medium of *brilliant words* that swirl *like dead leaves* across this land.

LC, 47

But Michaelis' role goes beyond that of the word game. Connie is soon having an affair with him, her first unfaithfulness to Clifford. She is now exposed to a new form of male aloneness which is not at all like that of Tommy Dukes. Michaelis' isolation is a part of his success, both material and sexual: *his isolation was a necessity to him; just as the appearance of conformity and mixing-in with the smart people was also a necessity*. Women see in his inner solitude a sort of hang-dog quality that arouses their compassion, which is why Connie yields to him. With him, and with all such in the book, success in the world and in bed are inseparable, but the success in the world is ultimately more significant to him. Connie's praise of his work, which he wrings from her, is to Michaelis *the last thin thrill of passion beyond any sexual orgasm*.

LC, 27

LC, 49

This is a sort of failure of manhood in itself, and it is symptomatic of a much deeper failure. In the presentation of the latter, Lawrence proceeds to make of sexual incompatibility the key to the forlorn condition of the world. Michaelis is subject to premature ejaculations, but he stays inside Connie while she brings *about her own crisis*. Lawrence declares that Michaelis is like many modern men in that *he was finished almost before he had begun. And that forced the woman to be active*. Connie does not mind this situation, rather it arouses in her a feeling of love because it seems to her that this is the *only real mode of intercourse* that Michaelis' isolation will permit him. But Michaelis does mind. He is almost brutal in telling her, finally, that he feels as if he has to hang on while she tears at him. This conflict is a fatal blow to their affair, and Connie is left with nothingness descended on her spirit.

LC, 51

It is not long after this that she meets Mellors. But before entering into this, the climactic relationship, it will be good to consider how Clifford functions as a male figure in this third form of the novel. It is a far more outstanding function than in the previous versions. He serves all the purposes he has before, as foil to Mellors and as the ultimate symbol of the sterility of the modern world, but he is so much more thoroughly revealed in *Lady Chatterley's Lover* that he elicits more sympathy from the reader, and if we take into account that Lawrence himself was almost surely impotent when he wrote the book, we catch at times what may be a sort of horrified identification of the author with his character.

LC, 20

Clifford's ruling ambition, at first, is to be *a first-class modern writer* of fiction, and he succeeds in gaining a reputation, though his stories are in truth only clever and empty. So we have another male conquest which amounts to nothing, and this one has been achieved at a great cost to Connie, for Clifford rises to his best in this endeavor at the time when Connie is totally immersed in tending him, as wife, nurse and all. But when her health begins to break down, through nervous affliction, Clifford is forced to bring in a professional nurse to care for him. This Mrs. Bolton of *Lady Chatterley's Lover* is still, as before, the widow devoted to the memory of her manly husband, but this time she is also a resurrection of the overpowering female figure done with a vengeance, and she and Clifford develop a curious attachment which is half play at being lovers and half a simulated mother-and-son bond.

A change now comes over Clifford. Art had sent him inward to find contentment and had brought him nothing. He now turns outward to industry, and with Mrs. Bolton as the woman behind him, he is soon a dazzling success, an industrial magnate given over to all that Gerald Crich is. At one point, even, he almost has himself and a few others convinced, but never Connie, that his achievements with the mines will bring back his sexual powers so that he can father a child with Connie. His greatest business acumen does not really materialize, however, until he learns late in the novel that Connie will leave him. To receive the comfort of Mrs. Bolton for this shock, he becomes like a child indeed, clinging to her bosom and begging her for kisses, *sinking*   LC, 273 *back to a childish position that was really perverse.* But now *his very passivity and prostitution to the Magna Mater gave him insight into material business affairs, and lent him a certain remarkable inhuman force.* With this, two attacks of Lawrence's on the modern world are unleashed together in a combination the like of which was never achieved elsewhere in his work. The desecration of England by the industrialist has found its agent in the utter physical impotence which came to Clifford truly as no accident but as an outward sign of an inward fate. And this triumph of the destroyer is joined now with a new surrender to the power of the dominant mother, the total situation forming the most scathing commentary possible on male achievement in the modern world. Industrialist and artist alike are impotent, and England in the hands of either is doomed.

While this last portrait of "mother and son" that Lawrence was to delineate in fiction may be thrust as far as possible into a bad light by the narrator, there is still something in the extreme bitterness of the picture to suggest that Lawrence felt a fair measure of self to be contained in it. The novelist heaps every possible bit of scorn upon his creation, down to the last scene when Connie humiliates Clifford to the core by confessing how she has carried on with Mellors under his

LC, 278   very nose, reducing him to *the silence of imbecile obstinacy* in which his only revenge is to refuse to give her a divorce — Frieda had begun her affair with Ravagli not long since, and Lawrence knew it. But it is not the deceived and outraged husband that leaves his mark through Clifford so much as it is the helpless and arrested son. It is a remarkable last portrait of a son and lover for Lawrence to have painted.

          When all that this array of male identities has to offer is gathered
LC, 60   within the radius of the novel, Connie can only *sift the generations of men* and still, after the manner of the prophet Jeremiah, fail to locate one real man in the *byways of Jerusalem*. The central purpose of all this preparation, of course, is to contribute to the meaning of Mellors in his special relation to Lady Chatterley and to England. And, as already pointed out, the deepest emotional identification of the author is with him. He first appears to Connie striding out of the wood like
LC,   *a swift menace.* He possesses *that curious kind of protective authority*
43 & 82   which is a property of the real male and which Connie gladly obeys when she begins to feel his spell. Not only that, but she senses in him an experience and a vision so wide and deep that she can surrender to him all responsibility for herself. This comes as a great solace to Connie, for Clifford is already well along toward what finally drives her into Mellors' arms. Clifford's growing success with the mines, when it does not have the effect of deluding him into thinking he can beget his own child, leads him to talk of permitting a substitute father of Connie's choosing but raising the child as his own. His reasoning,
LC, 104   which to Connie is a terrifying maze of *weird lies,* is that his success and his very life are dedicated only to her and to the future. This talk is to her a *declaration of idolatry,* and in actuality *the cruelty of utter impotence.* Authorial comment at this point shows that to Lawrence this sort of idealized relation to woman is the last capitulation of male strength: *What man with a spark of honor would put this ghastly burden of life-responsibility upon a woman, and leave her there; in the void?*

          The experience and vision of Mellors that give him a natural dominion over women, and men as well, Lawrence carefully builds up through presentation of his hero's native capabilities in conjunction with the course of events in his life. Successful as a scholarship student, he could have gone on to some form of adult success such as the other males chase so eagerly. But having begun as a clerk, he threw over the position and turned to blacksmithing at a colliery — like many of Lawrence's heroes, he has a way with horses. He goes back to the dialect, renouncing standard English. To a degree, this retreat to the common sphere of life is due to his disgust with the middle-class love of money and getting ahead, but it is connected even more to his

frustration with middle-class sexual mores. His first love, obviously LC, 187
modeled on Jessie Chambers, allows him to take her, but she adores
him only when they are talking and petting. Sexual intercourse itself
is repulsive to her. Mellors' second love affair amounts to the same
situation. And then comes Bertha Coutts, of his own class, who breaks
down in him the sexual reserve imposed by the previous women.
He and she copulate, and quarrel, with real abandon. But even the
sexual compatibility soon breaks down, in an important parallel to
Connie's recent experience with Michaelis, for the reason that Bertha
will not cooperate with Mellors in the achievement of simultaneous
orgasm, but waits till he is finished and then clutches at him as the
instrument of her own isolated pleasure. Mellors comes to loathe her
for this, condemns the habit as lesbian, stops sleeping with her, and
at last escapes by joining the army in 1915. She goes to live with a
collier not far off, until she erupts into the story to reclaim her husband
in the later part of the novel. There can be no doubt that this marriage
is based to some extent on the negative side of Lawrence's own union
with Frieda, with the high-born woman given the commonest class in
the fiction.

Mellors goes away to become a well-traveled man like his creator.
He has military service in Egypt and in India. He forms a close bond
overseas with a colonel who sees to it that he is commissioned, a bond
that to most readers displays overtones of homosexuality but is another
of Lawrence's persistent efforts to make the case that this sort of
closeness between men is not to be confused with perverted sex, and
that it is vital to any sort of restoration of unity among mankind.
Mellors learns out there across oceans that the failure of modern
civilization is linked indissolubly with the loss of blood contact between individuals, for instance, like the *gulf impassable* between classes LC, 14
exemplified by Clifford and the village inhabitants, which Lawrence
characterizes as a *denial of the common pulse of humanity.* Mellors
experiences some reawakening of fleshly communication not only
between himself and his colonel but in *the bodily awareness* that comes LC, 259
to prevail between him and the men under his command. The crowning lesson to Mellors is that real civilization, beyond this *industrial* LC, 206
epoch, this *black mistake,* must be grounded on a *natural physical* LC, 259
tenderness, to be encouraged *even between men; in a proper manly
way.* The complementary relation between man and woman that he
comes to believe in, but until he meets Connie despairs of ever knowing, this man defines as *being warm-hearted in love,* as *fucking with* LC, 193
a warm heart.

After the death of his mentor, and an illness seemingly brought
on by a grief that is nearly the end of Mellors himself, he comes back

to England, more determined than ever not to join the middle-class world, nor that of the colliers either. The wood, with its comparative isolation for a gamekeeper, is the nearest thing he can devise to a little

LC, 110   ark in which he can buffet the tide of his degenerate day, in *that bitter privacy of a man who at last wants only to be alone.* When Connie comes to break this privacy, when she first sees Mellors stripped to the waist and washing himself, in this third version of the novel, it is the achieved aloneness of the man that she finds so magnetic: the

LC, 62   *perfect, white, solitary nudity of a creature that lives alone, and inwardly alone.*

We have before us again, then, a man who knows that greatness of soul lies in the delicate balance between the capability of being perfectly alone and participating at the same time in the warm-hearted solidarity of mankind. But Lawrence does not find this ideal of independence versus mutuality any easier to resolve than he ever had or ever would, and some of the scenes that attempt to resolve it bring disturbing implications now and then. A scene that does not arouse any such perplexity is the fullest rendition yet of the fir-grove passion. This nearly perfect moment of love offers some enlightenment on what may be otherwise a puzzle. We recall that Connie practiced a self-induced orgasm with Michaelis that had the consent of the narrative voice, apparently because of her lover's inadequacy, but that the same practice of Bertha Coutts with Mellors is savagely denounced, apparently because Mellors offers her the opportunity of a proper sort of climax and she spurns it. The fir-grove scene clarifies what the novel seeks to define as the correct sort of intercourse, reminding us of a less successful attempt at the same clarification in *The Plumed Serpent.* Connie's participation is not subdued exactly. But if it is not passive, it is submissive in the right degree to Mellors' initiative, so that the lovers reach a simultaneous climax which is a source of infinite satisfaction to them both, and to Connie it brings an adoration for Mellors' power that is at the same time a yearning for pregnancy and a near assurance that it has been achieved.

Another sexual scene, much later on, is as difficult to reconcile with the exemplified tenderness of the fir grove as a similar scene in *Women in Love* is with other events of that novel. This is when Connie is about to go abroad for a little while, there to discover that travel is of no avail to a new life. Mellors is angry at the world in general that she must go, and on their last night together subjects

LC, 231   her to a *sensuality sharp and searing as fire. . . . When the sensual flame of it pressed through her bowels and breast, she really thought she was dying.* Lawrence describes this as an act of *burning out the shames, the deepest, oldest shames, in the most secret places,* and as a

process necessary to abolish the fear of the sheer physical and sensual
self harboring deep in the soul. Only in this way, Lawrence insists, can
two people really share the ultimate of touch, the communication of the
last and final nakedness, and learn to do so without shame.   LC, 232

Although Lawrence is not explicit as to physical acts in this
scene — and this in itself is a curious departure from the norm of the
book — he is surely referring to anal intercourse, as in a similar episode
in *Women in Love.* This in itself will be enough to repel a great many
readers. But more important, thematically, is what the scene is supposed to accomplish in culminating the relationship between the two
lovers, a relationship that is meant to promise the remaking of the
world under renewed male guidance. Obviously it ought to be the
heart of the novel. It is difficult, under this heading, to see how the
scene accomplishes its purpose. If Connie was not cleansed of all
contamination from the decadent male world in the fir-grove scene
— to choose only the most conspicuous example — certainly the whole
force of that scene, and others, leads us to believe that she was. Certainly she has no doubts whatever about the utter commitment of the
sensual relation between herself and Mellors, and no shame attaches
to it. If there has been any hanging back at all, it is in Mellors, but
most of the terms in which this is posited are social, not sensual. That
is, Mellors nurses a hatred against the modern world for keeping him
and Connie apart, and for many other reasons. This is the sort of
anger visible in him on the night when he orders Connie to the bedroom to begin this adventure in sodomy, to which she submits like *a*   LC, 231
physical slave, supposedly convinced that it is restorative. But the
reader may be inclined to think that Mellors is simply taking his frustration with the human race out on Connie, and there is nothing in
the scene to remove this suspicion. It is if anything confirmed by what
takes place next morning, when Connie reminds him that the real
basis of their union is *tenderness,* which she pointedly distinguishes   LC, 235
from the physical congress of the night just past, and Mellors answers
her with no more than a silent kiss. The strongest impression left by
the scene is that Mellors' misanthropy is on a rampage and that Connie's appeal is truly against this.

One of the most remarkable scenes in the novel, however, is a
previous one in which the misanthropy falls into equilibrium with
the other key elements. In preparation for this scene, Connie excitedly
describes her approaching trip to the Continent as a prelude to the
two lovers setting off together for a new life in one of the colonies.
Mellors, who has been to several of them and found them wanting,
is not very optimistic. Right after this talk they meet again in their
hut in the wood during a thunderstorm. To Connie this is *like being*   LC, 202

in a little ark in the Flood: the hut, like the wood itself, is that little vessel in which the lone couple must discover the purpose of the creative cosmos toward the future of man. Mellors denounces priggishness as the capital sin. Mankind has forgotten that *the root of sanity is in the balls.* This had led to the worship of money, not of life. He declares that the love of money will bring men to destroy one another. At first he contemplates with glee this *extermination of the human species and the long pause that follows before some other species crops up.* It is as though the Flood has swept man away.

LC, 203

LC,
203–204

Connie is uneasy with this thought. She thinks she is going to have a child. Laying her cheek against his belly, she begs him to say that he wants the child, and her action soon brings to life in him another consciousness, in which he tries to correlate acceptance of the child with the faint hopes in the common people that Lawrence had expressed. Mellors thinks that one might do something with the colliers, if one could only talk to them. And he delivers to Connie the message he would have for them. Men are to live no longer for money, but for the sake of the vividness of life. The first reform Mellors urges is that men wear red trousers, to make woman aware that they are men. This reform, at least, has been carried out since Lawrence's time, with little effect of the sort he expected. But it is understandable that he should associate, in his own day, the drabness of male clothing with industrial blight. Mellors' other recommendations, on this occasion, have a true enough ring of prophetic warning: to "undevelop," according to a phrase of our day, and to cut the birthrate in an already overcrowded world.

Alone Mellors can do nothing, and we know full well that the novel contains no other men to help him. Sailing away to leave it all is one answer, right enough, but he declares that *the Colonies aren't far enough. The moon wouldn't be far enough.* Even if the ark came to rest out there in space, one could still look back on the world of ruin where men have been transformed into *labour-insects.* So the greatest of distance offers no way for the pioneering individual to save man from his technological doom. A man and a woman, and their child, can only live their little life here. And in token of their own freedom, confined to the ark of the wood though it may be, Mellors and Connie dance naked in the rain.

LC, 206

The essence of this scene is the same as that of the set of circumstances on which the novel ends. The lovers are temporarily separated, with Mellors waiting for his divorce to be decreed final. Connie is staying with her sister in Scotland, hoping that Clifford will eventually release her. When spring comes, and the baby is born, the lovers expect to be together again, on a farm of their own, the nearest to an ark of salvation that the world affords. And it will be here in England, the distance having been renounced. The book closes with a letter from Mellors to Connie. About the industrial world he repeats nearly all that he had to say before, but he ends on a note of real tenderness, affirming that his only lasting belief is in *the little flame* of love between them, which can burn just as brightly in this period of enforced continence as it did during their most sensual encounters. The flame seems to flicker, in Mellors' way of describing it, as a tiny but inextinguishable steering lamp for the ark of the lovers drifting on the dark flood of the modern world, not toward some Ararat far off but, if anywhere, to some corner of England, after the subsiding of the waters. LC, 282

A never-completed bit of fiction from this same period finally gives us a glimpse of the "regenerate man" for whom Lawrence began to reach out in "The Flying Fish" and in *Lady Chatterley's Lover.* This is the "Dream of Life" fragment, which Lawrence may well have written around the time he was starting the third version of his Lady Chatterley novel. It begins as autobiography, with a recollection of the lusty colliers of Lawrence's youth as against those who have knuckled under to female authority and thereby fulfilled the dream of their grandmothers, having become "good" husbands. So the piece begins with disappointment in the male and small hope of his reassertion.

The narrative portion starts with Lawrence as persona leaving his native village on *a soft, hazy October day,* to walk past the familiar mines grown unfamiliar now with the inevitable multiplication of machinery, and on to an old quarry where the expedition into the author's past opens into a visionary future, the same quarry we have met with before. As a boy he had loved this quarry for many reasons: part of it was open and warm and full of flowers, but part was fearful and dark too, and there you could see flowers *that no one ever looked upon.* Pursuing his childish desire, now, *to pass through a gate* here into a *more silent world,* the narrator penetrates to a remote corner of the quarry, lies down, and falls asleep in *a little crystalline cavity in the rock, all crystal, a little pocket or womb of quartz.* PH, 822 PH, 824

A little comparison and reflection make it easy to see that this is one of those bits of early life and background that proceed in recurrence out of the depths of Lawrence's imagination to symbolize much in his art. In his immediate memory arise the juxtaposition of light and dark so meaningful to him and the discovery of the flowers of life as the first explorer to reach them. He used to play there with a sweetheart of earliest childhood, who later recalled that they *had shared so many joys and sorrows* in the neighborhood of the quarry. CB, vol. 1, 32

DR,
vol. 12,
146 &
ML, 953

VG, 48

PH, 827

PH, 829

PH, 832

Jessie Chambers remembered with emotion a visit to this place in Lawrence's company. His father was born in a cottage in a quarry, we remember, apparently this one. The Mrs. Holroyd of Lawrence's play, with her intricate responses to her husband's death in the mine, was associated with this area. The quarry makes its appearance in *The Virgin and The Gipsy* as the home of the gipsy, where Yvette begins to open to him *like a mysterious early flower*. It was, in brief, a vessel for rebirth by a voyage through time, a rebirth into magnificent manhood.

This is what occurs a thousand years after the persona falls asleep. Men of a strong new race bathe and massage him till he comes back to life, men with *formal, peaceful faces and trimmed beards, like old Egyptians*. As he returns with them to their village, near sundown, the fresh world lies before him. *On the slopes to the left were big, rectangular patches of dark plough-land. And men were ploughing still. On the right were hollow meadows, beyond the stream, with tufts of trees and many speckled cattle being slowly driven forwards. And in front the road swerved on, past a mill-pond and a mill, and a few little houses, and then swerved up a rather steep hill. And at the top of the hill was a town, all yellow in the late afternoon light, with yellow, curved walls rising massive from yellow-leaved orchards, and above, buildings swerving in a long oval curve, and round, faintly conical towers rearing up. It had something at once soft and majestical about it, with its soft yet powerful curves, and no sharp angles or edges, the whole substance seeming soft and golden like the golden flesh of a city.*

And I knew, even while I looked at it, that it was the place where I was born, the ugly colliery townlet of dirty red brick. Even as a child, coming home from Moorgreen, I had looked up and seen the squares of miners' dwellings, built by the Company, rising from the hill-top in the afternoon light like the walls of Jerusalem, and I wished it were a golden city, as in the hymns we sang in the Congregational Chapel.

Men now lead a ritual life. Rational man has given way to intuitive man. In the central square of the village *they were dancing the sun down, and dancing as birds wheel and dance, and fishes in shoals, controlled by some strange unanimous instinct. It was at once terrifying and magnificent, I wanted to die, so as not to see it, and I wanted to rush down, to be one of them. To be a drop in that wave of life.*

Time is now reborn in the cadence of the heart and the blood, not in the measuring of days by arithmetic. Space is reborn as the vast region where the human meets the divine and re-enacts in rhythmic cycle the ceremony of struggle and atonement. It is the pattern of imaginative experience that we meet everywhere in the writings of Lawrence. And the pieces of which the vision is knit are characteristic. In spite of his constant movement through the world, Lawrence continued always under the spell of feelings imposed by the fixed place and time of early life. The distant and perfected future holds in store the village that his childhood imaginings made golden in the light of chapel hymns: Eastwood become New Jerusalem — or, to repeat Aldous Huxley's phrase, Eastwood become the *Village of the Dark* HL, xxix *God.* The men of this piece of writing are Lawrence's own Midlanders, men like his father, speaking the dialect a thousand years in the future, after the cultivated English of his mother has gone silent forever: the father reincarnate and restored to power. But while so many of the elements of this vision are the hauntings of childhood, Lawrence bought to it also elements of his absorption with time and place far from Eastwood. The reawakening in the "tomb" of the quarry recalls the marvel of life in death he had recently seen in Etruscan tombs, which had made the idea of resurrection seem so potent. The dancers have learned their rhythms from the Hopi and Santo Domingo and Taos Indians. And all imaginings are borne inward to action and scene in that depth of Lawrence cosmology where the whole world — homeland and strange land — is Atlantis or the Crete of Minos or ancient Egypt or Etruria or pre-Aztec America or England. But Lawrence could go no further toward a real fictional reconstruction of a transformed England. He had tried in Mexico to imagine a world after the flood and he was not at all satisfied with the result. At home he could portray with great ability the latter days and the saving remnant. That was reality to him. The future was an idea, and an idea required a different sort of fabling.

NOTES

[1] When plans were underway for a London production of the play, which finally did come about in May 1927, Lawrence wrote music for it. The manuscript is in the Dartmouth College library. *See also* KL, 302.

[2] Although Lawrence wrote the story about a month before he began his last visit to the British Isles, chances are that he revised it to incorporate his firsthand experience with northern islands in August 1926. *See* SR, 151–153.

[3] The original for the character was Michael Arlen, a writer of Armenian origin whose real name was Dikran Kouyoumdjian and whom Lawrence had known since Bloomsbury days. Arlen had considerable success in the Twenties with novels like *The Green Hat* (1924). *See* ML, 1023, for Lawrence's report of meeting him again in 1927 and his description of him in terms much like those applied to Michaelis in *Lady Chatterley's Lover.*

14

Nothing Matters but the Longest Journey

The foregoing line, from one version of a late Lawrence poem, "The Ship of Death," sums up admirably the counter movement to the lovers cultivating a farm in England and holding out as in an ark until the subsiding of the waters across a wasted land. The *longest journey* was, of course, the journey of death, and to sustain him against the certainty of its approach, Lawrence also at this period created a series of symbolic journeys into time, space, and eternity in the Mediterranean. These soon came to outweigh the concurrent vision of the Ark and the Flood in Britain, reaching out through *Etruscan Places* and *The Escaped Cock* and *Apocalypse* and a whole set of poems like "The Ship of Death" to round out Lawrence's last vision of the Mediterranean world where his quest for the meaning of existence had found its first true expansion years before.

CP, 960

At no better place could he have begun this final search than the Etruscan tombs. As mentioned in the last chapter, Lawrence had first seized on the idea of writing about the Etruscans in the spring of 1926, several months before Lady Chatterley came along to occupy his attention. But a far earlier background to his fascination with this vanished race must be brought to mind. His later turning to them might be said to fulfill a beginning made in 1914 toward understanding the mystery of the ancients through the remains of their art, when he saw in the Egyptian and Assyrian sculpture at the British Museum something of *the tremendous unknown forces of life* that those races appeared to have enjoyed. But Lawrence did not become archeological in outlook for a long time, and never to any great degree. Discounting the bit of archeology he took up in Mexico, he never attempted until this late excursion into the Etruscan past anything like an arche-

ML, 291

ological study of those early races who embodied for him the ideal of the *Minoan distance*.

His first significant treatment of the Etruscans, however, was stimulated not by archeology but by an atmosphere of place — Tuscany in the fall of 1920. A poem written there, "Cypresses," revolves upon the metaphor *of slender, flickering men of Etruria* swaying in **CP, 297** his mind like the tall cypresses before his eyes. Those Etruscans, with their still-undeciphered tongue, appeared to Lawrence to have been masters of *dark thought,/For which the language is lost,* and he was **CP, 296** already wondering whether he might be able to recover some of their *delicate magic of life* by invoking their spirit out of the tombs. For **CP, 298** more than six years after writing the poem, he had persevered at the task it set by seeking to reaffirm the spirit of Montezuma against modern American denial. He was back now to continue his quest by reawakening the Etruscans out of the oblivion they had suffered from the Romans. The travel sketches resulting from this effort are the fountainhead of most of his other last works.

Besides the intervention of *Lady Chatterley's Lover,* it was partly Lawrence's health that caused about a year's delay in his tour of some of the Etruscan tomb sites. But he seems also to have been waiting for the right person to accompany him, some man sympathetic with his views and agreeable to be with. This man became available in his now fast friend Earl Brewster. Lord Berners, a rich Englishman, would have been glad to drive them about in his Rolls-Royce, but Lawrence found this idea distasteful. *Better tramp it our two selves,* he wrote **ML, 967** Brewster.

Which is what they did, now and again turning to the commonest forms of transportation for longer distances. The real expedition began in Rome, where they examined Etruscan objects in the museum of the Villa di Papa Giulia and probably in other museums, and continued from there to Cerveteri, a few miles up the coast, on April 6, 1927. The same day, after several hours at the nearby tombs, they made their way on north to Tarquinia, to stay for two days, then to the site of the vanished Etruscan city of Vulci, and finally to Volterra. Lawrence was back at the Villa Mirenda by Monday night, April 11.

This brief tour was intended to be followed by more extensive investigation later on. But the traveler began writing his sketches, **LS, 87** just the same, a couple of weeks after returning to Florence, and pro- **LS, 90** duced six of them by the beginning of July. As it turned out, due to ill health, the pressure of other works, and the small enthusiasm of publishers, Lawrence never wrote any further sketches. The existing ones were not published in book form till after his death. Still there

is no sense of handling a fragment in *Etruscan Places.* This last travel
work of Lawrence's, like the earlier *Sea and Sardinia,* conveys that
feeling of a superior intelligence penetrating quickly and thoroughly
to the heart of a place and its civilization, in this case a long-vanished
one.

The sudden awakening to the truth approach is common, as we
have noticed, in much of Lawrence's travel writing. So is it here:
EP, 1   *Myself, the first time I consciously saw Etruscan things, in the museum
at Perugia, I was instinctively attracted to them.* The ancient Romans
were not. They thought the Etruscans *vicious.* The narrator thus sets
himself against the traditional thought of the western world concerning his ancient heroes. He believes the Romans could not understand
their neighbors because the Roman order of power was totally dif-
EP, 29   ferent and inferior: the Romans lived by *brute force,* the Etruscans
by a *delicate sensitiveness* to the processes of life and death.

Lawrence's travel books always knit together a skillful blend of
some remote and alluring past with the vivid movement of the present.
The opportunity afforded for this in the circumstances of *Etruscan
Places* was an especially happy one. The traveler looks at the April
landscape with an ever-present comparison in mind between it and
what he feels the countryside must have been like several centuries
before Christ under Etruscan dominion. Much is gone of that time
when intense cultivation of the land still kept a harmony with nature,
but some things yet remain to let one know that a noble and vital
population has passed this way. Not only the Etruscans, but the early
Greeks besides. The latter seem to hover about the asphodels that
the travelers spy on their way from the railway station out to the
tombs at Cerveteri. Most moderns are disappointed, says the traveler,
EP, 8   that the Greeks selected such a *sparky, assertive flower* as the flower
of death. But the choice was perfect, for the flower *has a certain reck-
less glory, such as the Greeks loved.* The traveler's eager acceptance
of the flower of death is one small commitment of emotions to the
great power of death, preceding many of far larger scope in these
sketches.

The population through this whole region also calls up many
parallels with the ancient dwellers. This year may have been during
the height of that period when the Mussolini government was going
all out to make Italy seem as Roman as possible, but such residual
traits of olden times as the people exhibit more often appear Etruscan
than Roman to the keen eye of the traveler, if not more ancient still
than Etruscan. The faun is still visible in a Maremma shepherd who
shows up briefly at a little cave of a tavern, a rare example of a breed
of true male that must soon become extinct even here. The women

VULCI, ITALY

*Behind us to the right stood
the lonely black tower of the castle* (EP, 92)

EP, 7 seem more Etruscan in nature than anything else, somewhat this side of the faun in human development. They go about with the *noiselessness and inwardness, which women must have had in the past, ... something that can be lost, but can never be found out.*

These preliminary observations bring us prepared to the first tombs in Cerveteri, where at once the fundamental Lawrence is at work to reconcile and atone the great mystery of death with the beauty of life. He loves the Etruscans because of what he takes to be their simple yet profound affirmation of life and death as one joyous whole. In the first place, the Etruscans eschewed great monumental things — that was Roman. As Lawrence had said some years before of the Homeric Greeks, the greatness was in the man, and his house was a modest dwelling. The Etruscans were like that. Their houses and their temples too were small, wooden, and gaily painted. Their cities they built on high places, for defense naturally, but nearly always they sought out two hills side by side: one for the city of life, the other, which they tried to make look just as pleasant as the first, for the city of the dead. Always the Etruscans cultivated this easy concourse between life and death, a culminating appeal to Lawrence at this later stage of his life. Once actually arrived among the tombs at Cerveteri, he can look back over many years of travel among many racial expressions of death and find about him at present that elusive *Minoan distance* which makes the Etruscan feeling for death superior to all he

EP, 9 has known heretofore: *There is a queer stillness and a curious peaceful repose about the Etruscan places I have been to, quite different from the weirdness of Celtic places, the slightly repellent feeling of Rome and the old Campagna, and the rather horrible feeling of the great pyramid places of Mexico, Teotihuacan and Cholula, and Mitla in the south; or the amiably idolatrous Buddha places in Ceylon. There is a stillness and a softness in these great grassy mounds with their ancient stone girdles, and down the central walk there lingers still a kind of loneliness and happiness. True, it was a still and sunny afternoon in April, and larks rose from the soft grass of the tombs. But there was a stillness and a soothingness in all the air, in that sunken place, and a feeling that it was good for one's soul to be there.*

At this point, and often elsewhere in *Etruscan Places,* Lawrence refers to the tombs as *homes of the dead,* and he means this in an exact sense. Apparently he had some authority for feeling this way from the actual attitudes and beliefs of the Etruscans themselves. Not only in the location of their city of the afterlife did they attempt to create as near as possible an image of this life. The tombs were constructed and furnished in a lifelike manner, with the bodies of the great at Cerveteri laid out in stone sarcophagi, and all around them

CERVETERI, ITALY

There is a stillness and a softness
in these great grassy mounds with their ancient stone girdles (EP, 9)

on the walls lively painted scenes. As Lawrence understood this,

EP, 12   *death, to the Etruscan, was a pleasant continuance of life, with jewels and wine and flutes playing for the dance. It was neither an ecstasy of bliss, a heaven, nor a purgatory of torment. It was just a natural continuance of the fullness of life.* Lawrence hints several times at what at least one later Etruscan scholar identifies as a religious belief

TE, 125   of that culture expressed in the joyous frescoes: that when the tomb was closed the scenes actually came to life to form the environment of a new postmortem existence for the dead person. The most jubilant of these frescoes date from the earlier periods, before too much contact with the Romans brought about a degeneration — as Lawrence would have it — of Etruscan culture, and they represent, as does everything

EP, 10   in the tombs beginning with their structural design, what he calls *the natural beauty of proportion of the phallic consciousness.* That the Etruscans put great stress on phallic worship is evident from the *cippi,* or little phallic pillars found in abundance in connection with the tombs.

These glimpses into the religion of the long-extinct people to whom he felt he belonged by nature became for Lawrence a reconciliation with death in his own experience. He went to the Etruscan tombs as a medieval Christian might have gone to a monastery to prepare for the next world. But intimate as death may have seemed with life here, it was not a matter, among the Etruscans, of carrying on the next life on the premises of the necropolis itself. A journey of death was involved, and this too was compatible with Lawrence's brand of theology. In the tombs of the high-born dead many provisions had been made for their journey to the underworld. Carvings on the pillars and walls show articles they would need, and also

EP,   sometimes *the dog who is man's guardian even on the death journey.*
11–12   All sorts *of amazing impedimenta* were placed near the coffins: jewels,
EP,   dishes, tools, weapons, and then, always, *the little bronze ship of*
10–11   *death,* the vessel to bear the soul, not as among the Greeks and Romans to a Hades of thirsty shades, with a happy few permitted to sail on to the Blessed Isles, but to a place of ease and feasting for all the worthy and heroic. These Etruscan ships of death, with most of their accoutrements, were the pattern for Lawrence's own, which he was already building.

What principle of immortality was Lawrence evolving, then, that might be different in any sense from the continuance of the spirit of the dead in the living, the immortality he had most consistently affirmed up to now? The symbolism in *Etruscan Places* takes on several new ramifications. One is an elaboration of the "ark" theme in such a way as to yield a new variant to this well-established order of symbolism. Near the doorway of some tombs at Cerveteri were house-like or boxlike structures. This appears to have been the woman's emblem, as the little phallic pillar, the *cippo,* was the man's. Lawrence makes the connection between these and his ship-of-death/ship-of-rebirth construct by bringing in the motif of the Ark. The little boxes are indeed boatlike, like *the Noah's Ark box we had as chil-*   EP, 14 *dren, full of animals.* The symbol then expands in Lawrence's sensibility to surround the furthest implications of tomb and womb significance, including an etymological link among the different longings for restoration that take in both the womb of rebirth and the long voyage in search of the same consummation. It is a fanciful etymology, perhaps, in any event of poetic not scientific worth, of the Latin word *arx.* From early in this sketch Lawrence mentions now and then the stronghold, the citadel, high up in the center of each Etruscan city. By taking citadel with ark in both senses, he adds to what may have been a phallic tower on a high place the sense of the yonic as well as the idea of a vessel that bears life. The sense is double: of carrying life till it can issue forth into the world, and of carrying it on a voyage through dangerous waters to its end. The little house or box at the doorway of the Etruscan tomb is *the Ark, the arx, the womb. The womb of all the world, that brought forth all the creatures. The womb, the arx, where life retreats in the last refuge. The womb, the ark of the covenant, in which lies the mystery of eternal life, the manna and the mysteries.* And then, within two pages, drawing his sketch to a close, the keen-eyed traveler catches in the handsome faces of the local women some of *the lustre* of the Etruscans EP, still shining. They still possess, to some degree, what has been dese- 16–17 crated in the tombs, *the mystery of the unrifled ark.*

    Three of the six sketches, comprising more than half of the text of *Etruscan Places,* center on Tarquinia, the next large site up the coast from Cerveteri and one of the richest of all. Here, for two days, Lawrence and Brewster visited at least seventeen of the more than twenty-five tombs then opened, dividing their time between the underground of the tombs and the upper world of the spring-soft Italian countryside, which Lawrence still insisted on seeing, and with marvelous effect, as Etruscan. The best-preserved frescoes were in these tombs at Tarquinia, dating from early to late in the history of the ancient city. From one to another Lawrence carries out his eloquent re-creation of these paintings, in a manner reminiscent of the first time he ever came under the spell of religious imagery on dim walls, in the mountain chapel of Bavaria long ago, only now with an infinitely

EP, 46   greater skill and perception, all the while feeling *divided between the pleasure of finding so much and the disappointment that so little remains.*

EP,
38 & 40   As he descends into a tomb, he does *not seem to be underground at all, but in some gay chamber of the past. . . . And gradually the underworld of the Etruscans becomes more real than the above day of the afternoon.* But at times the proximity of the Etruscan remains brings another effect, and with this something of the great variety of Lawrence's response to the past and present through place. At such a moment he can look out across the double hills such as always constituted the topography of an Etruscan city and think of them in this

EP, 27   way: *The two hills are as inseparable as life and death, even now, on the sunny, green-filled April morning with the breeze blowing in from the sea. And the land beyond seems as mysterious and fresh as if it were still the morning of Time.* It is a magnificent feeling to have this sort of vivifying contact with the past and present both above and below ground, while seeking out assurances on death and immortality among the shades of the Etruscans in the rapturous Hades of their tombs.

One of the qualities that make Lawrence's imaginative recapture of the past so satisfying to read is a sort of two-fold nostalgia which can only exist in a writer if he possesses, as Lawrence did, the faculty of almost total recall. The nostalgia is two-fold because it presents in the light of memory two levels of the past, both illuminated by that sense of discovery and of inevitable loss working together which produces nostalgia. The thorough and spontaneous recall that brings up before the mind of the writer any detail he needs also lays out a flow of narrative which creates with great immediacy the fragment of life just lived to completeness and now vanished forever. That quality of nostalgia we find in all of Lawrence's best travel writing, in *Sea and Sardinia* particularly. With *Etruscan Places* it is the same, but that distant past which the traveler is in the process of unearthing and identifying carries also the full content of the emotion hovering about the certainty that he is unveiling an all-but-forgotten past to which he belongs but which he can only enter through symbol in the flow of the printed word or in contemplation. A phrase drifts through the text now and again confirming to the conscious mind of the pilgrim what his language is perpetually engaged in creating. He speaks out-

EP, 87   right of *the poignancy of perfect things long forgotten* in Etruscan
EP, 101   stones, of their *peculiar weighty richness,* or at one point where the
EP, 92   country is now empty, of that *peculiar, almost ominous, poignancy of places where life has once been intense.*

NEAR VULCI, ITALY

The ancient bridge, built in the first place
*by the Etruscans of Vulci, of blocks of black **tufo**,*
goes up in the air like a black bubble, so round and strange . . . ,
with the poignancy of perfect things long forgotten (EP, 87)

One of the best moments of this sort of nostalgic recall comes in Lawrence's description of the Tomb of the Leopards at Tarquinia. As he writes he attempts to see the scene live again as it did before his eyes a few weeks past. The narrative flows along in the present tense as though this might be the description of a procession in a village, out of *Sea and Sardinia* perhaps, but what Lawrence is pre-

EP, 38 senting is a scene of the tomb as if in movement: *On come the dancers and the music-players, moving in a broad frieze towards the front wall of the tomb, the wall facing us as we enter from the dark stairs, and where the banquet is going on in all its glory.* There are some three pages of this reconstruction, all of it molded to the purpose stated at

EP, 39 one point in the passage: *You cannot think of art, but only of life itself,* in looking at these painted scenes. The immediacy is all there, and yet much of the glow arises from your knowing, along with the traveler himself, that the movement is of two forms of the past, in one's own dwindling life, and in one's soul companions of long ago.

In Tarquinia, Lawrence continues to reach for the same effect on the surface of the present that he seeks in the burial chambers. He does so, for instance, on the evening of the first day spent in the area. And here he makes the far-off past merge with the present day to a degree almost unparalleled elsewhere in the book. He and Brewster watch the peasants coming in from the fields, peasants as in every age given over to intense cultivation of the soil. A moment's watching

EP, 58 is sufficient for the past to begin to obtrude upon the present. *On a fine evening like this,* in Etruscan times, *the men would come in naked, darkly ruddy-coloured from the sun and wind.* There would be singing and piping, salutes on passing the gay little temple, young nobles on horseback riding by, and all the whirl of life. Using sometimes past, sometimes conditional, and sometimes a straight present tense, Law-rence brings out a little scene in which the great magistrate, the Lu-cumo, passing along the street in his magnificent chariot, stops to pronounce justice upon the plea of a citizen. This section is a miniature of the return to the village after a thousand years in "A Dream of Life." The future there is the equal of the past here, the resplendent life gone but returned. But then, after the magistrate rides on, we fall back into the drabness of the present, to peasants in modern times, and again to the metal tables of the cafe where the travelers sit watching.

So discovery proceeds on several planes at once, always with the mystery of life among the Etruscans as the aura enveloping the whole march of the prose. But more occurs than the exposing to view of a mystery. The mystery has its symbols, extant still in Etruscan ruins, and Lawrence takes great pains to interpret these. He had declared several years before, in his "Foreword" to *Fantasia of the*

VOLTERRA, ITALY

Strange, dark old Etruscan heads of the city gate,
even now they are featureless they still have a peculiar,
out-reaching life of their own (EP, 101)

FU, 6   *Unconscious,* his belief in *a science in terms of life,* antediluvian in origin — that is, from the period before the glaciers melted and the seas rose to cover Atlantis and such places — a science that the Etrus-
FU, 7   cans and others remembered in *symbolic forms.* In much of the
EP,   burial sculpture, for example, the reclining man *holds in his hand the*
29–30   *sacred* **patera,** *or* **mundum,** *the round saucer with the raised knob in the centre.* This object must represent *the round germ of heaven and earth,* the *indivisible God* that yet divides and goes on dividing, *unborn and undying.* In effect, the man is holding in his hand his immortal soul, which is synonymous with the highest god.

    A great many symbols do not yield their meaning as easily as this one. Lawrence insists that in the life-science at the dawn of his-
EP, 66   tory, each symbol had *an exact esoteric meaning,* and that it aroused a particular emotion. But he does not expect always to recover this meaning. For that matter, neither could the Etruscan artist, for he too, though closer to the mystic source than any modern could hope to be, came long after the prime of the ancient way. He could only be *more or less aware* of *the profundity of the symbolic meaning* of what he was working with, but that awareness was the whole sum of his art and gave him his quickness in contrast to the deadness of most modern artists.

    Therefore Lawrence seldom suggests exact interpretation. In the Tomb of the Bulls he pores over the heraldic beasts of a gable-surface painting, one a lion with a goat's head sprouting from its shoulders — a *chimera.* Of this he can make nothing precise, only to say that whatever it is, it has the kind of symbolic force that makes of the famous Chimaera of Arezzo *one of the most fascinating bronzes in the world.* In the Tomb of the Augurs he calls attention to the same limitations of modern insight, refuting the likelihood that a wrestling match portrayed there is only a sport. A man with a crooked staff presides over the contestants. Birds fly above. A man just beyond the wrestlers guides by a sort of leash rod a ferocious dog attacking the genitals of a hooded man. Lawrence's insistence that this is a
EP, 71   scene symbolic of some kind of *raging, attacking element,* and not simply a barbarous sport, is based on the absence of spectators and a nearby scene depicting the controller of the dog in a kind of victory dance. In another endeavor at elucidating ancient symbols, Lawrence
EP, 107   moves closer to what might be thought "exact" equivalence. *The wings of the water-deities* may *represent evaporation towards the sun.* The arching tail of the dolphin may stand for torrents, the two images together representing *the come-and-go of the life-powers.* But still, by this interpretive scheme, the "exactness" of representation was

ETRUSCAN MUSEUM, FLORENCE

The famous bronze Chimaera of Arezzo . . . ,
which Benvenuto Cellini restored,
and which is one of the most fascinating bronzes
in the world. (EP, 66)

designed to arouse a complex of emotions of which moderns are no longer capable, not to produce a simple and automatic personification.

In a further undertaking, the pilgrim on occasion moves in through the symbolism to what he takes ancient prophecy to have been, the Etruscans having had a reputation for being seers. He approaches this subject through symbols of water as opposed to those of the air, and then advances to what the *auspex* or the *haruspex* might have perceived. This is an especially important passage, for it tells us what Lawrence thought about the kind of psychological insight on which the poet and the prophet both depend. The *auspex* stood on a high spot and observed the flight of birds as if they were impulses in the breast of man. The *haruspex* traced out the convolutions in the still warm organs of sacrificed animals. Both then made their predictions according to a forgotten science. But they were only doing, says Lawrence, what men still do in deciding a course to the future, finding their own form of access to inner power. The passage merits quoting in full:

EP, 55   *If you live by the cosmos, you look in the cosmos for your clue. If you live by a personal god, you pray to him. If you are rational, you think things over. But it all amounts to the same thing in the end. Prayer, or thought or studying the stars, or watching the flight of birds, or studying the entrails of the sacrifice, it is all the same process, ultimately: of divination. All it depends on is the amount of* **true,** *sincere, religious concentration you bring to bear on your object. An act of pure attention, if you are capable of it, will bring its own answer. And you choose that object to concentrate upon which will best focus your consciousness. Every real discovery made, every serious and significant decision ever reached, was reached and made by divination. The soul stirs, and makes an act of pure attention, and that is a discovery.*

Etruscan Places, as we have seen, is made up of alternate or interwoven sections of exploration into the past in the underworld of the tombs, and of observation of several sorts above ground. The book
EP, 49   is a quest for *the wandering huge vitalities of the world* on both of these planes. But it never overlooks the everyday, as in the portraits of people met in passage: as of Albertino, for instance, a manly lad
EP, 25   of fourteen with his *wistfulness, and trustfulness, and courage,* who is really the force behind the management of the inn in Tarquinia where the travelers stay, instead of his parents. Or there is Luigi, the herdsman turned baker's helper, who guides Lawrence and Brewster to the site of Vulci, a young man with the wildness of the open still about him. Finally, there is the young German student of archeology, the

"scientific" spirit as against the poetic spirit of the narrator, the man in search of "facts" who attributes no meaning to anything else.

Beyond individuals, from time to time, come observations of what the current politics of Italy creates among the populace, the best example of which is the evening in Volterra when the Italians, a people who can *never be wholeheartedly anything,* welcome a new   EP, 100 fascist official to the town with much noise and motion and a suppressed *jeering.* Or there are such splendid moments in the presence   EP, 99 of nature as that on the cliffs at Volterra at sunset, when the everyday verges on the miraculous: *All the vast concavity of the west roars*   EP, *with gold liquescency, as if the last hour had come, and the gods were*   103–104 *smelting us all back into yellow transmuted oneness.*

Everything in the book, ultimately, has its bearing upon a dual movement to come to rest and to proceed, either to stay and belong or to pass on in isolation. This is at one point expressed simply as the opposition between residing in the Etruscan area and traveling on. It is a glimmer of Rananim once more, or a Kiowa Ranch near the Mediterranean: *to live here, and have a house on the hills, and a horse*   EP, 97 *to ride, and space.* But the antitheses of mobility and fixity must be brought together, the traveler feels. This may be accomplished with some satisfaction by beholding what appears to shine forth from the art of the Etruscans. In that world each *isolated individual thing* had   EP, 68 its being, but at the same time a man on a horse, say, was a creature *surging along on a surge of animal power that burned with travel,*   EP, *with the passionate movement of the blood, and which was swirling*   68–69 *along on a mysterious course, to some unknown goal.* So that Etruscan immersion in the allness of the universe went hand in hand with a high degree of individuality, and of movement and stillness together.

It is not until we carry this sort of symbolic process to the accommodation of life with death, Lawrence's prime purpose in visiting the Etruscan tombs, that we can best appreciate the subtlety of it. The many contraries, in the final analysis, express the soul, which for the narrator *means that mysterious conscious point of balance*   EP, 56 *or equilibrium between the two halves of the duality.* With vividness on either hand, the soul goes into the egg, a symbol held up in display by many a fiery Etruscan man of the paintings, and in the egg awaits rebirth. But while the soul is the burning point between contraries, it is itself single and indivisible, a state which Lawrence would have to be its immortality. It is also, he proceeds to say, its own altar of sacrifice, life and death together. While it offers itself endlessly to annihilation, it is simultaneously at the task of engendering itself without end. It can offer itself with faith to the process of destruction

VOLTERRA, ITALY

*The **Badia** or Monastery of the Camaldolesi, sad-looking,*
destined at last to be devoured by Le Balze,
its old walls already splitting and yielding (EP, 103)

because it knows it can never be extinguished but will always return. Immortality, then, to the pilgrim in Lawrence, was the undying spark at the point of contact between the cosmic coming and going, a spark beyond the comprehension of a continuity conceived only as survival of the individual ego in the form of a spirit, "saved" or escaped from the material world.

In all these ways, then, the pilgrim in *Etruscan Places* sought out among the Etruscan ruins the *great sense of journeying* which alone   EP,110 could bring him through the final stages of his own journey and shape for him a form of immortality and afterlife adequate to his imaginative needs.

A work devoted to the same purposes as *Etruscan Places* and connected with it in a particular fashion is *The Escaped Cock* — or to give it the blander title under which it has long appeared, *The Man Who Died*. There are two forms of this fine piece of fiction: a short   AC,433 story written before any of the Etruscan sketches, within about two weeks after Lawrence's return to the Villa Mirenda, and the novella produced by making some changes in the short story and adding a second part, in the summer of 1928. The first "Escaped Cock" was a preparation for writing the Etruscan sketches, chronologically as well as in more important ways, for Lawrence turned from the story immediately to the sketches. My reason for not discussing it before *Etruscan Places* is that it will be easier to show how the definitive tale spans the complex of responses to life and death that Lawrence was undergoing all through this period. We need to remind ourselves also, perhaps, that this is the time of the final shaping of *Lady Chatterley's Lover* and the last stage of development in Lawrence's work of the phallic mystery.

The background of the first "Escaped Cock" is vital to a knowledge of its significance. On the Sunday morning of their arrival in Volterra,   RC,123 April 10 — Palm Sunday, not Easter as Brewster later recalled — Lawrence and he saw in a shop window a toy either of a rooster emerging from an egg or of a rooster escaping from a man. Brewster remarked, according to his own account, that someone ought to write a story about the Resurrection and entitle it "The Escaped Cock." Lawrence is supposed to have replied that he had thought of writing such a story but he seems to have had no title in mind. When he men-   ML,975 tioned having done the story, in a letter to Brewster a few weeks later, he identified the toy as the source of the title, though he did not give Brewster credit for thinking of it.

In any case, is was a coincidence of the sort that can suggest great things to a writer like Lawrence. The Etruscan tour happened to coincide with the Easter season, and the chance discovery of a toy

VOLTERRA, ITALY

They say these covered-wagon journeys are peculiar to Volterra,
found represented in no other Etruscan places . . . .
There is a great sense of **journeying:**
as of a people which remembers its migrations. (EP, 110)

emblematic of death and resurrection appears to have added a climactic touch to the symbolism of the tombs. An imaginative difficulty of vast importance was thereby brought to a head. How the magnificence of life could be lengthened into death was to be the burden of the Etruscan writings, but this involved the hard task of grafting the forgotten way of the ancients onto the Christ identity that Lawrence could not help professing. The problem was two-fold: in what way to conceive of immortality in terms of this phenomenal world, and in what way to deal with, once more, the old difficulty of how much to join with others as against how much to separate oneself from them, and what this proportion must be to allow for a real male identity. Lawrence spoke of this duality just now as the *sympathetic flow* ML,974 versus the *combative,* and his mood at one moment dictated that the combative had been undervalued. Still, at another moment, he plainly felt that aloneness might mean complete isolation. He wrote Mabel Dodge Luhan on Good Friday that he was *suffering from a change of* LT,325 *life, and a queer sort of recoil, as if one's whole soul were drawing back from connection with everything. This is the day they put Jesus in the tomb — and really, those three days in the tomb begin to have a terrible significance and reality to me. And the Resurrection is an unsatisfactory business — just noli me tangere and no more.* What better way to work out that "terrible reality" than to make the coming forth of the Son of Man like an Etruscan afterlife, a continuance of the glory of this life. And yet, how could a mutuality of human experience be reconciled with the withdrawal or elevation above the common man brought on by any sort of resurrection, how could any kind of unison be reached after the terrible isolation imposed by death? Death left the soul *combative.* How could the *sympathetic* be restored?

In the short story "The Escaped Cock" Lawrence did not accomplish both of these ends. He thought he had accomplished the first, that is, that Jesus was wholly reborn when on awaking he found *what* ML,975 *an astonishing place the phenomenal world is, far more marvellous than any salvation or heaven.* Lawrence did not yet know in full that a discovery of the phenomenal world cannot leave humanity out of account and hope to come near perfection.

With all this in mind, we can proceed to trace the course of Lawrence's feeling from short story to novella. In so doing, I will draw to some degree on conclusions advanced by Gerald Lacy in his definitive edition of *The Escaped Cock.*

All through the Etruscan experience, as we have seen, Lawrence had felt powerfully the surging of the Mediterranean springtime above the tombs. He felt it likewise when he returned to the Villa Mirenda, where he did much of his writing in an outdoors that he could turn into the organic framework for his story of a resurrected god: the olive terraces, the tender young wheat, the flowers, the figtrees in new leaf, many of them described in the story as they are in the sketch "Flowering Tuscany," written this same spring. All this becomes Jesus' phenomenal world, and he begins to discover it in peasant surroundings similar to those in which Lawrence wrote. It was a setting forth from the England of Lady Chatterley to an Italy made over as the Holy Land.

At first Jesus finds himself between worlds, that is between death and life. He has come back from death, pushed away the rock before his tomb through the unconscious workings of the will to live. But he cannot see that the greenness around him has ever belonged as he has to that which has died — he does not yet possess the consciousness of a vegetation deity, whose very divinity is based on this knowledge. All he can take account of now is that he is utterly alone and utterly disillusioned. It is not at all, at this point, a satisfying aloneness of independence.

The magnificent orange and black cock is to be for him the restorative link with the phenomenal world. The bird belongs to an earth-slow and earth-dense peasant, who has kept him tied by the leg until he broke his cord and escaped over the courtyard wall just as Jesus was rising from the dead. As he walks away from his sepulchre he meets the fleeing cock and the owner chasing him, and in his great indifference, by a mere reflex gesture, Jesus aids in the recapture of the cock. The peasant takes Jesus in, and as he lies recuperating in the sunshine of the courtyard, he watches the vibrant life of the cock, diminished by his tether but still raging with vitality. But still Jesus cannot see that living is any longer his affair. Nor is contact with mankind. *Noli me tangere* is a state beyond which he sees no reason to strive.

Now another potential edges in and takes the plot in a direction on which Lawrence insists as the resolution of Jesus' post-resurrection condition in this form of the story. This is an elaboration of the other part of Jesus' enigmatic *noli me tangere* assertion in the Gospel of John: *I am not yet ascended to my father.* Lawrence turns this into a confrontation between the two ways of life whose contradiction has always plagued him. Jesus meets Mary Magdalene twice in the garden near his tomb. The first time he expresses a new, if slight, interest in existence. He might come to live with her: *"Later,"* he says, *"when I am healed, and I am with my Father."* But her very eagerness to have him and to sacrifice herself is repellent, and makes him change his mind almost instantly. On his second meeting with Mary Magdalene, Jesus' mother is there also, standing at a distance, and the plea of Mary Magdalene is for him to return to his mother and to all of his

EC, 113

followers, to become a "savior" again, a spiritual lover of mankind and a leader to spiritual salvation. This is a climactic moment for Jesus in that he is rejecting for good the role for which he was formerly willing to give his life, and along with that — indeed the two are inseparable — he is rejecting the *pietà* mentality of mankind and the Madonna and Child image which between them have kept the human soul in subjection for so long to a pernicious sort of female domination. It is a turning away from the mother to seek out a male identity in some marvelous distance. For Jesus' answer to Mary Magdalene is, *"I must ascend to my Father. . . . Now I belong to my* EC, 116 *Father, though I know not what he is, nor where he is."*

This is a new direction in the resurrected life that now seems to rule out any personal contact with others. Jesus feels no *connection of touch* with any human. None of them has rid himself of *staleness* and EC, 117 *littleness* by going through death and resurrection, and none is therefore worthy of the aristocratic intimacy that this experience alone can make one worthy of. What sort of lonely immortality is it, then, that Jesus has wrought for himself? Lawrence defines it as *the immortality of being alive without fret,* or in a more telling phrase, Jesus has *discovered the inner world of insouciance, which is immortality.* It is what Lawrence could re-create, at the moment, of what he held to be the Etruscan view of life, but with the pilgrim mobility as adjunct. Jesus' new profession of faith is, *"I will wander the earth and say nothing; . . . I will wander like an iris walking naked within the inner air, well within the Father, and I shall be in the outer air as well."* The Father and the phenomenal world are synonymous. What we have here is a further cycle of one of Lawrence's earliest credos, from the "foreword" to *Sons and Lovers* and the "blood-religion letter": that the flesh and not spirit is the eternal substance and the true source of immortality. But this is a far cry from one aspect of that earlier credo, in which woman was the indispensable link between man and the cosmic source.

The Jesus of *The Escaped Cock,* both in the story and later in the novella, buys the flamboyant rooster from the peasant and goes away to become a healer. He "ascends" into the physical world, not into heaven. At length his rooster challenges another and kills it, thereby winning the right to the barnyard kingdom of his fallen rival. Jesus leaves him there and proceeds on his way, the *vast complexity* EC, 120 *of wonders* of the world before him. His adventure ends here in the short story, in full cognizance that the *infinite whirl* of the material universe is not to be "saved" from anything. It is sufficient to itself.

In the last pages of the story, however, a possible modification of Jesus' aloof *insouciance* is hinted at. *If a man would wash himself with* EC, *death,* he could then be prepared to *meet a woman erect and quite* 117&118

uncovered and encompassed by the Father as the iris is. But Lawrence is so intent on vivifying the quest for male integrity and male inde-

ML, 974   pendence in its *combative* sense that he has little wish at present to pursue any kind of man-woman togetherness. Even the relationship

EC, 118   suggested subdues the woman totally to the father fixation: *the great fulfillment is to be with the Father, and the whole body encompassed.*

The stage was set, at least, for the completion of what was already well begun, a transformation of the traditional Jesus into a pagan fertility god by inventing for him a consort and taking him through a myth-like narrative embodying the departure and return of the god as in the symbolism of a mystery religion. When Lawrence amplified the short story into a novella more than a year after writing the story and after completing the third and most phallic version of *Lady Chatterley's Lover,* he made changes in his protagonist, in modifying the story to turn it into the first half of the longer tale, changes which are not obtrusive in the text but which point to a fundamental differ-

EC, 142   ence. The Jesus of the novella discovers more *resoluteness* and *swaying* in the material creation to which he wakes, and less *raging* and *violence.* This change is one bit of the drift in the new protagonist

EC, 27   away from *compulsion* in human contact and towards *gentle reverence,* or the *tenderness* of *Lady Chatterley's Lover.* But more radical differences emerge between the two versions of Jesus. The later one knows from the beginning that his *noli me tangere* attitude will cease when he has truly achieved his lone integrity and can mingle with another person without losing it. The Father is no longer his all-containing metaphor for the phenomenal world. Most of the mystical Father language is, in fact, dropped in the novella, and the *inner air* self-enclosedness of the male with it. The reborn male now knows that when he has achieved a whole self, he will find the complementary non-possessive nature in a woman. The internal insouciance obtainable by the flowering in isolation is no longer an all-inclusive immortality

EC, 30   but only *one sort of immortality.* Lawrence will soon touch on another sort, as he makes inner preparation for the longest journey by associat-

EC, 34   ing Jesus' setting forth with a repudiation of the fear of death: *It was fear, the ultimate fear of death, that made men mad. So always he must move on, for if he stayed, his neighbours wound the strangling of their fear and bullying round him.* The travel instinct had reached a new declaration of purpose. And the other sort of immortality that Lawrence's last fictional version of Jesus will reach is a sexual apotheosis that includes a transit between the world of time and that of eternity.

Part Two of *The Escaped Cock* begins in a little Etruscan-inspired temple that stands on another plot of Lawrence's Italy, the Fiascherino seaside where he had known a season of his greatest happiness with

Frieda. But we might also say that it is the Holy Land of "Hymns in a Man's Life" — one of *those places that never existed on earth.* The PX, 600
priestess of the temple here, who will be Isis incarnate, has dedicated seven years of her life to Isis-in-Search, the goddess who wanders in quest of the scattered pieces of Osiris' body, so that she may reassemble him and bring him to life to fertilize her womb. As the priestess portrays her, Isis has located all of the dismembered Osiris except for *the last reality, the final clue to him, the genitals that alone could* EC, 38
bring him really back to her. The priestess could have had her pick of such great men as Mark Antony and Julius Caesar, but she waits for the ultimate sexual reality in the man-god who has been reborn.

The Jesus who comes along seeking shelter from the priestess is Lawrence's last fleshing out of the dark stranger through whom he began his quest in 1912. He is now *dark-faced, with a black pointed* EC, 40
beard, like an Etruscan or one of Lawrence's Midlanders in the fragment narrating rebirth in 2927. The cavity which has been symbolic of rebirth over and over figures again here. The priestess grants Jesus shelter in a little cave near her temple, and when she is called by a slave to observe from his scars while he sleeps that he is a malefactor, what she truly sees in him is *the tip of a fine flame of living.* This is the EC, 43
beginning of her bringing him out of the cave in which his sensual life is still entombed. When she invites him into the temple to pay homage to Isis, she begins to see that he is her long-sought Osiris.

The dilemma for the dark stranger is whether he wishes to submit to *touch* again. Men have killed him with their touch. He has dared EC, 46
the touch of death, can he dare the touch of life from woman? He can be Osiris, he decides, but only if Isis will heal him with the tormenting yet tender fire of her touch. In recounting this experience which Jesus consents to endure, Lawrence draws every possible parallel between crucifixion into death and the crucifixion into life of a sexual union. The awakening Osiris enters the temple with Isis, ready to know the *soft, strange courage of life,* totally unlike his *courage of death.* Terror, EC, 53
pain and grief run through the stirring soul. The priestess of Isis massages all his scars, on his hands and feet and deep in both his sides where the spear went completely through. He is fearful that she can never stroke death out of him, but slowly she does, rubbing all his lower body, including *the slain penis and the sad stones,* the organs EC, 56
still missing from Osiris. Desire, the first true desire of the man's life, begins to burn, desire like another sort of death before resurrection. The new Osiris now borrows words from the Gospels. Looking down at the woman, he intones, *"On this rock I build my life!"* And when he EC, 57
feels *the blaze of his manhood and his power rise up in his loins, magnificent,* he cries out *"I am risen!"*

This scene has been considered by some a howler of a failure, not to mention the accusation of some Christians that it is the crowning blasphemy in a thoroughly blasphemous tale. All we need consider here is the question of whether the scene is ludicrous. There is a reasonable enough point of view by which it is not, but that point of view is so far outside most literary tradition that many people refuse to adopt it. If the same matter of the "little death" of sexual intercourse, complete with "resurrection," is couched in the language of "wit," then it is acceptable or laudable or even called a flash of genius, according to our tradition. Or again, the language of secular love, providing it is indirect enough, can be and always has been employed to designate some sort of divine love: for example, between the divinity and the creature in the Canticles as interpreted by Jewish and Christian orthodoxy, or in the mystical poetry of St. John of the Cross. But in these indirectness is all. There may be phallic "symbols" all around, but there must never be the phallus itself. This is just the kind of tradition Lawrence was attempting to overcome, for of course he felt that all of the traditional "witty" and "symbolic" ways of demonstrating that physical fertility is the true basis of all life, whether of body or soul, were mentally imposed and substituted the hollow conceit for the actuality. Everyone knows that ritual intercourse was the source of the godly power to preserve the world in divine consorts like Isis and Osiris. If you believe that such ancient fertility religions are still of value to us, as Lawrence believed, then you have every good reason to devise your "myth" just as Lawrence did, and every good reason to accuse your detractors of judging the result by the standards of a way of thinking foreign to an equally valid set of standards by which the story is written.

Spring burgeons over the land and in the hearts of the godly lovers. The risen Osiris keeps an aura of beauty and splendor about him which is yonic and which is reminiscent of the "rose" of Heaven in Dante, that divine organ by which the Virgin Mary is queen of the cosmos. Law-

EC, 58 rence is simply more direct about it all. The new Osiris feels *the great rose of space* around him, a heavenly contact restored between man and woman, phallic and yonic in perfect conjunction.

By now Lawrence has set up also another world besides the greater world in which Isis and Osiris carry out their ceremonial life. This is the petty world of property, greed and suspicion, the estate which is ruled over by the priestess' mother and a Roman overseer, and which has the little temple cut off on its promontory. Inevitably this corrupt world encroaches upon and attempts to smother the greater world. That Jesus has somehow escaped Roman "justice" is eventually known to all on the estate. The overseer plots to seize him while he sleeps and return him to the Romans.

A change comes about now, too, in the world of living touch between Jesus and the priestess. She is pregnant, and hangs back a little from him. This is the normal cycle of the natural world: *The* EC, 59 *spring was fulfilled, a contact was established, the man and the woman were fulfilled of one another, and departure was in the air.* The male deity is primed for travel, for the departure that always must complete the return, and vice versa. *"I am a man, and the world is open,"* says EC, 60 Jesus to the priestess. He manages to outwit his enemies, stealing a boat from under their noses and rowing away. The phallic serpent sleeps, it is a gestation time for the mother of the ongoing world, and Jesus-Osiris has embarked upon his journey. But he will be back in due time, for this is a cyclical world of the coming and going of the god. The apotheosis of the male traveler could hardly be more neatly rounded out.

The Lawrences' stay at the Villa Mirenda near Florence lasted from the spring of 1926 until the early summer of 1928. From the fall of the first year on, as we have seen, it was a period spanned by the three versions of *Lady Chatterley,* punctuated from time to time by the other works we have looked into. It is a well-known story that Lawrence near the end of this period published the third version of *Lady Chatterley* himself and made a fair amount of money for the first time in his life, before the seizures, the burning and the piracy began in Britain and the United States. It was also near the time of beginning his novel that Lawrence took up painting as a serious pursuit. That activity eventually brought him into conflict with the same variety of censorship that the novel aroused.

As to Lawrence's emotional involvement with place and travel during these years, the day-to-day context surrounding his looking back and forth in his writing from England to the Mediterranean, and from past to present to future, is a host of longings and changing intentions toward several places. In addition to the wish to sail the Mediterranean like Odysseus there was always the desire to be at the ranch in New Mexico: but then again . . . a revulsion from America. He thought of going to Libya with Earl Brewster on something like the Etruscan excursion. Egypt is also mentioned as a residential possibility, and once Greenland, as a place to visit. On two or three occasions Lawrence brought up the idea of spending a year in Ireland. And increasingly he spoke of leaving Italy for good. He went on a prolonged visit to Austria and Germany during this time, part of which brought the Lawrences to Irschenhausen, Bavaria, once more, to the same house where they had lived in 1913. Here he felt revive briefly the old sense of freedom and openness in that landscape.

And so the impulses ran, as always, back and forth. Lawrence

ML, 951 could also protest, with vehemence, *I begin to hate journeys — I've journeyed enough.* But then he could be equally vociferous about going

ML, 980 off on a journey with a vengeance: *I shall go out into the world again, to kick it and stub my toes.* The opposition of mobility versus fixity

ML, 989 was complicated, in July 1927, by what Lawrence called a *bronchial hemorrhage:* tubercular, of course, and truly the beginning of the end for him. One effect of his realized but unadmitted illness was to bring a greater desire than ever to travel. He contemplated sailing around the world again, either in the same direction as before or the other way, either with Frieda or with her and the Brewsters. From New York

ML, they could go west: *We might afterwards sail to China and India from*
1018 *San Francisco — there's always that door out. Let's do it! Anything, anything to shake off this stupor and have a bit of fun in life. I'd even go to Hell, en route.*

Lawrence was too sick to travel far. After giving up the Villa Mirenda, he spent most of the summer and early fall of 1928 at Gsteig bei Gstaad, a mountain spot in Switzerland that was supposed to improve his health. Here, in August, as mentioned earlier, he finished the second half of *The Escaped Cock.*

If it was incumbent upon such a Christ-centered man as Lawrence to write a "gospel" after his own fashion, so was it to write an "apocalypse" as well. His opportunity came through an acquaintance named Frederick Carter, who had written a great deal and done drawings on the mystical import of the Book of Revelations. Lawrence had first read a manuscript of his in Chapala, Mexico, and had visited him in Shropshire in early 1924. They were in touch again by August 1929, and in early October Lawrence read another manuscript of Carter's, for which he promised to do an introduction. The first one that he began proved much too long in the end for such a purpose. So Lawrence wrote another of suitable length for Carter and planned to bring out the longer piece as an independent book, as his own interpretation of the symbolism of Revelations, less astrological than Carter's. He did not finish this work until about two months before he died. It appeared posthumously under the title *Apocalypse.* Lawrence's reading of the last and most obscure book of the New Testament offers much insight on the final state of his symbology of time and space and distance.

Just as Lawrence meant to rescue the figure of Jesus from his traditional moralistic and spiritual image and restore him to a passional role, so did he mean to unearth the profound old pagan symbolism glossed over by a moralistic Jewish-Christian in the Revelations. With both gospel and apocalypse he was recovering from the old book, the Bible, what he had recovered from the artifacts of the Etruscan tombs. The Bible, however, was something that had been with Lawrence from his earliest youth, and the introduction he fashioned for *Apocalypse* is a succinct account, here close to the end of his life, of his whole experience with symbolism, going back to the Biblical start of it.

Lawrence speaks of being so drenched with the Bible in his childhood that it *became an influence which affected all the processes of* emotion and thought. But he lost interest as soon as he began to mature, because it was the Bible *morally* and *dogmatically* expounded to which he was continually exposed. Once the meaning of a book, the Bible or any other, is fixed, the book dies for him. But he has taken up the Bible in later life, and discovered that it goes far beyond anything that interpreters of his youth could have told him. It has now become for him one of those few books that *make a man question his own identity.* This means, in dealing specifically with the Apocalypse, that what used to be understood as some kind of rigid allegory turns out to be a fathomless symbolism of the sort in which one can discover his own cosmic nature. Through exploration of this symbolism, Lawrence articulated his fullest rejection of the worst side of his puritan background, the narrow and literalistic pietism, while at the same time he gave one of his fullest expansions to the mystical side of puritanism, the drama of the individual soul reaching the universal harmony in its own manner by direct approach to cosmic realities.

The rejection comes first, by a peeling away of what is to Lawrence the objectionable surface of the Apocalypse. On this level it is a book of the "humble" rising up in envy against the rich and powerful, the Romans or their later equivalent, who may have the upper hand and wallow in opulence at present, but in the afterlife they will writhe in the fire and brimstone of hell while the elect luxuriate for eternity in a heaven of gold and precious stones like a *jeweller's paradise.* This is not only envy of riches but a deep lust for revenge, according to Lawrence, and it makes the Apocalypse repugnant to him. As a Judas was inevitable, given a Christ who based all on love and denied power, or rather postponed power to the next world, so was an Apocalypse, a *book of thwarted power-worship,* bound to succeed the Gospels. To Lawrence, of course, the glorification of true inner power in great men is a natural urge of the human race and will not be denied. When Jesus rejected earthly power, he left the way open for it to fall into the hands of the devil, and then to creep back into the ending of the New Testament after all in a ghastly form. If the masses are not

Margin references: AP, 3 — AP, 4 — AP, 89 — AP, 86

granted one kind of power to exalt, they will seize another. All through
the passages of *Apocalypse* dealing with the love and power controversy, Lawrence often approaches the texture of arguments presented
in Dostoevsky's "Grand Inquisitor" section of *The Brothers Karama-
zov:* the masses are incapable of the renunciation and individual wholeness directly reliant on God. Their paltriness must be completed in a
glorious authority which wields all varieties of power, economic as
well as any other, so that weak men may eat their bread under the
aegis of what Dostoevsky calls "miracle, mystery and authority." Most
of these echoes of Dostoevsky Lawrence picked up again and con-
solidated in an introduction he wrote for Koteliansky's translation of
"The Grand Inquisitor" at about the time he was writing *Apocalypse.*

AP, 26   Still, Lawrence confesses to *a dual feeling . . . with regard to the
Apocalypse,* for it seems to him to contain, especially in the first part,
AP, 23 something still of *the true and positive power-spirit.* John of Patmos,
AP, 33 in spite of himself, was to some degree *in touch with great old symbols*
of the pagan world. The vision of Jesus with a face like the sun and
AP, 25 holding seven stars is, for instance, the old *cosmic lord, standing among
the seven eternal lamps of the archaic planets.* The throne of God,
the four horsemen, the voices of thunder, the Magna Mater in both
her beneficent and malefic aspects, the elaborate symbolism of numbers — all this still carries with it some of the pagan splendor that
John was presumably out to suppress, and Lawrence goes far afield
to link up this symbolism with that gleaned from so many other sources
in his long absorption with what he took to be the remotest paganism.
At this time he read once again Burnet's *Early Greek Philosophy,*
from which he quotes on a few occasions in *Apocalypse.* Those pre-
Socratic thinkers belonged far more to the old instinctive world than
to the rational world that Plato introduced. Like the Etruscans they
AP, 102 were a last wave of the archaic past, steeped in *the oldest religious
conception of the cosmos,* bringing it down from the Chaldeans to
John of Patmos' age. This writer naturally had Old Testament sources
to call on, too, such as Ezekiel, whose symbolism was also borrowed,
however, from the tradition of the Chaldeans. All this added up, for
Lawrence, to a confirmation of what he saw in *the Minoan distance,*
and in one of the earliest religious documents to which he had
been exposed.

    Furthermore, he had adapted for his own use a theory which
helped to unify this wealth of symbolism in the Apocalypse, and which
lent to the work an individual character such as it must have if it was
to serve any purpose in the pilgrim's quest for atonement with the
cosmos. Lawrence had borrowed the theory several years before this
time from a book by James Pryse called *The Apocalypse Unsealed.*
Pryse held that the Apocalypse was the "revelation" in symbols of an

initiation rite into one of the mystery religions. He went so far as to claim that John was an adept who made the book sound Christian so as to stealthily preserve the secrets of his cult from exposure and destruction by the fanatical new sect, and also to plant the seeds of animism that they might one day again grow to overwhelm the detested moralism of Christianity. To Lawrence, although he followed Pryse to a great degree, John was no adept but just a curious mixture of a man who did not realize how much paganism he was leaving in the many-layered work that he was revising, nor to what extent he was by nature in sympathy with it. Pryse's ideas were for Lawrence altogether what his sources usually were, a point of departure for his imagination. And this time he attempted to draw from his imaginative flight his most comprehensive and symbolically precise view of the single soul journeying off into the cosmos to find union with the eternal spirits of time and space. This was to be *an escape from the tight little cage of* AP, 28 *our universe,* escape into *the great Chaldean star-spaces, instead of* AP, 36 *being pinched up in a Jewish tabernacle* — or we may say, in Lawrence's case, in a tight little fundamentalist chapel.

The escape was to come about through the body of man magnified to the sphere of the stars. In the famous seven seals *we are witnessing* AP, 60 *the opening and conquest of the great psychic centres of the human body. The old Adam is going to be conquered, die, and be reborn as the new Adam: but in stages: in sevenfold stages.* With the riding out of the four horsemen on the opening of the fourth seal, the seeker after a new life begins the death process. The second horse, being red, signifies war in *the inner world of the self.* The black horse announces AP, 63 the wasting away and the coming sacrifice of the body, and finally the fourth, the pale horse, indicates that the *dynamic self is dead,* and that we must *enter the Hades or underworld of our being.* And then, with the last three seals, the cycle is brought full circle. In its journey through the underworld, the longest journey, the soul must divest itself of the last vestige of the old life. But still it retains, down below, the *final flame-point of life,* and *at the very instant of extinction,* with the AP, 66 breaking of the seventh seal, the soul *becomes a new whole cloven flame of a new-bodied man with golden thighs and a face of glory.* It is the vitality of this life and the greater life it reflects that Lawrence sets up against the hereafter salvation which the Christian author was trying to read into the old initiation, but which is to Lawrence no more than a hope for heaven in the future by one who finds it impossible to "die" and then come fully to life here and now. This passage and others like it are preparatory to the ending of *Apocalypse,* to that magnificent hymn to life with which Lawrence chose to end his last book.

This basic ceremony suggests to Lawrence what seem to him self-evident truths. It points to great cycles which control everything.

AP, 54   He declares that *our idea of time as a continuity in an eternal straight line has crippled our consciousness cruelly*. The truer way of measurement is reflected not only in the initiation rites but in the whole form

AP, 54–55   of apocalypse, whose method is *to set forth the image, make a world, and then suddenly depart from this world in a cycle of time and movement and event, an epos*. To be sure, we might already know, after long perusal of recurring patterns in Lawrence, that the creative and

AP, 93   the destructive both reign within the cycle: *the god of the beginning of an era is the evil principle at the end of that era*. And this element of his thought brings Lawrence at several junctures in the book into confrontation again with the old matter of male ascendancy and of female susceptibility both to error and to possessiveness. He cannot speak about the old life without catching a glimpse once more of the

AP, 72   mother nemesis: *The great Moon and mother of my inner waterstreams, in so far as she is the old, dead moon, is hostile, hurtful, and hateful to my flesh, for she still has a power over my old flesh*. Turning his attention from mother to mate, Lawrence finds support in such

AP, 94   ancient myths as that of Andromeda that *no one is coiled more bitterly in the folds of the old Logos than woman,* in the superseded way of life, and that she *has no power of escape till man frees her*.

Still, whatever the stresses imposed by the coming and going of cyclical time, the great freedom of universal motion remains, and Lawrence improvises through many pages on the marvels of symbolism to be found in the potentialities of such movement. It can bear the imagi-

AP, 116   nation *into dim regions of the soul aeons and aeons back*. It can encompass the whole concept of the Creation praising its Maker: this is what Lawrence sees behind the four creatures surrounding the

AP, 104   throne of God. They are descended from *the four great creatures amid the wheels of the revolving heavens* in Ezekiel, and their myriad eyes identify them as *the stars of the trembling heavens for ever changing and travelling and pulsing* in praise of their Creator.

This long journey through the symbolism of the ancient world as the summation of a lifetime search and an accommodation with death at times produced also for Lawrence another principal aspect

AP, 114   of cosmology that he liked to ponder. That *old, flaming love of life* in now forgotten paganism had always been accompanied by *the strange shudder of the presence of the invisible dead*. And perhaps the last thing that concerned Lawrence on earth before the power to create began to slip from him was the "presence" of being even in the utmost "invisibility" of the soul in death. His great poem "Bavarian Gentians," written a few months before he died, considers this dark blue flower as a torch of darkness for the soul descending into the underworld, down and down the stairs of the longest journey to attend

the nuptials of Persephone and Pluto. The darkness below is the deepest conceivable, but the absence of light is not here held in the traditional manner to be a horror. Quite the opposite. In this *darkness* CP, 697
invisible enfolded in the deeper dark the flower torches shed rays of gloom on the god and goddess, and on the attendant soul now come to the culmination of its last voyage. This soul has discovered immortality through knowledge that the dark of the gentian constitutes life itself, and that the nature of life is to be in constant flow between the eternal sources of the underworld and the flowering and fading world above.

But the poem that must stand at the end of this investigation of what travel meant to Lawrence's life and work is "The Ship of Death," the title itself indicating how much Lawrence thought of his life as actual and as symbolic voyage. Before going into this poem, however, we need a brief summary of Lawrence's movements in his last couple of years to gather what we can of how place and travel affected him to the last.

During the stay at Gsteig bei Gstaag in Switzerland, which was never much to Lawrence's liking and did not bring any improvement in his health, he and Frieda made arrangements to spend the coming winter with the Richard Aldingtons and Brigit Patmore on the island of Port-Cros, just off the French coast near Toulon. They occupied an old fort made over into a dwelling on the highest point of the island, with an excellent view all around. But there was much rain, and Lawrence had not for a long time been fond of islands in any case. A month of Port-Cros was all he could take. He settled for the winter in a hotel in nearby Bandol, but not with any positive desire to do so, for he was feeling again that there was *nowhere to go, in Europe.* Aside from the ML, 1102
more distant places that were always calling, Spain came up as a possibility, as it had done occasionally before. Lawrence wanted to go there in the spring of 1929, because he now thought of it as *a man's* ML, 1112
country. What this plan led to was a trip to Mallorca that lasted from mid-April till mid-June of 1929. At times Lawrence liked this spot well enough, but then again he declared, *I feel old and sullen ghosts* ML, 1152
on the air, and am rather frightened. So the restlessness never ceased, and hopes for new places in the letters veer about between such extremes as India and Lake Garda or Lerici again, as if for a new start after all these years. None of these hopes materialized. The Lawrences ended by spending most of the summer in Germany and going back again to Bandol, where this time they rented the Villa Beau Soleil for the winter that was to be Lawrence's last. It was an urgent question now to find the place easiest on his health, for he did retain the illusion that health would sooner or later come back to him, in the right place.

And the spirit of adventure was still there, for from his villa on a
ML, 1205   promontory he could still look out across the bay and *still love the
Mediterranean, it still seems young as Odysseus, in the morning.* It
ML, 1206   was a comfort against civilization: *When the morning comes, and
the sea runs silvery and the distant islands are delicate and clear, then
I feel again, only man is vile.* Africa was in that direction, a beckon-
ing mystery that he would never see. As the winter went on, the last
desperate hopes that some journey would lead to health settled briefly,
as they had over and over for years, on the ranch in New Mexico, or
ML, 1242   anywhere *really thrilling* that he could sail away to, including some
fantastic place, as in the rueful remark *I sort of wish I could go to
ML, 1221   the moon.* Where he was finally forced to go was to a sanitorium in
Vence, near Nice, in February. But even in his greatly weakened condition a hospital could not hold him long. He left on March 1 to creep
to the Villa Robermond, also in Vence, which Frieda had just rented.
He died there the day after he came.

Three versions of "The Ship of Death" are printed in the de Sola
Pinto and Roberts edition of Lawrence's poems. The shortest and
probably the first written speaks of the destination of death only as
CP, 961   a *wonder-goal.* The next version, apparently still unsatisfactory to
the poet, approaches death in a manner less encouraging than "Bavar-
ian Gentians" does, by a complete lapsing into darkness and no more
CP, 960   than a question as to whether that peace may also contain *procreation.*
But in its third form the poem goes much further than either of these.

The voyage of the "Ship of Death" begins with enchanted recog-
CP, 716   nition that autumn has come for the soul and just as the apples *bruise
themselves an exit* as they fall, so must the soul slip out of *the fallen
self* and take *the long journey towards oblivion.* But the soul must
already have built its ship of death for the voyage. From here Lawrence proceeds to narrate and to chant what he envisions as the soul's
experience. The frightened soul feels the first cold blowing in through
CP, 718   the body. *The dark and endless ocean* will soon flood in through the
wounds. The preparation of the *little ark* goes forward, the details of
which are drawn perhaps from ancient Egyptian practice and certainly
from Etruscan artifacts which show the belief in such a vessel to have
CP, 719   been deeply ingrained in that culture. *With its store of food and little
cooking pans/and change of clothes,* the *ark of faith* will be ready to
brave *the sea of death.* But no steering of the ship is possible, for soon
it enters a realm without direction and without vision. The little vessel
is simply gone between the darkness above and the darkness below.
It is the end, it is oblivion.

The last two sections of the poem sound another note, and only
in this version. They show Lawrence returning to a pattern of death
and rebirth such as he had employed from the start of his career as

MEDITERRANEAN COAST

I still love the Mediterranean,
it still seems young as Odysseus, in the morning (ML, 1205)

wanderer and poet, but another intensity of imagery comes into play in this poem, revealing a strenuous effort by the poet to make his symbolism serve a purpose it has never been burdened with before. Formerly, death and rebirth had been a dual experience coming to pass in this world with symbolism called in from eternity to give it expression, even up through *Apocalypse*. But the actual end of life in our sphere now confronts the poet, and while he will not directly profess that he is conjuring up a vision of immortality based on the survival of the individual in an afterlife — that is, the kind of immortality that he has so frequently expostulated against — the potency of metaphor is such that he appears to be straining toward just this end. *And yet out of eternity, a thread/separates itself on the blackness.* These two lines follow the surrender to oblivion. And this thread, a thread of light,

CP, 720   leads into dawn, *the cruel dawn of coming back to life.* The little ark of the soul drifts through, still pale and cold, but then *the flood subsides,* the body reappears in what seems like Aphrodite on her sea shell, the ship comes home, *and the frail soul steps out, into her house again.*

In all this sweep of imagery Lawrence never lets go of the discourse as figure of speech. That is, he does not give up the appearance of referring to a cycle of experience within this life in the same sort of language so often employed before. And yet the implication is always there, fortified by the nearness of death in brute fact, that the poet is reaching for some kind of power in the metaphorical construct that will transform his poem into a transcendent actuality. Which is hardly surprising. A man with so vivid a sense of existence as Lawrence finds it next to impossible to conceive of extinction of the personality, no matter how much he may protest against that sort of immortality. It is not a profession of faith, but it is a natural turning to the prophetic power of poetry. We can only leave it at that, as Lawrence did with the end of his journey in view.

This thought suggests a few others on a strain of feeling in Lawrence which ran so far under the surface as to be rarely evident. His life was one long witness to the simple marvel of being conscious in the flesh, and few men with no faith in a blissful afterlife have died as well as he did. Yet he was anything but a mere optimist. We remember that he often described his outlook as tragic. By this he meant, as we have seen, different things at different times. But perhaps it always had something to do with glorification and disillusion together, forming a quality which underlies many others in Lawrence and which may have provided much of the essential antithesis without which a temperament such as his could hardly exist. Such a quality is at least suggested in many of the preceding pages, but it seems to deserve a closer look and to be a pertinent issue for a brief concluding section of this book.

Epilogue

One bright fall evening about sundown, my wife and I got off a train in a village in Switzerland. Like Lawrence some fifty years earlier, we had come from Germany: across the Boden See to Konstanz, up the Rhine to Schaffhausen, and from there we had set out to cross Switzerland along his route. The village where we were stopping for the night was Eglisau, also an overnight halt for Lawrence, and he had arrived on just such an evening as this, not by train but on foot. He had found this village, enclosed by hills on the Rhine, to be *a small, forgotten,* TI, 124 *wonderful world that belonged to the date of isolated village communities and wandering minstrels,* and had pretended to himself in a youthful fantasy that he was also *a sort of romantic, wandering* TI, 126 *character.*

A traveler who wished to indulge in such a daydream would have found it still easy to do so this half a century later, for not much had changed in Eglisau. The only appreciable loss was the old wooden covered bridge long since replaced by one of stone arching high over the water. The vineyards and the swift river reflecting *the tall village-* TI, 124 *front* with its lights held the same spirit as before. The inn that Lawrence remembered as "The Golden Stag" looked unchanged, and it was still the heart of activity in the evening. Probably Lawrence had the name a little wrong. It was now at any rate simply the "Gasthaus Hirschen," with no "golden" attached, although there was a stag of gilt paint on the door to the *gaststube.* This discrepancy being a tiny fact of no practical importance, even to set it down among the reams of notes taken on Lawrence's trail might have seemed pedantic, except for the course of thought it soon led to concerning Lawrence as a traveler arriving in this village.

In his walking that afternoon years ago, he had crossed a land-scape south of Schaffhausen that he thought *lifeless and hopeless,* until, approaching Eglisau, he had *dropped sharply into the Rhine valley again, suddenly, as if into another glamorous world.* On first thought you might have taken this shift of views for over-romanticizing, even though this village on the brim of the river was indeed lovely when compared with the country north of here. But later that evening you saw that a deeper quality of Lawrence's wayfaring was at work in all this, and it was the idea of the stag that brought it home to you.

Beyond the vineyards around the village the hills were wooded. This place must once have been a haunt of stags, whose memory had lingered in curious ways. Besides the one on the *gaststube* door, a stag emblem was the trademark of a *quelle* of *mineralwasser* whose head-quarters was next to the "new" bridge. But it was not until you left the lower village and went up the slope to look around the small, flattened space of the churchyard that you came across something more than a picturesque and commercialized vestige of the stag. On a prominent old tomb by the church door a running stag was carved, and below it was a paraphrase of the first verse of the Forty-Second Psalm:

> *Mein Seel nach dem Leben durst*
> *Wie ein Hirsch nach Wasser durst*

My soul thirsts for life/as a stag thirsts for water. It was not that Lawrence had seen this inscription, or if he did he had left no record of it. It was only that the verse expressed to perfection the passion in him that responded to changing mood and changing atmosphere in such a way as to produce a self adapted to drink in the maximum obtainable from each moment's life.

And yet this thought, so far, was deceptive. Thirst could be slaked but thirst came back. A man suffered from thirst, yet who could look on thirst as a mere curse to be relieved by the blessing of fullness? A man could love his thirst as well as hate it, and the same with drinking his fill. Or he could do what it appeared to you from long study of his work that Lawrence had done. A life so intense was bound to have been much haunted by this dual sense of the potentiality of existence. Lawrence found and lost over and over again what he was searching for in life. He knew that this was to be his fate, but he accepted it with gladness, and sometimes, too, bitterness. He made from it as mean-ingful a life, and as meaningful a death, as anyone could. He was able to do this because he came to understand that to thirst and to be filled were opposites whose whole significance was in the conflict between them. He stated and developed this antithesis in most of his works, from "The Crown" with its struggle between the lion and the unicorn to the late-written "Notes for *Birds, Beasts and Flowers,*" in which he agreed with Heraclitus that the universe would perish if strife should *pass away from among the gods and men . . . for in the ten-* **PH, 67** *sion of opposites all things have their being.* Lawrence came to live by this belief.

Therefore he could say with conviction, in 1922: *Travel seems to* **ML, 713** *me a splendid lesson in disillusion — chiefly that.* He wrote this in a letter on a ship in the Pacific, in transit from the Old World of the past, after the rebirth through the Red Sea, toward the most demanding of all his New Worlds, America. He knew essentially that any new continent would not for long fill his thirst after greatness of male being: he foresaw, and he accepted, the *disillusion.* But that the lesson would be *splendid* as well he also foresaw, and he would not truly have had it any other way. To consent and to prevail in a never-ceasing rhythm of disappointment and glorification may constitute, in effect, the essence of tragedy, and may establish, in this which Lawrence claimed was *essentially a tragic age,* the tragic nature of one of the greatest **LC, 5** travelers through that age.

Index

[419]